Government Impact on Sustainable and Responsible Supply Chain Management

Atour Taghipour
Normandy University, France

IGI Global
PUBLISHER of TIMELY KNOWLEDGE

A volume in the Advances in Logistics, Operations, and Management Science (ALOMS) Book Series

Published in the United States of America by
IGI Global
Information Science Reference (an imprint of IGI Global)
701 E. Chocolate Avenue
Hershey PA, USA 17033
Tel: 717-533-8845
Fax: 717-533-8661
E-mail: cust@igi-global.com
Web site: http://www.igi-global.com

Library of Congress Cataloging-in-Publication Data

Names: Taghipour, Atour, 1974- editor.
Title: Government impact on sustainable and responsible supply chain management / edited by: Atour Taghipour.
Description: Hershey PA : Information Science Reference, [2023] | Includes bibliographical references. | Summary: "The purpose of this book is to provide the new and innovative ways to adoption to integrate the social and environmental analysis into global value chains and to adapt the law that regulates corporate responsibility for the observance of sustainability and human rights in the supply chain"-- Provided by publisher.
Identifiers: LCCN 2023019752 (print) | LCCN 2023019753 (ebook) | ISBN 9781668490624 (hardcover) | ISBN 9781668490662 (paperback) | ISBN 9781668490631 (ebook)
Subjects: LCSH: Business logistics. | Sustainable engineering. | Industrial policy. | Social responsibility of business.
Classification: LCC HD38.5 .G6827 2023 (print) | LCC HD38.5 (ebook) | DDC 658.5--dc23/eng/20230601
LC record available at https://lccn.loc.gov/2023019752
LC ebook record available at https://lccn.loc.gov/2023019753

This book is published in the IGI Global book series Advances in Logistics, Operations, and Management Science (ALOMS) (ISSN: 2327-350X; eISSN: 2327-3518)

British Cataloguing in Publication Data
A Cataloguing in Publication record for this book is available from the British Library.

For electronic access to this publication, please contact: eresources@igi-global.com.

Advances in Logistics, Operations, and Management Science (ALOMS) Book Series

John Wang
Montclair State University, USA

ISSN:2327-350X
EISSN:2327-3518

Mission

Operations research and management science continue to influence business processes, administration, and management information systems, particularly in covering the application methods for decision-making processes. New case studies and applications on management science, operations management, social sciences, and other behavioral sciences have been incorporated into business and organizations real-world objectives.

The **Advances in Logistics, Operations, and Management Science** (ALOMS) Book Series provides a collection of reference publications on the current trends, applications, theories, and practices in the management science field. Providing relevant and current research, this series and its individual publications would be useful for academics, researchers, scholars, and practitioners interested in improving decision making models and business functions.

Coverage

- Operations Management
- Computing and information technologies
- Organizational Behavior
- Networks
- Marketing engineering
- Decision analysis and decision support
- Finance
- Production Management
- Services management
- Information Management

IGI Global is currently accepting manuscripts for publication within this series. To submit a proposal for a volume in this series, please contact our Acquisition Editors at Acquisitions@igi-global.com or visit: http://www.igi-global.com/publish/.

The Advances in Logistics, Operations, and Management Science (ALOMS) Book Series (ISSN 2327-350X) is published by IGI Global, 701 E. Chocolate Avenue, Hershey, PA 17033-1240, USA, www.igi-global.com. This series is composed of titles available for purchase individually; each title is edited to be contextually exclusive from any other title within the series. For pricing and ordering information please visit http://www.igi-global.com/book-series/advances-logistics-operations-management-science/37170. Postmaster: Send all address changes to above address.

Titles in this Series

For a list of additional titles in this series, please visit: http://www.igi-global.com/book-series/advances-logistics-operations-management-science/37170

Black Women's Formal and Informal Ways of Leadership Actualizing the Vision of a More Equitable Workplace
Audrey D. Bowser (Arkansas State University, USA) Kimberley M. Davis (University of Arkansas at Pine Bluff, USA) and Natalie Ann-Marie Johnson-Leslie (Arkansas State University, USA)
Information Science Reference • © 2023 • 300pp • H/C (ISBN: 9781668438275) • US $215.00

Considerations and Characteristics of the Millennial Leader in Today's Global Society
Tymon M. Graham (TMGraham Consulting, LLC, USA)
Business Science Reference • © 2023 • 300pp • H/C (ISBN: 9781668447116) • US $240.00

The Economics of Talent Management and Human Capital
Sharif Uddin Ahmed Rana (Paris Graduate School and World Talent Economy Forum, Malaysia) and Adrian David Cheok (Imagineering Institute, Malaysia)
Business Science Reference • © 2023 • 300pp • H/C (ISBN: 9781668466414) • US $235.00

Entrepreneurship Ecosystems and Their Opportunities and Challenges
Mohammed El Amine Abdelli (University of Brest, France) Shajara Ul-Durar (University for Creative Arts, UK) and Hala Wasef Hattab (British University in Egypt, Egypt)
Business Science Reference • © 2023 • 300pp • H/C (ISBN: 9781668471401) • US $250.00

Strategies and Applications of Islamic Entrepreneurship
Ahmad Rafiki (Universitas Medan Area, Indonesia) Alfatih Gessan Pananjung (Bahrain Institute of Banking & Finance, Bahrain) and Muhammad Dharma Tuah Putra Nasution (Universitas Pembangunan Panca Budi, Indonesia)
Business Science Reference • © 2023 • 300pp • H/C (ISBN: 9781668475195) • US $250.00

Cybersecurity Measures for Logistics Industry Framework
Noor Zaman Jhanjhi (Taylor's University, Malaysia) and Imdad Ali Shah (Taylor's University, Malaysia)
Information Science Reference • © 2023 • 310pp • H/C (ISBN: 9781668476253) • US $250.00

Transport and Logistics Planning and Optimization
Jaouad Boukachour (University of Le Havre, France) and Abdelhamid Benaini (University of Le Havre, France)
Business Science Reference • © 2023 • 330pp • H/C (ISBN: 9781668484746) • US $250.00

IGI Global
PUBLISHER of TIMELY KNOWLEDGE

701 East Chocolate Avenue, Hershey, PA 17033, USA
Tel: 717-533-8845 x100 • Fax: 717-533-8661
E-Mail: cust@igi-global.com • www.igi-global.com

Editorial Advisory Board

Table of Contents

Detailed Table of Contents

This chapter uses the German supply chain act as a lens to examine the impact on corporate social responsibility (CSR) of China's belt and road initiative (BRI) and global supply chain management techniques. China's BRI seeks to improve infrastructure, trade, and investment links with various nations. This chapter describes the BRI and how it may alter global supply chains in ways that raise or lower risks and possibilities related to sustainability and human rights. The chapter analyzes China's potential to advance green and socially responsible business practices along the BRI. A novel Chinese interpretation of the German supply chain act and its potential application inside the BRI are discussed. The chapter highlights the importance of worker rights and environmental preservation as it addresses the potential of technologies like blockchain inside the BRI framework to improve transparency, accountability, and traceability. The chapter also emphasizes the financial advantages of ethical supply chain management.

During recent years, the supply chain act was adapted to deal with human rights abuses and environmental protection in supply chains, as a way to motivate companies to integrate corporate responsibilities in their decisions. This directive can intervene without being transposed into national laws in other countries, where the actors of the supply chain exist. The act provides penalties for companies that don't have plans for respecting human rights and environmental protection. For this reason, companies need to have information channels to report possible breaches of the law. One of the critical supply chains is the food supply chain, which needs to assure food safety, in addition to other requirements determined by law, across the global supply chain, by coordinating food related businesses in each supply chain. In this study, the authors will analyse different companies, which transformed their supply chain following different crises and adapting new supply chain management laws. The example studies in this research can be used by other companies in their supply chain transformation.

Contemporary managerial thinking and practices have been developed in an economic context dominated by industrial logic. This logic conceals the imposing weight of services. Logistics is an activity that is undergoing major changes due to new technologies and managerial innovations. The advent of the supply chain service (SSCM), as a dual concept combining both traditional supply operations and the coordination of various resources, with a view to customer satisfaction, while integrating constraints of time, capacity, shared resources, and co-production, has turned logistics research upside down. The purpose of this chapter is to establish a qualitative analysis of the impact of MCSS practices on the performance of the service company. The theoretical analysis and the review of interviews show that

Republic of Serbia. The aim of the chapter is focused on highlighting both positive and limiting factors (the real situation), with the author's wish that the recommendation of good practice and the results of this research be implemented in Serbia.

Foreword

The Supply Chain Act, is a German law that comes into force on January 1, 2023. The law regulates corporate responsibility for the observance of human rights in the supply chain for the first time. The law on corporate due diligence in supply chains was published in the Federal Law Gazette on July 22, 2021 after the parliamentary procedure had been completed. In fact, according to this evolutionary law, companies need to identify, analyze, and prioritize the risks in their supply chains and new policies must be established based on these results. New measures are taken to prevent or minimize violations of human rights and damage to the environment. The companies also need to set up the grievance channels for people in the supply chains for regular reporting on supply chain practices. The Supply Chain Act gives consumers the security that companies are managed based on fair production. From 2023, the law will initially apply to companies with at least 3,000 employees in Germany, and from 2024 also to companies with at least 1,000 employees. The law strengthens human rights and environmental protection. These include, among other things: protection against child labor, forced labor and discrimination; women and supply chains; protection against land grabbing; occupational health and safety; right to fair wages; right to form trade unions; protection against environmental violations.

This book studies Government Impact on Sustainable and Responsible Supply Chain Management. The book features a collection of contributions related to the sustainability and responsibility. It further explains the ways in which these contributions can affect industries. Covering topics related to Government Impact on Sustainable and Responsible Supply Chain, this premier reference source is an excellent resource for governments, business leaders and executives, supply chain managers, logistics specialists, students and faculty of higher education, librarians, researchers, and academicians.

The parts of the book are well-linked and integrated altogether and offer a holistic and overarching perspective of sustainability. Hence, readers of this book will benefit extensively from this approach and the intertwined theoretical and applied approach followed when covering various aspects of supply chain sustainability. I am confident that this book will be very popular amongst academics and practitioners. In addition, it will be extremely valuable to both undergraduate and postgraduate students reading for supply chain management. To conclude, this book is a welcome addition. I recommend it highly to anybody interested to the topic of Government Impact on Sustainable and Responsible Supply Chain Management.

Sharareh Taghipour
Toronto Metropolitan University, Canada

Preface

A supply chain comprises different actors existing in different countries. Some actors are suppliers, some producers and some customers. Clothes are supplied from Asia to all planets; coffee beans are supplied from South America; cocoa is produced in Africa. In this regard, protecting the rights of people who produce goods in different countries is essential. As an example, the Supply Chain Act, is a German law that comes into force on January 1, 2023. The law regulates corporate responsibility for the observance of human rights in the supply chain for the first time. The law on corporate due diligence in supply chains was published in the Federal Law Gazette on July 22, 2021 after the parliamentary procedure had been completed. In fact, according to this evolutionary law, companies need to identify, analyze, and prioritize the risks in their supply chains and new policies must be established based on these results. New measures are taken to prevent or minimize violations of human rights and damage to the environment. The companies also need to set up the grievance channels for people in the supply chains for regular reporting on supply chain practices. The Supply Chain Act gives consumers the security that companies are managed based on fair production. From 2023, the law will initially apply to companies with at least 3,000 employees in Germany, and from 2024 also to companies with at least 1,000 employees. The law strengthens human rights and environmental protection. These include, among other things: protection against child labor, forced labor and discrimination; women and supply chains; protection against land grabbing; occupational health and safety; right to fair wages; right to form trade unions; protection against environmental violations.

A Description of the Target Audience

The target audience of this book will be composed of professionals and researchers working in the governmental and private organizations in the field of supply chain management, operations management, logistics, operations research. Moreover, the book will provide insights and support executives concerned with the management of expertise, knowledge, information and organizational development in different types of work communities and environments.

A DESCRIPTION OF EACH CHAPTER

Chapter 1: A French Guide for Businesses and Governments to Integrate the Concept of Sustainable Development into Their Supply Chains

The term sustainable development, as a new form of development that meets the needs of the present without compromising the ability of future generations to meet theirs. In this context, sustainable development needs to be at the crossroads between three pillars: the economic pillar, the social pillar and the environmental pillar (Martin, 2014). But, the question is raised: how do companies integrate the notion of sustainable development internally into their supply chain process. To answer this question, based on a literature review, we are interested in two points in particular. First, we will see the implementation of sustainable development in the production process and the change in costs, then in terms of the new internal systems of Corporate Social Responsibility. The results of this work can be used by governments, companies and researchers to integrate sustainable development in their decisions.

Chapter 2: The Role of Government Regulations on Business Practices in China: Impact and Lessons for Global Sustainability

As a growing major economic global power, China is currently dealing with pressing environmental issues necessitating the adoption of sustainable business practices. This review highlights the importance of sustainability and examines the role of Chinese regulations in driving sustainable business practices. Recognizing the pressing need to address environmental challenges, China has implemented a range of regulations aimed at fostering sustainability. The article emphasizes the significance of these regulations within Chinese industries. By analyzing a variety of regulations, this review provides valuable insights into the mechanisms through which Chinese companies are incentivized to adopt sustainable practices and provides a deeper understanding of the regulatory frameworks that shape sustainability efforts in China. The findings highlight the importance of integrating sustainability into business operations and demonstrate how Chinese regulators play a central role in encouraging companies to embrace sustainable strategies.

Chapter 3: Resilient Sustainable Supply Chain Management

Companies must respond to the growing expectations of their stakeholders, but also conduct their activities according to an ambitious responsible development approach, which means addressing the social and environmental practices associated with the development of its products. This commitment covers not only its own internal practices but also those of its suppliers. It involves identifying, managing and optimizing sustainable practices in the supply network. Working towards this has become an extension of the responsibility commitment, and is a key component of the overall business model and structure. However, supply chain management needs to deal with many difficulties to coordinate the actors of the supply chain. One of these difficulties is a wider range of risks. These include political, economic, social, environmental, legal and technological risks. The objective of this paper is to highlight, through the theoretical literature, some of the challenges and difficulties of supply chains and to constitute the strategies of resilience sustainable supply chain practices.

Chapter 4: Government Engagement in Green Supply Chain Management of Food and Beverage Companies

This case study-based chapter investigates the influence of government regulations on the green supply chain management practices of five renowned companies which are classified in group A by Carbon Disclosure Project (CDP): Ajinomoto Group, Asahi Group, Coca-Cola Company, Barry Callebaut, and Danone. Considering their commitment to sustainability and presence in the high-impact sector of food and beverages, this chapter analyzes the impact of government interventions on these companies' supply chains. Their CDP responses, sustainability reports, and relevant literature were qualitatively analyzed using the cross-case analysis method to investigate collaborative strategies enabling low-carbon transitions in these companies. Based on the analysis, environmental sustainability dimensions were devised that demand substantial engagement with governments and regulatory authorities. Implications of the study are manifold as it not only provides recommendations for effective government-industry partnerships in the food sector but also provides the basis for further research in this area.

Chapter 5: The Integration of China's Belt and Road Initiative into Global Supply Chains: New Pathways for Social and Environmental Responsibility

This chapter uses the German Supply Chain Act as a lens to examine the impact on Corporate Social Responsibility (CSR) of China's Belt and Road Initiative (BRI) and global supply chain management techniques. China's BRI seeks to improve infrastructure, trade, and investment links with various nations. This chapter describes the BRI and how it may alter global supply chains in ways that raise or lower risks and possibilities related to sustainability and human rights. The chapter analyzes China's potential to advance green and socially responsible business practices along the BRI. A novel Chinese interpretation of the German Supply Chain Act and its potential application inside the BRI are discussed. The chapter highlights the importance of worker rights and environmental preservation as it addresses the potential of technologies like blockchain inside the BRI framework to improve transparency, accountability, and traceability. The chapter also emphasizes the financial advantages of ethical supply chain management.

Chapter 6: The Evolution of Food Supply Chain Management in China

During recent years, the Supply Chain Act was adapted to deal with human rights abuses and environmental protection in supply chains, as a way to motivate companies to integrate corporate responsibilities in their decisions. This directive can intervene without being transposed into national laws in other countries, where the actors of the supply chain exist. The Act provides penalties for companies that don't have plans for respecting human rights and environmental protection. For this reason, companies need to have information channels to report possible breaches of the law. One of the critical supply chains is the food supply chain, which needs to assure food safety, in addition to other requirements determined by law, across the global supply chain, by coordinating food related businesses in each supply chain. In this study, we will analyze different companies, which transformed their supply chain following different crises and adapting new supply chain management laws. The example studies in this research can be used by other companies in their supply chain transformation.

Chapter 7: A Framework for Exploring the Global Performance of Service Supply Chain Management: A Qualitative Study

Contemporary managerial thinking and practices have been developed in an economic context dominated by industrial logic. This logic conceals the imposing weight of services. Logistics is an activity that is undergoing major changes due to new technologies and managerial innovations. The advent of the Supply Chain Service (SSCM), as a dual concept combining both traditional supply operations and the coordination of various resources, with a view to customer satisfaction, while integrating constraints of time, capacity, shared resources and co-production, has turned logistics research upside down. The purpose of this paper is to establish a qualitative analysis of the impact of MCSS practices on the performance of the service company. The theoretical analysis and the review of interviews show that SSCM approaches differ and that company performance is viewed differently depending on each SSCM practice and also depending on the multiple facets of this performance. Based on this qualitative review, several observations are identified.

Chapter 8: Big Data Supply Chain Management and Its Legal Context

The new digital tools can significantly improve the performance of supply chains. That means, the digitalization has the potential to provide companies with a range of practices to significantly reduce costs, increase product availability, improve access to information, and enhance responsiveness, collaboration, supply chain visibility, and resilience. One of the potentials of the digitalization is to explore big data. In fact, the quantitative explosion of data gave birth to Big Data in order to find new ways of analyzing and exploring the data. It offers the possibility to treat and analyze a huge amount of data in order to make conclusions and take decisions. Benefits such as cost reducing, better managing or even precise forecasting are possible with the big data. But a lot of companies have faced big problems such as data leaking, privacy violation. This paper will study big data supply chain management and its legal context based on a literature review and gives future directions for governments, companies and researchers.

Chapter 9: Digital Marketing Based on Machine Learning

The scan hole assessment revealed that some care was given to the behavior of marketers in relation to ML devices and their selection and use to aid critical and operational management. Examination introduced spotlights the choice and reception of ML-driven scientific devices by three particular gatherings: showcasing offices, media organizations, and promoters. The discoveries feature are as - the significant job of canny explanatory instruments in the creation and arrangement of showcasing methodologies, the absence of information about developing innovations, for example, ML and man-made consciousness, the likely use of ML devices in advertising, and; 4) the low degree of reception and using ML-driven scientific devices in promoting the board. A system comprising empowering agents as well as a procedure map was created to assist associations with recognizing the chances and effectively executing ventures that are arranged toward the sending and appropriation of the scientific ML instruments in advanced promoting.

Chapter 10: Drivers of Sustainable Supply Chain Management using Internet of Things Based Blockchain Technology

Information technologies are transforming conventional supply chain management (SCM) business practices and positively influencing sustainability. In particular, Blockchain Technology and the Internet of Things (IoT) are two important examples that play a significant role in sustainable supply chain management (SSCM). This chapter reviewed the impact of these technologies on SSCM separately and with their combination of forward and reversed supply chains. Academics and practitioners have studied the effects of these technologies on sustainability separately earlier, but integrating these technologies can lead to different insights and disclose several opportunities. Besides, the chapter highlights essential factors in developing blockchain and IoT to know the modern trends for industry automation, challenges, and future research opportunities on supply chain sustainability. Finally, the chapter presents an IoT-based service-oriented blockchain architecture for supply chain information systems that manifest the information-driven sustainability of the supply chain operation.

Chapter 11: A Mobile Social App for Better Life of Poor People Based on Perceived Similarity and Trust Using Supply Chain Management

As an attempt to collaborate the digital world with the physical one, we maintain track of the journey of dairy products, clothes, watches, bags, etc any type of material from producer to consumer. We can use the strength of internet technology and its extensive network, by which individuals can assist one other with only a click from their phone, to satisfy the growing need for advances in donation facilities and services. The suggested system for stuff donation aims to give needy people an online platform for giving clothes, books, or any unneeded things. Users can sign up for this system by providing the required information. Once registered, users can add a post either for giving donations or for requesting a donation. Using our app we can supply all the items outside of the country. Today, supply chain management is one of the most important usable ways for NGO to earn competitive benefits.

Chapter 12: Building Resilient Supply Chains to Natural Disasters

Firms may face internal or external risks. While internal risks can be managed with the firm's existing tangible or intangible resources, some of the external risks are not problems that firms can overcome with their own resources. When faced with these risks, firms can only try to minimize their losses. Natural disasters can be referred to as such external risks. This study examines the impact of earthquake, a type of natural disaster, on firms and supply chains. Earthquakes affect not only the firm or the country directly affected by the disaster, but also all supply chains, which have become more complex and sophisticated due to globalization. In order to create resilient supply chains, the shares of global firms during the earthquake process are analyzed and recommendations are developed.

Chapter 13: The Implementation of the Agenda 2030 on Sustainable Development: Focus on the Republic of Serbia

The 2030 Agenda for Sustainable Development is a plan with global implications, and the international community expects the nations that have signed it to devote all of their resources. The subject of the chapter is research on the Implementation of the Agenda 2030 on Sustainable Development, in the Republic of Serbia. The accomplishment of the sustainable adopted goals, which aim to promote honorable labor, an inclusive economy, and other aspects that might lead to a better society is crucial for Serbia. The main goal of the chapter is to establish, based on certain indicators, whether and to what extent the Republic of Serbia has embarked on the path of sustainable development. Since almost half of the time allotted for achieving sustainability goals has already passed, the author wishes to emphasize the urgency of ensuring the necessary preconditions for the implementation of Agenda 2030 in the Republic of Serbia and progress towards achieving it, in cooperation with the public and private sectors, the academic community, civil society organizations, and citizens.

Chapter 14: The Role of Government in Promoting Sustainable Procurement

This book chapter examines the crucial role of government in promoting sustainable procurement, which is an important tool for achieving sustainable development goals. The chapter provides an overview of sustainable procurement, its benefits, and challenges, and discusses the potential for government to use procurement policies to promote sustainability. The chapter highlights the importance of government leadership, legal frameworks, and institutional capacity for the effective implementation of sustainable procurement practices. The chapter also provides examples of successful sustainable procurement initiatives from around the world and identifies key lessons learned. The chapter concludes with recommendations for government action to promote sustainable procurement, including the need for strategic planning, stakeholder engagement, and ongoing monitoring and evaluation.

Chapter 15: Analysis of the Sustainability of Supply Chains and Value Chain Management: Economy in the Republic of Serbia

The philosophy of the supply chain concept is aimed at the greatest possible alignment of key business functions of all links in the distribution chain in the process of organizing goods and information flows. Applying the concept of an integrated supply chain between multiple organizations further increases the importance of operational logistics activities, improves process optimizations, and confirms the importance of logistics performance for profitability. Emphasis is placed on the sustainability of the supply chain in Serbia, but also on the broader context of the value chain of economic sectors in the Republic of Serbia. The aim of the chapter is focused on highlighting both positive and limiting factors (the real situation), with the author's wish that the recommendation of good practice and the results of this research be implemented in Serbia.

A CONCLUSION OF HOW THE BOOK IMPACTS

The book is written to cover the interests of a wide variety of audiences ranging from academic researchers, students and practitioners. It features a collection of contributions related to the government impact on sustainable and responsible supply chain management.

This work is an excellent book that pool together the literature related to application of sustainability and responsibility in supply chains, and presents some new methods and approaches as well. This book is clearly written and makes good use of tables and diagrams to illustrate the government impact on sustainable and responsible supply Chain management.

I recommend this book for a variety of audiences: professors, researchers, students and practitioners who are interested to obtain a good understanding of the current state of the government impact on sustainable and responsible supply Chain management.

Atour Taghipour
Normandy University, France

REFERENCES

Cauchois, R., Taghipour, A., Kang, D., Zoghlami, N., & Abed, M. (2017). Advanced Solutions for a Supply Chain with Stochastic Information. *Journal of Advanced Management Science, 5(*1).

Loivet, W., Taghipour, A., & Kang, D. S. (2020). The Rise of Green Supply Chain Management: Between Complexity and Necessity. Journal of Economics. *Business and Management*, *8*(1), 1–7.

Sahraoui, A., Tran, N. K., Tliche, Y., Kacem, A., & Taghipour, A. (2023). Examining ICT Innovation for Sustainable Terminal Operations in Developing Countries: A Case Study of the Port of Radès in Tunisia. *Sustainability (Basel)*, *15*(11), 9123. doi:10.3390u15119123

Taghipour, A. (2014). Improving the Plan of a Manufacturing Network with Non-Integrated Business Units. [IJAL]. *International Journal of Applied Logistics*, *5*(2), 1–11. doi:10.4018/ijal.2014040101

Taghipour, A., Abed, M., & Zoghlami, N. (2015, May). Design for remanufacturing respecting reverse logistics processes: A review. In 2015 4th International Conference on Advanced Logistics and Transport (ICALT) (pp. 299-304). IEEE. 10.1109/ICAdLT.2015.7136602

Taghipour, A., Fooladvand, A., Khazaei, M., & Ramezani, M. (2023). Criteria Clustering and Supplier Segmentation Based on Sustainable Shared Value Using BWM and PROMETHEE. *Sustainability (Basel)*, *15*(11), 8670. doi:10.3390u15118670

Taghipour, A., & Frayret, J. M. (2011a). A new heuristic search with local optimization to manage a supply chain. *Meta*, 15.

Taghipour, A., & Frayret, J. M. (2011b). Supply chain coordination planning: A review. Work paper, École polytechnique de Montréal.

Taghipour, A., Khazaei, M., Azar, A., Rajabzadeh Ghatari, A., Hajiaghaei-Keshteli, M., & Ramezani, M. (2022). Creating shared value and strategic corporate social responsibility through outsourcing within supply chain management. *Sustainability (Basel)*, *14*(4), 1940. doi:10.3390u14041940

Taghipour, A., Khazaei, M., Azar, A., Rajabzadeh Ghatari, A., Hajiaghaei-Keshteli, M., & Ramezani, M. (2022a). Creating Shared Value and Strategic Corporate Social Responsibility through Outsourcing within Supply Chain Management. *Sustainability (Basel)*, *14*(4), 1940. doi:10.3390u14041940

Taghipour, A., Murat, S., & Huang, P. (2021). E-Supply Chain Management: A Review. International Journal of e-Education, e-Business, e-. *Management Learning*, *11*(2), 51–61.

Taghipour, A., Ramezani, M., Khazaei, M., Roohparvar, V., & Hassannayebi, E. (2023). Smart Transportation Behavior through the COVID-19 Pandemic: A Ride-Hailing System in Iran. *Sustainability (Basel)*, *15*(5), 4178. doi:10.3390u15054178

Taghipour, A., Rouyendegh, B. D., Ünal, A., & Piya, S. (2022b). Selection of suppliers for speech recognition products in IT projects by combining techniques with an integrated fuzzy MCDM. *Sustainability (Basel)*, *14*(3), 1777. doi:10.3390u14031777

Tliche, Y., Taghipour, A., & Canel-Depitre, B. (2020). An improved forecasting approach to reduce inventory levels in decentralized supply chains. *European Journal of Operational Research*, *287*(2), 511–527. doi:10.1016/j.ejor.2020.04.044

Acknowledgment

The editor would like to acknowledge the help of all the people involved in this project and, more specifically, to the authors and reviewers that took part in the review process. Without their support, this book would not have become a reality.

First, the editor would like to thank each one of the authors for their contributions. Our sincere gratitude goes to the chapter's authors who contributed their time and expertise to this book.

Second, the editor wishes to acknowledge the valuable contributions of the reviewers regarding the improvement of quality, coherence, and content presentation of chapters. Most of the authors also served as referees; we highly appreciate their double task.

Atour Taghipour
Normandy University, France

Chapter 1
A French Guide for Businesses and Governments to Integrate the Concept of Sustainable Development Into Their Supply Chains

XiaoWen Lu
Normandy University, France

Atour Taghipour
Normandy University, France

ABSTRACT

Sustainable development is a new form of development that meets the needs of the present without compromising the ability of future generations to meet theirs. In this context, sustainable development needs to be at the crossroads between three pillars: the economic pillar, the social pillar, and the environmental pillar. But the question is raised: how do companies integrate the notion of sustainable development internally into their supply chain process? To answer this question, based on a literature review, the authors are interested in two points in particular. First, they will see the implementation of sustainable development in the production process and the change in costs, then in terms of the new internal systems of corporate social responsibility. The results of this work can be used by governments, companies, and researchers to integrate sustainable development in their decisions.

INTRODUCTION

The environment is the essence of human life. Air, water, oxygen, fauna and flora are part of our hemisphere and are essential to life. They are important resources, which is why they must be respected and taken into consideration as a whole. This is why we talk about sustainable development. Indeed, sustain-

DOI: 10.4018/978-1-6684-9062-4.ch001

able development is made up of several indicators, such as: gross national product, human development index, indicator of economic and social well-being, etc., but its primary goal is to strive to meet the needs of the present without compromising the ability to meet those of future generations (Brundtland WCED report, 1987). However, this concept is only beginning to come into fashion at the end of the 20th century. Indeed, in the 1960s, this notion of sustainable development was not as important as it is today. Industrialists and politicians focused instead on mass production, with innovation and money-making as a priority (Taghipour, 2014). It was only in the 1970s that mentalities began to change. Humans are gradually becoming aware of the degradation of the environment (Taghipour, 2020). In the 1980s, researchers highlighted the depletion or even the extinction of certain natural resources necessary for our survival as well as for industries. It was only in the 80s and 90s that society became aware of sustainable development and that new industrial and political governance emerged. Therefore, environmental protection and human living conditions are intertwined. However, few manufacturers feel concerned by this problem. As a result, a few years later at the Stockholm conference, the link between rising population growth and ever-increasing needs is mentioned, since these two notions influence industrialization, which aims to be ever more competitive. This endangers the environment since the need is stronger than the available resources.

It was not until the early 2000s that the sustainable environment became mandatory in companies. Indeed, the sustainable development movement is gaining momentum. Faced with developments and changes in society, the sustainable environment can be an enriching opening for companies, since they will care about people and put them at the center of their concerns, which will give a new air to management, opening new debates. However, it is a complex concept, since it implies for a company to position itself between its short-term constraints and its long-term vision. By engaging in sustainable development, companies must be economically viable, socially responsible and environmentally sound (Dubuisson-Quellier, 2009). This is why many of them are committed to a CSR (Corporate Social Responsibility) approach. As a result, companies constrained by these laws will take the opportunity to review their communication and gain notoriety. CSR aims to enable companies to better respond to the challenges they face such as the demand for transparency, the climate, or supply (Cauchois et al., 2017). Measuring the environmental impact will allow companies to better identify and anticipate the risks they face in order to identify opportunities, which in the long term will enhance their image (Taghipour et al., 2014). As a result, in order to reduce their environmental impact, companies have had to improve their Supply Chain and their production process (Colin, 2005). In the 1960s, organizations faced logistical problems in the field, so they had to find solutions to facilitate the transport of flows between territories (Savy, 2011). In addition, marketing greatly influences the quantities to be sold or transported. Indeed, over time consumption has changed; consumers increasingly tend to look for "rare" "personalized" and "quality" goods and in order to create the need, marketers create attractive advertisements (Gabriel, 2003). As a result, companies must adapt to the growing quantities. Supply chain management will therefore allow companies to take into consideration several logistics tools in order to group together several functions of the organization in a single management system (Akono and Fernandes, 2009). The main objective of this new operation is therefore to gain in effectiveness (these are the results obtained according to the objectives that the company has set itself) and in efficiency (the result obtained by a company on its productivity) (Benko, 2001). We can therefore qualify the Supply Chain as being a chain linking different functions of a company in order to be as efficient as possible in terms of transport, costs, etc. The primary objective is therefore to optimize supply flows (Taghipour et al., 2021), in order to reduce the complexity of the company and optimize flows (Taghipour and Frayret, 2011a & 2011b). Therefore, the main objective of a company is to make profit, cash and create value. According to PORTER, to achieve this optimally, companies must choose or combine two strategies:

- Pricing strategy: concerns companies seeking to sell in "volume" (large quantities) by reducing their prices in order to sell their products at a lower price. Companies will therefore play on prices by developing economies of scale (e.g. Ryanair, Aldi, etc.)
- Quality strategy: concerns companies that seek to produce and sell "high quality" products and thus play on quality to sell their more expensive products (e.g. luxury French brands, perfumery, lingerie, etc.).

This is why it seems important to us to take an interest in: How do companies integrate the notion of sustainable development internally into the production process?

For this we are interested in two points in particular. First, we will see the implementation of sustainable development in the production process and the change in costs, then in terms of the new internal systems (CSR).

THE IMPLEMENTATION OF SUSTAINABLE DEVELOPMENT IN THE PRODUCTION PROCESS AND COST CHANGES

The Change of the Raw Materials

In industries, the use of raw materials is fundamental in the production process. They will be used in the manufacture of a semi-finished or finished product, these require a major transformation to achieve the expected result. It is therefore a major pole in terms of costs because there is a lot of loss and waste. This point represents a significant cost to the company so it would be interesting to know the composition of the raw materials, to know which ones consume the least and especially which ones pollute the least in this process. It is then that we can focus on the context of industrial ecology (Diemer and Labrune, 2007). It is characterized as "the set of practices intended to reduce industrial pollution" according to ROBERT FROSCH.

This concept will consider new manufacturing processes that can reduce industrial pollution. Moreover, the major problem comes from the fact that human activity cannot be separated from natural resources to produce. Thus, the production of goods and services will always have an impact on the ecosystem. There are two visions to this complex situation, the first is scientific vision and the second is economic vision (Meunier and Zéroual, 2006). Indeed, for scientists the environment is coming to the depletion of its resources, it is therefore impossible to continue to proceed in the same way. For economists, it is necessary to meet the needs of the growing population. The situation being linked, it is urgent to find a correlation between these two visions. The today's objective is therefore to present the concept of sustainable development in a society that is hyper-industrialized. It is therefore necessary to optimize energy and material consumption, to reduce waste directly at the source (Sirieix and Le Borgne, 2016). What that makes people understand today is that it is necessary to know how to consume better and less. Finally, we understand that the best solution would be to organize the production process with an internal recycling concept within the company. Indeed, re-using off-cuts, waste, would allow the production process to be more efficient and thus cost less (Yang et al., 2017). Indeed, by reusing material already purchased, this should make it possible to considerably reduce costs and thus optimize the value chain. Thus, for some companies it is good to change this dimension because the production process is the one that consumes the most in terms of energy, but also the one that is the most possible to improve thanks to sustainable development. In this case, we can say that it is necessary to put in place industrial processes that allow this change or the improvement of raw materials. We can take the example of the transformation of petroleum-based raw materials, which can be changed into polymeric materials (these are materials such as starch or proteins which are much more respectful of the environment than materials from oil base). Other materials "pollute" more, this is the case of iron materials that companies will have to change to platinum. In reality, companies will have to do the cost calculations to know if it is a real advantage to consider a change of equipment. This is called "eco-efficiency", which makes it possible to calculate the correlation between the environmental value and the impact of economic activities. Thus, we understand from this research that the most important thing is that companies have the possibility of changing the way they produce, while the environment cannot evolve and "change" or "produce more" resources (Nadia et al., 2020).

This is why we understand that change must come internally, and in particular by installing new machines that allow recycling, or by changing raw materials. In addition to the raw materials to be changed, recycled, there is the principle of recycling of the finished products which must also be constantly improved. This means that semi-finished products must be consigned so companies can re-use products already used in previous sales. All this is beneficial not only in terms of costs but also ecologically.

Another very important point is "productivism", this is defined as the modernization of production in general. Thus, there is some improvement mainly through innovation; productivism combines new technologies and the rationalization of production (Merimi and Taghipour, 2021). This aspect considers different dimensions such as the environment, health and social. Thus, with this new "productivist" model, there will be many more "sustainable", "ethical" or even "responsible" certifications. This technique is very present especially in the food industry. Nevertheless, productivism also extends to the industrial domain (Fouilleux and Goulet, 2012).

The Change of Transport

Transport is what pollutes the most in the Supply Chain, it is also the one with the highest costs. Indeed, this creates negative externalities in production as well as for the protection of the environment, which is impacted by modes of transport (Shin and Taghipour, 2021). In addition, the transport of goods is much more important than the transport of passengers so this creates a major imbalance, which pollutes all the more. This will therefore focus on freight transport, which involves the transport of goods. For this, European policy has sustainable development objectives for this type of transport. Thus, the notion of green development will be considered, it has the definition of "contributing to economic prosperity, social well-being, and this without harming the environment and human health," according to CEMT (Laville, 2009). The objective of European policies is therefore to reduce CO2 emissions as much as possible while taking economic activity into account. Therefore, the biggest decision initially would be to liberalize rail transport on the principle of market forces, in which case competition would be more important. In other words, the principle would be to "leave" the market to apply certain new rules, for example of a financial nature, in this case the policies could apply regulations on fuels and then allow a drop-in price, in this case industries could focus on an alternative mode of transport (non-road), and less polluting. In addition, changing the infrastructure would be necessary for a smooth running.

The choice of transport is therefore essential to limit the impacts on these two aspects (economic and environmental). In addition, this could make it possible to reduce the costs mainly and thus improve the optimization of the transport. In fact, transport is becoming a priority because, according to the book "Secure of supplies" of November 2000, the energy consumption of transport was very high because it represented 28% of CO2 emissions in 1998, but with increasing globalization, the transport pollution is still increasing. At the time, the report already showed us a 50% increase between 1990 and 2010. Nowadays, we understand that pollution has exceeded this peak. This is especially present because road transport is the most important, but companies need to minimize road transport (which alone accounted for 84% of CO2 emissions) to focus on rail transport, because it pollutes much less on the one hand and it would be much less expensive because there would be more goods in the same wagon. However, road transport is much more flexible than that plane, boat or even train. Indeed, road transport has adapted infrastructures that are easier to set up. While for other transport it is necessary to obtain infrastructures that allow faster and more efficient delivery. In this case, it is all transport that must change, for example putting more train terminals, or even services set up from other client-supplier companies. On the other hand, air travel has accelerated rapidly, partly because the population wants "exotic" goods in a limited time. This is the principle of globalization. Thus, it is necessary to reduce this transport which is very expensive, but also one of the most polluting. We then understand that rail transport seems the most suitable for long-distance trade. It was also during the conference in Gothenburg, that this subject came to the fore, it was then that in 2012, the decision to establish many railway lines was voted. Thus, new structures have been put in place, but it must always be more important, because our consumption is too.

At another time, it is necessary to change the mode of consumption of the population, we are used to receiving "foreign" products for a fairly short period. Thus, for all companies to take sustainable development as essential to their operation, non-polluting or less polluting transport should be considered. In other words, the speed of delivery by polluting transport should be considered as "unfair competition" or else a system of penalties should be established for the company, and rewarding so-called "clean" transport. Thus, we understand that the change of raw materials but also of the production process seems necessary to optimize costs and integrate the concept of sustainable development into the company. This change therefore allows a reduction in costs but which will initially lead to a change which could be costly. In addition, consumers are increasingly vigilant about the manufacture of the product, its origin and its respect for the environment. Thus, improving the production process will improve the image of the company or increase sales and customer loyalty.

NEW INTERNAL SYSTEMS (RSE)

Changing Consumer Mindset

Consumption has undergone various changes over the years and centuries. Indeed, in the days of Taylor and Ford, companies mass-produced standardized goods. The objective is to increase productivity yields. As a result, consumers settled for utilitarian and standard goods. However, at the end of the 20th century, new goods appeared, more numerous and more diversified, following the appearance of supermarkets and hypermarkets in the 1960s, which brought France into the era of mass distribution. Large-scale distribution has led to an upheaval in terms of organization, relationship with customers, assortment but also the price. This is an innovative concept from a commercial point of view, aiming to adapt the distribution to the changes in its environment, in particular concerning the evolution of consumption (Fraisse, 1996). To achieve this, companies wish to offer an offer adapted to consumer expectations by seeking to anticipate their needs (Daumas, 2006).

This American concept of supermarket and self-service, which appeared at the time of the Thirty Glorious (A three-decade period that began with the reconstruction of post-war France in 1945), had difficulty establishing itself in French culture. However, over the years, it has become commonplace, in particular due to the fact that consumers are more urban, but also more in a hurry. Moreover, they do not seek quality in their purchases but an attractive and low price (Mahfod et al., 2019). At that time, the country was in reconstruction following the Second World War, so consumers attached importance to the prices of goods (Capron and Quairel-Lanoizelée, 2020). But as the world is confronted with climatic changes linked to global warming. Associations such as Greenpeace will conduct campaigns to raise awareness among the population, especially large companies. Indeed, this association is financed by donations, and seeks to protect the environment (fight against pollution, deforestation, support sustainable fishing and energy transition, etc.). As a result, these new campaigns to fight for the environment will impact consumers on their consumption habits, and certain companies on their way of producing. Indeed, consumers will seek to consume better and will be concerned about the ethics of the products they consume. This phenomenon has also been reinforced with the appearance of organic but also following the Coronavirus health crisis. They are ready to consume less but better, and therefore to pay more for quality products that respect the environment and act for a better world, for them and future generations. Consumption mentalities are changing and are increasingly oriented towards solidarity (local consumption). Some companies will engage in a CSR approach, more responsible towards the environment in order to fight against the disappearance of the natural resources necessary for their production, or to return a positive brand image in line with the values of its consumers but also its employees (Paradas, 2011).

Implementation of a CSR Approach

A company aims to make cash, but without its employees this would not be possible. Indeed, employees occupy an important place within organizations. They have economic power over the company due to the know-how they make available to it. This is why it is necessary for companies to take employees into consideration in the production process. Indeed, poor management as well as values in opposition to the image conveyed by the company can lead to turnover, an increase in the rate of absenteeism, strikes or even burn outs, which would generate additional costs. It is therefore necessary for companies to be aware of the shared values expected of their employees. In addition, companies are subject to environmental regulations such as: anti-pollution of air, water, soil but also concerning waste management. This is why some companies engage in a CSR approach. Indeed, this CSR (corporate social responsibility) approach has appeared in order to denounce predatory behavior with regard to the environment but also the health of workers and their working conditions due to the rapidity of the diffusion of new technologies and the rational factors (Taghipour and Merimi, 2021). The emergence of this theme is due to the search of our modern societies for new benchmarks in the face of the upheavals with which they are confronted, such as: globalization, the threat of ecological resources, the development of the information society, etc. This approach therefore constitutes new economic, social and ecological rules (Vosooghidizaji et al., 2020 & 2022). Consequently, the concept of CSR corresponds to the implementation of sustainable development by companies, and the ISO 26000 standard makes it possible to represent the guidelines of this approach at the international level (Cadet, 2010).

CSR therefore offers a new vision that can evolve over time. It's not something innate. This process is built. CSR therefore allows companies to better respond to the challenges they face such as: the demand for transparency, the climate, or supply. Measuring its environmental impact will allow companies to better identify the risks it faces and therefore better control them in order to try to identify new opportunities (Essid and Berland, 2011). In the long term, this will represent an advantage for the company, particularly with regard to its image (Tliche et al. 2019 and 2021). Indeed, this allows it to develop its competitiveness by internally retaining its best employees. However, in this approach, large companies are subject to more and more regulations such as extra-financial reporting requiring them to publish information on their environmental and social impacts, or duty of vigilance set up in 2017 aimed at preventing environmental, social or even governance risks.

The goal sought by companies that practice CSR is therefore to have a positive impact on society, but also to respect the environment, while being economically viable. By committing to CSR, companies must voluntarily integrate the legal dimensions imposed by implementing good practices, adapted to their company. It is therefore an internal co-construction in which action must be taken on three levels: human rights, the environment and ethics. CSR is therefore the most responsible approach for companies that undertake to do their best, by questioning their responsibility. They may have to ask themselves different questions such as: How to recruit employees in a less unequal way? How to reduce the impact of their activity on the environment? How to promote its economic impact?

To do so, companies can hire people with disabilities or promote local employment in order to have a positive impact on society. In order to limit their environmental impact, they can use clean technologies, such as wind turbines or recycling (Temri, 2011). Regarding the economic impact, companies can generate virtuous actions through the transparency of payments or the fair distribution of their profits among stakeholders. These three criteria allow companies to understand the risks and thus maintain the overall performance of the company (Taghipour, and Beneteau-Piet, 2020). But the more the company respects its commitment, the more its brand image will be favored in the eyes of consumers and stakeholders. Nevertheless, it is increasingly important for companies to be able to measure their environmental impacts and for this some of them use cleaner technologies and manufacture green products and services (Loivet et al., 2020).

Indeed, initially in order to establish the environmental concept within the company, this one must in ensure its planning (Taghipour, 2018) thanks to the tools such as: EMAS (Economy management and audit scheme) or via the eco -concept or the ISO 14000 law Indeed, the ISO 14000 law makes it possible to translate the convictions of companies into effective actions for the planet. It defines the criteria for effective environmental management (Taghipour et al., 2015).

For this, companies can use more environmentally friendly means of production such as drones to monitor protected areas and have access to information, however despite their usefulness these new technologies are not very ecological, they are not made up of recycled component (El-Nemr et al, 2017 et 2021). Nevertheless, there are certain technologies called eco-technologies. Indeed, these consist of technologies but avoid the formation of pollutants during the production processes and make it possible to reduce the discharge of all polluting substances into the environment, such as: wind turbines, recycling, solar panels and etc. These new technologies will complement or even replace human labour. This is why in our production system we still have to anticipate these changes in technology and thus be able to adapt the know-how of our employees to them. Indeed, new technologies have a life cycle, which consequently establishes a life cycle of knowledge.

Indeed, when a new technology develops, it is necessary at the same time to develop knowledge in line with it in order to be able to understand it and work on it. However, after a while there will be a breaking point. This point indicates that the technology will change, in other words, a new one appears. Therefore, at the breaking point employees will abandon the knowledge and skills they have acquired to develop new ones. Therefore, innovation is nothing more than the reuse of old skills combined with new ones, and this alliance will allow companies to combine skills with resources. Consequently, if companies engage in a CSR approach and opt for new production methods that are more respectful of the environment, its organization will change and its employees will have to be trained or at least made aware of these new methods, in order to create a co-construction internally.

Provide Business Ethics

Companies engaged in a CSR approach undertake to be more respectful of the environment, but this represents a cost for them. Nevertheless, nowadays consumers are more and more concerned about the products they consume. They seek quality and prefer to pay more to acquire a product worthy of their ethics.

As a result, CSR will thus allow the company to enhance its brand image, both internally with its employees, collaborators, investors and in the eyes of its consumers. Nevertheless, care must be taken with greenwashing. This is why, in order to prevent consumers or investors from making mistakes, there has been a ceremony taking place in Paris for a few years now, called the "Pinocchio Prize". This prize is awarded by the association "Les Amis de la Terre" created in 1970 to protect people and the environment, with the aim of illustrating but also denouncing the negative impacts of certain French companies, which are in total contradiction with the terms "sustainable development" or even "green marketing" which they use abundantly. This prize makes it possible to "promote" companies deemed guilty, in order to expose them to criticism so that they assume their so-called "sustainable" behavior. In other words, it is the prize awarded to the "biggest liar". The companies nominated during this ceremony see their image tarnished in the eyes of consumers and their stakeholders.

This is why it is important for a company to be honest, so as not to tarnish its reputation. A company must ensure that it is in line with the values it shares. Therefore, a committed company will have to invest in wind turbines, solar panels, etc., to stand out and meet its commitments. But this investment will not be in vain since its sales will increase since its "green" products (which have not polluted during their production or which are made of recycled or organic products) correspond to consumer expectations.

CONCLUSION

Globalization is the functioning process of our society. Indeed, the use of the IDPP (International Division of the production process) promotes international transport and cheaper labor. However, this has a very significant ecological impact, but the ethical aspect is also addressed in this context. Indeed, on a "Marketing" level, it is preferable initially to praise the ecological qualities of a company but also those of respect for human rights (example: Nike has faced various problems, which have pushed the company to change its marketing but also its way of managing).

Thus, marketing allows companies to obtain a certain legitimacy. Indeed, it makes it possible to redefine the social environment of the company. Previously, the objective of a company was mainly the creation of earnings, wealth in terms of production essentially. We then found ourselves in the context of mass consumption, which today no longer makes sense. Nowadays the population is more concerned about its environment and does not support organizations that boast of their mass production qualities. This is why consumers prefer to support a smaller but environmentally friendly activity (such as SMEs for example) (Paradas, 2006).

Marketing, and in particular nowadays "GREEN Marketing" is therefore a tool allowing companies to express their values. Nevertheless, the brand image they reflect must be in line with the values they advocate in their communications but also with their commitments.

However, you still have to be careful, since all the companies that say they respect their environment or are committed to a CSR approach do not respect the concept. Indeed, some companies practice greenwashing, that is to say they say they respect the CSR approach but when they take an interest in them by questioning their employees, we realize that there is a real lack of responsibility on their part. As a result, companies practicing greenwashing are not being honest with consumers. They mislead them regarding their environmental performance or the environmental benefits of their products. Nevertheless, greenwashing will have negative consequences for the companies concerned, such as the decline or even the loss of confidence among consumers and green investors.

Large companies tend to practice more greenwashing than SMEs, since they have more resources and a stronger reputation. Consequently, the repercussions will be less since their consumers are loyal to their products (consumption habits). However, some consumers are tired of being deceived by large groups, which is why some choose to consume less but better. In addition, in order to prevent consumers or investors from being "deceived", there is the "Pinocchio Prize" which is awarded to "so-called green" companies, which practice green marketing in their communication and which claim to be committed, but in the end, who are in total contradiction between what they say they are and what they are. This prize makes it possible to denounce companies that "cheat" and thus allow consumers, investors, or even the stakeholders of a company to no longer be mistaken.

The environment has become an important factor to consider. It is therefore necessary for companies to take it into consideration in their production system. Investing in eco-technologies can be interesting. This represents a cost but subsequently can make it possible to make savings on the direct costs of the companies with regard to production costs (wind turbines, solar panels (lower electricity costs). However, without having to invest Importantly, companies can initially engage in a CSR approach. However, for this to work, this approach must be desired by the company and the latter must commit to respecting its commitments. Thus, internally employees will be satisfied and proud to work in a respectful company. They will be more efficient and externally consumers will tend to pay more to obtain a healthy and quality product. Consequently, the company will increase its brand image, its notoriety and thus its sales.

Thus, we understand that the integration of an approach towards sustainable development is necessary within companies because it not only allows better optimization of costs, a "technological advance" which could make it possible to meet future government requests but also could restore their brand image and feel closer to the consumer. It is a costly approach at first but could allow a real "leap" in the industrial sector.

REFERENCES

Akono, D., & Fernandes, V. (2009). Impacts du développement durable sur les organisations logistiques. *Revue management et avenir*, (6), 241-255.

Benko, G. (2001). *Développement durable et systèmes productifs locaux. POMRNIER, P. Réseaux d'entreprises et territoires. Regards sur les systemes productifs locaux*. La Documentation Française.

Cadet, I. (2010). La norme ISO 26000 relative à la responsabilité sociétale: une nouvelle source d'usages internationaux. *Revue internationale de droit économique*, (4), 401-439.

Capron, M., & Quairel-Lanoizelée, F. (2020). *L'entreprise dans la société*. La Découverte.

Cauchois, R., Taghipour, A., Kang, D., Zoghlami, N., & Abed, M. (2017). Advanced solutions for a supply chain with stochastic information. *Journal of Advanced Management Science, 5*(1).

Colin, J. (2005). Le supply chain management existe-t-il réellement? *Revue française de gestion*, (3), 135-149.

Daumas, J. C. (2006). Consommation de masse et grande distribution: Une révolution permanente (1957-2005). *Vingtieme Siecle (Paris, France), 91*(3), 57–076. doi:10.3917/ving.091.76

Diemer, A., & Labrune, S. (2007). L'écologie industrielle: quand l'écosystème industriel devient un vecteur du développement durable. *Développement durable et territoires. Économie, géographie, politique, droit, sociologie*.

Dubuisson-Quellier, S. (2009). La consommation engagée. *Lectures, Les livres*.

El-Nemr, N., Canel-Depitre, B., & Taghipour, A. (2021). The determinants of hotel room rates in Beirut: A hedonic pricing model. International Journal of Trade. *Economics and Finance, 12*(2), 33–42.

El-Nemr, N., Canel-Depitre, B., & Taghipour, A. (2017, September). Determinants of hotel room rates. In *Marketing Trends Congress. Luxury Industries Conference London 2017*, London, England.

Essid, M., & Berland, N. (2011). Les impacts de la RSE sur les systèmes de contrôle. *Comptabilité-contrôle-audit, 17*(2), 59–88. doi:10.3917/cca.172.0059

Fouilleux, È., & Goulet, F. (2012). Firmes et développement durable: Le nouvel esprit du productivisme. *Etudes Rurales*, (190), 131–146. doi:10.4000/etudesrurales.9708

Fraisse, R. (1996). In Robert Rochefort, La Societe Des Consommateurs. Quinzaine Litteraire, 26-26.

Gabriel, P. (2003). Le marketing comme moyen de légitimation des, entreprises dans une perspective de développement durable. *Décisions marketing*, 67-76.

Laville, É. (2009). *L'entreprise verte: le développement durable change l'entreprise pour changer le monde*. Pearson Education France.

Loivet, W., Taghipour, A., & Kang, D. S. (2020). The rise of green supply chain management: Between complexity and necessity. *Journal of Economics. Business and Management, 8*(1), 1–7.

Mahfod, J., Canel-Depitre, B., & Taghipour, A. (2019). Quality function deployment-ELECTRE in supplier evaluation. *Journal of Advanced Management Science, 7*(4).

Martin, J. Y. (Ed.). (2014). *Développement durable?: Doctrines, pratiques, évaluations*. IRD Éditions.

Merimi, M., & Taghipour, A. (2021). Accelerating the digitalization of the supply chain: An empirical research about COVID-19 crisis. In *Digitalization of Decentralized Supply Chains During Global Crises* (pp. 1–24). IGI Global. doi:10.4018/978-1-7998-6874-3.ch001

Meunier, C., & Zéroual, T. (2006). Transport durable et développement économique. *Développement durable et territoires. Économie, géographie, politique, droit, sociologie.*

Nadia, E. N., Beatrice, C. D., & Atour, T. (2020). Luxury hotels' eco-friendly activities & customers' preferences and willingness to pay for green hotels. *Journal of Advanced Management Science, 8*(1).

Paradas, A. (2006). Perception du développement durable par des dirigeants de petites entreprises: résultats d'enquêtes. *actes du 8ème Congrès international francophone en entrepreneuriat et PME, Fribourg, Suisse.*

Paradas, A. (2011). Développement durable en petites entreprises: de la sensibilisation à l'engagement. *La Revue des sciences de gestion*, (1), 129-137.

Savy, M. (2011). *Le transport de marchandises*. Editions Eyrolles.

Shin, M., & Taghipour, A. (2021). Supply Chains Digital Transformation: Automated Underground Logistics Systems. *Underground Construction, 6*(2), 7. doi:10.18178/joebm.2021.9.2.651

Sirieix, L., & Le Borgne, G. (2016). *Vers de nouveaux modèles de consommation?* (No. hal-01595649).

Taghipour, A. (2014). *Production Network Planning Based on Constraint Relaxation and Discount Approach* (Vol. 2). Lecture Notes on Information Theory.

Taghipour, A. (2018). A Contemporary Approach to Plan Independent Logistics Actors. In *Contemporary Approaches and Strategies for Applied Logistics* (pp. 337–364). IGI Global. doi:10.4018/978-1-5225-5273-4.ch014

Taghipour, A. (Ed.). (2020). *Demand Forecasting and Order Planning in Supply Chains and Humanitarian Logistics*. IGI Global.

Taghipour, A., Abed, M., & Zoghlami, N. (2015, May). Design for remanufacturing respecting reverse logistics processes: A review. In 2015 4th International Conference on Advanced Logistics and Transport (ICALT) (pp. 299-304). IEEE. 10.1109/ICAdLT.2015.7136602

Taghipour, A., & Beneteau-Piet, C. (2020). Sustainable supply chain management performance. *International Journal of Innovation, Management and Technology, 11*(6), 165–169. doi:10.18178/ijimt.2020.11.6.897

Taghipour, A., & Frayret, J. M. (2011a). A new heuristic search with local optimization to manage a supply chain. *Meta*, 15.

Taghipour, A., & Frayret, J. M. (2011b). Supply chain coordination planning: A review. *Work paper, École polytechnique de Montréal.*

Taghipour, A., Glaa, B., & Zoghlami, N. (2014, May). Network coordination with minimum risk of information sharing. In *2014 International Conference on Advanced Logistics and Transport (ICALT)* (pp. 184-188). IEEE. 10.1109/ICAdLT.2014.6864115

Taghipour, A., & Merimi, M. (2021). Digital Transformation of Supply Chains during Crisis: COVID-19. In *11th Annual International Conference on Industrial Engineering and Operations Management, IEOM* (pp. 7493-7501).

Taghipour, A., Murat, S., & Huang, P. (2021). E-supply chain management: A review. International Journal of e-Education, e-Business, e-. *Management Learning, 11*(2), 51–61.

Temri, L. (2011). Innovations technologiques environnementales dans les petites entreprises: Proposition d'un modèle d'analyse. *Innovations (Paris), 34*(1), 11–36. doi:10.3917/inno.034.0011

Tliche, Y., Taghipour, A., & Canel-Depitre, B. (2019). Anticipation of Demand in Supply Chains. In *Hierarchical Planning and Information Sharing Techniques in Supply Chain Management* (pp. 1–45). IGI Global.

Tliche, Y., Taghipour, A., & Canel-Depitre, B. (2021). Exploring a Downstream Demand Inference Strategy in a Decentralized Two-Level Supply Chain. In *Demand Forecasting and Order Planning in Supply Chains and Humanitarian Logistics* (pp. 1–65). IGI Global. doi:10.4018/978-1-7998-3805-0.ch001

Vosooghidizaji, M., Taghipour, A., & Canel-Depitre, B. (2020). Information Asymmetry in Supply Chain Coordination: State of the Art. *Journal of Industrial and Intelligent Information Vol, 8*(2).

Vosooghidizaji, M., Taghipour, A., & Canel-Depitre, B. (2022). Coordinating corporate social responsibility in a two-level supply chain under bilateral information asymmetry. *Journal of Cleaner Production, 364*, 132627. doi:10.1016/j.jclepro.2022.132627

Yang, S., Taghipour, A., & Canel-Depitre, B. (2017, August). Cost optimization of reverse logistics: A review. In *Proceedings of the 7th International Conference on Information Communication and Management* (pp. 158-161). ACM. 10.1145/3134383.3134393

Chapter 2
The Role of Government Regulations on Business Practices in China:
Impact and Lessons for Global Sustainability

Youssef Elhaoussine
Beijing Normal University-Hong Kong Baptist University United International College, China

YiJiao Du
Beijing Normal University-Hong Kong Baptist University United International College, China

Huanchen Jia
Beijing Normal University-Hong Kong Baptist University United International College, China

ABSTRACT

As a growing major economic global power, China is currently dealing with pressing environmental issues necessitating the adoption of sustainable business practices. This review highlights the importance of sustainability and examines the role of Chinese regulations in driving sustainable business practices. Recognizing the pressing need to address environmental challenges, China has implemented a range of regulations aimed at fostering sustainability. The chapter emphasizes the significance of these regulations within Chinese industries. By analysing a variety of regulations, this review provides valuable insights into the mechanisms through which Chinese companies are incentivized to adopt sustainable practices and provides a deeper understanding of the regulatory frameworks that shape sustainability efforts in China. The findings highlight the importance of integrating sustainability into business operations and demonstrate how Chinese regulators play a central role in encouraging companies to embrace sustainable strategies.

DOI: 10.4018/978-1-6684-9062-4.ch002

INTRODUCTION

The concept of sustainability has garnered significant attention in recent years as businesses and organizations recognize the imperative to reduce their environmental impact and contribute to a more sustainable future. In today's business environment, companies have a heightened obligation to make their supply chains more sustainable (Taghipour et al., 2021). Such initiatives can lead to numerous benefits, including cost reductions, improved reputation, increased customer loyalty, and compliance with regulations. By embracing sustainability, companies also ensure long-term access to resources while minimizing negative impacts on the environment and communities. Additionally, the growing demand from consumers and investors for sustainable products and practices further emphasizes the need for businesses to prioritize sustainability (Taghipour and Merimi, 2021).

This global trend has not escaped the attention of governments worldwide. Governments are increasingly advocating for businesses and their supply chains to adopt sustainable practices for several reasons. Firstly, the unsustainable use of natural resources and the rise in pollution levels pose significant threats to the environment. They are keen for businesses to adopt more sustainable practices to minimize their environmental impact and contribute to the protection of the ecological system on which society and the public rely. Secondly, sustainable supply chains can enhance operational efficiency and reduce costs for businesses. By encouraging the adoption of sustainable practices, governments aim to improve the competitiveness of local businesses and foster economic growth. Thirdly, governments expect businesses to act responsibly and consider the impact of their operations on communities and workers (Taghipour et al., 2014). By promoting sustainable supply chains, governments aim to ensure that businesses create value without causing harm to the public. Finally, sustainability is now a global issue, and countries and their governments have obligations toward international initiatives and commitments such as the Paris Agreement or the Kyoto Protocol, which aim to reduce greenhouse gas emissions and protect the environment.

The role of governments in promoting sustainable supply chains is hence critical and can take various forms. Governments could play a key role in establishing regulations and standards for businesses to follow. These regulations and standards help ensure that businesses adopt sustainable practices and minimize the negative impact of their operations on the environment and society. Additionally, governments can utilize tax incentives to encourage businesses to adopt sustainable practices. Tax incentives can reduce the cost of implementing sustainable practices and provide rewards for companies that actively reduce their environmental impact. Examples include tax credits or rebates for companies investing in renewable energy projects or utilizing environmentally friendly materials. Furthermore, governments can also provide financial support and encouragement for the development of new sustainable technologies or processes. They can allocate funding to universities or directly to companies to facilitate research and development in sustainable technologies and processes.

China, as a leading manufacturing country coping with environmental issues, has implemented various regulations to promote sustainability in businesses and supply chains. In the following review, several Chinese regulations that aim to promote, enforce, or monitor sustainable development across industries and their supply chains will be presented. These regulations serve as examples of how the Chinese government is actively incentivizing companies to embrace sustainability and contribute to a more environmentally friendly and socially responsible business landscape.

China's significant progresses towards sustainable development position the country as an exemplary model for other nations seeking to implement sustainable business practices. With its comprehensive set of regulations and policies aimed at addressing environmental challenges, conserving energy, and managing resources efficiently, China effectively demonstrates its commitment to sustainability. The successful application of these practices in Chinese businesses highlights the feasibility and benefits of incorporating sustainability into various industries. As a result, China's experiences and achievements in sustainable development serve as valuable lessons and inspiration for other countries striving to adopt similar approaches. By sharing their best practices and lessons learned, China can play a key role in guiding and supporting other nations in their journey towards sustainable business practices and a more sustainable future for all.

Therefore, this article aims to highlight the importance of sustainability in business, focusing on Chinese regulations. It sheds some light on the pressing environmental and social challenges faced by China and emphasizes the need for integrating sustainable practices into business operations. Through a comprehensive review of various Chinese regulations, the article explores their role in promoting sustainable business practices, including environmental protection, energy conservation, resource management, and social responsibility. By describing and examining the effectiveness of these regulations and their impact on Chinese companies, it provides valuable insights into the power of regulations in driving sustainability.

This article uses a qualitative research approach to explore and analyse a sample of selected national and regional Chinese regulations promoting sustainable business practices, which proved to be successful. The methodology employed involves a review of existing literature and official government sources to gather comprehensive information on the regulations and their impact. By synthesizing and examining multiple sources of data, the article offers an overview of the regulatory landscape and its effectiveness in driving sustainability in China. The research methodology also involves critically evaluating the implementation of these regulations, examining case studies, and assessing their outcomes.

BACKGROUND

Sustainable Business Practices Through the Supply Chain

The journey towards a sustainable supply chain requires a dedicated commitment to implementing sustainable practices and fostering collaboration with suppliers, customers, and stakeholders (Taghipour and Frayret, 2011b). Through the adoption of various strategies, businesses can enhance the sustainability of their supply.

A key element in achieving sustainability goals is sustainable sourcing. This involves collaborating closely with suppliers to obtain materials and products in an environmentally friendly and socially responsible manner. By establishing sustainability standards, such as waste and emission reduction or the use of renewable energy sources, businesses can work hand in hand with their suppliers to implement sustainable practices (omit reference).

Another noteworthy strategy for promoting sustainability is lean manufacturing. The adoption of lean manufacturing practices, which also emphasize waste reduction and efficiency maximization, enables businesses to minimize their environmental impact (Taghipour and Frayret, 2011a). By optimizing resource utilization, minimizing emissions, and improving energy efficiency, businesses can decrease their ecological footprint (Mahfod et al., 2019). Embracing lean manufacturing principles not only bolsters sustainability efforts but also leads to cost savings and heightened competitiveness.

Transportation is of course an obvious contributor to the carbon footprint of many businesses, making it a critical area for improvement (Taghipour et al., 2015). Implementing environmentally friendly transportation methods, such as using hybrid vehicles or investing in alternative fuel technologies, allows businesses to reduce emissions and mitigate their environmental impact.

Sourcing, value chain management, and transportation are integral aspects of managing the supply chain sustainably. These components contribute to the development of Sustainable Supply Chain Management (SSCM), which is essential for businesses committed to environmental, social, and economic responsibility (Cauchois et al., 2017). The field of SSCM has witnessed remarkable growth, leading to the emergence of numerous theories and models aimed at achieving sustainability within supply chain operations (Merimi and Taghipour, 2021). By understanding these frameworks, businesses can enhance their sustainability efforts and make meaningful contributions to a more sustainable future.

The Triple Bottom Line (TBL) model is one of the most widely used frameworks in SSCM. It considers the three dimensions of sustainability - economic, social, and environmental and emphasizes the importance of balancing these dimensions in supply chain management (Elkington, 1997; Taghipour and Beneteau-Piet, 2020). The TBL model is used to assess the sustainability of supply chain practices and to guide sustainability initiatives, such as sustainable sourcing and sustainable production (Neri et al., 2021). One of the strengths of the TBL model is that it provides a comprehensive framework for sustainability, taking into account economic, social, and environmental factors. However, its weakness is that it may not be feasible for businesses to balance all three dimensions equally, as some may be more important or relevant in specific contexts (Neri et al., 2021).

The eco-efficiency model is another widely used framework in SSCM. It aims to reduce the environmental impact of supply chain activities while increasing economic efficiency. The eco-efficiency model is based on the idea that businesses can improve sustainability by reducing waste and increasing resource efficiency while maintaining or improving economic performance (DeSimone and Popoff, 2000). The strength of the eco-efficiency model is that it provides a clear and straightforward approach to sustainability, focusing on reducing the environmental impact of supply chain activities. Its weakness is that it may not fully take into account social and ethical considerations in supply chain management.

The Sustainable Value Chain (SVC) model is a framework that considers sustainability in the entire supply chain, from procurement to end-of-life. The SVC model focuses on creating sustainable value by improving sustainability performance across the entire supply chain, rather than just within individual businesses (Govindan et al., 2014). One of the strengths of the SVC model is that it provides a holistic approach to SSCM, considering the entire supply chain. Its weakness is that it may be difficult to implement in practice, as it requires collaboration and coordination between multiple businesses in the supply chain.

The Life Cycle Assessment (LCA) model is a tool used to evaluate the environmental impact of products and services over their entire life cycle, from raw materials procurement to disposal (Goffetti et al., 2022). The LCA model helps businesses identify areas of their supply chain that have the greatest environmental impact and provides a basis for implementing sustainability initiatives. The strength of the LCA model is that it provides a comprehensive understanding of the environmental impact of supply chain activities, allowing businesses to make informed decisions about sustainability initiatives. Its weakness is that it may be time-consuming and resource-intensive to conduct a full LCA.

The Role of Governments

Governments can create a more sustainable future by working with businesses and encouraging them to adopt sustainable practices (Vosooghidizaji et al., 2022). Their role in promoting sustainable supply chains is crucial.

Governments have a key role in setting regulations and standards for businesses to follow. Regulations and standards help to ensure that businesses adopt sustainable practices and minimize the negative impact of their operations on the environment and society. Governments can also use tax incentives to encourage businesses to adopt sustainable practices. Tax incentives can be used to reduce the cost of implementing sustainable practices, and to reward companies for reducing their environmental impact.

Governments, as consumers, have a significant impact on the market by choosing to purchase goods and services from businesses that adopt sustainable practices. By requiring suppliers to meet certain sustainability criteria, governments can encourage businesses to improve their sustainability performance. Furthermore, Governments can provide funding and support for R&D in sustainable technologies and practices. By investing in new technologies, governments aim to accelerate the transition to a more sustainable future. Finally, governments can partner with businesses to promote sustainable practices. For example, governments may collaborate with companies to develop sustainability guidelines or work together to support local communities affected by the operations of businesses.

Governments around the world have implemented, therefore, various regulations aimed at promoting sustainability in businesses and their supply chains. The European Union implemented the famous REACH (Registration, Evaluation, Authorization, and Restriction of Chemicals) Regulation which requires companies to assess and manage the risks of the chemicals they use in their products. The regulation aims to protect human health and the environment from the potential hazards of chemicals. (European Chemical Agency, 2021). The United States implemented the Energy Policy and Conservation Act (EPCA) which aims to improve energy efficiency and reduce energy consumption in the United States. The act requires companies to meet certain energy efficiency standards for various products, such as appliances and lighting. (U.S. Department of Energy, n.d.). At a higher level, the United Nations proposed the United Nations Global Compact which is a voluntary initiative that encourages companies to adopt sustainable and socially responsible practices. Companies that join the Global Compact are required to follow ten principles in areas such as human rights, labour, and the environment. (United Nations Global Compact, n.d.)

Non-compliance with sustainability regulations exposes companies to various negative consequences. Companies that disregard sustainability regulations face significant consequences across various aspects of their operations. Firstly, non-compliance can result in financial losses, such as increased costs, fines, and penalties, which can strain a company's resources and hinder its financial performance. Secondly, legal and regulatory repercussions can arise, including legal actions and penalties imposed by regulatory authorities, which can harm the company's reputation and have long-lasting financial implications. Additionally, companies that neglect sustainability may experience a loss of market opportunities, as customers and stakeholders increasingly prioritize sustainable products and services, potentially leading to a decline in market share and competitiveness.

Moreover, non-compliant companies may encounter challenges related to employee morale and retention. In an era where employees seek alignment between their personal values and organizational practices, companies that fail to prioritize sustainability may struggle to attract and retain top talent, thus affecting their human capital and potential for innovation. Furthermore, disregarding sustainability can diminish a company's brand value and reputation, as customers and stakeholders perceive such actions as irresponsible and untrustworthy. This can lead to decreased customer loyalty, negative public perception, and a potential decline in market value.

SITUATION IN CHINA

Challenges in China

Sustainable business practices have also gained significant importance in China amidst mounting environmental and social challenges. The country faces issues like air and water pollution, resource depletion, and income inequality. The environmental challenges in China encompass air and water pollution, deforestation, and soil degradation, primarily stemming from the rapid growth of its industrial sector. Addressing these concerns necessitates a comprehensive approach to environmental protection, entailing the development and implementation of effective regulations and policies.

Furthermore, China confronts substantial obstacles in energy conservation, driven by the escalating energy consumption resulting from rapid industrial expansion and population growth. To combat these challenges, a comprehensive strategy encompassing the adoption of energy-efficient technologies and practices is essential. Additionally, the country grapples with limited access to vital raw materials such as oil, coal, and minerals. Factors contributing to this limitation include declining domestic reserves, global competition, and rising extraction costs. To address these constraints, China must adopt an all-encompassing approach to resource management, including the formulation and execution of policies and technologies that promote efficient resource utilization and recycling.

The Chinese government has been actively promoting corporate sustainability and responsibility to mitigate the environmental impact of industrial activities and foster sustainable development. These efforts include implementing stricter emissions controls, promoting the use of green technologies, and investing in renewable energy sources. Additionally, the government has introduced sustainability reporting requirements and sustainability standards to encourage companies to adopt sustainable practices and promote a sustainable supply chain. Furthermore, resource utilization policies have been implemented to enhance resource efficiency and encourage the use of sustainable materials. These initiatives collectively aim to reduce environmental harm, promote energy conservation, and improve overall sustainability in China.

Sustainability of the Supply Chain in China

Promoting sustainable business practices in China heavily relies on ensuring the sustainability of its supply chains. A sustainable supply chain encompasses the complete life cycle of a product, from sourcing raw materials to manufacturing, distribution, and disposal. Recognizing the significance of sustainable supply chain management in mitigating environmental impact and ensuring the long-term viability of businesses has gained increasing traction in recent years.

To encourage the sustainability of supply chains in China, the government has instituted a range of regulations and initiatives. These endeavours are designed to tackle critical sustainability challenges such as resource depletion and pollution. Notably, regulations have been introduced to facilitate responsible sourcing of raw materials and encourage the adoption of energy-efficient production processes.

While progress has been achieved, establishing fully sustainable supply chains in China still presents challenges. Overcoming these hurdles requires addressing concerns such as compliance across a vast and diverse supplier base, managing intricate logistics networks, and striking a delicate balance between economic growth and environmental preservation. Nonetheless, these challenges also open doors for innovation and collaboration. By leveraging technological advancements, nurturing partnerships, and actively engaging with stakeholders, Chinese businesses can overcome these obstacles, building resilient and sustainable supply chains that drive long-term success.

REVIEW OF REGULATIONS IN CHINA

China to Promote Green, Low-Carbon Development in Shandong Province

The regulation introduced by the State Council on November 2nd, 2022 aims to promote green and low-carbon high-quality development in Shandong province (The State Council, 2022). Shandong is a significant industrial base and strategic area for economic development. The purpose of this regulation is to replace old growth drivers with new ones, focusing on innovation-driven strategic development. It seeks to encourage green and high-end development in traditional pillar industries while restraining the haphazard development of energy-intensive, high-emission, and low-level projects. The regulation also emphasizes the clean and efficient utilization of fossil fuels. It applies to almost all industries in Shandong, with a particular focus on chemical, coloured metals, building materials, spinning, and light industries. The objective is to establish pilot zones for green and low-carbon high-quality development in Shandong by 2027.

The circular has received a positive response from energy groups and investment groups. By early 2022, the proportion of new energy and renewable power generation in Shandong had increased by 17.6% compared to 2017 (Lan, 2022). State-owned enterprises, such as Shandong Energy Group Co Ltd and Shandong Development & Investment Holding Group Co Ltd, have taken the lead in implementing the circular. They are involved in the construction of wind-electricity bases and "green electricity in Shandong" projects, respectively. To implement the regulation, companies need to incorporate innovation into their operations and mechanisms, as well as actively promote a green and low-carbon supply chain. However, adjusting the current energy structure poses challenges, especially considering China's dependence on foreign energy sources, which has increased by 5.7% since 2012 (National Bureau of Statistics, 2022). Despite the potential of Shandong as an experimental pilot zone, accomplishing the mission of green transformation may require more time.

To concretely implement the circular, Rizhao City in Shandong has established a three-year plan from 2023 to 2025. The regime aims to make significant progress in constructing a modern economic system and achieving substantial low-carbon development, leading to improved living quality for citizens (Rizhao, 2023). In this regard, the fishing industry is encouraged to engage in deep-sea green cultivation, promoting competence in marine plantations. This initiative aligns with the establishment of the deep-sea creature research center and collaborations between research institutions and ocean cultivation enterprises (Li & Xu, 2019). By expanding deep-sea cultivation, the regime contributes to green fishing and the sustainable development of aquaculture.

China's Efforts to Curb Over-Packaging: A Comprehensive Approach

The circular published by the State Council on September 8th, 2022, underscores China's commitment to addressing the issue of over-packaging. Aimed at establishing a whole-chain administration system on over-packaging by 2025, this regulation recognizes the resurgence of over-packaging issues caused by the rapid development of the online shopping industry. The circular emphasizes the need for corresponding laws, regulations, standard systems, and industrial management improvements during the three-year period. By curbing excessive packaging, the regulation seeks to promote sustainable packaging practices and reduce environmental impact (The State Council, 2022).

To implement the circular, various stakeholders in the supply chain are involved. Packaging companies are encouraged to innovate in packaging technology and develop independent packaging materials. Product manufacturers are guided to avoid over-packaging and adhere to relevant packaging standards. Sales companies are required to refrain from selling over-packaged products and actively monitor compliance with packaging regulations. Efforts have also been made to promote the use of degradable and reusable packaging materials in the express delivery sector, as stated in the provisional regulation for express delivery approved by the State Council in 2018 (The State Council, 2018).

Despite the challenges posed by the existing value chain in excessive packaging, China has been actively addressing the issue since the early 2000s. The requirements for restricting excessive packaging in the food and cosmetics industries were first introduced in 2009, and an updated version was released in 2021 with higher packaging standards. These requirements set guidelines for various aspects of packaging, including contents, interspace ratio, single piece, package layers, and necessary special coefficient of a commodity (State Administration for Market Regulation & National Standardization Administrative Committee, 2021).

Provinces across China have been taking action in line with the State Council's guidance. For instance, the Administration of Market Regulation in Jiangsu province has been regulating over-packaging since August 2021. As of June 2022, the procurement of packaging materials meeting standards in the province reached 96.7%, and the proportion of packaging aligned with standardized operations reached 98.7% (Huang et al., 2022). In a notable initiative, SF Express placed 7.2 million recycling packaging boxes in Jiangsu, contributing to 2.8 million instances of packaging reuse.

While progress has been made, it is acknowledged that there is a need for exclusive laws on package regulation to effectively address the issue of over-packaging. Existing regulations are scattered across various superior laws, making it essential to elevate the regulation of packaging practices to a lawful level (The State Council, 2022).

Deepening Institutional Reform in the Electrical and Electronics Industry in China

The circular published by the State Council in 2022 focuses on deepening institutional reform in the electrical and electronics industry in China. The purpose of this reform is to remove institutional barriers that hinder the high-quality development of the industry and promote industrial upgrading. Several measures have been introduced to achieve these objectives. The circular streamlines the energy conservation assessment system and establishes a unified green products certification and labelling system. The National Administration of Market Regulation is responsible for inspecting corporate factories, corporate credibility, and product quality before certifying firms. Certified products enjoy benefits such as priority procurement and potential local bonus policies. Furthermore, the circular aims to ensure the healthy development of the electrical and electronics recycling industry by validating taxation allowance policies on the disposal of dilapidated electronics (The State Council, 2022).

The implementation of the reform has encountered challenges, particularly for moderate and small enterprises in the electronics and electrical industry of the Pearl River Delta. These enterprises face difficulties in undergoing green transformation due to factors such as lower susceptibility to energy-saving policies, lack of internal motivation, shortage of personnel with expertise, lack of supervision, and insufficient awareness. These challenges impede the adoption of energy-saving practices and hinder the sustainability of energy-saving efforts.

Currently, large state-owned firms are more inclined to follow national green manufacturing regulations and receive financial support, often relying on subsidiaries for implementing green initiatives. However, the circular recognizes that a long-term solution requires the involvement of moderate and small firms. To support their green reformation efforts, better financing mechanisms are needed. The Bank of China has taken the lead in offering customized differentiated green financing products to cater to the needs of smaller enterprises.

Regarding the recycling subsidiary, the circular in 2022 takes a more low-key approach and emphasizes the promotion of green self-upgrading among enterprises. This shift reflects the recognition that distributing subsidiaries is not a sustainable long-term solution for the transformation of the electrical and electronics industry. Previous research by Gu et al. (2016) highlights the limitations of the government's subsidiary policy. The "waste electrical and electronic products processing fund" implemented in 2012, which collects fees from producers to subsidize formal dismantling companies, poses financial pressure on the government and intensifies confusion in the recovery process. Backyard dismantling companies, operating informally, tend to offer lower fees but higher profit margins, posing challenges for formal recycling companies (Gu et al., 2016).

In conclusion, institutional reform in the electrical and electronics industry requires further refinement. The circular recognizes that the subsidiary policy is not a sustainable solution and poses challenges for both the industry and the government. Efforts are needed to overcome barriers faced by moderate and small enterprises, improve financing mechanisms, and promote sustainable practices in the industry.

Taxation Law of the People's Republic of China on Environment Protection

The Taxation Law of the People's Republic of China on Environment Protection was passed on December 25, 2016, and first modified on October 26, 2018. This law aims to protect and improve the environment, reduce pollutant emissions, and advance the construction of an ecological civilization. According to the law, taxpayers who directly emit taxable pollutants (including air pollutants, water pollutants, solid waste, and noise) into the environment within China's jurisdiction are required to pay taxes in compliance with this taxation law. However, if business entities and other operators emit taxable pollutants in a lawfully established centralized sewage treatment, they are exempt from taxation (Taxation Law of the People's Republic of China on Environment Protection, 2018).

The purpose of this law is to incentivize environmental responsibility and reduce pollution by implementing a taxation system. It aims to encourage companies to adopt environmentally friendly practices and technologies, improve resource efficiency, and promote sustainable development. The law serves to protect the environment and the well-being of the general population by imposing taxes on polluting activities and encouraging companies to minimize their environmental impact (Taxation Law of the People's Republic of China on Environment Protection, 2018).

The Taxation Law of the People's Republic of China on Environment Protection is aimed at individuals, companies, and other entities that emit taxable pollutants within the country's jurisdiction. It covers a wide range of industries and sectors, including manufacturing, energy, transportation, and construction. By targeting those responsible for pollutant emissions, the law seeks to regulate and control pollution at its source (Taxation Law of the People's Republic of China on Environment Protection, 2018).

The implementation of the Taxation Law of the People's Republic of China on Environment Protection has had significant implications for the industry. Companies subject to the law have had to take several measures to comply with its requirements. The law has prompted the adoption of greener practices, such as investing in emission reduction projects, improving resource efficiency, and utilizing low-carbon technologies. These changes have led to a positive impact on employment, as companies create more jobs to meet the demands of implementing environmentally friendly practices (Zhao et al., 2023).

Studies have shown that the taxation law has stimulated green management innovation among heavy-polluting listed enterprises in Shanghai and Shenzhen. Enterprises have proactively embraced environmental risk management, resulting in increased resource efficiency and lower costs. As a result, more employment opportunities have been generated (Zhao et al., 2023).

The taxation law has also promoted the development of green competitiveness among enterprises. It has encouraged companies to invest in technologies and practices that reduce environmental pollution, leading to improved environmental performance and lower risks of bankruptcy. Furthermore, the law has incentivized companies to enhance their operational management and adopt sustainable practices (Deng et al., 2021).

The effectiveness of the taxation law on environmental protection has been positive in terms of promoting environmental responsibility, resource efficiency, and employment. However, some challenges remain. The current tax rate and allowance criteria could be further improved to provide clearer guidelines and a more industry-specific grading system. This would ensure fairness and enhance the motivation for companies to manage their waste effectively (Standing Committee of the National People's Congress, 2018; Deng et al., 2021).

In summary, the Taxation Law of the People's Republic of China on Environment Protection has been instrumental in promoting environmental responsibility, reducing pollution, and fostering the development of green competitiveness among enterprises. It has encouraged the adoption of greener practices, investment in emission reduction projects, and improved resource efficiency. While the law has yielded positive results, there is room for further refinement to enhance its effectiveness and fairness.

Guangzhou Vessel Emission Control by Subsidy: Promoting Sustainable Shipping Practices

The Guangzhou Vessel Emission Control by Subsidy is a city-wide regulation introduced by the Guangzhou Port Authority with the aim of reducing port ship pollution emissions and improving the quality of the atmosphere and water environment (Guangzhou Port Authority, 2022). This regulation provides subsidies and incentives to shipping enterprises that engage in clean energy adoption, the construction of ship water pollutant reception facilities, and the renovation of vessels to use clean energy sources. The subsidies vary based on the degree of compliance, with increased subsidy levels for ships powered by liquefied natural gas (LNG) and higher ship power ratings.

The purpose of this regulation is to encourage shipping enterprises in Guangzhou to transition towards cleaner and more sustainable practices. By providing financial incentives, the regulation aims to promote the adoption of clean energy sources and the implementation of measures that reduce ship-related pollution. The focus is on protecting and improving the environment by reducing emissions and enhancing the overall sustainability of shipping activities in the port (Guangzhou Port Authority, 2022).

The Guangzhou Vessel Emission Control by Subsidy primarily targets shipping enterprises operating in the Guangzhou port. The regulation encourages these enterprises to invest in clean energy alternatives and upgrade their vessels to meet higher environmental standards. By doing so, the law seeks to control and mitigate the pollution caused by ships in the port area (Guangzhou Port Authority, 2022).

The implementation of the Guangzhou Vessel Emission Control by Subsidy regulation has had significant implications for the shipping industry in Guangzhou. Shipping enterprises had to undertake various measures to comply with the requirements of the regulation, including adopting clean energy technologies, building ship water pollutant reception facilities, and renovating vessels to use clean energy sources. These changes have had both benefits and challenges for the companies involved.

While the transition to cleaner practices may involve initial investment costs and adjustments to existing business operations, the subsidies provided by the regulation have served as incentives for shipping enterprises. The financial support has facilitated the reorganization of supply chains and business lines towards more sustainable practices. As a result, shipping enterprises have been encouraged to establish connections and partnerships with green energy providers, leading to increased collaboration within the industry (Guangzhou Port Authority, 2022).

The introduction of this regulation has also attracted the attention of major brokers and financial institutions in China. The policies and incentives related to sustainable shipping practices have influenced investment and financing decisions in the industry. For example, Jianglong Shipbuilding, a prominent industry leader, has received increased financial funding from major brokers in mainland China, which has further supported the adoption of sustainable practices. This indicates that the regulation has not only impacted the operational aspects of the industry but also influenced the financial sector's involvement in supporting sustainable shipping.

While specific data on the results of the regulation may be limited, the incentives and subsidies provided have incentivized shipping enterprises to adopt cleaner energy sources and reduce emissions. It is expected that the implementation of this regulation will lead to a reduction in port ship pollution emissions and contribute to the overall improvement of the atmosphere and water environment in Guangzhou. Ongoing monitoring and assessment by the Guangzhou Port Authority will likely inform any necessary updates or expansions to the regulation to further enhance its effectiveness in achieving the desired environmental goals (Guangzhou Port Authority, 2022).

In summary, the Guangzhou Vessel Emission Control by Subsidy regulation has played a significant role in promoting sustainable shipping practices in the Guangzhou port. By providing subsidies and incentives, the regulation encourages shipping enterprises to adopt clean energy sources, implement measures to reduce pollution and contribute to the overall improvement of the environment. While challenges and initial adjustments may be involved, the regulation has spurred collaboration within the industry and attracted financial support from major brokers. Continuous evaluation of the regulation's impact will guide further improvements and expansions to ensure its effectiveness in achieving environmental objectives.

Subsidies for Promoting New Energy Vehicles in 2022: Driving the Transition to Sustainable Transportation

The Subsidies for Promoting New Energy Vehicles in 2022 is a policy introduced by the Chinese government to support the growth of the new energy vehicle market and foster high-quality development within the industry (Ministry of Industry and Information Technology et al., 2021). With the rise of domestic brands like BYD and the establishment of large-scale factories by global industry leader Tesla in Shanghai, the government recognizes the potential of the new energy vehicle sector and aims to provide incentives to further expand its scale.

The purpose of this regulation is to encourage the adoption of new energy vehicles by offering subsidies to buyers, thereby stimulating demand and propelling the industry forward. The government aims to replace fuel-powered cars with new energy vehicles, promoting a shift towards sustainable transportation and reducing carbon emissions. The subsidies provided are determined based on factors such as the type of new energy vehicle, fast-charging technology, and energy-saving rate. Owners of vehicles with higher percentages of new energy utilization, advanced charging technology, and greater energy-saving capabilities are eligible for more substantial benefits (Ministry of Industry and Information Technology et al., 2021).

The Subsidies for Promoting New Energy Vehicles in 2022 target both private consumers, businesses and public service companies. By encouraging these entities to replace conventional fuel-powered cars with new energy vehicles, the regulation seeks to control and reduce the use of fossil fuels, promoting a cleaner and more sustainable transportation ecosystem. The focus is on protecting the environment and promoting the growth of the new energy vehicle industry (Ministry of Industry and Information Technology et al., 2021).

The implementation of the Subsidies for Promoting New Energy Vehicles in 2022 has yielded positive results for the industry. In 2022, there were 5.35 million new energy vehicles registered nationwide, representing an increase of 2.4 million vehicles or 81.48% compared to the previous year. This substantial growth indicates the effectiveness of the subsidy policy in driving the adoption of new energy vehicles (Ministry of Industry and Information Technology et al., 2021).

The policy has not only impacted the sales of new energy vehicles but also influenced the entire upstream supply chain. Companies involved in the production of components and materials for new energy vehicles, such as lithium ore, electrolytes, and electrode materials, have experienced significant growth. In the A-share market, 74 companies operating in this industry, with a focus on raw materials like cobalt-nickel ore and phosphate ore, have been listed. The third quarterly report data shows that 70 of these listed companies recorded positive net profits in the first three quarters, with 26 companies doubling their net profits compared to the previous year. These greener enterprises, bolstered by subsidy policies, have outperformed traditional fossil fuel industries like oil and coal, gaining a larger market share (Securities Times, 2022).

The application of this regulation required companies and individuals to transition from conventional fuel-powered vehicles to new energy vehicles. While there may have been challenges and constraints in terms of initial investment costs and infrastructure development, the subsidies provided by the government served as incentives for car owners and companies to make the transition. The benefits of reduced operating costs, environmental advantages, and government support have motivated the adoption of new energy vehicles and contributed to the industry's growth (Ministry of Industry and Information Technology et al., 2021).

Looking ahead, the government may continue to update or expand the subsidy policy based on ongoing evaluation and the evolving needs of the industry. The increasing market demand and positive outcomes from the implementation of the Subsidies for Promoting New Energy Vehicles in 2022 reflect a promising future for the new energy vehicle industry and a greener supply chain.

Measures to Promote the High-Quality Development of Green and Low-Carbon Industry in Shenzhen City: Fostering Sustainable Growth

The Measures to Promote the High-quality Development of Green and Low-carbon Industry in Shenzhen City were introduced by the people's government of Shenzhen to actively advance carbon peak and carbon neutrality. The regulation seeks to accelerate the development of green and low-carbon industries while fostering the establishment of sustainable production processes and lifestyles (General Office of the People's Government of Shenzhen Municipality, 2022).

The purpose of this law is to create a conducive environment for the growth of green and low-carbon industries in Shenzhen City. It aims to facilitate the transition towards sustainable practices by promoting the utilization of environmentally friendly technologies and reducing carbon emissions. The regulation encourages the integration of academic research into industrial applications by acting as a facilitator between universities and companies. It also introduces a new assessment method for state-owned companies, motivating them to become role models in their respective industries. The law focuses on protecting the environment and promoting the adoption of green and low-carbon practices in production and daily life (General Office of the People's Government of Shenzhen Municipality, 2022).

The Measures to Promote the High-quality Development of Green and Low-carbon Industries in Shenzhen City primarily target companies involved in green and low-carbon industries. The law intends to control and guide the behaviour of these companies, encouraging them to adopt sustainable practices and contribute to the city's overall environmental goals. Additionally, the regulation promotes cooperation between different firms by facilitating their relocation to specific industrial parks, fostering collaboration and knowledge sharing within the industry (General Office of the People's Government of Shenzhen Municipality, 2022).

The implementation of these measures has received positive responses from the industry in Shenzhen City. Companies have actively engaged with the government's efforts to promote green and low-carbon development. The collaboration between universities and businesses has facilitated the quick transfer of academic research outcomes into practical applications within industries, expediting the development of innovative technologies and solutions. By aligning state-owned companies with the objectives of the regulation, the government has encouraged these entities to lead by example and inspire others to adopt green and low-carbon practices (General Office of the People's Government of Shenzhen Municipality, 2022).

The transition to green and low-carbon industries may present challenges for companies, including the need for investment in new technologies, equipment, and training. However, the benefits of adopting sustainable practices and complying with the regulation are significant. Companies operating in green and low-carbon industries can enjoy enhanced reputations, improved access to government support, and increased competitiveness in the market. Furthermore, the concentration of low-carbon companies in designated industrial parks fosters collaboration, synergy, and knowledge sharing, creating a conducive environment for innovation and growth (General Office of the People's Government of Shenzhen Municipality, 2022).

To assess the overall impact of the regulation, further data and information are required regarding the specific outcomes and achievements in terms of carbon emissions reduction, industry growth, and the adoption of sustainable practices. The government may consider updating or expanding the regulation based on ongoing evaluations and the evolving needs of the industry. The Measures to Promote the High-quality Development of Green and Low-carbon Industry in Shenzhen City demonstrate Shenzhen's commitment to sustainable development and the transition to a greener and more environmentally friendly economy.

Guaranteeing the Development of the Yangtze River Delta: Promoting Joint Protection and Governance

The regulation titled "Guaranteeing the Development of the Yangtze River Delta" was introduced by The Supreme People's Court of The People's Republic of China, in collaboration with the courts of Shanghai, Jiangsu, Anhui, and Zhejiang provinces. The purpose of this regulation is to promote joint protection and governance of the ecological environment in the Yangtze River Delta, which is renowned as the most developed area in China (The Supreme People's Court of The People's Republic of China, 2021).

This law aims to shift the area's development approach from a sole economic perspective to a more balanced focus on both economic and environmental aspects. It seeks to establish a comprehensive legal and regulatory framework to safeguard the region's ecological environment. The regulation defines the rights and responsibilities of individuals and companies operating within the Yangtze River Delta, ensuring their compliance with environmental laws and regulations. By doing so, it aims to protect and preserve the region's ecological resources and promote sustainable development (The Supreme People's Court of The People's Republic of China, 2021).

The regulation primarily targets businesses operating in the Yangtze River Delta region. It is aimed at controlling the behaviour of these companies and ensuring their adherence to environmental laws and regulations. By imposing fines and penalties for non-compliance, the law aims to deter actions that harm the ecological environment. This regulatory initiative serves to protect the natural resources and ecosystems of the Yangtze River Delta and promote the overall well-being of the region and its inhabitants (The Supreme People's Court of The People's Republic of China, 2021).

The implementation of this regulation has received significant attention and compliance from businesses operating in the Yangtze River Delta. In response to the regulatory requirements, companies have had to make significant changes in their practices to align with the environmental protection guidelines. The clearer definition of laws and regulations has made it easier to identify and penalize instances of non-compliance. As a result, the punishment for anti-regulation behaviour by firms has become more severe. Notably, the Trial of "Illegal Pollutant Emissions to Yangtze River" resulted in a company being ordered to pay 520 million yuan in environmental remediation costs and fines, marking the highest fine imposed on enterprises at that time (Nanjing Intermediate People's Court of Jiangsu Province, 2021).

To comply with the regulation, companies in the Yangtze River Delta have implemented measures for the proper disposal and recycling of pollutants. The fear of facing substantial fines has compelled businesses to take responsibility for their environmental impact and prioritize sustainable practices. As a result, there has been a noticeable shift in common practices within the industries, with an emphasis on greening the supply chain. The regulation has encouraged companies to adopt environmentally friendly approaches, contributing to the overall sustainability and ecological well-being of the area (Nanjing Intermediate People's Court of Jiangsu Province, 2021).

While specific data on the overall impact and effectiveness of the regulation is not available, the significant fine imposed on non-compliant enterprises highlights the seriousness with which the government is enforcing the law. It demonstrates the government's commitment to promoting a sustainable environment in the Yangtze River Delta. As the regulation progresses, the government may update or expand it based on ongoing evaluations and the evolving needs of the region.

DISCUSSION

This review has investigated the role and effectiveness of Chinese regulations in driving sustainable business practices. Through the implementation of an array of policies and measures, the Chinese government has demonstrated an unwavering commitment to addressing environmental challenges and fostering resource efficiency. The regulations discussed in this review have served as catalysts, compelling Chinese companies to embrace sustainability and yielding noteworthy progress in terms of environmental protection and sustainable development.

The effectiveness of these regulations becomes evident when observing the significant strides made by Chinese industries in adopting sustainable practices. Companies have wholeheartedly recognized the intrinsic value of integrating sustainability into their operations, propelled by both regulatory compliance and the pursuit of long-term profitability. The regulations have created an enabling environment for innovation and technological advancements in crucial areas such as energy conservation, waste management, and resource utilization.

One of the fundamental strengths of the Chinese regulatory approach lies in its comprehensiveness. The government has implemented a wide range of regulations that address various facets of sustainability, encompassing environmental protection, energy conservation, and resource management. This multifaceted approach ensures that companies are held accountable across multiple dimensions of sustainability, fostering a holistic transformation towards a greener and more sustainable economy.

Looking ahead, the valuable experience gained from China's sustainable regulations can serve as a reference for other countries grappling with similar environmental challenges. With its unparalleled levels of industrialization, China has effectively showcased the feasibility and advantages of implementing sustainable business practices in a relatively short time.

Moreover, international collaboration and knowledge sharing are important for advancing sustainable practices on a global scale. China can draw inspiration from the experiences of other countries and continually refine its regulatory approach. By adopting best practices and embracing innovative solutions from around the world, China can further fortify its sustainability agenda and solidify its position as a global leader in sustainable development.

Likewise, other countries can find inspiration in China's regulatory framework and tailor it to suit their unique contexts. The Chinese experience underscores the importance of a proactive and comprehensive regulatory approach, underpinned by unwavering government commitment and stakeholder engagement. By tailoring their regulations to align with sustainability goals, countries can create an environment that nurtures responsible business practices and expedites the transition towards a more sustainable future.

RECOMMENDATIONS AND FUTURE RESEARCH DIRECTIONS

Following the success of many national and regional regulations, the Chinese government should continue to enhance and enforce sustainable business practices through more accurate, robust and comprehensive regulatory frameworks. Clearer guidelines and standards for sustainability reporting, supply chain management, and environmental impact assessments should be established in order to track results and keep records. Continuing providing businesses with clear guidelines and incentives for sustainable practices will keep driving the adoption of environmentally and socially responsible business practices.

In addition, collaboration among government agencies, industry stakeholders, and academia is crucial for advancing sustainable business practices. Knowledge-sharing platforms, workshops, and partnerships should be encouraged to facilitate the exchange of best practices, innovative solutions, and research findings. This collaborative approach will foster a collective understanding of sustainability challenges and lead to the development of effective strategies and solutions.

The collaborations will also provide technological solutions to comply with new regulations targets. Continued investment in research and development is essential for propelling sustainable business practices forward. Emphasis should be placed on the development and adoption of innovative technologies, such as renewable energy solutions, waste management systems, and circular economy models. The government can incentivize businesses to invest in sustainable technologies and provide support for research institutions and startups focused on sustainability.

Furthermore, recognizing that sustainability is a global challenge, China can play a crucial role in promoting international collaboration and knowledge exchange. By actively engaging with other nations, sharing experiences, and participating in global sustainability initiatives, China can contribute to the development of global standards, policies, and practices. This cooperation can benefit Chinese businesses by opening up international markets, enhancing their reputation, and creating opportunities for knowledge transfer.

Future research in the field of sustainable business practices in China should focus on assessing the long-term impacts and effectiveness of implemented regulations, studying the economic implications of sustainable practices on businesses, and evaluating the social and environmental benefits achieved through sustainable supply chains. Additionally, understanding consumer perceptions and behaviors towards sustainable products and services, as well as the role of education and awareness in promoting sustainable business practices, are important areas for investigation.

REFERENCES

Cauchois, R., Taghipour, A., Kang, D., Zoghlami, N., & Abed, M. (2017). Advanced solutions for a supply chain with stochastic information. *Journal of Advanced Management Science, 5*(1).

Deng, J., Tang, Y., & Zhang, T. (2021). The Deeping Research on the Enterprise's Green Competitiveness under the "Environmental Protection Tax Law" in China. *Technoeconomics & Management Research, 7*, 51–55.

DeSimone, L. D., & Popoff, F. (2000). *Eco-efficiency: the business link to sustainable development.* MIT Press.

Elkington, J. (1998). Partnerships from cannibals with forks: The triple bottom line of 21st-century business. *Environmental Quality Management*, *8*(1), 37–51. doi:10.1002/tqem.3310080106

European Chemical Agency. (2021). REACH – Regulation (EC) No 1907/2006. ECHA. https://echa.europa.eu/regulations/reach

General Office of the People's Government of Shenzhen Municipality. (2022, December 30). *Notice of the General Office of Shenzhen Municipal People's Government on the Issuance of Several Measures to Promote the High-Quality Development of Green and Low-Carbon Industries in Shenzhen--Policy and Regulations.* General Office of the People's Government of Shenzhen Municipality. http://www.sz.gov.cn/cn/xxgk/zfxxgj/zcfg/content/post_10364326.html

Goffetti, G., Böckin, D., Baumann, H., Tillman, A. M., & Zobel, T. (2022). Towards sustainable business models with a novel life cycle assessment method. *Business Strategy and the Environment*, *31*(5), 2019–2035. doi:10.1002/bse.3005

Govindan, K., Azevedo, S. G., Carvalho, H., & Cruz-Machado, V. (2014). Impact of supply chain management practices on sustainability. *Journal of Cleaner Production*, *85*, 212–225. doi:10.1016/j.jclepro.2014.05.068

Gu, Y., Wu, Y., Xu, M., & Zuo, T. (2016). Waste Electrical and Electronic Equipment (WEEE) Recycling for a Sustainable Resource Supply in the Electronics Industry in China. *Journal of Cleaner Production*, *127*, 331–338. doi:10.1016/j.jclepro.2016.04.041

Guangzhou Port Authority. (2022, September 19). Notice on the Issuance of the Implementation Measures of Guangzhou Port Ship Emission Control Subsidy Funds. Guangzhou Port Authority. https://www.gz.gov.cn/gfxwj/sbmgfxwj/gzsgwj/content/post_8576369.html

Huang, H., Liu, X., Lu, X., Li, J., & Lu, L. (2022). 250g tea with a 1kg package, it is time to get at the root of over-packaging. *Xinhua Daily*, 1–3.

Lan, H. (2022). *Grab the opportunity of low carbon and speed up energy transformation*, 5. Shandong Provincial State-owned Assets Supervision and Administration Commission.

Li, R., & Xu, C. (2019). Develop deep-sea green cultivation, and establish deep-sea creature research center. *Fisheries Science & Technology Information*, *46*(06), 350.

Mahfod, J., Canel-Depitre, B., & Taghipour, A. (2019). Quality function deployment-ELECTRE in supplier evaluation. *Journal of Advanced Management Science*, *7*(4).

Merimi, M., & Taghipour, A. (2021). Accelerating the digitalization of the supply chain: An empirical research about COVID-19 crisis. In *Digitalization of Decentralized Supply Chains During Global Crises* (pp. 1–24). IGI Global. doi:10.4018/978-1-7998-6874-3.ch001

Ministry of Industry and Information Technology, Ministry of Finance, Development and Reform Commission, & Ministry of Science and Technology. (2021, December 31). *Notice on the financial subsidy policy for the promotion and application of new energy vehicles in 2022.* China Government Network. https://www.gov.cn/zhengce/zhengceku/2021-12/31/content_5665857.htm

Nanjing Intermediate People's Court of Jiangsu Province. (2021, March 10). Nanjing Intermediate People's Court - Nanjing Trial Network. NJFY. https://www.njfy.gov.cn/www/njfy/xwzx_mb_a39210310136710.htm

National Bureau of Statistics. (2022, October 8). *The 14th Report on Achievements of Economical Society Development.* Information Disclosure, National Bureau of Statistics. http://www.stats.gov.cn/xxgk/jd/sjjd2020/202210/t202

Neri, A., Cagno, E., Lepri, M., & Trianni, A. (2021). A triple bottom line balanced set of key performance indicators to measure the sustainability performance of industrial supply chains. *Sustainable Production and Consumption*, *26*, 648–691. doi:10.1016/j.spc.2020.12.018

Rizhao. (2023). A 3-Year PLAN to Promote Green, Low-Carbon Development. *Rizhao Daily*, 1–15. doi:10.28662/n.cnki.nrzrb.2023.000051

Securities Times. (2022, November 9). Insights on the new energy vehicle value chain: The improvement of the upper steam and the rise of the track in thermal management. *Securities Times.* https://baijiahao.baidu.com/s?id=1748972321314236306&wfr=spider&for=pc

Standing Committee of the National People's Congress. (2018, October 26). *Taxation Law of the People's Republic of China on Environment Protection.* State Taxation Administration. http://www.chinatax.gov.cn/chinatax/n610/c5178958/content.html

State Administration for Market Regulation, & the National Standardization Administrative Committee. (2021, August 10). *Requirements of Restricting Excessive Package—Foods and Cosmetics.* China GB Standard. https://openstd.samr.gov.cn/bzgk/gb/newGbInfo?hcno=30366DF41D69DA50E3EEABC0CE18A241

Taghipour, A., Abed, M., & Zoghlami, N. (2015, May). Design for remanufacturing respecting reverse logistics processes: A review. In *2015 4th International Conference on Advanced Logistics and Transport (ICALT)* (pp. 299-304). IEEE. 10.1109/ICAdLT.2015.7136602

Taghipour, A., & Beneteau-Piet, C. (2020). Sustainable supply chain management performance. *International Journal of Innovation, Management and Technology*, *11*(6), 165–169. doi:10.18178/ijimt.2020.11.6.897

Taghipour, A., & Frayret, J. M. (2011a). A new heuristic search with local optimization to manage a supply chain. *Meta*, 15.

Taghipour, A., & Frayret, J. M. (2011b). *Supply chain coordination planning: A review.* Work paper, École Polytechnique de Montréal.

Taghipour, A., Glaa, B., & Zoghlami, N. (2014, May). Network coordination with minimum risk of information sharing. In *2014 International Conference on Advanced Logistics and Transport (ICALT)* (pp. 184-188). IEEE. 10.1109/ICAdLT.2014.6864115

Taghipour, A., & Merimi, M. (2021). Digital Transformation of Supply Chains during Crisis: COVID-19. *In 11th Annual International Conference on Industrial Engineering and Operations Management.* IEOM.

Taghipour, A., Murat, S., & Huang, P. (2021). E-supply chain management: A review. International Journal of e-Education, e-Business, e-. *Management Learning*, *11*(2), 51–61.

Taxation Law of the People's Republic of China on Environment Protection. (2018). *Environmental Protection Tax Law of the People's Republic of China.* State Taxation Administration. http://www.chinatax.gov.cn/chinatax/n610/c5178958/content.html

The State Council. (2018, March 27). *A Provisional Regulation For Express Delivery.* The State Council, The People's Republic of China. https://www.gov.cn/zhengce/content/2018-03/27/content_5277801.htm

The State Council. (2022). *China to deepen institutional reform in the electrical and electronics industry.* The State Council. english.www.gov.cn/policies/latestreleases/202209/23/content_WS632d9fdac6d0a757729e06e0.html

The State Council. (2022). *China to further curb over-packaging*. The State Council. english.www.gov.cn/policies/latestreleases/202209/08/content_WS6319ae19c6d0a757729dfc18.html

The Supreme People's Court of The People's Republic of China. (2021, November 2). *Authoritative Release - The Supreme People's Court of The People's Republic of China.* Supreme People's Court of the People's Republic of China. https://www.court.gov.cn/fabu-xiangqing-329821.html

United Nations Global Compact. (n.d.). *About the Global Compact.* UN. https://www.unglobalcompact.org/what-is-gc

U.S. Department of Energy. (n.d.). *Energy Policy and Conservation Act (EPCA).* USDE. https://www.energy.gov/laws-policies/energy-policy-and-conservation-act-epca

Vosooghidizaji, M., Taghipour, A., & Canel-Depitre, B. (2022). Coordinating corporate social responsibility in a two-level supply chain under bilateral information asymmetry. *Journal of Cleaner Production*, *364*, 132627. doi:10.1016/j.jclepro.2022.132627

Zhao, Z., Cheng, Z., Wu, F., & Lv, D. (2023). Impact of China's Environmental Protection Tax Law on Corporate Employment. *Zhongguo Renkou Ziyuan Yu Huanjing*, *33*(1), 61–73.

ADDITIONAL READINGS

do Paço, A. M. F. (2009). *Adam Werbach, Strategy for Sustainability. A Business Manifesto: Harvard Business Press.* Published in July. doi:10.100712208-009-0039-4

Schoettli, J. (2018). *The blue economy 3.0: the marriage of science, innovation and entrepreneurship creates a new business model that transforms society.* Xlibris..

KEY TERMS AND DEFINITIONS

Carbon Neutrality: Carbon neutrality refers to achieving a balance between the amount of carbon emissions produced and the amount of carbon removed from the atmosphere. It involves reducing emissions and offsetting remaining emissions through methods such as carbon offset projects or carbon capture and storage.

Circular Economy: The circular economy is an economic system aimed at minimizing waste and maximizing resource efficiency. It promotes the continual use, recycling, and repurposing of materials, reducing reliance on finite resources and minimizing environmental impact.

Corporate Sustainability: Corporate sustainability involves integrating economic, environmental, and social considerations into business strategies to create long-term value while minimizing adverse effects on the environment and society.

Environmental Compliance: Environmental compliance refers to adhering to environmental laws, regulations, and standards set by governing bodies to ensure that businesses operate within prescribed environmental limits and requirements.

Environmental Footprint: An environmental footprint refers to the impact of an individual, organization, or product on the environment. It includes the consumption of resources, energy use, greenhouse gas emissions, and waste generation, providing a measure of environmental sustainability.

Environmental Impact Assessment: Environmental impact assessment is a process that evaluates the potential environmental consequences of proposed projects or activities to inform decision-making and identify mitigation measures.

Environmental Regulations: Environmental regulations are rules and laws established by governments to protect the environment, promote sustainable practices, and mitigate the negative impacts of industrial activities.

Life Cycle Assessment (LCA): Life Cycle Assessment is a systematic evaluation of the environmental impacts of a product, process, or service throughout its entire life cycle, from raw material extraction to disposal. It considers various factors, including resource use, energy consumption, emissions, and waste generation.

Resource Management: Resource management involves planning, monitoring, and optimizing the use of natural resources to ensure their sustainable availability for current and future generations.

Social Responsibility: Social responsibility refers to the ethical and voluntary actions taken by individuals, organizations, or companies to contribute to the well-being of society and the environment. It involves addressing social issues, promoting community engagement, and acting in a socially and environmentally responsible manner.

Sustainable Business Practices: Sustainable business practices refer to strategies and actions adopted by companies to minimize negative environmental and social impacts while maintaining long-term profitability.

Sustainable Supply Chain: A sustainable supply chain focuses on integrating environmental and social considerations into every stage of the product lifecycle, from sourcing raw materials to manufacturing, distribution, and end-of-life disposal.

Triple Bottom Line: The triple bottom line is a framework that considers three dimensions of sustainability: economic, social, and environmental. It emphasizes the need for businesses and organizations to account for not only financial performance but also their social and environmental impacts.

Chapter 3
Resilient Sustainable Supply Chain Management

Atour Taghipour
Normandy University, France

Yassamine Belrhazi
Normandy University, France

Nouhaila Damoum
Normandy University, France

ABSTRACT

Companies must respond to the growing expectations of their stakeholders, but also conduct their activities according to an ambitious responsible development approach, which means addressing the social and environmental practices associated with the development of its products. This commitment covers not only its own internal practices but also those of its suppliers. It involves identifying, managing, and optimizing sustainable practices in the supply network. Working towards this has become an extension of the responsibility and commitment, and is a key component of the overall business model and structure. However, supply chain management needs to deal with many difficulties to coordinate the actors of the supply chain. One of these difficulties is a wider range of risks. These include political, economic, social, environmental, legal, and technological risks. The objective of this chapter is to highlight, through the theoretical literature, some of the challenges and difficulties of supply chains and to constitute the strategies of resilience sustainable supply chain practices.

INTRODUCTION

Over the past decades, thanks to globalization, international companies have multiplied. Between 1995 and 2007, the number of transnational companies doubled from 38,000 to 79,000, and the number of international/multinational companies tripled, from 265,000 to 790,000. In this regard, almost 80% of managers believe that the number of cooperative relationships with third parties will increase in the

DOI: 10.4018/978-1-6684-9062-4.ch003

coming years (United Nations. July 2008). Following globalization, competition between companies has turned into a competition between supply chains. Amongst the factors of competitiveness, sustainability, as a multidimensional factor that further than economic outcome, focuses on the efficient use of resources and achieving a return on investment, became crucial and a critical component of a company's long-term profitability and competitiveness (Elkington, 1997).

Indeed, the network between companies to create and distribute value in the form of products or services is defined as supply chain. It represents the steps required to deliver a product or service to customers. Improving supply chain management is the main challenge in all sectors to have an integrated global network, which is crucial in the creation and the distribution of value. In this regard, one of the main difficulties is to manage the risk, to ensure the adaptation of sustainability in all phases of its supply chain, whatever the types of products offered or the way they are manufactured, distributed and disposed at the end of their life (Taghipour and Beneteau-Piet, 2020). Since each company is part of a larger network, it is important to manage the relationships that require action beyond the company's boundaries. Each company's network, or stakeholders, play a central role in the effectiveness of the supply chain. They can be customers, providers, manufacturers, suppliers and vendors, who refer to both inside and outside the organization (Taghipour et al., 2014). Organizations must not only satisfy the desires and expectations of the stakeholders, but also avoid actions that can negatively impact future generations and their needs and actual employees (Golinelli and Volpe, 2012). Unfortunately, some companies outsourced their activities from the countries with low income, or low regulatory controls in order to avoid the strict financial, environmental and social regulations of production. For example, companies sourcing raw materials from countries could unintentionally abuse their suppliers' employees who work under inhumane conditions.

Supply chain management is difficult. One of the main reasons in addition to the complexity, is the risks that treat supply chains. In fact, the globalized companies are less performant in the risk management According to Robert W. Moffat, Jr. Senior Vice President and Executive Director IBM Systems and Technology Group, 69% of companies formally track risk, but only 31% manage performance and risk together. In this regard, a lack of standardized processes, insufficient data, and inadequate technology as their top barriers to effective risk management (Merimi and Taghipour, 2021).

Definition of Sustainable Supply Chain Management

In recent years, the concept of sustainable supply chain management (SSCM) has gained significant attention as organizations strive to minimize their environmental impact, ensure social responsibility, and enhance their economic performance. Sustainable supply chain management, as defined by Seuring and Muller (2008), is the management of all processes, activities, and relationships in a way that economic, social, and environmental objectives are balanced while supply chain creates long term value for customers. The concept of SSCM is premised on the idea that organizations should not only focus on economic goals but also address the social and environmental impacts of their supply chains (Nadia et al., 2020).

Sustainable supply chain management can also be defined as the integration of environmental, social, and economic considerations into all stages of the supply chain process to minimize the negative impacts and maximize the positive impacts of the supply chain. As noted by Carter and Rogers (2008), SSCM involves "identifying and managing the social, environmental, and economic impacts of a product or service from raw material extraction through to end-of-life disposal or reuse." The goal of SSCM is to achieve sustainable development by balancing the three dimensions of sustainability: economic, social, and environmental (Christopher and Peck, 2004).

There are several aspects to SSCM, including:

1. **Environmental sustainability:** This aspect of SSCM involves minimizing the environmental impact of the entire supply chain, including reducing greenhouse gas emissions, minimizing waste and pollution, conserving natural resources, and promoting the use of renewable energy.

"Environmental sustainability in supply chain management refers to managing the environmental impacts of all activities involved in the production and delivery of goods and services." - Seuring and Muller (2008)

2. **Social sustainability:** This aspect of SSCM involves promoting fair labor practices, human rights, and social justice throughout the supply chain. This includes ensuring safe and healthy working conditions for employees, preventing the use of child labor and forced labor, and promoting diversity and inclusion.

"Social sustainability in supply chain management means creating and maintaining fair and equitable relationships with all stakeholders throughout the supply chain." (Walker et al., 2014)

3. **Economic sustainability:** This aspect of SSCM involves ensuring the economic viability of the entire supply chain, including promoting ethical business practices, ensuring fair and transparent pricing, and promoting long-term relationships with suppliers.

"Economic sustainability in supply chain management involves ensuring that the supply chain operates in a manner that is financially viable, ethical and supports the long-term interests of all stakeholders." - Pagell and Wu (2009)

4. **Governance:** This aspect of SSCM involves implementing effective governance structures and processes to ensure that sustainability goals are achieved throughout the supply chain. This includes establishing policies and procedures, monitoring and reporting on sustainability performance, and engaging stakeholders.

"The governance of sustainable supply chains refers to the policies, procedures and processes established by a company to ensure that sustainable practices are integrated throughout the supply chain." - Sarkis et al. (2010)

SCM is about aligning economic, environmental, and social objectives and finding solutions that work for all stakeholders involved in the supply chain (Cauchois et al., 2017). By integrating environmental, social, and economic sustainability into their supply chain management practices, companies can create more sustainable and resilient supply chains that benefit all stakeholders, including the environment, society, and economy. As Stahl et al. (2012) state, "SSCM is an ongoing process of aligning supply chain activities with the triple bottom line of economic, social, and environmental sustainability, while finding innovative solutions that generate value for all stakeholders involved."

Supply Chain Challenges: PESTEL Analysis

To achieve sustainability, supply chain management must with different difficulties and challenges among them PESTEL can point out to a business strategy analysis framework, which stands for political, economic, sociological, technological, environmental and legal, covers the macro-environmental factors that can influence (positively or negatively) a company. The following paragraph analyses these challenges by giving some examples:

Social

Human exploitation is a one of challenges that can take many forms (child labor, unsafe working conditions, excessive working hours and low wages), however it can be difficult to detect. The number of people in modern slavery worldwide is estimated to be 40.3 million, according to the International Labor Organization's (ILO) Global Slavery Index 2018. Several sectors are affected by the risk of forced labor. Among them are: textiles, food and agriculture, electronics, construction and household hospitality are particularly affected. According to the ILO, modern slavery generates more than 150 billion dollars in illegal profits (Béatrice Héraud, 2016 in Novethic.fr):

- $99 billion from commercial sexual exploitation ;
- $51 billion is from trafficking for economic exploitation;
- $34 billion in construction, manufacturing, mining and utilities;
- $9 billion in agriculture (including forestry and fishing);
- $8 billion is saved by private households not paying or underpaying forced domestic workers.

This phenomenon continues to be a problem in many developing countries, creating a scandal for global brands that source from these factories. In this regard, each year, the direct and indirect costs of occupational accidents and diseases has been estimated at 2,800 billion dollars. Almost every 15 seconds, a worker loses his or her life worldwide as a result of a work-related accident or illness. Regularly, there are scandals in labour-intensive and low-wage industries with indecent working and safety conditions (long hours, non-compliant safety standards for buildings, handling of chemicals and toxic products without adequate protection...). An example is the factories of the subcontractors of the big textile brands are hidden in buildings not intended for this type of use and the safety of the buildings and the prevention of fires are not respected (El-Nemr et al., 2017)

Over the years, the working conditions cause serious cracks for the workers.

"There was no air conditioning, no fans. The electricity often went out. We had no breaks except to go to the bathroom. Most of the time, we didn't even have time to eat, and when we did, we had to swallow the food quickly, behind the sewing machine. Officially, the workday started at 8 am and ended at 5 pm. But I often worked overtime, until 10 pm. Sometimes until 3 am. I worked 7 days a week. Without rest or holidays", reports one of the victims of modern slavery.

Companies need to understand that they have a responsibility to assess and monitor their supply chains. A 2017 survey by the Chartered Institute of Procurement and Supply (CIPS) found that only 6% of UK business leaders were confident that their supply chains were not affected by modern slavery.

Economic

A World Bank study found that corruption was the biggest obstacle to development and economic growth. Some companies, both local and foreign, bribe public officials to turn a blind eye to troublesome laws or offer large rewards to obtain licenses and contracts and/or evade taxes and duties. Since the rules of some countries are unclear and their application is left to the goodwill of officials, companies are free to negotiate. Most of them do not pay their tax and customs obligations and bribe officials to obtain advantages. Smuggling, black market operations and falsification of accounts encourage tax evasion. The World Bank has reported that the high cost of bribing public officials encourages many companies to reduce their tax obligations by not reporting all of their sales, costs and payroll. Naturally, this results in substantial revenue loss to the government. The poor pay the price by paying more taxes and receiving fewer social benefits. A World Bank study showed that only 40% of small and medium-sized enterprises pay taxes and that many individuals do not file their tax returns (Sajdik, 2011).

Thus, globalization is among the main challenges related to supply chains. Globalization is a cost generator. Nearly 40% of supply chain executives report large profit margins. However, this profit growth is not necessarily tied to cost reductions. In fact, more than one-third of executives report increased costs due to international sourcing, increased sales or inflation. However, these higher costs are less prevalent in high-performing supply chains. These findings suggest that globalization has contributed more to increased revenues than to improved efficiency (Robert W. Moffat, www.lesaffaires.com).

Environmental

Environmental problems are a major concern in supply chain management. The production, transportation, and disposal of goods can have a significant impact on the environment, contributing to climate change, pollution, and resource depletion (Taghipour, 2014). One of the most significant environmental problems in the supply chain is greenhouse gas emissions. The transportation of goods, particularly over long distances, can result in significant carbon emissions, which contribute to global warming. Additionally, the production and disposal of goods can also lead to carbon emissions, particularly if these activities rely on fossil fuels.

Another environmental problem is waste generation. Many products are packaged in non-recyclable or non-biodegradable materials, which can result in a significant waste generation. This waste can contribute to environmental pollution, particularly if it is not disposed of properly. The disposal of hazardous waste, such as electronic waste, can also have significant environmental impacts, as these materials can leach toxic chemicals into the environment.

Deforestation is another environmental problem in the supply chain. Many products, such as palm oil and soy, are sourced from areas where deforestation is prevalent. This can have a range of negative environmental impacts, including the loss of biodiversity and carbon storage.

To illustrate, one example of environmental problems in the supply chain is the case of Walmart's sustainability efforts. In 2005, Walmart launched its sustainability program, which aimed to reduce greenhouse gas emissions, reduce waste, and promote sustainable sourcing practices in its supply chain.

As part of this program, the company set ambitious goals to reduce its greenhouse gas emissions and increase its use of renewable energy. Walmart also worked with its suppliers to reduce waste and improve sustainable sourcing practices. Through these efforts, Walmart was able to reduce its greenhouse gas emissions and save billions of dollars in costs.

Another example is the case of Unilever's sustainable sourcing efforts. In 2010, Unilever launched its Sustainable Living Plan, which aimed to reduce its environmental footprint and promote sustainable sourcing practices in its supply chain. As part of this plan, Unilever set ambitious goals to reduce its greenhouse gas emissions, reduce waste, and promote sustainable sourcing practices for agricultural commodities such as palm oil and tea. Unilever also worked with its suppliers to improve sustainable sourcing practices, and by 2020, 80% of its agricultural raw materials were sustainably sourced. Through these efforts, Unilever was able to reduce its environmental footprint and improve its reputation as a sustainable company.

In conclusion, environmental problems in the supply chain can have significant impacts on a company's operations and reputation. Companies must take steps to reduce their environmental footprint, including reducing greenhouse gas emissions, reducing waste generation, and promoting sustainable sourcing practices. By taking a proactive approach to these issues, companies can build responsible and sustainable supply chains that can withstand environmental scrutiny. As sustainability expert, Paul Polman, notes: "The business case for sustainability is clear - it is essential for long-term success and for creating a more sustainable future for all."

Technological

The use of technology in supply chain management has been a game-changer, offering new opportunities for efficiency and innovation. It has transformed the way we manage supply chains, offering new opportunities for efficiency and innovation. It has also brought new challenges, particularly in terms of cybersecurity, legacy systems, and the pace of technological change.

One of the most significant technological problems in the supply chain is cybersecurity. As the world becomes more interconnected, the risk of cyber threats increases. Companies that manage sensitive data, such as financial information or personal data, are particularly vulnerable to cyber-attacks. According to Bruce Schneider (2013), in the words of cybersecurity "the internet is no longer a web that we connect to. Instead, it's a computerized, networked, and interconnected world that we live in."

As Steve Morgan (2021), the founder of Cybersecurity Ventures, warns that "Cybercrime damages are predicted to cost the world $6 trillion annually by 2021, up from $3 trillion in 2015." Companies must take proactive steps to protect their systems and data from cyber threats, such as implementing robust security protocols and investing in robust cybersecurity measures to protect themselves from cybercriminals. This includes implementing security protocols, conducting regular security audits, and investing in cybersecurity training for employees.

To illustrate, one example of technological problems in the supply chain is the case of Target's data breach in 2013. Target experienced a massive data breach that compromised the personal information of millions of customers. The breach was caused by a cyberattack on Target's payment system, which was not properly secured. As a result, Target suffered significant financial losses and damage to its reputation. In response, the company invested heavily in cybersecurity measures to prevent future breaches.

Another technological problem in the supply chain is the reliance on legacy systems. Many companies continue to use outdated technology, which can be prone to errors and inefficiencies. This can create bottlenecks in the supply chain, causing delays and increasing costs. According to Geoffrey Moore, a technology expert, "without big data, you are blind and deaf and in the middle of a freeway." Companies must invest in modern technology solutions, such as cloud-based supply chain management software, to improve efficiency and reduce the risk of errors.

The rapid pace of technological change is another challenge in supply chain management. As new technologies emerge, companies must adapt quickly to remain competitive. According to Scott Brinker (2020), in the words of technology strategist, "the pace of technology change is so fast that if you don't innovate and stay ahead, you'll be disrupted by those who do." This can require significant investment in research and development, as well as a willingness to take risks and embrace change.

In conclusion, technology has transformed the supply chain, offering new opportunities for efficiency and innovation. However, it has also brought new challenges, particularly in terms of cybersecurity, legacy systems, and the pace of technological change. Companies must invest in robust cybersecurity measures, modern technology solutions, and a culture of innovation to overcome these challenges and remain competitive. As former CEO of IBM, Lou Gerstner, famously stated: "The last thing you want to do is become complacent and static. You need to be constantly questioning the status quo."

Political

Political problems in the supply chain can arise from a variety of factors, including changes in government policies, political instability, and international conflicts. These issues can disrupt supply chains, increase costs, and create reputational risks for companies. As political scientist, Ian Bremmer (2005), notes: "Politics is increasingly driving economics, and that includes supply chains."

One of the political problems that can impact the supply chain is changes in government policies. As policies shift, companies may face new regulations, tariffs, or trade barriers that disrupt their operations. As a former U.S. Secretary of Commerce, Penny Pritzker, notes: "Companies need to be prepared for changes in government policies, and that includes understanding the risks and opportunities of different scenarios." Companies must monitor political developments and have contingency plans in place to mitigate the impacts of policy changes. Political instability can also create risks in the supply chain. "Political instability is a growing challenge for companies that operate globally." Moisés Naím (1994)

Political unrest, civil war, or terrorism can disrupt supply chains and increase costs. Companies must assess political risks in the countries where they operate and have contingency plans in place to deal with political disruptions (Taghipour, 2018).

International conflicts can also create risks in the supply chain. According to Joseph Nye (2011), "international relations can have significant impacts on the global economy, including supply chains." Conflicts between countries can lead to trade barriers, sanctions, or other disruptions that impact supply chains. Companies must monitor international relations and have contingency plans in place to mitigate the impacts of conflicts.

Moreover, political problems in the supply chain can also have reputational impacts, particularly in the age of social media. Companies that are seen as engaging in unethical or illegal practices in their supply chains can face public backlash and damage to their reputation. It is essential to be transparent and proactive in managing political risks in their supply chains, communicating their policies and practices to stakeholders, and demonstrating their commitment to responsible and sustainable practices.

In conclusion, political problems in the supply chain can have significant impacts on a company's operations and reputation. Companies must monitor political developments, assess political risks, and have contingency plans in place to mitigate the impacts of political disruptions. By taking a proactive approach to these challenges, companies can build resilient supply chains that can mitigate political disruptions. As former U.S. Secretary of State, Madeleine Albright, famously stated: "There is no doubt that a company's success depends on its ability to navigate the complex web of political, economic, and social forces that shape the global landscape."

However, it is also important to note that political problems in the supply chain are often complex and interconnected. For example, changes in government policies may be influenced by international relations, domestic politics, or economic considerations. According to Francis Fukuyama (2015), "politics is not just about policy, it's also about power and influence." Companies must take a holistic approach to managing political risks in the supply chain, collaborating with suppliers, and engaging with stakeholders to promote sustainable and responsible practices.

Moreover, political problems in the supply chain can also create opportunities for companies that are prepared to adapt and innovate. As former U.S. Trade Representative, Charlene Barshefsky (2001) explains "the disruptions in the supply chain can create opportunities for companies that are agile and innovative." Companies that are able to respond quickly to political disruptions, such as by diversifying their supply chains or developing new products, can gain a competitive advantage.

Legal

Legal problems in the supply chain can arise from a variety of factors, including non-compliance with laws and regulations, violations of human rights, and breaches of contract. These issues can lead to legal liabilities, reputational risks, and financial losses for companies. According to Hart and Zingales (2017), "the supply chain is a complex web of legal relationships, and companies must ensure that they are compliant with all relevant laws and regulations."

One legal problem that can impact the supply chain is non-compliance with labor laws and regulations. For example, companies that use forced labor, child labor, or engage in other forms of labor exploitation can face legal liabilities and reputational risks. In recent years, there have been several high-profile cases of companies facing legal action over labor violations in their supply chains, including lawsuits against clothing brands for using sweatshop labor and tech companies for exploiting foreign workers. It is essential for companies to ensure that their supply chains are free from labor abuses and that they are compliant with all relevant labor laws and regulations (El-NEMR et al., 2021).

Another legal problem that can impact the supply chain is violations of human rights. For example, companies that use suppliers who engage in human rights abuses, such as human trafficking, can face legal liabilities and reputational risks. In recent years, there have been several cases of companies facing legal action over human rights violations in their supply chains, including lawsuits against chocolate companies for using suppliers who engage in child labor and seafood companies for using suppliers who engage in forced labor. It is essential for companies to ensure that their supply chains are free from human rights abuses and that they are compliant with all relevant human rights laws and regulations.

Moreover, legal problems in the supply chain can also arise from breaches of contract. For example, if a supplier fails to deliver goods or services on time or fails to meet quality standards, this can create legal liabilities and financial losses for companies (Mahfod et al., 2019). In recent years, there have been several cases of companies facing legal action over breaches of contract in their supply chains, including lawsuits against auto companies for failing to ensure that their suppliers met environmental and labor standards. It is essential for companies to have clear contractual terms with their suppliers and to ensure that they are compliant with all relevant laws and regulations.

One example of legal problems in the supply chain was the case of Nike's labor practices in the 1990s. In the 1990s, Nike faced a public backlash over allegations of labor abuses in its supply chain, including the use of sweatshop labor and child labor. The company faced legal action and was forced to pay millions of dollars in settlements. Nike subsequently implemented a series of reforms to address these issues, including adopting a code of conduct for its suppliers and establishing a monitoring program to ensure compliance with labor standards.

Another example is the case of Apple's labor practices in the early 2010s. In the early 2010s, Apple faced criticism over labor abuses in its supply chain, including the use of forced labor and poor working conditions. The company faced legal action and was forced to implement a series of reforms, including improving working conditions in its factories and conducting audits of its suppliers to ensure compliance with labor standards.

In conclusion, legal problems in the supply chain can have significant impacts on a company's operations and reputation. Companies must ensure that they are compliant with all relevant laws and regulations, and that their supply chains are free from labor abuses, human rights violations, and breaches of contract. By taking a proactive approach to these issues, companies can build responsible and sustainable supply chains that can withstand legal scrutiny. According to Cass Sunstein (2002), "companies that operate in a complex legal environment must navigate a variety of legal risks, and that includes risks in the supply chain.

Ways to Improve Supply Chain Sustainability

Supplier

As already mentioned, the company cannot function in a sustainable way if its partners, who always have an influence on the company and the brand image are not fully integrated. To guarantee a sustainable supply chain, the company must have maximum visibility of all the links and processes, starting from the producing and delivery of the raw material. In this case, the supply chain needs to have strategies for appropriate risk mapping, implementation of a vigilance plan, evaluations and regular social audits. Conside a large international manufacturer working with many subcontractors all over the world, who have their direct suppliers and each of these last suppliers have their own suppliers and so on. In this case, it will be so complicated to know exactly whether or not they are exploiting their employees. So, supply chain managers have difficulty determining non-compliance with policies and procedures.

To manage the supply chains, with this regard, on the one hand, a company can develop its own policies and codes of conduct for suppliers, as well as a variety of monitoring and audit mechanisms to enforce these codes against any type of corruption, including poor working conditions in factories in the global supply chain. The underlying assumption is that the information gathered through factory audits will be used by labor rights NGOs to pressure global brands to reform their sourcing practices (Improving Work Conditions in a Global Supply Chain). On the other hand, the company may ask the respect of the international standards from these suppliers, such as, the standards of the International Organization for Standardization (ISO) that shows the environmental measures of companies, Duty of Vigilance in France (2017), Modern Slavery Act adopted by the United Kingdom (2015), Transparency in Supply Chain Act in California (2010), GATS that has a quality assurance system and conducts regular audits of the internal device responsible for controlling the various types of global risks, or the very recent law in Australia (2018) require companies of a certain size more transparency to prevent the risks of forced labor in their supply chain. In addition, the Human Capital Practices Global Reporting Initiative or Sustainability Accounting Standards Board represent global standards regarding child and forced labor issues. Similarly, the company may require ESG (Environmental, Social and Governance) reporting from a third-party who has verified the carbon footprints of its supply chain to do business. When a company fails to take appropriate action to eradicate human exploitation from its supply chains, its shareholders can also bring a legal claim against the directors. Indeed, companies' actions on the ground influence their partners in at-risk countries to eradicate all forms of global outsourcing corruption.

Manufacturer

In general, companies need inventory for two reasons: to satisfy the estimated demand in the future using distribution centers or because of the uncertainty in demand and lack of an appropriate forecasting method (Taghipour, 2020; Tliche et al., 2019). The optimization of the latter can be a fundamental factor in reducing costs, waste and pollution, as warehouses and the operations related to them account for approximately 13% of all greenhouse gas emissions related to the supply chain (Yang et al., 2017). They consume energy due to heating/cooling and lighting and emit a specific amount of GHGs relative to the mix of energy sources in the region (green, coal). For many companies, inventory management is one of the major constraints in the supply chain (Loivet et al., 2020). It is necessary to align forecasts with inventory thanks to Big Data and behavioural analysis. This solution allows to have a stock volume continuously adapted to the buying habits of the consumers. Transportation is also at the heart of logistics forecasting (Shin and Taghipour, 2021). Managing supplier requirements through a vast distribution and transportation network is very complicated. The company must have up-to-date information about delivery times, modes of transportation, etc. to know when to reorganize its inventory (Vosooghidizaji et al., 2020). An updated and enriched database can turn serious supply chain problems into creative problem-solving opportunities (Taghipour et al., 2015).

In addition, organizations could adopt a zero-waste strategy, an effective approach to disposing of its by-products. For example, waste could be used as raw material by other businesses. Beverage bottles from bars and restaurants can be recycled and used as raw material by beverage companies. Bars and restaurants can make a small profit from the container deposit fees, and contribute significantly to the reduction of GHG emissions caused by waste disposal.

Thus, in the face of rising commodity prices, cost control is a very important element in the supply chain (Vosooghidizaji et al., 2022). It must be able to adapt quickly to changing market conditions and have variable cost structures as revenues increase and decrease. Flexibility is their antidote to cost volatility and chain performance.

Distributor

Many options are available to reduce transportation-related carbon emissions. Among them:

- Load trucks to the point where there is no more space available.
- Adopting electric vehicles.

- Using IoT (smart devices) helps minimize the environmental cost of transportation by encouraging drivers to drive at lower speeds.
- Use transportation pooling (consolidating, storing and delivering packages from multiple companies by a single carrier) as a solution to limit fuel consumption, CO2 and air pollutant emissions, and more generally to reduce the environmental impact of transportation.

Retailer

Companies that actively practice sustainability focus on reusable packaging. According to the European Union, only 1% of plastics are biodegradable. The typical effective recycling rate for plastics is low. They are tough, so they can live for a long time in the wild and frequently enter the food chain, posing a danger to the environment and human health. Despite their well-known drawbacks, companies frequently use them as packaging materials because they are inexpensive. Biodegradable packaging materials should be used by companies aiming for a sustainable supply chain (Taghipour, 2020). They can select environmentally friendly packaging materials.

In the same way, the digitalization of the supply chain helps companies to develop ecological production processes, seeking to develop short circuits to save energy and the circular economy to save materials (Taghipour and Merimi, 2021). It dematerializes, digitizes work procedures and offers new services like e-administration and e-payment. These new services allow the reduction of paper consumption and facilitate inter-organizational exchanges.

Customer

In order to reap the benefits of Green Supply Chain Management, customers need to be aware of the efforts that are being made within the company. It is important to publish reports describing the new environmental processes that have been put in place, which can then be taken up by the press, encourage other companies, attract new customers and thus increase the company's profitability. Research shows that 33% of consumers prefer to buy from brands that offer "green", environmentally friendly products and services, the brands that propose clear marketing about sustainable packaging.

CONCLUSION

In conclusion, sustainable supply chain management is a crucial aspect of modern business operations. As Tom Linton, Chief Procurement and Supply Chain Officer at Flex, stated, "sustainability is no longer a 'nice-to-have' but a 'must-have' for businesses to remain competitive in today's market." It is a holistic approach that integrates environmental, social, and economic considerations into every stage of the supply chain, offering numerous benefits for businesses and society as a whole.

One of the key benefits of sustainable supply chain management is cost savings. As Sara Enright, Senior Manager of Sustainability at BSR, notes, "implementing sustainable practices in the supply chain can help companies reduce costs, increase efficiency, and improve profitability." By reducing waste, optimizing transportation and logistics, and using energy-efficient technologies, businesses can lower their operating expenses and improve their bottom line (Taghipour and Frayret, 2011a).

Another important benefit of sustainable supply chain management is risk reduction (Taghipour at al., 2021). As Benjamin Ware, Senior Director of Global Social and Environmental Responsibility at Walmart, notes, "by managing social and environmental risks in the supply chain, companies can reduce the likelihood of supply chain disruptions, reputational damage, and legal liabilities." By implementing responsible sourcing practices, promoting fair labor practices, and engaging with suppliers and stakeholders, businesses can mitigate risks and build long-term resilience.

Furthermore, sustainable supply chain management can enhance brand reputation and customer loyalty. As Cindy Hoots, Global Vice President of Procurement and Supply Chain at Whirlpool, notes, "sustainability is increasingly becoming a differentiator for brands, with consumers and stakeholders demanding greater transparency and accountability." By communicating their sustainability efforts to customers and stakeholders, businesses can build trust and loyalty and gain a competitive advantage in the marketplace.

However, as Jose Lopez, former Executive Vice President of Operations at Nestle, notes, "implementing sustainable supply chain management is not without its challenges." Businesses may face resistance from suppliers, customers, and even their own employees. The lack of transparency and traceability in some supply chains also presents a significant barrier to achieving sustainability goals. Therefore, businesses must take a collaborative approach to sustainable supply chain management (Tliche et al., 2021), as noted by Shannon Bouton, Chief Operating Officer at McKinsey Center for Business and Environment: "achieving sustainability requires companies to work with their suppliers and other stakeholders to identify areas for improvement and develop innovative solutions that benefit everyone involved."

In summary, sustainable supply chain management is a crucial aspect of modern business operations, as noted by Paul Simpson, CEO of CDP: "companies that fail to integrate sustainability into their supply chain management risk falling behind and becoming irrelevant." By implementing sustainable practices, businesses can achieve cost savings, risk reduction, and enhance brand reputation, while contributing to the achievement of environmental, social, and economic sustainability. While there are significant challenges to implementing sustainable supply chain management, businesses can overcome these by taking a collaborative approach, leveraging technology and data, and committing to ongoing monitoring and reporting of their sustainability performance. As the world continues to face significant environmental and social challenges, sustainable supply chain management will only become more important in the years ahead (Taghipour and Frayret, 2011b).

REFERENCES

Barshefsky, C. (2001). Trade policy for a networked world. *Foreign Affairs*, *80*(2), 134–146. doi:10.2307/20050070

Bremmer, I. (2005). Managing risk in an unstable world. *Harvard Business Review*, *83*(6), 51–54. PMID:15938438

Brinker, S. (2020). Martech 5000—Really 8,000, but who's counting?. *Marketing technology landscape supergraphic*.

Cauchois, R., Taghipour, A., Kang, D., Zoghlami, N., & Abed, M. (2017). Advanced solutions for a supply chain with stochastic information. *Journal of Advanced Management Science, 5*(1).

Christopher, M., & Peck, H. (2004). *Building the resilient supply chain.*

El-Nemr, N., Canel-Depitre, B., & Taghipour, A. (2021). The determinants of hotel room rates in Beirut: A hedonic pricing model. International Journal of Trade. *Economics and Finance*, *12*(2), 33–42.

El-Nemr, N., Canel-Depitre, B., & Taghipour, A. (2017, September). Determinants of hotel room rates. In *Marketing Trends Congress. Luxury Industries Conference London 2017*. ACM.

Elkington, J. (1997). The triple bottom line. *Environmental management: Readings and cases, 2*, 49-66.

Fukuyama, F. (2015). After neoconservatism. In *Paradoxes of Power* (pp. 130–139). Routledge.

Golinelli, G. M., & Volpe, L. (2012). *Consonance, value, sustainability. Toward sustainable enterprise.* Cedam.

Hart, O., & Zingales, L. (2017). *Companies should maximize shareholder welfare not market value.* ECGI-Finance Working Paper, (521).

Loivet, W., Taghipour, A., & Kang, D. S. (2020). The rise of green supply chain management: Between complexity and necessity. *Journal of Economics. Business and Management*, *8*(1), 1–7.

Mahfod, J., Canel-Depitre, B., & Taghipour, A. (2019). Quality function deployment-ELECTRE in supplier evaluation. *Journal of Advanced Management Science, 7*(4).

Merimi, M., & Taghipour, A. (2021). Accelerating the digitalization of the supply chain: An empirical research about COVID-19 crisis. In *Digitalization of Decentralized Supply Chains During Global Crises* (pp. 1–24). IGI Global. doi:10.4018/978-1-7998-6874-3.ch001

Morgan, S. (2021). *Report: Cyberwarfare in the C-suite*. Cybercrime Magazine.

Nadia, E. N., Beatrice, C. D., & Atour, T. (2020). Luxury hotels' eco-friendly activities & customers' preferences and willingness to pay for green hotels. *Journal of Advanced Management Science, 8*(1).

Naím, M. (1994). Latin America: The second stage of reform. *Journal of Democracy*, *5*(4), 32–48. doi:10.1353/jod.1994.0057

Nye, J. S. (2011). Power and foreign policy. *Journal of Political Power*, *4*(1), 9–24. doi:10.1080/2158379X.2011.555960

Pagell, M., & Wu, Z. (2009). Building a more complete theory of sustainable supply chain management using case studies of 10 exemplars. *The Journal of Supply Chain Management*, *45*(2), 37–56. doi:10.1111/j.1745-493X.2009.03162.x

Rogers, J. (2008). Sustainability and the'world class' city: what is being sustained and for who? In World Cities and Urban Form: Fragmented, Polycentric, Sustainable? (pp. 57-70). Routledge.

Sajdik, M. (2011). Rendre la justice sur le terrain: Les défis de la lutte contre la corruption aux niveaux national et international. *Chronique ONU*, *49*(4), 19–21. doi:10.18356/4170e8b4-fr

Sarkis, J., Gonzalez-Torre, P., & Adenso-Diaz, B. (2010). Stakeholder pressure and the adoption of environmental practices: The mediating effect of training. *Journal of Operations Management*, *28*(2), 163–176. doi:10.1016/j.jom.2009.10.001

Seuring, S., & Müller, M. (2008). From a literature review to a conceptual framework for sustainable supply chain management. *Journal of Cleaner Production*, *16*(15), 1699–1710. doi:10.1016/j.jclepro.2008.04.020

Shin, M., & Taghipour, A. (2021). Supply Chains Digital Transformation: Automated Underground Logistics Systems. *Underground Construction*, *6*(2), 7. doi:10.18178/joebm.2021.9.2.651

Stahl, B., Cerinšek, G., Colombo, F., & Taisch, M. (2012). Development of competence for sustainable manufacturing by using serious games. *Transactions of FAMENA*, *36*(4), 63–72.

Sunstein, C. R. (2002). *Risk and reason: Safety, law, and the environment*. Cambridge university press.

Taghipour, A. (2014). *Production Network Planning Based on Constraint Relaxation and Discount Approach* (Vol. 2). Lecture Notes on Information Theory.

Taghipour, A. (2018). A Contemporary Approach to Plan Independent Logistics Actors. In *Contemporary Approaches and Strategies for Applied Logistics* (pp. 337–364). IGI Global. doi:10.4018/978-1-5225-5273-4.ch014

Taghipour, A. (Ed.). (2020). *Demand Forecasting and Order Planning in Supply Chains and Humanitarian Logistics*. IGI Global.

Taghipour, A., Abed, M., & Zoghlami, N. (2015, May). Design for remanufacturing respecting reverse logistics processes: A review. In *2015 4th International Conference on Advanced Logistics and Transport (ICALT)* (pp. 299-304). IEEE. 10.1109/ICAdLT.2015.7136602

Taghipour, A., & Beneteau-Piet, C. (2020). Sustainable supply chain management performance. *International Journal of Innovation, Management and Technology*, *11*(6), 165–169. doi:10.18178/ijimt.2020.11.6.897

Taghipour, A., & Frayret, J. M. (2011a). A new heuristic search with local optimization to manage a supply chain. *Meta*, 15.

Taghipour, A., & Frayret, J. M. (2011b). Supply chain coordination planning: A review. *Work paper, École polytechnique de Montréal.*

Taghipour, A., Glaa, B., & Zoghlami, N. (2014, May). Network coordination with minimum risk of information sharing. In *2014 International Conference on Advanced Logistics and Transport (ICALT)* (pp. 184-188). IEEE. 10.1109/ICAdLT.2014.6864115

Taghipour, A., & Merimi, M. (2021). Digital Transformation of Supply Chains during Crisis: COVID-19. In *11th Annual International Conference on Industrial Engineering and Operations Management, IEOM* (pp. 7493-7501). IEEE.

Taghipour, A., Murat, S., & Huang, P. (2021). E-supply chain management: A review. International Journal of e-Education, e-Business, e-. *Management Learning*, *11*(2), 51–61.

Tliche, Y., Taghipour, A., & Canel-Depitre, B. (2019). Anticipation of Demand in Supply Chains. In *Hierarchical Planning and Information Sharing Techniques in Supply Chain Management* (pp. 1–45). IGI Global.

Tliche, Y., Taghipour, A., & Canel-Depitre, B. (2021). Exploring a Downstream Demand Inference Strategy in a Decentralized Two-Level Supply Chain. In *Demand Forecasting and Order Planning in Supply Chains and Humanitarian Logistics* (pp. 1–65). IGI Global. doi:10.4018/978-1-7998-3805-0.ch001

Vosooghidizaji, M., Taghipour, A., & Canel-Depitre, B. (2020). Information Asymmetry in Supply Chain Coordination: State of the Art. *Journal of Industrial and Intelligent Information, 8*(2).

Vosooghidizaji, M., Taghipour, A., & Canel-Depitre, B. (2022). Coordinating corporate social responsibility in a two-level supply chain under bilateral information asymmetry. *Journal of Cleaner Production*, *364*, 132627. doi:10.1016/j.jclepro.2022.132627

Walker, P. H., Seuring, P. S., Sarkis, P. J., & Klassen, P. R. (2014). Sustainable operations management: Recent trends and future directions. *International Journal of Operations & Production Management*, *34*(5). doi:10.1108/IJOPM-12-2013-0557

Yang, S., Taghipour, A., & Canel-Depitre, B. (2017, August). Cost optimization of reverse logistics: A review. In *Proceedings of the 7th International Conference on Information Communication and Management* (pp. 158-161). ACM. 10.1145/3134383.3134393

Chapter 4
Government Engagement in Green Supply Chain Management of Food and Beverage Companies

Muhammad Salman Asif
https://orcid.org/0000-0001-9769-910X
Western Sydney University, Australia

Dilupa Nakandala
https://orcid.org/0000-0003-1535-5288
Western Sydney University, Australia

Henry Lau
Western Sydney University, Australia

Hilal Hurriyet
Western Sydney University, Australia

ABSTRACT

This case study-based chapter investigates the influence of government regulations on the green supply chain management practices of five renowned companies which are classified in group A by Carbon Disclosure Project (CDP): Ajinomoto Group, Asahi Group, Coca-Cola Company, Barry Callebaut, and Danone. Considering their commitment to sustainability and presence in the high-impact sector of food and beverages, this chapter analyzes the impact of government interventions on these companies' supply chains. Their CDP responses, sustainability reports, and relevant literature were qualitatively analyzed using the cross-case analysis method to investigate collaborative strategies enabling low-carbon transitions in these companies. Based on the analysis, environmental sustainability dimensions were devised that demand substantial engagement with governments and regulatory authorities. Implications of the study are manifold as it not only provides recommendations for effective government-industry partnerships in the food sector but also provides the basis for further research in this area.

DOI: 10.4018/978-1-6684-9062-4.ch004

Government policies and regulations play a crucial role in shaping sustainable and responsible supply chain management practices within companies. In this context, food supply chains are historically known for their high environmental impacts and challenges in the implementation of environmentally friendly practices. The food sector highly contributes to land and ocean waste, environmental deterioration, and greenhouse gas emissions. Major hotspots in typical food supply chains include farming, manufacturing, packaging, and transportation, and these hotspots need to be managed in collaboration with relevant members of the supply chain (Asif et al., 2022). Therefore, all stakeholders, including governments and NGOs, are responsible for combating climate change.

Recently, many international bodies and governments have taken steps to enhance the environmental performance of food supply chains. For example, the farm-to-fork strategy initiated by the European Union (EU) calls for a reduction in fertilizer use and promotes organic farming (Garske et al., 2020). Furthermore, environmental bodies such as the Sustainable Packaging Coalition (SPC) and Sustainable Agriculture Initiative (SAI) platform provide guidance on best practices, benchmark cases, and certifications to reduce the environmental impact of interested companies. Some government-led programs, such as China's national plan to promote eco-agriculture have raised the demand for eco-friendly products and thus improved the resource conservation and pollution impact in their agricultural sector (Xu et al., 2020).

This case study-based chapter focuses on analyzing the impact of government interventions on the supply chains of five prominent companies: Ajinomoto Group, Asahi Group Holdings, Coca-Cola Company, Barry Callebaut, and Danone. These companies have been selected for their significant presence in the world of food and beverages, and their commitment to sustainability. By examining the strategies adopted by these companies and the influence of government policies on their supply chain management, we gained valuable insights into how governments can drive sustainable practices and the resulting benefits for businesses and societies. The chapter includes a cross-case study analysis followed by a discussion of the results obtained and how they pave future research directions. Finally, the chapter concludes with some valuable recommendations for practitioners, researchers, and policymakers.

BACKGROUND

To review the global policies and regulations on reducing the environmental impact of food companies, we analyzed the literature on government policies and regulations shaping the environmental performance of food companies and the importance of supply chain collaborations with respect to internal and external stakeholders.

Literature on Government Policies and Regulations

Government policies and regulations play a critical role in improvising the sustainability initiatives of food companies as they can provide a set of standards and regulatory frameworks to guide companies towards sustainable practices. Such government policies usually incentivize companies for adopting green practices through tax credits and grants for sustainable initiatives (Guo et al., 2018). Therefore, government policies can act as a promoter of innovation and technology in the food industry. On the other hand, regulations can also drive the implementation of green practices by imposing non-compliance penalties and fines to ensure the prioritization of sustainability in any food business model (Albertini, 2013; Habib & Bhuiyan, 2017).

The study of Gunningham (2013) also implies that government policies including emission standards and waste reduction regulations provide equal opportunities for food companies while ensuring the consistency of sustainability efforts across the food sector. At the same time, these regulations also provide a roadmap for transparent and traceable supply chains by directing the companies to report their environmental performance and allowing the stakeholders to assess and compare their performance (Blanco et al., 2016).

Governments can also mandate the companies to gain important environmental certifications such as ISO-14001 or Climate Active certifications. ISO-14001 (Environmental Management System) provides a standard framework for businesses to implement and monitor sustainability practices across the supply chains. Meanwhile, these standards promote industrial symbiosis and effective collaborations among internal and external parties to achieve regional goals of carbon neutrality or net-zero emissions (Bravi et al., 2020; Castka & Balzarova, 2018). Moreover, these standards also benefit the consumers and shareholders as they realize the commitment of a company towards sustainability leading to improved reputation and competitive advantage for the company.

The study by Bohnsack et al. (2015) highlighted the role of government interventions in shaping the Corporate Social Responsibility (CSR) of food companies and how they catalyze the integration of sustainability into corporate governance. Furthermore, the comprehensive study of Knudsen et al. (2015) explored the CSR practices of food firms across environmental, social, and economic dimensions and suggested the positive influence of institutional and governmental pressures on these practices. While regulations help in maximizing the positive environmental outcomes for companies, they also forbid them from unethical practices such as greenwashing. Various studies have explored the motivations for greenwashing, the role of governments in preventing misleading marketing tactics, and the need for stringent policies on enabling trustworthy environmental disclosures (Kolcava, 2023; Nishitani et al., 2021; Sun & Zhang, 2019).

Literature on Green Supply Chain Management

Various studies have explored different aspects of GSCM and its implementation. The study of Cauchois et al. (2017) discussed advanced solutions for managing supply chains with stochastic information and suggested robust strategies including flexibility and adaptability to handle uncertainties in environmental factors and achieve sustainability goals. Similarly, the study of Loivet et al. (2020) highlighted the critical GSCM practices to address the growing complexity of supply chains and external pressure to integrate sustainability and green initiatives throughout the supply chain. To promote GSCM, the supplier selection process plays a cornerstone role and various frameworks have been developed to implement a sustainable supplier selection process. The study by Mahfod et al. (2019) explored the application of quality function deployment and ELECTRE in supplier evaluation and emphasized the importance of considering environmental criteria in the supplier selection process. Latest shifts in consumer trends also call for the integration of environmental sustainability factors across the value chain. For instance, the study of Nadia et al. (2020) sheds light on the value customers place on sustainability and how it influences supply chain decisions in the hospitality sector.

With the growing need for sustainability, businesses are adopting environmentally sound technologies and transforming into digital supply chains. A major shift in this trend was observed during COVID-19 when businesses deliberately implemented digital technologies in supply chains to survive in an uncertain environment (Merimi & Taghipour, 2021). Digitalization not only improves the environmental performance of firms but also helps in developing more resilient, sustainable, and responsive supply chains. Another study by Shin and Taghipour (2021) revealed the positive impacts of advanced technologies, such as robotics and automation, in streamlining logistics operations and reducing environmental deterioration. E-supply chain management has also emerged in recent years but the challenges associated with the integration of e-business practices in supply chain operations need further investigation for building efficient e-supply chains (Taghipour et al., 2021). Furthermore, digitalization and automation require seamless integration of the organisation's Enterprise Resource Planning (ERP) system with cutting-edge technologies (artificial intelligence, machine learning, internet-of-things and cloud computing) to achieve operational excellence and optimize business processes (Asif, 2018).

Literature on Collaborations in Supply Chains

Existing literature has explored various aspects of supply chain collaborations – mainly operational and strategic collaborations. Marquès et al. (2010) analysed Vendor Managed Inventory (VMI) through the lens of organisational operations and collaborations, whereas, the latest study by Omar et al. (2020) and Asif and Gill (2022) implied the use of a blockchain platform to decentralise the information, enhance trust and transparency, and generate auditable transactions in VMI operations. Moreover, the concept of Collaborative Risk Management (CRM) has also emerged over the past years (Friday et al., 2018) and risk-sharing contracts have enabled food firms to create more value for their products and services while reducing financial losses (Cao et al., 2021; Li et al., 2015; Wakolbinger & Cruz, 2011). Collaborative Planning, Forecasting, and Replenishment (CPFR) also promise trust development, transparent information sharing, and mutual loss and profit sharing among supply chain entities (Eksoz et al., 2014; Hollmann et al., 2015). The positive impact of collaborations on risk management has been historically explored through the concept of SCRM which includes constructs and frameworks for joint risk management in the supply chains (Ali & Shukran, 2016; Christopher & Peck, 2004; Tang, 2006). Furthermore, exploring the challenges and strategies related to information sharing in supply chains, the study of Taghipour et al. (2014) highlighted the importance of risk mitigation and establishing trust in collaborative networks. Another study has explored various decision-making models on supply chain coordination planning and emphasized the importance of synchronization and collaboration among supply chain partners (Taghipour & Frayret, 2011).

Numerous literature studies have found that a firm's internal collaborations and its collaborations with suppliers and customers have a positive effect on the mitigation of environmental risks (Asif et al., 2020; Chen et al., 2013). However, it is argued that internal collaborations are not sufficient to combat the climate crisis and that external stakeholders need to be engaged to reap the widespread benefits of the sustainability (Laukkanen et al., 2021; Tolkamp et al., 2018). For instance, based on a survey of 122 Italian firms, the study of Dangelico and Pontrandolfo (2015) found that a firm's image performance (perceived reputation) is positively affected by its collaborations with non-business actors including governments and NGOs. Furthermore, the concept of Green Supply Chain Collaborative Innovation (GSCCI) has been highlighted in a recent study (Hong et al., 2019). The study revealed that collaborative innovations among organizations, governments, and institutions positively affect the sustainability capabilities and green innovation performance of a firm. A collaborative environment effectively integrates the sustainability laws and regulations that influence the internal and external engagements of a firm. On the other hand, stringent regulations can have widespread consequences impacting the economic, social, and environmental performance of a firm (Niesten et al., 2017).

However, very limited studies have taken the effect of government collaborations on environmental risk mitigation strategies specific to the food and agriculture industry. Various operational constraints are critical in food supply chains particularly in the sourcing, processing, storage, and distribution (Zhu et al., 2018). Resultantly, many researchers and governments support the sourcing of locally grown fresh food to avoid the global challenges that exist in the food supply chains (Nakandala & Lau, 2019). A Pakistan-based study on agricultural water usage has suggested the need for legislation on water use by the private sector through licensing and tariffs based on volumetric water use instead of fixed charges (Nizami et al., 2021). Moreover, the study of Li et al. (2015) has argued that collaborative practices of risk information sharing and risk sharing mechanisms with external stakeholders can escalate our goals of net-zero. Similarly, the study of Dewick et al. (2017) explored the power dynamics of UK dairy industry and emphasized the need for substantial institutional and governmental interventions to achieve triple bottom-line goals.

Therefore, a significant research gap exists in terms of identifying the benefits of such government-industry partnerships from real-world companies. Following the cross-case analysis method proposed by Yin (2009), our study tends to fill this gap by highlighting the sustainability dimensions requiring a high degree of engagement with governments and regulatory authorities.

Theoretical Context

To understand the influence of external actors such as governments and institutional bodies on the adoption of sustainable practices in the food sector, we studied existing theories and concepts. In this regard, the institutional theory applies as the foundation of this study as it implies the role of policies and regulations in shaping the performance dynamics of a firm (Shibin et al., 2020). Furthermore, stakeholder theory helps in examining the influence of internal and external stakeholders in shaping the sustainability strategies of a firm. On the other hand, stakeholder theory also helps in understanding how government regulations and policies are influenced by critical stakeholders (consumers, NGOs, and industry partnerships) (Asif et al., 2020). Another important theory aligned with our study is the resource dependence theory which analyzes how the food industries are dependent upon governmental resources, incentives, and collaboration for practicing sustainable business strategies (Dania et al., 2018).

RESEARCH METHOD

For this book chapter, we have used the four-step method proposed by Yin (2009): (1) Case studies selection, (2) collecting case study evidence, (3) analyzing case study evidence, and (4) Discussion of case study evidence.

Case Studies Selection

Carbon Disclosure Project (CDP) is an independent body working with governments and policymakers to promote environmental disclosures. In 2020, 252 companies reported their environmental data under the food, beverage, and tobacco sector. We selected the 5 top performing 'A' category companies as reflected through the CDP rating. We used other inclusion and exclusion criteria to shortlist these 5 companies – sufficient disclosure on their collaborations with the government, their global sustainability leadership role, and their substantial influence on government policies and regulations.

Collecting Case Study Evidence

As suggested by Yin (2009), case study researchers should follow certain formal procedures during data collection to ensure quality control throughout the process. We followed the three principles of data collection as explained below:

The first principle refers to triangulation which is the rationale for using multiple sources of evidence. It is believed that the case studies using multiple sources of evidence were highly rated as compared to those relying on a single source of evidence (Heale & Twycross, 2018). Moreover, multiple sources of evidence allow the researcher to address a broader range of business issues. Triangulation of data allows us to reach a convincing and accurate conclusion as it is based on several sources of information corroborating the same finding (Yin, 2009). Although, CDP disclosures of these companies from 2019 to 2021 serve as the primary source of case study data, but we also incorporated annual sustainability and CSR reports of these companies, their websites, and government reports to strengthen the findings of our study.

Following the second principle of data collection, we created a case study database that includes raw data and artifacts related to each company obtained from multiple sources. The third principle then suggests maintaining a chain of evidence to increase the reliability of the information in a case study. This will allow the readers or future researchers to work backward and identify the specific data and evidence that leads to the findings of the study. Therefore, we rigorously maintained the quality of analysis by following the renowned case study research framework of Yin (2009).

Analyzing Case Study Evidence

We followed the analytical approach in developing the case study protocol. Such case study-based research requires the expertise of the case analyst to enforce rigorous empirical thinking, supported by sufficient evidence and consideration of multi-dimensional interpretations. Therefore, to analyze each company, we first provide an overview of that company followed by an explanation of their sustainability strategies and collaborations with the government.

Asahi Group Holdings

The beverage industry plays a crucial role in the consumer market and Asahi Group is a prominent player due to the diverse product range they offer. Asahi Group, established in Japan in 1889, offers a large variety of liquor products and food items. They have always recognized the importance of sustainability and have implemented various sustainability programs across their supply chains as well as influenced the sustainability policies at the government level (Global, 2020).

Sustainability Goals of Asahi

The Asahi Beverage Group strives to forecast any event of outrageous climatic catastrophe, and its consequences on their product supply chains and organizational tasks. In 2018, with the intent of achieving net zero CO_2 emissions by 2050, they developed Asahi Carbon Zero Plan (CDP, 2019-2022). The company has developed thoughtful medium and long-term targets for climate change, including a 40% reduction in emissions by 2025, and a further 30% reduction in scope 3 emissions by 2030. Asahi is continuously implementing action plans to achieve these targets – reducing energy use in their facilities, transitioning to renewable energy sources, reducing and recycling waste, and developing cogeneration facilities to reduce the environmental burden (Asahi, 2021). These action plans align with the global standards to mitigate climate change and transform Asahi into a carbon-neutral brand.

Sustainable Agricultural Practices

Asahi Group is focused on identifying and utilizing sustainable agricultural raw materials to promote biodiversity and preserve natural resources for future generations (Global, 2020). Through government partnerships, Asahi Group promotes sustainable agricultural practices and develops regional priorities for sustainable sourcing of ingredients. The collaborations and government oversights help the company to maintain environmentally and socially responsible supply chains and provide a benchmark for other companies to follow.

Water Conservation

Water conservation is another example of Asahi's sustainability initiatives in collaboration with local authorities. Initiatives such as 'water neutrality' aims at reducing water usage in operations and recycling water waste from manufacturing plants. Such collaborative approaches help the company to improve groundwater extraction, protect water resources on land, and mitigate the effect of water scarcity. Furthermore, to give back to the community, Asahi Group has developed Asahi Forest in Hiroshima to protect biodiversity while nourishing the forest with the same amount of water as they use in their manufacturing operations. Working alongside with Japanese government, the company has also achieved a 90% water recycling rate in 2021 in its breweries and reduced its overall water consumption by 9% compared to 2020 (Global, 2021).

Sustainable Packaging

To develop a circular economy and address the detrimental impact of packaging on natural resources, they developed a '3R+Innovation' initiative. The initiative allowed the company to reduce the weight of plastics, increase the use of recycled products, and decrease the use of labels on their products. Their goal is to use all recycled materials for their plastic containers by 2030, and by 2050, they want to achieve 100% conversion to biodegradable materials and use PET for all their business-wide packaging needs (Asahi, 2021).

In response to the government regulations, Asahi has joined the Science Based Targets initiative (SBTi) to demonstrate their eagerness in achieving the global target of capping the global temperature rise to 1.5° C by 2030. SBTi ensures that the environmental aims and objectives of a firm align with the scientific data for achieving global climate change targets Initiative (Initiaive, 2023). They also joined RE100 in 2020 mandating them to accelerate the renewable energy usage in all their operations and ultimately fulfilling all their energy needs through renewables by 2050. Taking part in such sustainability initiatives allows the company to leverage government resources and expertise and drive a widespread positive change. Asahi's commitment to carbon emissions reduction is also consistent with the Japanese government's 2030 targets to reduce corporate emissions by 46% compared to base levels of 2013 (Global, 2021).

COCA-COLA Beverages

Coca-cola has made significant efforts over the past two decades to enhance its sustainability practices across all its supply chains. Their major practices include water stewardship, sustainable packaging, and the use of renewable energy in all their facilities. Some of their initiative involving government collaborations are explained below:

Water Stewardship

Water stewardship is the key sustainability focus for Coca-Cola. Water scarcity is considered a global issue and Coca-Cola is ambitious to give back the same amount of water to the community as it uses in its manufacturing processes and products (Padhee & Nandan, 2021). Therefore, the company has implemented various water conservation measures, collaborated with local governments and communities, and taken part in various watershed protection initiatives (Coca-Cola, 2022). Moreover, through their collaborations with the government, Coca-Cola has made efforts to replenish water sources and promote clean water access, resulting in a 68% replenishment of total water used in their beverages globally (Global, 2020). Such initiatives reflect the company's commitment to saving water resources and mitigating water scarcity-related risks.

Sustainable Packaging

In collaboration with important stakeholders, Coca-Cola has introduced innovative packaging solutions including the manufacturing of paper and plant bottles, contributing to sustainable packaging and circular economy goals. The company is also focused on transitioning to 100% recyclable packaging by 2025 (CDP, 2019a). Coca-Cola has been greatly supported by local governments during these initiatives as they gained various financial incentives, tax credits, and grants considering the size and impact of Coca-Cola on global climate change issues. In terms of waste management, the company has reported a collection of over 1.4 million metric tons of used packaging material since 2010, resulting in a 22% increase in the global recycling rate of the company since 2015 (Coca-Cola, 2022). Hence, Coca-Cola has also contributed to the United Nations Sustainable Development Goals (UN SDGs) on clean water and sanitation.

Reducing Greenhouse Gas Emissions

Coca-Cola is striving to reduce its greenhouse gas emissions and fulfilling its energy needs through renewable sources. Coca-Cola has invested hefty amounts in their renewable energy projects – installing wind farms and solar panels for their facilities and using electric vehicles for logistics needs. Moreover, the company's Science Based Targets plan to lessen the ozone-depleting substances by 25% across their value chains by 2030, addressing the growing concern of ozone mitigation in a few regions (Global, 2020).

Public-private partnerships have proved to be very beneficial for the triple bottom line of Coca-Cola. Such partnerships have facilitated knowledge sharing, providing funding opportunities and joint ventures to address the impacts of climate change. Furthermore, government partnerships have allowed the company to acquire innovative technological resources for pilot tests in its operations. Apart from collaborations with external entities, Coca-Cola closely works with its farmers to promote sustainable agriculture while empowering local communities to play their role in combating global environmental issues (CDP, 2019-2022). Figure 1 shows how people and communities drive the sustainability focus of Coca-Cola by highlighting key strategic areas that require collaborations with external parties.

Figure 1. Sustainability areas that engage Coca-Cola with communities and extended stakeholders

Danone Foods

Danone's sustainability strategies are aligned with its organizational structure and focus on waste and water management, eco-efficiency, corporate governance, and supply chain management. While shifting towards environmental sustainability in their business models, Danone also strategically manages the implications on social and economic dimensions of business.

Water Management at Danone

Danone has taken a life cycle perspective to manage water conservation across their operations – measuring water footprint by taking all stages of the product life cycle into account (Asif et al., 2022; CDP, 2019b). Research and benchmarking helped Danone to consider both pollution and resource depletion aspects in its water management approach. Danone Waters (the company's water unit) has developed a regionalized water pressure index and a water consumption indicator to ensure the conservation of underground water around their plants (D. Group, 2022).

Eco-Efficiency Indicators

Danone establishes realistic goals and long-term plans to promote its energy management initiatives across its supply chains. In 2008, Danone developed the 'lean plant' program with quantitative goals of reducing energy consumption by 20%, packaging weight by 10%, water usage by 30%, and achieving an 80% waste recovery rate across their plants in the next five years (Global, 2021). In the same year, Danone also announced reducing its GHG emissions by 30% in five years and achieved its target quite efficiently in 2012.

Supply Chain Management Indicators

One of the famous programs Danone implemented to monitor the sustainability progress of their suppliers was called 'RESPECT'. The program included awareness and training on sustainable business practices and supplier audits conducted through an independent body, SEDEX. Danone also ensured compliance of all their global suppliers with relevant government regulations and actively tracked and managed non-compliance activities (CDP, 2019-2022).

Corporate Governance and CSR at Danone

The annual sustainability reports of Danone suggest that the company engages with internal and external stakeholders to achieve the common goal of becoming a net-zero economy. The company categorized their stakeholders into four groups – social, public, economic, and professional associations (D. Group, 2022). From 2006 to 2015, Danone developed various protocols and contact methods to ensure frequent interaction with all their stakeholders. Various studies have fortified the importance of addressing social, economic, and environmental challenges and creating value for their own business through sustainability initiatives (Guoyou et al., 2013; Velter et al., 2022). Danone's business strategy aligns with this notion as they strive to avail any opportunities for creating shared value and driving positive change.

All the mentioned sustainability initiatives of Danone wouldn't have been that successful without their high degree of collaboration with local governments and authorities. For instance, Danone's adoption of life cycle management and water consumption indices aligned with their local government guidelines on water usage and pollution control. Similarly, supplier incentivization programs and stakeholder engagement practices reflect the company's compliance with government policies in the corporate governance (Global, 2020).

Barry Callebaut

Barry Callebaut is one of the largest chocolate manufacturers highly committed to its corporate social responsibility and 'Forever Chocolate' sustainability strategy. This strategy drives sustainability initiatives across their operations, including challenges in their cocoa supply chains, sustainable procurement, and collaborative practices towards achieving net-zero emission targets. Following are some of the noteworthy sustainability practices, that demonstrate Barry Callebaut's degree of engagement with government and other stakeholders.

Forever Chocolate: Sustainability Strategy

The company's sustainability strategy called 'Forever Chocolate' is based on 4 critical challenges common to cocoa supply chains: farmer poverty, child labour, sustainable sourcing, and carbon and forest footprint. The company has set up multiple medium and long-term goals to address these challenges by 2025 (CDP, 2019-2022). The strategy reflects the importance of environmentally conscious stakeholders including farmers, employees, consumers, and local communities to achieve the CSR goals. Moreover, by engaging with the government, Barry Callebaut demonstrates its commitment to addressing regional challenges in the cocoa sector (Callebaut, 2022). Such stakeholder engagements help the company to leverage collaborative efforts, drive policy changes, and lead towards a resilient cocoa supply chain.

Sustainable Sourcing and Supply Chain Transparency

While implementing a variety of environmental certifications and sustainability programs, Barry Callebaut has developed a Cocoa Horizons Foundation to promote sustainable practices that enable the conservation of land and water, as well as improve the livelihood of cocoa farmers. With sustainable sourcing practices in place, the company takes pride in ensuring transparency and traceability in its value chain and enabling the customers to trace and identify the source of ingredients in any chocolate they buy (Global, 2020). Barry Callebaut is also a key participant in World Cocoa Foundation's CocoaAction program which is a joint venture among governments and chocolate companies. CocoaAction aims to accelerate sustainability and industrial symbiosis among chocolate manufacturers to enhance the overall productivity of the chocolate sector (Foundation, 2023). Figure 2 shows the performance of sustainable material sourcing and selling in Barry Callebaut over the recent five years (2016-2021) based on the data reported by the company (Global, 2020).

Figure 2. Sustainable selling and sourcing performance of Barry Callebaut (2016-2021) (Global, 2020)

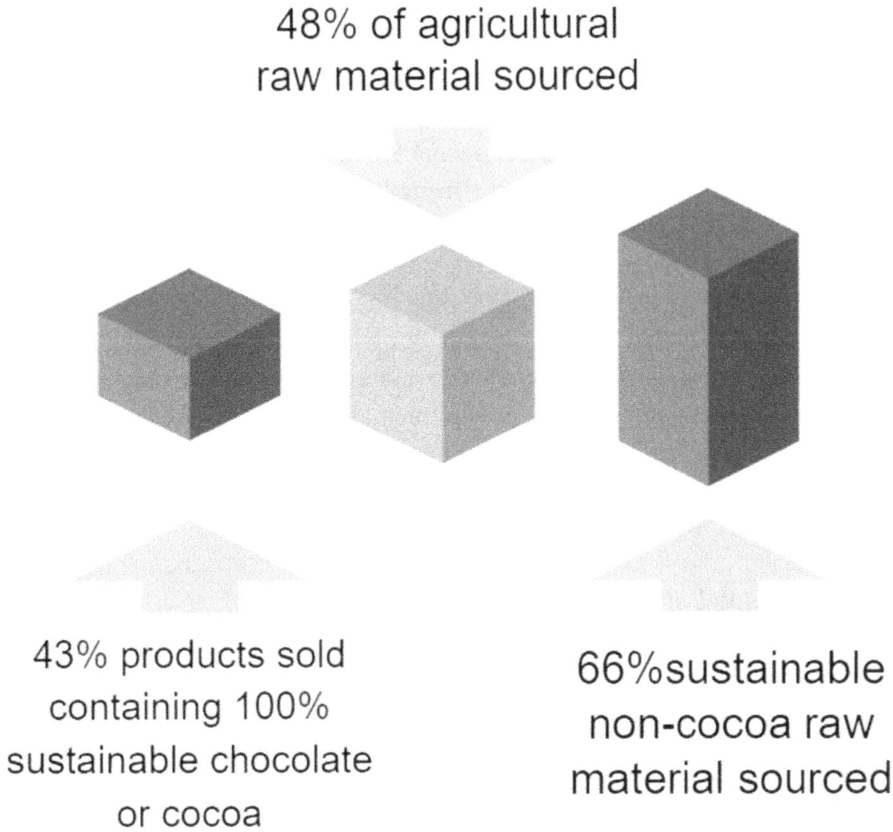

Environmental Collaborations and Partnerships

Besides engaging with the key stakeholders in their supply chains, Barry Callebaut actively participates in government-led initiatives including the International Cocoa Initiative (ICI), the Sustainable Trade Initiative (IDH) and the CocoaAction program. These collaborations are working for the company in terms of business productivity and sustainable community development. To support the triple bottom line, Barry Callebaut has also developed a Sustainability Bond Framework that provides sustainability bonds to finance environmentally sound processes and technologies (Callebaut, 2022). This framework aligns well with the international standards for green and social bonds and reflects the high moral values of the company. For Barry Callebaut, one of the metrics to measure success is the annual percentage increase in sustainable sourcing which they report to the CDP and their local authorities (Global, 2021).

Ajinomoto Group

Ajinomoto is a food company dealing in the production of various food, fine chemicals, medicines, and health-related products. In their global operations, the company follows their ultimate sustainability goal of developing a 'Recycling-Oriented Society' to ensure harmony between the environment and the public (Global, 2020). Following is an analysis of Ajinomoto's sustainability strategies including their environmental and governance initiatives.

Environmental Strategies

Over the last decade, Ajinomoto has collaborated with its key stakeholders and developed a few environmental objectives to enhance its sustainability performance. Ajinomoto is motivated to achieve a low-carbon society by reducing GHG emissions throughout the life cycles of its products. The company also ensures the availability of food resources, environmental protection, and water conservation for future generations (CDP, 2019-2022). Moreover, Ajinomoto encourages efficient resource usage by following the 3R principle – reducing, reusing, and recycling waste from all stages of the product life cycle. For up-to-date compliance with applicable laws and regulations, they have developed a business-wide environmental management system that triggers any non-compliance for timely actions (A. Group, 2022).

As part of the governance strategy, Ajinomoto has established a strategic risk management and crisis management system to address any social or environmental concerns before they cause damage. Also, the company ensures consistency between their climate change strategy and the government's climate change policies through regular monitoring and assessments by the in-house environmental committee (Global, 2021).

Ajinomoto's Partnerships With the Government

Although Ajinomoto collaborates with all its key stakeholders, three partnerships with governmental bodies are paving the way to become a carbon-neutral company. Firstly, Ajinomoto has been actively participating in the maintenance of environmental information clarification, carried out by the Ministry of the Environment in Japan. Ajinomoto mainly uses data from the CDP to understand their impact on climate change and report it independently to the Ministry (CDP, 2019-2022). Secondly, Ajinomoto partnered with the local Ministry of Economy, Trade, and Industry (METI) in their pilot program for improving enterprise-wide energy efficiencies. Ajinomoto's expertise and input were sought by METI during the implementation of the pilot program, showcasing the company's leadership role in reducing environmental burdens alongside the government departments. Last, but not least, Ajinomoto also collaborates with the Japan Food Industry Association, especially providing data for investigations on food losses and the environmental impact of food logistics (A. Group, 2022).

Ajinomoto's win-win environmental strategies and multifaced collaborations with government institutions reflect its dedication to protecting the environment and the social well-being of surrounding communities.

RESULT AND DISCUSSION

This book chapter provides a comprehensive analysis of government-industry collaborations in the food sector through case examples of five notable companies from the food and beverage sector. The findings show a substantial role of government collaborations during the development and implementation of sustainable practices and highlight the importance of government-industry partnerships in achieving sustainable global food supply chains. In the following sections, we will present a cross-case analysis to identify common sustainability approaches and highlight the critical implications of the study.

Cross-Case Analysis

As suggested by Yin (2009), the credibility of cross-case analysis depends on the research boundaries and categories under which different cases are analyzed. Therefore, to identify the overarching themes and patterns in the impact of governments on sustainability initiatives of food companies, we compare the responses of five companies under five broad categories.

Organizational Restructuring and Strategic Focus

To transform into sustainable organizations, all five companies have undergone some organizational restructuring and aligned their strategic focus with the sustainability requirements of their stakeholders including the governments. These optimizations in their organizational structure fortify their environmental stewardship and eco-friendly commitments. For instance, Danone optimized its supply chain by divesting from non-core businesses and focusing on sustainable growth areas including fresh dairy products, beverages, and biscuits (D. Group, 2022). Similarly, Coca-Cola altered its business model to demonstrate its attention to regenerative practices, the use of biodegradable materials, and promoting biodiversity. Moreover, Asahi Group also demonstrated their aggressive approach to environmental sustainability through programs like Asahi Carbon Zero, renewable energy adoption, water resource conservation, and sustainable packaging (Global, 2020). Awareness campaigns and sustainability training also maximize the impact of green initiatives and allow the firms to play their role in building environmentally conscious societies (Ali & Shukran, 2016). Organizations often undergo changes in their business model to expand their online operations as they lower the scope 1 and scope 2 emissions of a firm. For most of the analyzed companies, government engagements were observed during the implementation of carbon taxes, innovative technologies, environmental risk management, community trainings, and energy efficiency plans.

Environmental Practices for Resource Management

Analysis revealed that sustainable resource management often requires engagement with external stakeholders. Ajinomoto Group has implemented various strategies for resource conservation in line with their government policies and regulations. Reduction in their environmental impact through improved energy efficiency, reduced water consumption, and sustainable packaging was driven by external stakeholder pressure and highlighted the company's commitment to environmental stewardship (CDP, 2019-2022). Additionally, online retailing and marketing have been employed by most companies to allow resource sharing. For example, all the partners share the same values, resources, and customers on e-commerce websites, also called virtual stores (Amblee & Bui, 2011). This benefits in eliminating carbon emissions through efficient use of resources.

The companies under analysis have also demonstrated their efforts towards Closed-Loop Supply Chains (CLSC) and the latest CLSC models have considered waste management and resource recovery as part of the loop to enable a circular economy (Miemczyk et al., 2016; Sgarbossa & Russo, 2017). Moreover, firms practice industrial symbiosis to reduce waste from their value chains resulting in resource efficiency. Industrial symbiosis enables a circular economy by allowing firms to transfer their waste or by-products to another firm as their production inputs (Yazan et al., 2020). Therefore, the implementation of industrial symbiosis and CLSC also promote regenerative practices, recyclable products, and biodegradable raw materials (Asif et al., 2020).

Most of the companies mentioned the usage of recyclable products and biodegradable packaging but from their own perspective. Some of them focused on using biogas and natural fuels instead of petroleum oils as energy resources in their working plants. A few of the companies drove their plastic usage to a minimum number as it cast carbon emissions to the environment (CDP, 2019-2022).

Governance Structure and Stakeholder Engagement

To achieve sustainability objectives, it is paramount for food companies to engage with their stakeholders and establish an effective governance structure within their organization. Stakeholder engagement and corporate governance were central to Danone's approach, with specific procedures established for managing relationships with various stakeholder categories. Danone has categorized its stakeholders into social, public, economic, and professional associations to streamline contact frequencies and establish effective methods of interaction (Global, 2020). This approach not only helps the company to actively engage with governments but also helps them to promote education and awareness campaigns on sustainability issues. Such partnerships also disseminate information about sustainable practices and changing consumer trends.

Joint certification programs and collaborative LCAs were also practiced in some of the analyzed companies as they allow the firms to involve stakeholders in managing emissions across their value chains (CDP, 2019a). Moreover, by efficient integration of stakeholder expectations in environmental strategies and initiatives, firms can gain a competitive advantage in the novel sustainability market, and ultimately enhance their financial performance too.

Supply Chain Management and Sustainable Procurement

Government collaborations have pushed companies to monitor and improve the sustainability performance of their supplier tiers – not just the direct suppliers but the chain of suppliers. To develop green supply chains, Barry Callebaut actively participates in government-led initiatives such as the International Cocoa Initiative and the CocoaAction program of the World Cocoa Foundation. These partnerships have allowed the company to promote community development and enable sustainable production and consumption in cocoa-producing countries. Similarly, Ajinomoto Group's sustainable agricultural practices, including organic production methods, are influenced by their local government to ensure sustainable farming practices in their region. In response to immense institutional pressure on green packaging and sustainable material sourcing, companies are striving to transform their supply chains to avoid carbon penalties and taxes (Guo et al., 2018).

Barry Callebaut took steps forward to provide organic consumables and committed to providing social and economic benefits to suppliers that can provide carbon-neutral raw materials (CDP, 2019a). Food companies also undertake technological commitments and sustainable innovations in collaboration with key stakeholders including governments and 3rd party logistics providers. Innovative technologies such as Blockchain Technology (BCT) and Internet-of-Things (IoT) help companies to record emissions from all parts of their supply chain, making them more competitive in the sustainability market (Schmidt & Wagner, 2019).

Sustainable Transportation and Energy

Transportation and energy consumption are the key hotspots in food supply chains. From the analysis of five benchmark companies, we found that fuel efficiency measures, collaborative transport initiatives, and fuel taxes are practiced to reduce carbon emissions from their transportation operations. For instance, Ajinomoto Group has implemented eco-friendly transportation methods (electric and hybrid vehicles) to reduce GHG emissions from their logistics. The company also complies with relevant laws and regulations on energy conservation and integrates such regulations in its 3R approach (Reduce, Reuse, and Recycle) for the waste management (Global, 2020). Asahi Group also demonstrated optimization in their transportation routes and hefty investments in renewable energy as part of their 2050 Asahi Carbon Zero plan. Therefore, such initiatives in collaboration with governments lead to a reduction in GHG emissions, promoting biodiversity, and conservation of natural resources.

Collaborative transport also impedes carbon emissions as it allows companies to reduce empty mileage across borders. Moreover, through collaborations, companies can make better use of container space and manage the share of the freight risk with other companies (Williams et al., 2008). Following the principles of reverse logistics and green procurement also showcase the firm's attention to global regulations as it impedes waste and pollution from escaping the supply chain loop (Asif et al., 2022).

FINDINGS AND IMPLICATIONS

The findings of a cross-case analysis are argued to be more robust than the single-case analysis (Yin, 2009). An important point in conducting cross-case synthesis is that the examination of case-case patterns strongly depends on the arguments and interpretations of the authors. Therefore, following the cross-case analysis, we identified major sustainability practices, strategies, and initiatives that reflect companies' collaborations with their relevant governments. Table 2 shows all such collaborative practices and strategies aligned with the eight themes (sustainability dimensions) we developed for government-industry environmental collaborations.

Table 1. Selected themes and relevant green practices, initiatives, and strategies

Environmental Sustainability Dimensions	Relevant green practices/initiatives/strategies
Environmental Stewardship	Eco-friendly commitments, Industrial symbiosis, use of biodegradable materials, regenerative practices, in-house energy efficiency
Sustainable Agriculture	Sustainable cultivational practices, promoting biodiversity, sustainable material sourcing, organic production
Incentives and Taxes	Changing consumer behavior and trends, fuel tax, carbon tax
Waste Management	Fuel efficiency, recyclable products, green packaging, technological commitments
Environmental Disclosures	Published reports, CDP disclosures, Environmental Risk Management
Green Supply Chains	Collaborative LCAs, green procurement, reverse logistics, green transportation
Sustainable Energy	Managing trade-offs, renewable energy transitions, energy efficiency, sustainability innovations
Educations and Awareness training	Online retailing and marketing, awareness campaigns, joint certification programs

These eight environmental sustainability dimensions uncover the successful practices and strategies companies have implemented in collaboration with the stakeholders including their relevant governments and authorities. For instance, sustainable energy implies the management of trade-offs in renewable transitions, optimizing energy consumption in key operations, and investing and participating in collaborative energy innovations and pilot programs. Similarly, environmental disclosures demand sharing of sustainability information with government institutions and 3rd parties and managing environmental risks pertaining to the global climate change and energy crisis.

Implications of the Study

From a comprehensive analysis of the sustainability practices of five benchmark companies and the results of their collaborative efforts with relevant governments, we identified eight key themes. Figure 3 shows the themes or sustainability dimensions found at the intersection of business sustainability strategies and government collaborations as reported in CDP disclosures.

Figure 3. Environmental sustainability dimensions for government-industry collaborations

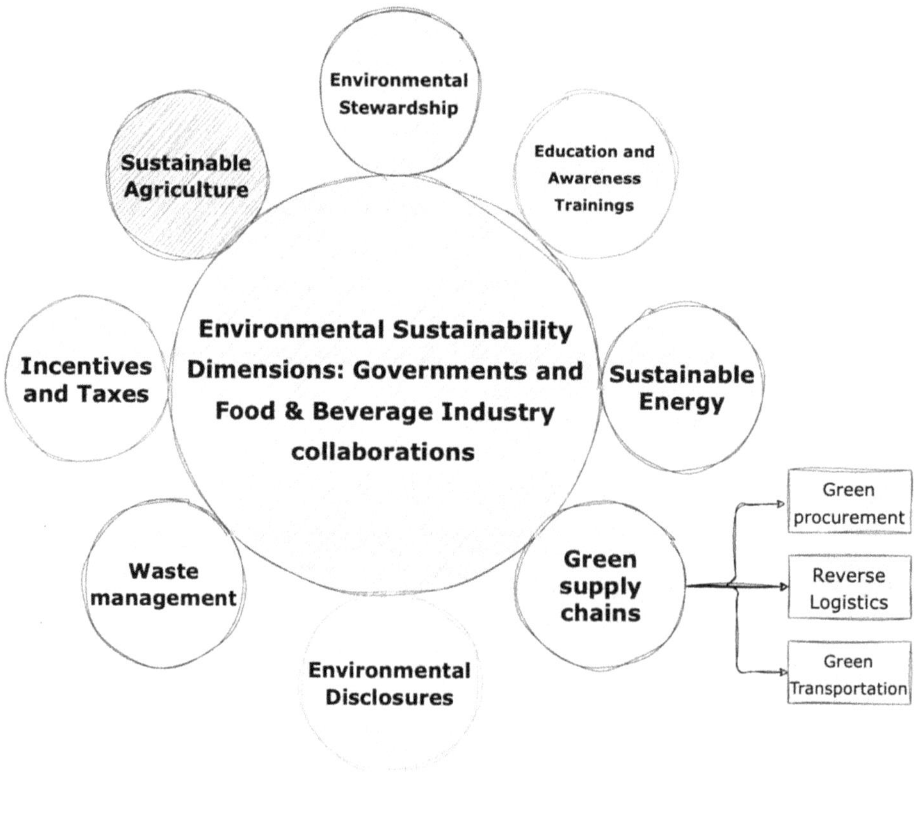

The cross-case analysis results showcase the significant influence of government engagements and partnerships on the sustainability initiatives of the five examined food companies. These collaborations have transformed the business strategies and actions in major environmental aspects of sustainability including environmental stewardship, green supply chains, education and awareness, waste management, and sustainable agriculture. Government engagements not only provide regulatory frameworks, high-level goals, and incentives guiding the companies in their sustainability efforts but also highlight the importance of collaborative efforts in achieving a more sustainable food industry.

Implications of this study are also critical for food companies, especially Small and Medium Enterprises (SMEs) that are striving to contribute towards global net-zero emission targets. From the findings of this research, companies can identify the environmental sustainability dimensions relevant to their business operations and ways to engage with relevant authorities to promote sustainability across these dimensions. Moreover, the implications are highly practical as it offers real case examples that can serve as benchmarks for other companies in the sector. Companies can learn from the efforts of these renowned companies to enhance their own sustainability performance. The findings can also help the companies in understanding the regulatory landscape as they identify the compliance requirements and leverage policy frameworks to drive their environmental initiatives in an effective manner.

Furthermore, the study confirms the importance of sustainability reporting. Food companies can take guidance from this study to improvise their sustainability reporting by aligning it with recognized frameworks, such as CDP, and sharing their disclosures with governments and regulatory bodies to gain sustainability incentives and brand reputation. Policy implications of the study are also noteworthy, guiding policymakers in formulating supportive regulations and frameworks. The study provides major environmental sustainability dimensions where governments and policymakers can establish productive relationships with local companies and escalate their progress towards Sustainable Development Goals (SDGs).

In contrast, there are various theoretical implications of the study. Mainly, the findings of the study contribute to the theoretical understanding of the impact of government interventions on sustainable practices in the food and beverage sector. The sustainability strategies identified in the study offer insights into the effective collaborations between the food industry and governments, providing the roadmap for developing collaborative strategies in other industrial sectors facing similar sustainability challenges. The findings and methodology of the study may also inspire future researchers to investigate how partnerships can be fostered and leveraged to drive sustainability practices in other industries as well.

LIMITATIONS AND RECOMMENDATIONS

To enhance the robustness of the study, the authors carefully assessed the limitations of the study and provide the following recommendations for future research.

Cross-Sector Studies

Future researchers can expand the research beyond the food and beverage sector by including other high-impact industries, such as chemicals, textiles, and automotive to compare the government interventions across diverse sectors. This can reveal sector-specific challenges and more opportunities for sustainable growth.

Policy Evaluation

This study has qualitatively analyzed the impact of government policies and regulations on five companies only and the authors understand the limitations related to the generalizability of the study. Further research is required to effectively evaluate the efficiency of government regulations in shaping the sustainability performance of a firm. This could include investigating the inconsistencies between policy objectives and actual outcomes, analyzing the drivers and barriers to policy implementation, and exploring the impact of enforcement mechanisms. Moreover, quantitative research studies can measure the environmental outcomes of government policies and regulations by assessing emission reductions, resource efficiencies, and financial performance a firm undergoing collaborative sustainability strategies.

Comprehensive Comparative Analysis

Future researchers can use a larger sample of food and beverage companies to provide a better understanding of the impact of policies and regulations across distinct parts of food supply chains. Furthermore, this study only encompasses the environmental sustainability dimensions and further research is required to expand the scope in terms of social and economic sustainability dimensions. Common social sustainability dimensions to research include community engagement, fair trade, labour laws, and others that help in developing a better understanding of government influence across the triple bottom line of a company.

Longitudinal Studies

Although our study assessed the CDP disclosure of five companies from 2019 to 2021, detailed time-series research can offer more insights into the evolution of government policies and their impact on sustainability initiatives. Examining the changes in policy, regulations, and business practices over extended periods can highlight the latest trends, challenges, and success factors in achieving relevant SDGs.

Global Perspectives

The five companies analyzed in this study were selected based on their global operations and their government collaborations were analyzed independent of any regional boundaries i.e., regional variables were beyond the scope of the study. Future researchers can conduct comparative studies across different regions and countries to demonstrate the variations in cultural context, government policies, and political dynamics influencing the sustainability initiatives of a firm.

CONCLUSION

By examining the CDP disclosure and sustainability reports of five global food and beverage companies, we identified some of the best environmental strategies and initiatives and the subsequent influence of government policies and regulations. The study followed the reliable cross-case analysis method to highlight the common sustainability dimensions of five companies and generalized the findings of the study for wider applications. Understanding the role of governments across these sustainability dimensions is an important contribution of the study. By investigating the influence of collaborations on success of the sustainability practices, the study argued the positive impact of government-industry collaborations across eight sustainability dimensions including green supply chain management, environmental disclosures, environmental stewardship, and others. Therefore, the study provides valuable insights into how governments can drive sustainable practices and the resultant long-term advantages for businesses and society. Finally, the study provides critical theoretical and practical implications along with further recommendations to pave the way for future research in the government-industry sustainability collaborations domain.

REFERENCES

Albertini, E. (2013). Does environmental management improve financial performance? A meta-analytical review. *Organization & Environment*, *26*(4), 431–457. doi:10.1177/1086026613510301

Ali, I., & Shukran, K. (2016). Managing supply chain risks and vulnerabilities through collaboration: Present and future scope. *Journal of Developing Areas*, *50*(5), 335–342. doi:10.1353/jda.2016.0027

Amblee, N., & Bui, T. (2011). Harnessing the influence of social proof in online shopping: The effect of electronic word of mouth on sales of digital microproducts. *International Journal of Electronic Commerce*, *16*(2), 91–114. doi:10.2753/JEC1086-4415160205

Asahi. (2021). *Annual sustainability report*. Ashai.

Asif, M. S. (2018). An appraisal of issues faced by manufacturing companies, when selecting an enterprise resource planning (Erp) system. *International Journal of Business and General Management*, *7*(1), 1–8.

Asif, M. S., & Gill, H. (2022). Blockchain technology and green supply chain management (GSCM)–improving environmental and energy performance in multi-echelon supply chains. IOP Conference Series: Earth and Environmental Science. IOP Publishing. doi:10.1016/j.jclepro.2020.124191

Asif, M. S., Lau, H., Nakandala, D., Fan, Y., & Hurriyet, H. (2020). Adoption of green supply chain management practices through collaboration approach in developing countries–From literature review to conceptual framework. *Journal of Cleaner Production*, *276*, 124191. doi:10.1016/j.jclepro.2020.124191

Asif, M. S., Lau, H., Nakandala, D., Fan, Y., & Hurriyet, H. (2022). Case study research of green life cycle model for the evaluation and reduction of scope 3 emissions in food supply chains. *Corporate Social Responsibility and Environmental Management*, *29*(4), 1050–1066. doi:10.1002/csr.2253

Blanco, C., Caro, F., & Corbett, C. J. (2016). The state of supply chain carbon footprinting: Analysis of CDP disclosures by US firms. *Journal of Cleaner Production*, *135*, 1189–1197. doi:10.1016/j.jclepro.2016.06.132

Bohnsack, R., Kolk, A., & Pinkse, J. (2015). Catching recurring waves: Low-emission vehicles, international policy developments and firm innovation strategies. *Technological Forecasting and Social Change*, *98*, 71–87. doi:10.1016/j.techfore.2015.06.020

Bravi, L., Santos, G., Pagano, A., & Murmura, F. (2020). Environmental management system according to ISO 14001: 2015 as a driver to sustainable development. *Corporate Social Responsibility and Environmental Management*, *27*(6), 2599–2614. doi:10.1002/csr.1985

Callebaut, B. (2022). *Forever Chocolate Progress Report 2021/2022*. Barry Callebaut. https://www.barry-callebaut.com/en-AU/group/forever-chocolate/sustainability-reporting/forever-chocolate-progress-report-202122

Cao, S., Bryceson, K., & Hine, D. (2021). Collaborative risk management in decentralised multi-tier global food supply chains: An exploratory study. *International Journal of Logistics Management*, *32*(3), 1050–1067. doi:10.1108/IJLM-07-2020-0278

Castka, P., & Balzarova, M. A. (2018). An exploration of interventions in ISO 9001 and ISO 14001 certification context–A multiple case study approach. *Journal of Cleaner Production*, *174*, 1642–1652. doi:10.1016/j.jclepro.2017.11.096

Cauchois, R., Taghipour, A., Kang, D., Zoghlami, N., & Abed, M. (2017). Advanced solutions for a supply chain with stochastic information. *Journal of Advanced Management Science, 5*(1).

CDP. (2019a). Cascading Commitments: Driving ambitious action through supply chain engagement. In: CDP Carbon Trust. CDP.

CDP. (2019b). MAJOR RISK OR ROSY OPPORTUNITY; Are companies ready for climate change? *CDP Carbon Trust*. CDP. https://6fefcbb86e61af1b2fc4-c70d8ead6ced550b4d987d7c03fcdd1d.ssl.cf3.rackcdn.com/cms/reports/documents/000/004/588/original/CDP_Climate_Change_report_2019.pdf?1562321876

Chen, J., Sohal, A. S., & Prajogo, D. I. (2013). Supply chain operational risk mitigation: A collaborative approach. *International Journal of Production Research*, *51*(7), 2186–2199. doi:10.1080/00207543.2012.727490

Christopher, M., & Peck, H. (2004). *Building the resilient supply chain*. Emerald Insight.

Coca-Cola. (2022). *Refresh the world. Make a difference*. Coca-Cola. https://www.coca-colacompany.com/content/dam/journey/us/en/reports/coca-cola-business-and-sustainability-report-2022.pdf

Dangelico, R. M., & Pontrandolfo, P. (2015). Being 'green and competitive': The impact of environmental actions and collaborations on firm performance. *Business Strategy and the Environment*, *24*(6), 413–430. doi:10.1002/bse.1828

Dania, W. A. P., Xing, K., & Amer, Y. (2018). Collaboration behavioural factors for sustainable agri-food supply chains: A systematic review. *Journal of Cleaner Production*, *186*, 851–864. doi:10.1016/j.jclepro.2018.03.148

Dewick, P., Foster, C., & Webster, S. (2017). Facilitating a more sustainable food and farming sector in the UK. In *System Innovation for Sustainability 3* (pp. 46–58). Routledge. doi:10.4324/9781351279369-3

Eksoz, C., Mansouri, S. A., & Bourlakis, M. (2014). Collaborative forecasting in the food supply chain: A conceptual framework. *International Journal of Production Economics*, *158*, 120–135. doi:10.1016/j.ijpe.2014.07.031

Friday, D., Ryan, S., Sridharan, R., & Collins, D. (2018). Collaborative risk management: A systematic literature review. *International Journal of Physical Distribution & Logistics Management*, *48*(3), 231–253. doi:10.1108/IJPDLM-01-2017-0035

Garske, B., Stubenrauch, J., & Ekardt, F. (2020). Sustainable phosphorus management in European agricultural and environmental law. *Review of European, Comparative & International Environmental Law*, *29*(1), 107–117. doi:10.1111/reel.12318

Global, C. (2020). CDP Climate Change. In Yearly. United Kingdom: Carbon Disclosure Project.

Global, C. (2021). CDP Climate Change. In Yearly. United Kingdom: Carbon Disclosure Project.

Ajinmoto Group. (2022). *Ajinomoto Group ASV Report 2022*. Ajinmoto. https://www.ajinomoto.co.jp/company/en/ir/library/annual/main/08/teaserItems1/01/linkList/0/link/ASV%20Report%202022_E_A4.pdf

Danone Group. (2022). *Integrated Annual Report - Danone's Sustainability Performance*. Danone Group. https://www.danone.com/content/dam/danone-corp/danone-com/rai/2022/danone-integrated-annual-report-2022.pdf

Gunningham, N. (2013). Managing the energy trilemma: The case of Indonesia. *Energy Policy*, *54*, 184–193. doi:10.1016/j.enpol.2012.11.018

Guo, Y., Xia, X., Zhang, S., & Zhang, D. (2018). Environmental regulation, government R&D funding and green technology innovation: Evidence from China provincial data. *Sustainability (Basel)*, *10*(4), 940. doi:10.3390u10040940

Guoyou, Q., Saixing, Z., Chiming, T., Haitao, Y., & Hailiang, Z. (2013). Stakeholders' influences on corporate green innovation strategy: A case study of manufacturing firms in China. *Corporate Social Responsibility and Environmental Management*, *20*(1), 1–14. doi:10.1002/csr.283

Habib, A., & Bhuiyan, M. B. U. (2017). Determinants of monetary penalties for environmental violations. *Business Strategy and the Environment*, *26*(6), 754–775. doi:10.1002/bse.1947

Heale, R., & Twycross, A. (2018). *What is a case study?* (Vol. 21). Royal College of Nursing.

Hollmann, R. L., Scavarda, L. F., & Thomé, A. M. T. (2015). Collaborative planning, forecasting and replenishment: A literature review. *International Journal of Productivity and Performance Management*, *64*(7), 971–993. doi:10.1108/IJPPM-03-2014-0039

Hong, J., Zheng, R., Deng, H., & Zhou, Y. (2019). Green supply chain collaborative innovation, absorptive capacity and innovation performance: Evidence from China. *Journal of Cleaner Production*, *241*, 118377. doi:10.1016/j.jclepro.2019.118377

Science Based Targets. (2023). *Ambitious Corporate Climate Action*. Science Based Targets. https://sciencebasedtargets.org/

Knudsen, J. S., Moon, J., & Slager, R. (2015). Government policies for corporate social responsibility in Europe: A comparative analysis of institutionalisation. *Policy and Politics*, *43*(1), 81–99. doi:10.1332/030557312X656016

Kolcava, D. (2023). Greenwashing and public demand for government regulation. *Journal of Public Policy*, *43*(1), 179–198. doi:10.1017/S0143814X22000277

Laukkanen, M., Manninen, K., Huiskonen, J., & Kinnunen, N. (2021). Sustainable Value Creation for Advancing Sustainability Transition: An Approach to Integrate Company-and System-Level Sustainability. In Business Models for Sustainability Transitions: How Organisations Contribute to Societal Transformation (pp. 89-121). Springer.

Li, G., Fan, H., Lee, P. K., & Cheng, T. (2015). Joint supply chain risk management: An agency and collaboration perspective. *International Journal of Production Economics*, *164*, 83–94. doi:10.1016/j.ijpe.2015.02.021

Loivet, W., Taghipour, A., & Kang, D. S. (2020). The rise of green supply chain management: Between complexity and necessity. *Journal of Economics. Business and Management*, *8*(1), 1–7.

Mahfod, J., Canel-Depitre, B., & Taghipour, A. (2019). Quality function deployment-ELECTRE in supplier evaluation. *Journal of Advanced Management Science, 7*(4).

Marquès, G., Thierry, C., Lamothe, J., & Gourc, D. (2010). A review of vendor managed inventory (VMI): From concept to processes. *Production Planning and Control*, *21*(6), 547–561. doi:10.1080/09537287.2010.488937

Merimi, M., & Taghipour, A. (2021). Accelerating the digitalization of the supply chain: An empirical research about COVID-19 crisis. In *Digitalization of Decentralized Supply Chains During Global Crises* (pp. 1–24). IGI Global. doi:10.4018/978-1-7998-6874-3.ch001

Miemczyk, J., Howard, M., & Johnsen, T. E. (2016). Dynamic development and execution of closed-loop supply chains: A natural resource-based view. *Supply Chain Management*, *21*(4), 453–469. doi:10.1108/SCM-12-2014-0405

Nadia, E.-N., Beatrice, C.-D., & Atour, T. (2020). Luxury hotels' eco-friendly activities & customers' preferences and willingness to pay for green hotels. *Journal of Advanced Management Science, 8*(1).

Nakandala, D., & Lau, H. C. (2019). Innovative adoption of hybrid supply chain strategies in urban local fresh food supply chain. *Supply Chain Management*, *24*(2), 241–255. doi:10.1108/SCM-09-2017-0287

Niesten, E., Jolink, A., de Sousa Jabbour, A. B. L., Chappin, M., & Lozano, R. (2017). Sustainable collaboration: The impact of governance and institutions on sustainable performance. *Journal of Cleaner Production*, *155*, 1–6. doi:10.1016/j.jclepro.2016.12.085

Nishitani, K., Nguyen, T. B. H., Trinh, T. Q., Wu, Q., & Kokubu, K. (2021). Are corporate environmental activities to meet sustainable development goals (SDGs) simply greenwashing? An empirical study of environmental management control systems in Vietnamese companies from the stakeholder management perspective. *Journal of Environmental Management*, *296*, 113364. doi:10.1016/j.jenvman.2021.113364 PMID:34399553

Nizami, A., Ali, J., & Nguyen-Khoa, S. (2021). Government-industry partnership for sustainable water use: Insights from Pakistan. *Sustain. Ind. Water Use Perspect. Incent. Tools*, *115*, 115–126. doi:10.2166/9781789060676_0115

Omar, I. A., Jayaraman, R., Salah, K., Debe, M., & Omar, M. (2020). Enhancing vendor managed inventory supply chain operations using blockchain smart contracts. *IEEE Access : Practical Innovations, Open Solutions*, *8*, 182704–182719. doi:10.1109/ACCESS.2020.3028031

Padhee, S., & Nandan, D. (2021). Design of Automated Visual Inspection System for Beverage Industry Production Line. *TS. Traitement du Signal*, *38*(2), 461–466. doi:10.18280/ts.380225

Schmidt, C. G., & Wagner, S. M. (2019). Blockchain and supply chain relations: A transaction cost theory perspective. *Journal of Purchasing and Supply Management*, *25*(4), 100552. doi:10.1016/j.pursup.2019.100552

Sgarbossa, F., & Russo, I. (2017). A proactive model in sustainable food supply chain: Insight from a case study. *International Journal of Production Economics*, *183*, 596–606. doi:10.1016/j.ijpe.2016.07.022

Shibin, K., Dubey, R., Gunasekaran, A., Hazen, B., Roubaud, D., Gupta, S., & Foropon, C. (2020). Examining sustainable supply chain management of SMEs using resource based view and institutional theory. *Annals of Operations Research*, *290*(1-2), 301–326. doi:10.100710479-017-2706-x

Shin, M., & Taghipour, A. (2021). Supply Chains Digital Transformation: Automated Underground Logistics Systems. *Underground Construction*, *6*(2), 7. doi:10.18178/joebm.2021.9.2.651

Sun, Z., & Zhang, W. (2019). Do government regulations prevent greenwashing? An evolutionary game analysis of heterogeneous enterprises. *Journal of Cleaner Production*, *231*, 1489–1502. doi:10.1016/j.jclepro.2019.05.335

Taghipour, A., & Frayret, J.-M. (2011). Supply chain coordination planning: A review. *Work paper, École polytechnique de Montréal.*

Taghipour, A., Glaa, B., & Zoghlami, N. (2014). Network coordination with minimum risk of information sharing. *2014 International Conference on Advanced Logistics and Transport (ICALT).* IEEE. 10.1109/ICAdLT.2014.6864115

Taghipour, A., Murat, S., & Huang, P. (2021). E-supply chain management: A review. *International Journal of e-Education, e-Business, e-. Management Learning*, *11*(2), 51–61.

Tang, C. S. (2006). Perspectives in supply chain risk management. *International Journal of Production Economics*, *103*(2), 451–488. doi:10.1016/j.ijpe.2005.12.006

Tolkamp, J., Huijben, J., Mourik, R., Verbong, G., & Bouwknegt, R. (2018). User-centred sustainable business model design: The case of energy efficiency services in the Netherlands. *Journal of Cleaner Production*, *182*, 755–764. doi:10.1016/j.jclepro.2018.02.032

Velter, M., Bitzer, V., & Bocken, N. (2022). A boundary tool for multi-stakeholder sustainable business model innovation. *Circular Economy and Sustainability*, *2*(2), 401–431. doi:10.100743615-021-00103-3 PMID:34888576

Wakolbinger, T., & Cruz, J. M. (2011). Supply chain disruption risk management through strategic information acquisition and sharing and risk-sharing contracts. *International Journal of Production Research*, *49*(13), 4063–4084. doi:10.1080/00207543.2010.501550

World Cocoa Foundation. (2023). *CocoaAction Brasil*. World of Cocoa Foundation. https://www.worldcocoafoundation.org/initiative/cocoaaction-brasil-por/

Williams, H., Wikström, F., & Löfgren, M. (2008). A life cycle perspective on environmental effects of customer focused packaging development. *Journal of Cleaner Production*, *16*(7), 853–859. doi:10.1016/j.jclepro.2007.05.006

Xu, B., Chen, W., Zhang, G., Wang, J., Ping, W., Luo, L., & Chen, J. (2020). How to achieve green growth in China's agricultural sector. *Journal of Cleaner Production*, *271*, 122770. doi:10.1016/j.jclepro.2020.122770

Yazan, D. M., Yazdanpanah, V., & Fraccascia, L. (2020). Learning strategic cooperative behavior in industrial symbiosis: A game-theoretic approach integrated with agent-based simulation. *Business Strategy and the Environment*, *29*(5), 2078–2091. doi:10.1002/bse.2488

Yin, R. K. (2009). *Case study research: Design and methods, 5*. Sage.

Zhu, Z., Chu, F., Dolgui, A., Chu, C., Zhou, W., & Piramuthu, S. (2018). Recent advances and opportunities in sustainable food supply chain: A model-oriented review. *International Journal of Production Research*, *56*(17), 5700–5722. doi:10.1080/00207543.2018.1425014

KEY TERMS AND DEFINITIONS

Circular Economy: The circular economy is an economic model based on closed-loop systems that minimize waste, maximize resource efficiency, and promote the reuse, recycling, and recovery of resources during all of the product/service supply chain stages.

Corporate Social Responsibility: Corporate Social Responsibility or CSR acts as a business model encompassing the ethical and responsible actions that companies take to ensure the positive impact of their operations on society and the environment.

Environmental collaborations: Environmental collaborations include strategic alliances and partnerships among business stakeholders including governments, competitors, suppliers, and contractors to share green practices and jointly work towards environmental sustainability goals.

Environmental Stewardship: Environmental stewardship is a business concept referring to the responsible management of natural resources and the environment to ensure their long-term protection and preservation. To achieve this, businesses take action towards minimizing their negative environmental impacts, promoting ecological well-being, and conserving natural resources.

Green Supply Chain Management: Green supply chain management refers to the integration of environmentally friendly practices and strategies in all stages of the supply chain operations, including material sourcing, manufacturing, distribution, and end-of-life management of a product.

Industrial Symbiosis: It is defined as a collaborative approach in businesses and organizations to optimize resource utilization and minimize total waste. Organizations and businesses do so by exchanging materials, energy, and by-products to develop a mutually beneficial system that serves the goals of the circular economy.

Life Cycle Assessment (LCA): LCA helps in the systematic evaluation of the environmental damage from a product, process, or industry by taking account of the utilized materials, resources, energy, and released waste and emissions during the lifetime of a product or production cycle of a process or industry. Product LCAs consider environmental impacts across the lifetime of a product, including raw material sourcing, production, distribution, use, and end-of-life stages.

Net-Zero Targets: Net-zero targets are the high-level ambitious goals set by industries, organizations, and governments to balance their greenhouse gas emissions such as CO_2 by removing or offsetting the equivalent amount of emissions from the atmosphere. Entities working towards net-zero targets apply a combination of emission reduction strategies and carbon offset projects to achieve overall carbon neutrality.

Supply Chain Transparency: Supply chain transparency refers to the visibility and traceability of products throughout their movement in the supply chain and allows relevant stakeholders to understand the environmental and social impact of those products.

Chapter 5
The Integration of China's Belt and Road Initiative Into Global Supply Chains:
New Pathways for Social and Environmental Responsibility

Mohamad Zreik
https://orcid.org/0000-0002-6812-6529
Independent Researcher, Lebanon

ABSTRACT

This chapter uses the German supply chain act as a lens to examine the impact on corporate social responsibility (CSR) of China's belt and road initiative (BRI) and global supply chain management techniques. China's BRI seeks to improve infrastructure, trade, and investment links with various nations. This chapter describes the BRI and how it may alter global supply chains in ways that raise or lower risks and possibilities related to sustainability and human rights. The chapter analyzes China's potential to advance green and socially responsible business practices along the BRI. A novel Chinese interpretation of the German supply chain act and its potential application inside the BRI are discussed. The chapter highlights the importance of worker rights and environmental preservation as it addresses the potential of technologies like blockchain inside the BRI framework to improve transparency, accountability, and traceability. The chapter also emphasizes the financial advantages of ethical supply chain management.

1. INTRODUCTION

Supply chains have expanded in complexity and size as a result of globalization, and now frequently span multiple continents and involve numerous parties (Mangan & Lalwani, 2016). China's Belt and Road Initiative (BRI), a megaproject to improve regional integration and growth through infrastructure, commerce, and investment, is one key initiative with the potential to transform global supply chains.

DOI: 10.4018/978-1-6684-9062-4.ch005

The BRI has the potential to significantly impact businesses all over the world due to China's central role in global supply networks (Butt & Ali, 2020).

The growing awareness of the need to include social responsibility and environmental sustainability into supply chain management strategies inspired this chapter. Consumers, governments, and non-governmental organizations (NGOs) are all putting pressure on businesses to show they support these values. This shift is mirrored in recent legislation like Germany's Supply Chain Act, which requires businesses to uphold human rights and environmental standards in their operations (Horner & Alford, 2019; Cauchois et al., 2017).

Given this context, this chapter's primary goal is to investigate the BRI's effects on international supply chains and the possibilities it offers for bolstering Corporate Social Responsibility (CSR) initiatives. In particular, the chapter hopes to educate readers about the BRI, assess the initiative's potential effects on international supply chains, and explore ways in which it might be utilized to advance ecologically and socially responsible business policies.

The chapter also aims to clarify the role of emerging technologies, particularly blockchain, in increasing supply chain transparency and explain how the principles of the German Supply Chain Act can be used within the BRI framework. By doing so, the chapter intends to provide useful information and advice to a wide audience, including policymakers, managers, researchers, and logistics, operations, and supply chain specialists. As advocates for a more environmentally and socially conscious global economy, we see this investigation as not only opportune but essential.

In 2013, Chinese President Xi Jinping introduced the BRI, a global development plan with lofty goals. The effort, widely regarded as the most extensive infrastructure undertaking of the 21st century, seeks to improve commercial, cultural, and governmental connections across a large swath of the globe by funding the construction of an extensive system of railroads, highways, pipelines, and power grids (Zreik, 2021).

'Belt' in BRI stands for 'Silk Road Economic Belt,' a network of land links that will link China to Central Asia, Eastern Europe, and Western Europe (Dave & Kobayashi, 2018). It's a tribute to the historical Silk Road, which allowed for a thriving flow of products and ideas between the East and West. The 'Road' element, in contrast, alludes to the '21st Century Maritime Silk Road,' a massive sea corridor linking China's coastal regions with Africa and the Mediterranean (Summers, 2016; El-Nemr, Canel-Depitre, & Taghipour, 2017).

Nearly two-thirds of the world's population and one-third of global GDP are represented by the roughly 70 countries involved in the BRI (Lin, 2022). The initiative's goals include boosting China's global standing and strategic might while simultaneously easing economic development and easing regional integration.

The BRI is more than just a physical construction project. It promotes all-around regional cooperation and growth by touching on such varied spheres as energy, trade, policy coordination, financial services, and interpersonal interactions. It could have a dramatic effect on cross-border trade and the structure of global supply networks. Because of these factors, the BRI has emerged as a central topic of discussion regarding the future of global supply chain operations, particularly in the areas of social responsibility and environmental sustainability.

2. UNDERSTANDING THE BELT AND ROAD INITIATIVE

2.1. Definition and Objectives of BRI

Sometimes referred to as the "project of the century," Chinese President Xi Jinping introduced the BRI in 2013 (Rana & Ji, 2020). The Silk Road was an ancient trading route that connected Asia, Africa, and Europe, and the BRI borrows its name from this route to symbolize China's desire to modernize these channels (Miller, 2019).

The initiative has two main parts: the overland 'Silk Road Economic Belt,' which spans Central and Western Asia and leads to Europe; and the '21st Century Maritime Silk Road,' which follows the coastlines of China, Southeast Asia, Africa, and Europe (Chan, 2018). Collectively, these corridors represent the two-way communication between East and West that the BRI hopes to foster.

The BRI has many fundamental purposes, including economic, geopolitical, and diplomatic ones. Its primary objective is to spur economic growth by the building and improvement of a vast system of transportation and utility infrastructure, including roads, railroads, ports, airports, pipelines, and power plants. The goals of the BRI include improving cross-continental communication, boosting international trade, and easing international investment (Githaiga et al., 2019).

At the same time, China's geopolitical goal of becoming a dominant actor in international affairs is embodied in the BRI. China aims to strengthen diplomatic ties, boost regional security, and form a global commercial network more centered on China by funding infrastructure projects in underdeveloped countries.

Many people see the BRI as an opportunity to advance regional policy coordination, trade liberalization, financial cooperation, and cross-cultural understanding. Therefore, the BRI represents China's dream of a more interconnected world, where economic growth benefits everyone and helps maintain global peace and stability.

2.2. Geographical Scope and Impact

The BRI has a massive geographic reach, encompassing around 70 nations throughout Asia, Africa, and Europe. About 65% of the world's population resides in these countries; they also account for about 40% of global GDP and an estimated 75% of the world's energy reserves (Zreik, 2022).

The BRI's 'Silk Road Economic Belt' spans the Eurasian continent, linking China, Central Asia, Russia, and Europe. The China–Mongolia–Russia Corridor, the China–Central Asia–West Asia Corridor, and the China–Indochina Peninsula Corridor all fall under the purview of this section (Kunavut, Okuda, & Lee, 2018). On the other side, the "21st Century Maritime Silk Road" is a vast maritime network that connects China's coastal areas to those of Southeast Asia, South Asia, Africa, and Europe.

The BRI's global reach will have far-reaching consequences. The BRI has the potential to greatly improve trade and investment flows among member nations by constructing a large infrastructure network that connects previously isolated regions. Within the BRI framework, this is especially helpful because it has the potential to boost economic growth, lessen poverty, and advance regional integration in developing nations (Liu & Dunford, 2016).

Furthermore, billions of dollars have already been committed to infrastructure projects across the BRI countries as a result of the BRI's impetus (Li, 2020). This has expanded China's worldwide economic clout and altered the economic profiles of numerous nations, especially in Asia and Africa.

Because of its expansive scope, the BRI raises a number of complex issues, such as the financial risks inherent in building such massive infrastructure, political concerns over sovereignty and national security, and environmental worries over the construction and industrialization processes. Solving these problems calls for a methodical strategy that takes into account both the financial gains from the BRI and the imperatives of social responsibility and environmental sustainability.

2.3. Key Sectors Involved in the BRI

The BRI is distinguished from other infrastructure projects by the wide variety of industries it involves. The BRI's goal is to build a massive network of physical links, and this goal relies heavily on infrastructure and building. Transportation and communication infrastructure, including roads, railways, ports, airports, and telecommunication networks, must be improved and new ones built. The initiative has sparked a flurry of construction projects, which in turn has increased the need for skilled labor and funding. In order to meet this demand, Chinese businesses, especially state-owned enterprises, have been working hard to implement projects in all of the BRI countries.

Commerce and trade play an important role in the BRI as well. The initiative's stated goal is to improve economic ties between participating nations by constructing necessary infrastructure and enacting trade-friendly governmental measures. Businesses in several sectors, including manufacturing, agriculture, and consumer goods, stand to gain from the BRI's efforts to streamline customs procedures, reduce trade obstacles, and boost cross-border cooperation (Hahm & Raihan, 2018).

The BRI includes the energy industry as well. Investments in conventional energy infrastructure like oil and gas pipelines and power plants make up a sizable portion of the BRI's overall portfolio. The importance of sustainable development is highlighted, and a transition to a green and low-carbon economy is signaled, via the inclusion of renewable energy projects (Rafique et al., 2022).

Given the massive capital expenditures required by the numerous BRI projects, financial services are crucial to their successful implementation. Financial institutions like as commercial banks, insurers, and investment organizations play an important part in funding BRI endeavors. Specifically, to aid in the funding of BRI projects, China has formed new financial institutions including the Asian Infrastructure Investment Bank (AIIB) and the Silk Road Fund (Callaghan & Hubbard, 2016).

Technology and innovation have been incorporated into the BRI framework to keep up with the worldwide trend toward digital transformation. The initiative encourages high-tech solutions to environmental problems, transportation challenges, and other infrastructure needs. Through the Digital Silk Road, which aims to promote collaboration in areas including e-commerce, smart cities, and big data, there is a concentrated effort to improve digital connectivity (Naughton, 2020).

The BRI also places an emphasis on fostering human connections through cultural and touristic activities. The BRI intends to stimulate the tourism sector through the improvement of transport links and the expansion of tourist infrastructure. Cultural events and exchanges are also encouraged to help BRI citizens get to know one another and develop lasting bonds of friendship.

The problem lies in ensuring that these sectors flourish in a socially and environmentally responsible manner as the BRI grows. A solid familiarity with global supply chains and the varied settings of the BRI countries is necessary for striking a balance between rapid economic growth and sustainable development.

3. CHINA'S POSITION IN THE GLOBAL SUPPLY CHAIN

3.1. Role of China in Global Trade and Manufacturing

China has been a major actor in international trade and manufacturing over the past few decades. The country's large labor force, competitive production capabilities, and smart governmental actions targeted at boosting the economy have all played a role in this shift (Li & Wang, 2012).

China's position in international trade is crucial. China has a pivotal role in international trade as the world's largest exporter and the world's second-largest importer (Zreik, 2023). It exports a diverse array of goods, from machinery and electronics to textiles and medical supplies (Shih, 2020). Its enormous consumer market and production base necessitate a wide range of imported items to meet their varying demands. China's desire to further consolidate its position in global commerce is reflected in the Belt and Road Initiative's emphasis on increasing trade connectivity.

China is the world's largest industrial nation and is often simply called the "world's factory." It has become a superpower by capitalizing on its large labor force and expanding its industrial infrastructure (Keane et al., 2020). Manufacturing in this country is extremely varied, with many different types of items being made there. These include electronics, autos, steel, textiles, and consumer goods. Investment in high-tech manufacturing fields like robotics, aerospace, and biotechnology has allowed China to begin climbing the value chain (Malkin, 2022).

China's global economic and manufacturing leadership positions it with significant responsibilities. It plays a crucial role in propelling several global supply chains toward more environmentally and socially conscious methods of operation. As a world leader, the country must do its part to promote more sustainable practices in international commerce and industry.

Chinese trade and manufacturing policies should reflect the importance placed on labor rights, environmental protection, and corporate social responsibility as these concerns continue to attract increased international attention. In the context of the Belt and Road Initiative, this is especially important since it presents China with an opportunity to lead the way in promoting environmentally friendly and socially just trade and production methods worldwide.

3.2. Challenges and Opportunities in Integrating BRI into Global Supply Chains

The ambitious scale, diverse participant countries, and complex dynamics of global trade and industry all create problems and opportunities for the BRI's integration into global supply chains.

The vastly different political, economic, and social systems in BRI countries present a major obstacle (Huang, 2016). Understanding these nuances and working diplomatically to bridge them is essential for establishing productive cross-border cooperation. Large-scale infrastructure projects linked with the BRI also pose significant financial risks, such as concerns over the debt sustainability of the participating countries (Hurley, Morris, & Portelance, 2019). There are also significant difficulties associated with issues of openness, leadership, and community effect.

In addition, international laws and regulations, like as those pertaining to labor rights, environmental protection, and corporate social responsibility, must be met in order to successfully incorporate the BRI into global supply chains. Given the varying legal systems and enforcement capacities of different countries, ensuring that BRI projects adhere to these standards might be difficult (Banik & Lin, 2019).

However, there are also tremendous advantages to incorporating the BRI into global supply systems. Enhanced economic connectedness is a possibility that could have a major impact. The BRI can make it easier and more efficient for products, services, and investments to move across nations by improving infrastructure and lowering trade obstacles. This has the potential to promote regional cohesion, job creation, and economic expansion.

The BRI is a chance to reform global supply networks in a way that prioritizes environmental and social responsibility. China can affect the "greenness" and "fairness" of global supply chains by incorporating ideals of environmental sustainability and social responsibility into BRI projects. This includes supporting renewable energy, fighting for workers' rights, and fostering ethical business practices.

Adding the BRI to global supply chains also has the potential to boost innovation and new technologies. Because of the BRI's focus on digital connection and technical cooperation, cutting-edge technologies like blockchain, AI, and the Internet of Things may become more prevalent in international supply chains (Catalano, 2023). This has the potential to increase openness, boost productivity, and inspire novel approaches to doing business.

Therefore, a well-rounded strategy that takes into account both the difficulties and the potential benefits of incorporating the BRI into global supply chains is necessary. It necessitates an openness to change and innovation, as well as a dedication to responsibility and sustainability on the part of all parties involved.

4. BRI AND CORPORATE SOCIAL RESPONSIBILITY (CSR)

4.1. Overview of CSR and its Importance in Global Supply Chains

By practicing what is known as "Corporate Social Responsibility," businesses acknowledge that their actions have consequences for people beyond just themselves. This goes beyond merely meeting legal obligations, and instead entails making voluntary pledges to advance societal well-being and environmental sustainability.

Over time, the meaning of "corporate social responsibility" has expanded greatly. At first, this term was most often used to refer to the charitable efforts of large businesses (Carroll & Shabana, 2010). Nonetheless, modern understandings of CSR cover a far wider range of issues, such as ethical business practices, employee rights, environmental preservation, sustainable sourcing, community development, and open governance (Crane et al., 2019).

The significance of CSR in the context of international supply chains cannot be emphasized. Suppliers, producers, distributors, and customers all play important roles in global supply chains (Ponte & Sturgeon, 2014; El-Nemr, Canel-Depitre, & Taghipour, 2021). There can be serious social and environmental consequences at every link in this chain. Thus, it is essential to integrate CSR concepts at each level to guarantee ethical and long-term operations.

Socially responsible actions in supply chains can take many forms. Businesses can, for instance, safeguard their supply chains by instituting fair labor policies that protect workers from abuse and defend their rights (Yang, Taghipour, & Canel-Depitre, 2017). They can also adopt sustainable sourcing rules to guarantee that all of the components they use are safe for the environment and obtained in a moral manner. Businesses can ensure their goods are produced in a sustainable manner by cutting down on waste and carbon emissions.

CSR is not only the ethical thing to do; it's also a smart business move. Today's shoppers care more than ever before about how their purchases will affect the world around them. As a result, customers are more likely to stick with businesses that they perceive to be socially responsible. Further bolstering a company's competitiveness, ethical and sustainable practices can cut costs, reduce risks, and improve efficiencies across the board (Epstein & Buhovac, 2014).

CSR assumes greater significance in the BRI framework. The BRI has the potential to significantly affect many communities and ecosystems due to its enormous geographical scope and its inclusion of a wide range of sectors. China and the other BRI countries can ensure that this historic endeavor results in not just economic growth, but also social advancement and environmental sustainability, by incorporating CSR concepts into BRI projects.

4.2. Potential of BRI to Enhance CSR Practices

Given its size and scope, the Belt and Road Initiative has great potential to improve CSR practices in global supply chains. Given the breadth of the proposed infrastructure and trade networks and the diversity of the stakeholders engaged, this effort presents a rare opportunity to encourage ethical business practices.

To begin with, the BRI can serve as a means to harmonize corporate social responsibility standards amongst a wide range of countries. Having a single set of CSR principles under the BRI can make compliance easier and promote wider adoption of these practices given the diversity of legislation and norms across different nations (Banik & Lin, 2019; Vosooghidizaji, Taghipour, & Canel-Depitre, 2022). As two of the most important parts of CSR, labor rights and environmental protection each have their own set of rules around the world, this might be especially useful.

Second, sustainability may be easily integrated during the planning and construction phases of the BRI's infrastructure projects. Sustainable resources, waste reduction, and minimal emissions are all examples of ecologically responsible building methods (Vosooghidizaji, Taghipour, & Canel-Depitre, 2020). Sustainable results can be prioritized in the selection of projects by, for example, emphasizing renewable energy and green mobility.

Thirdly, the BRI can affect CSR practices by increasing visibility and responsibility in international supply chains. By integrating digital technologies like blockchain into the BRI framework, it can improve traceability and guarantee that only ethical and environmentally friendly procedures are used along the whole supply chain. Consumers may feel more secure in the things they buy if they know where they came from and that they are ethically sound (Centobelli et al., 2022).

In addition, the BRI can advance CSR through easing international collaboration and the dissemination of information regarding CSR best practices. This includes collaborative platforms for businesses to share their CSR experiences and learn from one another, cross-border training programs for workers, and cooperative research and development in sustainable technologies.

However, it is essential to stress that conscious effort and strategic planning would be required to realize the BRI's potential to improve CSR standards. Establishing CSR requirements for BRI projects, creating monitoring and enforcement procedures, and encouraging a responsible mindset among all BRI participants are all necessary steps. A comprehensive approach to CSR requires the participation of a wide range of non-business actors, such as governments, NGOs, and local communities (Mao, 2023; Tliche, Taghipour, & Canel-Depitre, 2021).

The genuine spirit of a "community of shared future for mankind" can be reflected in the BRI if its potential is used to improve CSR practices, leading to a more sustainable and fair global economy.

4.3. The Role of BRI in Promoting Socially Responsible Practices

The BRI is a massive undertaking involving a wide variety of countries and industries, and as such, it can play a crucial part in encouraging ethical business practices. As part of this mission, it seeks to promote worker rights, community well-being, ethical corporate practices, and economic progress for all in its extensive service area (Banik & Lin, 2019).

Respect for workers' rights is a cornerstone of ethical business. The BRI's many infrastructure projects have the potential to generate millions of new job opportunities in the nations that take part in it (Iqbal, Rahman, & Sami, 2019). Priority should be given to initiatives that ensure fair labor practices like living wages, safe working conditions, and the ability to bargain collectively. In order to protect employees' rights and promote decent employment, the BRI can serve as a model by mandating that all projects adhere to International Labor Organization standards (Tliche, Taghipour, & Canel-Depitre, 2019).

The BRI can also encourage ethical business practices by protecting local populations. Large-scale infrastructure projects often have far-reaching social effects, such as the relocation of residents and the disruption of local economies. The BRI can reduce negative effects and guarantee locals benefit from the projects by using rigorous social impact assessment processes and providing for meaningful dialogue with communities (Khan et al., 2018).

Socially responsible activities also include engaging in ethical corporate behavior. Because of its focus on commerce and finance, the BRI has the potential to advance moral standards by championing openness, responsibility, and equal opportunity in business dealings. Businesses participating in BRI projects should be encouraged to implement anti-corruption measures, receive business ethics training, and use strong governance structures (Lee & Shen, 2020; Loivet, Taghipour, & Kang, 2020).

At last, the BRI can help advance one of the cornerstones of responsible development: economic equality. Making sure the advantages of trade and infrastructure development are shared fairly is crucial to the BRI's goal of shared prosperity. This includes bolstering small and medium-sized businesses, establishing policies to minimize inequality within and across nations, and promoting inclusive growth initiatives (Wolf, 2021).

The BRI can help make the global economy more sustainable and equitable by encouraging these types of socially responsible practices. Noting that governments, industry, civil society, and international organizations will all need to work together toward this goal is essential. Socially responsible behaviors are not an endpoint, but rather a journey that necessitates a dedication to constant learning and progress.

5. INTERSECTING GERMAN SUPPLY CHAIN ACT AND BRI: A PATH TOWARDS RESPONSIBLE SUPPLY CHAINS

5.1. Overview of the German Supply Chain Act

The Supply Chain Act or "Lieferkettengesetz", is a game-changing piece of legislation that advances the cause of corporate responsibility and transparency. Its purpose is to monitor German firms' supply chains for compliance with human rights and environmental regulations (Çelik & Schmid, 2022).

Risk assessments for potential human rights and environmental abuses within supply chains are mandatory under the act. Suppliers lower down the supply chain are included in this as much as the company's direct suppliers are (Rühmkorf, 2023).

The organization must take reasonable precautions to address recognized risks and correct any violations that may have occurred. Depending on the severity of the problem, this could mean working with suppliers to change their practices, adjusting purchasing procedures, or severing relations with noncompliant suppliers altogether.

The statute contains provisions for grievance processes in addition to these duties of due diligence. This means that businesses must set up ways via which victims can report any infractions, and must conduct thorough investigations into such claims (Taghipour & Merimi, 2021). Companies that fail to meet their due diligence requirements face penalties under the act, such as fines and disqualification from government contracts.

The OECD Guidelines for Multinational Enterprises and the United Nations Guiding Principles on Business and Human Rights serve as inspiration for Germany's Supply Chain Act (Campos, 2022). Germany has taken the lead in fostering corporate accountability and responsibility by converting these worldwide principles into obligatory national legislation (Mahfod, Canel-Depitre, & Taghipour, 2019).

The measure has far-reaching consequences that go beyond Germany's borders. Because of the interconnected nature of global supply networks, the law will affect firms outside of Germany that provide goods or services to German ones. It paves the way for other nations to follow suit and adds to the worldwide push for more ethical and environmentally friendly supply chains. In addition, it provides a helpful template for incorporating social and environmental responsibilities into the BRI, which is the focus of this chapter.

5.2. Integrating Principles of German Supply Chain Act in BRI

The BRI might be strengthened by adopting concepts from the German Supply Chain Act, adding to the global movement toward more responsible and sustainable supply chains. Such an integration has the potential to have far-reaching effects, given the breadth of the BRI and the prominence of Chinese businesses in global supply chains.

Human rights and environmental concerns within supply networks are given increased attention in the German Supply Chain Act. The BRI projects can easily use this idea. For instance, BRI infrastructure projects involving Chinese firms may necessitate that those firms perform due diligence on their suppliers and contractors to guarantee that they adhere to all applicable human rights and environmental regulations (Hughes et al., 2020).

The act's provisions for complaint processes can be implemented, too, inside the BRI structure. Workers and local populations who are impacted by BRI projects should have a way to report any violations they observe. After receiving such reports, an in-depth investigation must be conducted, followed by corrective measures.

Projects funded by the BRI may incorporate the act's emphasis on transparency and accountability. Information concerning Chinese firms' supplier networks and due diligence procedures, for instance, could need to be made public. This would increase the openness of BRI projects and make it easier for various groups to monitor and regulate firms (Gertz & Evers, 2020).

The BRI's mission to foster collaboration that is "open, green, and clean" is well-suited to the incorporation of these ideals (Colley & van Noort, 2022). However, this type of integration would call for a lot of work and cooperation from all parties involved. Companies in China, BRI countries, global bodies, and non-governmental organizations are all included. For enterprises to understand and meet their duties, there must be strong procedures for monitoring and enforcement, as well as measures to enhance their ability.

5.3. Implications of this Integration for the Global Supply Chain

The ideas of the German Supply Chain Act might have far-reaching effects on supply chains around the world if they were incorporated into the BRI. Given the BRI's global scope, such an integration would undoubtedly alter the dynamics of international trade and industry, raising the bar for corporate transparency and responsibility.

The possibility for a global convergence on uniform sustainability standards is one of the most far-reaching effects that could result. Various nations from Asia, Europe, Africa, and Latin America are participating in the BRI (Oliveira & Myers, 2021). A more uniform set of norms for human rights and environmental responsibility throughout a substantial sector of the global economy would result from these countries adopting the concepts of the German Supply Chain Act. This would improve global corporate responsibility standards and make them more accessible to multinational corporations (Merimi, M., & Taghipour, 2021).

Improving the visibility and auditability of global supply chains is a further significant aspect. German law mandates that businesses evaluate their suppliers and be transparent about their supply chains in accordance with the objectives of the German Supply Chain Act (Baid & Jayaraman, 2022). If these ideas were included into the BRI, supply chain transparency would rise dramatically, helping buyers, investors, and government agencies make better choices.

The application of these guidelines may also affect productivity and creativity. Brand reputation, customer loyalty, and operational risks can all improve when a company practices social and environmental responsibility to a high standard. In addition, the need to find novel solutions to achieve these stringent requirements could inspire the creation of novel materials and methods of production (Miethlich et al., 2023).

Last but not least, this sort of amalgamation could aid international initiatives to accomplish the SDGs set forth by the United Nations. Goal 8 (Decent Work and Economic Growth), Goal 12 (Responsible Consumption and Production), and Goal 13 (Climate Action) are all in line with the concepts of the German Supply Chain Act. China and other BRI countries could make significant contributions to global sustainability if they incorporated these concepts into the BRI.

6. THE ROLE OF EMERGING TECHNOLOGIES IN ENHANCING SUPPLY CHAIN TRANSPARENCY

6.1. Potential of Blockchain Technology for BRI

Integrating the BRI into global supply chains has the potential to greatly increase efficiency, transparency, and trustworthiness if blockchain technology is implemented. Blockchain's distributed ledger technology makes it possible to keep records of transactions in a way that is both immutable and transparent, simplifying many of the processes involved in international trade and supply chain management (Al-Rakhami & Al-Mashari, 2022; Taghipour, & Beneteau-Piet, 2020).

Blockchain's capacity to improve supply chain traceability is one of its primary advantages. Given the BRI's expansive breadth, spanning multiple nations and sectors, monitoring the movement of commodities can be difficult. Companies may more easily track things from their point of origin to their final destination with the use of blockchain technology, which provides a shared and unchangeable record of transactions (Wang et al., 2020). With this improved traceability, the legitimacy of supply chains can be protected from things like forgery and fraud. Consumers may be able to check the product's origins, which may encourage more mindful purchasing decisions.

Blockchain could potentially improve supply chain management and international trade. Manufacturers, shippers, customs agencies, and banking institutions all have their own processes and documentation to deal with while engaging in international trade (Chang, Iakovou, & Shi, 2020). To minimize waste and mistakes, blockchain technology can unify several separate databases into one. Blockchain's smart contracts functionality can automate many of the transactions, which in turn expedites operations and lowers costs (Nadia, Beatrice, & Atour, 2020).

Additionally, blockchain has the potential to improve BRI project accountability and transparency. Thanks to blockchain's immutable record, everything from contract awards to budget disbursements can be tracked reliably and transparently. Corruption can be prevented and accountability for all parties can be ensured if this is implemented (Shin, & Taghipour, 2021).

Finally, the concepts of the German Supply Chain Act can be integrated into the BRI with the use of blockchain technology. As was previously mentioned, the act mandates that businesses perform supplier due diligence and offer grievance methods. Blockchain technology can help with these procedures by keeping supplier evaluations and complaints in an immutable, auditable ledger.

6.2. Benefits of Blockchain for Traceability and Accountability

The revolutionary potential of blockchain technology in improving traceability and accountability, two key parts of managing and maintaining sustainable supply chains, has attracted a lot of attention (Paliwal, Chandra, & Sharma, 2020; Taghipour, A., & Frayret, 2011a). Blockchain's ability to create an immutable, transparent, and distributed ledger of transactions would greatly enhance the efficiency and openness of BRI supply chains.

One of blockchain technology's most appealing features is the improved traceability it provides. Traceability, in the context of global supply chains, is the process by which products can be followed from their inception to their final destination (Sunny, Undralla, & Pillai, 2020). Traceability can be difficult to maintain in the BRI due to its complexity and global reach. Blockchain technology's immutable, distributed ledger of all product transactions and interactions in chronological order helps streamline this process. This capacity can help verify sustainability credentials or ethical labor practices along the supply chain, which can help avoid counterfeiting and ensure product authenticity. Since blockchain-based traceability provides auditable evidence of sustainable and ethical behaviors, it can greatly contribute to corporate social responsibility (Saberi et al., 2019).

Another crucial part of sustainable supply chains that blockchain can help with is accountability. Blockchain is built to offer an immutable record of transactions that is accessible to all nodes in the network, increasing transparency and lowering the likelihood of conflicts (Puthal et al., 2018). By using blockchain technology, BRI projects can have their agreements, contracts, and associated transactions recorded and immutable. This openness guarantees that all parties can be held to account for their promises, which helps prevent fraud. A business participating in a BRI project, for instance, may utilize blockchain to attest to the fact that it has paid its bills and complied with all applicable environmental standards.

Smart contracts built on the blockchain have the potential to automate the enforcement of agreements, leading to greater transparency and accountability (Chang, Chen, & Lu, 2019). When certain circumstances are met, the transactions in these programmable contracts are carried out automatically. Not only does this feature remove the need for middlemen, but it also guarantees adherence to the terms of any contracts involved.

6.3. Other Emerging Technologies and Their Role

The BRI and its incorporation into global supply chains can be made more sustainable, efficient, and transparent with the help of blockchain technology and other emerging technologies. Technology like AI, IoT, and big data analytics all fall within this category.

Supply chain operations under the BRI framework can benefit from AI's advanced machine learning and predictive analytics capabilities. Artificial intelligence (AI) has many potential applications in business, including but not limited to demand forecasting, logistics optimization, and inventory management. In addition, AI can help spot red flags in the supply chain, such as unethical or unsustainable behaviors, so that businesses may quickly and effectively address them (Holbeche, 2023).

Another technological advancement with the potential to alter BRI-related supply chains is IoT. Internet of Things (IoT) sensors and trackers allow for real-time inventory tracking, improving supply chain transparency and accountability. In addition, IoT devices may track environmental metrics like energy use and garbage output to help businesses reduce their negative impact on the planet (Ranganathan et al., 2022; Taghipour & Frayret, 2011b).

The fields of AI and IoT are intrinsically linked to big data analytics. Big data analytics can shed light on the massive amounts of data produced by modern supply chains, especially those as large as those involved with the BRI. Better decision-making, the ability to spot patterns and foretell the future are all possible outcomes thanks to these tools. To further the goal of sustainability and accountability, big data analytics can also be used to evaluate the social and environmental effects of supply chains (Taghipour, Murat, & Huang, 2021).

Additive manufacturing techniques like 3D printing could also have an impact on the BRI. 3D printing has the potential to lessen the environmental effect of supply chains by allowing for on-demand manufacture close to the point of consumption (Garrett, 2014).

7. BUSINESS CASE FOR SOCIALLY RESPONSIBLE SUPPLY CHAIN MANAGEMENT IN BRI

7.1. Benefits of CSR for Business Performance and Competitiveness

What we call "Corporate Social Responsibility" (or "CSR") is the ethical behavior of a firm towards society, and it includes anything from promoting safe working conditions and protecting the environment to investing in local neighborhoods and giving back to charitable causes (Snider, Hill, & Martin, 2003). In recent years, corporate social responsibility has emerged not only as a moral imperative, but also as a strategic instrument that can improve a company's performance and competitiveness. Given the

BRI's scope and capacity to influence corporate culture around the world, this is an especially pertinent consideration.

CSR has the potential to greatly improve a company's image, making it one of the key advantages. Building goodwill among consumers, investors, and the general public is possible when businesses demonstrate dedication to ethical practices and social issues. This has the dual benefit of increasing consumer loyalty and luring ethical investors, both of which can boost a company's bottom line (Taghipour, 2014).

Companies who invest in CSR often find that they have an advantage in the war for talent. Younger workers in particular place a high priority on working for environmentally and socially conscious businesses. Companies can increase their competitiveness by attracting and retaining top people through public displays of CSR (Jones, Comfort, & Hillier, 2005).

In addition, CSR has the potential to improve business operations and cut expenses. Energy efficiency and trash reduction are only two examples of ecologically sustainable initiatives that can help businesses save money. Potential risks and costs related to environmental harm or labor rights breaches can also be sidestepped (Taghipour, Glaa, & Zoghlami, 2014).

As an added benefit, CSR can help spark creative thinking. In order to fulfill their social and environmental obligations, businesses must frequently create novel goods, procedures, or organizational structures (Taghipour, Abed, & Zoghlami, 2015). More sustainable technology or solutions may be developed as a result, giving businesses an advantage.

Companies involved in the BRI can benefit from CSR in a number of ways, including gaining a better understanding of the regulatory, cultural, and social landscapes of the nations involved. Companies with strong commitments to social and environmental responsibility are more likely to establish positive relationships with local communities and comply with the regulations of various nations. This has the potential to lessen dangers and tensions, making BRI projects more likely to succeed and last.

7.2. Case Studies of Successful Integration of CSR in BRI

Numerous global initiatives have been sparked by the BRI, with several standouts illustrating the effective incorporation of CSR techniques. These examples can be used as a guide for how to proceed with other BRI-related endeavors.

The PPA project in Greece, which oversees the port of Piraeus, is one such example. Since Chinese shipping giant COSCO Shipping assumed control of the Piraeus Port, its growth has skyrocketed, making it one of the world's busiest (Van der Putten & Meijnders, 2015). The company's dedication to corporate social responsibility is, however, particularly impressive. COSCO has made substantial investments in eco-friendly technologies and instituted stringent waste management requirements to lessen the port's negative effects on the natural environment. It has also made investments in the neighborhood by supporting local initiatives like job creation and infrastructure improvement. Because of COSCO, the port's economic performance has improved and the port's social and environmental sustainability have been enhanced (Pallis & Vaggelas, 2017).

The Jakarta–Bandung High-Speed Railway project in Indonesia is yet another example of a Chinese–Indonesian business partnership. The project stands out because of its commitment to eco-friendly building methods and active participation from the neighborhood (Negara & Suryadinata, 2018). The creators of the project have pledged to mitigate the negative effects on the environment as much as possible. This includes taking measures to manage garbage and prevent contamination, such as using tunnels. In addition to compensating residents for land usage and funding community development initiatives from the get-go, they have actively engaged with local communities. This has helped win over residents and reduce negative societal effects (Hong, 2014; Taghipour, 2018).

The third example is the BRI's crown jewel, the China-Pakistan Economic Corridor (CPEC). The Port Qasim coal-fired power station is just one example of the many CPEC projects that have incorporated corporate social responsibility into their daily operations (Taghipour, 2020). The Port Qasim power plant project, for example, has included investments in cutting-edge technologies to cut emissions and save local species. It also includes a community development fund that helps finance things like schools, hospitals, and roads (Radford et al., 2021).

These examples illustrate how CSR initiatives can enhance the economic, social, and environmental outcomes of BRI projects. They show that CSR is more than simply a moral imperative; it's also a strategic instrument that may improve project success, stakeholder engagement, and long-term viability. They offer helpful examples and lessons for other BRI-affiliated businesses and stakeholders, pleading with them to make CSR a central part of their operations.

8. CONCLUSION

Opportunities and difficulties meet at the crossroads of China's BRI and global supply networks. As has been emphasized throughout this chapter, this integration has far-reaching and varied consequences that cut across fields and regions. In spite of all the moving parts, one thing shines out: the BRI's potential to rethink CSR and environmental sustainability in international supply chains.

Since the BRI is so large and ambitious, it has the ability to change not only economic but also social and environmental norms across the world via altering supply networks. Economic growth and development can be boosted in the participating countries as a result of the initiative's focus on infrastructure development, trade facilitation, and investor attractiveness. However, social and environmental factors must be taken into account alongside economic progress. CSR is a framework for striking this delicate equilibrium between profit, people, and the planet.

The BRI has tremendous potential to strengthen CSR policies and procedures. Companies can increase their commercial success and competitiveness while simultaneously maintaining ethical standards and reducing negative social and environmental impacts by incorporating CSR into their BRI initiatives. Corporate social responsibility has the potential to improve a company's image, employee loyalty, productivity, and creativity. They can reduce risks and tensions by better understanding the BRI countries' complex regulatory, cultural, and social environments.

In addition, the principles of the German Supply Chain Act provide a relevant foundation for incorporating CSR into the BRI. This law compels due diligence in supply chains to preserve human rights and environmental norms. Although the Act was passed in Germany, the concepts it contains are international and can help steer businesses involved in the BRI toward more ethical and ecological methods of operation. This fusion can be bolstered by the promise of emerging technologies like blockchain to increase supply chain transparency, traceability, and accountability.

However, for this potential to be actualized, cooperation between national and international governments, businesses, and non-governmental groups is essential. Governments should foster policy conditions that reward ethical and environmentally sound behavior. Businesses should make CSR a priority by implementing policies and procedures that increase sustainability and openness in the supply chain. Responsible actions need to be monitored and advocated for by civil society and international organizations.

Redefining corporate social responsibility and environmental sustainability is a unique opportunity made possible by the BRI's incorporation into global supply chains. It's a chance to construct not just transportation infrastructure like highways and trains, but also a more ethical and environmentally friendly global economy. All relevant parties must work together, viewing CSR not as a burden but as a means to an objective (sustainable development). This chapter has aimed to shed light on the topic in order to help guide future discussions and policymaking on this vital topic.

REFERENCES

Al-Rakhami, M., & Al-Mashari, M. (2022). Interoperability approaches of blockchain technology for supply chain systems. *Business Process Management Journal.*

Baid, V., & Jayaraman, V. (2022). Amplifying and promoting the "S" in ESG investing: the case for social responsibility in supply chain financing. *Managerial Finance.*

Banik, D., & Lin, K. (2019). Business and morals: Corporate strategies for sustainable development in China. *Business and Politics*, *21*(4), 514–539. doi:10.1017/bap.2019.26

Butt, A. S., & Ali, I. (2020). Understanding the implications of Belt and Road Initiative for sustainable supply chains: An environmental perspective. *Benchmarking*, *27*(9), 2631–2648. doi:10.1108/BIJ-04-2020-0143

Callaghan, M., & Hubbard, P. (2016). The Asian infrastructure investment bank: Multilateralism on the silk road. *China Economic Journal*, *9*(2), 116–139. doi:10.1080/17538963.2016.1162970

Campos, A. R. (2022). The role of companies in promoting human rights. In *The Palgrave Handbook of ESG and Corporate Governance* (pp. 167–187). Springer International Publishing. doi:10.1007/978-3-030-99468-6_9

Carroll, A. B., & Shabana, K. M. (2010). The business case for corporate social responsibility: A review of concepts, research and practice. *International Journal of Management Reviews*, *12*(1), 85–105. doi:10.1111/j.1468-2370.2009.00275.x

Catalano, G. (2023). *The Duality of Digital Standard-Setting: Geopolitical Coopetition in a Multipolar World* [Master's thesis, Norwegian University of Life Sciences].

Cauchois, R., Taghipour, A., Kang, D., Zoghlami, N., & Abed, M. (2017). Advanced solutions for a supply chain with stochastic information. *Journal of Advanced Management Science, 5*(1).

Çelik, E., & Schmid, S. N. (2022). Global Justice Advocacy, Trade Unions, and the Supply Chain Law Initiative in Germany. *New Global Studies*, *16*(1), 91–111. doi:10.1515/ngs-2022-0005

Centobelli, P., Cerchione, R., Del Vecchio, P., Oropallo, E., & Secundo, G. (2022). Blockchain technology for bridging trust, traceability and transparency in circular supply chain. *Information & Management*, *59*(7), 103508. doi:10.1016/j.im.2021.103508

Chan, M. H. T. (2018). The belt and road initiative–the new silk road: A research agenda. *Journal of Contemporary East Asia Studies*, *7*(2), 104–123. doi:10.1080/24761028.2019.1580407

Chang, S. E., Chen, Y. C., & Lu, M. F. (2019). Supply chain re-engineering using blockchain technology: A case of smart contract based tracking process. *Technological Forecasting and Social Change*, *144*, 1–11. doi:10.1016/j.techfore.2019.03.015

Chang, Y., Iakovou, E., & Shi, W. (2020). Blockchain in global supply chains and cross border trade: A critical synthesis of the state-of-the-art, challenges and opportunities. *International Journal of Production Research*, *58*(7), 2082–2099. doi:10.1080/00207543.2019.1651946

Colley, T., & van Noort, C. (2022). China's Belt and Road Strategic Narratives up to the Second Belt and Road Forum. In *Strategic Narratives, Ontological Security and Global Policy: Responses to China's Belt and Road Initiative* (pp. 47-67). Cham: Springer International Publishing. 10.1007/978-3-031-00852-8_3

Crane, A., Matten, D., Glozer, S., & Spence, L. J. (2019). *Business ethics: Managing corporate citizenship and sustainability in the age of globalization*. Oxford University Press.

Dave, B., & Kobayashi, Y. (2018). China's silk road economic belt initiative in Central Asia: Economic and security implications. *Asia Europe Journal*, *16*(3), 267–281. doi:10.100710308-018-0513-x

El-Nemr, N., Canel-Depitre, B., & Taghipour, A. (2017, September). Determinants of hotel room rates. In *Marketing Trends Congress*. Luxury Industries.

El-Nemr, N., Canel-Depitre, B., & Taghipour, A. (2021). The determinants of hotel room rates in Beirut: A hedonic pricing model. International Journal of Trade. *Economics and Finance*, *12*(2), 33–42.

Epstein, M. J., & Buhovac, A. R. (2014). *Making sustainability work: Best practices in managing and measuring corporate social, environmental, and economic impacts*. Berrett-koehler publishers.

Garrett, B. (2014). 3D printing: New economic paradigms and strategic shifts. *Global Policy*, *5*(1), 70–75. doi:10.1111/1758-5899.12119

Gertz, G., & Evers, M. M. (2020). Geoeconomic competition: Will state capitalism win? *The Washington Quarterly*, *43*(2), 117–136. doi:10.1080/0163660X.2020.1770962

Githaiga, N. M., Burimaso, A., Wang, B., & Ahmed, S. M. (2019). The belt and road initiative: Opportunities and risks for Africa's connectivity. *China Quarterly of International Strategic Studies*, *5*(1), 117–141. doi:10.1142/S2377740019500064

Hahm, H., & Raihan, S. (2018). The Belt and Road Initiative: Maximizing benefits, managing risks—A computable general equilibrium approach. *Journal of Infrastructure. Policy and Development*, *2*(1), 97–115. doi:10.24294/jipd.v2i1.140

Holbeche, L. (2023). *The agile organization: how to build an engaged, innovative and resilient business*. Kogan Page Publishers.

Hong, Y. (2014). China's eagerness to export its high-speed rail expertise to ASEAN members. *The Copenhagen Journal of Asian Studies*, *32*(2), 13–36. doi:10.22439/cjas.v32i2.4756

Horner, R., & Alford, M. (2019). The roles of the state in global value chains. In *Handbook on global value chains* (pp. 555–569). Edward Elgar Publishing. doi:10.4337/9781788113779.00044

Huang, Y. (2016). Understanding China's Belt & Road initiative: Motivation, framework and assessment. *China Economic Review*, *40*, 314–321. doi:10.1016/j.chieco.2016.07.007

Hughes, A. C., Lechner, A. M., Chitov, A., Horstmann, A., Hinsley, A., Tritto, A., & Douglas, W. Y. (2020). Horizon scan of the belt and road initiative. *Trends in Ecology & Evolution*, *35*(7), 583–593. doi:10.1016/j.tree.2020.02.005 PMID:32521242

Hurley, J., Morris, S., & Portelance, G. (2019). Examining the debt implications of the Belt and Road Initiative from a policy perspective. *Journal of Infrastructure. Policy and Development*, *3*(1), 139–175.

Iqbal, B. A., Rahman, M. N., & Sami, S. (2019). Impact of belt and road initiative on asian economies. *Global Journal of Emerging Market Economies*, *11*(3), 260–277. doi:10.1177/0974910119887059

Jones, P., Comfort, D., & Hillier, D. (2005). Corporate social responsibility and the UK's top ten retailers. *International Journal of Retail & Distribution Management*, *33*(12), 882–892. doi:10.1108/09590550510634611

Keane, M., Yu, H., Zhao, E. J., & Leong, S. (2020). *Chinas Digital Presence in the Asia-Pacific: Culture, Technology and Platforms*. Anthem Press. doi:10.2307/j.ctv20pxxzt

Khan, M. K., Sandano, I. A., Pratt, C. B., & Farid, T. (2018). China's Belt and Road Initiative: A global model for an evolving approach to sustainable regional development. *Sustainability (Basel)*, *10*(11), 4234. doi:10.3390u10114234

Kunavut, K., Okuda, A., & Lee, D. (2018). Belt and road initiative (BRI): Enhancing ICT connectivity in China-Central Asia corridor. *Journal of Infrastructure. Policy and Development*, *2*(1), 116–141. doi:10.24294/jipd.v2i1.164

Lee, H. L., & Shen, Z. J. M. (2020). Supply chain and logistics innovations with the Belt and Road Initiative. *Journal of Management Science and Engineering*, *5*(2), 77–86. doi:10.1016/j.jmse.2020.05.001

Li, J., & Wang, X. (2012). Energy and climate policy in China's twelfth five-year plan: A paradigm shift. *Energy Policy*, *41*, 519–528. doi:10.1016/j.enpol.2011.11.012

Li, M. (2020). The Belt and Road Initiative: Geo-economics and Indo-Pacific security competition. *International Affairs*, *96*(1), 169–187. doi:10.1093/ia/iiz240

Lin, J. Y. (2022). China's Belt and Road Initiative: The rationale and likely impacts of the new structural economics perspective. *Journal of International Business Policy*, *5*(2), 259–265. doi:10.105742214-022-00138-9

Liu, W., & Dunford, M. (2016). Inclusive globalization: Unpacking China's belt and road initiative. *Area Development and Policy*, *1*(3), 323–340. doi:10.1080/23792949.2016.1232598

Loivet, W., Taghipour, A., & Kang, D. S. (2020). The rise of green supply chain management: Between complexity and necessity. Journal of Economics. *Business and Management*, *8*(1), 1–7.

Mahfod, J., Canel-Depitre, B., & Taghipour, A. (2019). Quality function deployment-ELECTRE in supplier evaluation. *Journal of Advanced Management Science, 7*(4).

Malkin, A. (2022). The made in China challenge to US structural power: Industrial policy, intellectual property and multinational corporations. *Review of International Political Economy*, *29*(2), 538–570. doi:10.1080/09692290.2020.1824930

Mangan, J., & Lalwani, C. (2016). *Global logistics and supply chain management*. John Wiley & Sons.

Mao, C. (2023). North–South development competition and the quality and sustainability of Chinese and Japanese trans-national infrastructure initiatives. *Journal of International Development*, *35*(2), 331–346. doi:10.1002/jid.3694

Merimi, M., & Taghipour, A. (2021). Accelerating the digitalization of the supply chain: An empirical research about COVID-19 crisis. In *Digitalization of Decentralized Supply Chains During Global Crises* (pp. 1–24). IGI Global. doi:10.4018/978-1-7998-6874-3.ch001

Miethlich, B., Beliakova, M., Voropaeva, L., Ustyuzhina, O., & Yurieva, T. (2023). Internal Corporate Policy: CSR and Employee Satisfaction. *Employee Responsibilities and Rights Journal*, *35*(1), 127–141. doi:10.100710672-022-09406-5

Miller, T. (2019). *China's Asian dream: Empire building along the new silk road*. Bloomsbury Publishing.

Nadia, E. N., Beatrice, C. D., & Atour, T. (2020). Luxury hotels' eco-friendly activities & customers' preferences and willingness to pay for green hotels. *Journal of Advanced Management Science, 8*(1).

Naughton, B. (2020). Chinese Industrial Policy and the Digital Silk Road. *Asia Policy*, *15*(1), 23–40. doi:10.1353/asp.2020.0006

Negara, S. D., & Suryadinata, L. (2018). *Indonesia and China's Belt and Road Initiatives: Perspectives, issues and prospects*. ISEAS-Yusof Ishak Institute. doi:10.1355/9789814818605

Oliveira, G. D. L., & Myers, M. (2021). The tenuous co-production of China's Belt and Road Initiative in Brazil and Latin America. *Journal of Contemporary China*, *30*(129), 481–499. doi:10.1080/10670564.2020.1827358

Paliwal, V., Chandra, S., & Sharma, S. (2020). Blockchain technology for sustainable supply chain management: A systematic literature review and a classification framework. *Sustainability (Basel)*, *12*(18), 7638. doi:10.3390u12187638

Pallis, A. A., & Vaggelas, G. K. (2017). A Greek prototype of port governance. *Research in Transportation Business & Management*, *22*, 49–57. doi:10.1016/j.rtbm.2016.12.003

Ponte, S., & Sturgeon, T. (2014). Explaining governance in global value chains: A modular theory-building effort. *Review of International Political Economy*, *21*(1), 195–223. doi:10.1080/09692290.2013.809596

Puthal, D., Malik, N., Mohanty, S. P., Kougianos, E., & Das, G. (2018). Everything you wanted to know about the blockchain: Its promise, components, processes, and problems. *IEEE Consumer Electronics Magazine*, *7*(4), 6–14. doi:10.1109/MCE.2018.2816299

Radford, A., Geddes, J. A., Gallagher, K., & Larson, B. A. (2021). Open-source methods for estimating health risks of fine particulate matter from coal-fired power plants: A demonstration from Karachi, Pakistan. *Environmental Impact Assessment Review*, *91*, 106638. doi:10.1016/j.eiar.2021.106638

Rafique, M. Z., Schneider, N., Shahzad, U., & Song, M. (2022). High-tech industries, financial expansion, and low-carbon energy deployment along the Belt and Road Initiative. *Sustainable Development (Bradford), 30*(6), 1779–1795. doi:10.1002d.2347

Rana, P. B., & Ji, X. (2020). *China's Belt and Road Initiative*. Springer Singapore. doi:10.1007/978-981-15-5171-0

Ranganathan, V., Kumar, P., Kaur, U., Li, S. H., Chakraborty, T., & Chandra, R. (2022). Re-inventing the food supply chain with IoT: A data-driven solution to reduce food loss. *IEEE Internet of Things Magazine, 5*(1), 41–47. doi:10.1109/IOTM.003.2200025

Rühmkorf, A. (2023). The German Supply Chain Law: A First Step Towards More Corporate Sustainability. *European Company Law, 20*(1).

Saberi, S., Kouhizadeh, M., Sarkis, J., & Shen, L. (2019). Blockchain technology and its relationships to sustainable supply chain management. *International Journal of Production Research, 57*(7), 2117–2135. doi:10.1080/00207543.2018.1533261

Shih, W. C. (2020). Global supply chains in a post-pandemic world. *Harvard Business Review, 98*(5), 82–89.

Shin, M., & Taghipour, A. (2021). Supply Chains Digital Transformation: Automated Underground Logistics Systems. *Underground Construction, 6*(2), 7. doi:10.18178/joebm.2021.9.2.651

Snider, J., Hill, R. P., & Martin, D. (2003). Corporate social responsibility in the 21st century: A view from the world's most successful firms. *Journal of Business Ethics, 48*(2), 175–187. doi:10.1023/B:BUSI.0000004606.29523.db

Summers, T. (2016). China's 'New Silk Roads': Sub-national regions and networks of global political economy. *Third World Quarterly, 37*(9), 1628–1643. doi:10.1080/01436597.2016.1153415

Sunny, J., Undralla, N., & Pillai, V. M. (2020). Supply chain transparency through blockchain-based traceability: An overview with demonstration. *Computers & Industrial Engineering, 150*, 106895. doi:10.1016/j.cie.2020.106895

Taghipour, A. (2014). *Production Network Planning Based on Constraint Relaxation and Discount Approach* (Vol. 2). Lecture Notes on Information Theory.

Taghipour, A. (2018). A Contemporary Approach to Plan Independent Logistics Actors. In *Contemporary Approaches and Strategies for Applied Logistics* (pp. 337–364). IGI Global. doi:10.4018/978-1-5225-5273-4.ch014

Taghipour, A. (Ed.). (2020). *Demand Forecasting and Order Planning in Supply Chains and Humanitarian Logistics*. IGI Global.

Taghipour, A., Abed, M., & Zoghlami, N. (2015, May). Design for remanufacturing respecting reverse logistics processes: A review. In *2015 4th International Conference on Advanced Logistics and Transport (ICALT)* (pp. 299-304). IEEE. 10.1109/ICAdLT.2015.7136602

Taghipour, A., & Beneteau-Piet, C. (2020). Sustainable supply chain management performance. *International Journal of Innovation, Management and Technology*, *11*(6), 165–169. doi:10.18178/ijimt.2020.11.6.897

Taghipour, A., & Frayret, J. M. (2011a). A new heuristic search with local optimization to manage a supply chain. *Meta*, 15.

Taghipour, A., & Frayret, J. M. (2011b). *Supply chain coordination planning: A review*. Work paper, École polytechnique de Montréal.

Taghipour, A., Glaa, B., & Zoghlami, N. (2014, May). Network coordination with minimum risk of information sharing. In *2014 International Conference on Advanced Logistics and Transport (ICALT)* (pp. 184-188). IEEE. 10.1109/ICAdLT.2014.6864115

Taghipour, A., & Merimi, M. (2021). Digital Transformation of Supply Chains during Crisis: COVID-19. In *11th Annual International Conference on Industrial Engineering and Operations Management, IEOM* (pp. 7493-7501). IEOM Society.

Taghipour, A., Murat, S., & Huang, P. (2021). E-supply chain management: A review. International Journal of e-Education, e-Business, e-. *Management Learning*, *11*(2), 51–61.

Tliche, Y., Taghipour, A., & Canel-Depitre, B. (2019). Anticipation of Demand in Supply Chains. In *Hierarchical Planning and Information Sharing Techniques in Supply Chain Management* (pp. 1–45). IGI Global.

Tliche, Y., Taghipour, A., & Canel-Depitre, B. (2021). Exploring a Downstream Demand Inference Strategy in a Decentralized Two-Level Supply Chain. In *Demand Forecasting and Order Planning in Supply Chains and Humanitarian Logistics* (pp. 1–65). IGI Global. doi:10.4018/978-1-7998-3805-0.ch001

Van der Putten, F. P., & Meijnders, M. (2015). China, Europe and the maritime silk road. Clingendael Institute.

Vosooghidizaji, M., Taghipour, A., & Canel-Depitre, B. (2020). Information Asymmetry in Supply Chain Coordination: State of the Art. *Journal of Industrial and Intelligent Information, 8*(2).

Vosooghidizaji, M., Taghipour, A., & Canel-Depitre, B. (2022). Coordinating corporate social responsibility in a two-level supply chain under bilateral information asymmetry. *Journal of Cleaner Production*, *364*, 132627. doi:10.1016/j.jclepro.2022.132627

Wang, M., Wu, Y., Chen, B., & Evans, M. (2020). Blockchain and supply chain management: A new paradigm for supply chain integration and collaboration. *Operations and Supply Chain Management: An International Journal*, *14*(1), 111–122. doi:10.31387/oscm0440290

Wolf, S. O. (2021). *China-Pakistan Economic Corridor of the Belt and Road Initiative*. Springer.

Yang, S., Taghipour, A., & Canel-Depitre, B. (2017, August). Cost optimization of reverse logistics: A review. In *Proceedings of the 7th International Conference on Information Communication and Management* (pp. 158-161). ACM. 10.1145/3134383.3134393

Zreik, M. (2021). The Potential of a Sino-Lebanese Partnership through the Belt and Road Initiative (BRI). *Contemporary Arab Affairs*, *14*(3), 125–145. doi:10.1525/caa.2021.14.3.125

Zreik, M. (2022). Contemporary geopolitics of Eurasia and the Belt and Road Initiative. *Eurasian Research Journal*, *4*(1), 7–26. doi:10.53277/2519-2442-2022.1-01

Zreik, M. (2023). Analytical study on Foreign Direct Investment Divestment Inflows and Outflows in Developing Economies: Evidence of China. *Chinese Economy*, 1–16. doi:10.1080/10971475.2023.2193118

Chapter 6
The Evolution of Food Supply Chain Management in China

XiaoWen Lu
Normandy University, France

Atour Taghipour
Normandy University, France

ABSTRACT

During recent years, the supply chain act was adapted to deal with human rights abuses and environmental protection in supply chains, as a way to motivate companies to integrate corporate responsibilities in their decisions. This directive can intervene without being transposed into national laws in other countries, where the actors of the supply chain exist. The act provides penalties for companies that don't have plans for respecting human rights and environmental protection. For this reason, companies need to have information channels to report possible breaches of the law. One of the critical supply chains is the food supply chain, which needs to assure food safety, in addition to other requirements determined by law, across the global supply chain, by coordinating food related businesses in each supply chain. In this study, the authors will analyse different companies, which transformed their supply chain following different crises and adapting new supply chain management laws. The example studies in this research can be used by other companies in their supply chain transformation.

INTRODUCTION

The Concept of a Food Supply Chain

One of The main objectives of food supply chain management is to assure the safety of food across the global supply chain. This is possible thanks to the coordination of food related businesses. These businesses form a sequence of economic activities involved in the movement of food from production to consumption, including pre-production and post-consumption activities. The actors of a food supply chain are a group of interdependent companies working closely together to create and deliver value in

DOI: 10.4018/978-1-6684-9062-4.ch006

the form of foods for final customers. The actors of a food supply chain are farmers, manufacturers, warehouses, vendors, wholesalers, and retailers. The integration between these parties are essential to the success of the food supply chain. Each actor of the food supply chain is in charge of a process such as production, processing, distribution, consumption and disposal. In the food supply chain, food changes its identity from farmer to consumer in a domino-like fashion. In addition to the product flow, there are two other flows in a food supply chain: information flow and financial flow (Tliche et al., 2019 & 2021). Financial flow moves from consumers to producers in the reverse process, also in a domino-likc fashion (Yang et al., 2017).

The management of a food supply chain adapts the principle of push and pull integration. In a food supply chain, producers generally push products using a forecasting system and consumers pull foods by determining their demands. Here are key characters of a traditional food supply chain:

- Corporate relations in the supply chain are often framed in opposite positions, which raises some inter-organizational suspicions. Relationships are made by way of competition, even oppositional, whereby every company seeks to buy as economically and to sell as extensively as possible (Nadia et al., 2020).
- Agriculturalists, smallholders and others concerns are preserved as interchangeable and exploitable providers, often working in constrained markets or under short-term bonds led them generally to suffer the risks (Stevenson and Pirog, 2013).
- The benefits and profits from the retailing of finished foodstuffs are unevenly distributed through the supply chain, with food processors and marketers usually receiving a disproportionately higher share (Taghipour, 2020).
- Actions are gradually located and organized on a national and international measure, with food production, processing and marketing sited according to short-term financial advantages for those parties who control the chain (Taghipour et al., 2015).

Securing the food supply chain is a permanent challenge, whatever the level of decision-making and political regime. There are two ways to secure a supply chain. The first is to adapt the principles of sustainability for different decision-making processes in supply chains (Xuewen, 2007). In this case, the companies apply self-adopted policies (Taghipour and Beneteau-Piet, 2020). The second, consists in setting up control of flows by authorities such as the supply chain Act, and it can be applied whatever the country in which the actors of supply chain exist. In the following section we study more different examples of the companies, which adapted their strategy to be proactive in the management of their supply chains.

The McDonald's Food Supply Chain is the Key of his Success in the Worldwide

McDonald's Corporation is the world's largest chain of fast food restaurants. Its net sales break down by type of restaurant. This company had 37,295 franchises at the beginning of 2022 and 2,736 directly operated restaurants. Its international turnover represents 61.8% of its total turnover. In 2015, McDonald's supply chain ranked No. 2 in the Gartner Supply Chain Top 25 list, before Amazon. McDonald's has held the No. 2 spot for three years in a row. Managing McDonald's supply chain requires filling the needs of a corporation with more than 36,000 restaurants that serve 69 million customers daily in 100 countries along with meeting the company's goal of never being out of an item in a customer order.

McDonalds doesn't make any of its products. It bonds with suppliers to meet this enormous requirement. So, their suppliers are like a part of McDonalds' three-legged stool—the other two being the customers and the company employees. McDonalds' suppliers include Tyson Food, Fresh Express, Sunny Fresh Farms, General Mills, Dean Foods, Newman's Own, Kraft Foods, Golden State Foods, Dannon, Coca-Cola, McCormick, and many more. They supply bakery supplies, meat, poultry, fish, produce, and dairy (Team, 2014).

The supply chain management strategy is one of the reasons the company developed from its start in 1955 to a global institution. His global supply chain needs to ensure an impressive amount of materials from beef to a restaurant operating supplies make it to each location; McDonald's supply chain also must fill the company's demand to specialize menus according to preferences of local customers and source products locally.

PROBLEMATIC

The Problem of China's Food Supply Chain

The Importance of Food Safety in China

China has experienced a high rate of food incidents in recent years. According to statistics, the production of counterfeit medicines in China has caused the death of at least 200,000 people. The proportion of counterfeit drugs represents 15% of total drug production. Nearly 100,000 lawsuits related to food quality have been filed in the courts of the People's Republic of China in recent years. Food supply chain is also treated by different types of risk: global pandemics, natural tragedies, unfavourable weather, rising foodstuff costs, contract violations or cyber security issues, etc. They are all the dangers troubling the food manufacturing today (El-Nemr et al., 2017; El-Nemr et al., 2021). Over the last five years, Chinese clients have had to struggle with everything from polluted milk to expired meat, growing serious problems concerning the food safety for consumption. Establishing the food supply chain is the key to ensure a food product quality in today's markets (Mahfod et al., 2019). Combatting tainted and modified foods within the supply chain needs to be a top priority, though, as a major incident can have a long-lasting negative impact on the brand.

Food safety issues can be divided into two aspects: reaching quality standards, and eliminating uncertainties (Cauchois et al., 2017). The first is needed to ensure food quality that is safe to eat, the second that consumers believe it is safe to eat – a sense of food security.

Because the food safety problem is very sensitive in China and the Chinese people care so much about the safety of their food (Yasuda, 2015). The food supply chain management has a significant importance in the food industry. It can destroy an enterprise or make a brand become a hot number. Because food processing is too complex to easily understand, there is a strong challenge for foreign companies to adapt to China's food supply chain. To increase confidence in food or to show the consumers the safety of the product could help the company to have a good image for all the aspects (Loive et al., 2020).

For the majority of consumers, just certifying meeting standards at every stage of the food supply chain can solve the food quality theme. Classifying an exploitation plan for controlling every move of the food processing succession will need manpower and financing (Taghipour, 2014). Second, identifying how to use punishing indemnities is also part of the process of balancing consumer interests against food industry lobbying and gaining legislative and government support.

A food supply chain has a domino-like phenomenon, when one part of the food supply chain is affected, the whole food supply chain is affected, which is often manifested through having a bad reputation or else. The trouble is bad reputations aren't lost that easily.

The Development of Regulation in China

The solutions of food safety issue always depend on government power to accomplish its responsibilities – by the supervision of food suppliers, or protecting the legal rights of consumers (Zhou and Jin, 2013). Some of the foreign firms always take the problem of china's food safety as the results of corruption, local obstructionism or weak state capacity. However, the China's government develops a national food safety policy that can effectively integrate divers' interests within a common framework of governance to manage over 240 million farmers, 1 million processors, and many millions of distributors. In this part, we try to study the China Food and Drug Administration (CFDA), which is a Chinese governmental association who supervises the regime of china's food safety. This association is not the only association, which supervises China's food safety; we can also point out to the Ministry of Health, the General Administration for Quality Supervision, Inspection, and Quarantine (AQSIQ). But, the main power belongs to the CFDA since March 2013. During these years, the CFDA has improved the food supply chain in different ways, like a new food recall regulation and some new licenses for all distributors, retailers and food service establishments, despite different barriers related to the reorganizing the regulations, or survey the post-marketing of products and entities.

Requirements of a Food Supply Chain

Short Supply Chain

In the world, people prefer a short food supply chain, like sending products from the farms directly to the families so as to guarantee the freshness and safety, plus reducing uncertain information (Vosooghidizaji et al., 2020 & 2022). In China, the degree of processing of agricultural products is still quite complex, and the food supply chain is still too long (Taghipour et al. 2014). However, in many cases, a short food supply chain not only will be useful for the food safety or food quality problem, but also can solve the problem of regional development.

Cloud-Based Traceability

Traceability is the ability to follow the movement of a food product through the stages of production, processing, and distribution (Dabbene et al., 2014). From two points of view traceability in the food supply chain can be useful. First, it is to improve food safety and consumer confidence. Second, to provide timely, accurate information exchange between trading partners (Jourdan, 2014). The need of food traceability is obvious, however, to achieve an end-to-end traceability across the supply chain, more progress is essential in developing a technical solution, which can coordinate the actors of the supply chain, which is justifiable from the cost perspective (Taghipour and Merimi, 2021). As an example, we can name the Radio Frequency Identification (RFID) technology, which is the most used tool to develop traceability systems in food supply chains (Taghipour, 2018).

By tracking ingredients, it can be understood that they come from multiple suppliers, each with their different techniques, procedures, data systems and coding structures in different countries (Martindale, 2010). Cloud-based traceability applications can capture data from all of these sources, translate it into common formats and integrate it into appropriate applications for processing. Cloud-based traceability could be immediately visible to all supply chain participants. Cloud technology can help companies to go farther than ever. It will break down the geographical barriers to manage across the food supply chain, as a new trend in supply chain management (Merimi and Taghipour, 2021).

Cold Supply Chain

Because of the various features of the food supply chain, the food supply chain has a higher demand for the equipment. So, for building an efficient food supply chain, we cannot neglect the facilities that are used for the food supply chain.

THE CASE OF MCDONALD'S FOOD SUPPLY CHAIN IN CHINA

The McDonald's Food Supply Chain is the Key of his Success

McDonald's is known for its legendary supply chain management. McDonald's supply chain ranked No. 2 in the 2015 Gartner Supply Chain Top 25 list, second only to Amazon. McDonald's has held the No. 2 spot for three years in a row. Managing McDonald's supply chain requires filling the needs of a corporation with more than 36,000 restaurants that serve 69 million customers daily in 100 countries along with meeting the company's goal of never being out of an item in a customer order. McDonalds doesn't make any of its products. It bonds with suppliers to meet this enormous requirement. So, their suppliers are like a part of McDonalds' three-legged stool—the other two being the customers and the company employees. McDonalds' suppliers include Tyson Food, Fresh Express, Sunny Fresh Farms, General Mills, Dean Foods, Newman's Own, Kraft Foods, Golden State Foods, Dannon, Coca-Cola, McCormick, and many more. They supply bakery supplies, meat, poultry, fish, produce, and dairy.

The supply chain management strategy is one of the reasons for the company's successes, from its start in 1955 to a global institution. Its global supply chain ensures an impressive amount of materials from suppliers to customers, McDonald's supply chain also must fill the company's demand to specialize menus according to preferences of local customers and source products locally.

McDonald's Supply Chain Methodology

McDonald's largest distributor, the Martin-Brower Company LLC, is tasked with delivering supplies to nearly all of the company's 15,000 locations in North America. Each centre of distribution handles 250 to 700 restaurants, providing warehousing, transportation, and logistics services to each. Most restaurants get two or three deliveries per week, with one delivery truck able to completely stock the establishment. Delivery times are coordinated to not interrupt breakfast or lunch service because customers may not enter if they see the truck in the parking lot. Drivers call on the route to be sure the restaurant has workers there to take delivery when it arrives, reducing the time trucks are in the parking lot by up to 30%. The company also uses the roller and stand of delivery that move from the truck into the restaurant. Inventory is turned over every four days at a McDonald's restaurant. The company can do this because of relationships they've formed with their suppliers, many of which still maintain the relationship that started with McDonald's Corporation founder Ray Kroc. McDonald's "System" philosophy is often described as a three-legged stool. One of the legs is a McDonald's employee, a second leg is the owner/operators that run the restaurants, and the third leg is a McDonald's supplier partner. The stool is only as strong as its three legs. This means that the company employees, the owner/operators and the suppliers, each support the weight of McDonald's equally. For one to prosper, everyone must prosper. Kroc's System has stood the test of time because leaders within the System have continued to honour a "System First" approach where solutions always include the consideration, "What's best for the System?"

The Crisis of McDonald's Food Supply Chain Management in China

When McDonald's is looking to China - where consumers see foreign brands as offering better food quality - for long-term growth given the size of its population, growing middle class and rapid economic growth. This crisis of food safety is not only happening to McDonald's, but also to Yum Brands Inc., which owns the KFC and Pizza Hut chains.

In the 2014 July, Chinese police arrested six staff from McDonald's supplier OSI Group Inc., which used expired meat and doctored food production dates. This scandal of the improper meat created by a supplier (Shanghai Husi Food, a subsidiary of American-based OSI group), and McDonald's was suffered by a negative influence to sales at all their outlets during several months in the 2014, which led to McDonald's' annual net income dropped 15% to $4.7 billion - making 2014 one of the worst years in the company's history.

When McDonald's intended to capture China's mass markets within a short period of time, the company built its food supply chain with its actors, which trust in 100%, located in the American or European market, without studying profoundly new markets. The company ignored that it was also a new challenge for their partners. So, when worthy-trust partners worked with inexperienced or untrustworthy local suppliers and made the huge trouble with the food safety problem, they finally knew the building of a right supply chain in their new market should be done as the first thing in the strategy.

After a big scandal with one of its suppliers in China, McDonald's decided to continue its supply with its 50-year long business partner (OSI, the food-processing group). The company switched its supply to an OSI-owned plant in Henan province. McDonald's still believes that the quality of meat is better than the local supplier and confirms that the company will ensure high quality of meat in the future.

After the failure of supplier management in China, McDonald's had to look no further than find the trusted System. So, McDonald's shifted to the other long-term supplier partners such as Keystone Foods and Cargill Inc. to re-establish a stable source of supply in China in the short time. This is how McDonald operates to face a crisis in the supply chain: quickly acting with established strategic suppliers that are committed to McDonald's success. This is not the first time McDonald's suppliers have come to the rescue of other suppliers. In the 2004 Avian Flu crisis, McDonald's suppliers stepped up to meet McDonald's assured supply goals in Asia during crises, assuring supply when virtually all of McDonald's competitors ran out of chicken.

China has already become McDonald's third largest market by the number of outlets and the number one market for KFC-parent Yum. McDonald's currently has over 2,000 restaurants in Mainland China.

The Changes of McDonald's Supply Chain Strategy in China

Finding appropriate supply chain partners and developing mechanisms for building trust, transparency and decision-making.

Create a Transparent Supply Chain

Since 2004 the company has decided to adopt a new strategy toward more transparency is the extension of a strategy adapted by the company from 2004, by withdrawing from the "Super Size" menus and adding a range of salads. Following this strategy, the company has decided to publish the composition and nutritional quality of its products on the packaging. To do that, using a system of easy-to-understand icons and bar graphs, the packaging of products includes precise information on their composition and nutritional quality, such as level of calories, fat, sugar, fibre. Increased transparency scored McDonald's a major public relations victory in Europe. The company's supply chain transparency was singled out for praise by the Elliott Review, in the British government's official investigation into the horsemeat scandal.

Centralization

The centralized strategy allows McDonald's to control and supervise its product quality in food supply chain management than the decentralized approach, especially when advanced quality control methods cannot be applied due to limited physical/human resources as well as when the testing technologies and procedures can be systematically influenced or altered. However, organizing a more centralized food supply chain will require more time and financial resources, and not all companies will be able to build a company-owned supply chain (Taghipour et al, 2021). For these companies, there are a number of other viable options for establishing strong partnerships, as well as for exerting vertical control among legally independent firms in a supply chain, such as developing the so-called supplier code of conduct, utilizing supplier certification programs, and enforcing high quality standards with a strict monitoring and control system (Shin and Taghipour, 2021).

Traceability

The company constantly tracks everything from daily point-of-sale data for each item, restaurant stock levels and its marketing plans for promotional items or local menus to distribution centre shipments and inventories. The company handles the major suppliers. The operation requires knowing who is responsible for planning each task and carrying out those plans. The supply chain also needs to anticipate future demands and changes in sales volume (Taghipour and Frayret, 2011a & 2011b).

We believe that MacDonald's has its own system to realise the traceability, but how could we use the traceability to rebuild our consumer's trust. Maybe cooperating with the mobile app and the QR code, when the consumer buys the product, scanning the QR code they can know all the process of production.

A New System of Audit

Conducting regular audits is another good way to make sure suppliers are complying with your standards. Visit, on-site, with your suppliers to get an inside look into the conditions in which your products are being sourced. Scheduling a regular audit procedure and understanding your suppliers' weak spots will strengthen your overall sourcing strategies.

McDonald's monitors more its Chinese suppliers and sends more quality control specialists to all meat production facilities. The firm has also created a new role to oversee food safety governance in China and has launched a hotline to report food safety issues. And the half of the audits would be done unannounced and would be carried out by third party auditors and internal teams.

THE CASE OF COFCO

Presentation of the COFCO

China National Cereals, Oils and Foodstuffs Corporation, founded in 1949, COFCO is a global service provider of agricultural products and diversified food services, including agricultural products trading, logistics and storage, raw materials processing, biofuels, branded food production and sales, among others. COFCO provides grain and foods to consumers of one fourth of the global population.

COFCO boasts a wide range of branded products and service portfolios, such as Fortune edible oil, Great Wall wine, China Tea products, Le Conte chocolate, Tunhe tomato products, Joycome meat products, Snow-Lotus cashmere, Cereal Way fast noodle, Lohas fruit and vegetable juice, Joy City shopping mall, Yalong Bay resorts, Gloria hotels, COFCO-Aviva Life Insurance, COFCO Trust, etc.

The COFCO's Food Supply Chain Management

As China's biggest integrated oil and food supplier, COFCO is committed to developing a global supply chain and full control of quality and traceability across the entire supply chain; as well as to international cooperation for food security, stable supply of food and health and safety. They cooperate with PwC and Asure Quality to further enhance the development of food safety.

COFCO knows globalization, regulatory change, resource scarcity and food fraud in China are the issues we need to face, meanwhile the suppliers need to deal with downward cost pressure which leads to increased risks throughout the supply chain.

COFCO tries to acquire the best practices from these international top industries like PwC and AsureQuality, which will also facilitate innovative solutions for COFCO across its whole food supply chain, including food security, safety and quality. Making use of innovative solutions, COFCO can achieve the goals of attaining robust food safety standards and managing profitability and that will be a key cornerstone of success for food companies.

The growing wealth of China's urbanized consumers and its middle class are changing food demand dynamics and creating greater expectations not just of safety, but of quality, choice and aesthetics. A key challenge for the food industry is how best to manage food safety across the global supply chain while ensuring regulatory compliance. There is increasing awareness and concern regarding food security, safety, quality and sustainability; and a demand for performance improvement and transformation across the food supply chain (Smith, 2008).

In response to the supply and demands of the global market, COFCO is committed to creating an agricultural and Food Company with an integrated value chain that connects farms to the household by its global expansion strategy and new business model.

CONCLUSION

The situation and demand in China are unique, brought about by the country's rapid social advancements and the urbanization of its people. Providing safe and reliable quality food to more than 1.3 billion people on a daily basis presents many challenges and opportunities. In this work, we studied the case of McDonald's and China National Cereals, Oils and Foodstuffs Corporation and we showed that in the case of crises, how these companies found a way to turn crisis into opportunities. As these examples, there are so many examples of the Chinese companies that got their success by establishing an excellent food supply chain.

REFERENCES

Cauchois, R., Taghipour, A., Kang, D., Zoghlami, N., & Abed, M. (2017). Advanced solutions for a supply chain with stochastic information. *Journal of Advanced Management Science, 5*(1).

Dabbene, F., Gay, P., & Tortia, C. (2014). Traceability issues in food supply chain management: A review. *Biosystems Engineering, 120*, 65–80. doi:10.1016/j.biosystemseng.2013.09.006

El-Nemr, N., Canel-Depitre, B., & Taghipour, A. (2021). The determinants of hotel room rates in Beirut: A hedonic pricing model. International Journal of Trade. *Economics and Finance*, *12*(2), 33–42.

El-Nemr, N., Canel-Depitre, B., & Taghipour, A. (2017, September). Determinants of hotel room rates. In *Marketing Trends Congress. Luxury Industries Conference London 2017*. HAL.

Jourdan, A. (2014). McDonald's to boost China supplier audits after food safety scandal. *Reuters*.

Loivet, W., Taghipour, A., & Kang, D. S. (2020). The rise of green supply chain management: Between complexity and necessity. *Journal of Economics. Business and Management*, *8*(1), 1–7.

Mahfod, J., Canel-Depitre, B., & Taghipour, A. (2019). Quality function deployment-ELECTRE in supplier evaluation. *Journal of Advanced Management Science, 7*(4).

Martindale, W. (2010). Food supply chain innovations. *Aspects of Applied Biology*, *102*, 1–6.

Merimi, M., & Taghipour, A. (2021). Accelerating the digitalization of the supply chain: An empirical research about COVID-19 crisis. In *Digitalization of Decentralized Supply Chains During Global Crises* (pp. 1–24). IGI Global. doi:10.4018/978-1-7998-6874-3.ch001

Nadia, E. N., Beatrice, C. D., & Atour, T. (2020). Luxury hotels' eco-friendly activities & customers' preferences and willingness to pay for green hotels. *Journal of Advanced Management Science, 8*(1).

Shin, M., & Taghipour, A. (2021). Supply Chains Digital Transformation: Automated Underground Logistics Systems. *Underground Construction*, *6*(2), 7. doi:10.18178/joebm.2021.9.2.651

Smith, B. G. (2008). Developing sustainable food supply chains. *Philosophical Transactions of the Royal Society of London. Series B, Biological Sciences*, *363*(1492), 849–861. doi:10.1098/rstb.2007.2187 PMID:17766237

Stevenson, G. W., & Pirog, R. (2013). Values-based food supply chains: Strategies for agri-food enterprises-of-the-middle. *Techincal Report. Accessed*, (June), 22.

Taghipour, A. (2014). *Production Network Planning Based on Constraint Relaxation and Discount Approach* (Vol. 2). Lecture Notes on Information Theory.

Taghipour, A. (2018). A Contemporary Approach to Plan Independent Logistics Actors. In *Contemporary Approaches and Strategies for Applied Logistics* (pp. 337–364). IGI Global. doi:10.4018/978-1-5225-5273-4.ch014

Taghipour, A. (Ed.). (2020). *Demand Forecasting and Order Planning in Supply Chains and Humanitarian Logistics*. IGI Global.

Taghipour, A., Abed, M., & Zoghlami, N. (2015, May). Design for remanufacturing respecting reverse logistics processes: A review. In *2015 4th International Conference on Advanced Logistics and Transport (ICALT)* (pp. 299-304). IEEE. 10.1109/ICAdLT.2015.7136602

Taghipour, A., & Beneteau-Piet, C. (2020). Sustainable supply chain management performance. *International Journal of Innovation, Management and Technology*, *11*(6), 165–169. doi:10.18178/ijimt.2020.11.6.897

Taghipour, A., & Frayret, J. M. (2011a). A new heuristic search with local optimization to manage a supply chain. *Meta*, 15.

Taghipour, A., & Frayret, J. M. (2011b). *Supply chain coordination planning: A review.* Work paper, École polytechnique de Montréal.

Taghipour, A., Glaa, B., & Zoghlami, N. (2014, May). Network coordination with minimum risk of information sharing. In *2014 International Conference on Advanced Logistics and Transport (ICALT)* (pp. 184-188). IEEE. 10.1109/ICAdLT.2014.6864115

Taghipour, A., & Merimi, M. (2021). Digital Transformation of Supply Chains during Crisis: COVID-19. In *11th Annual International Conference on Industrial Engineering and Operations Management, IEOM* (pp. 7493-7501). IEEE.

Taghipour, A., Murat, S., & Huang, P. (2021). E-supply chain management: A review. International Journal of e-Education, e-Business, e-. *Management Learning*, *11*(2), 51–61.

Team, T. (2014). McDonald's faces declining sales in Asia after China food scandal. *Forbes*.

Tliche, Y., Taghipour, A., & Canel-Depitre, B. (2019). Anticipation of Demand in Supply Chains. In *Hierarchical Planning and Information Sharing Techniques in Supply Chain Management* (pp. 1–45). IGI Global.

Tliche, Y., Taghipour, A., & Canel-Depitre, B. (2021). Exploring a Downstream Demand Inference Strategy in a Decentralized Two-Level Supply Chain. In *Demand Forecasting and Order Planning in Supply Chains and Humanitarian Logistics* (pp. 1–65). IGI Global. doi:10.4018/978-1-7998-3805-0.ch001

Vosooghidizaji, M., Taghipour, A., & Canel-Depitre, B. (2020). Information Asymmetry in Supply Chain Coordination: State of the Art. *Journal of Industrial and Intelligent Information, 8*(2).

Vosooghidizaji, M., Taghipour, A., & Canel-Depitre, B. (2022). Coordinating corporate social responsibility in a two-level supply chain under bilateral information asymmetry. *Journal of Cleaner Production*, *364*, 132627. doi:10.1016/j.jclepro.2022.132627

Xuewen, T. (2007). *The Sustainability of Food Supply Chain in China: Review and Comment.* Rural Development Institute of Chinese Academy of Social Sciences.

Yang, S., Taghipour, A., & Canel-Depitre, B. (2017, August). Cost optimization of reverse logistics: A review. In *Proceedings of the 7th International Conference on Information Communication and Management* (pp. 158-161). ACM. 10.1145/3134383.3134393

Yasuda, J. K. (2015). Why food safety fails in China: The politics of scale. *The China Quarterly*, *223*, 745–769. doi:10.1017/S030574101500079X

Zhou, J., & Jin, S. (2013). *Food safety management in China: A perspective from food quality control system*. World Scientific. doi:10.1142/8689

Chapter 7
A Framework for Exploring the Global Performance of Service Supply Chain Management:
A Qualitative Study

Badr Bentalha
National School of Business and Management, Sidi Mohammed Ben Abdellah University, Morocco

ABSTRACT

Contemporary managerial thinking and practices have been developed in an economic context dominated by industrial logic. This logic conceals the imposing weight of services. Logistics is an activity that is undergoing major changes due to new technologies and managerial innovations. The advent of the supply chain service (SSCM), as a dual concept combining both traditional supply operations and the coordination of various resources, with a view to customer satisfaction, while integrating constraints of time, capacity, shared resources, and co-production, has turned logistics research upside down. The purpose of this chapter is to establish a qualitative analysis of the impact of MCSS practices on the performance of the service company. The theoretical analysis and the review of interviews show that SSCM approaches differ, and that company performance is viewed differently depending on each SSCM practice, and also depending on the multiple facets of this performance. Based on this qualitative review, several observations are identified.

INTRODUCTION

The development of services appears to be a major predisposition of economies both in macro-economic terms, through the domination of the tertiary sector, and in micro-economic terms, due to the nature of the tasks performed within companies or the nature of the products and services offered. Faced with the challenges of competitiveness, optimizing the Service Supply Chain (SSC) is becoming one of the key factors in the performance of service companies, in terms of customer satisfaction and loyalty, profitability, sales and market share. Service Supply Chain Management (SSCM) is a cross-functional process,

DOI: 10.4018/978-1-6684-9062-4.ch007

encompassing the steering dimensions of demand, capacity and resources, customer and supplier relations, the ordering process, service performance, and information and technology (Ellram et al., 2004).

Performance refers to the degree to which results are achieved in relation to the efforts made and resources absorbed. It is based on the concepts of effectiveness and efficiency. Its measurement is therefore multi-variable, covering several levels. Performance is a difficult notion to define, and a comparison of possible translations reveals this conceptual difficulty. Performance cannot be reduced to a single dimension that would encompass all the others. On the contrary, it is necessary to recognize the coexistence of several dimensions, for which there is no single optimum that would impose itself on all stakeholders. Performance becomes "global" when the company strives to satisfy the expectations of investors and other stakeholders. Supply chain performance measurement focuses on improving the operation of production support processes and increasing productivity.

The aim of this work is to establish a qualitative analysis of the impact of SSCM practices on the overall performance of the service company. The theoretical analysis carried out and the review of the interviews conducted show that SSCM approaches are many and varied, and that the overall performance of the company is apprehended unequally according to each SSCM practice. On the basis of this qualitative review, we have identified a number of possible observations and considered a number of avenues for further reflection.

1. CONCEPTUAL AND THEORETICAL FRAMEWORK

1.1. Supply Chain Management Concept and Approach

Lambert et al. (1998) define a supply chain (SC) as a sequence of associated companies supplying products and services to the market. Mentzer et al (2001) define a SC as a set of three or more organizations directly involved in the upstream and downstream flow of goods, services, finance and/or information from supplier to consumer. Supply Chain Management (SCM) emerged in the 1980s and gained widespread acceptance in the 1990s (Bentalha, 2023). The objective of SCM is customer satisfaction. This inspires the supply chain to encompass independent partners with a single global strategy. Market developments since the early 1980s have led to a profound rethinking of classic centralized and hierarchical organizational models, and to talk of the emergence of a new structural paradigm.

Building and managing a supply chain is all about facilitating the marketing of products (Bouhtati et al., 2022). The imperatives of performance and the challenges of competitiveness require inter- and intra-organizational management of these chains. This managerial and contractual duality has broadened the concept of "*integrated logistics*" towards a more open understanding, Supply Chain Management, in which the entire organization of the company undergoes changes, beyond its current structures, to enable greater flexibility. In this way, several managerial parameters are combined in supply chain management. The complexity of this management is also greater when it comes to managing service supply chains.

In contrast to manufacturing products, services have unique and specific characteristics. Firstly, service is intangible, although many service processes can be considered tangible in terms of results. Secondly, services are heterogeneous. Services are tailored to the unique needs of customers in a changing business environment. So it's difficult to automate them (Hemilä & Vilko, 2015). Also, there is simultaneity between delivery and consumption of the service (Boon-itt et al., 2017). Perishability refers to the difficulty of reselling, storing and transporting services due to their immediate and contextual nature. Services are also characterized by strong customer involvement. Due to duality, customers are both suppliers of service inputs and consumers of service outputs (Aitken et al., 2016). This strong customer involvement is accompanied by strong interaction with staff. Finally, there is a solid difficulty in assessing the quality dimension.

The structural uniqueness of a service supply chain is essentially due to its specific characteristics. For this reason, several authors have clearly distinguished integrated supply chains specifically for services, calling them Servicc Supply Chains (SSC). Thus, Baltacioglu et al (2007) define the SSC as a network of suppliers, service providers, consumers and other support units that perform the functions of transacting the resources required to produce services, transforming these resources into core or support services, and delivering these services to customers. Key members of the service supply chain are suppliers, service providers, customers and other partners. SSCs usually involve the customer as an active participant in the production process (Hmioui et Bentalha, 2020). The service provider is the central unit in the service supply chain and functions as the core business, usually the pivot in the supply chain (Bentalha et al., 2020). When providing services to the customer, suppliers of physical products must supply the service provider, while service provider's supply related services as part of the services provided to the customer.

Ellram et al (2004), defined SSCM as follows: "*the management of information, processes, capacity, service performance and funds, from supplier to end customer*". These authors defined seven service and SSCM processes (Table 1):

Table 1. Service supply chain processes according to Ellram et al. (2004)

Process type	Related activities
Supplier relationship management	Supplier selection and contracting, supplier relationship management through: coordination, cooperation, commitment, information sharing and feedback.
Capacity and resource management	Resource and capacity planning, resource scheduling. Resources are organized effectively and efficiently, and operate at optimum levels.
Demand management	Forecasting, matching forecast demand with available capacity.
Information and technology management	Adoption of technologies to support and collaborate within the supply chain to improve SSC operations for competitive advantage in their businesses.
Customer relationship management	Maintain and develop long-term relationships with customers by continually developing customer information and trying to understand what they want.
Service performance management	Customer segmentation, tracking, improving customer satisfaction
Order Process Management	SSC systems should all be taken into account when managing, measuring, modifying and rewarding service performance in order to improve organizational performance to achieve the organization's strategic objectives and promote its mission and values.

Source: Adapted from Ellram et al. (2004)

Service supply chains have several specific features. A first characteristic of SSCMs is the strong presence of customers. The customer always plays several roles, as co-designer, co-producer, co-deliverer and quality controller of the service. As a result, customers evaluate not only the final "*result*" of the process, but also the way in which the service has been delivered and the quality of their personal experience (Grönroos & Ojasalo, 2004). A second feature of SSCM is the fragmentation of service processes between different actors. Often, the various SSC partners are directly involved in the operations of the service process, including the processing of customer inputs and direct interaction with the customer. A third characteristic of SSCMs is the strong presence of personnel (Bentalha & Hmioui, 2022). Indeed, services tend to be much more labor-intensive than manufacturing (Fitzsimmons & Fitzsimmons, 2010). Automation is difficult to introduce in a service environment (Bentalha, 2022). As a result, labor often represents a significant portion of the operating costs of an SSC operation (Hmioui et al, 2019; Taghipour et al., 2021).

1.2. The Contours of Global Performance

Performance has always been an ambiguous concept. The concept of performance can be defined, for a company, as the level of achievement of results in relation to the efforts made and resources consumed. It is largely based on the notions of effectiveness and efficiency. Performance also relates to the company's vision, strategy and objectives. It's a concept that gives rise to many divergences. It is therefore a vast and vague concept, imbued with managerial or socio-psychological ideology, explaining a natural tendency of achievement or success in several sectors of activity (Grenier and Martin, 2013). It's also a polysemous (Issor, 2017) and polytheistic (Bourguignon, 1997) concept, given that the lexeme performance belongs to the vocabulary of several disciplinary fields. In the field of management, performance has always been an ambiguous notion. It can be defined "as the achievement of organizational objectives, whatever the nature and variety of these objectives. This achievement can be understood in the strict sense or in the broad sense of the process that leads to the result (action)" (Bourguignon, 2000).

The one-dimensional approach to performance is a limited vision that was soon abandoned. For Dixon et al (1990), an organization's performance is no longer expressed solely in terms of profit and cost, as in the Taylorian era, when it was expressed solely in terms of profitability (financial performance), but also in terms of other criteria such as quality, lead time and innovation. Performance has thus become multi-criteria: strategic, competitive, socio-economic, financial, economic, commercial, organizational, social and societal.

Global performance is defined as "*the combination of financial, social and societal performance*" (Germain and Trébucq, 2004) or "*the aggregation of economic, social and environmental performance*" (Baret, 2006). It takes the form of multi-criteria, multi-actor indicators, rather than a single measure such as product and service quality, employee motivation, productivity, customer satisfaction, plant safety, etc. Reynaud (2003) proposes a three-dimensional definition of overall corporate performance: social performance (equal treatment, respect for human rights, good working conditions, etc.), economic performance (market share, profitability, profitability, etc.) and environmental performance (pollution reduction, plant safety, product safety, use of renewable resources, etc.). Capron and Quairel (2006) consider global corporate performance to be "*a holistic conception that seeks to designate an integration of performances in a synthetic approach. This integration may imply coherence between the three dimensions, with causal models linking different factors from different dimensions*". From this perspective, the organization is assigned multiple goals, profit being just one of them (Alla et al., 2023). Global performance is defined as the satisfaction of multiple stakeholders, with three main goals: economic, social and environmental.

1.3. The Impact of SSCM Practices on Global Performance: A State-of-the-Art Review

The theoretical and conceptual analysis of the supply chain management service and global performance enabled us to explore the theme under study (Hmioui & Bentalha, 2021). We completed this exploration with a literature review of works related to SSCM practices (Table 2).

Table 2. Theoretical summary of SSCM practices

	Practices	Authors
Common SSCM practices	Information exchange and sharing practices	Choon Tan et al. (2002, p. 622); Sahay & Mohan (2003, p. 590); Li et al. (2005, p. 621); Li et al. (2006, p. 110); Zhou & Benton (2007, p. 1352); Chow et al. (2008, p. 669); Roth et al. (2008, p. 84); Sezen (2008, p. 236); Sharma et al. (2008, p. 257); Brulhart & Moncef (2010, p. 39); Cook & Heiser (2011, p. 109); Jabbour et al. (2011, p. 24); Vanichchinchai & Igel (2011, p. 3407); Sundram et al. (2011, p. 838); Ibrahim & Ogunyemi (2012, p. 450); Karimi & Rafiee (2014, p. 3); Marinagi et al. (2015, p. 477); Kaliani Sundram et al. (2016, p. 1449); Carter et al. (2016, p. 116); Banerjee & Mishra (2017, p. 253); Al-Doori, (2019, p. 245); Bag et al. (2020, p. 6)
	Partnership management practices in supplier relations	Donlon (1996, p. 58); Mentzer et al. (1997, p. 638); Tan et al. (1998, p. 9); Alvarado & Kotzab (2001, p. 187); Wisner (2003, p. 10); Sahay & Mohan (2003, p. 590); Chen & Paulraj (2004, p. 122); Li et al. (2005, p. 621); Li et al. (2006, p. 110); Burgess et al. (2006, p. 718); Da Silveira & Arkader (2007, p. 152); Chow et al. (2008, p. 669); Sharma et al. (2008, p. 257); Brulhart & Moncef (2010, p. 39); Vanichchinchai & Igel (2011, p. 3407); Sundram et al. (2011, p. 838); Jabbour et al. (2011, p. 24); Ibrahim & Ogunyemi (2012, p. 450); Deshpande (2012, p. 4); Chin et al. (2014, p. 259); Zimmermann & Foerstl (2014, p. 38); Kaliani Sundram et al. (2016, p. 1449); Phan et al. (2020, p. 178); Macchion et al. (2020, p. 8);
	Practices of partnership management of customer relations and demand	Mentzer et al. (1997, p. 638); Tan et al. (1998, p. 9); Zhou & Benton (2007, p. 1352); Brulhart & Moncef (2010, p. 39); Jabbour et al. (2011, p. 24); Sundram et al. (2011, p. 838); Ibrahim & Ogunyemi (2012, p. 450); Karimi & Rafiee (2014, p. 3); Chin et al. (2014, p. 259); Spina et al. (2014, p. 4); Chin et al. (2014, p. 259);Kaliani Sundram et al. (2016, p. 1449); Banerjee & Mishra (2017, p. 253); Zailani et al. (2019, p. 5); Phan et al. (2020, p. 178);
	Resource and capacity management practices	Alvarado & Kotzab (2001, p. 187); Van Hoek (2001, p. 26); Wisner (2003, p. 10); Chen & Paulraj (2004, p. 122); Sharma et al. (2008, p. 257); Martin & Patterson (2009, p. 2456); Zimmermann & Foerstl (2014, p. 38); Banerjee & Mishra (2017, p. 253); Macchion et al. (2020, p. 8);
	Risk management practices	Min & Mentzer (2004, p. 67); Ritchie & Brindley (2007, p. 311); Wagner & Bode (2008, p. 316); Kaliani Sundram et al. (2016, p. 1449); Phan et al. (2020, p. 178);
Specific SSCM practices	Service delivery and performance management practices	Youngdahl (1996, p. 32); Gunasekaran et al. (2001, p. 84); Lenny Koh et al. (2007, p. 124); Zhou & Benton (2007, p. 1352); Sezen (2008, p. 236); Chow et al. (2008, p. 673); Ramanathan (2010, p. 954); Cao & Zhang (2011, p. 165); Agus (2011, p. 137); Cho et al. (2012, p. 804); Lotfi et al. (2013, p. 475); Fu et al. (2013, p. 299); Zimmermann & Foerstl (2014, p. 38); Spina et al. (2014, p. 4); Karimi & Rafiee (2014, p. 3); Sillanpää (2015, p. 267); Anand & Grover, 2015, p. 154); Shahin et al. (2016, p. 13-15); Taschner, (2016, p. 1790); Carter et al. (2016, p. 116); Yang & Lirn (2017, p. 900); Elgazzar & Elzarka, (2017, p. 124-125); Wahdan & Emam (2017, p. 142); Aliakbari Nouri et al., (2018, p. 164); Leończuk et al. (2019, p. 102); Shahin & Jamshidian (2020, p. 7); Rahman (2020, p. 24)
	Service cash-flow management practices	Lenny Koh et al. (2007, p. 124); Sundram et al. (2011, p. 838); Mishra & Sharma (2014, p. 113); Shahin et al. (2016, p. 13-15); Yang & Lirn (2017, p. 900); Aliakbari Nouri et al., (2018, p. 164); Shahin & Jamshidian (2020, p. 7);
	Service development, knowledge management and innovation practices	Kathawala & Abdou (2003, p. 144); Jin (2006, p. 105): Chow et al. (2008, p. 673); Wong et al. (2013, p. 567); Zimmermann & Foerstl (2014, p. 38); Sillanpää (2015, p. 267); Shahin et al. (2016, p. 13-15); Carter et al. (2016, p. 116); Banerjee & Mishra (2017, p. 253); Elgazzar & Elzarka, (2017, p. 124-125); Yusuf & Shehu (2017, p. 114); Aliakbari Nouri et al., (2018, p. 164); Bag et al. (2020, p. 6);

Source: Author

We can see that there are several practices linked to the management of service supply chains. This topic has received a great deal of interest from researchers, especially in the last ten years. Thus, we have divided the management practices of service supply chains into two levels: practices specific to SSCM and practices common to all supply chains.

Despite the growing attention paid to service supply chain management by practitioners and academics alike, the performance measurement of these chains remains largely unexplored. Most service companies realize that, in order to evolve a chain, performance management parameters need to be integrated. A review of performance measurement issues in service supply chains has been carried out. Vickery et al (2003) studied the relationship between SSC integration strategy and performance by applying information integration to product supply chain management. Jin (2006) examined the SSCM model of customer satisfaction and business performance of civil aviation services in China. Sengupta et al. (2006) found that SSCM has high relevance to business performance. Indeed, the service supply chain function is the key to using service to leverage supply chain management and operations to meet diversified customer demand through service integration. The authors focus on SSC performance measures (Taghipour, 2020). A distinction is made between the operational and financial performance of these chains. The former is attributed directly to perceived customer satisfaction (Alla et al., 2022a). It concerns measures of costs and profits in relation to competitors. The results show that these differ between the manufacturing and service sectors. Information sharing and the level of customization (relative to competitors) are much higher for operational performance in the service sector. Field & Meile (2008) empirically examined the relationship between supplier relationships and supply chain performance with a sample of 108 financial services processes. The results show that, after controlling for supplier efficiency and responsiveness, information use, electronic information sharing and supplier type (internal and external), better supplier relationships are associated with satisfaction with overall chain performance activities. Also, some research on logistics service supply chains focuses on supplier performance evaluation (Yao & Liu, 2009), supplier selection (Yu, 2003) and supplier coordination mechanism (Cui & Liu, 2009).

Fu et al. (2013) explored high-performance work systems and how they influence professional services supply chain performance, and tested the relationship between professional services supply chain performance and organizational performance. They found that staff motivated and supported by service supply chain management and human resource management can improve the company's professional SSC effectiveness and organizational performance. The role of supply chain management processes in achieving competitive advantage in the service sector has been widely discussed. However, due to the lack of valid measurement scales, the effects of SSCM process capability cannot be determined. Boonitt et al. (2017) developed measurement scales for constructing SSCM process capability. The scales were first developed on the basis of a literature review and refined using the Q-sort method. Wang et al. (2018) showed the primary role of interpersonal relationships in service chains as a lever for performance improvement. Ounnar & Pujo (2018) discussed the fact that supply chains involve a large and growing number of logistics actors. This poses the problem of global steering that takes into account the interests of each and every one. This complexity implies solutions that are difficult to optimize in a hierarchical, centralized way.

Numerous studies have presented the facets of global performance in logistics service chains (Hmioui et al., 2020; Bentalha et al., 2021). We have chosen to follow the framework of the Balanced Scorecard by presenting these works divided into four dimensions (Table 3).

Table 3. Outline of a theoretical synthesis of SSCM global performance items

Dimensions	Authors
Financial dimension	Gunasekaran et al. (2001, p. 84); Tan et al. (2002, p. 623); Ellram et al., (2004, p. 27); Chen & Paulraj (2004, p. 145); Li et al. (2006, p. 111); Bhagwat & Sharma (2007, p. 53-54); Brulhart & Moncef (2010, p. 46); Cao & Zhang (2011, p. 165); Giannakis (2011, p. 360); Cho et al. (2012, p. 804); Green et al. (2012, p. 293); Solakivi (2014, p. 19); Zimmermann & Foerstl (2014, p. 38); Okongwu et al. (2015, p. 702); Sillanpää (2015, p. 267); Wahdan & Emam (2017, p. 142); Elgazzar & Elzarka, (2017, p. 124-125); Aliakbari Nouri et al., (2018, p. 164); Leończuk et al. (2019, p. 89).
Stakeholder performance	Tixier, et al. (1996, p. 113); Beamon & Chen (2001, p. 3200); Gunasekaran et al. (2001, p. 84); Tan et al. (2002, p. 623); Cassivi (2006, p. 250); Bhagwat & Sharma (2007, p. 53-54); Lenny Koh et al. (2007, p. 124); Livolsi (2007, p. 105); Chow et al. (2008, p. 32); Field & Meile (2008, p. 2); Ahn et al. (2010, p. 804); Brulhart & Moncef (2010, p. 46); Agus (2011, p. 137); Hoa Vo & Bironneau (2011, p. 5); Cao & Zhang (2011, p. 174); Yalabik & Fairchild (2011, p. 519); Ciliberti et al. (2011, p. 887); Cho et al. (2012, p. 804); Iraten (2014, p. 143); Selviaridis & Norrman (2014, p. 154); Solakivi (2014, p. 19); Mishra & Sharma (2014, p. 113); Sillanpää (2015, p. 267); Okongwu et al. (2015, p. 702); Song et al. (2016, p. 611); Shahin et al. (2016, p. 13-15); Muduli et al. (2016, p. 177); Huo et al. (2016, p. 134); Taschner, (2016, p. 1790); Lemtaoui & Rochdi (2017, p. 3); Wahdan & Emam (2017, p. 142); Yang & Lirn (2017, p. 900); Hussain & Al-Aomar (2017, p. 1); Boon-itt et al. (2017, p. 10); Elgazzar & Elzarka, (2017, p. 124-125); Aliakbari Nouri et al., (2018, p. 164); Leończuk et al. (2019, p. 89); Shahin & Jamshidian (2020, p. 7); Rahman (2020, p. 24); Ozbekler & Ozturkoglu (2020, p. 1514); Muhammad & Gul-E-Rana (2020, p. 2); Tseng et al. (2020, p. 980).
Supply chain dimension	Youngdahl (1996, p. 32); Tixier, et al. (1996, p. 113); Gunasekaran et al. (2001, p. 84); Beamon & Chen (2001, p. 3200); Tan et al. (2002, p. 623); Hausman (2004, p. 62); Tanriverdi (2006, p. 73); Lenny Koh et al. (2007, p. 124); Livolsi (2007, p. 105); Bhagwat & Sharma (2007b, p. 53-54); Chow et al. (2008, p. 32); Brulhart & Moncef (2010, p. 46); Hoa Vo & Bironneau (2011, p. 5); Agus (2011, p. 137); Cao & Zhang (2011, p. 174); Boonitt & Pongpanarat (2011, p. 218); Johnston et al. (2012, p. 58); Cho et al. (2012, p. 804); Akinlar & Fraunhofer (2014, p. 10); Solakivi (2014, p. 19); Khanchanapong et al. (2014, p. 199); Mishra & Sharma (2014, p. 113); Zimmermann & Foerstl (2014, p. 38); Okongwu et al. (2015, p. 702); Sillanpää (2015, p. 267); Chopra & Meindl (2015, p. 181); Taschner, (2016, p. 1790); Shahin et al. (2016, p. 13-15); Filippini & Forza (2016, p. 21); Diallo et al. (2016, p. 1278); Mello et al. (2016, p. 92); Manders et al. (2017, p. 975); Yang & Lirn (2017, p. 900); Elgazzar & Elzarka, (2017, p. 124-125) ; Hong et al. (2017, p. 263); Chen et al. (2017, p. 1145); Boone & al. (2018, p. 170); Rojo et al. (2018, p. 642); Aliakbari Nouri et al., (2018, p. 164); Zhou et al. (2018, p. 199); Leończuk et al. (2019, p. 102); Basheer et al. (2019, p. 276); Li et al. (2019, p. 575); Shahin & Jamshidian (2020, p. 7); Xie et al. (2020, p. 715); Rahman (2020, p. 24); Dai et al. (2020, p. 3).
Learning, growth and innovation dimension	Beamon & Chen (2001, p. 3200); Kathawala & Abdou (2003, p. 144); Danskin et al. (2005, p. 92); Tanriverdi (2006, p. 73); Plessis (2007, p. 97); Livolsi (2007, p. 105); Bhagwat & Sharma (2007b, p. 53-54); Chow et al. (2008, p. 32); Yang et al., (2009, p. 6) ; Mukaddes et al. (2010, p. 227). Brulhart & Moncef (2010, p. 46); Agus (2011, p. 137); Boonitt & Pongpanarat (2011, p. 220); Zailani & Kumar (2011, p. 203); Wisner et al. (2012, p. 514); Sampson & Spring (2012, p. 34); Johnston et al. (2012, p. 287) ; Ambe (2014, p. 281); Mishra & Sharma (2014, p. 113); Okongwu et al. (2015, p. 702); Chopra & Meindl (2015, p. 53); Shahin et al. (2016, p. 13-15); Lemtaoui & Rochdi (2017, p. 3); Elgazzar & Elzarka, (2017, p. 124-125); Boon-itt et al. (2017, p. 8); Aliakbari Nouri et al., (2018, p. 164); Leończuk et al. (2019, p. 89); Chanegrih & Creusier (2019, p. 184) ; Xie et al. (2020, p. 715); Rahman (2020, p. 24).

Source: Author

2. RESEARCH METHODOLOGY

Qualitative studies aim to respond to and study variables measured on a nominal or ordinal, i.e. non-metric, scale. They aim to analyze how people construct and interpret the social situation in which they are engaged. This social reality is constructed on the basis of past experience and acquired knowledge. The qualitative approach scrutinizes the process rather than the result (Guilbert, 2007). In qualitative research, the aim is to understand the meanings that individuals give to their own lives and experiences. From a qualitative perspective, knowledge is a shared construction between researcher and participant (Anadon & Savoie-Zajc, 2009). Meaning and interpretation are thus elaborated by and in social interactions, where political and social aspects affect the actors' points of view. As a result, the myth of neutrality is debunked, and the study of human realities becomes a space of multiple knowledge in which rationality and the discourse of causality give way to interpretation and consensus (Lamsiah & Bentalha, 2022).

To collect qualitative data, we adopted a series of semi-structured interviews. Comments are analyzed qualitatively by means of a qualitative content analysis. The 10 interviews lasted an average of 45 minutes each. Our interviewees were asked to express themselves using an open-ended questionnaire (Alla et al., 2022b). They were also asked to give us their views on the evolution of the tourism market (as an intermediary in this market), their future, current projects, and so on. The aim was to discover, as far as possible, their strategic orientations. The ten interviewees are experts in logistics service chains with a variety of profiles (Table 4).

Table 4. Interviewee profiles

N°	Industry	Position	Sex	Workforce	Experience	Length of interview
1	Pharmaceuticals and health	Logistics manager	M	250	12 ans	36 min
2	Insurance	Administrative manager	M	850	16 ans	45 min
3	Banking	General services manager	W	500	3 ans	29 min
4	Transport	Logistics Manager	M	80	10 ans	38 min
5	Accounting	Administrative manager	M	10	12 ans	33 min
6	Education	Educational Director	M	20	8 ans	49 min
7	Hospitality	Sales manager	M	60	11 ans	51 min
8	Public administration	Administrative executive	W	40	9 ans	31 min

Source: Author

Opinions and comments are first processed statistically using TROPES and IRAMUTEQ. As far as software for analyzing textual data is concerned, the list is relatively short. To present the results, we'll start with a thematic study of the topics covered in the various notices. We will then proceed to an overall analysis of all the comments.

3. RESULTS AND DISCUSSION

Statistical analysis via IRAMUTEQ of the comments enables us to identify panoply of fundamental items for assessing the level of impact of SSCM practices on performance. We first looked for the most repeated occurrences in the interviews in Table 5.

Table 5. List of items with high occurrence

Items	occurrences
Customer	88
Service	50
Management	42
Logistics	30
Sscm	28
Sales	25
Practice	24
Supplier	24
Relationship	22
Subject	22
Enable	21
information	21
deadline	21
quality	20
term	19
risk	17
possible	17
customers	17
capacity	17
chain	16
satisfaction	15
company	15
delivery	14

Source: Results of the statistical study

The manual grouping of the above items enabled us to extract 15 main dimensions for measuring the degree of SSCM practices from the interviews conducted (Table 6).

Table 6. Supply chain management practices

	Items	Score		%	
Information exchange and sharing	General information	38	75	4,64%	9,16%
	Collaboration and coordination	37		4,52%	
partnership management of supplier relations	Quality of relationship	24	69	2,93%	8,42%
	Nature of the relationship	45		5,49%	
customer and demand management	Relationship management practices	134	279	16,36%	34,07%
	Effectiveness of the relationship	145		17,70%	
resource and capacity management	Resources and capabilities	84	95	10,26%	11,60%
	Capacity management	11		1,34%	
risk management	Risk factors	28	32	3,42%	3,91%
	Risk management	4		0,49%	
knowledge management	Knowledge	6	24	0,73%	2,93%
	Knowledge management	18		2,20%	
service delivery and performance management	Service management practices	73	184	8,91%	22,47%
	Service performance	111		13,55%	
financial flow management	Financial flow management	49	49	5,98%	5,98%
service development and innovation	Innovation management	12	12	1,47%	1,47%
		819		100%	

Source: Results of the statistical study

While it's true that the above nine functions are all crucial to the effectiveness of SSCM practices, our study shows that customers are only moderately involved in the most advanced functions of the purchasing process, namely information exchange and sharing, and supplier relationship management. However, the customer and his satisfaction are central to the other items. Nevertheless, customer and demand management practices, and practices linked to service delivery and performance management remain key, with 34.07% and 22.47% respectively.

We then proceeded to analyze the determinants of overall performance in the interviews conducted. The manual grouping of performance-related items enabled us to design Table 7:

Table 7. Service company global performance items

	Items	Score	%
Return on assets	Processes, materials, networks, etc.	34	9,86%
Value creation	Value, coordination, collaboration	38	11,01%
Sales performance and growth	Sales, listening, follow-up, consumption	52	15,07%
Cash flow improvement	Financial, payment, due date, etc.	27	7,83%
On-time delivery	Delay, time, date, responsiveness, etc.	51	14,78%
Flexibility	Flexibility, adapt, change, reactivity, etc	29	8,41%
Service quality	Improvement, quality, etc	22	6,38%
Customer satisfaction	Satisfy, need, etc	27	7,83%
Innovation	Innovate, new, etc	14	4,06%
Cost control	Control, load, etc.	5	1,45%
Social performance	Social, employee, human, etc	44	12,75%
Social performance	Societal, society	2	0,58%
		819	100,00%

Source: Results of the statistical study

While it's true that the different facets of performance are all important, we can see that sales performance is relatively first with 15.07%. This is followed by deadline management (14.78%) and social performance (12.75%). We also note that societal performance is relatively marginalized (0.58%).

From this exploratory study, we can affirm that the more the customer is involved in the SSCM process, the greater his contribution to value creation will be. We have several observations to make:

Firstly, there is a strong predominance of the operational aspect of SSCM. SSCM practices can be divided into two broad categories according to the perception of those surveyed. The primary ones (customer and demand management, service delivery and performance management), the complementary ones (information exchange and sharing, partnership management of supplier relations, resource and capacity management and financial flow management) and the secondary ones (risk management, knowledge management, service development and innovation). Indeed, SSCM is by definition multidimensional, integrated, and correlated with organizational performance and, above all, constitutes a new field for scientific research, given its empirical importance.

Secondly, environmental performance was relatively marginalized in the various interviews conducted. Indeed, the themes of sustainable development, ethics and society are not among the major concerns of the various players in the service supply chain (Taghipour & Beneteau-Piet; Bentalha et al., 2023). We have noted that little importance is given to this aspect of performance. Environmental considerations are embryonic, and service companies seem to be relatively far behind industrial companies in environmental considerations (Hmioui et al., 2017). This may be explained by the low level of inventory, the importance of intangibles or the simultaneous presence of the customer at the time of the service.

Commercial performance is also highly coveted by service companies. Indeed, sales efficiency, delivery and deadlines, and customer satisfaction are frequent themes in the various discourses. Typically commercial considerations are much discussed by respondents. This theme seems to be more favored and abundant in discussions and analysis items. At this level, it should be pointed out that there is also a great deal of interest in social performance, given its importance in service activities.

Finally, we can say that there is a certain imbalance and misalignment between the managerial literature on SSCM and some of our findings. For example, the question of innovation is crucial for several researchers, but relatively little stated in the interviews. The same is true of cost control and risk management. This scientific "gap" calls on us to delve deeper into our qualitative analysis and try to bridge this gap using other qualitative methods.

CONCLUSION

The search for performance has always been a preoccupation of Supply Chain Management. At the academic level, the interest of researchers, particularly Anglo-Saxons, in this relationship is relatively recent (Bentalha et al., 2019). The study we conducted shows a strong relationship between the SCM of the service company and its performance. Also, there is a great conceptual divergence, between the different authors around the notions of performance, supply chain management of service and in the interpretation of the causality of the relationship. Today's competitive and uncertain environment is putting great pressure on the quality-price ratio of service companies. For this reason, SCM seems to be a global performance parameter.

The strategic aspect of performance is relatively marginalized to the detriment of more operational and tactical aspects. Also, the indicators used are, in most cases, metric and quantitative in nature, pushing statistical analysis more than behavioral or modeling analysis. Finally, the performance indicators considered represent a wide diversity and transversally of approaches, attesting to and confirming the multi-variable nature intrinsic to SSCM.

Our aim is to contribute to a better understanding of SSCM and its contribution to overall corporate performance. For this reason we have established a qualitative study via interviews. At the same time, we can derive future research perspectives from the conceptual model of SSC or the causal relationship between SSCM and corporate performance, the use of network theory, service-oriented architecture, value chain theory, total quality management, customer value innovation theory, trust equilibrium, knowledge management, and more.

REFERENCES

Agus, A. (2011). Supply chain management, supply chain flexibility and business performance. *Journal of Global Strategic Management.*, *5*(1), 134–145. doi:10.20460/JGSM.2011515818

Ahn, S. H., Lee, Y. H., & Hwang, M. K. (2010). A framework for measuring performance of service SCM. The *40th International Conference on Computers & Indutrial Engineering, 62*(3), 801-818. 10.1109/ICCIE.2010.5668196

Aitken, J., Childerhouse, P., Deakins, E., & Towill, D. (2016). A comparative study of manufacturing and service sector supply chain integration via the uncertainty circle model. *International Journal of Logistics Management*, *27*(1), 188–205. doi:10.1108/IJLM-03-2014-0047

Akinlar, S., & Fraunhofer, I. M. L. (2014). *Logistics 4.0 and challenges for the supply chain planning and IT.* IIS. https://www.iis.fraunhofer.de/content/dam/iis/tr/Session%203_5_Logistics_Fraunhofer%20IML_Akinlar.pdf

Al-Doori, J. A. (2019). The impact of supply chain collaboration on performance in automotive industry: Empirical evidence. *Journal of Industrial Engineering and Management, 12*(2), 241–253. doi:10.3926/jiem.2835

Aliakbari Nouri, F., Shafiei Nikabadi, M., & Olfat, L. (2019). Developing the framework of sustainable service supply chain balanced scorecard (SSSC BSC). *International Journal of Productivity and Performance Management, 68*(1), 148–170. doi:10.1108/IJPPM-04-2018-0149

Alla, L., Bentalha, B., & Bouhtati, N. (2022a). Assessing Supply Chain Performance in the Covid 19 Context: A Prospective Model. In *2022 14th International Colloquium of Logistics and Supply Chain Management (LOGISTIQUA)* (pp. 1-6). IEEE.

Alla, L., Bentalha, B., & Elyoussfi, A. (2023). Intelligence territoriale et positionnement stratégique des regions au Maroc: Le cas de la région de Fès Meknes en perspective. *Le concept de l'intéligence en sciences juridiques, économiques et sociales*, 215-237.

Alla, L., Bentalha, B., Megzari, G., & Hmioui, A. (2022b). The effects of COVID-19 on supply chains: A qualitative analysis. *Reconfigurations du tourisme en contexte de la crise du Covid-19: Quelles démarches pour quelles résiliences au Maroc et ailleurs, 1* (1), pp.130-153

Alvarado, U. Y., & Kotzab, H. (2001). Supply chain management: The integration of logistics in marketing. *Industrial Marketing Management, 30*(2), 183–198. doi:10.1016/S0019-8501(00)00142-5

Anadon, M., & Savoie-Zajc, L. (2009). L'analyse qualitative des données. *Association pour la recherche qualitative, 28*(1). [En ligne] www.recherche-qualitative.qc.ca/revue.html consulté le 07/01/2020

Anand, N., & Grover, N. (2015). Measuring retail supply chain performance: Theoretical model using key performance indicators (KPIs). *Benchmarking, 22*(1), 135–166. doi:10.1108/BIJ-05-2012-0034

Bag, S., Wood, L. C., Xu, L., Dhamija, P., & Kayikci, Y. (2020). Big data analytics as an operational excellence approach to enhance sustainable supply chain performance. *Resources, Conservation and Recycling, 153*(1), 104559. doi:10.1016/j.resconrec.2019.104559

Baltacioglu, T., Ada, E., Kaplan, M. D., And, O. Y., & Kaplan, Y. C. (2007). A New Framework for Service Supply Chains. *Service Industries Journal, 27*(2), 105–124. doi:10.1080/02642060601122629

Banerjee, M., & Mishra, M. (2017). Retail supply chain management practices in India: A business intelligence perspective. *Journal of Retailing and Consumer Services, 34*(1), 248–259. doi:10.1016/j.jretconser.2015.09.009

Baret, P. (2006), L'évaluation contingente de la Performance Globale des Entreprises: Une méthode pour fonder un management sociétalement responsable? 2ème journée de recherche du CEROS, 1-24.

Basheer, M. F., Siam, M. R. A., Awn, A. M., & Hussan, S. G. (2019). Exploring the role of TQM and supply chain practices for firm supply performance in the presence of information technology capabilities and supply chain technology adoption: A case of textile firms in Pakistan. *Uncertain Supply Chain Management*, *7*(1), 275–288. doi:10.5267/j.uscm.2018.9.001

Beamon, B. M., & Chen, V. C. P. (2001). Performance analysis of conjoined supply chains. *International Journal of Production Research*, *39*(14), 3195–3218. doi:10.1080/00207540110053156

Bentalha, B. (2022). Smart Technologies for a Sustainable Service Supply Chain: A Prospective Perspective. *Journal of Environmental Issues and Climate Change*, *1*(1), 77–89. doi:10.59110/jeicc.v1i1.81

Bentalha, B. (2023). Les fondements théoriques du supply chain management: Une analyse critique. *Alternatives Managériales Economiques*, *5*(2), 1–22.

Bentalha, B., & Hmioui, A. (2022). Smart Service Supply Chain and Just Walk Out Technology: A Netnographic Approach. In *Innovations in Smart Cities Applications Volume 5: The Proceedings of the 6th International Conference on Smart City Applications* (pp. 223-236). Cham: Springer International Publishing. 10.1007/978-3-030-94191-8_18

Bentalha, B., Hmioui, A., & Alla, L. (2019). The digitalization of the supply chain management of service companies: a prospective approach. In *Proceedings of the 4th International Conference on Smart City Applications* (pp. 1-8). ACM. 10.1145/3368756.3369005

Bentalha, B., Hmioui, A., & Alla, L. (2020). Digital service supply chain management: current realities and prospective visions. In *Innovations in Smart Cities Applications Edition 3: The Proceedings of the 4th International Conference on Smart City Applications 4* (pp. 808-822). Springer International Publishing. 10.1007/978-3-030-37629-1_58

Bentalha, B., Hmioui, A., & Alla, L. (2021). The global performance of a service supply chain: a simulation-optimization under arena. In *Innovations in Smart Cities Applications Volume 4: The Proceedings of the 5th International Conference on Smart City Applications* (pp. 489-502). Springer International Publishing. 10.1007/978-3-030-66840-2_37

Bentalha, B., Hmioui, A., & Alla, L. (2023). Green Transportation Balanced Scorecard: A VIKOR Fuzzy Method for Evaluating Green Logistics Initiatives. In *Digital Technologies and Applications: Proceedings of ICDTA'23,* (pp. 916-925). Cham: Springer Nature Switzerland. 10.1007/978-3-031-29857-8_91

Bhagwat, R., & Sharma, M. K. (2007). Performance measurement of supply chain management: A balance scorecard approach. *Computers & Industrial Engineering*, *53*(1), 43–62. doi:10.1016/j.cie.2007.04.001

Boon-itt, S., Wong, C. Y., & Wong, C. W. Y. (2017). Service supply chain management process capabilities: Measurement development. *International Journal of Production Economics*, *193*, 1–11. doi:10.1016/j.ijpe.2017.06.024

Boone, T., Ganeshan, R., Jain, A., & Sanders, N. R. (2018). Forecasting sales in the supply chain: Consumer analytics in the big data era. *International Journal of Forecasting*, *35*(1), 170–180. doi:10.1016/j.ijforecast.2018.09.003

Boonitt, S., & Pongpanarat, C. (2011). Measuring service supply chain management processes: The application of the Q-sort technique. *International Journal of Innovation, Management and Technology, 2*(1), 217–221.

Bouhtati, N., Hmioui, A., Alla, L., & Bentalha, B. (2022). Logistique et performance touristique: Une étude comparative des principales destinations en Afrique. *Alternatives Managériales Economiques, 1*, 116–132.

Bourguignon, A. (1995). Peut-on définir la performance? *Revue Française de Comptabilité*, (juillet-août), 61–66.

Bourguignon, A. (1997). Sous les pavés la plage… ou les multiples fonctions du vocabulaire comptable: l'exemple de la performance. *Comptabilité - Contrôle - Audit, tome 3*(1), 89-101. . doi:10.3917/cca.031.0089

Bourguignon, A. (2000). *Performance et contrôle de gestion, encyclopédie de comptabilité, contrôle de gestion et audit*. Ed Economica.

Brulhart, F., & Moncef, B. (2010). L'impact des pratiques de SCM sur la performance de l'entreprise: Une étude empirique dans le contexte français. Finance Contrôle Stratégie. *Association FCS, 13*(1), 33–66.

Burgess, K., & Singh, P. J. (2006). A proposed integrated framework for analysing supply chains. *Supply Chain Management, 11*(4), 337–344. doi:10.1108/13598540610671789

Cao, M., & Zhang, Q. (2011). Supply chain collaboration: Impact on collaborative advantage and firm performance. *Journal of Operations Management, 29*(3), 163–180. doi:10.1016/j.jom.2010.12.008

Capron, M. & Quairel, F. (2006). Évaluer les stratégies de développement durable des entreprises: l'utopie mobilisatrice de la performance globale. *Revue de l'organisation responsable, 1*(1), 5-17. doi:10.3917/ror.001.0005

Carter, C. R., Kosmol, T., & Kaufmann, L. (2016). Toward a Supply Chain Practice View. *The Journal of Supply Chain Management, 53*(1), 114–122. doi:10.1111/jscm.12130

Cassivi, L. (2006). Collaboration planning in a supply chain. *Supply Chain Management, 11*(3), 249–258. doi:10.1108/13598540610662158

Chanegrih, T., & Creusier, J. (2019). L'élargissement du lean aux acteurs de la supply chain : Vers plus de performance? *Logistique & Management, 27*(3), 182–191. doi:10.1080/12507970.2019.1586457

Chen, I. J., & Paulraj, A. (2004). Understanding supply chain management: Critical research and a theoretical framework. *International Journal of Production Research, 42*(1), 131–163. doi:10.1080/00207540310001602865

Chen, X., Xi, Z., & Jing, P. (2017). A Unified Framework for Evaluating Supply Chain Reliability and Resilience. *IEEE Transactions on Reliability, 66*(4), 1144–1156. doi:10.1109/TR.2017.2737822

Chin, T. A., Hamid, A. B. A., Raslic, A., & Heng, L. H. (2014). The Impact of Supply Chain Integration on Operational Capability in Malaysian Manufacturers. *Procedia: Social and Behavioral Sciences, 130*(1), 257–265. doi:10.1016/j.sbspro.2014.04.030

Cho, D. W., Lee, Y. H., Ahn, S. H., & Hwang, M. K. (2012). A framework for measuring the performance of service supply chain management. *Computers & Industrial Engineering*, *62*(3), 801–818. doi:10.1016/j.cie.2011.11.014

Choon Tan, K., Lyman, S. B., & Wisner, J. D. (2002). Supply chain management: A strategic perspective. *International Journal of Operations & Production Management*, *22*(6), 614–631. doi:10.1108/01443570210427659

Chow, W., Madu, C., Kuei, C., Lu, M., Lin, C., & Tseng, H. (2008). Supply chain management in the U.S. and Taïwan: An empirical study. *Omega*, *36*(5), 665–679. doi:10.1016/j.omega.2006.01.001

Ciliberti, F., de Haan, J., de Groot, G., & Pontrandolfo, P. (2011). CSR codes and the principal-agent problem in supply chains: Four case studies. *Journal of Cleaner Production*, *19*(8), 885–894. doi:10.1016/j.jclepro.2010.09.005

Cook, L., Heiser, D., & Sengupta, K. (2011). The moderating effect of supply chain role on the relationship between supply chain practices and performance: An empirical analysis. *International Journal of Physical Distribution & Logistics Management*, *41*(2), 104–134. doi:10.1108/09600031111118521

Cui, A. P., & Liu, W. (2009). Study on capability coordination in logistics service supply chain with options contract. *Chin. J. Manage. Sci.*, *17*(2), 59–65.

Da Silveira, G., & Arkader, R. (2007). The direct and mediated relationships between supply chain coordination investments and delivery performance. *International Journal of Operations & Production Management*, *27*(2), 140–158. doi:10.1108/01443570710720595

Dai, B., Nu, Y., Xie, X., & Li, J. (2020). Interactions of Traceability and Reliability Optimization in a Competitive Supply Chain with Product Recall. *European Journal of Operational Research*, *290*(1), 116–131. doi:10.1016/j.ejor.2020.08.003

Danskin, P., Englis, B. G., Solomon, M. R., Goldsmith, M., & Davey, J. (2005). Knowledge management as competitive advantage: Lessons from the textile and apparel value chain. *Journal of Knowledge Management*, *9*(2), 91–102. doi:10.1108/13673270510590245

Deshpande, A. R. (2012). Supply Chain Management Dimensions, Supply Chain Performance and Organizational Performance: An Integrated Framework. *International Journal of Business and Management*, *7*(8), 2–19. doi:10.5539/ijbm.v7n8p2

Diallo, C., Venkatadri, U., Khatab, A., & Bhakthavatchalam, S. (2016). State of the art review of quality, reliability and maintenance issues in closed-loop supply chains with remanufacturing. *International Journal of Production Research*, *55*(5), 1277–1296. doi:10.1080/00207543.2016.1200152

Dixon, J. R., Nanni, A. J., & Volmann, T. E. (1990). *The new performance challenge: measuring operations for world class competition*. Dow Jones-Irwin.

Donlon, J. P. (1996). Maximizing value in the supply chain. *Chief Executive*, *117*, 54–63.

Elgazzar, S., & Elzarka, S. (2017) Supply chain management in the service sector: an applied framework. In: *ABRM - AASTMT 2nd International Conference (Entrepreneurship, Supply Chain Management & Information Systems),* 121 – 134.

Ellram, L. M., Tate, W. L., & Billington, C. (2004). Understanding and Managing the Services Supply Chain. *The Journal of Supply Chain Management, 40*(4), 17–32. doi:10.1111/j.1745-493X.2004.tb00176.x

Ellram, L. M., Tate, W. L., & Billington, C. (2007). Services Supply Management: The Next Frontier for Improved Organizational Performance. *California Management Review, 49*(4), 44–66. doi:10.2307/41166405

Field, J. M., & Meile, L. C. (2008). Supplier relations and supply chain performance in financial services processes. *International Journal of Operations & Production Management, 28*(2), 185–206. doi:10.1108/01443570810846892

Filippini, R., & Forza, C. (2016). The Impact of the Just-in-Time Approach on Production System Performance: A Survey of Italian Industry. *A Review and Outlook. A Journey through Manufacturing and Supply Chain Strategy Research,* (19–39). Springer. doi:10.1007/978-3-319-31104-3_2

Fitzsimmons, J., & Fitzsimmons, M. (2010). *Service Management: Operations. Strategy, and Information Technology* (7th ed.). McGraw-Hill.

Fu, N., Flood, P. C., Bosak, J., Morris, T., & O'Regan, P. (2013). Exploring the Performance Effect of HPWS on Professional Service Supply Chain Management. *Supply Chain Management, 18*(3), 292–307. doi:10.1108/SCM-04-2012-0118

Germain, C., & Trébucq, S. (2004), La performance globale de l'entreprise et son pilotage: quelques réflexions, pp. 35-41. Semaine sociale Lamy.

Giannakis, M. (2011). Conceptualizing and managing service supply chains. *Service Industries Journal, 31*(11), 1809–1823. doi:10.1080/02642069.2010.503879

Green, K. W. Jr, Zelbst, P. J., Meacham, J., & Bhadauria, V. S. (2012). Green supply chain management practices: Impact on performance. *Supply Chain Management, 17*(3), 290–305. doi:10.1108/13598541211227126

Grenier, C., & Martin, V. (2013). Performance des organisations et bien-être des usagers: Quels modes de pilotage et d'intervention? *Management & Avenir, 61*(3), 129–145. doi:10.3917/mav.061.0129

Grönroos, C., & Ojasalo, K. (2004). Service productivity. *Journal of Business Research, 57*(4), 414–423. doi:10.1016/S0148-2963(02)00275-8

Guilbert, L. (2007). Ethnologie collaborative: Elaboration et analyse d'espaces de médiation en contexte de migration. *Recherches Qualitatives, 4*(1), 14–36.

Gunasekaran, A., Patel, C., & Tirtiroglu, E. (2001). Performance measures and metrics in a supply chain environment. *International Journal of Operations & Production Management, 21*(1/2), 71–87. doi:10.1108/01443570110358468

Hausman, H. (2004). Supply chain performance metrics. In *The practice of supply chain management: Where theory and application converge* (pp. 61–73). Springer. doi:10.1007/0-387-27275-5_4

Hemilä, J., & Vilko, J. (2015). The development of a service supply chain model for a manufacturing SME. *International Journal of Logistics Management, 26*(3), 517–542. doi:10.1108/IJLM-01-2014-0001

Hmioui, A., Alla, L., & Bentalha, B. (2017). *Impact des pratiques de la RSE sur la performance commerciale des entreprises touristiques: Cas des établissements hôteliers de Fès. Le tourisme au Maghreb: Économie et Management, Laboratoire de recherche en entrepreneuriat et management des organisations.* ENCG de Fès.

Hmioui, A., & Bentalha, B. (2020). Service Supply Chain Management et performance commerciale: Esquisse d'une synthèse théorique. *Revue ame, 2,* 1-21.

Hmioui, A., & Bentalha, B. (2021). Service supply chain management: A literature review. *International Journal of Logistics Systems and Management, 40*(3), 332–353. doi:10.1504/IJLSM.2021.120253

Hmioui, A., Bentalha, B., & Alla, L. (2020). Service supply chain: A prospective analysis of sustainable management for global performance. In 2020 *IEEE 13th International Colloquium of Logistics and Supply Chain Management (LOGISTIQUA)* (pp. 1-7). IEEE. 10.1109/LOGISTIQUA49782.2020.9353940

Hoa Vo, T. L., & Bironneau, L. (2011). Systèmes d'information et gestion globale de la chaîne logistique: un état de l'art. 2ème journée thématique SILOGIN - Système d'information, logistique, innovation, Nantes, France.

Hong, J., Zhang, Y., & Shi, M. (2017). The impact of supply chain quality management practices and knowledge transfer on organisational performance: An empirical investigation from China. *International Journal of Logistics, 21*(3), 259–278. doi:10.1080/13675567.2017.1394992

Huo, B., Ye, Y., Zhao, X., & Shou, Y. (2016). The impact of human capital on supply chain integration and competitive performance. *International Journal of Production Economics, 178*(1), 132–143. doi:10.1016/j.ijpe.2016.05.009

Hussain, M., & Al-Aomar, R. (2017). A model for assessing the impact of sustainable supplier selection on the performance of service supply chains. *International Journal of Sustainable Engineering, 11*(6), 366–381. doi:10.1080/19397038.2017.1414898

Ibrahim, S. E., & Ogunyemi, O. (2012). The effect of linkages and information sharing on supply chain and export performance: An empirical study of Egyptian textile manufacturers. *Journal of Manufacturing Technology Management, 23*(4), 441–463. doi:10.1108/17410381211230394

Iraten, S. (2014). La Supply Chain management un levier pour améliorer la performance de l'entreprise. *Revue Reformes Economiques et Intégration En Economie Mondiale, 17*(1), 135–159.

Issor, Z. (2017). La performance de l'entreprise: un concept complexe aux multiples dimensions. *Projectics / Proyéctica / Projectique, 17*(2), 93-103. . doi:10.3917/proj.017.0093

Jabbour, A. B. L., Filho, A. G. A., Viana, A. B. N., & Jabbour, C. J. C. (2011). Measuring supply chain management practices. *Measuring Business Excellence, 15*(2), 18–31. doi:10.1108/13683041111131592

Jin, L. Y. (2006). Service Supply Chain Management, Customer Satisfaction and Business Performance. *Chinese Journal of Management Science, 14*(1), 100–106.

Johnston, R., Glark, G., & Shulver, M. (2012). *Service operations and management* (4th ed.). Pearson.

Kaliani Sundram, V. P., Chandran, V., & Awais Bhatti, M. (2016). Supply chain practices and performance: The indirect effects of supply chain integration. *Benchmarking*, *23*(6), 1445–1471. doi:10.1108/BIJ-03-2015-0023

Karimi, E., & Rafiee, M. (2014). Analyzing the Impact of Supply Chain Management Practices on Organizational Performance through Competitive Priorities (Case Study: Iran Pumps Company). International Journal of Academic Research in Accounting, Finance and Management Sciences, 4(1), 1-15. doi:10.6007/IJARAFMS/v4-i1/503

Kathawala, Y., & Abdou, K. (2003). Supply chain evaluation in the service industry: A framework development compared to manufacturing. *Managerial Auditing Journal*, *18*(2), 140–149. doi:10.1108/02686900310455137

Khanchanapong, T., Prajogo, D., Sohal, A., Cooper, B., Yeung, A., & Cheng, T. (2014). The Unique and Complementary Effects of Manufacturing Technologies and Lean Practices on Manufacturing Operational Performance. *International Journal of Production Economics*, *153*(1), 191–203. doi:10.1016/j.ijpe.2014.02.021

Lambert, D. M., Cooper, M. C., & Pagh, J. D. (1998). Supply Chain Management: Implementation Issues and Research Opportunities. *International Journal of Logistics Management*, *9*(2), 1–20. doi:10.1108/09574099810805807

Lamsiah, A., & Bentalha, B. (2022). Economic Diplomacy and Economic Intelligence Amalgamation: The Moroccan-Nigerian Economic Exchange as a Case Study. *Alternatives Managériales Economiques*, *4*(4), 582–603.

Lemtaoui, M., & Rochdi, M. H. (2017). Le management de la chaine logistique entre efficience et réactivité. *Revue d'Etudes en Management et Finance d'Organisation*, *2*(6), 1–13.

Lenny Koh, S. C., Demirbag, M., Bayraktar, E., Tatoglu, E., & Zaim, S. (2007). The impact of supply chain management practices on performance of SMEs. *Industrial Management & Data Systems*, *107*(1), 103–124. doi:10.1108/02635570710719089

Leończuk, D., Ryciuk, U., Szymczak, M., & Nazarko, J. (2019). Measuring Performance of Adaptive Supply Chains. In A. Kawa & A. Maryniak (Eds.), *SMART Supply Network. EcoProduction (Environmental Issues in Logistics and Manufacturing)*. Springer. doi:10.1007/978-3-319-91668-2_5

Li, S., Ragu-Nathan, B., Ragu-Nathan, T. S., & Subba Rao, S. (2006). The impact of supply chain management practices on competitive advantage and organizational performance. *Omega*, *34*(2), 107–124. doi:10.1016/j.omega.2004.08.002 PMID:17876965

Li, S., Rao, S., Ragunathan, T., & Ragunathan, B. (2005). Development and validation of a measurement instrument for studying supply chain management practices. *Journal of Operations Management*, *23*(6), 618–641. doi:10.1016/j.jom.2005.01.002

Livolsi, L. (2007), Le Supply Chain Management: synthèse et propositions. *Actes de la XVIIIème Conférence Internationale de Management Stratégique de l'AIMS*. Grenoble.

Lotfi, Z., Sahran, S., Mukhtar, M., & Zadeh, A. T. (2013). The relationship between supply chain integration and product quality. *Procedia Technology*, *11*(2), 471–478. doi:10.1016/j.protcy.2013.12.217

Macchion, L., Moretto, A., Caniato, F., Danese, P., & Vinelli, A. (2020). Static supply chain complexity and sustainability practices: A multitier examination. *Corporate Social Responsibility and Environmental Management*, *27*(6), 2679–2691. doi:10.1002/csr.1992

Manders, J. H. M., Caniëls, M. C. J., & Ghijsen, P. W. T. (2017). Supply chain flexibility. *International Journal of Logistics Management*, *28*(4), 964–1026. doi:10.1108/IJLM-07-2016-0176

Marinagi, C., Trivellas, P., & Reklitis, P. (2015). Information quality and supply chain performance: The mediating role of information sharing. *Procedia: Social and Behavioral Sciences*, *175*(1), 473–479. doi:10.1016/j.sbspro.2015.01.1225

Martin, P. R., & Patterson, J. W. (2009). On measuring company performance within a supply chain. *International Journal of Production Research*, *47*(9), 2449–2460. doi:10.1080/00207540701725604

Mello, M. H., Gosling, J., Naim, M. M., Strandhagen, J. O., & Brett, P. O. (2016). Improving coordination in an engineer-to-order supply chain using a soft systems approach. *Production Planning and Control*, *28*(2), 89–107. doi:10.1080/09537287.2016.1233471

Mentzer, J. T., DeWitt, W., Keebler, J. S., Min, S., Nix, N. W., Smith, C. D., & Zacharia, Z. G. (2001). Defining Supply Chain Management. *Journal of Business Logistics*, *22*(2), 1–25. doi:10.1002/j.2158-1592.2001.tb00001.x

Mentzer, J. T., Rutner, S. M., & Matsuno, K. (1997). Application of the means-end value hierarchy model to understanding logistics service value. *International Journal of Physical Distribution & Logistics Management*, *27*(9/10), 630–643. doi:10.1108/09600039710188693

Min, S., & Mentzer, J. T. (2004). DEVELOPING AND MEASURING SUPPLY CHAIN MANAGEMENT CONCEPTS. *Journal of Business Logistics*, *25*(1), 63–99. doi:10.1002/j.2158-1592.2004.tb00170.x

Muduli, K., Barve, A., Tripathy, S., & Biswal, J. N. (2016). Green practices adopted by the mining supply chains in India: A case study. *International Journal of Environment and Sustainable Development*, *15*(2), 159. Advance online publication. doi:10.1504/IJESD.2016.076365

Muhammad, L., & Gul-E-Rana. (2020). Mediating role of customer forgiveness between perceived justice and satisfaction. *Journal of Retailing and Consumer Services*, *52*(1), 101886. doi:10.1016/j.jretconser.2019.101886

Mukaddes, A. M. M., Abul, C., Rashed, A., & Abdul, A. M. (2010). Developing an Information Model for Supply Chain Information Flow and its Management. *International Journal of Innovation and Technology Management.*, *1*(2), 226–231.

Okongwu, U., Brulhart, F., & Moncef, B. (2015). Causal linkages between supply chain management practices and performance. *Journal of Manufacturing Technology Management*, *26*(5), 678–702. doi:10.1108/JMTM-01-2013-0002

Ounnar F. (2018). *Une formulation multicritère pour le choix de prestataires de services logistiques dans un réseau partenarial auto-organisé*. Logistique & Management. doi:10.1080/12507970.2018.1528902

Ozbekler, T. M., & Ozturkoglu, Y. (2020). Analysing the importance of sustainability-oriented service quality in competition environment. *Business Strategy and the Environment*, *29*(1), 1504–1516. doi:10.1002/bse.2449

Phan, T., Doan, X., & Nguyen, T. (2020). The impact of supply chain practices on performance through supply chain integration in textile and garment industry of Vietnam. *Uncertain Supply Chain Management*, *8*(1), 175–186. doi:10.5267/j.uscm.2019.7.006

Plessis, M. D. (2007). Knowledge management: What make complex implementations successful? *Journal of Knowledge Management*, *11*(2), 91–101. doi:10.1108/13673270710738942

Rahman, M. (2020). Performance Measurement of Service Supply Chain Management of Steel Industry on Dealers' Perspective -The Case of Bangladesh. 22. *International Journal of Research in Humanities and Social Studies*, *7*(1), 22–28.

Ramanathan, R. (2010). The moderating roles of risk and efficiency on the relationship between logistics performance and customer loyalty in e-commerce. *Transportation Research Part E, Logistics and Transportation Review*, *46*(6), 950–962. doi:10.1016/j.tre.2010.02.002

Reynaud, E. (2003). *Développement durable et entreprise: vers une relation symbiotique, Journée AIMS, Atelier développement durable*. ESSCA Angers.

Ritchie, B., & Brindley, C. (2007). Supply chain risk management and performance: A guiding framework for future development. *International Journal of Operations & Production Management*, *26*(3), 303–322. doi:10.1108/01443570710725563

Rojo, A., Stevenson, M., Lloréns Montes, F. J., & Perez-Arostegui, M. N. (2018). Supply chain flexibility in dynamic environments. *International Journal of Operations & Production Management*, *38*(3), 636–666. doi:10.1108/IJOPM-08-2016-0450

Roth, A., Cattani, K., & Froehle, C. (2008). Antecedents and performance outcomes of global competence: An empirical investigation. *Journal of Engineering and Technology Management*, *25*(1-2), 75–92. doi:10.1016/j.jengtecman.2008.01.003

Sahay, B. S., & Mohan, R. (2003). Supply chain management practices in Indian industry. *International Journal of Physical Distribution & Logistics Management*, *33*(7), 582–606. doi:10.1108/09600030310499277

Sampson, S. E., & Spring, M. (2012). Customer Roles in Service Supply Chains and Opportunities for Innovation. *The Journal of Supply Chain Management*, *48*(4), 30–50. doi:10.1111/j.1745-493X.2012.03282.x

Selviaridis, K., & Norrman, A. (2014). Performance-based contracting in service supply chains: A service provider risk perspective. *Supply Chain Management*, *19*(2), 153–172. doi:10.1108/SCM-06-2013-0216

Sengupta, K., Heiser, D. R., & Cook, L. S. (2006). Manufacturing and Service Supply Chain Performance: A Comparative Analysis. *The Journal of Supply Chain Management*, *42*(4), 4–15. doi:10.1111/j.1745-493X.2006.00018.x

Sezen, B. (2008). Relative effects of design, integration and information sharing on supply chain performance. *Supply Chain Management*, *13*(3), 233–240. doi:10.1108/13598540810871271

Shahin, Arash & Jamshidian, Mehdi. (2020). *Indicators of Supply Chain Management (SCM): Performance and Supplier Selection*. Online conference logistic, Tahran, Iran.

Shahin, A. & Mehrparvar, H. & Karbasian, M. (2016). *An Integrated Framework for Selecting Performance Indicators Based on ELECTRE Method and SMART Criteria With a Case Study in Single Level Bidirectional Service Supply Chain*. Social Science Research Network.

Sharma, M. J., Moon, I., & Bae, H. (2008). Analytic hierarchy process to assess and optimize distribution network. *Applied Mathematics and Computation*, *202*(1), 256–265. doi:10.1016/j.amc.2008.02.008

Solakivi, T. (2014). *The connection between supply chain practices and firm performance-Evidence from multiple surveys and financial reporting data*. Turku School of Economics.

Spina, D., Di Serio, L. C., Brito, L., & Duarte, A. (2015). The Influence of Supply Chain Management Practices in the Enterprise Performance. *American Journal of Management*, *15*(2), 54–63.

Sundram, V. P., Ibrahim, A. R., & Govindaraju, V. G. R. (2011). Supply chain management practices in the electronics industry in Malaysia: Consequences for supply chain performance. *Benchmarking*, *18*(6), 834–855. doi:10.1108/14635771111180725

Taghipour, A. (Ed.). (2020). *Demand Forecasting and Order Planning in Supply Chains and Humanitarian Logistics*. IGI Global.

Taghipour, A., & Beneteau-Piet, C. (2020). Sustainable supply chain management performance. *International Journal of Innovation, Management and Technology*, *11*(6), 165–169. doi:10.18178/ijimt.2020.11.6.897

Taghipour, A., Murat, S., & Huang, P. (2021). E-supply chain management: A review. International Journal of e-Education, e-Business, e-. *Management Learning*, *11*(2), 51–61.

Tan, K. C., Kannan, V. R., & Handfield, R. B. (1998). Supply chain management: Supplier performance and firm performance. *International Journal of Purchasing and Materials Management*, *34*(3), 2–9.

Tan, K. H., & Steven, B. (2002). Supply chain management: A strategic perspective. *International Journal of Operations & Production Management*, *22*(6), 614–631. doi:10.1108/01443570210427659

Tanriverdi, H. (2006). Performance effects of information technology synergies in multibusiness firms. *Management Information Systems Quarterly*, *30*(1), 57–77. doi:10.2307/25148717

Taschner, A. (2016). Improving SME logistics performance through benchmarking, Benchmarking. *Benchmarking*, *23*(7), 1780–1797. doi:10.1108/BIJ-03-2015-0029

Tixier, D., Mathe, H., & Colin, J. (1996). *La logistique d'entreprise: vers un management plus compétitif*. Éditions Dunod.

Tseng, M.-L., Chen, C.-C., Wu, K.-J., & Tan, R. (2020). Eco-efficient sustainable service supply chain management hierarchical model based on qualitative information and quantitative data. *Management of Environmental Quality*, *31*(4), 961–984. doi:10.1108/MEQ-08-2019-0179

Van Hoek, R. I. (2001). The contribution of performance measurement to the expansion of third party logistics alliances in the supply chain. *International Journal of Operations & Production Management, 21*(1-2), 15–29. doi:10.1108/01443570110358431

Vanichchinchai, A., & Igel, B. (2011). The impact of total quality management on supply chain management and firm's supply performance. *International Journal of Production Research, 49*(11), 3405–3424. doi:10.1080/00207543.2010.492805

Vickery, S. K., Jayaram, J., Droge, C., & Calantone, R. (2003). The Effects of an Integrative Supply Chain Strategy on Customer Service and Financial Performance: An Analysis of Direct versus Indirect Relationships. *Journal of Operations Management, 21*(5), 523–539. doi:10.1016/j.jom.2003.02.002

Wagner, S. M., & Bode, C. (2008). An empirical examination of supply chain performance along several dimensions of risk. *Journal of Business Logistics, 29*(1), 307–325. doi:10.1002/j.2158-1592.2008.tb00081.x

Wahdan, M. A., & Emam, M. A. (2017). The Impact of Supply Chain Management on Financial Performance and Responsibility Accounting Agribusiness Case from Egypt. *Accounting and Finance Research, 6*(2), 136. doi:10.5430/afr.v6n2p136

Wang, B., Kang, Y., Childerhouse, P., & Huo, B. (2018). Service supply chain integration: The role of interpersonal relationships. *Industrial Management & Data Systems, 118*(4), 828–849. doi:10.1108/IMDS-02-2017-0062

Wisner, J. D. (2003). A structural equation model of supply chain management strategies and firm performance. *Journal of Business Logistics, 24*(1), 1–26. doi:10.1002/j.2158-1592.2003.tb00030.x

Xie, Y., Yin, Y., Xue, W., Shi, H., & Chong, D. (2020). Intelligent supply chain performance measurement in Industry 4.0. *Systems Research and Behavioral Science, 37*(1), 711–718. doi:10.1002res.2712

Yalabik, B., & Fairchild, R. J. (2011). Customer, regulatory, and competitive pressure as drivers of environmental innovation. *International Journal of Production Economics, 131*(2), 519–527. doi:10.1016/j.ijpe.2011.01.020

Yang, C.-S., & Lirn, T.-C. (2017). Revisiting the resource-based view on logistics performance in the shipping industry. *International Journal of Physical Distribution & Logistics Management, 47*(9), 884–905. doi:10.1108/IJPDLM-05-2017-0184

Yang, C.-S., & Lirn, T.-C. (2017). Revisiting the resource-based view on logistics performance in the shipping industry. *International Journal of Physical Distribution & Logistics Management, 47*(9), 884–905. doi:10.1108/IJPDLM-05-2017-0184

Yao, J., & Liu, L. (2009). Optimization analysis of supply chain scheduling in mass customization. *International Journal of Production Economics, 117*(1), 197–211. doi:10.1016/j.ijpe.2008.10.008

Youngdahl, W. E. (1996). An investigation of service-based manufacturing performance relationships. *International Journal of Operations & Production Management, 16*(8), 29–43. doi:10.1108/01443579610125769

Yu, T. (2003). Supplier selection in constructing logistics service supply chain. Syst. Eng.-. *Theory into Practice, 23*(5), 49–53.

Yusuf, R., & Shehu, A. U. (2017). The review of supply chain management systems and firm performance. *International Journal of Management Research and Reviews*, *7*(2), 113–122.

Zailani, S., Iranmanesh, M., Foroughi, B., Kim, K., & Hyun, S. S. (2019). Effects of supply chain practices, integration and closed-loop supply chain activities on cost-containment of biodiesel. *Review of Managerial Science*, *14*(1), 1299–1319. doi:10.100711846-019-00332-9

Zhou, H., & Benton, W. Jr. (2007). Supply chain practice and information sharing. *Journal of Operations Management*, *25*(6), 1348–1365. doi:10.1016/j.jom.2007.01.009

Zimmermann, F., & Foerstl, K. (2014). A Meta-Analysis of the "Purchasing and Supply Management Practice–Performance Link". *The Journal of Supply Chain Management*, *50*(1), 37–54. doi:10.1111/jscm.12051

Chapter 8
Big Data Supply Chain Management and Its Legal Context

Atour Taghipour
Normandy University, France

XiaoWen Lu
Normandy University, France

ABSTRACT

The new digital tools can significantly improve the performance of supply chains. That means, the digitalization has the potential to provide companies with a range of practices to significantly reduce costs, increase product availability, improve access to information, and enhance responsiveness, collaboration, supply chain visibility, and resilience. One of the potentials of the digitalization is to explore big data. In fact, the quantitative explosion of data gave birth to big data in order to find new ways of analyzing and exploring the data. It offers the possibility to treat and analyze a huge amount of data in order to make conclusions and take decisions. Benefits such as cost reducing, better management, or even precise forecasting are possible with the big data. But a lot of companies have faced big problems such as data leaking and privacy violation. This chapter will study big data supply chain management and its legal context based on a literature review and gives future directions for governments, companies, and researchers.

INTRODUCTION

The arrival of the internet can be considered as the beginning of digitization. However, real digitalization has started with the integration of digital technologies into business processes with the aim of improving them. In reality, digitalization transforms all core businesses into advanced forms. It is a process that aims to improve the performance of the processes of an organization.

DOI: 10.4018/978-1-6684-9062-4.ch008

The globalization of industries formed supply chains, which represent all processes required to deliver a product or service to customers (Nadia et al., 2020). To manage these processes in harmony the supply chain management was born as a solution to manage the interaction between global companies and to offer the companies multi factors of competitiveness. However, the growth of the international business has created strong competition in the market. In addition, supply chain management also needs to deal with the difficulties that face supply chain managers and researchers, including complexity, conflicting objectives, dynamic environment and sources of risks, in addition to making their supply chains more competitive (Taghipour and Frayret, 2011).

With the introduction of the technology, many changes and improvements have occurred. The companies saw a great opportunity with the development of all the technologies during the past decades to take a competitive advantage and to surpass the competition. First, with the internet, companies could access information and develop their website to add value to their products and services in order to attract clients. Then the digitalization and the digital transformation, which allowed the companies to transcend their own concept and reach step by step more efficiency (Taghipour and Merimi, 2021).

Today, in this competitive environment, it is necessary to use technology to develop a new business model, and thus maintain a sustainable competitive advantage (Saeed and Kersten, 2019). The goal of every company is to optimize workflows and satisfy the customer's needs in terms of quality, quantity, price and delivery time (Taghipour et al., 2021). The transformation of a traditional supply chain into a digital supply chain means digitalizing an integrated system that interconnects all actors to avoid the loss of time and money, improving business performance and being environmentally friendly (Devins et al., 2017). According to a Forbes Insights survey, 65% of managers want to transform their business models in the digital age. Therefore, it is necessary to know how emerging technologies can be used in these processes to gain a competitive advantage. In this context, one of the emerging technologies is Big Data, which can offer a series of benefits in terms of capacity to collect and analyze information. Big-data is the tool that can help a company reach a near perfect functioning (Farouk and Zhen, 2019). This article, after exploring the big data in the context of supply chain management, studies characteristics as well as the benefits of such a tool and its utilization in a legal context to define a way of application of the bigdata that won't be against the countries' regulations.

SUPPLY CHAIN MANAGEMENT

Definitions of Supply Chain Management

Before 2000 - Amongst the first definitions of supply chain management we can mention the one defined by kranz (1996) as all efforts involved in producing and delivering a product from suppliers to customers. The main observation from this definition is that the supply chain is to manage all the actions from the acquisitions of the goods until the delivery to the customer. Quinn (1997) defines supply chain management as the activities associated to move goods from the raw materials to the end user. The supply chain encompasses all the steps from buying the product, production, inventory management, transportation and even storage (Prajogo and Sohal, 2013). According to other authors such as Copacino (1997), supply chain management refers to the art of managing the flow from source to user. Contrary to the previous definitions, Johnson and woods (1996) assume that the supply chain management is larger than logistics and it is not only a matter of managing flux and physical objects. But, the interaction between the actors is a very important issue, which can be seen, especially in the case of a possible conflict, that may result in a failure in the optimization (Taghipour and Frayret, 2011). So, an appropriate linkage between members has a great impact on improving the global performance, in the terms of the reduction of cost and the maximization of profit, through the coordination between actors (Larson et al., 1998).

After 2000 - Here are some different definitions of Supply Chain Management in recent years: "Supply chain management (SCM) is the management and oversight of a product from its origin until it is consumed." (TechnoPedia, 2018); "The design, planning, execution, control, and monitoring of supply chain activities with the objective of creating net value, building a competitive infrastructure, leveraging worldwide logistics, synchronizing supply with demand, and measuring performance globally." (Association of Supply Chain Management, 2015); "Supply chain management is the management of the flow of goods and services." (Nabil Abu El Ata et al., 2017).

The main observation from these definitions is that management is possible if we include the dimension of information (Vosooghidizaji et al., 2020). However, the information is often confidential and most of the companies do not want to share their critical knowledge. Paradoxically, sharing of information is needed to add value through the entire process of the supply chain (Merimi and Taghipour, 2021). The information sharing is the main enabler to coordinate the actors and to create optimum solutions to deliver the product of the service to the final customers (Vosooghidizaji et al., 2022).

Levels of the Supply Chain

Supply Chain Management includes all the actors in the logistics chain, from the producers of raw materials to the final consumer, including all the possible intermediaries (processors, wholesalers, transporters, distributors, etc.) (Taghipour et al., 2015). It defines all the resources, methods and tools intended to manage the global supply chain as efficiently as possible. The Supply Chain has three levels:

The first one is strategic, it is used to define products and offered services, dimensioning of the industrial and logistics tool and negotiation of contracts and partnerships with suppliers and customers (Mahfod et al., 2019). The second is tactical, which develops sales forecasts, planning, scheduling and calculation of requirements, establishing supply rules and inventory management rules (Taghipour, 2020). The last one is operational, which consists in managing customer orders, scheduling operations, managing contingencies and order execution: production, distribution and billing. The coherence of tools, processes and daily practices with the Supply Chain strategy will allow the company to guarantee its efficiency in the face of market needs.

In this regard, supply chain management propose different approaches to better manage the whole supply chain, including demand forecasting, materials planning (Manufacturing Resources planning II), distribution management, stock level optimization, warehouse and location management, supplier relationship management (SRM), purchasing and supply chain management as well as flow traceability (Taghipour, 2018).

Each time the global situation changes: new market expectations, new competitors, new links between companies and their partners, supply chain management must be readapted to the new environment. Today, only those companies that adapt to change very quickly and implement the most cost-effective operational solutions succeed. In this regard, supply chain integration offers multiple advantages such as higher reactivity, respect of the quantity ordered, delivered to the right location with the respect of the time, a significant decrease in costs, a clear improvement in quality and customer service, and better performance. That is possible by optimizing the resources and reducing the costs through the integration and streamlining the processes (Yang et al., 2017). So, implementing true supply chain management is based on efficient information systems, which allows the companies to acquire new competitive advantages.

Supply Chain Management: Past and Present

Supply chain management has undergone a lot of evolution since its beginnings with military logistics. Production companies started to implement logistics systems to gain efficiency in mass production (Taghipour, 2014). Supply chain management has evolved significantly over the last century. Each stage of the supply chain has undergone several evolutions. The processes of procurement, transportation and manufacturing have changed significantly. From the introduction of new handling techniques to the use of ships for long distances, and from containerization to digitalization, global supply chains are both more complex and more efficient than ever before.

Over the years, most companies have focused on the effectiveness and efficiency of independent business functions. However, as a new way of doing business, more and more companies are beginning to realize the strategic importance of planning, controlling and designing the entire supply chain. To help companies leverage the synergies of cross-functional and cross-organizational supply chain integration and coordination, and subsequently make better supply chain decisions, supply chain models need to evolve over time (Shin and Taghipour, 2021).

Supply chain management in the past - Before the industrial revolution, supply chains existed, but in a simpler way. For example, the way a shoemaker, a farmer or a blacksmith was procuring the raw material or the tools. Then, little by little, with mass manufacturing, mechanization, the development of means of transportation, etc., companies began to organize the supply of raw materials and set up what we call today the supply chains. Also, thanks to inventions like the internal combustion engine, electric power generation and mass communication technologies, things really exploded and the interrelationships became more important. In this regard, logistics and transportation was the most important field of supply chains. Many universities offer courses in this field to meet the needs of the labor market. However, subjects such as logistics, physical procurement and supply chain management were not discussed and remained unknown.

The technology was not part of the relationship. Even after the discovery of the computer, it took a long time before companies were interested in this technology to simplify their exchanges and gain in productivity and efficiency. The traditional way of placing orders with the necessary quantities with suppliers remained the most practiced for a long time until the 2000s when a change began to be made at the management level.

Supply chain management today - Supply chain management after the 2000s was beginning to become the most popular model in many countries around the world. This model became a chain that encompasses the planning and management of all activities related to supply and production, as well as all activities related to logistics.

It was from the year 2010 that a real change took place, the world experienced an unprecedented technological revolution and supply chain management did not escape this. Digitization affects all areas of human life, including the supply chain. The digitization of the Supply Chain means the dematerialization of information processing. This digitization offers better management of data flows as well as unparalleled reliability of information related to the Supply Chain. For optimal management of production flows, the digitization of flows (physical logistics flow or just-in-time logistics) is therefore essential. Companies quickly understood that it was necessary to orient themselves and invest in the digitalization of the supply chain in order to remain competitive and survive the various challenges (Almeida et al., 2013). Today the majority of large companies have automated their production and supply processes. This digitalization of supply chain management includes:

- Emerging technologies (AI, Cloud, Blockchain etc.)
- Big data analysis
- Robotics
- Change management
- Digital competencies

Complexity Inside the Supply Chain

Supply chain is a complex system. There are many actors that produce many products and a big amount of data. The supply chain is also operating in a dynamic environment. As an example, the customer demand may change during the course of the planning or supplier capability evolve over time (Blecker et al., 2015). These two aspects are two of the main difficulties of supply chain management. The difficulty of the management can be increased by considering other factors. First of all, the internal organization which means the factors inside the company that can harden the supply chain process (Serdarasan, 2013). As an example, we can mention non-synchronized functions in a company, the structural deficit, non-harmonized decisions, information gap and a shortened product life cycle. The other factor is the uncertainty, which cannot be eliminated by companies, such as a global pandemic. As a result, it can be said that the supply chain has a lot of variables to consider and the question that arises is if a digital tool can improve the efficiency of supply chains.

Why Digitalize the Supply Chain?

A digital supply chain offers significant advantages for planning and managing operations. These benefits include:

On the Environmental and Social Level

Today the choice of an environmental strategy based on sustainable development, increasingly defines a company's prospects in the competitive marketplace (Taghipour and Beneteau-Piet, 2020). The digitalization of the supply chain helps companies to develop ecological production processes, seeking to develop short circuits to save energy and the circular economy to save materials. It dematerializes, digitizes work procedures and offers new services like e-administration and e-payment. These new services allow the reduction of paper consumption, facilitate inter-organizational exchanges but also substitute travel and transport which generate CO2 emissions and therefore reduce gas emissions (which can represent more than 90% of the carbon footprint of a company), waste and pollution. As a result, customers have become much more environmentally conscious. A recent IBM study found that nearly 80% of consumers indicate that sustainability is important to them and 60% are willing to change their purchasing habits to reduce environmental impact. Keep in mind that anticipating human activity, including purchasing habits and generational lifestyles, makes the decision easier (Barney, 2012).

On the Economic Level

These revolutionary transformations are expected to boost the national and international economy as companies adapt to supply chain crises, such as Covid-19 and the Russia-Ukraine conflict (Nadia et al., 2021). They are seen as the most effective way to improve business resiliency, overcome shipping bottlenecks, and address product shortages that are of primary concern. For example, computer processing of various market information enables companies to improve sales processes, anticipate future market trends, optimize production and drive accurate and timely operations (El-Nemr et al., 2017).

On the Business Transformation Level

Digital customers -Traditional customer service methods often boil down to the manual use of overly complex checklists. This becomes increasingly complicated when a company requests new information about its customers. As a result, the error rate can be as high as 70% due to human error, which leads to poor customer management. Companies can increase the level of customer satisfaction while keeping up with current trends. Digitization ensures a digital customer history by collecting data and reusing it to fill out new forms and thus offer the best services. Trend mining is able to filter a large amount of data, get accurate predictions and make the right decisions. According to the survey of the global manufacturing consulting firm Mckinsey and Company: customer satisfaction can be increased by 33% and costs reduced by 25-35% by digitizing customer service. The speed of access to information introduced by digitization allows customers to compare product prices and see the opinions of others.

Digital production and logistics systems - It is about integrating digitalization with automatons and robotics to speed up the production and logistics process, and to collect the corresponding data in real time. It allows to:

- Give reliable access to all information anywhere and anytime using any device.
- Automate data transfer and communication between the supplier, the company and the consumer. Information must be present at all times, either before production or after sales, since the ability to meet customer demand and satisfaction cannot be achieved without the exchange and flow of information.
- Automate the processes.
- Be flexible in the face of problems thanks to the prediction of possible risks and the adaptation to the disruptions and rapid changes that customers demand every day throughout the chain.

In other words, a robust digital infrastructure can increase the ability to easily respond to demand, especially when it is unplanned. For example, geolocation shippers provide real-time data on product location and increase supply chain visibility and transparency. Similarly, for production, real-time information helps to better manage and therefore avoid breakdowns, including knowing how, how much and when to produce (Li et al., 2006).

Big Data

Big data is more than ever in our daily lives. Companies understood the huge advantages and benefits they could get owing to the use of big data. But, what exactly is big data? What are its characteristics? How can it be used and what are the benefits of big data?

Ward and barker (2013) state that the term big data is shared between academia, industry and the media and there is no single unified definition and there is a lack of a consistent definition related to big data. This makes clear that big data can have different definitions, characteristics, goals and benefits following the sectors in which it is used. So, we can assume that big data is complex to define. According to Baro et al., (2015) the big data is first of all characterized by the size of it. Initially it is a data, but what makes it being called big is its complexity (Loivet et al., 2020). This source also stated that the complexity of big data comes from the main aspect. Widely used notions to describe the complexity of big data are the three "Vs": volume, variety, and velocity. "Big Data is a term used to describe information assemblages that make conventional data, or database, processing problematic due to any combination of their size (volume), frequency of update (velocity), or diversity (variety)" (O'Reilly Radar Team, 2012). Veracity is a fourth "V" sometimes added to describe a big data challenge.

Big data is then also characterized by the nature of this amount of data. As we are trying to see the impact of big data in supply chain/purchase, it's also interesting to have a definition which goes toward this sector. Big data could then be defined as a way to have access to an amount of crucial information that can be used to define a supply strategy maximizing efficiency (Tliche et al., 2021).

Benefits of Big Data

Big data makes possible the treatment of thousands and thousands of data in real time so that the companies identify some similarities or disparities between these data and then manage to create optimization regarding their supply chain. Big data absolutely needs computers or machines with advanced analytic models to analyze the data, but in return valuable knowledge can be obtained, such knowledge is useful to predict, for example a behavior or the demand of a product (Singh and Reddy, 2014). In this regard, Big data analytics is the application of advanced analytic methods on big data to extract valuable knowledge, by identifying trends, detecting patterns, assessing scenarios and gleaning invaluable information to facilitate data-driven supply chain decision-making (Xu et al., 2021).

Right after forecasting, the companies plan their operations. In this regard, accuracy of forecasting is crucial to provide optimal plans to actors of the supply chain (Tliche et al., 2019). Big data is the best tool that helps the companies to take their planning decisions based on the most accurate forecasting. Owing to big data, it's possible to understand the customers' behavior, in other words, the demand and its characteristics.

How to Use Big Data

The research made by Sharma et al., (2016) reveals that there are several steps of deployment of the big data. First of all, the data distillation where features are obtained for disorganized texts or values, for obtaining similar characters or components. Then, there is the model deployment, comprising feature choosing, sampling and accumulation, transformation, model appraisal, model rectification and model benchmarking. Then there is the validation and deployment, to confirm that the model works in the real world. This step involves obtaining fresh data, executing using the model, and comparing results with real data. After that comes the real time scoring where real time systems will use the same hardware but not the same data. Finally, there is the model refresh. Due to the fact that the data is always changing, it is necessary to refresh the data and also the model on which it is built (Wang et al., 2015).

Tools That Can Be Used to Deal With the Bigdata

Xplenty - Xplenty is a software that allows the integration of processes using the data that will be analyzed on the cloud. The interface of the software remains intuitive and can be useful for sales, purchase, marketing, support and developers.

Adverity - Adverity is a software that will be useful for marketers. This system is fully-automated and will integrate data from more than 600 sources. It permits marketing services to have an overview of all the data in a single view, without any efforts. Furthermore, this data can be seen in real-time.

Cloudera - Cloudera is an open source, free and simple software. It allows its users to collect, to process, to manage, to model and to distribute the data.

Rapidminer - Rapidminer is a software used by scientists. It presents a lot of similarities with the previous software. The free version allows you to deal with 10 000 data.

Other tools - Big data is a domain where you can encounter a lot of software that will permit you to deal with all the data. Otherwise, it will be impossible for companies to analyze all this amount of information. Dataddo, Apache Hadoop, Apache Cassandra, Knime, Datawrapper, MongoDB, Lumify, HPCC, Storm, Apache Samoa, Talend, Qubole, Tableau, R, Oracle Data Mining and so many, are tools that will allow to deal with that mass of data.

Big Data to Soften the Complexity?

As we saw earlier, the supply chain is a complex system that has to consider a multitude of criteria and information to decide. This complexity can impact the efficiency of the decisions. In this context, big data is the use of advanced quantitative and qualitative analysis to a vast volume of structured and unstructured data. Such analyses include predictive analytics (Schoenherr and Speier-Pero, 2015), business analytics, big data analytics and supply chain analytics (Wang et al. 2016). The use of big data in the supply chain really can reduce the complexity of the supply chain (Cauchois et al., 2017). Indeed, big data analytics is an essential tool for predicting business trends or an unanticipated demand, and we stated before that uncertainty is one of the drivers that increase the complexity of the supply chain (Tiwari et al., 2018). Big data can be used to optimize the supply chain for example by predicting and forecasting the future demand of goods. If the suppliers know more precisely the demand, they will be able to optimize the sourcing and storage to reduce costs. Cost reduction is at the heart of the supply chain function. Big data can make the process easier in many areas such as raw material procurement. It can be applied to identify an existing trend and pattern. Big data can help in a faster and more accurate forecasting which will permit to the suppliers a better decision and less risks (Taghipour et al., 2014). Big data is also useful in manufacturing. Toyota claims to avoid nearly 80% of defect's prior to building the physical prototype using big data (Big data Insight Group 2012).

Legal Context

Today we are in a society where the privacy of data is taken seriously by everyone. Data privacy consists of ensuring the confidentiality of personal data by implementing all protective measures and rules that meet regulatory and ethical requirements. In this context, protecting privacy in the case of big data means keeping information safe and planning a measured response if an incident occurs. A lot of company's like Fakebook or Google have been sued fora data leak of thousands of conversations or information. This is in this context that big data must adapt and evolve and some challenges that have to be faced (Chen et al., 2013). First of all, big data must respect the privacy of people. It must not reveal the identity of those concerned with the data. Privacy is defined by the International Telecommunications Union as the "right of individuals to control or influence what information related to them may be disclosed". Privacy can concern individuals as well as companies but, in any case, it must be respected and the company who does not respect it can be sued and pay a compensation (Zwitter, 2014). So, the companies of the supply chains that use big data must make sure that the data is secured and assume that the security of the data is the responsibility of the company using the big data (Kuner et al. 2012).

The company also has to make sure that it respects the law about the principle of fairness and lawfulness (Bredenoord et al., 2015). These principles state that the company that processes the data has to be clear with the people about the way their data will be used and for what purpose. It also states that this process of data has to be based on consent.

During recent years, there have been a series of laws regarding big data and they keep multiplying over the years. As the big data is regulated, companies have no other choice but to adopt the usage of their big data policy to the law.

Finally, the decision makers must integrate big data in their supply chain management decisions. Big data facilitates efficient decision making by analyzing a huge amount of data and concluding decisions that will fit perfectly to the situation. However, big data does not have a critical mind and subjective aspect and it is entirely objective. However, the final decision should always be taken by the humans.

CONCLUSION

To conclude, it can be said that big data, a tool presenting a lot of benefits in terms of data analysis, accuracy, volume, velocity and variety is really useful to the supply chain management field. As the supply chain management requires existing data to forecast, it is necessary to adapt to the existing law and regulation imposed by the governments. Such laws are often subjective and do not correspond to the field of big data which is objective and rational. That's why big data should always be a tool and not a full entity that takes decisions on its own because it does not possess a critical mind only possessed by the suppliers or the humans. In this regard, what we can propose as future lines of research are the development of the research related to the real time processing and more focus on data privacy due to new regulations.

REFERENCES

Abu el Ata, N., Drucbert, A., Abu el Ata, N., & Drucbert, A. (2017). Case# 3: Managing Operational Risk: Global Supply Chain. *Leading from Under the Sword of Damocles: A Business Leader's Practical Guide to Using Predictive Emulation to Manage Risk and Maintain Profitability*, 191-196.

Almeida, F. L. F., & Calistru, C. (2013). The main challenges and issues of big data management. *International Journal of Research Studies in Computing*, *2*(1). Advance online publication. doi:10.5861/ijrsc.2012.209

Association for Supply Chain Management. (2015). *What is supply chain management?* ASCM. https://www.ascm.org/scm/#:~:text=What%20is%20supply%20chain%20management,information%2C%20physical%20distribution%20and%20cash

Barney, J. B. (2012). Purchasing, Supply Chain Management and Sustained Competitive Advantage: The Relevance of Resource-based Theory. *The Journal of Supply Chain Management, 48*(2), 3–6. doi:10.1111/j.1745-493X.2012.03265.x

Baro, E., Degoul, S., Beuscart, R., & Chazard, E. (2015). Toward a literature-driven definition of big data in healthcare. *BioMed Research International, 2015*, 2015. doi:10.1155/2015/639021 PMID:26137488

Blecker, T., Kersten, W., & Meyer, C. (2015). *Development of an Approach for Analyzing Supply Chain Complexity*. Hamburg University of Technology.

Bredenoord, A. L., Mostert, M., Isasi, R., & Knoppers, B. M. (2015). Data sharing in stem cell translational science: Policy statement by the international stem cell forum ethics working party. *Regenerative Medicine*, *10*(7), 857–861. doi:10.2217/rme.15.42 PMID:26506014

Cauchois, R., Taghipour, A., Kang, D., Zoghlami, N., & Abed, M. (2017). Advanced solutions for a supply chain with stochastic information. *Journal of Advanced Management Science, 5*(1).

Chen, J., Chen, Y., Du, X., Li, C., Lu, J., Zhao, S., & Zhou, X. (2013). Big data challenge: A data management perspective. *Frontiers of Computer Science*, *7*(2), 157–164. doi:10.100711704-013-3903-7

Copacino, W. C. (1997). *Supply chain management: The basics and beyond* (1). CRC Press.

Devins, C., Felin, T., Kauffman, S., & Koppl, R. (2017). The Law and Big Data. *Cornell Journal of Law and Public Policy*, *27*(2), 3. https://scholarship.law.cornell.edu/cjlpp/vol27/iss2/3

El-Nemr, N., Canel-Depitre, B., & Taghipour, A. (2017, September). Determinants of hotel room rates. In *Marketing Trends Congress. Luxury Industries Conference London 2017*. Research Gate.

Farouk, A., & Zhen, D. (2019). Big data analysis techniques for intelligent systems. *Journal of Intelligent & Fuzzy Systems*, *37*(3), 3067–3071. doi:10.3233/JIFS-179109

Johnson, J. C., & Wood, D. F. (1990). *Contemporary logistics*. Macmillan.

Kranz, S. (1996). *What is it?* Purchasing Today.

Kuner, C., Cate, F. H., Millard, C., & Svantesson, D. J. B. (2012). The challenge of « big data » for data protection. *International Data Privacy Law*, *2*(2), 47–49. doi:10.1093/idpl/ips003

Larson, P. D., & Rogers, D. S. (1998). Supply Chain Management: Definition, Growth and Approaches. *Journal of Marketing Theory and Practice*, *6*(4), 1–5. doi:10.1080/10696679.1998.11501805

Li, S., Ragu-Nathan, B., Ragu-Nathan, T., & Subba Rao, S. (2006). The impact of supply chain management practices on competitive advantage and organizational performance. *Omega*, *34*(2), 107–124. doi:10.1016/j.omega.2004.08.002 PMID:17876965

Loivet, W., Taghipour, A., & Kang, D. S. (2020). The rise of green supply chain management: Between complexity and necessity. *Journal of Economics. Business and Management*, *8*(1), 1–7.

Mahfod, J., Canel-Depitre, B., & Taghipour, A. (2019). Quality function deployment-ELECTRE in supplier evaluation. *Journal of Advanced Management Science Vol*, *7*(4).

Nadia, E. N., Beatrice, C. D., & Atour, T. (2020). Luxury hotels' eco-friendly activities & customers' preferences and willingness to pay for green hotels. Journal of Advanced Management Science Vol, 8(1).
Merimi, M., & Taghipour, A. (2021). Accelerating the digitalization of the supply chain: An empirical research about COVID-19 crisis. In Digitalization of Decentralized Supply Chains During Global Crises (pp. 1-24). IGI Global.

Nadia, E. N., Beatrice, C. D., & Atour, T. (2021). The Determinants of Hotel Room Rates in Beirut: A Hedonic Pricing Model. *International Journal of Trade, Economics and Finance, 12*(2).

O'Reilly Radar Team. (2012). *Planning for big data: A CIO's handbook to the changing data landscape* (E. Dumbill, Ed.; 1st ed.). O'Reilly Media Inc.

Prajogo, D., & Sohal, A. (2013). Supply chain professionals. *International Journal of Operations & Production Management*, *33*(11/12), 1532–1554. doi:10.1108/IJOPM-08-2010-0228

Quinn, F. J. (1997). What's the buzz. *Logistics Management*, *36*(2), 43–47.

Saeed, M., & Kersten, W. (2019). Drivers of Sustainable Supply Chain Management: Identification and Classification. *Sustainability (Basel)*, *11*(4), 1137. doi:10.3390u11041137

Schoenherr, T., & Speier-Pero, C. (2015). Data science, predictive analytics, and big data in supply chain management: Current state and future potential. *Journal of Business Logistics*, *36*(1), 120–132. doi:10.1111/jbl.12082

Serdarasan, S. (2013). A review of supply chain complexity drivers. *Computers & Industrial Engineering*, *66*(3), 533–540. doi:10.1016/j.cie.2012.12.008

Sharma, D. K., Pradhan, R., Kumar, V., & Gupta, Y. (2016). *Big data and analytics. Work paper*. GLA University India.

Shin, M., & Taghipour, A. (2021). Supply Chains Digital Transformation: Automated Underground Logistics Systems. *Underground Construction*, *6*(2), 7. doi:10.18178/joebm.2021.9.2.651

Singh, D., & Reddy, C. K. (2014). A survey on platforms for big data analytics. *Journal of Big Data*, *2*(1), 8. Advance online publication. doi:10.118640537-014-0008-6 PMID:26191487

Taghipour, A. (2014). *Production Network Planning Based on Constraint Relaxation and Discount Approach* (Vol. 2). Lecture Notes on Information Theory.

Taghipour, A. (2018). A Contemporary Approach to Plan Independent Logistics Actors. In *Contemporary Approaches and Strategies for Applied Logistics* (pp. 337–364). IGI Global. doi:10.4018/978-1-5225-5273-4.ch014

Taghipour, A. (Ed.). (2020). *Demand Forecasting and Order Planning in Supply Chains and Humanitarian Logistics*. IGI Global.

Taghipour, A., Abed, M., & Zoghlami, N. (2015, May). Design for remanufacturing respecting reverse logistics processes: A review. In *2015 4th International Conference on Advanced Logistics and Transport (ICALT)* (pp. 299-304). IEEE. 10.1109/ICAdLT.2015.7136602

Taghipour, A., & Beneteau-Piet, C. (2020). Sustainable supply chain management performance. *International Journal of Innovation, Management and Technology*, *11*(6), 165–169. doi:10.18178/ijimt.2020.11.6.897

Taghipour, A., & Frayret, J. M. (2011). Supply chain coordination planning: A review. *Work paper, École polytechnique de Montréal.*

Taghipour, A., & Frayret, J. M. (2011). A new heuristic search with local optimization to manage a supply chain. *Meta*, 15.

Taghipour, A., Glaa, B., & Zoghlami, N. (2014, May). Network coordination with minimum risk of information sharing. In *2014 International Conference on Advanced Logistics and Transport (ICALT)* (pp. 184-188). IEEE. 10.1109/ICAdLT.2014.6864115

Taghipour, A., & Merimi, M. (2021). Digital Transformation of Supply Chains during Crisis: COVID-19. In *11th Annual International Conference on Industrial Engineering and Operations Management, IEOM* (pp. 7493-7501).

Taghipour, A., Murat, S., & Huang, P. (2021). E-supply chain management: A review. International Journal of e-Education, e-Business, e-. *Management Learning*, *11*(2), 51–61.

Techopedia.com. (2018). What is an Artificial Neural Network (ANN)? *Technopedia.* https://www.techopedia.com/definition/5967/artificial-neural-network-ann

Tiwari, S., Wee, H., & Daryanto, Y. (2018). Big data analytics in supply chain management between 2010 and 2016: Insights to industries. *Computers & Industrial Engineering*, *115*, 319–330. doi:10.1016/j.cie.2017.11.017

Tliche, Y., Taghipour, A., & Canel-Depitre, B. (2019). Anticipation of Demand in Supply Chains. In *Hierarchical Planning and Information Sharing Techniques in Supply Chain Management* (pp. 1–45). IGI Global.

Tliche, Y., Taghipour, A., & Canel-Depitre, B. (2021). Exploring a Downstream Demand Inference Strategy in a Decentralized Two-Level Supply Chain. In *Demand Forecasting and Order Planning in Supply Chains and Humanitarian Logistics* (pp. 1–65). IGI Global. doi:10.4018/978-1-7998-3805-0.ch001

Vosooghidizaji, M., Taghipour, A., & Canel-Depitre, B. (2020). Information Asymmetry in Supply Chain Coordination: State of the Art. *Journal of Industrial and Intelligent Information, 8*(2).

Vosooghidizaji, M., Taghipour, A., & Canel-Depitre, B. (2022). Coordinating corporate social responsibility in a two-level supply chain under bilateral information asymmetry. *Journal of Cleaner Production*, *364*, 132627. doi:10.1016/j.jclepro.2022.132627

Wang, G., Gunasekaran, A., Ngai, E. W., & Papadopoulos, T. (2016). Big data analytics in logistics and supply chain management: Certain investigations for research and applications. *International Journal of Production Economics*, *176*, 98–110. doi:10.1016/j.ijpe.2016.03.014

Wang, X., White, L., & Chen, X. (2015). Big data research for the knowledge economy: Past, present, and future. *Industrial Management & Data Systems*, *115*(9). Advance online publication. doi:10.1108/IMDS-09-2015-0388

Ward, J. S., & Barker, A. (2013). Undefined by data: a survey of big data definitions. *arXiv preprint arXiv:1309.5821*.

Xu, J., Pero, M. E. P., Ciccullo, F., & Sianesi, A. (2021). On relating big data analytics to supply chain planning: Towards a research agenda. *International Journal of Physical Distribution & Logistics Management*, *51*(6), 656–682. doi:10.1108/IJPDLM-04-2020-0129

Yang, S., Taghipour, A., & Canel-Depitre, B. (2017, August). Cost optimization of reverse logistics: A review. In *Proceedings of the 7th International Conference on Information Communication and Management* (pp. 158-161). 10.1145/3134383.3134393

Zwitter, A. (2014). Big Data ethics. *Big Data & Society*, *1*(2), 205395171455925. doi:10.1177/2053951714559253

Chapter 9
Digital Marketing Based on Machine Learning

Damodharan Palaniappan
Marwadi University, India

Yatri Davda
V.V.P. Engineering College, India

T. Premavathi
Marwadi University, India

ABSTRACT

The scan hole assessment revealed that some care was given to the behavior of marketers in relation to ML devices and their selection and use to aid critical and operational management. Examination introduced spotlights the choice and reception of ML-driven scientific devices by three particular gatherings: showcasing offices, media organizations, and promoters. The discoveries feature are as - the significant job of canny explanatory instruments in the creation and arrangement of showcasing methodologies, the absence of information about developing innovations, for example, ML and man-made consciousness, the likely use of ML devices in advertising, and; 4) the low degree of reception and using ML-driven scientific devices in promoting the board. A system comprising empowering agents as well as a procedure map was created to assist associations with recognizing the chances and effectively executing ventures that are arranged toward the sending and appropriation of the scientific ML instruments in advanced promoting.

1. INTRODUCTION

As of late, broad advancement data as well as correspondence innovations in the private and open areas started the development of another computerized showcasing condition. Because of the multiplication of data innovation, an immense measure of information is as of now created. It has been determined that there are 2.5 bytes of information per day, and this quantity increases as the Internet of Things begins

DOI: 10.4018/978-1-6684-9062-4.ch009

(IoT). It is also evaluated that during the past two years 90 per cent of the world's accessible knowledge was generated. The age, access and use of value-data is a prerequisite and exact business choices. Exponential and unhindered inventive progress expanded worldwide. This original copy was planned and reaffirmed by Malik Jahan Khan, partner manager. Therefore, take advantage of new ways to present the Board by implementing new information.

Advanced showcasing rose as a characteristic reaction by organizations to use and advantage from the critical buyer focus on the Internet. Different kinds of associations, including organizations, medical clinics, schools, proficient affiliations, chambers and NGOs, utilize advanced advertising as a major aspect of their showcasing techniques and sending programs. A portion of these associations can likewise work their own web-based business stage; however, they generally utilize the Internet as a channel/medium inside their correspondence procedure. These associations regularly satisfy the job of customers or promoters – likewise alluded to as brands. Different classes of associations additionally work in the advanced promoting space. Advanced offices make and actualize promoting techniques for the associations in the principal gathering and utilize computerized showcasing as their very own major aspect advertising methodology. Associations in the third gathering, to be specific media, are utilized by computerized offices (or the promoters straightforwardly) to speak with their intended interest group (S. Angra and S. Ahuja 2017, Cauchois, R., Taghipour, A., Kang, D., Zoghlami, N., & Abed, M., 2017).

The Internet condition empowers organizations to become familiar with shoppers through a couple of snaps in the fitting expository device. The best bit of leeway of advanced showcasing over other advertising devices and channels is its quantifiability. The advanced impression of each Internet client contains a lot of information that can fill in as contribution for promoting investigation. Manual securing and investigation of the information has been tedious and just barely directed. Diagnostic apparatuses are at present utilized in showcasing the board to systemize forms, smooth out the dynamic, and robotize work. These refined systematic instruments use AI (ML) to gain from recorded information and help plan future exercises all the more adequately. The ML apparatuses can be used in numerous parts. The examination introduced in this article centres explicitly around their utilization in showcasing investigation towards improving vital and operational choices in advertising the board. Utilizing an interdisciplinary methodology, the exploration investigates the capability of ML in advertising examination, the level of execution of the innovation, just as the mentalities of promoting organizations and showcasing supervisors towards dynamic use of these instruments.

2. LITERATURE OVERVIEW

2.1. Significance of Data Analysis in Strategic Planning

Analytical apparatuses smooth out vital arranging and assist associations with settling on operational choices quicker and all the more effectively. In the past, crucial arrangements were usually based on information and data acquired in the association. It is important to see crucial arrangements as a dynamic, constantly changing process in the current unique age. Whether the process is used to examine previous opportunities and to anticipate future opportunities, the essential arrangements are reinforced by cutting-edge exams and explanatory instruments that use continuous IT development. The key arranging process that utilizes IT devices must incorporate at any rate the accompanying four stages: (1) arranging; (2) introducing a vital thought; (3) calibrating the key thought; (4) building up a key arrangement. The main stage is trailed by two extra stages, in particular the (1) execution stage that changes the key plans into down to earth exercises and the (2) data bolster stage that gives data about the current and future association status (T. Davenport, A. Guha, D. Grewal, and T. Bressgott 2020; El-Nemr, N., Canel-Depitre, B., & Taghipour, A., 2017).

Huge amounts of data are required in these stages to make a complete diagram of the analyzed region and consolidate realities that may adversely influence the arranging procedure. Assessment of the successful execution of showcasing procedures likewise shapes some portion of organizations' vital administration forms. Numerous associations disregard this stage or totally overlook it, which can prompt disappointments in future key arranging. The assessment of the executed key arrangement helps change the dynamic procedure, distinguish inadequacies at all phases of the vital arranging and show steps in future arranging. In the present innovation period information-based instruments ought to be utilized to smooth out the key procedure, increment the odds of a fruitful, result orientated technique usage and improve authoritative adequacy. Based on adequate information volumes and enormous figuring power, current diagnostic apparatuses can anticipate for example customer purchasing conduct, the reaction to item presentation and the plausible accomplishment of a created key arrangement.

The preparing of large information present chances and transformational potential for some ventures. As the volume of information expands, profound learning gets significant, permitting the usage of prescient diagnostic arrangements. Expository instruments of this sort can be made to learn and improve. Informational indexes that structure the contribution for promoting examination can be arranged quickly, in this way sparing weeks, months or now and then long periods of people's manual endeavours. Current publicity has entered the AI and ML periods that greatly alleviate the major associations' procedures and strengthen the crucial dynamics. Connecting advertising examination and progressed investigative apparatuses makes the way for another reality where all can ''inhale life'' keen onequipment and projects by showing them how to learn and in this manner making lives simpler to individuals. Artificial intelligence can possibly be utilized in all aspects of our lives and its present application is only the start (El-NEMR, N., CANEL-DEPITRE, B., & TAGHIPOUR, A., 2021). Choosing the privilege explanatory apparatus that will meet the necessities of information examination is indispensable to guarantee rate of return and the additional estimation of the produced data.

When building up the best advertising procedure the consideration of capable staff ought to be moved from customary logical apparatuses to cutting edge and concentrated diagnostic instruments. This is particularly significant in showcasing, where many possibly applicable measurements should be thought of. Scientific instruments in advertising can possibly:

- Get to the information as vital resources;
- Envision information into clear structures;
- Give a diagram of existing and likely clients;
- Increment the viability of showcasing choices;
- Center around proactivity towards customers;
- Make customized offers to explicit purchasers;
- Adjust the advanced condition to the inclinations of explicit clients;
- Take part continuously conversations with buyers;
- Increment the adequacy of promoting exercises (counting on the web and disconnected correspondence); and
- Center around pointers of organization achievement.

2.2. ML-Based Analytical Tools in Marketing

In order to comprehend and model ML contains various tools that allow a PC or computer to learn. After some time, learning new capabilities will extend the system execution. The rationale for flexible systems is structured by ML devices. Of order to accomplish quantifiable numerical strategies, the mechanical capacities in present data systems include a computerised limit. The extension of advances in programming that capture ML standards hence results in bigger amounts of clever expository systems. Its use not only saves companies substantial costs over the long run, but also simplifies purchasers' lives. A special problem – human or counterfeit – is addressed by the use of neural systems. ML may be considered as a superficial manipulation of information that maintains one data layer. Top to bottom realizing, which is a piece of ML, handles a few layers of information at the same time. In this manner, arrangements grasping top to bottom taking in can get new data from which they make extra layers to be handled along these lines. In view of this methodology, prescient investigation gets conceivable (J. Mark. Res., 2018; Loivet, W., Taghipour, A., & Kang, D. S., 2020).

The use of inside and out learning can uncover connections between factors that were avoided ML. Along these lines, inside and out learning adds to a progressively productive dynamic procedure with entrancing ramifications for hypothesis and business practice. Inside and out learning takes a shot at the rule that the system is taken care of with information, the information is prepared, and the system additionally thinks about other information in its choice. At present, independent vehicles fill in as a delineation (Mahfod, J., Canel-Depitre, B., & Taghipour, A., 2019). The system is given beginning information to process, yet when its reasonable tests and utilization began, more information are gathered, permitting articles to be perceived and reactions created. Hence, notwithstanding the first settings, the system gathers the information it utilizes when settling on different information gathered. The connection among cost and request in the lodging market by taking a gander at online commercials has been inspected (J. Ciuffo, 2019; Merimi, M., & Taghipour, A. 2021; Nadia, E. N., Beatrice, C. D., & Atour, T., 2020).

ML is utilized to distinguish sets of copy commercials that allude to a similar lodging unit. A misleadingly insightful chatbot has been created and conveyed to convey exceptionally exact programmed answers by utilizing an information base and supporting the day in and day out help accessibility of client assistance focuses (contact focuses). The chatbot builds the adequacy of help benefits and robotizes the related procedure in the computerized condition. In order to forecast the perception level of business sites, ML models are constructed. A tilting Hashtag application is developed to provide web-based life business customers, which uses MLs and various techniques (Shin, M., & Taghipour, A., 2021) to build drifting and relevant hashtags for customer content to reach the target audience. A concept was developed and presented using ML to accurately detect the presentation and offer of drugs by illicit internet traffickers through Twitter.

In a further study the information mining, text mining, ML and insights are used to deconstruct customer behaviour on the site and to provide two behaviour patterns which rely on the scheme and number of URLs. A quantitative research investigates the use of enormous information and information by Dubai associations to enhance their customers' knowledge and service, and to improve investor appreciation. The quality of ML and extensive information in anticipation of the events in the portable exchange business while changing their cellular phones was highlighted. Constant Bidding (RTB) as a methodology in show promoting building computerization, combination, and advancement has been broke down (K. Jarek and G. Mazurek, 2019).

An approach to precisely distinguish tweets advertising the unlawful online offer of controlled substances has been created. In order to allow on-line advertisers in the context of "burning'," "spinner" and "blurring" major events combined to understand the importance of the developed online data (Taghipour, A., & Frayret, J. M., 2011a), the created ML model is used for this purpose. It is hypothesised that techniques can segregate customer data with essential accuracy from online writings. Understanding the objective of customers on internet web-based living diversions (for example, for buying a loft, rental a car or travelling somewhere) offers unbelievable possibilities for enhanced promotion. An advanced factual graphical design for arrangement information and a bidirection of ML model based on contingent irregular fields (CRFs). (R. T. Rust, 2020; Taghipour, A., Murat, S., & Huang, P., 2021).

2.3. Sending ML-Based Analytic Toolwithin DigitalizedMarketings

Digitally showcasing being generally measuredlike umbrellas terms, comprisingweb-based promoting, net advertising as well as versatile promoting. It tends to be characterized as showcasing that uses advanced advances (equipment, programming, correspondence advances) for the arrangement of promoting systems. The instruments used in computerized promoting incorporate statistical surveying, surveying, different types of publicizing, internet searcher showcasing, bulletins and online life advertising. Showcasing examination is a characteristic piece of successfully utilizing any of these devices. Each of the three kinds of associations (publicists, organizations, media) need the mindfulness and capacity to work with a lot of information to separate important data and increment the viability of their computerized showcasing activities. It tends to be reasoned that ML can, in light of broad information handling, give the data important to the dynamic procedure of showcasing authorities. The utilization of ML-driven devices into advanced showcasing presents different new difficulties and openings (M. Riikkinen, H. Saarijärvi, P. Sarlin, and I. Lähteenmäki, 2018; Taghipour, A., & Frayret, J. M., 2011b). Among the greatest advantages of utilizing these devices in advertising are:

2.3.1. Optimal Execution

Machines perform consistently at 100% in light of the fact that they can't be upset or occupied.

2.3.2. Faster Dynamic

Machine dynamic time is controlled by the accessible information. After a brisk computation, machines can choose (very quickly. The choice isn't influenced by abstract factors, for example, emotions, individual inclinations, assessments, and so on

2.3.3. Automatization of Unsurprising Exercises

ML can viably robotize routine exercises. For instance, in computerized promoting, ML can help with age of normal reports on publicizing efforts in online networking showcasing.

2.3.4. Reducing Blunder Rates

Dispensing with mistakes ordinarily brought about by human elements. Machines play out an undertaking by continually following the predefined method.

2.3.5. Digital Collaborators

Individual human colleagues are now normally utilized. ML-driven systems can deal with confused errands and upgrade every day schedules (J. Sterne 2017, Taghipour, A., 2014).

2.3.6. Exploring Regions Inaccessible to People

In numerous zones an individual can't play out the necessary undertakings for different reasons. For instance, people can't plunge into the most profound territories of seas or procedure a lot of information that are produced each moment over the net. Machines may be adapted to virtually every scenario and even the most difficult quantitative factual operations can be handled by processing. Execution of ML applied to showcasing logical instruments has no undeniable disservices. Be that as it may, contingent upon the sort of hardware, there are a few concerns or constraining components for its powerful use:

2.3.7. Creativity

A significant part of the choices and utilization of promoting depends on inventiveness. Imagination brings about joining a few boundaries that are local to people, with feelings, instinct, and sympathy having a critical impact. These three segments will be extremely hard to reproduce by machines (J. Paschen, J. Kietzmann, and T. C. Kietzmann, 2019; Taghipour, A., Glaa, B., & Zoghlami, N., 2014).

2.3.8. Moral and Moral Standards

It is the ability to make people human, to convey sentiments, to understand morality and ethics. It is questionable if machines are never able to do this or can be thought of in later stages. There are valid concerns regarding whether machines are now operating on a valid basis for individuals and inside moral and good limits when the advancement proceeds (Q. André et al., 2018).

2.3.9. Consumer Inclinations

Clients would prefer consistently not to collaborate with a robot or programming. It is in this manner anticipated that, sooner rather than later, the requirement for association with a person will stay particular, with shoppers having more prominent trust in such correspondence.

2.3.10. ML instruments can't be workingexcept human intercession:

within the up and coming 10years, human personalities may be in any case be expected to work with ML machines as well as create as well as enhance such innovation (G. Stalidis, D. Karapistolis, and A. Vafeiadis, 2015; Taghipour, A., Abed, M., & Zoghlami, N., 2015).

2.3.11. Algorithms Cannot be Right

Choices dependent on MLs' numerical counts and measurements can bring about wrong activities taken, due to staff directions or information. Any propelled data systems are expected fundamentally to serve individuals. As people groups' necessities change and advance after some timings, thismay bring about ML-related instruments couldn't giving the ideal outcomes in the current arrangement. Robotized reactions to online life demand or consequently created limits if there should arise an occurrence of misery with the buying procedure can fill in as models (Предприемачество, 2018; Taghipour, A., 2018).

2.3.12. ML as Well as Business

Such techniques which may in part supplant human working force within computerized showcasing. For instance, programmed transferring of posts via web-based networking media, computerized article peruse support, and so on. In any case, noted these systems may not perform appropriately without human help (H. Conick, 2017; Taghipour, A., 2020).

3. RESEARCH GAP AND AIMS

The last study in AI and ML focused on how systems and applications that are driven by ML can be improved in the light of explicit inquiries, solving problems, enhancing dynamics, understanding target markets, predicting shoppers' conduct and increasing interchange capabilities, promoting new dispatch of items, smoothing up advanced inside publicity procedures or improved grooves. In any event, the investigation failed to investigate and talk about the problems of choice and reception by partners, including publicity organisations and other promoters of these systematic gadgets driven by ML. Almost no is thought about showcasing experts' information on, and mentality towards these apparatuses, just as the reception and usage of the devices for both key and operational administration.

This exploration hole shapes the establishment of the examination portrayed here. A more profound investigation of significant assets and work with optional information uncovered that various data systems that grasp the standards of ML are accessible to showcasing administrators and organizations. In any case, these organizations and people have been delayed in receiving and using these systems. This examination centersaround distinguishing the purposes behind the moderate utilization of ML in computerized advertising and proposing potential arrangements. The primary point of the examination is to recognize potential uses of ML diagnostic devices in the promoting field. Auxiliary targets are to

- Research the job of systematic apparatuses during the time spent getting ready, executing, and assessing computerized showcasing procedures;
- Decide how chosen advanced promoting elements use advertising investigation and logical instruments;
- Distinguish the degree of familiarity with important phrasing, for example, large information, information the executives, Machine LearningotherwiseArtificial Intelligence; also
- Discover how ML-rooted devices are utilized in the computerized advertising condition.

4. METHODOLOGY

4.1. Exploration Types as Well as Samples Selections

Qualitating examination, utilizing technique for inside and out meetings, was utilized to pick up understanding into the manner in which ML is basically utilized in promoting. Computerized presentations of specialists who spoke to (1) publicist companies; (2) delegate organisations; and (3) media space organisations in Slovakia were selected as members of the conference with the following important models in mind: The interviewee is a director of the Pay per Click (PPC) or Search Engine Optimization (SEO) or Real-time Bidding (RTB) campaign improvement or enhancement, who has worked for a number of years at advanced promotion for all levels. A total of nine responders, for example, encountered three professionals from each of these three meetings. Discoveries via inside and out meetings demonstrate the current circumstance in the region of utilizing ML-driven scientific devices by associations that are dynamic in the field of computerized showcasing. Quantitative exploration, utilizing a normalized survey, was directed to affirm the discoveries and increase more bits of knowledge into the distinguished issues.

4.2. In-Depth Interviews

The procedure of inside and out meetings comprised of three stages: (1) planning; (2) usage; (3) information handling. The readiness stage included characterizing the meeting structure, defining beginning guidelines for respondents, planning research questions, giving sound account procedures, and choosing an appropriate domain for the meetings. The evaluated length of the meeting was 60 minutes. Preceding each meeting, the respondent was approached to sign an assent structure. The meetings depended on a pre-characterized structure and directed. In any case, respondents were allowed the chance to propose extra points and offer remarks that originate from the progression of the discussion. Prior to the meetings, members were mentioned to communicate their emotions and convictions and to give just obvious data. They were offered the confirmation that there are no off-base responses, that answers are viewed as classified, that reactions won't be connected to people, and that Specifically for research reasons the auditory chronicle of the meeting and the prepared notes made by the specialist shall be used. The interviewees were also taught that the results of the test might be presented in composed and spoken structures.

Notwithstanding the underlying and last guidelines, the meeting convention contained 19 open inquiries. Afew scenarios, discussion went into territories which aren't recorded within readied situation, along these lines distinguishing new chances and dangers related with the potential outcomes of promoting examination and ML-driven expository apparatuses. The inquiries were separated into the accompanying four headings:

4.2.1. General Data

The explanation for this portion was that they said that the responses fulfilled the determination rules set out in the system and characterised the key exercise technique.

4.2.2. Market investigation as well as explanatory apparatuses:

The segment inspected the observation and genuine utilization of promoting examination and scientific instruments by and by.

4.2.3. Awareness Level in Regards to Huge Information and Information the Board

Questions around there inspected the degree of mindfulness and suspicions related with large information and their use in advertising.

2.4. ML as well as AI Useful Applications

Respondent communicated insight as well as feelings onto difficulties regarding Machine Learning innovation as well as the applications prospects in the field of computerized showcasing.

4.3. Questionnaires

The consequences of the meetings were utilized as reason for building up a survey to confirm the outcomes on a bigger example. The poll contained 15 inquiries: 11 shut finished inquiries, three rate scales questionings, as well asone opened/finished inquiry. To arrive at the particular gathering of advertising pros, the poll was circulated online by means of four unique channels.

Figure 1. Processing about preparations, implementations, as well as evaluations regarding digitalized market strategies

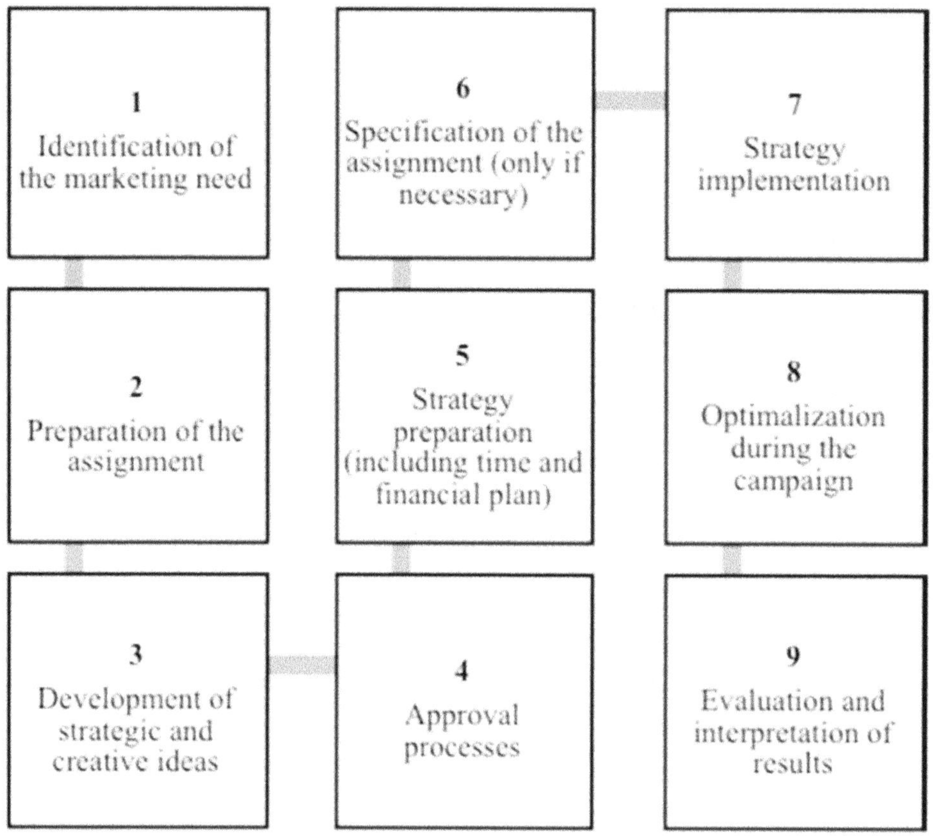

Sum of 58 replies were studied using enlightening insights from sophisticated exhibition authorities and C-level executives from firms engaged in computerised promotion. The discussions took place within and outside of the quantitative exploration programme between 15 June and 30 July 2018. The survey was conducted on the four channels indicated earlier between 06 August and 15 August 2018 and was then carried out shortly. The results were collected from 21 August to 10 September 2018. After the information assortment was completed, information was processed and evaluated on the findings and the readiness to explore results were carried out (finished on 14 October 2018).

5. FINDINGS

5.1. The Process of Preparation, Implementation and Evaluation of Digital Marketing Strategies

In view of the data acquired, a model of the planning procedure, the usage and the assessment of computerized showcasing systems (Figure 1) was created. Office, media, and sponsors' laborers are to a great extent following the previously mentioned nine-advance model. Be that as it may, various advances were accentuated by various respondents. In view of their reactions, the accompanying advances are considered as generally significant for various associations:

5.1.1. Agencies

Steps 3, 5, 7, 8, and 9 are the most urgent. During the time spent promoting correspondence, organizations are the agents of customer assignments (for this situation, publicists), so the means to plan, actualize, upgrade, and assess advertising efforts are generally significant for them.

5.1.2. Media

They cause to notice stages 7, 8, and 9 and give media spaces all through the entire procedure. Their fundamental intrigue is to accomplish acceptable following outcomes, (for example, the quantity of flag ads, mouse activities, and so forth.). Thusly, the means of actualizing, streamlining, and assessing efforts are generally significant for the media. On the off chance that the battle accomplishes great outcomes, the likelihood of future requests from the office or sponsor increments.

5.1.3. Advertisers

Steps 1, 2, 4, and 9 were for the most part talked about. A particular brand item should obviously characterize what it plans to accomplish with a showcasing effort and effectively decipher its objectives to the office or media that are the agent of the correspondence procedure. Another significant advance for the sponsor is the assessment of the crusade, giving important data about future showcasing correspondence systems. The subsequent quantitative examination affirmed that advertising investigation and work with programming systematic instruments fundamentally influence the way toward getting ready promoting techniques. The five most unequivocal elements for creating promoting procedures are: 1) know-how from past battles (85%); 2) showcasing examination (considers and accessible information) (79%), diagnostic programming apparatuses (64%), emotional dynamic – 28%, genuine beliefs and experience (26%). Obviously, information and instruments help to separate important data from respondents and are seen as basic during the time spent creating promoting systems.

5.2. View of Marketing Analysis and Analytical Tools

In the second arrangement of inquiries in the top to bottom meetings, the aim was to discover how respondents see showcasing examinations and expository devices and how they actualize these instruments in computerized advertising forms in their organization (Taghipour, A., & Beneteau-Piet, C. 2020; Taghipour, A., & Merimi, M., 2021). The main inquiry concentrated in transit respondents use showcasing examination during the time spent arranging and executing computerized promoting procedures. The accompanying remarks represent the circumstance around there:

- Data about showcasing effort target gathering,
- Portion size location,
- Data about contender promoting exercises,
- Current patterns in computerized advertising in the neighbourhood showcase.

Figure 2. Outline of the most regularly utilized diagnostic devices in advanced showcasing
Source (Hubspot)

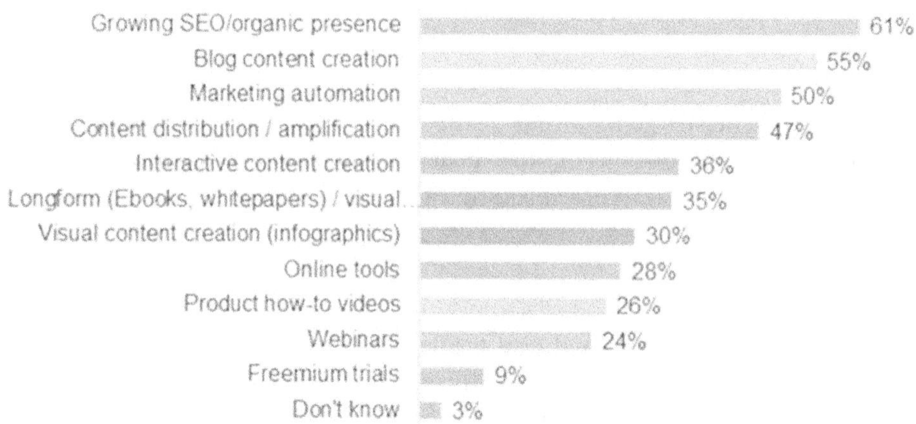

- Location of important watchword search volume,
- Data about potential promoting correspondence intercession,
- Forecast of recurrence of showing the ideal showcasing message to the client,
- Segment data about the objective gathering, and
- Recognizable proof of circumstances where buys are generally normal.

The discoveries represented that showcasing investigation fills in as a wellspring of data and are utilized by respondents for extremely significant zones of getting ready and actualizing computerized promoting methodologies. This was trailed by the inquiry: ''What are the wellsprings of this data?'' The motivation behind this inquiry was to check where the respondents are looking and getting to the essential data. The appropriate responses appeared in Figure 2 were for the most part rehashed: The term ''wellspring of showcasing data'' can be viewed as any data about the market, section, item, target gathering or rivalry that has been gotten from inward sources and from paid or unpaid outsider assets. It is critical to understand that, in spite of the wellspring of this data, it is typically important to work with investigative devices that help during the time spent gathering, sectioning, assessing and deciphering the gathered information (Tliche, Y., Taghipour, A., & Canel-Depitre, B., 2019). When asked the following study inquiry: ''Do you utilize scientific instruments during the time spent making advertising techniques?'' all respondents addressed yes. Any action on the Internet is quantifiable through computerized advancements and the gathered outcomes are utilized to settle on increasingly successful choices in future exercises.

Advanced promoting experts are very much aware of this and they use quantifiability as one of the most significant upper hands of their organization. The different diagnostic instruments accessible available can be incorporated into the arrangement, usage and assessment of computerized advertising efforts. The decision of the particular instrument is dependent upon business needs. The inquiry: ''Please show what devices you use and what reason do they serve?'' started conversations about the most generally utilized explanatory apparatuses and affirmed that the promoting offices center around execution, while media organizations are centered around assessment, and publicist are centered around appointing advanced advertising procedures. Figure 3 records the announced systematic apparatuses, a short particular, and the element that utilizes the device.

The apparatuses are positioned by recurrence of event. The rundown contains scientific devices that are most every now and again utilized by respondents. Huge numbers of the referenced instruments are all inclusive and their utilization was affirmed by respondents from every one of the three elements (office, media, publicist) (Tliche, Y., Taghipour, A., & Canel-Depitre, B., 2021). Every respondent consistently utilizes a normal of 16 explanatory instruments with scientific capacities that spread practically all regions of advanced advertising. Respondents from every one of the three elements said that 60% of the way toward making and actualizing an advanced showcasing system is finished by explanatory apparatuses and information, while 40% is done through exercises, for example, conceptualizing, making commercials, making visuals, and so forth. All accept that different devices are utilized rarely, or the interviewee didn't refer to them because of the restricted time committed to the meeting.

The significance of information examination in promoting was affirmed on the bigger example. One of the inquiries in the survey decided if showcasing administrators see advanced promoting as a science or a workmanship. 40% of respondents chose the principal alternative, 19% chose the second, 41% were impartial, perceiving that both these definitions are valid and in balance. Another inquiry posed to how information are gathered and prepared in organizations. Just 9% of organizations don't gather significant information on clients and markets however they are intending to begin doing as such. 71% of organizations are gathering information inside. Of these, 16% uses outsider to help them with their preparing and examination. 19% of organizations utilize an outsider accomplice to likewise gather the information for their benefit. 2% of the respondents were uncertain how information are overseen in their organizations. Promoting chiefs are completely mindful that, in the present condition and markets, information assume a significant job in advanced advertising.

5.3. Level of Awareness of Big Data And ML

The top to bottom meetings distinguished respondents' recognition viewing terms, for example, enormous information and information the executives and how they see these terms. A portion of the remarks were:

5.3.1. Big Data

5.3.1.1. Respondent 1

''I consider the to be information as an immense measure of information from various sections of the online condition that organizations should gather and assess inside in light of the fact that that is the eventual fate of working together in the Internet condition.''

5.3.1.2. Respondent 2

''They are broadly enormous information that is crude, not divided at all, not handled at all.''

5.3.1.3. Respondent 3

''Every organization has some measure of information or has a few information accessible in some structure. Large information is an industry that forms these extraordinary sums of information, and inside this product accessible information are imagined.''

5.3.1.4. Respondent 4

''Countless Excel spreadsheets with a lot of information. High volumes of information are being gathered these days, yet when individuals don't have a clue how to utilize them, it is smarter to gather them less, yet to know the motivation behind their utilization.

5.3.1.5. Respondent 5

''Processing a lot of information utilizing various databases. Huge information are a generally excellent beginning and its preparing and understanding will be utilized to make AI as one of the ways to deal with advanced showcasing.''

Figure 3. Diagram of the most ordinarily utilized scientific apparatuses in advanced advertising

Analytical tool	**Specification**	**Agency**	**Media**	**Advertiser**
Google Analytics	An analytical tool that monitors users' activities on website.	✓	✓	✓
Google Data Studio	Visualizes collected data into graphs and infographics.	✓	✓	✓
Google AdWords	Advertising system for banner advertising and search engine advertising.	✓	✓	✓
Firebase	Provides information about using mobile and web applications.		✓	
Screaming-frog	A web browser that provides information about SEO settings.	✓	✓	
Facebook Ads Manager	Facebook social network advertising system.	✓	✓	✓
Facebook Insights	An internal analytical tool that includes profile and user information.	✓	✓	✓

These replies were fully or not entirely accepted by the four interviewers. The notion of vast information was acknowledged and understood by all responders. All of them were willing to describe the phrase in their own terms as, for example, a lot of previously natural facts and information. The next stage is to fragment and "understand" the huge information in each individual structure. All respondents agreed that it is important to abuse large-scale information, which is the ultimate destination of computerised promotion and many distinct companies. The respondents were also asked how the term "information of the board," strongly associated with huge information, was understood. Some of the comments were made:

5.3.2. Data Management

5.3.2.1. Respondent 1

''Data the board is an instrument to deal with this information.''

5.3.2.2. Respondent 2

''It is through information the executives that this information can be handled and changed over for their potential benefit. Since having information is incredible, everybody can have it, yet the inquiry is the way an individual can change that enormous information into something explicit. Step by step directions for utilising them (Vosooghidizaji, M., Taghipour, A., & Canel-Depitre, B., 2020), whether they can use them to focus, like our organisation, to look at or to focus negatively on or can accurately detect that there is still no super-structure in a certain treatment.''

5.3.2.3. Respondent 3

''You have a stage where the information is put away. Information ought to be given importance, rationale and assessed in like manner. This is upheld by programming that take a shot at information the executive's standards.''

5.3.2.4. Respondent 4

''Finding an association between information. Their right arrangement. Huge information are a fridge and information the executives.''

5.3.2.5. Respondent 5

''Data the board is a piece of working with enormous information.''

reactions of 4 different respondent halfway/totally bolstered such remarks. Gathered data uncovers that respondents some comprehension of information the board, yet they are significantly less sure with huge information. About portion of respondents see information the executives as an instrument for handling enormous information. Others either befuddled the ideas of large information and information the board, believed their substance to be the equivalent, or couldn't remark on the term as they don't get it. All respondents concurred that these days, one should focus on information the board (Vosooghidizaji, M., Taghipour, A., & Canel-Depitre, B., 2022). In any case, many conceded that extra instruction is required on the grounds that to completely grasp the open doors requires huge information. When asked how respondents and their organizations manage information, most respondents demonstrated that they utilize their own investigative devices or outsider information. Just one of the interviewees announced no action around there.

All respondents see information as a key resource that makes upper hand for the organization. Respondents who utilize systematic devices to recover information, fundamentally get the data from deals reports and chronicled advertising efforts. A few organizations secure information from outsiders, including colleagues and unreservedly accessible databases. In spite of the fact that it was not the basic role of the inquiry, the meetings uncovered that offices depend on outsider information, media organizations depend principally on their own information, and increasingly dynamic publicists utilize their very own mix information and information from outsiders. Despite seeing enormous potential for such movements in the future, a less dynamic promoter has not worked with information yet. The survey further influenced the opinions of respondents on the biggest obstacles to the use of information for improved presentations:

5.3.2.6. High Costs

Seven out of nine (78%) respondents felt that it is highly expensive to develop and update material in the section. Only a worldwide agency with an extensive turnover or a reasonable spending plan may pay for the Slovak show's fees. All respondents believed that, regardless of the cost of knowledge, such speculation had a relatively short compensation period. The respondents also expressed the idea that it was easier to build an information company from the start than to merge information arrangements into existing organisations, often non-bending.

5.3.2.7. Time Utilization

Most respondents knew that their present company or a prior boss was supported by modern systems. All respondents (100%) agreed that the means to update new techniques is slow and overcomes a pre-competitive phase on a regular basis. In view of their prior experience, respondents are concerned by the tiresome use of prepared approaches.

5.3.2.8. High Weight on Know-How

Digital advertising is an industry typically young, requiring much more fresh information, therefore compressing workers' teaching and training. Information-driven methods are a lot younger industry implemented in the modern globe of innovation. In order to combine innovation, numerical data and the worlds of advertising, new specialists from this field are necessary. This combination of skill is typically scarce, and people with such expertise in view of their highly learned value are expensive for the company. It might also be arranged for HR to educate, which so calls for time and costs.

5.3.2.9. Limited Slovak Advertise

Answers see the size and imaginable results of the nearby market as one of the problems in information execution. On the world, only scientific effort and information preparation are devoted to organisations. These offices go about as outsiders that give information preparing administrations to their customers or they sell legitimately gathered and handled information bundles. As per the interviewees, the presence of such an organization is ridiculous in Slovakia, on the grounds that the advanced advertising substances don't right now have the necessary assets to take care of the expenses of utilizing such an information organization. Another difficulty is the size of the population of Slovakia, the internet infiltration and additional costs linked to the constant refreshment of information collected, of which optimality routinely is linked to a treat that monitors data from the last 30 days alone.

The inside and out inquiries questions investigated the current utilization of showcasing examination and scientific instruments. While discussing scientific devices, the respondents guided the discussion into processing computerization, ML, as well as AI, becausepractical to advanced showcasing. Another question to be asked was: "What do you think about the AI term? Try to distinguish the AI and ML contrasts." In particular, respondents were told while submitting this question that their feelings and convictions were analysed, giving little attention to their education. While respondents in earlier queries have typically been certain of their replies, they need to be able to describe their answers more and their replies have been vague and contradicting. This is shown in the following reactions:

5.3.3. Artificial Intelligence

5.3.3.1. Respondent 1

''A machine, a component that thinks. It has a processor and accomplishes something.''

5.3.3.2. Respondent 2

''AI is something that is modified by an individual and accomplishes something that depends on certain standards that the man sets.''

5.3.3.3. Respondent 3

''AI is a superstructure, it's a Mercedes among ML. It can gain not just from contextual investigations that somebody gives it, however it can likewise instruct itself.''

5.3.3.4. Respondent 4

''AI ought to have the option to tackle issues all alone.''

5.3.3.5. Respondent 5

''AI is a calculation that sooner or later begins to settle on choices dependent on countless inferred, aberrant sources of info. Given that it is beginning to enter contributions starting here all alone, everyone can essentially discuss insight.'' In the present time, all respondents have previously experienced and think it is vital. However, the replies were different, indistinguishable and confusing. All respondents grossly understood the qualities, hardly no perception of the phrase with its written description was entirely trustworthy. The correct answers were not received or the essence of AI was only captured in part. In addition, the characteristics of the word ML were included.

5.3.4. Machine Learning

5.3.4.1. Respondent 1

''It can advance. It can learn and create.''

5.3.4.2. Respondent 2

"It learns on the basis of what it accomplishes, and then improves its workouts, more and more regularly. The first stage is to have AI and integrate ML with it so that AI can learn better, e.g. to talk to you based on certain facts.''

5.3.4.3. Respondent 3

''ML ought to be a procedure by which the procedure is improving here and there, that implies, it ought to have the option to create better outcomes after various arrangements.''

5.3.4.4. Respondent 4

''ML is increasingly unsurprising and just reacts to straightforwardly set information sources. Nonetheless, its particularity is that it has gotten a lot of information, or that it ''encountered'' many re-enacted circumstances, making its yield progressively precise and applicable.''

All participants acknowledged ML as an important feature of AI. Moreover, most responders made the point that ML is a kind of process which collects vast measurements of information on which the system is based. Again, the relevant answers are only partially in accordance with the definition stated in the writing. The AI and ML principles were confused by two of the responders. The interviewees made a far longer effort to figure their answers, in contrast with different inquiries. At the point when all posed the extra inquiry: ''Where did you catch wind of the referenced terms just because?'' most respondents referenced proficient advertising gatherings where the theme is as of now exceptionally well known.

Different reactions included Internet assets, articles on showcasing and innovation sites, messages after wilful membership to news via particular site as well as different education relaxing recordings. It follows that interviewees know the terms and conditions and have encountered them everywhere and thought about what they are talking about. The use of AI and ML for sophisticated kinds of showcasing and sentiments of interviewers were the focus of several concerns on how this application is portrayed. All interviewers agreed that AI and ML, in particular for innovation organised businesses, have unbelievable potential for enhanced showing and that process computerization and the ability to deal with plenty of information are the key issues.

Advanced showcasing industries utilize computerized innovation solely to process yields. The work is completed on PCs and tablets, including managerial exercises, correspondence and imaginative exercises, for example, drawing illustrations, sites and standards structure, extra photograph altering, and so on. In any event, conceptualizing, conference as well as orally yield isbeing recorded within electric configuration. The particular work of specialists permits an enormous piece of these procedures to be robotized. A few representatives are as of now being substituted via computerized programming for routine exercises, for example, getting ready normal reports, conveying produced content, paying membership support on informal communities, and even somewhat speaking with clients by means of email or robotized reactions on interpersonal organization.

Respondents saw the highest AI and ML capacity in robotic exercise and procedural systematisation. Computerized support is an informative and inventive combination of labour. As the responses stated, robots and programming are gradually taking the logical portion and persons would have to devote more time to creative work and vital dynamics. In addition, participants received some information on using an AI-based instrument in their business as part of the quantitative study that followed.

The examination uncovered that, despite the fact that the vast majority of the respondents comprehended what AI means and how it tends to be used (59%), a huge gathering of showcasing administrators despite everything need fundamental information about AI or have questions of its value. 31% of respondents are not fully certain about AI and 10% just have minimal information about the word AI. The three most frequent replies received were: (1) the robotization process (81 percent); (2) the optimization of advertising efforts in operations (71 percent); and (3) the data mining, including the connectivity of various systemic devices (52 percent). At the point when similar inquiries was posed, yet not constrained to their own organization, the main decision was the equivalent.

5.4. Utilizing ML in Practice

The interviewees were asked, in top-to-bottom meetings: "Can you classify diagnostic devices based on key AI standards?" In response to the respondents' comments, regular reference was made to accompanying devices: Google (AdWords, Search); Google Data Studio, YouTube; Ada Manager, Facebook; visit apps; automated purchase programming; Echobox; on line robot lessons; Mailchimp. Answerers are aware of sophisticated ML or AI-dependent display devices. Notwithstanding referencing advertising devices, respondents additionally recorded organizations that create designs cards, self-rulingly oversaw vehicles, and text interpreters. When solicited which from these instruments are utilized in their organization, respondents recorded indistinguishable apparatuses from in the past inquiry.

The reactions demonstrate that the instruments that depend on the standards of ML will for the most part influence the accompanying territories of computerized showcasing: • notice systems and the administration of notice crusades, • robotization of announcing forms, • halfway computerization of correspondence (particularly in composed structure, for example, messages or talk correspondence). Expository instruments can be utilized to recover information from the previously mentioned regions. This disposes of the requirement for human mediation and the product arrangements can perform characterized activities self-sufficiently. In regions where AI is hard to apply, respondents consider: • innovative procedures, • assembling and keeping up associations with colleagues. These zones for the most part work with information in a restricted or quite certain structure. These days, the improvement of thoughts or drawing pictures can likewise be robotized. Be that as it may, results produced by machines will presumably never be equivalent to those created from human conceptualizing. PCs will most likely always be unable to be enthusiastic, which altogether impacts the outcome (at times positively).

Another inquiry in the subjective review was: ''What exercises does your organization plan for ML sooner rather than later?'' If the respondent was ineffectively mindful of scientific apparatuses, showcasing investigation, huge information, information the board, and so forth and the respondent's organization bolsters the sending of ML-driven devices just barely, truth be told, extremely essential or no exercises are arranged. On the off chance that the respondents were completely mindful of the themes examined and works in a creative organization, the ML plans were all around created. Among the most regular zones where the respondents' organizations are arranging such exercises are: • report mechanization, • connecting a few showcasing investigative instruments, • assortment of information produced from promoting exercises, • robotization of the handling of gathered information, • advanced substance creations. The final question was: "Is it possible in future to replace human job with machines? If this is the case, by whatever means will it be shown?' Everyone interviewed agreed that human labour cannot be replaced without doubt by machinery and more likely than not. Be that as it may, there will in any case be territories where machines and mechanized programming won't have the option to completely control and oversee.

As indicated by the respondents, substitution will for the most part influence regions that work with information, just as monotonous work, (for example, week after week or month to month announcing of crusade results). Representatives who have done this tedious task in the past will have the choice of offering additional opportunities in the advanced showcase situation for vital and innovative movement. When the advanced promotion rate was requested to be replaced by machines within five years, the base measurement is 50% and the extreme is 95%. After the subjective examination, the poll aimed to detect the obstacles and hazards of ML and AI in the computerised promotion of ML-based apparatuses and the expected future work of this sector.

5.5. System for Success in Adopting ML within Digitalized Markets

The analysis and translation of results from both subjective and quantitative investigation have enabled the development of a system that aims to encourage the usage and selection of sophisticated ML-based diagnostic equipment. The system has two main segments: 1) enablers and executives, for example, who add to the environment and conditions when such a business may be launched and successfully completed, and 2) process map, such as a guidance for a four-stage process (Figure 4). The nonappearance of the empowering agent as well as following the recommended way may adversely influence the accomplishment of ML-driven apparatuses' appropriation. Right off the bat, the task needs top administration support. Because of its character (cost, cross-departmental reach and so forth.), reception of ML instruments can't be sought after without top chiefs' responsibility. There have been situations where ventures filled by standard representatives and lower level of the board were effective. Be that as it may, when all is said in done, a top-base driven inventive atmosphere is required for such complex venture to succeed. The organization's chiefs ought to likewise go about as pioneers who know about the significance of nonstop improvement, the commitment of definite investigation to the business and performance of their venture groups. They ought to present thoughts, receive new arrangements and test them.

Figure 4. Block diagram to successfully adopt ML into digitalized markets

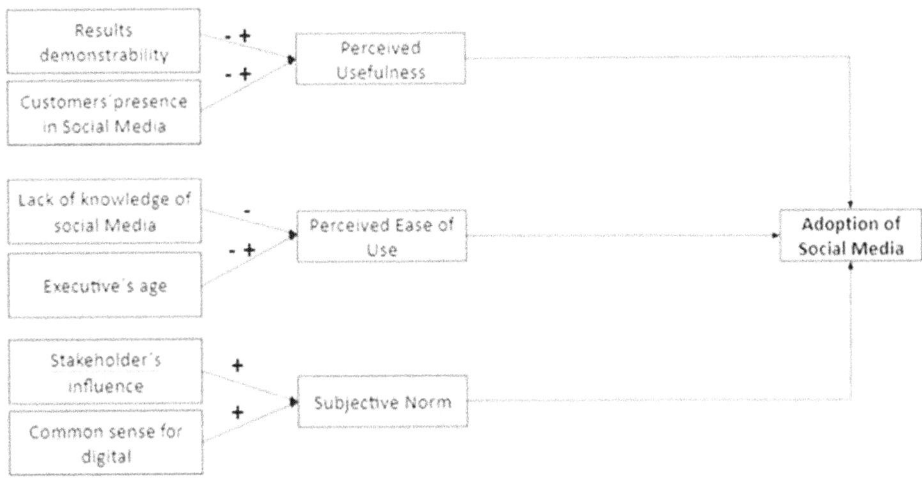

Furthermore, presenting creative arrangements, measures, and instruments should be inserted in the organization culture and associated with its seriousness and procedure effectiveness. Thirdly, it must be understood that progress structures the basis of its compulsory performance. A skilful CIO and other administrators at the C-level should always have a strong understanding of late mechanical developments and its commercial focals. It is favourable if the organisation has an in-house IT group with qualified experts and engineers and has established consistent and practical associations. Ultimately, the organization needs to cultivate visit and nitty gritty utilization of information for conveying its administrations, breaking down the effect of advertising methodologies, and for interior administration. Without this part, the activity to robotize information serious procedures and announcing would not be legitimate by hard information, proposing enormous time reserve funds and adequacy helps.

The procedure map (Figure 5) plots the stages and important strides for presenting mechanization of advanced promoting procedures and ML-driven investigative instruments into organizations. Following the procedure guide will control the association through the phases of the venture to focus on every essential viewpoint, empowering the minimization of hazard and expanding the opportunity of undertaking achievement. The procedures of usage and reception of ML-based explanatory instruments in advanced promoting are remembered for one of four primary stages. At the heart of the process map is the identifiable evidence of periodic, time-consuming forms that are mostly strengthened in the area of information research utilising the intensity of ML by clever programming arrangements. The procedure map expands on the information created by this exploration. The execution procedure, as sketched out in Figure 3, begins with the Education stage.

The hypothetical need to know how to use ML and AI to promote prevents organisations from reflecting on the progress made. It is advised that organisations collect and gain know-how.4 conceivably significant and open gatherings of information assets have been distinguished. Quality writing from checked companion explored sources ought to be utilized to normally channel off base or deceiving content. Advertising supervisors are used to taking an interest in meetings and talk to a major source of information. Moreover, important information may be discovered on the online newspapers, video blogs, foundations' sites, and affiliations and their newsletters from the open web assets. Last but not least, several large, instructional, free and paid, open-line courses may be employed for information research, ML and AI by the essential employees.

The audit stage will begin with the distinctive evidence of processes which spend a lot of time on crucial employees. These methods can begin at any of the nine stages of computerised promotional methodology use and evaluations (Figure 1) are commonly associated with breaking down a lot of information. This investigation brings about the arrangement computerized showcasing efforts, understanding the conduct of customers, their response towards the correspondence message, items, and, when all is said in done, their inclinations. The distinct techniques should be classified as innovative or periodic. At now, ML's capacity to diagnose instruments resides in the roboticization of lengthy, routinely ineffective periodical exposure processes carried out by individuals. Each accepted method is disassembled in a grouping to individual breakthroughs. Then, behaviour and dynamic instances are detected.

These speak to the skill of every representative when managing the procedure, for instance the sources of info the person in question thinks about while creating a periodical exhibition report. Additionally, the inclinations of end clients of the item, the customer, should be recognized and thought of. At long last, before moving to the following stage, all information sources that are utilized in each procedure are distinguished and firmly broke down. A large portion of the stages would have their own APIs which can be utilized when building up the product arrangement. The Design stage begins with settling on the choice whether to include outer specialists and outsiders all the while. Following the group creation, the way toward planning, creating and discharging the product begins. Some of the time, existing items and arrangements may get picked and actualized, in different events this might should be altered and incorporated.

Figure 5. Periodic processing's through ML-based analytic tools

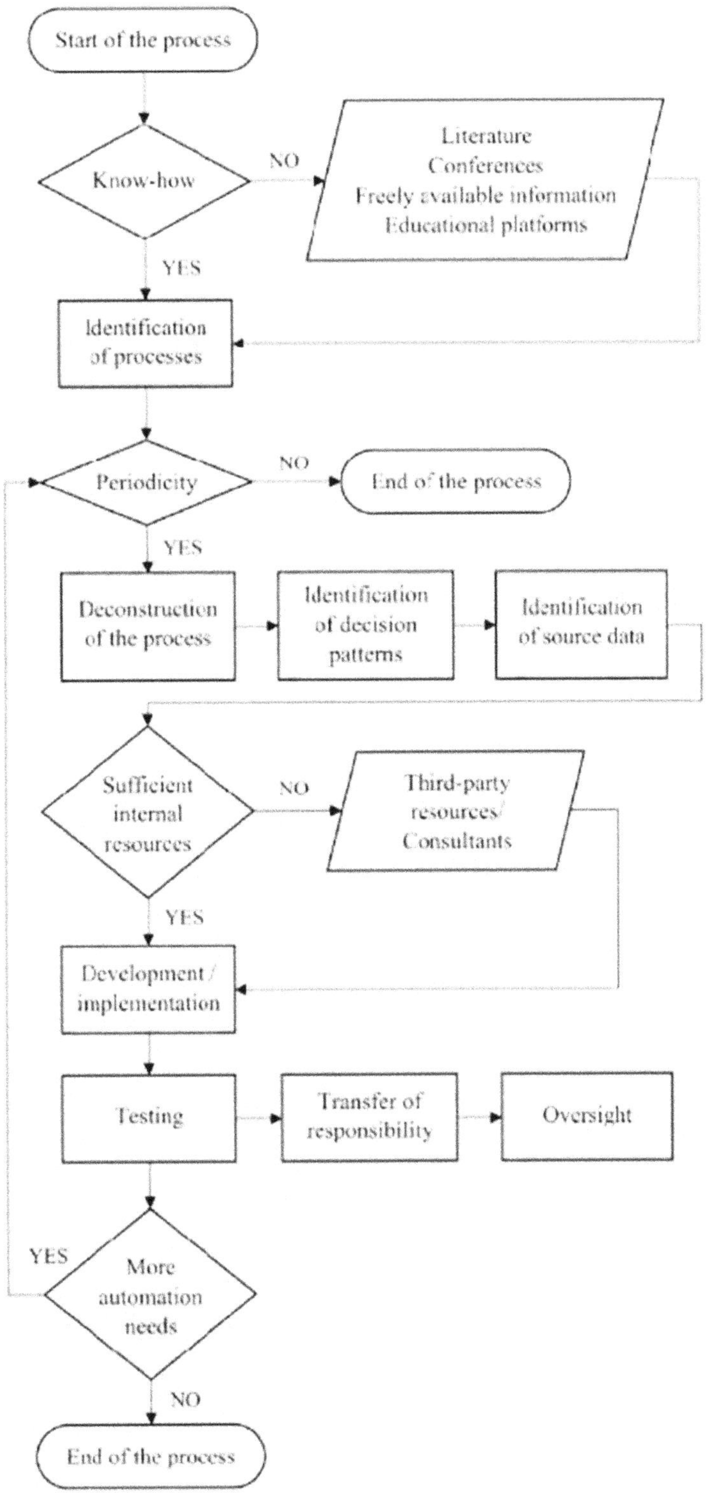

In other circumstances, the customer progress must satisfy the necessary requirements. The new arrangements must be tried and the task of using them transferred to devoted groups in the deployment phase. Supervisors should monitor their use, resolve and resolve future problems and address plausible ideas for improvement. In the case that in the audit phases further procedures which need to be considered and robotized have been drawn out, the procedure returns to assess if they are intermittent. It would also bode good to make them computer.

6. RESULT AND DISCUSSION

Based on all the acceptable answers, everyone can clearly say that examining is the basis on which to develop and execute a publicity approach. Each of the nine respondents confirmed that they work in a very almost consistent manner with information and employ an information examination. All responders agreed that no further steps would be taken without data collected from the research. The test and the logical device used to supply information is a basic component of preparedness and performance in stages 2 to 9. This is illustrated by the model (see figure 1).

Respondent affirmed reliance regarding advertisers onto promoting examination as well as logical devices, sincedata underpins dynamic in the advancement of digitalmarketing techniques. The expository apparatuses fill in as the primary wellspring of data for showcasing examination, on which advertising administrators base their key choices. Working with explanatory devices has numerous points of interest, for example, a diagram of contender exercises and market mapping; quickening the dynamic procedure; plausibility of bringing inner information into outsider expository instruments; probability of perception of acquired information; rich focusing on capacities; moment accessibility of data; the capacity to follow continuous information in progressing efforts; the capacity to distinguish space for upgrading progressing forms; the exactness of the watched boundaries; conceivable outcomes of target bunch division by social profiles; regularly helped diagnostic apparatus execution or natural UI (Yang, S., Taghipour, A., & Canel-Depitre, B., 2017).

Then again respondents alluded to inconveniences of utilizing these apparatuses, for example, information access can be constrained in explicit scientific devices (some expository devices require extra charges for full information get to); the execution of logical instruments is regularly costly; off base information (erroneously estimated) prompts distorted choices; the right utilization of systematic devices presses extra expertise, along these lines creating expensive extra staff preparing; the usage of diagnostic devices is frequently a confounded and tedious procedure; numerous explanatory devices use tests of respondents dependent on which picked up data win over the entire market (regularly it is sketchy whether an example is agent); diverse investigative devices utilize various measurements that are regularly not good with one another and extra figuring's are expected to accomplish a rundown result; the measurements are regularly balanced, as per who possesses the scientific device; the nonappearance of a complete perspective on the outcomes accomplished over every expository device utilized.

The conversation about the utilization of information and enormous information for showcasing examination can be summed up in the accompanying proclamation: huge organizations in the Slovak market will oversee and utilize information inside their exclusively evolved IT systems. This has been the consequences of headways in the innovative prospects of information situated methodologies and the diminishing expenses for the turn of events and execution of own product arrangements. Independent companies, then again, will likely not have enough cash to pay for the custom turn of events. The choice of executing normalized arrangements and applications can likewise demonstrate troublesome because of the decent variety of advanced showcasing exercises.

7. CONCLUSION AND IMPLICATIONS

In view of the replies from the respondents, the degree of acquaintance with ML and AI ideas and their current rate of application were identified in some cases in addition. Discussions on the present use of ML to advanced showcase forms and areas where ML may be used led to the conclusion that better usage of ML is to provide better information and robotic procedures. Roboticing, e.g. detailing, updating, and even correspondence with customers can be applied to a recurrent operation. While presenting imaginative advances, the attention is essentially on process computerization and information handling. These exercises are right now performed physically, albeit just insignificant scholarly information is required for these undertakings. Indeed, even in the making of computerized content, which seems, by all accounts, to be profoundly mentally escalated, respondents alluded to the mechanized interpretation of articles from outside media. The substantial bulk of Slovak-based computerised substances are derived from remote media and barely adapted to local market needs. In order to design and implement devices using inventive measures, including ML, the responders' organisations shall venture out to other innovation organisations. You see it as too costly and tiresome for self-improvement and they work with masters on the ground in this direction. In light of the consequences of this exploration, it very well may be expressed that ML as of now has a spot in crafted by promoting directors and computerized showcasing pros.

The subjective examination gave bits of knowledge into the manner in which respondents consider the utilization of ML in computerized promoting and how their organizations see the advantages and downsides of AI as well as ML devices. Experiences of sophisticated advertising specialists in Slovakia might be tested in the subsequent investigation in different nations throughout the world. The quantitative investigation which followed discovered that administrative administrators are still new to the issue and some of them are unclear even about the core concept and functioning of ML and AI. Regardless, most exhibiting chief executives are aware that ML and AI are the fate of computerised promotions and accept the distinctive reception and risk of executing ML-based gadgets. System speaks to commitment into existing group'sinformation that transcendently centresontoimprovement about mostly exceptional as well as keen advances at the same time as coming up short ontoattention on the organization as well as appropriation. This empowers experts via IT as well as advertising into comprehendingdifficulties about way toward executing ML-relied apparatus inassociation. System likewise can possibly uncover chances of such a venture and guide the association through the entire sending process.

REFERENCES

André, Q., Carmon, Z., Wertenbroch, K., Crum, A., Frank, D., Goldstein, W., Huber, J., van Boven, L., Weber, B., & Yang, H. (2018). Consumer choice and autonomy in the age of artificial intelligence and big data. *Customer Needs and Solutions*, *5*(1-2), 28–37. doi:10.100740547-017-0085-8

Cauchois, R., Taghipour, A., Kang, D., Zoghlami, N., & Abed, M. (2017). Advanced solutions for a supply chain with stochastic information. *Journal of Advanced Management Science, 5*(1).

Ciuffo, J., Jones, S. S., & Groom, F. M. (2019). Artificial Intelligence in Marketing. In Artificial Intelligence and Machine Learning for Business for Non-Engineers (pp. 71-76). CRC Press, Taylor & Francis Group. doi:10.1201/9780367821654-6

Conick, H. (2017). The past, present and future of AI in marketing. *Marketing News*, *51*(1), 26–35.

Davenport, T., Guha, A., Grewal, D., & Bressgott, T. (2020). How artificial intelligence will change the future of marketing. *Journal of the Academy of Marketing Science*, *48*(1), 24–42. doi:10.100711747-019-00696-0

Dimitrieska, S., Stankovska, A., & Efremova, T. (2018). Artificial intelligence and marketing. *Entrepreneurship*, *6*(2), 298–304.

El-Nemr, N., Canel-Depitre, B., & Taghipour, A. (2021). The determinants of hotel room rates in Beirut: A hedonic pricing model. International Journal of Trade. *Economics and Finance*, *12*(2), 33–42.

El-Nemr, N., Canel-Depitre, B., & Taghipour, A. (2017, September). Determinants of hotel room rates. In *Marketing Trends Congress*. Luxury Industries Conference.

Jarek, K., & Mazurek, G. (2019). Marketing and Artificial Intelligence. *Central European Business Review, 8*(2).

Loivet, W., Taghipour, A., & Kang, D. S. (2020). The rise of green supply chain management: Between complexity and necessity. Journal of Economics. *Business and Management*, *8*(1), 1–7.

Mahfod, J., Canel-Depitre, B., & Taghipour, A. (2019). Quality function deployment-ELECTRE in supplier evaluation. *Journal of Advanced Management Science, 7*(4).

Merimi, M., & Taghipour, A. (2021). Accelerating the digitalization of the supply chain: An empirical research about COVID-19 crisis. In *Digitalization of Decentralized Supply Chains During Global Crises* (pp. 1–24). IGI Global. doi:10.4018/978-1-7998-6874-3.ch001

Nadia, E. N., Beatrice, C. D., & Atour, T. (2020). Luxury hotels' eco-friendly activities & customers' preferences and willingness to pay for green hotels. *Journal of Advanced Management Science, 8*(1).

Paschen, J., Kietzmann, J., & Kietzmann, T. C. (2019). Artificial intelligence (AI) and its implications for market knowledge in B2B marketing. *Journal of Business and Industrial Marketing*, *34*(7), 1410–1419. doi:10.1108/JBIM-10-2018-0295

Riikkinen, M., Saarijärvi, H., Sarlin, P., & Lähteenmäki, I. (2018). Using artificial intelligence to create value in insurance. *International Journal of Bank Marketing*, *36*(6), 1145–1168. doi:10.1108/IJBM-01-2017-0015

Rust, R. T. (2020). The future of marketing. *International Journal of Research in Marketing*, *37*(1), 15–26. doi:10.1016/j.ijresmar.2019.08.002

Sheena, A., & Sachin, A. (2017). Machine learning and its applications: A review. In *International Conference on Big Data Analytics and Computational Intelligence (ICBDAC)* (Vol. 10).

Shin, M., & Taghipour, A. (2021). Supply Chains Digital Transformation: Automated Underground Logistics Systems. *Underground Construction*, *6*(2), 7. doi:10.18178/joebm.2021.9.2.651

Stalidis, G., Karapistolis, D., & Vafeiadis, A. (2015). Marketing decision support using Artificial Intelligence and Knowledge Modeling: Application to tourist destination management. *Procedia: Social and Behavioral Sciences*, *175*, 106–113. doi:10.1016/j.sbspro.2015.01.1180

Sterne, J. (2017). *Artificial intelligence for marketing: practical applications*. John Wiley & Sons. doi:10.1002/9781119406341

Taghipour, A. (2014). *Production Network Planning Based on Constraint Relaxation and Discount Approach* (Vol. 2). Lecture Notes on Information Theory.

Taghipour, A. (2018). A Contemporary Approach to Plan Independent Logistics Actors. In *Contemporary Approaches and Strategies for Applied Logistics* (pp. 337–364). IGI Global. doi:10.4018/978-1-5225-5273-4.ch014

Taghipour, A. (Ed.). (2020). *Demand Forecasting and Order Planning in Supply Chains and Humanitarian Logistics*. IGI Global.

Taghipour, A., Abed, M., & Zoghlami, N. (2015, May). Design for remanufacturing respecting reverse logistics processes: A review. In *2015 4th International Conference on Advanced Logistics and Transport (ICALT)* (pp. 299-304). IEEE. 10.1109/ICAdLT.2015.7136602

Taghipour, A., & Beneteau-Piet, C. (2020). Sustainable supply chain management performance. *International Journal of Innovation, Management and Technology*, *11*(6), 165–169. doi:10.18178/ijimt.2020.11.6.897

Taghipour, A., & Frayret, J. M. (2011a). A new heuristic search with local optimization to manage a supply chain. *Meta*, 15.

Taghipour, A., & Frayret, J. M. (2011b). *Supply chain coordination planning: A review*. Work paper, École polytechnique de Montréal.

Taghipour, A., Glaa, B., & Zoghlami, N. (2014, May). Network coordination with minimum risk of information sharing. In *2014 International Conference on Advanced Logistics and Transport (ICALT)* (pp. 184-188). IEEE. 10.1109/ICAdLT.2014.6864115

Taghipour, A., & Merimi, M. (2021). Digital Transformation of Supply Chains during Crisis: COVID-19. In *11th Annual International Conference on Industrial Engineering and Operations Management, IEOM* (pp. 7493-7501).

Taghipour, A., Murat, S., & Huang, P. (2021). E-supply chain management: A review. International Journal of e-Education, e-Business, e-. *Management Learning*, *11*(2), 51–61.

Tliche, Y., Taghipour, A., & Canel-Depitre, B. (2019). Anticipation of Demand in Supply Chains. In *Hierarchical Planning and Information Sharing Techniques in Supply Chain Management* (pp. 1–45). IGI Global.

Tliche, Y., Taghipour, A., & Canel-Depitre, B. (2021). Exploring a Downstream Demand Inference Strategy in a Decentralized Two-Level Supply Chain. In *Demand Forecasting and Order Planning in Supply Chains and Humanitarian Logistics* (pp. 1–65). IGI Global. doi:10.4018/978-1-7998-3805-0.ch001

Vosooghidizaji, M., Taghipour, A., & Canel-Depitre, B. (2020). Information Asymmetry in Supply Chain Coordination: State of the Art. *Journal of Industrial and Intelligent Information, 8*(2).

Vosooghidizaji, M., Taghipour, A., & Canel-Depitre, B. (2022). Coordinating corporate social responsibility in a two-level supply chain under bilateral information asymmetry. *Journal of Cleaner Production, 364*, 132627. doi:10.1016/j.jclepro.2022.132627

Wirth, N. (2018). Hello marketing, what can artificial intelligence help you with? *International Journal of Market Research, 60*(5), 435–438. doi:10.1177/1470785318776841

Yang, S., Taghipour, A., & Canel-Depitre, B. (2017, August). Cost optimization of reverse logistics: A review. In *Proceedings of the 7th International Conference on Information Communication and Management* (pp. 158-161). ACM. 10.1145/3134383.3134393

Chapter 10
Drivers of Sustainable Supply Chain Management Using Internet of Things-Based Blockchain Technology

Kamalendu Pal
https://orcid.org/0000-0001-7158-6481
University of London, UK

ABSTRACT

Information technologies are transforming conventional supply chain management (SCM) business practices and positively influencing sustainability. In particular, blockchain technology and the internet of things (IoT) are two important examples that play a significant role in sustainable supply chain management (SSCM). This chapter reviewed the impact of these technologies on SSCM separately and with their combination of forward and reversed supply chains. Academics and practitioners have studied the effects of these technologies on sustainability separately earlier, but integrating these technologies can lead to different insights and disclose several opportunities. Besides, the chapter highlights essential factors in developing blockchain and IoT to know the modern trends for industry automation, challenges, and future research opportunities on supply chain sustainability. Finally, the chapter presents an IoT-based service-oriented blockchain architecture for supply chain information systems that manifest the information-driven sustainability of the supply chain operation.

INTRODUCTION

Commercial trading between different countries and across various continents has started since ancient times of human civilization. In the early days of civilization, cross-border trade happened mainly for goods such as rice gain, wheat, spices, textile, metals, petroleum products, and other essential commodities. Through the Silk Road, the Spice Route, and various other interconnected trade transportation networks,

DOI: 10.4018/978-1-6684-9062-4.ch010

human civilization has initiated trade patterns that have blossomed with industrialization (Bardhan, 2003) and globalization (Stiglitz, 2017).

While the central perception of global trade is simple and unchanged to move goods and money from point A in one country to point B in another country, however in reality, it is much more complex to deploy this business operational practice. In this way, the operational business practices include financing trade, tracking and tracing goods along supply chains, and verifying the quality of those goods through provenance and product pedigree. As global trade has grown in scale, operational business processes have become more numerous and complex. In addition, these business practices strain to accommodate the demands of increased trade volume among more participants – business financiers, partners as importers and exporters servicing different market segments, freight forwarders, customs and port authorities, regulatory governing bodies, and insurance providers. In this way, business communities realize and appreciate the concept of supply chain operations, their values, and their management.

Trends in supply chain management (SCM), such as the globalization of market economies, shorter product life cycles, digitalization, and multifaceted customer expectations, along with developments such as resource scarcity, stricter regulatory requirements, and a more long-term focus, have led to the evolution of highly complicated supply chains. Incorporating environmental and social responsibility issues into the management of supply chains is becoming increasingly relevant to the success of organizations and their supply chains. Organizations are considered accountable for their activities that affect the environment, society, and economy of their businesses, as well as those of their supply chain participants (Pal, 2018). As a result, sustainability within an organization's operations and the supply chain has become a contemporary issue and an important area of research (Pal, 2023).

The adoption of sustainability practices not only improves the environmental and social performance of organizations and their supply chains but also provides an opportunity for organizations to acquire a new set of competencies, which can help them to achieve a competitive advantage by undertaking sustainability initiatives within and outside of the organizational boundaries (Pal, 2023). In this way, some of the main agenda for sustainability are – economic stability, environment conservation, green operations (e.g., warehouse management, transport management, product design), and logistic optimization. At the same time, the supply chain operation team needs to look for continuous improvement in products and services, and enabling information technologies (e.g., radio frequency identification mechanism, internet of things, and appropriate data communication techniques) are essential drivers to achieve the strategic goals. Figure 1 represents a simple diagrammatic representation of supply chain sustainability drivers that can help to gain corporate strategic social values. In this way, business communities realize and appreciate the concept of supply chain operations, their values, and their management from ancient times. Supply chain management and operational issues are essential in corporate strategy formation and execution. In addition, industry-specific supply chain operation patterns demand more research agendas in today's globalized world (Auchois et al., 2017) (Loivet et al., 2020) (Merimi & Taghipour, 2021).

For example, in the textile industry, one of the significant hubs in Asia, most coffee beans are supplied from South America, and cocoa is produced in Africa. Protecting the rights of people who produce goods in different countries is essential. In fact, according to this globalized and evolutionary law, companies need to identify, analyze, and prioritize the risks in their supply chains. It includes new corporate policies and measures that need to be in place to prevent or minimize violations of human rights and damage to the environment. Companies also need to set up grievance channels for people in the supply chains for regular reporting on supply chain practices. The German Supply Chain Act gives consumers the security that companies are managed based on fair production, and many similar legislations are likely to follow in other nations. Businesses worldwide must prepare for these policies to impact their supply chain management strategy before they are enforced to avoid revenue-impacting delays.

In this way, the government's impact on sustainable and responsible supply chain management is studied by researchers (Pal, 2017) (Pal, 2022) (Shin & Taghipour, 2021) (Taghipour et al., 2021), with about a decade of experience as a director in automobile and high-tech industries, provides new and innovative ways to integrate social and environmental analysis into global value chains and adapt the law that regulates corporate responsibility for the observance of sustainability and human rights-related issues in the supply chain (Taghipour & Frayret, 2011) (Taghipour, 2014). In this way, science, technology, and innovation play an enormous role in realizing these ambitious goals to improve human living conditions. The process of creative destruction started by technological progress can help change economies and improve living conditions by increasing productivity, reducing production costs, making better accessibility for the public, and helping to raise real wages (Pal, 2023) (Taghipour et al., 2015) (Taghipour & Merimi, 2021) (Vosooghidizaji et al., 2022).

Figure 1. Main drivers of sustainable supply chain management

Given the rapid changes and the enhanced reliance on technology, how it changes work and working practice is highly salient for researchers of organizational psychology and organizational behavior.

In recent decades academics and practitioners have seen a rapid growth of interest in questions around digital technologies, including IoT and blockchain technology (Pal & Yasar, 2020), big data (Kitchin, 2014) (Pal, 2018) (Pal, 2019), algorithms (Amoore, 2018) (Crampton, 2016), social networks (Shelton et al., 2015), and the new spatial forms to which they give rise – the intelligent supply chain (Pal, 2022), the smart border (Amoore, 2006), and "code/space" (Kitchin & Dodge, 2011). Researchers have been well-positioned to offer insightful and necessary critiques of how these technologies reshape dominant epistemologies, relationships of power, and spatial practices while highlighting the agentive capacities of technological objects and systems (Ash et al., 2018).

The effects of technology throughout human history are well documented (Beniger, 1986) (Bradley & Nolan, 1998) (Bradley et al., 2016). The growth and advancement of civilization can be divided into three eras according to their respective core technological infrastructures: agricultural, industrial, and digital. Each of these eras has been profoundly affected by the ability to acquire new information and knowledge. However, they have all required and enabled new economic structures, social anthropologies (Bardhan & Roy, 2008), cultural transformations, work practices, and supply chain management models (Pal & Karakostas, 2014) (Pal & Yasar, 2020) (Pal, 2017).

Harnessing the frontier of technologies helps to mitigate the persistent gaps between developing and developed nations in getting and using existing technologies. It also creates and delivers innovations (including non-technological and new forms of social innovation), which could be transformative in creating sustainable development goals and producing more prosperous, inclusive, and healthy human societies. In this way, society gets required solutions and opportunities for sustainable development that are better, cheaper, faster, scalable, and easy to use. The extent of technological development impact has already ushered in the transformative implications of information and communication technologies (ICTs) in many countries worldwide. However, these new technologies are often threatening to outpace the capability of societies and policymakers to adapt to the changes they can create, giving rise to widespread anxiety and ambivalence or hostility to some technological advances.

In addition, the recent covid-19 pandemic has created ripples across all spheres of our lives, bringing the world to a standstill. Imposed lockdown disrupted the procurement of raw materials and the timely supply of goods, resulting in high product prices (Bhaskar et al., 2020). The increased demand for e-commerce products during the pandemic caused higher returns, which added inefficiencies in reverse logistics processes. It also shows the importance of both forward and reverse SC coordination and the vital role of information sharing between the SC players (Guo et al., 2020) (Thghipour, 2009) (Thghipour, 2014). Supply chain management (SCM) refers to the governance of SC facets while delivering products to customers and generating maximum customer value. Reverse logistics refers to handling products returned to the company with substantial losses. With companies constantly looking for cost reduction, on-time delivery, better product quality, and growing environmental concerns, the 'Sustainability' concept also got incorporated into the SC. Sustainability focuses on using limited resources to fulfill the current demand and leave adequate resources to meet future needs. It is based on the union of three central pillars: economic, social, and environmental sustainability. The Internet of Things (IoT) and blockchain technology are modern industry technologies that fulfill the sustainability pillars' demands. Hence, blockchain and IoT may be an excellent answer to iron out issues related to forward and reverse supply chains.

Blockchain technology brought its name because it requires every activity to be recorded in blocks and connected sequentially like a chain. Different nodes can access these blocks, making it a transparent system that makes the process safer. Some of the world's top companies are making blockchain an integral part of their strategic outlook. Blockchain can help with transaction settlement (smart contracts), cost reduction, providing better information, automation, audit transparency, and reducing human error (Choi et al. 2020). In addition, IoT technology is the collection of interconnected devices to exchange data requiring little human intervention. As a result, IoT can help with operational efficiencies and revenue growth to provide companies that can implement it with a competitive advantage (Liao & Wang 2019).

Industry 4.0 technologies can benefit the corporate world by digitizing SCs, reverse logistics, services, and customer relations (Manavalan and Jayakrishna, 2019). Blockchain, IoT, cloud computing, data science, and cyber-physical systems would enable the next industrial revolution with smart manufacturing as an integral part (Kusiak 2018). Poor data quality jeopardizes the company's operation and leads to faulty strategy formulation (Mahyuni et al., 2020). Industries prefer to wait than make an entire investment now because of complications in SC (D. Choi et al. 2020). Blockchain plays an essential part in rectifying this situation leading companies towards optimized and sustainable operations (Choi and Luo 2019). Blockchain applications make the SC system cost-effective, energy-efficient, and high-performance-oriented (Kim and Shin 2019; Yadav et al. 2020). Each transaction is permanently documented to reduce time delays significantly, additional costs, sustainability problems, and the human fallacy (Öztürk and Yildizbaşi 2020). Traceability and Transparency are the advantages of using blockchain technology (Bai and Sarkis 2020). Electronic industries are more concerned with integrating blockchain and robotics to bring visibility to SC (Gupta et al. 2020). The main innovative technological features of blockchain are safe transactions without intermediation, robustness, resilience, durability, open structure, pseudonymity, and process reliability (Astarita et al., 2020).

Moreover, sustainability is essential for accessing global markets and accomplishing high profits (Pal, 2021). For example, while sustainable shipment management was considered a cost in the past, now, thanks to modern technologies (e.g., IoT, radio frequency identification, blockchain, and cloud computing), it is possible to guarantee sustainable logistics. Indeed, using these emerging technologies, improving carbon emissions-related issues and saving resources is possible. One of the most critical requirements for sustainable supply chain management demands the Transparency of information and appropriate communication mechanisms between the supply chain business stakeholders. In order to earn these goals, it is essential to have adequate information and communication technology (ICT) standards that ensure the reliability of information systems architectures and foolproof security of operational data.

As to emerging technologies, the Internet of Things (IoT) and radio frequency identification (RFID) technology are heavily used in supply chain operations. These technologies can shake up an industry or enable a business model that creates an entirely new way of operations management, even though these technologies may be unfavorable to the users at the early stage (Pal, 2021). Besides, disruptive technologies dominate different industries with new, exciting features that are differentiated from existing technologies (Pal, 2019). Business models based on disruptive technologies are typically more efficient, productive, and convenient than those established on the incumbent technology (Pal, 2021). For example, the IoT has radically changed warehouse and inventory management by tightly coupling distribution centers, transportation, and customer relationship management (CRM) systems. As a result, IoT could reduce operational costs and provide more customized, responsive, and innovative customer service.

The recent emergence of the digitation of supply chain business processes is attracting massive attention from academics and practitioners (Lebosse et al., 2017) (Mbiatem et al., 2018) (Ren et al., 2016) (Thghipour & Frayrel, 2010) (Thghipour & Frayrel, 2013). The data exchanges between autonomous networks over untrusted channels are also significant. Blockchain technology opens new dimensions towards the data exchange mechanism, intelligent resource management, user access control, audibility, and chronology in stored transactions to ensure data security, privacy, and stakeholder trust. Besides, academics and practitioners are concentrating their research activities on two particular areas: (i) supply chain management-related sustainability issues and (ii) deploying emerging technologies (e.g., IoT, blockchain technology) to improve the supply chain business-partners collaboration. In doing so, they are ensuring broader business operations, Transparency, and traceability of resources along the supply chain networks by exchanging operational data.

Indeed, one of the most investigated topics is the use of blockchain for product tracking and tracing, and the evidence is available in the research literature (Bai & Sarkis, 2020) (Tang & Veelenturf, 2019). Specifically, the research literature has analyzed detection systems such as RFID, GPS technology, and IoT infrastructures (Bouzembrak et al., 2019) (Chanchaichujit et al., 2020) (Lam & Ip, 2019) (Ketzenberg et al., 2015) (Wognum et al., 2011). These systems have brought forward new ways of monitoring products and business processes, from the origin to the end consumer, regarding price, date, location, and quality assurance certificates. However, they suffer from many drawbacks related to security issues, standardization, interoperability, and distribution among the players on a large scale (Zhang & Kitsos, 2016) (Matharu et al., 2014). Blockchain technology can fill these inefficiencies by allowing goods management without intermediaries or trusted parties (Chang et al., 2020) (Min, 2019). The effectiveness of supply chain transactional performances can be improved by crediting to the distinctive features of blockchain. Indeed, to achieve adequate traceability, the visibility of the business process needs to have a unified, assured, and tamper-proof shared ledger that is globally accessible by all the stakeholders (Lezoche et al., 2020) (Kamble et al., 2020). Furthermore, optimizing the entire supply chain can take place through smart contracts to verify and permit actions by physical devices that collect information from the operational areas, enhancing the security of the IoT systems architectures (Pournader et al., 2020). Smart contracts help the system automation for particular actions based on the constant detection by the sensors along the supply chain operations, such as automatic financial payment after receipt of the required product (Habib et al., 2020) or appropriate management of anomalies along the shipment (Hasan et al., 2019).

Therefore, this chapter aims to test further insights for increasing the literature on improving sustainability issues using modern technologies. The rest of the chapter is structured as follows. Section 2 presents the overview of the modern technologies allowing goods tracking within supply chains. Section 3 highlights the discussions focusing on sustainability issues and managerial implications. Finally, Section 4 concludes the chapter with concluding remarks, limitations, and insights for future research.

BACKGROUND AND RELATED RESEARCH

This section presents an overview of sustainable development, the applications of sustainability in the context of SCM, and a review of recent research on the sustainability issues of Industry 4.0 and the impact of evolving technologies on supply chains.

Sustainable Development

The central concept of sustainability focuses on economic viability and the industry's role in implementing sustainable solutions for economic advantage. Academics and practitioners often consider the sustainable solution as a way to mitigate the limitations of linear production and consumption models for increasing resource use efficiency. At the same time, some of the researchers are debating on the conceptual view of *circular economics* (CE) and sustainability. The CE introduces better balances of sustainability's economic, environmental, and social aspects. Countries such as China promote CE as a cleaner production strategy that endorses efficient use of resources. At the same time, other regions, such as the European Union, Japan, and the USA, also consider it a waste management strategy (Ghisellini et al., 2016).

Economic system circularity was introduced with the law of thermodynamics as its fundamental principle (Pearce & Turner, 1990). Initially, this was conceptualized to describe matter and energy degradation to maintain the sustainability of the earth's natural resources. In these initial CE descriptions, the environment has three main functions: supply resources, provide a life support system, and offer a sink for emissions and waste. Unlike other economic functions with direct pricing, sometimes no direct price or market for environmental goods exists (what is the price of air and water quality?). However, recent Life Cycle Assessment (LCA) methods have tried to monetize environmental prices, indicating the loss of economic welfare as a result of environmental emissions (De Bruyn et al., 2018) (Weidema, 2015). In addition, environmental policies and consumer and producer responsibilities have been employed to mitigate the high consumption of resources (Ghisellini et al., 2016).

CE provides many advantages to industrial applications: (i) elongating an asset's usage cycle, (ii) improving asset utilization through sharing, (iii) asset reusing, recycling, and remanufacturing, (iv) regenerating and preserving natural resources by returning biological elements to their original ecosystem and avoid nutrients leakage from one system to another. In order to implement these advantages and value drivers, a framework named ReSOLVE - Regenerate, Share, Optimize, Loop, Virtualize, and Exchange has been introduced by the Ellen MacArthur Foundation (Ellen MacArthur Foundation, 2015).

However, CE and its basic conceptual principles are not without criticism (Prendeville et al., 2018): (i) First is the definition of CE. Practitioners are often unclear regarding the fundamental principles of CE. Some consider it a macro-level activity, while others consider it a micro-level intervention. (ii) Second, some principles may not necessarily benefit the environment. For example, infinite recycling of materials and energy will not be without efficiency loss; reuse of old technologies may result in higher energy consumption or sharing economy initiatives that may not be as environmentally viable as promoted. (iii) Third, very few businesses adopt CE-related strategies. Also, CE models often give more authority to businesses than consumers and social communities.

While CE can help companies realize business outcomes of implementing sustainable operations, the implementation scope and scale of CE efforts are currently limited. As new technologies emerge, novel business models can orient organizations towards enhancing sustainability outcomes through CE principles.

Industry 4.0

The term Industry 4.0 presents a promise of a new industrial revolution, which integrates advanced manufacturing methods with the Internet of Things to create interconnected manufacturing systems that communicate, analyze, and use the information to drive further intelligent action back in the physical world. Industry 4.0 originated from the German word Industrie 4.0, a set of connected cyber-physical objects capable of using Big Data analytics within the manufacturing and production domains (Vogel-Heuser & Hess, 2016). Industry 4.0 is part of the Industrial Internet of Things (IIoT) (Lom et al., 2016), and different characteristics have been assigned to Industry 4.0 to equip not only manufacturing systems with advanced data acquisition technologies but also value generation and service innovation (Kagermann, 2015).

In recent decades, Germany has developed a four-step strategic plan for transforming industries of the information age to industry 4.0: (i) building a network of CPSs, (ii) researching the 'smart factory' and 'intelligent production' concepts, (iii) integrating the elements of value chains on three levels of horizontal integration, vertical integration, and end-to-end integration, and finally (iv) achieving eight planning objectives. The proper planning objectives include standardization, efficient management, a reliable industrial infrastructure, safety and security, organization and work design, workforce training, creating a regulatory framework, and improving the efficiency of resources (Zhou et al., 2015).

Given that Industry 4.0 is such a broad topic, blockchain technology is evaluated to show its potential as one of the most recent elements. However, the importance of blockchain resides in its ability to enhance information integration across supply chains and between various business stakeholders, one of the main agendas of industry 4.0.

With so many potential opportunities to digitalize various aspects of the supply chain, business organizations must take a structural approach to strategic decision-making. In order to help the supply chain strategic decision-makers, this chapter presents a series of digitalization business scenarios covering inbound, internal, outbound, and end-to-end perspectives, as shown diagrammatically in Figure 2.

By breaking down the supply chain into a series of digital scenarios, the chapter has presented a framework for robust decision-making based on a clear understanding of what outcomes business corporations seek. In addition, this section highlighted maturity models for each scenario to help businesses think about which areas they want to focus on, assess their level of achievement to date, and prioritize their efforts. Besides, the framework starts by defining the practical application of digital technologies at the appropriate stage in the value chain. Finally, before assessing current and required capabilities in terms of technology and skills, the business benefits and challenges finish with assessing achievability.

Figure 2. A digital supply chain applications scenario

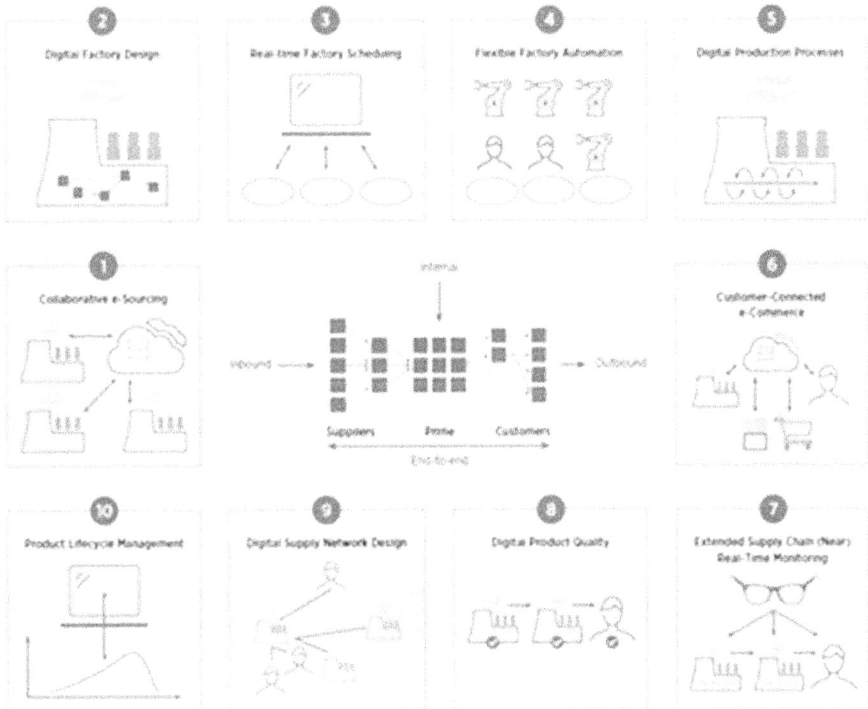

Collaborative Electronic Sourcing

Recent global events have presented new dimension of supply chain visibility into business and operations. In the face of disruption, organizations could not forecast demand, predict supply, and meet delivery schedules. As a result, organizations of all sizes need to speed up their transformation initiatives to increase flexibility, agility, and visibility for a more resilient supply chain. Digitizing supply chains through modern integration, automation, and secure and connected ecosystems makes it easy to manage information flows and uncover insights to ensure continued operations, even in the face of significant disruptions. The dominating options are electronic data interchange (EDI) and automated call-off are established forms of digital sourcing; businesses are trying to extend this to manage tiers beyond direct suppliers and to provide the option of initiative-taking warning systems.

Further, business organizations try to create deeper strategic engagement with supplier communities. In addition, business organizations need seamless connectivity among themself, by which automated replenishment from the supplier network (multiple tiers) with real-time business operation monitoring and predictive disruption analysis capabilities. At the same time, businesses must score how significant they consider the opportunities and advantages this operation practice could bring and the challenges and uncertainties. The proceeding step is to take the initiative to evaluate how mature the current enabling technologies are now and over the coming years and how well-developed their organizational skills, know-how, and attitudes are. By repeating this process for the other nine scenarios outlined below, businesses can develop concrete strategic business cases where they must concentrate their corporate resources to attain strategic goals.

Digital Factory Design

The digital economy represents the pervasive use of IT (hardware, software, applications, and data communication technologies) in different areas of the economy, including internal operations of organizations (business, government, and non-profit); transactions between organizations; and transactions between individuals, acting both as consumers and citizens, and organizations. Digital 3D modelling systems for factory design are becoming increasingly sophisticated. This process, coupled with the advent of flexible manufacturing systems and data connectivity, these advances stimulate a new paradigm in factory layout design, process, and material flows. As well as looking different, tomorrow's digital factory will significantly impact takt time, buffers, skills, and staffing. It should also be easily reconfigurable in response to change conditions.

Real-Time Factory Scheduling

How manufacturers run factories, as well as how they design them, will change dramatically, and this requires s form of digital business process re-engineering. The prize could significantly increase productivity, improve delivery performance, respond to change, and have fewer missed sales. However, making full use of the sensor-enabled, smart device, real-time opportunity with seamlessly joined-up ERP, MES, and cloud systems is not easy. Instead, it needs careful navigation to maximize business benefits and avoid costs and complexity.

Flexible Factory Automation

Ever-cheaper technology, collaborative robotics, and machine learning mean manufacturers are entering a new era of factory automation. The business benefits include lower variable costs, increased customization, labour saving, quality assurance, closer-to-make location, and improved health and safety. One crucial aspect is introducing equipment modularity and standards into the overall vision, supporting the necessary economies, and enabling flexible reconfiguration.

Digital Production Processes

The shift towards replacing 'subtractive' manufacturing processes (such as machining) with 'additive' processes (such as laser sintering and digital printing) has obvious benefits in cost, with even more significant opportunities in enabling new product designs and enhanced customization. In addition, these new techniques could bring about the disruptive reconfiguration of complete supply chains and industry sectors.

Customer Connected E-Commerce

At a minimum, companies should aim to extend e-commerce to optimize web-based order management, including personalized configuration, omnichannel access, and last-mile delivery. The latter is becoming a critical competitive differentiator, particularly in retail consumer goods, where 'last-mile' costs often outstripped the total cost of manufacturing and primary distribution. As a result, companies are now looking beyond stereotypical business operations and will use completely new business models based on customer-connected supply chains – constantly monitoring product usage and experience and tailoring the offering to suit.

Extended Supply Chain Monitoring

It involves the entire network, using data science, predictive analytics, real-time risk management, and dynamic resource optimization – enabled by distributed sensors and track-and-trace to create visualization optimize information systems integration, predict disruptions, and support dynamic decision-making.

Digital Product Quality

The vision for Total Quality Management (TQM) in the digital context involves end-to-end transparency, real-time root cause analytics, and initiative-taking resolution driven by customer connectivity. The challenge is to connect a series of 'traceability islands' back from customers, across internal operation networks, right through to suppliers. The potential benefits are considerable, from faster problem resolution, problem prevention, customer satisfaction, performance, compliance verification, and avoided warranties.

Digital Supply Network Design

It presents the opportunity at the total supply network level. This involves digital network design, modelling, and visualization tools that support a deeper understanding of fundamental dynamics and drivers covering the cost, responses, risk, resource access, and innovation. The tools also support rapid experimentation regarding possible future network options leading to breakthrough scenarios and faster transformation. This can lead to new network design principles and step changes in supply collaboration, site location, capacity, inventory, and customer response.

Product Lifecycle Management

There is a growing need to integrate product-based data systems with supply chain-based systems, aligned with a single vision for product lifecycle management (PLM) and value capture. These next-generation PLM systems can provide accurate, up-to-date product information accessible throughout the value chain and product lifecycle. This enables enhanced cross-function and cross-organizational involvement in the design, collaborative innovation, design for manufacture, procurement, platform-based design philosophies, quicker time-to-market, and improved portfolio management.

IoT for the Supply Chain Management

The vision behind the IoT is to create real-time connection and data communication with people or any business process along supply chain operation, anytime, anywhere, using any network. It facilitates overcoming the limitations of legacy systems and ways of data communication and processing. In this way, IoT systems embedded with industrial operations often consist of software, electronic components, actuators, sensors, detectors, and wireless connectivity that enable them to collect data from these objects can be defined as the "IoT". An IoT system has the following essential characteristics:

- IoT is a ubiquitous technology advancement that enables supply chain business-related objects to be connected to the internet via wired or wireless networks to communicate.
- Several wireless sensor networks are available for IoT devices, including near-field communication (NFC), Zigbee, radio frequency identification (RFID), Bluetooth, and Wi-Fi.
- The sensors can be connected to various technologies, including long-term evolution (LTE), general packet radio service (GPRS), and global system for mobile communication (GSMC).
- The efficiency of an IoT system is largely determined by three main components, each of which is vital to its day-to-day operation: (i) perception layer, (ii) network and middleware (Edge, Fog, and Cloud) layer, and (iii) application layer.

Nevertheless, cloud computing offers virtually unlimited storage and system capabilities to address many IoT-related challenges. Consequently, the phrase "cloud of things" (CoT) is used to allude to the fusion of IoT and cloud computing. The CoT is a paradigm for increasing productivity and improving system performance that is widely used by most industries and manufacturers. Several researchers discussed in their research (Pal, 2023) the use of the cloud to analyze vast amounts of data (i.e., Big Data) when data storage and processing are required.

With the advent of the IoT, vast amounts of data are generated in real-time, which poses a significant concern for traditional cloud computing network topologies (Fang & Ma, 2020). A traditional cloud infrastructure condenses all processing, storage, and networking into a limited set of data centers, and the distance between remote devices and remote data centers is relatively wide (Wang et al., 2010). Edge computing could address this challenge since it provides access to computing resources closer to IoT edge devices and may lead to a new ecosystem for IoT innovation (Jiang et al., 2020). In this way, architectural issues on IoT systems in automating supply chain operations play a significant role, and there are diverse types of layered architecture for supply chain industrial applications (Pal & Yasar, 2020).

IoT Systems Architecture

The layered architecture is designed to meet the requirements of various industries (e.g., manufacturing, retail), enterprises, societies, institutions, and governments. The functionalities of the various layers are (Pal, 2023): (i) edge layer: This is the hardware layer and consists of sensor networks, embedded systems, RFID tags, and readers or several types of sensors in different forms. Many of these hardware elements provide identification and information storage, information collection, information processing, communication, control, and actuation, (ii) access gateway layer: It takes care of message routing, publishing, and subscribing and performs cross-platform communication if required, (iii) the middleware layer interfaces the access gateway layer and the application layer. It is responsible for functions and takes care of issues like data filtering, data aggregation, semantic analysis, access control, and information discovery, such as EPC (Electronic Product Code) information service and ONS (Object Naming Service), and (iv) application layer that is responsible for delivering various applications to different users in IoT. Figure 3. represents a simplified IoT technology-based architecture for SCM.

About the technologies of IoT, (Jiang et al., 2020) presents the technology areas enabling the IoT: (i) identification technology: The purpose of identification is to map a unique identifier or UID (globally unique or unique within a particular scope) to an entity to make it retrievable and identifiable without ambiguity, (ii) IoT architecture challenges: Scalability, modularity, extensibility, and interoperability among heterogenous things and their environments are the essential design requirements for IoT, (iii) communication technology, (iv) network technology: The IoT deployment requires the development of suitable network technology for implementing the vision of IoT to reach out to objects in the physical world and to bring them into the internet, (v) software and algorithms, and (vi) hardware technology which includes intelligent devices with enhanced inter-device communication.

Figure 3. A layered IoT architecture for supply chain operation

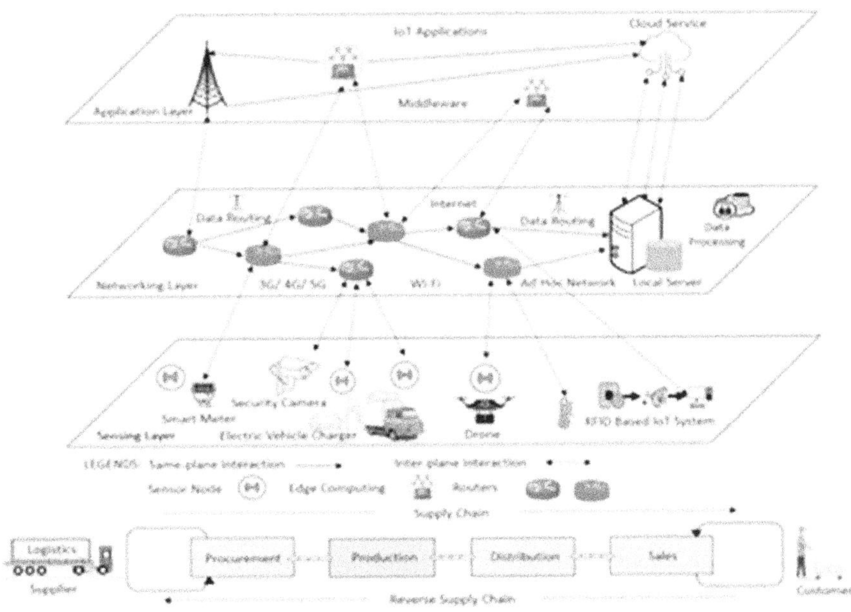

The other essential technologies necessary for the IoT-based sensing environment are: (i) data and signal processing technology, (ii) discovering and search engine technology, (iii) relationship network management technology in managing networks that contain a vast number of heterogeneous things, and (iii) power and energy storage technology, (iv) security and privacy technologies to maintain two significant issues in IoT system, and (iv) standardization which should be designed to support a wide range of applications and address standard requirements from a wide range of industrial SCM systems.

Review of Recent Literature

In this way, information technology enables effective supply chain management; and information sharing capability. This section presents a brief review of IoT technology and its uses in SCM's different application areas: (i) procurement process, (ii) make process, (iii) delivery process, (iv) return process, and (v) industry-specific deployment.

Table 1. Applications of IoT technology for supply chain operations

Procurement process: The request for materials and services by companies is the sourcing process. Planning source activities strategically across the supply chain is a sign of success. Yuvaraj and Sangeetha (Yuvaraj & Sangeetha, 2016) highlighted how to monitor goods anytime and anywhere by integrating RFID tags with GPS technology to track indoor and outdoor products in a supply chain environment. The impact of IoT on supplier selection was studied by Yu and colleagues (Ng & Wakenshaw, 2017). Also, several advantages of IoT regarding the sourcing process have been identified. For example, in analyzing the impact of the cost of sensors and notifications on the purchase cost of a unit, researchers (Decker et al., 2008) developed a simple linear cost model.
Make process: The operational areas that IoT applications can enhance and relevant to the supply chain make process involves factory visibility as in (Wang et al., 2016), management of innovative production networks as by (Veza & Gjeldum, 2015), intelligent design and production control as by (Zawadzki & Zywickl, 2016) systematic design of the virtual factory as by (Choi et al., 2015), smart factory in the petrochemical industry (Li, 2016), opportunities for sustainable manufacturing in industry 4.0 (Stock & Seliger, 2016).
Delivery process: The delivery function is one of the most significant logistics tasks. Logistics includes planning, storing, and controlling goods and services flows (Ballou, 2007). The delivery process in the supply chain concerns the warehouse, inventory, order management, and transportation. The main impact of IoT on the supply chain delivery process includes: (i) Warehousing function: the IoT enables timesaving of joint ordering via smart RFID tags (Angeles, 2005). IoT also achieves collaborative warehousing via using smart things and multi-agent systems. It also increases the safety and security of the supply chain (Liukkonen & Tsai, 2016). (ii) In order and inventory management: the IoT enables sharing of information and inventory accuracy (Bowman et al., 2009) using RFID tags. [iii] In transportation function: the IoT achieves accurate and timely delivery using sensors and networks (Fang et al., 2013). It also saves smartphone scanning and recording time (Li et al., 2014).
Return Process: A closed-loop supply chain model to meet the demand of sales collection centers using new and remanufactured products presented by researchers (Paksovy et al., 2016). The e-reverse logistic framework was designed by Xing et al. (Xing et al., 2012). Fang and other searchers proposed an integrated three-stage model for optimizing procurement, pricing, product recovery, and strategy of return acquisition (Fang et al., 2016).
Industry-specific deployment: IoT technology is also deployed in various supply chain applications. For example, a group of researchers used IoT for a pharmaceutical supply chain (Yan & Huang, 2009), and it has also been used for the construction industry (Shin et al., 2011), the petrochemical industry (Li, 2016), retail industry, and food supply chains (Verdouw et al., 2016).

The IoT technology can potentially *'connect the unconnected,'* It introduces a new concept that aims to enhance the forms of communication the individual supply chain business partners need today. In this way, it addresses many supplies chain operational challenges, including the enhanced business need to improve supply chain information transparency and introduce the integrity of production data and the identity of products. At the same time, IoT applications generate vast volumes of data along the supply chain operations, and often this data resides in silos, which are generally underutilized and present to extract real-time business insights information. These data silos can be considered trapped or hidden sources of potential business insights and value, which can be made available after appropriate processing steps. For example, appropriate processing steps can provide facilities with the shift from mass to customized products for specific customers. Finally, the research community highlights the requirements to establish interoperable data exchange standards among production business partners (Pal, 2021).

The other essential characteristics of these data silos are distributed in nature, and the service-oriented computing (SOC) paradigm presents an attractive solution for providing business services. These services are self-contained application systems used over industry-specific middleware architecture, capable of describing, publishing, locating, and orchestrating over dedicated data communication networks. These architectures are often used in large-scale data center environments. These architectures are often used in large-scale data center environments. However, data centers' consolidation and centralization produce a significant problem due to the increased distance between customers and relevant services for business. Besides, this arrangement creates different outcomes in high variability in latency and bandwidth-related issues. To address this issue, decentralized SOC architectures, namely cloudlets, have emerged, particularly regarding resource-intensive and interactive applications. Cloudlets are small-scale data centers near user applications and can mitigate low latency and high bandwidth guarantees.

Despite the potential, as mentioned earlier, IoT technology is also facing many challenges: (i) device reliability and durability, (ii) security and privacy issues, (iii) scalability and latency, and (iv) standardization. Device reliability and durability often relate to industrial operations (e.g., manufacturing, transportation, and retail business). These issues include remote access control, reliability, connectivity, and reliable services provision. The other significant challenge is security and privacy issues. It includes authentication and access control in industrial control systems security, data protection, privacy preservation under data protection regulations, and the protection and security of human, industrial assets, and critical infrastructures. Unfortunately, conventional security and privacy approaches are not extremely helpful to IoT-based industrial supply chain applications due to their dynamic topology and distributed nature. In addition, the present Internet architecture, with its server-based infrastructure, might be unsuitable for managing numerous devices and substantial amounts of data because individual servers may pose a single point of failure for cyber-attacks and physical damage.

Moreover, centralized information systems may pose a fragility for IoT deployments in the supply chain for traceability purposes. A centralized data hosting and control approach can lead to several business risks and operational issues related to data integrity, security, and privacy. For example, cloud-based solutions for monitoring IoT data may be subject to manipulation and privacy legislation issues that arise when exporting substantial amounts of confidential and susceptible information to external services in other jurisdictions (Kshetri, 2017) (Cam-Winget et al., 2016). Additionally, these solutions may cause opacity and increase information asymmetry between supply chain exchange partners. Blockchain technology can help to alleviate several of these problems.

Blockchain Technology

Blockchain is a new type of database. In this database, the data is saved in a block linked to other blocks in a chain creating the blockchain. This way, a blockchain is distributed data structure, a distributed ledger, in which the data is shared on a peer-to-peer network. The network members and nodes communicate and validate the data following a predefined protocol without a central authority. Distributed ledgers can be either decentralized, giving equal rights to all users, or centralized, providing specific users with special rights. In addition, blockchain is, by nature, a distributed ledger since each network node has a copy of the ledger. Depending on the right of the users, blockchain can be designed as a centralized or decentralized ledger. If blockchain is designed to share decision-making among multiple users, it is decentralized; if one central entity is the primary decision-maker, it is centralized.

Blockchain technology was popularized with the 'Bitcoin' cryptocurrency peer-to-peer network. Blockchains are created using cryptography in which each block – transaction, file of data – has a cryptographic hash and is linked to a previous block. Once a block is verified by a certain percentage of the network nodes, it is added to previous blocks and forms a blockchain, also known as a public ledger of transactions (Casado-Vara et al., 2018). Figure 4 represents a diagrammatic representation of a blockchain network.

Blockchain technology alters how administrative control is digitally regulated and maintained. In blockchains, data are converted to digital codes, stored in shared databases, have higher transparency, and limited risk of deletion and revision – immutability. Blockchain potential lies with every agreement, payment, and transactional activity having a digital record. These records may be validated and shared among individuals, machines, algorithms, and organizations. Intermediaries such as brokers, bankers, and lawyers are needed less often (Lansiti & Lakhani, 2017). Intermediaries function as intermediaries and oversee the accuracy and verification of transactions in different industries. With blockchain, trust is shifted from human and traditional agents for verifying transactions to computer codes.

Figure 4. A diagrammatic representation of a blockchain

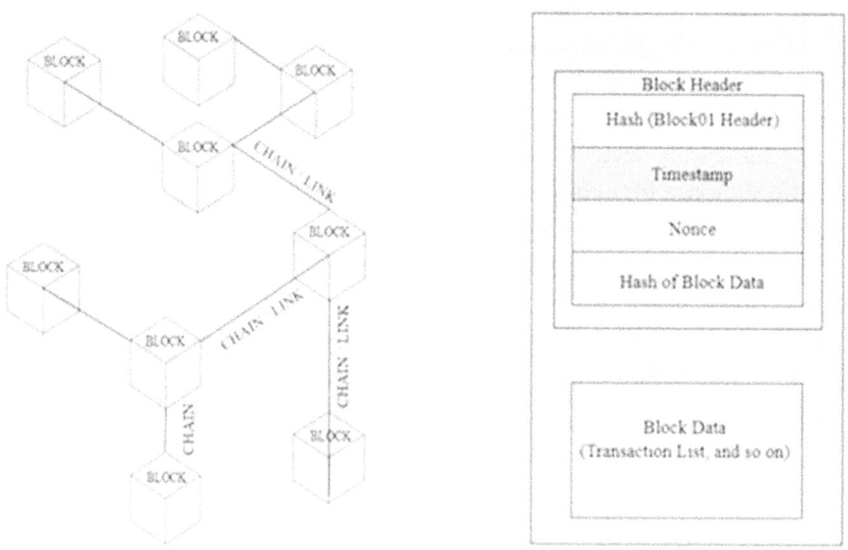

Blockchain technology appears in the commercial world with enormous promise. Bitcoin was an audacious idea: until cryptocurrencies came along, no one could transmit value at a distance without the permission and support of a third party. In this way, it is a simple but revolutionary idea of instant value transfer. For example, in the Bitcoin market, an individual has complete control over their Bitcoin balance. Unlike a bank balance, an individual's Bitcoin balance cannot be manipulated or viewed digitally. If the individual has the proper passcode, they can authorize entry on the blockchain ledger and transfer it to another individual's address (Athey et al., 2016). Among blockchain technology advantages are transparency, less risk of fraud, instantaneous transactions, privacy and security, financial data assurance, and no exchange costs (Sharma et al., 2017) (Crosby et al., 2016). In addition, blockchain technology can provide the following capabilities, which may be dependent on the platform needed to be used (Barton, 2018): (i) *Shared ledger*: a data structure that is distributed locally and shared between different participants; (ii) *Permissioning*: secure and authenticated transactions that ensure privacy and transparency of data; (iii) *Smart contract*: business terms are embedded in a database and are implemented with transactions; and (iv) *Consensus*: transactions are endorsed by relevant users that ensure the immutability and traceability of data.

Most existing blockchain researchers concentrate on Bitcoin and cryptocurrency-related industrial applications (Yli-Huumo et al., 2016). However, the technology can be employed in different industrial applications. Although blockchain is in its relative infancy, some consider it a general-purpose technology (GPT) with several key features of GPTs (Kane, 2017). GPTs such as the steam engine, electricity, and the internet result in innovation and productivity gains among multiple industries, leading to economic growth for years (Catalini & Gans, 2016), and this outcome is part of the blockchain promise; whether it comes to fruition is an open question.

Blockchain technology has attracted wide attention due to cryptocurrencies (e.g., bitcoin) (Nakamoto, 2008). Technically, a blockchain is managed by a network of nodes, and every node executes and records the transactions. A simple blockchain diagram is shown in Figure 3.

Industry users of the blockchain-based information system network use mining nodes to create new blocks, verified by algorithmic software for their information, and ultimately add them to a distributed P2P network. Blockchain technology uses the consensus algorithm to add a new block to the network and follow the steps below:

1. Blockchain network users use the cryptographic-based private key to sign a transaction and advertises the book to their peers.
2. Blockchain network peers validate the received transaction and advertise it over the blockchain network.
3. Involved users generally verify the transaction to meet a consensus algorithmic digital agreement.
4. The miner nodes add the valid transaction into a time-stamped block and broadcast it again into the blockchain network.
5. Next, verifying the advertised block and matching its hash with the previous block, the block in consideration adds to the blockchain network.

This way, consensus algorithms are one of blockchain technology's most essential and revolutionary aspects. For example, consensus algorithms use rules and verification methods to validate data that lets the blockchain network, including devices, agree about adding data to the blockchain network (Bashir, 2017).

One of the benefits of blockchain-based technology is to validate the block's trustfulness in a decentralized, trustless business operating environment without the necessity of the trusted third-party authority. In a blockchain-based P2P network environment, reaching a *consensus* on a newly generated block is challenging as the consensus may favour malicious nodes. This challenge can be mitigated by using dedicated *consensus* algorithms. Typical consensus algorithms are – proof of work (PoW), proof of stake (PoS), and practical byzantine fault tolerance (PBFT) (Bach et al., 2018).

In this way, blockchain can be defined as a decentralized, encrypted database distributed across a peer-to-peer network without a central authority to control and secure it. A consensus mechanism protects and validates the information stored in the Blockchain. Consensus algorithms refer to the different mechanisms used to reach an agreement and ensure security in a distributed system. This kind of system faces a fundamental problem similar to the Byzantine Generals Problem, which relies on achieving consensus in the presence of several faulty and malicious participants. As it is based on a decentralized and distributed network, Blockchain also needs such algorithms to handle data and reach consensus. There are several types of consensus algorithms used in a real-world implementation. The most common algorithms are Proof of Work, the first consensus algorithm implemented by the first Blockchain (Bitcoin), Proof of Stake, and Delegated Proof of Stake.

Blockchain technology can significantly transform many activities and operations in the supply chain that require increased attention from academics and practitioners (Pal, 2022). Numerous studies have reported significant advantages of blockchain technology in logistics and supply chain management (Kamble et al., 2019). These benefits include improvement in cybersecurity and protection (Kshetri, 2017), transparency and accountability (Kshetri, 2018) (Zou et al., 2018), traceability and fraud prevention (Biswas et al., 2018), and researchers highlight many other operational management issues. Blockchain technology can redefine, redesign, and remodel the characteristics of the relationships between all the players in the supply chain (Queiroz & Fosso Wamba, 2019).

Blockchain technology in SCM makes operation management safer, more transparent, traceable, and efficient (Aste et al., 2017) (Kshetri, 2018). Furthermore, blockchain technology can increase the cooperation between the members of SCM (Aste et al., 2017), with indirect positive effects on cost and efficiency in the supply chain. Blockchain technology can also enhance customers' trust, thanks to the traceability of goods throughout their journey across the supply chain (Biswas et al., 2017), and supports the prevention of product fraud and fakes across the supply chains (Chen, 2018), which has a positive impact in terms of cost reduction and efficiency.

BLOCKCHAIN-BASED IoT APPLICATION

This section presents some of the crucial challenges and the related application solutions of deploying blockchain technology, which designs for devices with permanent storage capability and computing capability on the minimal resources of IoT hardware. Some significant integration challenges can be found in the previous research (Reyna et al., 2018).

Blockchain and IoT Integration Challenges

Scalability: The blockchain size widens with an increasing number of connected devices because it needs to store and validate all the transactional information. This is a significant integration disadvantage as IoT networks are expected to contain many nodes that can generate big data in real time.

Security: The increasing number of security-related attacks on IoT networks and their ultimate impacts make securing IoT devices with blockchain technology essential. This integration characteristic may create a severe problem when IoT-based applications do not operate appropriately, and corrupted data arrives and remains in the blockchain. As a result, IoT devices need to be tested before their integration with blockchain because of the undetectable nature of this problem (Roman et al., 2013). Unfortunately, they are often hacked since their constraints limit the firmware updates, stopping them from actuating possible bugs or security breaches. Besides, updating devices one by one is challenging, as required in global IoT deployments in the production industry. Hence, run-time up-grading and reconfiguration mechanisms are needed in IoT devices to keep running over time (Reyna et al., 2018).

Anonymity and data privacy: Privacy is an essential concern in IoT applications. Massive amounts of privacy-sensitive data can be generated, processed, and transferred between device applications. Blockchain technology presents an ideal solution to address identity management in IoT to protect the person's identity when sending personal data that protects user data privacy instead of identities. User anonymity can be revealed by examining the address of the transaction advertised to every participant (He et al., 2018). The IoT devices secured data storage, and authorization of access is a significant challenge since accomplishing it requires integrating cryptographic security solutions into the device, considering limited resources.

Resource utilization and Consensus: Trusted authority in centralized architectures make sure consensus integrity, while in the decentralized environment, nodes of the blockchain network need to reach consensus by voting, which is a resource-intensive process. IoT devices are attributed to relatively low computing capabilities, power consumption, and wireless bandwidth. For example, blockchains that utilize PoW as a consensus mechanism need vast computational power and utilities a considerable amount of energy for the mining process. Computationally complex consensus algorithms do not apply to IoT scenarios, and limited resources should be allocated to find a possible agreement. However, PoS is more likely to be used in IoT, but none of these issues has yet been deployed in IoT as a commercial adoption (Atlam et al., 2018) (Danzi et al., 2018).

A distributed and decentralized blockchain architecture can reduce the overall cost of the IoT system compared to centralized architectures. However, a decentralized blockchain architecture suffers from a new type of resource-wasting, which challenges its integration with IoT. Resource requirements depend on the blockchain network consensus algorithm. Typically, solutions to this problem are to delegate these tasks to an unconstrained device or another gateway device capable of catering to the functionality. Otherwise, off-chain solutions are also useable in this situation, and off-chain moves information outside the blockchain to minimize the high latency in the blockchain could provide the functionality (Reyna et al., 2018).

Smart contracts: Devices can use smart contract techniques with addresses or guide them as application reactions to listening events. They provide a dependable and secure IoT feature, which records and manages their interactions. Working with smart contracts requires using oracles that consist of specific entities that provide real-world data in a trusted manner. Smart contracts should consider the heterogeneity and limitations presented in the IoT. Also, actuation mechanisms directly from smart contracts would help faster reactions with the IoT (Reyna et al., 2018).

IoT designers should select a solution based on their restrictions and requirements, the diversity of solutions for blockchain integration with IoT, and the diverse types of IoT devices and their applications. The following section presents the proposed IoT, blockchain, and SOC technologies architecture.

PROPOSED ENTERPRISE ARCHITECTURE

This section explains how service-oriented computing (SOC) technology will improve efficiencies, provide new business opportunities, address regulatory requirements, and improve transparency and visibility of global production activities. Figure 5 represents the proposed enterprise architecture, which consists of multilayered IoT, blockchain, and service-oriented computing. The IoT systems allow for capturing real-time production business process data from the plant-level operational environment. The enterprise architecture for distributed production (e.g., apparel) supply network used for the current research is shown in Figure 5. The architecture mainly consists of three layers: (i) IoT-based service, (ii) blockchain-based data control, and (iii) data storage and processing part.

IoT-Based Service Layer

The IoT technology development created many opportunities, such as interconnected and interoperable data collection and exchange devices. The data obtained from IoT devices can make production more convenient through numerous types of decision-making at all levels and areas of production business activities.

Blockchain-Based Data Controlling

The blockchain-based controlling part can potentially improve the IoT technology used in the production industry. The production industry is part of a complex and information-intensive supply chain comprising a set of globally connected and distributed organizations, including other critical infrastructures supporting world trade, such as transport and international border management.

Figure 5. Enterprise information system architecture for production (e.g., apparel) business

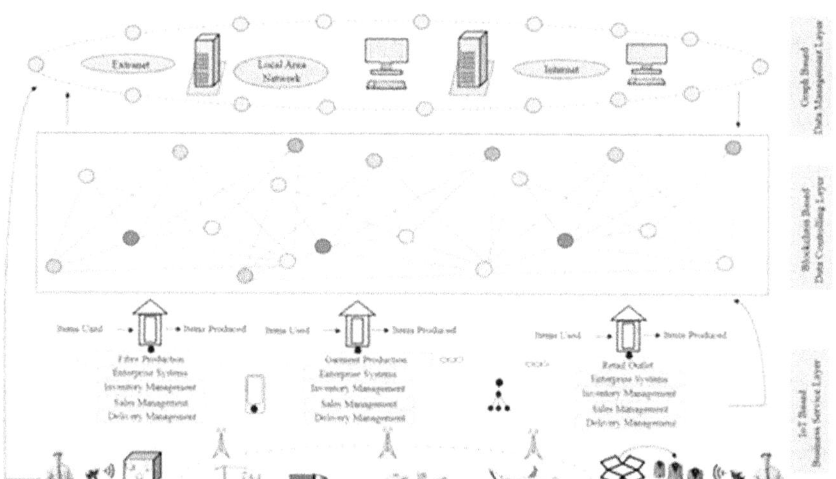

Production and its supply chain management are regarded as a domain where blockchains are good fits for distinct reasons. During the product's lifecycle, as it flows down the value chain network (from production to consumption), the data produced in each step can be present as a transaction, making a permanent history of the item of interest (i.e., product). Among other things, blockchain technology can effectively contribute to (i) recording every single asset (from product to containers) as it flows through the production chain nodes, (ii) tracking orders, receipts, invoices, payments, and any other official documents, and (iii) track digital assets (e.g., certifications, warranties, licenses, copyrights) in a unified way and parcels with physical assets, and others. Moreover, through its decentralized nature, the blockchain can effectively share information regarding the production step, delivery, and maintenance schemes of products between suppliers and vendors, bringing new collaboration opportunities in complex assembly lines.

The challenges in transportation modeling parameters, such as delays in delivery, loss of documentation, unknown source of products, and errors, can be minimized and even avoided by blockchain implementation. Integrating the production supply chain with blockchain benefits are enhanced environmental audit-related issues, minimized errors and delays, reduced transport costs, faster issue identification, increased trust (consumer and partner trust), and improved product transport and inventory management.

Data Management Layer

Industries use different blockchain platforms, and different data models are used on the platforms (e.g., Ethereum (Ethereum, 2021) adopted a key-value data model, while a few of them, like R3 Corda (Corda, 2021), use a relational data model). This characteristic emphasizes that no single blockchain platform is suitable for diverse types of data used in a wide range of product supply chain applications. For example, geolocation data recorded from supply chain transport vehicles may not be efficiently queried using a key-value store. Also, even though blockchain platforms such as Hyperledger Fabric (Hyperledger, 2021) use a pluggable storage model, service users must decide at development time which storage to use (e.g., either Level DB (Kim, 2016), or key-value store using CouchDB (CoucDB, 2021) (document store). Thus, special techniques are required for supporting multiple types of data stores such as key-value, document, SQL, and spatial data stores simultaneously in the same blockchain system. In the proposed architecture, a generic graph database model has been used.

FUTURE RESEARCH DIRECTIONS

Blockchain technology with the IoT applications is getting importance in production industry automation. Besides, data privacy issues remain a fundamental challenge for regulatory bodies. The European General Data Protection Regulation (GDPR) lays the foundation for users to control their data and information about any devices involved in collecting and processing this data. The main objective is to provide individual entities must have the authoritative power and control over their data assets and to be able to transfer their data without any unmitigated risk. Blockchains give the advantages of distributed ledgers that can securely manage digital transactions, where data centralization is unnecessary. In the future, this research will take the initiative of how blockchain technology can be used to develop an audit trail of data generated in IoT devices, providing GDPR rules to be verified on such a trail. This mechanism will help translate such rules into smart contracts to protect personal data transparently and automatically.

CONCLUSION

The stark prospects of climate change and its mounting economic and human costs are essential factors for the survival of humanity from disastrous consequences. Particularly business activities need to identify ways to minimize the penalties of disastrous consequences by acting appropriately rather than waiting for human prosperity to be overturned by rapidly advancing adversities. The world would be foolish to neglect this strong and strictly time-bound practical message to survive. Consequently, the adoption of sustainability practices not only improves the environmental and social performance of organizations and their supply chains but also provides an opportunity for organizations to acquire a new set of competencies, which can help them to achieve a competitive advantage by undertaking sustainability initiatives within and outside of the organizational boundaries. In this way, some of the main agenda for sustainability are – economic stability, environmental conservation, and green operations to minimize the carbon footprint. At the same time, the supply chain operation team needs to look for continuous improvement in products and services, and enabling information technologies (e.g., radio frequency identification mechanism, internet of things, and appropriate data communication techniques) are essential drivers to achieve the strategic goals. The government's impact on sustainable and responsible supply chain management is attracting huge interest from researchers, providing new and innovative ways to integrate social and environmental analysis into global value chains, and adapting the law that regulates corporate responsibility for the observance of sustainability and human rights-related issues in the supply chain. In this way, science, technology, and innovation play an enormous role in realizing these ambitious goals to improve human living conditions. The process of creative destruction started by technological progress can help change economies and improve living conditions by including productivity, reducing production costs, making better accessibility for the public, and helping to raise real wages. This chapter presents an introductory commentary on sustainability-related issues for business organizations.

In the last few decades, considerable attention has been focused on sustainability, and finding a balance between a business organization's environmental, economic, and social aspects is essential for achieving or supporting sustainable value. Sustainability performance defines as a company's performance in all dimensions and for all drivers of corporate sustainability. There are numerous models and indicators used for supply chain sustainability performance. This chapter highlights the trends of business process automation using modern information and communication technology as a driver for supply chain sustainability practices. In particular, this chapter presents a hybrid enterprise information systems architecture of IoT applications and a blockchain-based distributed ledger to support transaction services within a multi-party global production business network. However, standalone IoT systems face security and privacy-related problems. Finally, the chapter presents a hybrid IoT and blockchain technology architecture for automating supply chain information systems.

REFERENCES

Amoore, L. (2006). Biometric borders: Governing mobilities in the war on terror. *Political Geography*, *25*(3), 336–351. doi:10.1016/j.polgeo.2006.02.001

Amoore, L. (2018). Cloud geographies: Computing, data, sovereignty. *Progress in Human Geography*, *42*(1), 4–24. doi:10.1177/0309132516662147

Angeles, R. (2005). RFID technologies: Supply-chain applications and implementation issues. *Information Systems Management*, *22*(1), 51–65. doi:10.1201/1078/44912.22.1.20051201/85739.7

Ash, J., Kitchin, R., & Leszczynski, A. (2018). Digital turn, digital geographies? *Progress in Human Geography*, *42*(1), 25–43. doi:10.1177/0309132516664800

Athey, S., Parashkevov, I., Sarukkai, V., & Xia, J., (2016). *Bitcoin pricing, adoption, and usage: theory and evidence.* Stanford University.

Atlam, H. F., Alenezi, A., Alassafi, M. O., & Wills, G. (2018). Blockchain with Internet of Things: Benefits, challenges, and future directions. *International Journal of Intelligent Systems and Applications*, *10*(6), 40–48. doi:10.5815/ijisa.2018.06.05

Auchois, R., Taghipour, A., Kang, D., Zoghlami, N., & Abed, M. (2017). Advanced solutions for a supply chain with stochastic information. *Journal of Advanced Management Science*, *5*(1).

Bai, C., & Sarkis, J. (2020). A supply chain transparency and sustainability technology appraisal model for blockchain technology. *International Journal of Production Research*, *2020*(58), 2142–2162. doi:10.1080/00207543.2019.1708989

Bardhan, P., & Ray, I. (2008). The Contested Commons: Conversations Between Economists and Anthropologists. Blackwell Publishing.

Barhhan, P. (2003). *International Trade Growth and Development: Essays*. Wiley-Blackwell. doi:10.1002/9780470752777

Beniger, J. R. (1986). *The Control Revolution: Technological and Economic Origins of the Information Society*. Harvard University Press.

Bouzembrak, Y., Klüche, M., Gavai, A., & Marvin, H. J. P. (2019). Internet of Things in food safety: Literature review and a bibliometric analysis. *Trends in Food Science & Technology*, *2019*(94), 54–64. doi:10.1016/j.tifs.2019.11.002

Bowman, P., Ng, J., Harrison, M., Lopez, S., & Illic, A. (2009). Sensor based condition monitoring. B*uilding Radio frequency IDentification for the Global Environment, (Bridge) Euro RFID project.*

Bradley, S. P., & Nolan, R. L. (1998). *Sense and Respond: Capturing Value in the Network Era*. Harvard Business School Press.

Casado-Vara, R., Prieto, J., De la Prieta, F., & Corchado, J. M. (2018). How Blockchain improves the supply chain: Case study alimentary supply chain. *Procedia Computer Science*, *134*, 393–398. doi:10.1016/j.procs.2018.07.193

Catalini, C., & Gans, J. S. (2016). *Some simple Economics of the Blockchain*. National Bureau of Economic Research. doi:10.3386/w22952

Chanchaichujit, J., Balasubramanian, S. & Charmaine, N.S.M.(2020). A systematic literature review on the benefit-drivers of RFID implementation in supply chains and its impact on organizational competitive advantage. *Cogent Bus. Manag.*

Chang, Y., Iakovou, E., & Shi, W. (2020). Blockchain in global supply chains and cross border trade: A critical synthesis of the state-of-the-art, challenges and opportunities. *International Journal of Production Research*, *58*(7), 2082–2099. doi:10.1080/00207543.2019.1651946

Choi, S., Kim, B. H., & Noh, S. D. (2015). A diagnosis and evaluation method for strategic planning and systematic design of a virtual factory in smart manufacturing systems. *International Journal of Precision Engineering and Manufacturing, 16*(6), 1107–1115. doi:10.100712541-015-0143-9

Choi, T. M., Cai, Y. J., & Shen, B. (2019). Sustainable Fashion Supply Chain Management: A System of Systems Analysis. *IEEE Transactions on Engineering Management, 66*(4), 730–745. doi:10.1109/TEM.2018.2857831

Crampton, J. (2016). Assemblage of the vertical: Commercial drones and algorithmic life. *Geographica Helvetica, 7*(12), 137–146. doi:10.5194/gh-71-137-2016

Crosby, M., Pattanayak, P., Verma, S., & Kalyanaraman, V. (2016). Blockchain technology: Beyond Bitcoin. *Appl. Innov., 2*, 6–10.

Danzi, P., Kalor, A. E., Stefanovic, C., & Popovski, P. (2018). Analysis of the communication traffic for blockchain synchronization of IoT devices. In *2018 IEEE International Conference on Communications (ICC)*. IEEE. 10.1109/ICC.2018.8422485

De Bruyn, S., Ahdour, S., Bijleveld, M., de Graaff, L., Schep, E., Schroten, A., & Vergeer, R. (2018). Environmental Prices Handbook 2017: Methods and Numbers for Valuation of Environmental Impacts. CE Delft, Delft.

Decker, C., Berchtold, M. L., Chaves, W. F., Beigl, M., Roehr, D., & Riedel, T. (2008). Cost benefit model for smart items in the supply chain. The Internet of Things, 155–172. Springer. doi:10.1007/978-3-540-78731-0_10

Fang, C., Liu, X., Pardalos, P. M., & Pei, J. (2016). Optimization for a three-stage production system in the Internet of Things: Procurement, production and product recovery, and acquisition. *International Journal of Advanced Manufacturing Technology, 83*(5-8), 689–710. doi:10.100700170-015-7593-1

Fang, J., & Ma, A. (2020). IoT application modules placement and dynamic task processing in edge-cloud computing. *IEEE Internet of Things Journal, 8*(6), 12771–12781.

Fang, J., Qu, T., Li, Z. G., Xu, G., & Huang, G. Q. (2013). Agent-based gateway operating system for RFID-enabled ubiquitous manufacturing enterprise. *Robotics and Computer-integrated Manufacturing, 29*(4), 222–231. doi:10.1016/j.rcim.2013.01.001

Ghisellini, P., Cialani, C., & Ulgiati, S. (2016). A review on circular economy: The expected transition to a balanced interplay of environmental and economic systems. *Journal of Cleaner Production, 114*, 11–32. doi:10.1016/j.jclepro.2015.09.007

Gubbi, J., Buyya, R., Marusic, S., & Palaniswami, M. (2013). Internet of Things (IoT): A vision, architectural elements, and future directions. *Future Generation Computer Systems, 29*(7), 1645–1660. doi:10.1016/j.future.2013.01.010

Habib, M. A., Sardar, M. B., Jabbar, S., Faisal, C. M. N., Mahmood, N., & Ahmad, M. (2020). Blockchain-based Supply Chain for the Automation of Transaction Process: Case Study based Validation. In *Proceedings of the 2020 International Conference on Engineering and Emerging Technologies, ICEET 2020*, Lahore, Pakistan. 10.1109/ICEET48479.2020.9048213

Hasan, H., AlHadhrami, E., AlDhaheri, A., Salah, K., & Jayaraman, R. (2019). Smart contract-based approach for efficient shipment management. *Computers & Industrial Engineering*, *136*, 2019. doi:10.1016/j.cie.2019.07.022

He, Q., Guan, N., Lv, M., & Yi, W. (2018). On the consensus mechanisms of blockchain/dlt for internet of things. In *2018 IEEE 13th International Symposium on Industrial Embedded Systems (SIES)*. IEEE. 10.1109/SIES.2018.8442076

Jiang, J., Li, Z., Tian, Y., & Al-Nabhan, N. (2020). A review of techniques and methods for IoT applications in collaborative cloud-fog environment. *Security and Communication Networks*, *2020*, 1–15. doi:10.1155/2020/8849181

Kagermann, H. (2015). Change through digitization—value creation in the age of Industry 4.0. Management of Permanent Change, 23–45. Springer.

Kamble, S., Gunasekaran, A., & Arha, H. (2019). Understanding the Blockchain technology adoption in supply chains-Indian Context. *International Journal of Production Research*, *57*(7), 2009–2033. doi:10.1080/00207543.2018.1518610

Kamble, S. S., Gunasekaran, A., & Gawankar, S. A. (2020). Achieving sustainable performance in a data-driven agriculture supply chain:A review for research and applications. *International Journal of Production Economics*, *2020*(219), 179–194. doi:10.1016/j.ijpe.2019.05.022

Kane, E., (2017). *Is Blockchain a General Purpose Technology*?

Ketzenberg, M., Bloemhof, J., & Gaukler, G. (2015). Managing perishables with time and temperature history. *Production and Operations Management*, *2015*(24), 54–70. doi:10.1111/poms.12209

Kitchin, R., & Dodge, M. (2011). *Code/Space: Software and Everyday Life*. MIT Press. doi:10.7551/mitpress/9780262042482.001.0001

Kshetri, N. (2018). Blockchain's roles in meeting key supply chain management objectives. *International Journal of Information Management*, *39*(April), 80–89. doi:10.1016/j.ijinfomgt.2017.12.005

Lam, C. Y., & Ip, W. H. (2019). An Integrated Logistics Routing and Scheduling Network Model with RFID-GPS Data for Supply Chain Management. *Wireless Personal Communications*, *2019*(105), 803–817. doi:10.100711277-019-06122-6

Lansiti, Marco, & Lakhani, K. (2017). The truth about Blockchain. *Harvard Business Review*.

Lasi, H., Fettke, P., Kemper, H.-G., Feld, T., & Hoffmann, M. (2014). Industry 4.0. *Business & Information Systems Engineering*, *6*(4), 239–242. doi:10.100712599-014-0334-4

Lebosse, S., Taghipour, A., & Canel-Depitre, B. (2017). Quick response to fluctuations in supply chains: A review. *Journal of Advanced Management Science*, *5*(5), 394–400. doi:10.18178/joams.5.5.394-400

Lezoche, M., Panetto, H., Kacprzyk, J., Hernandez, J. E., & Alemany Díaz, M. M. E. (2020). Agri-food 4.0: A survey of the Supply Chains and Technologies for the Future Agriculture. *Computers in Industry*, *2020*(117), 103187. doi:10.1016/j.compind.2020.103187

Li, B., Yang, C., & Huang, S. (2014). Study on supply chain disruption management under service level dependent. *Journal of Networking*, *9*(6), 1432–1439. doi:10.4304/jnw.9.6.1432-1439

Li, D. (2016). Perspective for smart factory in petrochemical industry. *Computers & Chemical Engineering*, *91*, 136–148. doi:10.1016/j.compchemeng.2016.03.006

Liukkonen, M., & Tsai, T. N. (2016). Toward decentralized intelligence in manufacturing: Recent trends in automatic identification of things. *International Journal of Advanced Manufacturing Technology*, *87*(9-12), 2509–2531. doi:10.100700170-016-8628-y

Loivet, W., Taghipour, A., & Kang, D. S. (2020). The rise of green supply chain management: Between complexity and necessity. *Journal of Economics. Business and Management*, *8*(1), 1–7.

Lom, M., Pribyl, O., & Svitek, M. (2016). Industry 4.0 as a Part of Smart Cities, *Smart Cities Symposium Prague (SCSP)*, 2016. IEEE, 1–6. 10.1109/SCSP.2016.7501015

Matharu, G. S., Upadhyay, P., & Chaudhary, L. (2014). *The Internet of Things: Challenges & security issues.* In *Proceedings of the 2014 International Conference on Emerging Technologies, ICET 2014*, Islamabad, Pakistan. 10.1109/ICET.2014.7021016

Mbiatem, J., Taghipour, A., & Canel-Depitre, B. (2018). Supplier selection approaches for decision makers. In *Proceedings of the 8th International Conference on Information Communication and Management,* (pp. 108-112). ACM. 10.1145/3268891.3268895

Merimi, M., & Taghipour, A. (2021). Accelerating the digitalization of the supply chain: An empirical research about COVID-19 crisis. In *Digitalization of Decentralized Supply Chains During Global Crises* (pp. 1–24). IGI Global. doi:10.4018/978-1-7998-6874-3.ch001

Min, H. (2019). Blockchain technology for enhancing supply chain resilience. *Business Horizons*, *2019*(62), 35–45. doi:10.1016/j.bushor.2018.08.012

Nakamoto, S. (2008). *Bitcoin: A peer-to-peer electronic cash system.* Bitcoin.

Narayanan, A. (2015). Private Blockchain' is just a confusing name for a shared database. *Freedom to Tinker.* https://freedom-to-tinker.com/2015/09/18/private-blockchaini s-just-a-confusing-name-for-a-shared-database/

Ng, I. C., & Wakenshaw, S. Y. (2017). The Internet-of-Things: Review and research directions. *International Journal of Research in Marketing*, *34*(1), 3–21. doi:10.1016/j.ijresmar.2016.11.003

Paksoy, T., Karaoğlan, I., Gökçen, H., Pardalos, P. M., & Torğul, B. (2016). Experimental research on closed loop supply chain management with internet of things. *Journal of Economics Bibliograph.*, *15*(3), 1–20.

Pal, K. (2017). Supply Chain Coordination Based on Web Services. In H. K. Chan, N. Subramanian, & M. D. Abdulrahman (Eds.), *Supply Chain Management in the Big Data Era* (pp. 137–171). IGI Global Publication. doi:10.4018/978-1-5225-0956-1.ch009

Pal, K. (2017). Supply Chain Coordination Based on Web Services. In H. K. Chan, N. Subramanian, & M. D. Abdulrahman (Eds.), *Supply Chain Management in the Big Data Era*. IGI Global Publishing.

Pal, K. (2018). A Big Data Framework for Decision Making in Supply Chain. In P K Gupta, Tuner Oren, Mayank Singh (eds.) Predictive Intelligence Using Big Data and the Internet of Things. IGI Global Publication.

Pal, K. (2019). Algorithmic Solutions for RFID Tag Anti-Collision Problem in Supply Chain Management. *The 9th International Symposium on Frontiers in Ambient and Mobile Systems (FAMS).* Procedia Computer Science, 929-934.

Pal, K. (2019). Quality Assurance Issues for Big Data Applications in Supply Chain Management, in P K Gupta, Tuner Oren, Mayank Singh (eds). Predictive Intelligence Using Big Data and the Internet of Things. IGI Global Publication.

Pal, K. (2020). Internet of Things and Blockchain Technology in Apparel Supply Chain Management. In H. Patel & G. S. Thakur (Eds.), *Blockchain Applications in IoT Security*. IGI Global Publication.

Pal, K. (2021). Privacy, Security and Policies: A Review of Problems and Solutions with Blockchain-Based Internet of Things Applications in Manufacturing Industry. *Procedia Computer Science*, *191*, 176–183. doi:10.1016/j.procs.2021.07.022

Pal, K. (2021). Privacy, Security and Policies: A Review of Problems and Solutions with Blockchain-Based Internet of Things Applications in Manufacturing Industry [Elsevier.]. *Procedia Computer Science*, *191*, 176–183. doi:10.1016/j.procs.2021.07.022

Pal, K. (2023). Security Issues and Solutions for Resource-Constrained IoT Applications. Using Lightweight Cryptography, in Cybersecurity Issues, Challenges, and Solutions in the Business World. IGI Global Publication.

Pal, K., & Karakostas, B. (2014). A Multi Agent-Based Service Framework for Supply Chain Management. In *Proceedings of the 5th International Conference on Ambient Systems, Networks and Technologies (ANT14).* Procedia Computer Science.

Pal, K., & Yasar, A. (2020). Internet of Things and Blockchain Technology in Apparel Manufacturing Supply Chain Data Management. *Procedia Computer Science*, *170*, 450–457. doi:10.1016/j.procs.2020.03.088

Pal, K., & Yasar, A. (2023). Internet of Things Impact on Supply Chain Management, in *Proceedings of the 14th International Conference on Ambient Systems, Networks and Technologies (ANT23).* Procedia Computer Science.

Pearce, D. W., & Turner, R. K. (1990). *Economics of Natural Resources and the Environment*. JHU Press.

Pournader, M., Shi, Y., Seuring, S., & Koh, S. C. L. (2020). Blockchain applications in supply chains, transport, and logistics: A systematic review of the literature. *International Journal of Production Research, 2020*(58), 2063–2081. doi:10.1080/00207543.2019.1650976

Prendeville, S., Cherim, E., & Bocken, N. (2017). Circular cities: Mapping six cities in transition. *Environmental Innovation and Societal Transitions*.

Ren, Z., Taghipour, A., & Canel-Depitre, B. (2016). Information sharing in the supply chain under uncertainty. In *2016 6th International Conference on Information Communication and Management (ICICM)*, (pp. 67-71). IEEE. 10.1109/INFOCOMAN.2016.7784217

Reyna, A., Martin, C., Chen, J., Soler, E., & Diaz, M. (2018). On blockchain and its integration with IoT, Challenges and opportunities. *Future Generation Computer Systems*, *28*, 173–190. doi:10.1016/j.future.2018.05.046

Sharma, P. K., Moon, S. Y., & Park, J. H. (2017). Block-VN: A distributed Blockchain based vehicular network architecture in smart city. *Journal of Information Processing Systems*, *13*(1), 84.

Shelton, T., Poorthuis, A., & Zook, M. (2015). Social media and the city: Rethinking urban socio-spatial inequality using user-generated geographic information. *Landscape and Urban Planning*, *142*, 198–211. doi:10.1016/j.landurbplan.2015.02.020

Shin, M., & Taghipour, A. (2021). Supply Chains Digital Transformation: Automated Underground Logistics Systems. *Underground Construction*, *6*(2), 7. doi:10.18178/joebm.2021.9.2.651

Shin, T. H., Chin, S., Yoon, S. W., & Kwon, S. W. (2011). A service-oriented integrated information framework for RFID/WSN-based intelligent construction supply chain management. *Automation in Construction*, *20*(6), 706–715. doi:10.1016/j.autcon.2010.12.002

Stiglitz, J. (2017). *Globalization and its Discontents Revisited: Anti-Globalization in the Era of Trump*. Penguin.

Taghipour, A. (2009). Évaluation de la collaboration dans une chaîne d'approvisionnement. *Revue française de gestion industrielle, 28*(1), 26-42.

Taghipour, A. (2014). Improving the Plan of a Manufacturing Network with Non-Integrated Business Units. [IJAL]. *International Journal of Applied Logistics*, *5*(2), 1–11. doi:10.4018/ijal.2014040101

Taghipour, A. (2014). *Production Network Planning Based on Constraint Relaxation and Discount Approach* (Vol. 2). Lecture Notes on Information Theory.

Taghipour, A., Abed, M., & Zoghlami, N. (2015). Design for remanufacturing respecting reverse logistics processes: A review. In *2015 4th International Conference on Advanced Logistics and Transport (ICALT)*. IEEE. 10.1109/ICAdLT.2015.7136602

Taghipour, A., & Beneteau-Piet, C. (2020). Sustainable supply chain management performance. *International Journal of Innovation, Management and Technology*, *11*(6), 165–169. doi:10.18178/ijimt.2020.11.6.897

Taghipour, A., & Frayret, J. M. (2010). Negotiation-based coordination in supply chain: model and discussion. In *2010 IEEE International Conference on Systems, Man and Cybernetics*. IEEE. 10.1109/ICSMC.2010.5642397

Taghipour, A., & Frayret, J. M. (2011b). *Supply chain coordination planning: A review*. Work paper, École polytechnique de Montréal.

Taghipour, A., & Frayret, J. M. (2013). An algorithm to improve operations planning in decentralized supply chains. In *2013 International Conference on Advanced Logistics and Transport*. IEEE. 10.1109/ICAdLT.2013.6568442

Taghipour, A., Glaa, B., & Zoghlami, N. (2014). Network coordination with minimum risk of information sharing. In *2014 International Conference on Advanced Logistics and Transport (ICALT)*. IEEE. 10.1109/ICAdLT.2014.6864115

Taghipour, A., & Merimi, M. (2021). Digital Transformation of Supply Chains during Crisis: COVID-19. In *11th Annual International Conference on Industrial Engineering and Operations Management, IEOM* (pp. 7493-7501). IEEE.

Taghipour, A., Murat, S., & Huang, P. (2021). E-supply chain management: A review. *International Journal of e-Education, e-Business, e-Management, and e-Learning, 11*(2), 51-61.

Tan, J., & Koo, S. (2014). A survey of technologies in internet of things, in IEEE. *Computers & Society*, 269–274.

Tang, C. S., & Veelenturf, L. P. (2019). The strategic role of logistics in the industry 4.0 era. Transp. Res. Part E Logist. *Transport Reviews, 2019*(129), 1–11.

Verdouw, C. N., Wolfert, J., Beulens, A., & Rialland, A. (2016). Virtualization of food supply chains with the internet of things. *Journal of Food Engineering*, *176*, 128–136. doi:10.1016/j.jfoodeng.2015.11.009

Veza, I., Mladineo, M., & Gjeldum, N. (2015). Managing innovative production network of smart factories. *IFAC-PapersOnLine*, *48*(3), 555–560. doi:10.1016/j.ifacol.2015.06.139

Vogel-Heuser, B., & Hess, D. (2016). Guest editorial Industry 4.0–prerequisites and visions. *IEEE Transactions on Automation Science and Engineering*, *13*(2), 411–413. doi:10.1109/TASE.2016.2523639

Vosooghidizaji, M., Taghipour, A., & Canel-Depitre, B. (2022). Coordinating corporate social responsibility in a two-level supply chain under bilateral information asymmetry. *Journal of Cleaner Production*, *364*, 132627. doi:10.1016/j.jclepro.2022.132627

Wang, L., Laszewski, G. V., Young, K. M., & Tao, J. (2010). Cloud Computing: A Perspective Study. *New Generation Computing*, *28*(2), 137–146. doi:10.100700354-008-0081-5

Wang, T., Zhang, Y., & Zang, D. (2016) Real-time visibility and traceability framework for discrete manufacturing shopfloor. In Proceedings of the 22nd International Conference on Industrial Engineering and Engineering Management, (pp. 763–772). Springer. 10.2991/978-94-6239-180-2_72

Weidema, B. P. (2015). Comparing three life cycle impact assessment methods from an endpoint perspective. *Journal of Industrial Ecology*, *19*(1), 20–26. doi:10.1111/jiec.12162

Wognum, P. M., Bremmers, H., Trienekens, J. H., Van Der Vorst, J. G. A. J., & Bloemhof, J. M. (2011). Systems for sustainability and transparency of food supply chains—Current status and challenges. *Advanced Engineering Informatics*, *2011*(25), 65–76. doi:10.1016/j.aei.2010.06.001

Xing, B., Gao, W. J., Battle, K., Nelwamondo, F. V., & Marwala, T. (2012). e-RL: the Internet of things supported reverse logistics for remanufacture-to-order, *International Conference in Swarm Intelligence: Advances in Swarm Intelligence*, (pp. 519–526). IEEE.

Yan, B., & Huang, G. (2009). Supply chain information transmission based on RFID and internet of things in Computing. In: *Communication, Control, and Management, ISECS International Colloquium on*, (pp. 166–169). Springer.

Yli-Huumo, J., Ko, D., Choi, S., Park, S., & Smolander, K. (2016). Where is current research on Blockchain technology?—A systematic review. *PLoS One, 11*(10), 1–27. doi:10.1371/journal.pone.0163477 PMID:27695049

Yuvaraj, S., & Sangeetha, M. (2016). Smart supply chain management using internet of things (IoT) and low power wireless communication system. *Wireless Communication, Signal Processing and Networking, International Conference*, (pp. 555-558). Springer.

Zawadzki, P., & Zywicki, K. (2016). Smart product design and production control for effective mass customization in the industry 4.0 concept. *Management of Production Engineering Review, 7*(3), 105–112. doi:10.1515/mper-2016-0030

Zhang, Y., & Kitsos, P. (2016). *Security in RFID and Sensor Networks* (1st ed.). Auerbach Publications.

Zhou, K., Liu, T., & Zhou, L. (2015). Industry 4.0: towards future industrial opportunities and challenges. In: *2015 12th International Conference on Fuzzy Systems and Knowledge Discovery (FSKD).* IEEE.

KEY TERMS AND DEFINITIONS

Block: A block is a data structure used to communicate incremental changes to the local state of a node. It consists of a list of transactions, a reference to a previous block and a nonce.

Blockchain: In simple, a blockchain is just a data structure that can be shared by different users using computing data communication network (e.g., peer-to-peer or P2P). Blockchain is a distributed data structure comprising a chain of blocks. It can act as a global ledger that maintains records of all transactions on a blockchain network. The transactions are time-stamped and bundled into blocks where each block is identified by its *cryptographic hash.*

Cryptography: Blockchain's transactions achieve validity, trust, and finality based on cryptographic proofs and underlying mathematical computations between various trading partners.

Decentralized computing infrastructure: These computing infrastructures feature computing nodes that can make independent processing and computational decisions irrespective of what other peer computing nodes may decide.

Immutability: This term refers to the fact that blockchain transactions cannot be deleted or altered.

Internet of Things (IoT): The Internet of Things (IoT), also called the Internet of Everything or the Industrial Internet, is now a technology paradigm envisioned as a global network of machines and devices capable of interacting with each other. The IoT is recognized as one of the most critical areas of future technology and is gaining vast attention from a wide range of industries.

Provenance: In a blockchain ledger, provenance is a way to trace the origin of every transaction such that there is no dispute about the origin and sequence of the transactions in the ledger.

Supply Chain Management: A supply chain consists of a network of *key business processes* and facilities, involving end-users and suppliers that provide products, services, and information.

Warehouse: A warehouse can also be called a storage area, and it is a commercial building where raw materials or goods are stored by suppliers, exporters, manufacturers, or wholesalers, they are constructed and equipped with tools according to special standards depending on the purpose of their use.

Chapter 11
A Mobile Social App for Better Life of Poor People Based on Perceived Similarity and Trust Using Supply Chain Management

Ahmad Mhala
Marwadi University, India

Yatri Davda
V.V.P. Engineering College, India

Damodharan Palaniappan
Marwadi University, India

ABSTRACT

As an attempt to collaborate the digital world with the physical one, the authors maintain track of the journey of dairy products, clothes, watches, bags, etc.; any type of material from producer to consumer. The authors can use the strength of internet technology and its extensive network, by which individuals can assist one other with only a click from their phone, to satisfy the growing need for advances in donation facilities and services. The suggested system for stuff donation aims to give needy people an online platform for giving clothes, books, or any unneeded things. Users can sign up for this system by providing the required information. Once registered, users can add a post either for giving donations or for requesting a donation. Using their app, the authors can supply all the items outside of the country. Today, supply chain management is one of the most important usable ways for NGO to earn competitive benefits.

DOI: 10.4018/978-1-6684-9062-4.ch011

1. INTRODUCTION

Having a social life is important to village people, and mobile social applications (apps) cannot be absent in modern life. However, many mobile apps have trust issues more or less. To solve trust issues and promote online social life, a mobile social app specifically for poor people and NGOs is designed. The proposed way to solve trust issues between users is based on perceived similarity and trust (L. Jianglong and X. Min 2016, Cauchois, R., Taghipour, A., Kang, D., Zoghlami, N., & Abed, M. (2017)). The proliferation of Java has had a profound impact on how simple programs and complex applications are developed and distributed (El-Nemr, N., Canel-Depitre, B., & Taghipour, A. (2017, September)). The Java platform comes with a rich set of function libraries that ease the software developer's task and make the language suitable for developing programs in multiple application domains. In addition, Java applications consist of dynamically loaded pieces of code that can be downloaded over a network and linked at runtime (El-NEMR, N., CANEL-DEPITRE, B., & TAGHIPOUR, A. (2021), Loivet, W., Taghipour, A., & Kang, D. S. (2020)) as needed to provide an extensible programming environment. Another feature of his Java language that helped popularize is its portability. Java programs are compiled to platform-independent format. plat- form. Because much of the information needed to run bytecode is stored as symbolic references, and the JVM was designed with a very simple architecture, the bytecode format can be used on machines run by real microprocessors. Relatively simple compared to the complexity of the code. In addition, a large amount of documentation is available on both the Java Virtual Machine and the Java language. These facts make the decompilation process so easy that it threatens the interests of software developers and companies investing money in distributing Java-based software. decompilation is the process of converting object code into source code and is relevant for Java application security for a number of reasons. In fact, reverse engineering of executable code facilitates software piracy, allowing attackers to steal software intellectual property and obtain solutions to specific problems for reuse (and sometimes resale). Make it possible. In addition, such processes allow attackers to discover application vulnerabilities or obtain sensitive information (passwords, license numbers, credit card numbers) hidden in executable code. This opens up many security vulnerabilities. The Java Standard Software Development Kit includes a basic disassembler included in the standard development tools provided. Variables and methods contained in the class. Since the early days of Java, there are also many third party decompilers on the market that provide an easy way to get the source code from the classes that the compiled. At the same time, code obfuscation tools were developed with the aim of making the decompilation process more difficult.

2. PROJECT DOMAINS

Android studio: is the official integrated development environment (IDE) for Google's Android operating system, built on JetBrains' IntelliJ IDEA software and designed specifically for Android development (Developer Community, A. (n.d.). 24 December 2022)

Java programming language: Android is an open-source software platform and Linux-based operating system for mobile devices. The Android platform allows developers to write managed code using Java to manage and control the Android device (kanjilal, jaydip, Kanjilal, J., By, Kanjilal, J., Manoj Debnath -October 23, -, M. D., Robert Gravelle - April 26, -, R. G., Joydip Kanjilal - December 21, & -, J. K. 2021, June 8)

XML:XML stands for eXtensible Markup Language, which is a way of describing data using a text-based document. Because XML is extensible and very flexible (Mahfod, J., Canel-Depitre, B., & Taghipour, A. (2019)),

Figure 1. Contact data and donation details collections

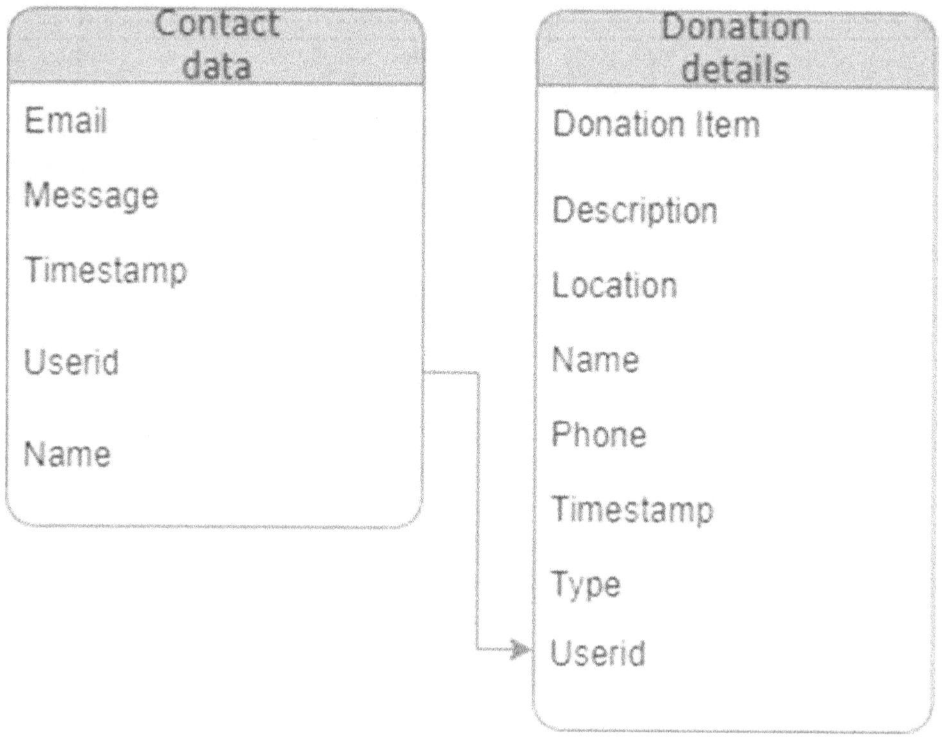

Figure 2. Admin and user collections

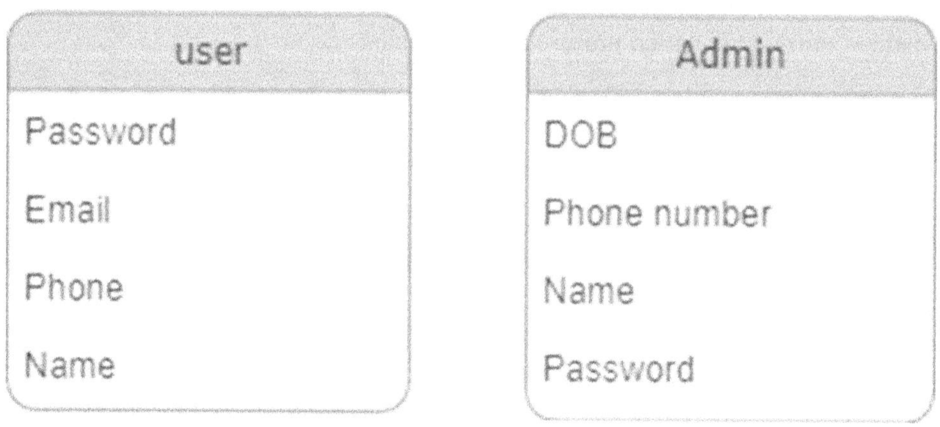

it's used for many different things, including defining the UI layout of Android apps (Google Developers 2023, Merimi, M., & Taghipour, A. (2021), Nadia, E. N., Beatrice, C. D., & Atour, T. (2020)).

Firebase (Google Developers 2023)

- Authentication (sign-in method)
- Firestore database (NoSQL database)

DATABASE

We have four collections, each collection has documents, and each document has fields as shown in Figure 1 and Figure 2.

IMPLEMENTED FUNCTIONALITY

The first page will be the main page which includes four pages, login, registration, login as admin, and contact us page by swiping right and left (K. L. Lentine, N. N. Lam, and D. L. Segev 2019, Shin, M., & Taghipour, A. (2021), Taghipour, A., & Frayret, J. M. (2011a))

- login page: after entering a valid username and password, the application checks if the entered email and password are valid and the password length is more than six characters, then will compare them with data in the database to check if the user is valid or not.
    - if yes, the user will be moved to the user dashboard page.
    - if not correct, the application will show a notification (user name or password invalid) (Taghipour, A., Murat, S., & Huang, P. (2021)).
- Register page: On this page, the user registers himself, after entering valid data, it will be saved in the database and then the user will be redirected to the dashboard page.

Figure 3. User login

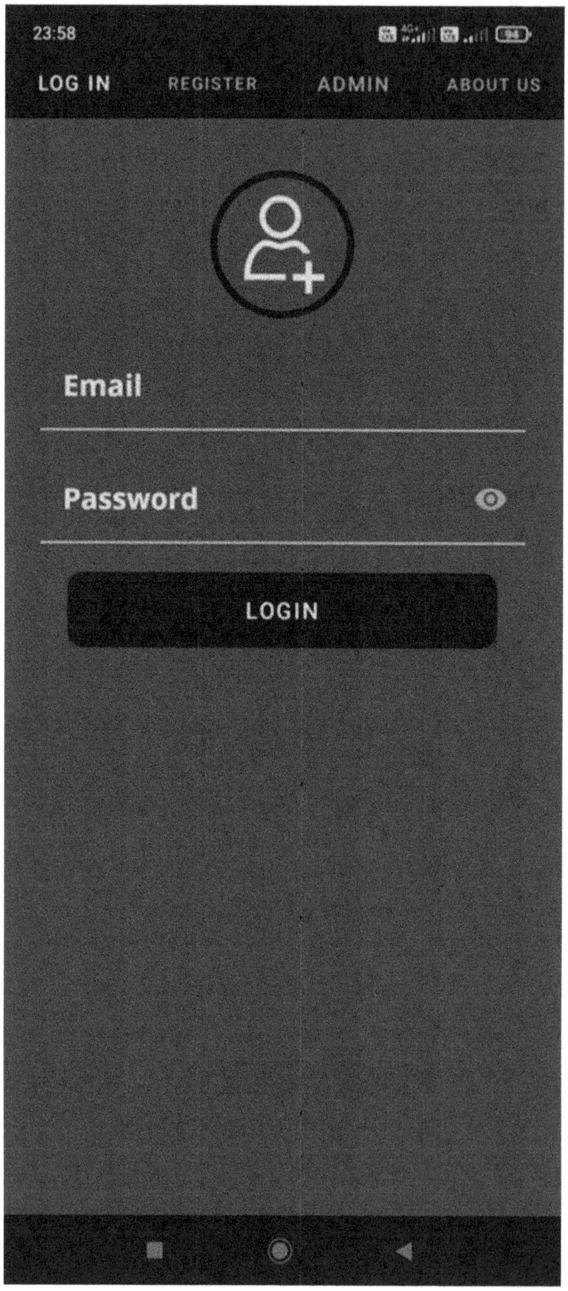

Figure 4. Register

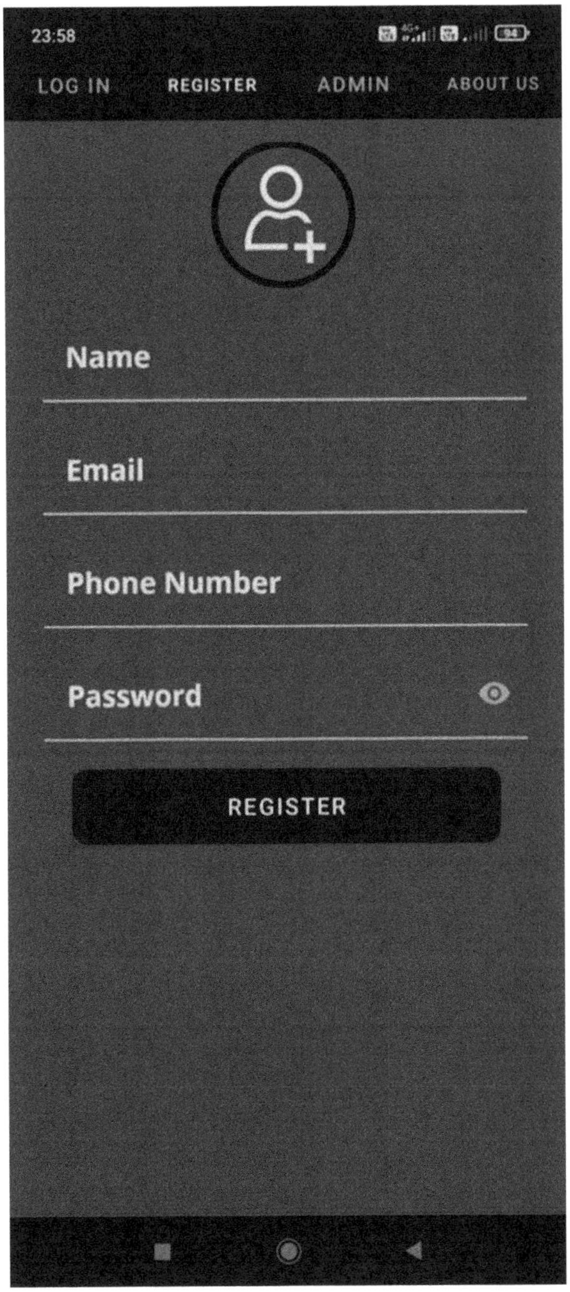

- Admin login page: On this page the admin login as an admin, after entering the data, the application checks if it is valid in the database. If yes, the admin will be redirected to the admin dashboard
- Contact us page (Figure 11)

  After the user login (Figure 3) or registers (Figure 4), he/she will be redirected to the dashboard page, and here the user has 8 activities
- User dashboard (Figure 6 and Figure 7):

- Donate: it is a page that allows users to add donations, user will enter important data and application takes his permission for location and after that all the data which is entered by user and his location will be sent and saved in the database.

Figure 5. Contact us

Figure 6. User dashboard

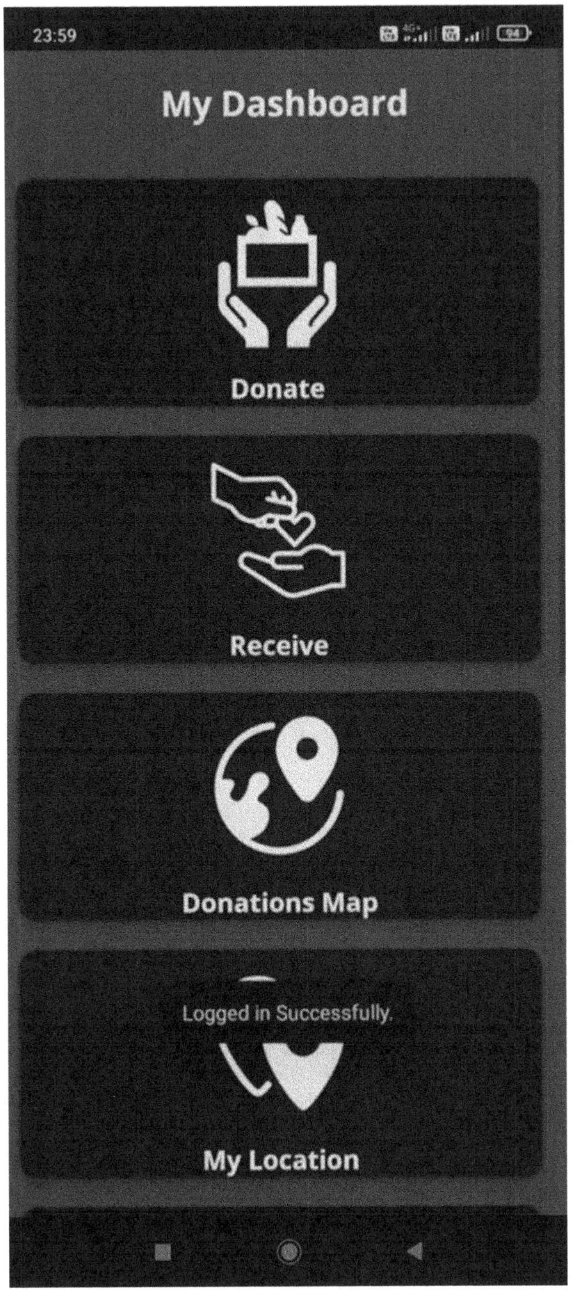

- Receive (Figure 13): in this page users are able to add requests for receiving a donation, the user enters important data and applications take his permission for location, after that all the data that is entered by the user and his location will be sent and saved.

Figure 7. User dashboard

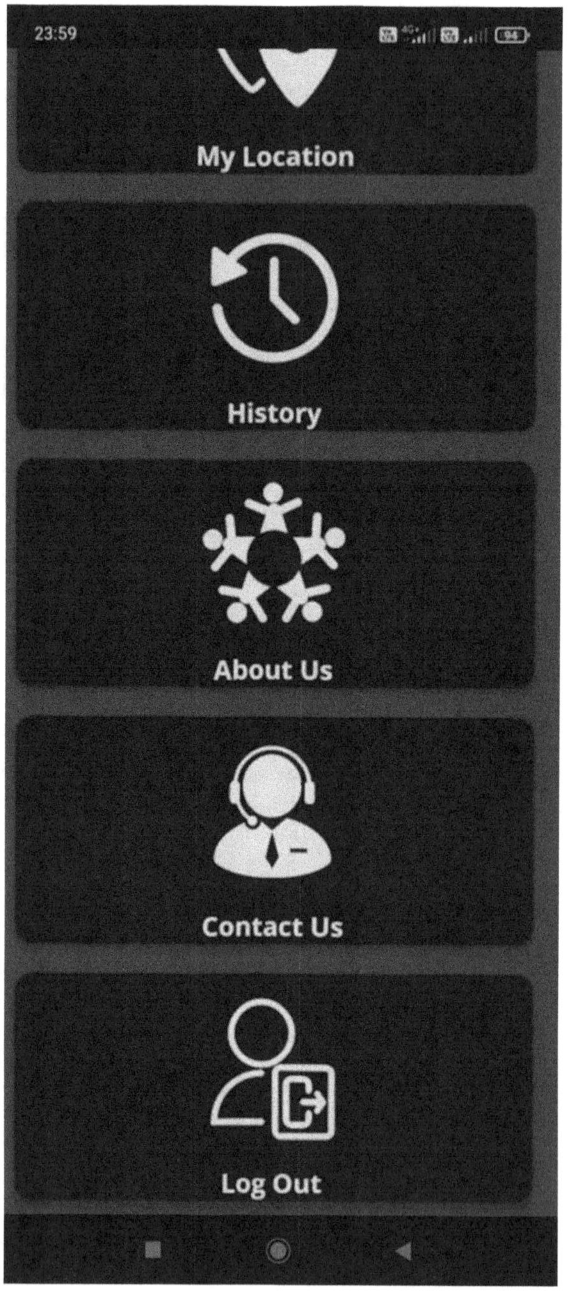

Figure 8. Donation map

- Donation Map (Figure 8) this page shows the map which includes receiving and giving donations requests. receive a donation is marked by a blue mark, giving a donation is marked by a green mark (Google Developers 2023, Taghipour, A., & Frayret, J. M. (2011b), Taghipour, A. (2014))
- History: shows the history (Figure 9) requests of the user, and the user can delete his request from here.
- About us (Figure 10)

- Contact us (Figure 5): is a page where the user can add any query, and then the data will be sent and saved in the database.

Figure 9. History for us

Figure 10. About us

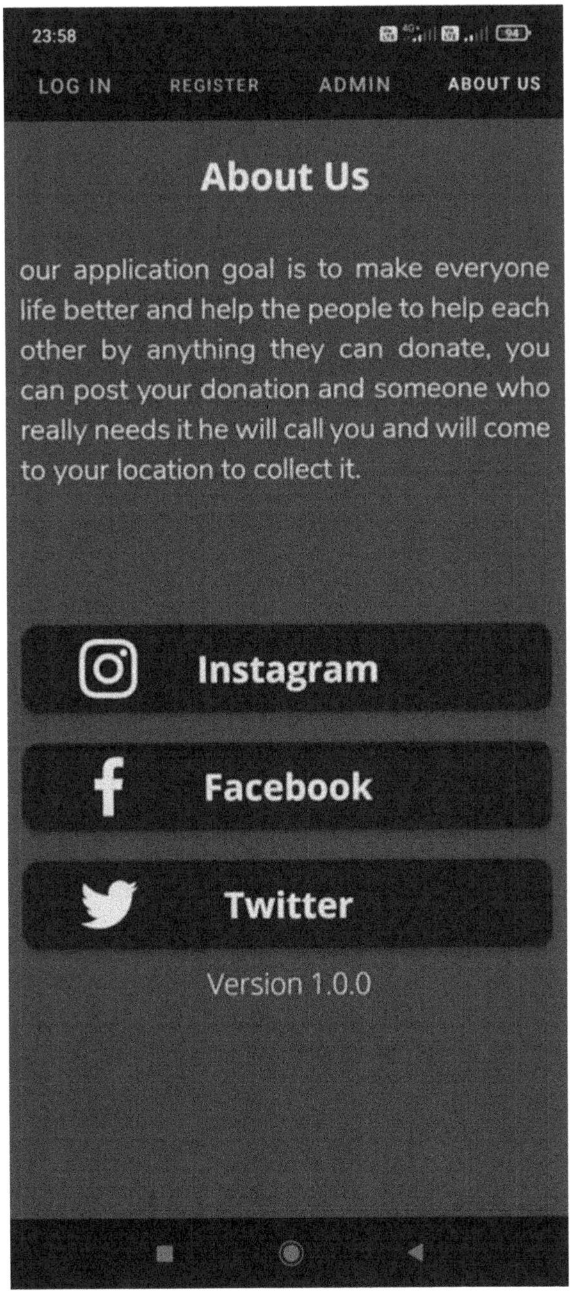

- location: it shows the user's location on the map
- Logout: after the user clicks on this button, he will be logged out and redirected to the main page
    - Admin login: After admin login, the admin will be redirected to the Admin dashboard page, where he will be able to go into two pages and he has a logout button also in this page.

Figure 11. Contact us

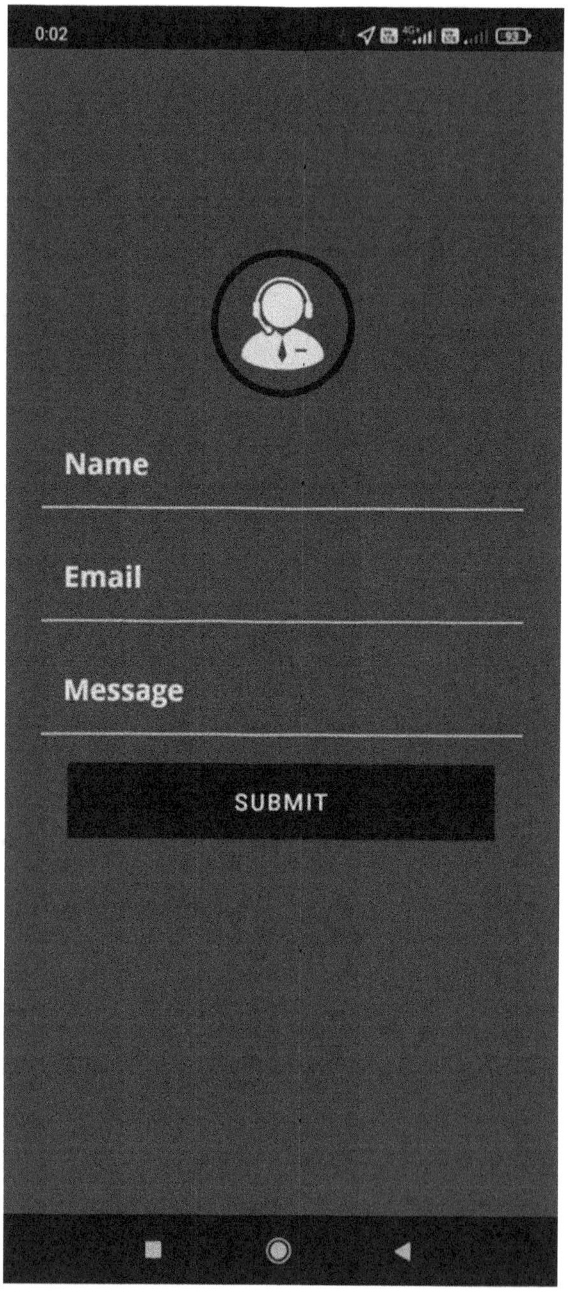

Figure 12. User location

- Donation map for admin: here the admin is able to see all the donations are on google Maps (Figure 12).
- History page for admin: the admin will be able to manage the history of all users.
- Logout: admin will be redirected to the main page
    - contact us: it has contact information

Figure 13. Admin receive

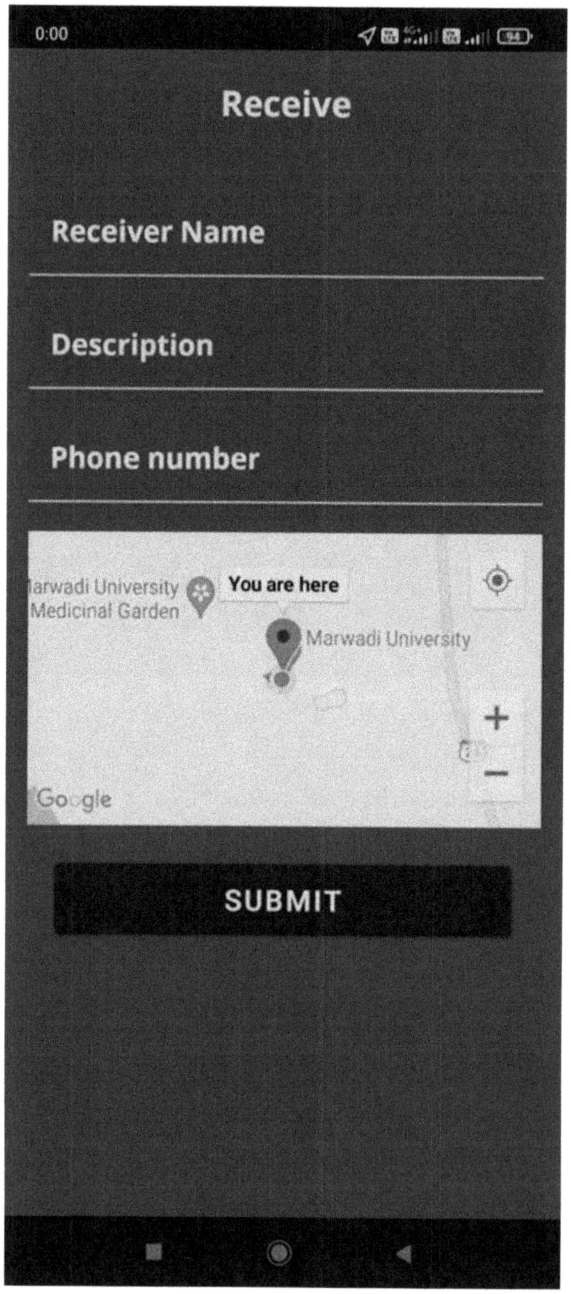

TESTING METHODS

- White box testing: White Box Testing is a software testing technique in which internal structure, design, and coding of software are tested to verify the flow of input- output and to improve design, usability, and security. In white box testing, code is visible to testers so it is also called Clear box testing, Open box testing, Transparent box testing, Code-based testing, and Glass box test (Taghipour, A., Glaa, B., & Zoghlami, N. (2014, May))

Following are important White Box Testing Techniques:

- Statement Coverage
- Decision Coverage
- Branch Coverage
- Condition Coverage
- Multiple Condition Coverage
- Finite State Machine Coverage
- Path Coverage
- Control flow testing
- Data flow testing

APPLICATION IMPLEMENTATION

- Github: https://github.com/Ahmad-Mhala/betterlife
- youtube: https://www.youtube.com/shorts/gV1zybCICW8

FUTURE SCOOP

- Notifications: to keep users informed about updates to their requests or donations, or about new requests or donations in their area (Taghipour, A., Abed, M., & Zoghlami, N. (2015, May), Taghipour, A. (2018), Taghipour, A. (Ed.). (2020)).
- Rating system: to allow users to rate each other based on the successful completion of a donation or request transaction.
- Search functionality: to allow users to search for specific items or keywords.
- Image upload: Allow users to upload images of the items they're donating or requesting to make it easier for others to see what they're offering.
- Rating/review system: Allow users to rate and review each other based on the quality of items donated or received.
- phone number authentication

ADVANTAGES AND DISADVANTAGES

1) Advantages:

   a) Increased reach: With the ability to accept dona- tions from anywhere in the world, donation appli- cations can help organizations expand their reach and attract more donors (Taghipour, A., & Beneteau-Piet, C. (2020), Taghipour, A., & Merimi, M. (2021)).
   b) Lower costs: By reducing the need for manual processes and paper-based systems, donation ap- plications can help organizations save money and reduce administrative costs.
   c) Increased accessibility: For donors with disabili- ties, or those who are unable to visit or- ganizations in person, donation applications can provide a more accessible way to make contributions.
   d) our application make it easy for people to donate to their favorite causes without having to physically visit the organization or write a check (Tliche, Y., Taghipour, A., & Canel-Depitre, B. (2019), Tliche, Y., Taghipour, A., & Canel-Depitre, B. (2021)).
2) Disadvantages:
   a) Technical issues: Technical problems such as ap- plication crashes, slow load times, and security breaches can deter donors from using the appli- cation and negatively impact the organization's reputation
   b) Dependence on technology: Donation applications rely on technology, which can be subject to out- ages, errors, and malfunctions. Organizations may need to have a backup plan in place in case the application is unavailable
   c) Phone number and email ID verification not valid, user can use fake information
   d) chat section is not available between users

LITERATURE REVIEW

Studies of supply chain management have called for more theory development (Kent and Flint, 1997; Mentzer and Kahn, 1995; Meredith, 1993; Melynk and Handfield, 1998; Wacker, 1998). Despite this call, there has been very limited progress in theory building in the field of supply chain management (Carter and Ellram, 2003). This is in part due to the relatively small number of existing studies in the logistics literature that have employed rigorous inductive approaches such as grounded theoretical methods or interpretation-based traditions (Flint et al., 2005; Svensson, 2000, Vosooghidizaji, M., Taghipour, A., & Canel-Depitre, B. (2020)).

It is important to note that research studies are not the only means of testing theories a priori, and interpretive field research using interviews and observations is not the only way to develop theories (Elsbach et al., 1999; DiMaggio, 1995; Weick, 1999; McGrath, 1982, Vosooghidizaji, M., Taghipour, A., & Canel-Depitre, B. (2022)). Conceptual theorizing methods balance inductive and deductive reasoning and inquiry, and can help scholars guide and direct management practice (Meredith, 1993).

Meredith (1993, p. 7) defines the conceptual framework of SSCM as "a collection of two or more related propo- sitions that explain an event, convey an understanding, or suggest a testable hypothesis." The methodology for achieving this theory construction involves integrating multiple studies, sum- marizing common elements, contrasting differences, and extending the existing studies in some way (Meredith, 1993, p. 8).

Wacker (1998, p. 368) also contributes to the integration of existing theories with logical deductions through the definition of variables and the development of particular predictions. These statements gen- erated by the conceptual framework are supported by the work of Handfield and Melnyk (1998, p. 323).

However, it is important to note that the field of supply chain management is rapidly evolving, and theories and practices are continually being refined and updated. The development of theories in supply chain management is a complex and ongoing process that requires a multidisciplinary approach and a deep understanding of the complexities and challenges facing organizations in managing their supply chains.

It is also crucial to consider the practical implications of the- ory development in supply chain management. Theories must be developed and refined in a manner that provides valuable insights and practical guidance for organizations. This requires a close collaboration between practitioners and academics, as well as a deep understanding of the real-world challenges facing organizations in managing their supply chains.

In conclusion, the development of theories in supply chain management is crucial for advancing the field and improving the management of supply chains. The integration of multiple studies, the definition of variables, and the development of predictions are important steps in this process. However, it is also important to consider the practical implications of theory development and to ensure that theories are developed in a manner that provides valuable insights and practical guidance for organizations.

CONCLUSION

In conclusion, the project developed an Android mobile app to help people donate items in an easy way. The project used Java programming language to code the system features and used SQL language to manage the system database (S. Pargaien, A. V. Pargaien, B. Chilwal, N. Tripathi, H. Joshi and H. Negi 2021, Yang, S., Taghipour, A., & Canel-Depitre, B. (2017, August)). The process of the mobile apps is demonstrated through logical design that includes a use case diagram, class diagram, activity diagram, and sequence diagram from the synthesis section. The system prototype had successfully achieved all project objectives and expected results. However, the prototype exists a lot of limitations and required better enhancement in the future.

REFERENCES

Anand, A. (2015). Securing android code using white box cryptography and ob-fuscation technique. *International journal of computer science and mobile1295computing 4*(4), 347–352.

Barak, B., Goldreich, O., Impagliazzo, R., Rudich, S., Sahai, A., Vadhan, S., & Yang, K. (2001). On the (im) possibility of obfuscating programs. Annual International Cryptology Conference. Springer.

Bhalerao, S., Agarwal, S., Borkar, S., Anekar, S., Kulkarni N., & Bhag- wat, S. (2019) *Supply Chain Management using Blockchain.* 2019 International Conference on Intelligent Sustainable Systems (ICISS), Palladam, India. . doi:10.1109/ISS1.2019.8908031

Capocasale, V., Musso, S., & Perboli, G. (2022). Interplanetary File System in Logistic Networks: a Review. *2022 IEEE 46th Annual Com- puters, Software, and Applications Conference (COMPSAC).* IEEE. 10.1109/COMPSAC54236.2022.00268

Cauchois, R., Taghipour, A., Kang, D., Zoghlami, N., & Abed, M. (2017). Advanced solutions for a supply chain with stochastic information. *Journal of Advanced Management Science, 5*(1).

Chan, J.-T., & Yang, W. (2004). Advanced obfuscation techniques for Java bytecode. *Journal of Systems and Software, 71*(1-2), 1–10. doi:10.1016/S0164-1212(02)00066-3

Chow, S., Eisen, P., Johnson, H., & Van Oorschot, P. C. (2002). A white-box des im-plementation for drm applications. *ACM Workshop on Digital RightsManagement*. Springer.

Cimato, S., De Santis, A., & Ferraro Petrillo, U. (2005). Overcoming the obfuscation of Java programs by identifier renaming. *Journal of Systems and Software, 78*(1). Elsevier BV. . doi:10.1016/j.jss.2004.11.019

Developer Community for Android. (n.d.). *Meet android studio &Android Developers*. Android. https://developer.android.com/studio/intro

El-Nemr, N., Canel-Depitre, B., & Taghipour, A. (2021). The determinants of hotel room rates in Beirut: A hedonic pricing model. International Journal of Trade. *Economics and Finance, 12*(2), 33–42.

El-Nemr, N., Canel-Depitre, B., & Taghipour, A. (2017, September). Determinants of hotel room rates. In Marketing Trends Congress. Luxury Industries Conference London 2017.

Hoenicke, J. 2002. Java optimize and decompile environment. *Source Forge*. ¡https://jode.sourceforge.net/¿

Jianglong, L., & Min, X. (2016). A Mobile Social App for College Students Based on Perceived Similarity and Trust. 2016 8th International Con- ference on Information Technology in Medicine and Education. ITME. doi:10.1109/ITME.2016.0090

Kanjilal, J. (2021, June 8). *How java is used in Android App Development*. Developer.com. https://www.developer.com/mobile/java-mobile/java-mobile- programming-for android/

Lentine, K., Lam, N. & Segev, D. L. (2019). Risks of Living Kidney Donation. *Clinical Journal of the American Society of Nephrology, 14*(4). Ovid Technologies (Wolters Kluwer Health). . doi:10.2215/CJN.11220918

Loivet, W., Taghipour, A., & Kang, D. S. (2020). The rise of green supply chain management: Between complexity and necessity. Journal of Economics. *Business and Management, 8*(1), 1–7.

Mahfod, J., Canel-Depitre, B., & Taghipour, A. (2019). Quality function deployment-ELECTRE in supplier evaluation. *Journal of Advanced Management Science, 7*(4).

Merimi, M., & Taghipour, A. (2021). Accelerating the digitalization of the supply chain: An empirical research about COVID-19 crisis. In *Digitalization of Decentralized Supply Chains During Global Crises* (pp. 1–24). IGI Global. doi:10.4018/978-1-7998-6874-3.ch001

Miecznikowski, J., & Hendren, L. (2002). Decompiling java bytecode: problems, traps and pitfalls. In: *Compiler Construction, 11th International Conference, 2304 of Lecture Notes in Computer Science*. Springer-Verlag.

Nadia, E. N., Beatrice, C. D., & Atour, T. (2020). *Luxury hotels' eco-friendly activities & customers' preferences and willingness to pay for green hotels. Journal of Advanced Management Science, 8*(1).

Panigrahi, S. S., Bahinipati, B., & Jain, V. (2019). Sustainable supply chain management: A review of literature and implications for future research. *Management of Environmental Quality*, *30*(5), 1001–1049. doi:10.1108/MEQ-01-2018-0003

Pargaien, S., Pargaien, A. V., Chilwal, B., Tripathi, N., Joshi, H., & Negi, H. (2021). Urge To Implement IOT For Monitoring and Preventing Blood Bank System Crisis. *2021 First International Conference on Advances in Computing and Future Communication Technologies (ICACFCT)*, Meerut, India. 10.1109/ICACFCT53978.2021.9837377

Rashmitha, M., Babu, R. J., Sumathi, B., Mories, M. S., Sravani, V., & Madhuri, C. R. (2021). Covid Contentment Contribution. *2021 5th International Conference on Electrical, Electronics, Communication, Computer Technologies and Optimization Techniques (ICEECCOT),* Mysuru, India. 10.1109/ICEECCOT52851.2021.9708001

Santoso, T., Ahmed, S., Goetschalckx, M., & Shapiro, A. (2005). A stochastic pro- gramming approach for supply chain network design under uncertainty [H. Mohammadi Bidhandi, M.Y.]. *European Journal of Operational Research*, *167*(1), 96–115. doi:10.1016/j.ejor.2004.01.046

Shin, M., & Taghipour, A. (2021). Supply Chains Digital Transformation: Automated Underground Logistics Systems. *Underground Construction*, *6*(2), 7. doi:10.18178/joebm.2021.9.2.651

Simchi-Levi, D., Chen, X., & Bramel, J. (2005). *The Logic of Logistics: Theory, Algorithms, and Applications for Logistics Management* (2nd ed.). Springer.

Taghipour, A. (2014). *Production Network Planning Based on Constraint Relaxation and Discount Approach* (Vol. 2). Lecture Notes on Information Theory.

Taghipour, A. (2018). A Contemporary Approach to Plan Independent Logistics Actors. In *Contemporary Approaches and Strategies for Applied Logistics* (pp. 337–364). IGI Global. doi:10.4018/978-1-5225-5273-4.ch014

Taghipour, A. (Ed.). (2020). *Demand Forecasting and Order Planning in Supply Chains and Humanitarian Logistics*. IGI Global.

Taghipour, A., Abed, M., & Zoghlami, N. (2015, May). Design for remanufacturing respecting reverse logistics processes: A review. In *2015 4th International Conference on Advanced Logistics and Transport (ICALT)* (pp. 299-304). IEEE. 10.1109/ICAdLT.2015.7136602

Taghipour, A., & Beneteau-Piet, C. (2020). Sustainable supply chain management performance. *International Journal of Innovation, Management and Technology*, *11*(6), 165–169. doi:10.18178/ijimt.2020.11.6.897

Taghipour, A., & Frayret, J. M. (2011a). A new heuristic search with local optimization to manage a supply chain. *Meta*, 15.

Taghipour, A., & Frayret, J. M. (2011b). *Supply chain coordination planning: A review.* Work paper, École polytechnique de Montréal.

Taghipour, A., Glaa, B., & Zoghlami, N. (2014, May). Network coordination with minimum risk of information sharing. *In 2014 International Conference on Advanced Logistics and Transport (ICALT)* (pp. 184-188). IEEE. 10.1109/ICAdLT.2014.6864115

Taghipour, A., & Merimi, M. (2021). Digital Transformation of Supply Chains during Crisis: COVID-19. In *11th Annual International Conference on Industrial Engineering and Operations Management, IEOM* (pp. 7493-7501). IEOM.

Taghipour, A., Murat, S., & Huang, P. (2021). E-supply chain management: A review. International Journal of e-Education, e-Business, e-. *Management Learning*, *11*(2), 51–61.

Tliche, Y., Taghipour, A., & Canel-Depitre, B. (2019). Anticipation of Demand in Supply Chains. In *Hierarchical Planning and Information Sharing Techniques in Supply Chain Management* (pp. 1–45). IGI Global.

Tliche, Y., Taghipour, A., & Canel-Depitre, B. (2021). Exploring a Downstream Demand Inference Strategy in a Decentralized Two-Level Supply Chain. In *Demand Forecasting and Order Planning in Supply Chains and Humanitarian Logistics* (pp. 1–65). IGI Global. doi:10.4018/978-1-7998-3805-0.ch001

Vosooghidizaji, M., Taghipour, A., & Canel-Depitre, B. (2020). Information Asymmetry in Supply Chain Coordination: State of the Art. *Journal of Industrial and Intelligent Information, 8*(2).

Vosooghidizaji, M., Taghipour, A., & Canel-Depitre, B. (2022). Coordinating corporate social responsibility in a two-level supply chain under bilateral information asymmetry. *Journal of Cleaner Production*, *364*, 132627. doi:10.1016/j.jclepro.2022.132627

Yang, S., Taghipour, A., & Canel-Depitre, B. (2017, August). Cost optimization of reverse logistics: A review. In *Proceedings of the 7th International Conference on Information Communication and Management* (pp. 158-161). ACM. 10.1145/3134383.3134393

Chapter 12
Building Resilient Supply Chains to Natural Disasters

Erdinç Koç
Bingol University, Turkey

ABSTRACT

Firms may face internal or external risks. While internal risks can be managed with the firm's existing tangible or intangible resources, some of the external risks are not problems that firms can overcome with their own resources. When faced with these risks, firms can only try to minimize their losses. Natural disasters can be referred to as such external risks. This study examines the impact of earthquakes, a type of natural disaster, on firms and supply chains. Earthquakes affect not only the firm or the country directly affected by the disaster, but also all supply chains, which have become more complex and sophisticated due to globalization. In order to create resilient supply chains, the shares of global firms during the earthquake process are analyzed and recommendations are developed.

INTRODUCTION

A disaster is defined by the United Nations Office for Disaster Risk Reduction (UNDRR) as "*A serious disruption of the functioning of a community or a society at any scale due to hazardous events interacting with conditions of exposure, vulnerability and capacity, leading to one or more of the following: human, material, economic and environmental losses and impacts*" (UNDRR, 2023). The Federal Emergency Management Agency (FEMA) defines a disaster as "*a non-routine event that exceeds the capacity of the affected area to respond to it in such a way as to save lives; to preserve property; and to maintain the social, ecological, economic, and political stability of the affected region*" (FEMA, 2003). In order for an event to be recorded as a disaster, the Centre for Research on Epidemiology of Disasters (CRED) requires the following four criteria to be met: (1) ten or more people have been recorded as dead, (2) 100 or more people have been affected, (3) a state of emergency has been declared, (4) an international call for assistance has been made (CRED, 2023). Although different types of disasters are defined by different organizations, three types are commonly used: natural, man-made and hybrid (Shaluf, 2007). Shaluf (2007) defines the first group of man-made disasters as the socio-technical group consisting of

DOI: 10.4018/978-1-6684-9062-4.ch012

technological, transportation, stadia or other public places failures and production failures. The second group, warfare, is divided into two subgroups: national and international. Hybrid disasters are used for situations where there are known floodplains, an active volcano, or housing or factories built in an avalanche zone. Other forms of disasters are briefly discussed because this study focuses mostly on natural disasters. Despite the fact that every disaster has unique characteristics, it is important to carefully consider disaster types that have traits in common with the difficulties explored in this study. Natural disasters are catastrophic occurrences brought on by the forces of nature. It's common to refer to natural disasters as *"Acts of God."* CRED categorizes natural disasters into six types: biological, climatological, extra-terrestrial, geophysical, hydrological and meteorological. The geophysical disaster type is divided into three subgroups: volcanic activity, earthquake and mass movement. Earthquake is divided into two subtypes: ground movement and tsunami. According to CRED data, 16543 natural disasters occurred worldwide between 1900 and 2023. Of these natural disasters, 1583 were earthquakes, and more than 31 million people lost their lives in the earthquake in the last century. Earthquakes that took place since the beginning of the 20th century caused 652,349 deaths in China, 225,170 in Haiti, 163,529 in Japan, 154,277 in Iran and 146,403 in Russia. In addition, it has been calculated that the earthquakes that took place in the same period caused 334 billion dollars of damage in Japan, 177 billion dollars in China, 142 billion dollars in Italy, 103 billion dollars in the USA and 45 billion dollars in Turkey.

While earthquakes result in individual losses of life and property, they also result in institutional losses. According to World Bank data, 740,000 businesses were affected by the disaster in Japan in 2011 (Fujita et al., 2012). Firms are impacted by losses at the corporate level and even in the supply chain from the moment of disaster. These losses include both tangible and intangible assets. Companies may also lose the skills of their human resources, supplier relationships, and supply chain network as intangible elements in disasters, in addition to tangible losses such facilities, machinery, and equipment, and stocks. The losses that the supply chain has to endure, on the other hand, cause upside and downside breaks. Automobile manufacturing decreased by 33% in the second quarter after falling by 25% in the first due to the tsunami disaster in Japan. The tsunami's effects extended beyond Japan; Thailand and China's Guangdong both had declines of 17% and 11%, respectively. Due to the inability to import intermediate goods from Japan, growth in the US dropped from 15% to 2% (Fujita et al., 2012). In light of these findings, it is obvious that supply chains today, with the advancement of information and transportation infrastructure, extend beyond national borders and are a phenomenon that must be assessed on a global scale (Taghipour & Beneteau-Piet, 2020; Merimi & Taghipour, 2021; Vosooghidizaji et al., 2022). This emphasizes the reality that a disaster in one area can have far-reaching consequences in other countries via supply chains. This chapter clearly defines the disruptions that catastrophes create to supply chains and the implications of these disruptions, as well as information on what has to be done to lessen the impact of these disruptions and make supply chains more resilient. This chapter uses a case study approach to explore the supply chain strategies and operations used by firms during previous disasters. Evaluations on the topic are also provided.

Supply Chain Resilience

Although the term of resilience can be evaluated from ecological, social, psychological, economic, and organizational viewpoints (Ponis, 2012; Ponomarov & Holcomb, 2009), this study looks at it from a supply chain perspective. Resilience is clearly defined as the ability of a system to return to its original state or a better state after disturbed (Christopher & Peck, 2004). Like all systems, firms may face risks that may interrupt their activities. The negativities encountered cause the operations of the firms to be stopped and the interruptions in the supply chains to occur. Negative situations that occur may arise from within the firm, as well as from outside the control area of the firms. One of the environmental risks that a business cannot manage is the risk of a disaster. Risks associated with the environment include political instability, changes in governmental policy, macroeconomic uncertainty, social uncertainties, and natural uncertainties (Martínez et al., 2020). However, the disaster that was experienced disrupts firm operations and has an impact on not just the concerned firm but also the supply chain in which it is involved. Events such as an accident, direct action, extreme weather or natural disasters are considered to be environmental risks, but in addition to affecting the focal company, they can also affect the entire supply chain due to the damage they cause to the flow in the value chain (Christopher & Peck, 2004).

Ponomarov & Holcomb, (2009) defined supply chain resilience as the ability of the supply chain to adapt to foresee unanticipated events, respond to disruptions, and sustain planned operational continuity. By providing supply chain resilience, the behavior of internal and external factors can be monitored, and the ability of the supply chain to respond to risks and make agile decisions can be improved, and thus the overall stability of the supply chain can be achieved (Meng et al., 2021). Tukamuhabwa et al. (2015) defines supply chain resilience as "*The adaptive capability of a supply chain to prepare for and/or respond to disruptions, to make a timely and cost-effective recovery, and therefore progress to a post-disruption state of operations-ideally, a better state than prior to disruption*". Another definiton of supply chain resilience defined by (Kamalahmadi & Parast, 2016) like "*The adaptive capability of a supply chain to reduce the probability of facing sudden disturbances, resist the spread of disturbances by maintaining control over structures and functions, and recover and respond by immediate and effective reactive plans to transcend the disturbance and restore the supply chain to a robust state of operations*".

Hosseini et al., (2019) explain supply chain resilience with a four-step pyramid as shown in Figure 1. In the first step, the manufacturer's stock of raw materials or intermediate goods and different supplier networks allow for increasing supply chain resilience. In the second step, the elements that enable increasing supply chain resilience are included in the absorptive, adaptive and restorative capacities and form the supply chain resilience capacity as a whole. Supply chains with high resilience capacity are less vulnerable and require less recovery effort. Supply chains with low resilience capacity are more vulnerable and require more recovery effort. Supply chain resilience is at the top of the pyramid as a function of supply chain vulnerability and recoverability.

In the literature, some characteristics are emphasised as the formative elements of supply chain resilience or the antecedents of supply chain resilience (Ponomarov & Holcomb, 2009). These characteristics are flexibility, velocity, visibility and collaboration (Jüttner & Maklan, 2011). Flexibility is defined as a firm's ability to adjust supply chain speed, destinations and delivery volumes (Lummus et al., 2003). Another characteristic, velocity, is defined as the interval in time. The time interval referred to is the time between the order placed by the focal firm to the first stage supplier in the supply chain and the delivery of the product to the customer (Christopher & Peck, 2004). Conducting an in-depth study on the concept of supply chain visibility, (Francis, 2008) defines supply chain visibility as "is the identity, location and status of entities transiting the supply chain, captured in timely messages about events, along with the planned and actual dates/times for these events". Collaboration means working together with individuals or firms on a business or project.

METHODOLOGY

The case study method is one of the social science research methods frequently used especially in the creation of new knowledge. With this method, which is used when there is not enough knowledge in the relevant field, the subject is examined in depth and it is tried to contribute to the formation of theory. In this study, Japanese firms are selected due to the earthquake that occurred in the Tohoku region of Japan in March 2011. As an island country, Japan has always kept the earthquake on its agenda as an external risk, taking into account its previous experiences. The earthquake first caused structural damage in the region. Subsequently, the tsunami caused serious destruction on the coastline. Finally, three reactors melted down at the Fukushima nuclear power plant due to the tsunami (Kumar & Havey, 2013). Global firms in the Japanese manufacturing sector were examined within the scope of this study. Symmetrical information sharing of global companies with the public is the reason for this preference. Since sufficient data were not shared about some of the companies examined, data were obtained from the companies shared below. Secondary data on the case studies used in the study were obtained from the companies' websites. The data presented for each case study were shared in chronological order. The activities of the companies related to the production and supply chain were shared, and the humanitarian aid and donations they made during the disaster period were evaluated outside the scope of the study, and their activities under these headings were not included in the study.

Toyota

Toyota, which was founded in 1937, is primarily engaged in the manufacture and sale of automobiles. As of March 31, 2022, the company has a capital of 635 billion yen. It also has production facilities on 5 continents with more than 70,000 employees. In historical order, Toyota has experienced the Nihonzaka Tunnel fire in 1979, the Great Hanshin Awaji (Kobe) earthquake in 1995, the Aisin Seki fire in 1997, the Chuetsu earthquake in 2007 and the Great East Japan earthquake in 2011 (Fujimoto et al., 2019). The earthquake on 11 March 2011, later called the Great East Japan Earthquake, and the subsequent tsunami caused loss of life and property in Iwate, Miyagi and Fukushima prefectures. The disaster also caused damage to Toyota's Miyagi, Iwate and Tohoku plants. After the crisis response meeting, Toyota announced that it will continue its activities with the priorities of protecting human life, assisting disaster victims and resuming production. In order to meet the priority of resuming production, Toyota started work on 15 March to find out the status of its secondary and downstream suppliers. It concluded that 659 of its secondary and downstream suppliers had suffered major damage from the disaster. In its assessment, the company concluded that there could be interruptions in the supply of 1260 components supplied, affecting 80 percent of global production. As information such as the status of suppliers whose facilities were damaged and inventory quantities were collected, it became clear that urgent measures were required for 500 components in order to continue production. The company announced that Tsutsumi and Kyushu factories started partial production on 28 March and all other factories in Japan started operations on 18 April, albeit at low levels. The company also stated that production volumes may increase from July for factories in Japan and August for overseas factories, but normalisation of the entire production process may take until November or December. In the statement made on 11 May, the number of 500 components, which were thought to be subject to supply disruptions, was reduced to 30, and it was shared that the anticipated increase in production volumes of factories in Japan for July would be realised in June (Toyota, 2011).

Sony

Founded in 1946 by Masaru Ibuka, Tokyo Telecommunications Engineering Company was renamed Sony in 1958. In 2022, it announced that it was restructured as Sony Group Corporation. games & network services, music, pictures, entertainment technology & services, imaging and sensing solutions, financial services are the main fields of activity of the company. Sony announced on 14 March 2011 that Tagajyo, which manufactures magnetic tapes in the Miyagi region; Tome, which manufactures optical devices; Shiroishi Semiconductor, which manufactures semiconductor lasers; Koriyama and Motomiya, which manufacture lithium ion batteries in the Fukushima region; and Kuki, which manufactures assembly equipment in the Saitama region, were affected by the Tohoku earthquake and tsunami and suspended production at these factories. On 22 March 2011, the Company announced that production was suspended due to planned and unplanned power cuts. In the statement, it was also stated that rescue plans were prepared for the factories affected by the earthquake and tsunami to resume their operations and that production was suspended for a while due to problems in the supply of raw materials or components in facilities that were not directly affected by the earthquake or tsunami. In its latest statement, The company announced on 6 April 2011 that its production facilities began production activities on various dates such as 15, 22, 28 March, and 6 April, and that there is no plant that has not begun production. Sony also announced that measures such as reallocating existing raw materials and components to facilities, using alternative components for components that cannot be supplied and expanding supply channels will be put into effect in order to reach full production capacity (Sony, 2011).

Honda

In 1946, Soichiri Honda started its activities by producing bicycles with auxiliary motors, and in 1963 it started automobile production. As of March 31, 2022, the company has reached a capitalization of 86 billion yen and has more than 27 million units sold. Honda announced on March 14, 2011 that it had decided to suspend production at its Saitama, Ogawa, Tochigi, Hamamatsu, Suzuka and Kumamoto plants. Although it was announced in the previous statement that production would be suspended until March 20, it was announced on March 18 that Saitama, Suzuka and Kumamoto plants would suspend production until March 23. The company also stated in the same statement that it will make decisions for operations after March 24 according to the supply of parts. On March 22, 2011, the third statement postponed the start of production at the factories mentioned in the second statement to March 27. After March 28, it was announced that the operations to be carried out will be decided according to whether or not components will be supplied from suppliers. On March 24, a fourth announcement was made that the Kumamoto plant, which produces motorcycles, resumed production on March 18, while production at the Saitama and Suzaka plants, which produce automobiles, will be suspended until April 3. In the same statement, the company announced that it has decided to move some of its operations such as automobile product development, production technology development and procurement from its automobile R&D center in Tochigi to Sayama, Suzuka and Wako. On March 31, the Company announced that it will start production in the factories where it will manufacture automobiles on April 11 and will continue its operations with 50% of its production plan due to supply problems (Honda, 2011).

Nissan

Founded as Jidosha Seizo Co., Ltd. in Yokohama in 1933, the company was renamed Nissan Motor Co., Ltd. in 1949. As of 2021, the company has net sales of 8.42 trillion yen and has 30 production facilities. In addition, as of 2022, the company has 134,000 employees on a global scale. On 10 March 2011, Nissan announced that it had suspended all operations at its Iwaki, Tochigi, Yokohama and Oppama plants and its Zama operations centre. In its fourth statement on March 13, the company announced the suspension of production at its Tochigi and Iwaki plants until March 18. In the same statement, it was shared that Oppama, Kyushu and Yokohama plants suspended production until March 16. On March 16, a fifth statement said that plants other than the Iwaki plant were able to repair their facilities or equipment, but that there were still problems with expected parts shipments from suppliers. In the same statement, it was announced that the Oppama, Tochigi and Yokohama plants will resume production activities on March 20. On March 20, in another statement, the company emphasized that it will take time for the supply chain to become operational again and announced that, with the exception of the Iwaki plant, all other plants will partially resume production as of March 21. This partial production includes the production of parts necessary for the continuation of overseas production and repairs. It was reported that vehicle production will continue as long as material stocks last. In the same statement, the company states that it does not remain indifferent to restoration calls from its suppliers and provides support. On March 30, it was announced that all factories, except the Iwaki plant, would return to normal operation from mid-April. On April 8, it was announced that 50% capacity would be achieved compared to last year, but on April 25, it was announced that 40% capacity had been reached. Although the company has stated that it will work at a more intensive pace to compensate for the delays experienced, the realization of this situation depends on the supply of components from suppliers (Nissan, 2011).

Mazda

Mazda Motor Corporation, founded in 1920, is primarily engaged in the production and marketing of passenger cars and commercial vehicles. The company, which has a capital of 284 billion yen, sells vehicles produced in 10 production facilities to more than 130 countries. With more than 48,000 employees, the company reached a sales volume of 1,250,000 units as of March 31, 2022. With its first statement on March 14, Mazda announced that it would suspend production activities at its Hiroshima and Hofu plants between March 14 and March 16, and that it would provide information about the situation after March 17. On March 15, the company made a second announcement that it was suspending production at its Hiroshima and Hofu plants until March 21. On March 18, the company announced that as of March 22, the Hiroshima and Hofu plants will partially resume vehicle production with existing inventory, along with the production of parts and spare parts for overseas production. According to the statement made by the company on March 24, it was announced that vehicle production was suspended with the current inventory at the Hofu plant as of March 22. It was also stated in the same statement that an announcement will be made at a later date regarding the normalization of both vehicle and parts production. On March 31, Mazda announced that as of April 4, it will resume limited vehicle production at its Hiroshima and Hofu plants with the current parts supply (Mazda, 2011).

DISCUSSION

Supply chain managers face risks that can adversely affect the supply chain. One of the most important of these risks is the disruptions in supply chains. Disruptions in industrial supply chains have the power to affect multiple sectors at once. A supply problem with a component such as hydrogen peroxide, which is used in areas such as semiconductor manufacturing, pulp and paper manufacturing, textiles, sewer and wastewater treatment, leather tanning and processing, photographic processing and fur dressing and dyeing, has the power to break multiple supply chains and disrupt production processes (Matsuo, 2015). Because of the role of intermediate goods in the production process, a disruption in their production would disrupt the orderly flow of goods and services. Disruptions or interruptions in the focus company that manufactures intermediate goods influence more than one industry, as well as intricate and complex supply chains. The disruption may also affect overseas countries through supply chains, leading to negative macroeconomic consequences (Carvalho et al., 2021). In other words, the negative repercussions of a natural disaster are seen not only in the region where it occurs, but also in regions that are not directly affected by the disaster through supply chains (Kashiwagi & Todo, 2020). Firms that move some of their production activities out of the country due to offshoring and outsourcing also face more risks. A disruption in the supply chain reduces the resilience of the entire supply chain and leaves it vulnerable. Supply chain disruptions can be caused by endogenous reasons as well as exogenous reasons. As an exogenous cause, disasters carry a high level of uncertainty given the direct and indirect effects they may cause (Drozdibob et al., 2022). Major supply chain disruptions are thought to be primarily caused by both natural and man-made disasters (Elluru et al., 2019; Kaur & Singh, 2019).

When natural disasters occur, managers need to make quick and difficult decisions (Madu & Kuei, 2014). As seen in the case studies, companies review their current situation within short time intervals and try to provide up-to-date information to their stakeholders and shareholders about their facilities and production facilities. When the case studies are analyzed, it is observed that companies share information with the public at intervals of a few days. In addition to providing information on when production facilities would be partially or fully restored, firms also tried to provide brief information about their suppliers and supply chains. The large operational areas of these firms and the large number of suppliers were considered as the reason for the firms' inability to share detailed information. Following the 2011 Tohoku earthquake, Toyota experienced a six-month downturn in its operations and revised its production strategy, regionalized its suppliers, and studied the weaknesses of its suppliers. As a result, it was able to resume operations two weeks after the earthquake in 2016 (Henrich et al., 2022).

With more than $210 billion in economic losses, the Great East Japan Earthquake and the subsequent tsunami disaster had a major impact on companies with facilities in the northeast region. In addition to the direct losses suffered by these firms, the disaster also adversely affected their ability to produce their products and services (Abe & Ye, 2013). Many factories at home and abroad, which use the intermediate goods produced by these facilities as inputs, are directly or indirectly affected by the disaster. As Japan-based Renesas suspended its production activities due to the earthquake, GM, Ford and Chrysler in the US had to suspend their automobile production activities (Park et al., 2013). As Renesas and the case studies analyzed in this study show, supply chain disruption does not only affect the focal firm. Especially international businesses that benefit from the advantages of globalization may be more vulnerable to supply chain disruptions. According to research conducted by Aon Risk Solutions, 28% of global companies experienced supply chain disruptions in 2011(Jesús Sáenz & Revilla, 2014). According to research conducted by MIT Network Scale, 60% of executives stated that they are not actively engaged in supply chain risk planning and management (Jesús Sáenz & Revilla, 2014). The fact that supply chain disruptions that cause so much damage to business processes are not within the active work areas of supply chain managers even in global companies or that risk plans for extraordinary situations have not been developed by these companies unfortunately shows that the issue is not given enough importance despite the destructive consequences.

CONCLUSION

This study is about building supply chain resilience in times of natural disasters. Losses during natural disasters are considered as external risks that cannot be eliminated but can be minimized for businesses and supply chains. In minimizing external risks, firms should harmonize their decisions from the strategic to the tactical level and should affirm their commitment to these decisions and operations. It will not only be sufficient for the focal firm in the supply chain to realize this, but all firms in the supply chain must have the ability to make the stated decisions. By increasing the effectiveness of the factors that will increase the resilience capacity of the supply chain, a more effective response to disruptions can be achieved.

The effects of the Great East Japan Earthquake on supply chains have been analyzed and the actions to be taken to create more resilient supply chains have been evaluated in this study. In this context, the case study method is used in the study and the statements made by Sony, Toyota, Nissan, Honda and Mazda to the public, that is, to both shareholders and stakeholders during the earthquake process are analyzed. It is clear from the case studies that the Great East Japan Earthquake caused significant problems for the Japanese manufacturing giants. Just-in-time production, which has increased its popularity and application areas especially in the last few decades, has started to be questioned with the earthquake. After the earthquake, it is seen that the manufacturers first stopped their manufacturing activities for the realisation of damage assessment studies. Subsequently, it is seen that the manufacturers who do not have raw material and intermediate product stock suspended their manufacturing activities or switched to partial production considering their existing inventories. In recent years, manufacturers that have implemented just-in-time production philosophy in all their facilities as much as possible have unfortunately been more affected by the disruptions in the supply chain. Although the disruptions in the supply chain vary from company to company, unfortunately, there are examples where even partial production is realised within a period of several months.

Disruptions in supply chains, especially in the supply chains of manufacturers operating in global markets, do not only affect the focal company or the country. The disruption directly affects all of the supply chain partners together with the firm. In particular, the disruption in the supply chains of some intermediate product manufacturers affects not only one sector but also many sectors at the same time. The disruption in the supply chain of Renasas Electronics, one of the pioneers of the semiconductor industry, caused production disruptions in many different sectors such as automotive, healthcare, communications and home buildings. Although (Scholten & Schilder, 2015) argues that working with suppliers for a long period of time ensures supply chain resilience due to increased visibility and speed, it is also seen in case studies that working with a limited number of suppliers during extraordinary periods such as natural disasters causes production disruptions. It is important to increase the number of suppliers and to gain the ability to work with suppliers from different geographical regions in order to prevent disruptions in supply chains and to cope with disaster situations where external risks such as earthquakes come to light.

Ono & Watanabe, (2015), taking into account previous disaster situations, suggest that supply chains should be evaluated under two headings to make them more resilient. Under the first heading, the stages of supply chain vulnerability in previous earthquakes should be analyzed to understand the current situation. Under the second heading, it is suggested that response and preparedness plans should be made in which employees, stock quantities and transportation facilities should be reviewed. Since there is insufficient publicly available information on the case studies analysed in this study, there is no data on the reactions of firms and where supply chain disruptions occurred in previous disaster periods. It can be stated that the sub-headings suggested in the second stage are realised by the firms throughout the process. It has been evaluated that all of the examined firms firstly focused on the safety of the employees, secondly on damage assessment and thirdly on the conditions under which the production will start by reviewing the inventory levels.

REFERENCES

Abe, M., & Ye, L. (2013). Building Resilient Supply Chains against Natural Disasters: The Cases of Japan and Thailand. *Global Business Review*, *14*(4), 567–586. doi:10.1177/0972150913501606

Carvalho, V. M., Nirei, M., Saito, Y. U., & Tahbaz-Salehi, A. (2021). Supply chain disruptions: Evidence from the great east japan earthquake. In Quarterly Journal of Economics, 136(2), 1255–1321. Oxford University Press. doi:10.1093/qje/qjaa044

Christopher, M., & Peck, H. (2004). Building the Resilient Suply Chain. *International Journal of Logistics Management*, *15*(2), 1–13. doi:10.1108/09574090410700275

CRED. (Centre for Research on the Epidemiology of Disasters). (2023). *Explanatory Notes.* CRED. https://www.emdat.be/explanatory-notes

Drozdibob, A., Sohal, A., Nyland, C., & Fayezi, S. (2022). Supply chain resilience in relation to natural disasters: Framework development. *Production Planning and Control*, 1–15. doi:10.1080/09537287.2022.2035446

Elluru, S., Gupta, H., Kaur, H., & Singh, S. P. (2019). Proactive and reactive models for disaster resilient supply chain. *Annals of Operations Research*, *283*(1–2), 199–224. doi:10.100710479-017-2681-2

FEMA (Federal Emergency Management Agency). (2003). *Citizen Corps*. FEMA.

Francis, V. (2008). Supply chain visibility: Lost in translation? *Supply Chain Management*, *13*(3), 180–184. doi:10.1108/13598540810871226

Fujimoto, T., Kato, Y., & Iwao, S. (2019). *The Evolution of Disaster-Response Capabilities: The Case of Toyota*.

Fujita, M., Nobuaki, H., Sagara, J., & Adam, B. (2012). *The economics of disaster risk, risk management, and risk financing*. World Bank. https://documents1.worldbank.org/curated/en/175611468044671950/pdf/793950BRI0drm000Box377374B00Public0.pdf

Henrich, J., Li, J. D., Mazuera, C., & Perez, F. (2022). *Future-proofing the supply chain with supply chains in the spotlight, three new long-term transformation priorities form a fresh focus for competitive advantage*. McKinsey.

Honda. (2011). *About the major earthquake in northeastern Japan*. Honda. https://global.honda/newsroom/news/2011/c110314eng.html

Hosseini, S., Ivanov, D., & Dolgui, A. (2019). Review of quantitative methods for supply chain resilience analysis. *Transportation Research Part E, Logistics and Transportation Review*, *125*, 285–307. doi:10.1016/j.tre.2019.03.001

Jesús Sáenz, M., & Revilla, E. (2014). *Creating More Resilient Supply Chains*. MIT Sloan Management Review. https://sloanreview.mit.edu/article/creating-more-resilient-supply-chains/

Jüttner, U., & Maklan, S. (2011). Supply chain resilience in the global financial crisis: An empirical study. *Supply Chain Management*, *16*(4), 246–259. doi:10.1108/13598541111139062

Kamalahmadi, M., & Parast, M. M. (2016). A review of the literature on the principles of enterprise and supply chain resilience: Major findings and directions for future research. *International Journal of Production Economics*, *171*, 116–133. doi:10.1016/j.ijpe.2015.10.023

Kashiwagi, Y., & Todo, Y. (2020). *Propagation of Positive Effects of Postdisaster Policies through Supply Chains: Evidence from the Great East Japan Earthquake and Tsunami*. ADB. doi:10.22617/WPS200003-2

Kaur, H., & Singh, S. P. (2019). Sustainable procurement and logistics for disaster resilient supply chain. *Annals of Operations Research*, *283*(1–2), 309–354. doi:10.100710479-016-2374-2

Kumar, S., & Havey, T. (2013). Before and after disaster strikes: A relief supply chain decision support framework. *International Journal of Production Economics*, *145*(2), 613–629. doi:10.1016/j.ijpe.2013.05.016

Lummus, R. R., Duclos, L. K., & Vokurka, R. J. (2003). Supply Chain Flexibility : Building a New Model. *Global Journal of Flexible Systems Managment*, *4*(4), 1–13. www.giftsociety.org

Madu, C. N., & Kuei, C. H. (2014). Disaster relief supply chain quality management (DRSCQM). *International Journal of Quality & Reliability Management*, *31*(9), 1052–1067. doi:10.1108/IJQRM-08-2013-0136

Martínez, C., Paraskevas, J. P., Grimm, C., Corsi, T., & Boyson, S. (2020). The Impact of Environmental Risks in Supply Chain Resilience. In *Supply Chain Management and Logistics in Emerging Markets* (pp. 11–39). Emerald Publishing Limited. doi:10.1108/978-1-83909-331-920201002

Matsuo, H. (2015). Implications of the Tohoku earthquake for Toyota's coordination mechanism: Supply chain disruption of automotive semiconductors. *International Journal of Production Economics*, *161*, 217–227. doi:10.1016/j.ijpe.2014.07.010

Mazda. (2011). Mazda production schedule update for 4 April onward in wake of major earthquake in northeast Japan. *Newsroom*. https://newsroom.mazda.com/en/publicity/release/2011/201103/110331a.pdf

Meng, S., Dong, W., Hu, H., & Li, Y. (2021). Analysis of supply chain's resilience in crowd networks. *International Journal of Crowd Science*, *5*(2), 166–184. doi:10.1108/IJCS-02-2021-0004

Merimi, M., & Taghipour, A. (2021). Accelerating the digitalization of the supply chain: An empirical research about COVID-19 crisis. In *Digitalization of Decentralized Supply Chains During Global Crises* (pp. 1–24). IGI Global. doi:10.4018/978-1-7998-6874-3.ch001

Ono, T., & Watanabe, K. (2015). Application of natural disaster information for supply chain resilience. *Journal of Disaster Research*, *10*(sp), 783–786. doi:10.20965/jdr.2015.p0783

Park, Y. W., Hong, P., & Roh, J. J. (2013). Supply chain lessons from the catastrophic natural disaster in Japan. *Business Horizons*, *56*(1), 75–85. doi:10.1016/j.bushor.2012.09.008

Ponis, S. T., & Koronis, E. (2012). Supply Chain Resilience: Definition Of Concept And Its Formative Elements. *Journal of Applied Business Research*, *28*(5), 921. https://www.cluteinstitute.com/. doi:10.19030/jabr.v28i5.7234

Ponomarov, S. Y., & Holcomb, M. C. (2009). Understanding the concept of supply chain resilience. *International Journal of Logistics Management*, *20*(1), 124–143. doi:10.1108/09574090910954873

Scholten, K., & Schilder, S. (2015). The role of collaboration in supply chain resilience. *Supply Chain Management*, *20*(4), 471–484. doi:10.1108/SCM-11-2014-0386

Son, B. G., Chae, S., & Kocabasoglu-Hillmer, C. (2020). Catastrophic supply chain disruptions and supply network changes: A study of the 2011 Japanese earthquake. *International Journal of Operations & Production Management*, *41*(6), 781–804. doi:10.1108/IJOPM-09-2020-0614

Sony. (2011). *Status of Sony group manufacturing operations in Japan affected pacific coast of Tohoku earthquake, tsunami and related power outages*. Sony. https://www.sony.com/en/SonyInfo/News/Press/201103/11-0322E/

Taghipour, A., & Beneteau-Piet, C. (2020). Sustainable supply chain management performance. *International Journal of Innovation, Management and Technology*, *11*(6), 165–169. doi:10.18178/ijimt.2020.11.6.897

Toyota. (2011). *The Great East Japan Earthquake*. Toyota. https://www.toyota-global.com/company/history_of_toyota/75years/text/leaping_forward_as_a_global_corporation/chapter5/section5/item1.html

Tukamuhabwa, B. R., Stevenson, M., Busby, J., & Zorzini, M. (2015). Supply chain resilience: Definition, review and theoretical foundations for further study. *International Journal of Production Research*, *53*(18), 1–32. doi:10.1080/00207543.2015.1037934

UNDRR. (United Nations Office for Disaster Risk Reduction) (2023). *Terminology Disaster*. UNDRR. https://www.undrr.org/terminology/disaster

Vosooghidizaji, M., Taghipour, A., & Canel-Depitre, B. (2022). Coordinating corporate social responsibility in a two-level supply chain under bilateral information asymmetry. *Journal of Cleaner Production*, *364*, 132627. doi:10.1016/j.jclepro.2022.132627

Chapter 13
The Implementation of the Agenda 2030 on Sustainable Development:
Focus on the Republic of Serbia

Biljana Stojan Ilic
Faculty of Project and Innovations Management "Petar Jovanovic" of Belgrade, Educons University, Serbia

Suncica Stankovic
Faculty of Business Economics and Entrepreneurship of Belgrade, Serbia

ABSTRACT

The 2030 agenda for sustainable development is a plan with global implications, and the international community expects the nations that have signed it to devote all of their resources. The subject of the chapter is research on the implementation of the agenda 2030 on sustainable development, in the Republic of Serbia. The accomplishment of the sustainable adopted goals, which aim to promote honorable labor, an inclusive economy, and other aspects that might lead to a better society, is crucial for Serbia. The main goal of the chapter is to establish, based on certain indicators, whether and to what extent the Republic of Serbia has embarked on the path of sustainable development. Since almost half of the time allotted for achieving sustainability goals has already passed, the authors wish to emphasize the urgency of ensuring the necessary preconditions for the implementation of Agenda 2030 in the Republic of Serbia and progress towards achieving it, in cooperation with the public and private sectors, the academic community, civil society organizations, and citizens.

DOI: 10.4018/978-1-6684-9062-4.ch013

INTRODUCTION

In 2015, the United Nations held a summit in New York in September, at which resolution A/RES/70/1 - Transforming our world: the 2030 Agenda for Sustainable Development (Forum for responsible business) was adopted. The Agenda for Sustainable Development until 2030 represents a strategy that has a universal character. The agenda consists of 17 goals, which are: world without poverty, world without hunger, health and well-being, quality education, gender equality, clean water and sanitary conditions, affordable energy from clean sources, dignified work and economic growth, industries - innovations - infrastructure, reducing inequality, sustainable cities, and communities, responsible consumption and production, preserving the climate, preserving the aquatic world, preserving life on Earth, peace-justice-strong institutions, partnering to the goal (Taghipour, 2014). The listed goals include three dimensions of sustainability: the economic category in terms of growth, the social dimension in terms of inclusion, and environmental protection as an ecological dimension (Figure 1). The United Nations agenda represents a global framework for achieving goals that are extremely important for the Republic of Serbia.

Figure 1. Sustainability and the three pillars of sustainable development
(Source: Holmberg & Sandbrook, 2019)

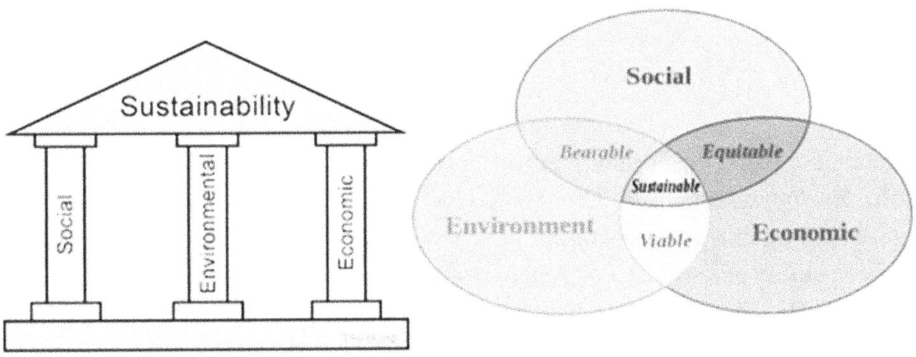

Considering its universality, the Republic of Serbia, by adopting Agenda 2030, also committed itself to the implementation of the goals. From then until today, teams of experts in Serbia have produced various reports, in which analyses of the situation and changes in previous years have been carried. In the chapter, the author wants to refer to the prepared documentation - especially from the Platform called "Sustainable Development for All" - which was made in 2020. The reports were related to Serbia's preparedness for the implementation of the 2030 Agenda, as well as to the development priorities of Serbia as a country. The chapter defines two goals. The first refers to the analysis of the situation in the Republic of Serbia - the situation concerning the achievement of the European level of democracy, the rule of law, and the quality of state institutions in terms of reaching European standards, while the second refers to the analysis of the competitiveness of the economy and productive sustainable business in the Republic of Serbia. In the chapter, the emphasis is placed on the facts of how much (necessary) progress was made in the previous two years in the implementation of the 2030 Agenda. The current situation in the Republic of Serbia, regarding the institutional framework for the implementation of the 2030 Agenda, is very unfavorable. The decision of the Government, adopted in 2015, established the

Interdepartmental Working Group for the implementation of the United Nations Agenda on Sustainable Development until 2030, which unfortunately ceased to operate after the establishment of the new Government of the Republic of Serbia in October 2020. Due to the various political turmoils that are currently happening, both in the world and in the area of the Western Balkans, representatives of interested parties are still insufficiently involved in the processes of implementing the 2030 Agenda. Even though certain processes, important for the implementation of the 2030 Agenda, have been started or implemented, including the mapping of sustainable development goals about existing planning documents and the establishment of a system for monitoring progress and reporting, many authors believe that Agenda 2030 is not given enough space and importance in public discourse. The reason for such an unfavorable situation for the implementation of sustainable development in Serbia must also be sought from the external environment. Serbia is a small country, which needs to preserve peace and stability and establish strong economic relations with other countries, both with the countries of Europe and the world. Unfortunately, due to unresolved political relations, which concern the internal organization of the state, Serbia suffered condemnations and punishments from the countries from which it needed help. The current framework for the implementation of most of the goals is only partially established, and in terms of reaching the nationalized sub-goals, defined by the non-state sector, significant challenges have been noted. What are the next steps and what would be the key recommendation and priority for Serbia at this moment, remain to be concluded based on the facts presented below.

BACKGROUND

The 2030 Agenda confirms the commitment of developed countries to allocate 0.7% of gross social income to help developing countries. This goal, which was set decades ago, has so far been achieved by a small number of countries. Cooperation in achieving the Sustainable Development Goals implies partnership responsibility and solidarity, exchange of knowledge and expertise, use of correct ecological technologies, more efficient financial policy, harmonization of standards for measuring results, harmonization of customs policies, promotion of international trade... (Blewitt, 2014; Taghipour et al., 2014; Taghipour, 2018),. The rapid flow of information and a series of joint decision-making mechanisms, which characterize the modern world, is the basis of the Sustainable Development Goals, but full success in achieving them can, first of all, be achieved only with a strong determination and commitment to global partnership and cooperation. All 17 sustainable development goals from Agenda 2030 are shown in Figure 2.

Figure 2. Sustainable development goals: Agenda 2030
Source: United Nations Platform

The first goal of sustainable development in the Agenda is related to poverty reduction. It is linked to the second and third goals, which are aimed at a world without hunger and good health. More than one billion tons of food is thrown away annually in the world, and in Serbia about more than two hundred thousand tons. Along with irrational consumption, there are also data on irrational production - so in 1990, to meet the needs of one person, about 8 tons of natural resources were needed, while in 2015, twelve tons were needed for that. The 2030 Agenda envisages that food waste will be halved and advocates sustainable and efficient use of natural resources, i.e. respecting the time it takes to renew them or develop substitutes (Sachs, 2015; Taghipour et al., 2015; Taghipour, 2020). By satisfying the basic human needs through the first three goals, one can move to a higher level regarding gender equality and quality education for all (Ruiz-Mallén, & Heras, 2020; Loivet et al., 2020). To achieve a better quality of life, the Agenda emphasized the importance of providing clean water and healthy sanitary conditions. The use of clean and renewable energy should also be available and promoted globally. In this way, not only would environmental pollution be reduced, which is mostly caused by the use of fossil fuels, but non-renewable natural resources would be preserved for future generations (Ilic et al., 2020; Cauchois et al., 2017). Decent work and economic growth, as well as an industry based on innovation and an organized infrastructure, would lead to a global reduction of inequality, which are the goals of the Agenda 2030, under numbers 8, 9, and 10. The development of sustainable cities and communities could be encouraged by the use of new technologies, but also by using renewable natural resources (solar energy, wind energy, wave energy). All this would contribute to the achievement of goal 13, which refers to climate change and actions undertaken in favor of climate factors. In this way, goals 14 and 15 from the Agenda could also be achieved, which set out the provision of life underwater, i.e. the preservation of water resources and the plant and animal life that lives in them, as well as the preservation of life on Earth, i.e. the preservation of the life of all living things beings. Responsible consumption and production would contribute to preserving the environment and raising people's quality of life, while the achievement of peace, justice, and strong institutions would lead to people's sense of security (Ilic & Djukic, 2022; Vosooghidizaji et al., 2022; Taghipour & Frayret, 2011a). Finally, goal 17 of the Sustainable Development Agenda advocates and refers to partnership, because only with joint efforts would humanity achieve some progress for a better tomorrow. Only together can we act synergistically in realizing the desired vision, i.e. a better future for current and future generations (Ilic, 2019)? Measures advocated by Agenda 2030, among others, such as recycling and management of municipal waste and chemicals, protect the environment, extend the sustainable use of what nature has to offer, influence the creation of new jobs, and reduce inequality at the regional level and within local communities (Djukic & Ilic, 2020a; Dobrescu, 2017; Nadia et al., 2020).

Functional institutions based on the principles of "good governance" and respect for the rule of law are necessary conditions for the realization and preservation of human rights, as well as other European and universal values. In this regard, it is of particular importance to achieve the Sustainable Development Goal (COR) number 16, which implies the building of functional and responsible institutions at all levels. COR 16 is compatible with the political and institutional priorities in the negotiation process between Serbia and the EU (Tliche et al., 2021). This also represents the nationalized goal 16 from the Agenda in terms of promoting a peaceful and inclusive society for sustainable development, ensuring access to justice for all, and building a functional and responsible institution at all levels (Ivic et al., 2021; Shin & Taghipour, 2021). As a candidate country for EU membership, Serbia undertook to implement a series of reforms that coincide with the essence of the development priority of sub-goal number 3, i.e. ensuring a healthy life and promoting well-being for people of all generations (Roehrl et al., 2020; Mahfod et al., 2019). Covered first of all by the fundamental cluster in the accession process, among which are the political criteria and chapters related to the judiciary and fundamental rights, justice, freedom, and security, the implementation of appropriate reforms, has primacy with the remaining obligations, considering that from the progress the entire course and dynamics of Serbia's negotiations for membership in Europe depend on these areas. Reforms in the areas of importance for this development priority have been carried out for several years and relate both to the adoption of appropriate legal and institutional solutions and to the ability to adequately apply the adopted solutions, strengthen institutions, and achieve tangible results in practice (Milovanovic et al., 2012). The report "Serbia 2030: development priorities - report of the non-state Sector" from 2020 indicates that the general state of the rule of law, the quality of institutions, and freedom of expression is at a low level, that the concept of responsibility in public administration is insufficiently developed, and that elements so-called "closed" states.

In the further text of the chapter, an assessment of Serbia's progress in achieving the development priority of sub-goal 16, under number 3, i.e. - ensuring a healthy life and promoting the rule of law at the national and international level, with equal access to justice for all - in the period after the publication of the mentioned report from 2020. years.

MAIN FOCUS: EUROPEAN STANDARD OF DEMOCRACY AND INCLUSIVE ECONOMY

Analysis of Reaching the European Level of Democracy and the Rule of Law in Serbia

The assessment of progress among global indicators for monitoring progress, in the report "Serbia 2030: development priorities - non-state Sector Report" was formed based on: an assessment of the annual report of the European Commission; on the global governance indicators (The Worldwide Governance Indicators - WGI); based on the Freedom House assessment, on the state of freedom and democracy;

based on the Rule of Law Index of the World Justice Project; as well as based on the Corruption Perception Index (CPI). The aforementioned sources served as benchmarks for assessing Serbia's progress in the area of the rule of law, good governance, and the functioning of democratic institutions in general, and represent the most relevant international indicators in the context of the nationalized goal of COR 16, i.e. development priority 3, promoting the rule of law at the national and international level. In addition to them, many other sources shed light on the situation and progress in certain areas of importance for this development priority. Below is an overview of the latest results for Serbia, using certain sources, both from official state platforms and from relevant literature (Republican Institute of Statistics of Serbia; Biermann et al., 2022; Ilic, 2019; Pradhan, 2019; Nilsson et al., 2016). Based on the assessment of the European Commission's annual report, it was determined that in the reporting period for two years, 2020-2022, there was no major progress in meeting the political criteria in the process of Serbia's accession to the European Union. In the report of the European Commission for Serbia from 2021, it is estimated that limited progress has been achieved when it comes to the political criteria of essential importance for development priority 3, namely in the reports on Reforms in Public Administration (RPA), the functioning of the judiciary, the fight against corruption, the fight against organized crime and freedom of expression.

Countries that are in the process of joining the European Union should meet several political and economic criteria to become EU members. Public administration reform, in addition to the rule of law and economic management, is singled out as one of the three pillars on which state reform rests in the process of European integration (Public administration reforms). Also, the assessment of readiness for membership in these areas remained unchanged in the Commission's report from 2020, and also about earlier reports, so in the domain of readiness for membership, one can speak of continuous stagnation. Despite the new strategic framework of RU for the period 2021-2030. year, which includes the adoption of accompanying, complementary public policy documents for certain areas of this reform, and the accelerated development of electronic administration as a response to the consequences of the crisis caused by the Coronavirus in 2021, it is still necessary to solve the key problems carried over from the previous period (Stojanovic et al, 2017). In other words, in the report from 2021, the Commission indicates once again that it is necessary to reduce the number of incumbents in the public administration by announcing vacancies for all positions currently held by persons in this status; enabling the Republic Secretariat for Public Policy (RSPP) to play a strong role in quality control for the effective implementation of the Law on the Planning System in Serbia; and establish a unique, comprehensive and transparent system for planning and managing Serbia's capital projects. The main recommendations of the Commission in the field of the functioning of the judiciary and the fight against corruption are also valid for the next period. In addition to continuing work on constitutional reform, it is reiterated that it is necessary to strengthen the independence of the judiciary and the prosecution through legal and constitutional amendments, including strengthening the role of the High Council of the Judiciary and the State Council of Prosecutors in preserving judicial independence and the autonomy of the prosecution.

When it comes to the fight against corruption, although the position of the Agency for the Prevention of Corruption has been improved by the new legal framework in Serbia, there is still a lack of results when it comes to investigations and processing of high-level corruption cases, while, on the other hand, we are still waiting for the adoption of a new national strategy for the fight against corruption (Ilic, 2022). In the field of freedom of expression in the Republic of Serbia, although the Action Plan for the implementation of the media strategy was adopted, a limited number of measures were implemented in the reporting period, while attacks on journalists (sometimes also by high-ranking officials) continued.

In this regard, a large number of media associations withdrew from the Working Group for the Safety of Journalists. In such circumstances, the priority remains the improvement of the overall environment for freedom of expression, by stopping threats and attacks on journalists, timely implementation of the media strategy, strengthening of media pluralism, as well as transparency and fairness of co-financing of media content of public interest, media ownership, and media advertising. (Trumm, 2018; Stojanovic, 2017). Finally, in the area of the fight against organized crime, it is necessary to work on previously identified shortcomings, which implies better results in the field of investigations, prosecutions, and judgments in cases of organized crime, including money laundering, as well as in the seizure and confiscation of assets obtained through criminal means. According to the World Governance Indicators (WGI), in 2020, according to the results of almost all indicators, Serbia regressed to a certain extent compared to 2019. Global (World) indicators of governance provide an assessment of the state of governance based on six composite indicators, namely: political stability and absence of violence, the effectiveness of government, quality of regulatory function, rule of law, control of corruption, and voting rights and accountability (Andjelic et al., 2022). These complex, aggregate indicators combine the views of a large number of respondents from the general population (citizens), businessmen, and experts, in all countries where they are measured. They are based on over 30 individual data sources produced by various research, non-governmental and international organizations, and the private sector. The following table provides an overview of the results for Serbia in the previous two years.

Table 1. World indicators for Serbia (WGI) for 2019 and 2020 according to percentile rank from 0 to 100 (with 0 being the lowest and 100 the highest rank)

	2019.	**2020.**
Corruption control	40,4	37,5
Effectiveness of government	54,3	54,3
Political stability/absence of violence	45,3	43,9
The quality of the regulatory function	60,6	57,2
The rule of law	48,1	47,6
Right to vote and responsibility	44,0	40,6

Source: The Worldwide Governance Indicators

Freedom House's latest reports for 2021 - "Freedom in the World", which assesses the level of freedom in states, i.e. "Nations in transit", as well as the level of democracy, speak of the unchanged status of Serbia, i.e. a slight drop in overall ratings. Serbia retained the status of a partially free country with an overall score of 64/100 (down from 66/100 compared to 2020), as well as the status of a transitional or hybrid regime with a score of 48/100 (down from 49/100). Among the key events in 2020, Freedom House ranks the parliamentary elections, marked by the boycott of opposition parties due to inadequate election conditions, and the reduction of the electoral threshold for the necessary votes to participate in the distribution of mandates as an attempt to weaken the announced boycott (Freedom House).

It is also stated that the civil protests against measures to combat COVID-19 were marked by the use of force against protest participants and journalists and that the public is not transparently informed when it comes to data on deaths due to coronavirus infection (David, 2020).

Table 2. Rule of law index for 2019 and 2020, according to eight constituent factors (0 means the least commitment to the rule of law, 1 means the highest commitment)

	2020.	2021.
Total score	0,50	0,49
The power control and authorities' actions	0,39	0,38
Absence of corruption	0,44	0,43
Government transparency	0,47	0,46
Fundamental rights	0,57	0,56
Work and safety	0,77	0,77
Law enforcement	0,48	0,47
The civil justice	0,51	0,50
Justice in criminal matters	0,40	0,39

Source: World Justice Project Rule of Law Index, 2021.

Similarly, the Rule of Law Index of the World Justice Project is also in a slight decline. Overall, Serbia's score for 2021 is lower compared to the previous one (drop from 0.50 to 0.49), although it is necessary to point out that in the overall ranking, Serbia has improved by one place (81st out of 139 countries). If you look at the individual factors that make up the entire index, it is mostly a slight decline compared to the previous (2020) examined year, and when it comes to the possibility of control of the executive power by the legislature, the judiciary, independent bodies, and civil society, it is also a slight decline. Likewise, in terms of the openness and transparency of the government, this index recorded a slight decline since 2016. The author points out that the Rule of Law Index in Serbia for 2022 remained unchanged compared to 2021 and amounts to 0.49 in the overall score, which places Serbia in 83rd place, compared to other countries in the world (World Justice Project, 2022.) According to the corruption perception index (CPI) of Transparency International, Serbia still has an unfavorable position. After falling by four places in 2019, from 87th to 91st place among 180 countries, a similar trend continued according to the latest results for 2020 - Serbia was in 94th place, due to a slight drop in the overall score. It is also the lowest score of Serbia according to this index from 2012 to 2020 (38/100).

Figure 3. Corruption perception index (2012-2020.)
Source: Transparency International, 2020.

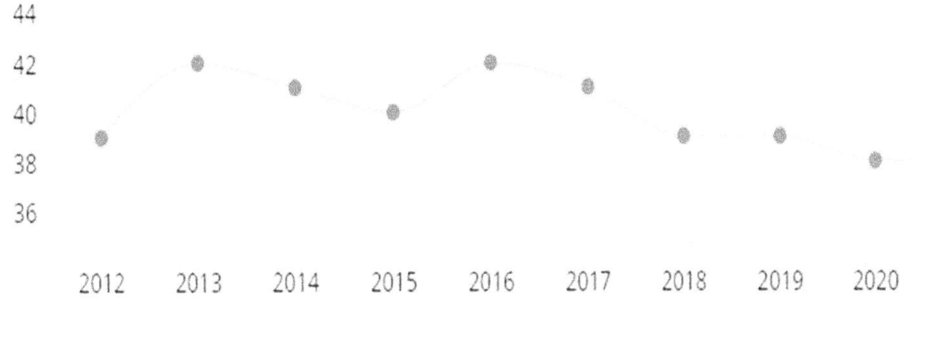

However, in 2023, Serbia has a CPI index of 36 out of 100 possible and has fallen to the 101st position. The latest score is also the worst in the last 11 years since the same assessment methodology has been applied, Transparency Serbia (TS) announced. At the same time, TS assessed that this decline, after decades of stagnation, was expected in a situation of open violation of numerous anti-corruption preventive laws. Serbia's index is seven points lower than the world average. Of the countries in the region, only Bosnia and Herzegovina is worse (with an index of 34), and Albania shares the 101st position with Serbia (Corruption Perception Index, CPI, 2022). In the group of countries of Eastern Europe and Central Asia (ECA), Serbia does not belong to those countries that are rapidly progressing or regressing, but the corruption perception index still places Serbia on the list of countries to watch (Countries to Watch). which represents the unfavorable situation of Serbia in Europe. Problems in the implementation of the rule of law and the erosion of democracy are cited as the biggest challenges in Serbia, while the COVID-19 pandemic additionally affected the risks of corruption due to insufficient access to information.

However, it should be pointed out that there are other indicators, research, and assessments, which can be used to monitor the realization or provide information about development priority 3, i.e. COR 16, for Serbia. For example, according to the political transformation index of the Bertelsmann Foundation, democracy in Serbia was marked as defective in 2020, with a score of 7, which ranks it at the bottom of the Eastern Europe region, and the same is the case with economic transformation, which is considered limited (Bradas et al., 2022). Among other things, the report for Serbia states that it is necessary to re-establish a system of checks and balances between the various branches of government. Compared to 2018, the results of this index indicate a downward trend in all dimensions (democracy, economy, governance). The public opinion surveys of the Balkan Barometer include, among other things, a series of questions about the functioning and control of the executive power, the independence of the judiciary, the position of independent institutions, and the susceptibility to corruption of various sectors of public policies and authorities. For example, according to this research for the year 2021, the perception of the effectiveness of the fight against corruption in Serbia is more positive compared to the previous year and is the only case of agreement of the majority of the population in the entire Western Balkan region (55%) (Bradas, 2021). However, despite the generally more positive perception, the attitudes of public opinion according to the same research are diametrically different when it comes to the susceptibility of certain sectors to corruption, so more than two-thirds of citizens agree that corruption affects the work of the judiciary in Serbia. On the other hand, according to the updated data of the Republic Institute of Statistics from 2021, of the total number of people who had at least one contact with a public official in the last 12 months, almost every tenth gave a bribe or was asked for a bribe (indicator 1, sub-goal 16.5). The latest Annual Report of the United Nations in Serbia for 2022 provides a detailed insight into the collective actions of 20 UN bodies working in Serbia. The goal of cooperation was to achieve the results of the Cooperation Framework 2021-2025, Sustainable Development Goals, through close cooperation with the Government of the Republic of Serbia, civil society, and partners. The main goal in 2022 was to support national development priorities in three key areas (United Nations, Serbia).

1. Green transformation and encouragement for Serbia to use the full potential of the green, sustainable, and inclusive economy;
2. Investing in human capital and placing social equality and the well-being of all at the center of policies and practices and;

3. Strengthening good governance and building trust through the rule of law and respect for human rights.

From the listed key areas, it can be seen that the area of strengthening good governance and building trust through the rule of law has not been left out, which means that in the future, Serbia as a country will advocate for better institutional frameworks, but that it will also not neglect to invest in human capital, which is the other (listed above) key area. The overall goal for the Republic of Serbia is to achieve the vision by 2025, in the spirit of the principle "Leave no one left behind".

Competitive Economy and Productive Jobs: Sustainable Inclusive Economy

Goal number eight from Agenda 2030 refers to decent work and economic growth. The nationalized sub-goal by the Republic of Serbia, 8.3, is related to the promotion of a development-oriented policy that supports productive activities, the creation of dignified jobs, entrepreneurship, creativity, and innovation, encouraging the formalization and growth of micro-enterprises, that is small and medium-sized enterprises, among other things, through access to financial services. Nationalized sub-goal 8.5 refers to the achievement of full employment productivity and decent work for all women and men. This sub-goal includes young people and people with disabilities, as well as achieving equality in their earnings. Until 2030, the previously listed items are planned for realization. However, what is the real situation in Serbia? Serbia, similar to the other countries of the Western Balkans, is a country with a relatively low standard of living and slow economic growth. According to data from the Report for 2021, entitled "Serbia 2030: development priorities - non-state sector report", the Gross Domestic Product (GDP) per capita, expressed in units of purchasing power parity - PPP, reaches only forty percent of the EU average, i.e. sixty percent of the average of the new member states (Central and Eastern Europe) (The European Commission, 2021). However, in nominal terms, which measure the ability of citizens to afford durable consumer goods, such as cars and mobile phones, or to travel, the situation is significantly worse, i.e. the GDP per capita of Serbia is only slightly more than twenty percent of the European one, i.e. fifty percent of the average of a new member state. If it is taken into account that in the ten years from 2010 to 2019, Serbia grew on average at a worryingly low rate of approximately two percent per year, it can be concluded that its position could not be significantly improved (The European Commission, 2020). Nevertheless, the author highlights the fact that economic growth has slightly accelerated in the last few years, according to certain indicators. After more than a decade of stagnation since the World Financial Crisis, economic growth rose to an almost "acceptable" four percent in 2018 and 2019 (Mnatsakanyan et al., 2021; Jandric & Molnar, 2018). Fiscal consolidation, attracting a large number of foreign direct investments, and increased investment in public infrastructure created conditions for better economic performance (Udovicki & Medic, 2021). Of course, this growth is far from the potential and necessary for Serbia to become a modern and developed economy modeled on EU countries. For example, in its 2019 study, the World Bank estimated that Serbia has the potential to grow by as much as 7% per year, which would mean that it doubles its GDP every 10 years (World Bank, 2019). The main reason for the stagnation of these estimates is insufficient and poorly productive employment in Serbia.

According to data from the 2021 report entitled "Serbia 2030: development priorities - non-state sector report", only 65% of the population in the age group from 20 to 64 is employed, while the European average is over seventy percent (Serbia 2030: development priorities). In addition, Serbia has very low average labor productivity, where it lags between twenty and fifty percent, compared to the new member states. As much as eighty percent of Serbia's GDP growth in the last five years is due to a simple increase in employment, while productivity grew (only) one percent per year. The structure of employment in the Republic of Serbia is unfavorable, with a large share of sectors with little added value and low productivity (Vrzina, 2022). Although there has been a partial re-industrialization in the last ten years, the productivity of the manufacturing industry has been declining. In addition, the service sector recorded employment growth, but with very limited productivity growth. Finally, Serbian agriculture, which is largely traditional, fragmented, and informal, is extremely low-productive on average, accounting for as much as twenty percent of employment. Taking into account the mentioned factors, it is not a big surprise that the expected earnings of the average household in Serbia can "cover" the average consumer basket only in the Belgrade region (Dimitrijevic, 2021). The average grade of progress according to the indicators of the achievement of sub-goals 8.3 and 8.5 proposed in the report "Serbia 2030: development priorities - report of the non-state sector" includes: The achieved employment rate of the population in the age group 20-64 years of 75%, with medial earnings that enable obtaining the average consumer baskets; Increase of total labor productivity by fifty percent and increase of labor productivity in the processing industry.

The authors point out that the achieved share of private investments in GDP (of at least 20%, and public investments of at least 5% of GDP) until 2022 is included in the average assessment of the achievement of sub-goals 8.3 and 8.5. However, due to the abundance of data, this indicator requires special research (Djukic et al, 2021). In the past period, there has been slight progress in achieving the goals measured by the first indicator of the labor force, that is, the employment of the population. According to the Labor Force Survey, in the second quarter of 2021, the employment rate for the age group from 20 to 64 was sixty-six percent (Republic Institute for Statistics of Serbia). This indicates a recovery of the labor market after the first "hit" of the COVID-19 pandemic in 2020, but also a slight improvement since the employment rate exceeds the pre-crisis level (about sixty-three percent in the second quarter of 2019). However, it is important to emphasize that amid the crisis, there was a significant drop in almost exclusively informal employment, which is made up of the vulnerable category of workers (Medic et al., 2020). According to CEVES estimates, the drop in informal employment at the end of March and mid-April 2020 (while the curfew was in effect) amounted to up to eighty percent compared to usual levels, while at the end of the second quarter employment was twenty percent lower, which means that there was a relatively quick recovery and a return to the level close to the pre-crisis (Udovicki & Medic, 2021). On the other hand, the unemployment rate for the same age group in the same period was slightly more than eleven percent (7.9% in the same quarter of 2020). However, for the sake of example, it should be noted that compared to formal employees, informal workers on average earn about thirty percent lower wages and in more than fifty percent of cases assess the financial position of their households as bad or mostly bad. According to the International Labor Organization (ILO) definition, informal workers are those who work in an unregistered firm, and also those who work in a registered firm, but without a formal employment contract and social and pension insurance (Declaration ILO, 1998). Informal employees also include unpaid "helping" members of the household. More often than the formally employed, the informally employed belong to vulnerable sociodemographic groups - the young, the elderly, as well as the less educated (Udovicki & Medic, 2021). The unemployment rate is calculated as the quotient of the number of unemployed and the number of active persons (employed plus unemployed) (Ivkovic & Jovic, (2018). In 2020, there was a decline in population activity, not an increase in employment, and therefore the unemployment rate was lower than in 2019 so that in 2021, the unemployment rate would return to the pre-crisis level. This is particularly significant because, according to the data of the Labor

Force Survey, the inactive and long-term unemployed population in the age group from 15 to 64 years, in the second quarter of 2021, numbers as many as one and a half million people, of which about four hundred thousand are the population is aged 25 to 45 years. In addition, from January 2021, the changed methodology of the Labor Force Survey is valid, whereby the most significant change is that persons who produce agricultural goods and services intended for personal consumption are excluded from the contingent of employees, i.e. without placement on the market (Labor Force Survey, 2021). In this way, compared to the previous methodology, the number of employees decreased, which mostly spilled over into the inactive contingent and a smaller portion into the unemployed contingent (Arandarenko, 2007). Unfortunately, Serbia is among the European countries with the lowest levels of activity and employment. There are still large gender differences in the labor market. There is a large difference between the employment rate of men and women, in the sense that a large number of women in Serbia are inactive, which potentially indicates the discouragement of women from looking for work. However, it should be pointed out that the median wage has increased partly due to the increase in the minimum wage, which as of January 1, 2021, is higher by 6.6% compared to the previous year. In 2021, a new Employment Strategy for the period 2021–2026 was adopted. However, there are no clear connections with education policy in the Strategy. In addition, the focus on the fulfillment of quantitative employment goals was maintained without the introduction of employment quality indicators, i.e. dignified work (Ilic et al., 2020). According to the Center for Democracy Foundation and the group of authors who participated in the drafting of the documents, there were no measures to remove obstacles to the inclusion of women in the labor market, such as the development of childcare and elderly care services (Bradas, 2020; Petovar, 2020). In addition, the Strategy did not envisage measures to strengthen the capacities of social partners and improve the capacities of the Social and Economic Union. Additionally, the measure proposed by the Association of Free and Independent Trade Unions to motivate employees to report more often to the National Employment Service is not mentioned in the Strategy. Finally, the employment policy was not viewed at all from the point of view of sustainable development (Sekulovic et al., 2020). Recent changes to the legislative framework have not completely resolved the status of freelancers. With the adoption of the Law on Amendments to the Law on Personal Income Tax and the Law on Amendments to the Law on Mandatory Social Security Contributions, the relatively favorable tax treatment of freelancers' income is introduced for income generated from 2015 to the end of 2021, while a certain part will be the change applies from 2022, which enabled freelancers who wanted to change their status to do so promptly (e.g. to become entrepreneurs or establish a limited liability company) (Zivkovic, 2022). Serbia is trying to preserve the stability of its economy and the trust of consumers and investors, as evidenced by the cumulative real GDP growth in the period 2020-2022. of about nine percent, i.e. better inflows of Foreign Direct Investments. According to the estimates of the Republic Institute for Statistics of Serbia, real GDP growth in 2022 amounted to slightly more than two percent, which was predicted in the projection of the National Bank of Serbia (National Bank of Serbia, 2023). In this way, in the years in which it was faced with the negative effects of multidimensional shocks, Serbia still tried to record economic growth.

Supply Chain Industry in Serbia and Focus on Sustainability

The Serbian industry is essentially at a turning point since it needs to work toward adopting sustainable techniques, or else it won't change in the coming years. Supply chains in Serbia will need to follow international trends in order to maintain their market leadership as e-commerce develops and becomes more and more popular, as well as as the number of deliveries rises (Vosooghidizaji, et al., 2020; Tliche et al., 2019). Recent papers (Taghipour et al., 2021; Taghipour & Beneteau-Piet, 2020; Merimi, & Taghipour, 2021; Taghipour & Frayret, 2011b) have written a lot about current supply chains. The COVID-19 epidemic generated an imbalance in supply and demand that Serbian logistics companies had to find a means to balance out in order to maintain their market dominance in 2022 (Taghipour & Merimi, 2021). Global output was slowed down in 2020 as a result of the pandemic and lockdown. Many governments started to stimulate the economy at the same time, and money swiftly moved from consumers' hands to businesses, which then spent it again. Many nations consumed products worth billions of dollars as a result of the collapse of domestic and global industry. Retailers depleted their own inventories in an effort to keep up with the trend as demand outpaced supply. In Serbia, this was the situation. However, the amount of delivery did not alter, that is, it remained the same, until the growth rate of e-commerce reverted to the level it was at prior to the pandemic. Serbian businesses have had to reconsider their methods of operation and adopt the escalating trends in supply chains and logistics in order to improve supply chain operations' efficiency, save expenses associated with logistics, and maintain consumers' satisfaction with on-time delivery. Following are the eight top sustainable supply chain trends that Serbia attempted to incorporate into its industrial practice in the wake of the pandemic (Ilic, 2019; Yang et al., 2017):

1. Focus on driver retention
2. Localization of the supply chain
3. Using advanced technology to create agile supply chains
4. Forecasting inventory and delivery needs
5. Implementation of crowdsourced deliveries and more logistics partnerships
6. Transition to last-mile delivery methods
7. Management of returned shipments in supply chains
8. Reducing the carbon footprint in order to achieve sustainable development

The issue with item number 1, which focuses on *keeping drivers*, is that there aren't enough trucks and drivers. For every nine positions, there is one qualified driver, according to Forbes. Due to escalating costs, small businesses in Serbia in this industry do not have much space to expand their capacities, which hinders them from purchasing new cars. In order to keep drivers in small businesses and give them better pay and working conditions, it is vital to maintain supply networks. The second item on the list is the *necessity of supply chains being shifted* to the local level in order for Serbian logistics businesses to provide quicker delivery alternatives. Unlike in the past when inventory and delivery management was carried out at the regional level. Retailers must *automate their operations*, integrate their systems and data, provide their employees new tools, and improve managers' insight into the supply chain in order to establish agile supply chains. Purchasing a supply chain optimization platform is necessary for all of this.

The fourth item on the list, "forecasting inventory and delivery needs," relates to the requirement for supply chain managers to forecast inventories and deliveries using current technology in order to be prepared for peak season. With the use of this technology, businesses can now make supply chain data more accessible than before. It is important to effectively manage several fleets while using crowd-sourced delivery and numerous logistical alliances. This is yet another crucial step in the direction of cost-cutting, satisfying consumer expectations, and preserving digital supply chains. Modern consumers must be pleased in terms of quicker and more transparent delivery as a result of the shift to "last-mile" delivery techniques. Whether it's small goods, furniture, medical equipment, or even solar-powered vehicles, logistics companies may now make this segment of the supply chain visible to all stakeholders by using modern technologies in last-mile delivery. Everyone must understand the procedure, and issues must be dealt immediately. The need that organizations who want to remain competitive must focus on returns management is referred to as the "focus on returns management" concept. The number of returned shipments really rises along with the quantity of online orders. Supply chains may now manage returned shipments automatically and transparently thanks to modern technologies. Work must be done to educate the workers in Serbian businesses that deal with logistics so they can use cutting-edge technology. *Sustainable development: decreasing the carbon* footprint is actually the most important point made because, in accordance with some data, the retail business is the largest generator of carbon emissions, accounting for more than 50% of industrial carbon emissions. According to recent studies, the growth of e-commerce would boost carbon emissions from product delivery by more than 30% by 2030. Retailers are starting to rely on their shippers to assist them cut, manage, measure, and report their carbon emissions - and even show consumers their reduction progress - as a result of consumer expectations for sustainable delivery and logistics and legal requirements.

Supply chains could expand market share and remain competitive in the future by incorporating green logistics techniques, notably through sustainable purchasing and shipping alternatives.

Issues, Controversies, Problems

The current situation regarding the institutional framework and coordination mechanism for the implementation of Agenda 2030 in Serbia, as already written, is not good. Although the Government Decision in 2015 established an Interdepartmental Working Group for the Implementation of the UN Sustainable Development Agenda (until 2030) - which had twenty-seven members (representatives of ministries, offices, commissariats, and coordinating bodies, the Republic Secretariat for Public Policies, the Republic Institute of Statistics and the Team for Social Inclusion and Poverty Reduction), due to a combination of unfavorable circumstances, the group stopped working in 2020. While it existed, the Interdepartmental Working Group had the task of proposing the process of adopting a national sustainable development strategy, unifying the views, and coordinating the activities of all competent ministries concerning the 2030 Agenda. In addition, it had several tasks related to monitoring: cooperating with the relevant ministries to monitor the implementation of the UN Sustainable Development Agenda and proposing the basis for statistical monitoring of goals and sub-goals. In the end, her task was also reporting: preparation of periodic reports on the implementation of the Agenda and continuous information of the permanent coordinator of the UN in the Republic of Serbia and the UN system about the results of the work of the Working Group and the implementation of goals and sub-goals. It is obvious that during the tenure of the temporary government, no interdepartmental body was established to coordinate the activities of the Government in connection with the implementation of the 2030 Agenda.

However, it is expected that the public and interested parties in the country can advocate for a new Interdepartmental Working Group. The working group is not the only body established to accomplish tasks related to the goals of sustainable development. Namely, with the support of the Government of Switzerland and the UN Development Program, the Focus Group of the National Assembly of the Republic of Serbia was established for the development of control mechanisms for the COR implementation process. The role of the Focus Group was to include supervision and support for the implementation of the 2030 Agenda in Serbia, and control of the work and activities of the Interdepartmental Working Group for the Implementation of the 2030 Agenda (while it existed). Also, the tasks of this group were:

adoption of laws governing the implementation of the 2030 Agenda, provision of additional funds for achieving COR - in the process of adoption of the Budget Law, and strengthening of awareness of the importance of the 2030 Agenda among members of the National Assembly. According to official news about the work of the Focus Group, it met in January and November 2021 (Bradas et al., 2022). At the meeting in January 2021, it was concluded that in the coming period, it is important to send a request to the competent Committee for Administrative-Budgetary and Mandate-Immunity Issues to adopt the proposal that future proposals of acts, which it adopts The National Assembly must have an overview of the analysis of the effects regarding the implementation of the Agenda 2030, as well as to initiate the adoption of the Declaration on COR in the National Assembly (National Assembly of the Republic of Serbia, 2021b).

Also, the importance of lowering the implementation of COR to the level of local self-governments, cooperation with secondary schools and colleges, and the promotion of Agenda 2030. However, no information is available on whether some of the proposed activities have been implemented. According to information published on the official website, at the meeting in November 2021. In 2016, the only draft resolution on commitment to achieving sustainable development goals was discussed in the UN (National Assembly of the Republic of Serbia, 2021b). Apart from those two bodies, in the Voluntary National, the report stated that an independent supervisory hub was established, consisting of the Protector of Citizens, the Commissioner for the Protection of Equality, the Commissioner for Information of Public Importance, and the Protection of Personal Data, and the State Audit Institution. Information about the work of this body is not publicly available. The role of the State Audit Institution was discussed in more detail at the meetings held during 2019 and 2020, but there is no information as to whether this institution has assumed responsibilities related to the goals of sustainable development (State Audit Institution 2019; 2020).

Certain ministries have a role in implementing the 2030 Agenda, such as the Ministry of Human and Minority Rights and Social Dialogue. In addition, the Ministry of Finance is an indispensable institution when it comes to implementing the 2030 Agenda and achieving the goals of sustainable development. On the Internet presentation of the Ministry of the Republic of Serbia, however, there is no information about whether and in what way this ministry deals with Agenda 2030 and whose jurisdiction it is. An additional problem in the assessment of the institutional framework is that information on institutions, working groups, and bodies that have competencies regarding the implementation of the 2030 Agenda is not consolidated and publicly available in one place. Non-state actors were not directly involved in official institutional bodies dealing with the achievement of the SDGs. Namely, while it existed, there were no representatives of civil society and other non-state actors in the composition of the Interdepartmental Working Group for the Implementation of the UN Agenda on Sustainable Development until 2030. Although it is one of the main principles on which Agenda 2030 rests, establishing cooperation with representatives of interested parties is not listed as one of the tasks of the Working Group. At the constitutive session, it was stated that the Working Group would be of an open type, but this was not implemented. It was accepted that the responsibility for the coherent implementation of the 2030 Agenda also exists at the local level and that related activities should be continued. The Permanent Conference of Cities and Municipalities and Civil Society Organizations dealing with the localization of the SDGs launched several projects that connect the SDGs and set priorities at the local level with local planning documents (Permanent Conference of Cities and Municipalities; Civil society organization). Guidelines have been published by the Republican Secretariat for Public Policy for the preparation of development plans for Local Self-Government Units that would be related to SDP, as well as guidelines for providing support for monitoring the realization of SDP in the field of environmental protection, nature protection, and climate change from Agenda 2030 at the local level (Radomirovic et al., 2020; Pavlovic-Krizanic, 2021).

When it comes to the workforce in Serbia, that is, human capital, the essence of the problem lies in the fact that the state must fulfill its legal obligation to collect taxes and contributions, but not in a discriminatory manner. The status of internet workers (freelancers) has not yet been fully regulated. It is also not good that the status of freelancers will not be resolved together with the Labor Law, which should thoroughly define workers and employers as well as their rights, given that it was not discussed before 2023 (Obradovic, 2021). By adopting the amendments to the Law on Financial Support for Families with Children, the position of female workers will be improved, which will have a positive effect on general employment and the level of wages, but some problems will still not be solved. In addition, in 2021, the Proposal for Amendments to the Law on Financial Support for Families with Children was adopted, the most important solution of which implies that the full monthly amount of maternity pay, i.e. pay during maternity leave, cannot be less than the minimum wage determined on the day of commencement exercising that right. This law repealed the provision that conditioned mothers of children with disabilities to choose between the allowance related to their earnings and the allowance to which their child is entitled. In addition, the rights of agricultural-insured women (women) will be equalized with the rights of other women giving birth in Serbia. However, the law has not completely removed the old provisions regarding leave for child care, which are contrary to the International Convention on Maternity Protection (Clark, et al., 2010). As stated by the Association "Moms are the law", there is still no minimum compensation for the period of child care, and that period is longer than maternity leave (Moms are the law). In addition, the Law still does not recognize the right to the parental allowance for the fifth child (Barisic & Brkic, 2021). Due to the increased volume of work in certain activities, the Law on Work Engagement will not contribute to the improvement of the dignity of work and employment in the economy (Wehrmann, 2010). The public debate on the Draft Law on employment due to the increased volume of work in certain industries was recently completed, which means that the adoption of this law could be expected soon. The basic idea is to extend the existing Law on Seasonal Workers, in addition to agriculture, to construction, catering and tourism, and other areas. The problem, however, is that the mentioned activities are not occasional. According to the trade union, the changes will threaten the rights of workers, who will be employed outside of the employment contract from now on. In addition, according to the draft of the new law, a foreigner who can enter Serbia without a visa can engage in work under the law without a work permit. An additional problem is that the National Alliance for Local Economic Development's analysis of the consequences and effects that this law can produce, according to experts, did not consult the Law on the Planning System of Serbia and two regulations (NALED). In the past period, there was no significant progress in achieving higher productivity. According to calculations based on the latest data from the Bureau of Statistics, the total labor productivity in 2020 in Serbia was around twelve thousand Euros, which is a drop of one percent compared to the previous year. When it comes to the processing industry, labor productivity in 2020 was around eleven thousand Euros, which represents a slight increase (0.2%) compared to 2019. However, the effect of the crisis caused by the COVID-19 pandemic should be taken into account, given that a state of emergency and curfew lasted for two months, from March to May (Ikram et al., 2020). Production fell, and thus added value, but most sectors maintained employment, which also affected the fall in VAT (Value Added Tax). This means that in this period it was not particularly relevant to observe productivity growth, especially not in the processing industry. On the other hand, at the level of the entire industry (manufacturing, mining, and energy), average labor productivity in the first two quarters of 2021 increased by almost six percent compared to the same period in 2019 (Penev, 2021). Serbia is one of the least productive countries in Europe, while its manufacturing industry, after North Macedonia, is also the least productive.

SOLUTIONS AND RECOMMENDATIONS

The establishment of institutional and coordination mechanisms is considered one of the important issues, considering the complexity of the 2030 Agenda itself, but it is accepted that how an will be established and adjusted institutional framework for the implementation of Agenda 2030 depends on the national context. The guidelines and recommendations often emphasize the necessity of cooperation with the civil sector and other representatives of interested parties, who should be heavily involved in the process of establishing and monitoring the achievement of SDG. Also, vertical coordination is seen as extremely important, because a large part of the responsibility for the implementation of the 2030 Agenda lies at the local level. That is why, for the consistency of its implementation, the issue of sharing responsibility at different levels is very important for authorities. It is estimated that around 65% of the goals of Agenda 2030 could not be fully realized without the contribution of regional and local authorities (it is believed that around 70% of the EU acquis is implemented at the local level) (Prorok et al., 2019). In the next decade, Serbia needs to shift its focus from competitiveness based on low labor and energy costs to competitiveness based on knowledge and productive jobs. In this regard, it is important to promote development-oriented policies that support productive activities, the creation of decent jobs, entrepreneurship, creativity, and innovation (sub-goal 8.3), to achieve full and productive employment and decent work for all women and men, including young people and persons with disabilities, as well as equal pay for work of equal value (sub-goal 8.5), and raise investments in research and development, improve technological capacities and encourage innovation - especially in the private sector (sub-goal 9.5). Priority activities aimed at accelerating progress towards reaching sub-goals 8.3 and 8.5: » Amend the current Employment Strategy 2021-2026. so that budget allocations for active employment measures are increased to 0.5% of GDP, as well as to define activities for the motivation of the inactive and employment of the long-term unemployed population; »regulate the status of workers on the Internet following the Constitution, the Labor Law and international conventions signed by Serbia. It is necessary to recognize their specific position, but not in a way in which they would be favored or discriminated against (eg tax-wise) compared to other employees. Consult examples of good practice from Europe and the world; »amend the Law on Employment due to the increased volume of work in certain industries before its adoption. The Law must be regulated following the Constitution, the Labor Law, and international conventions signed by Serbia; » the new ERP, set as a strategic goal an increase in the share of the manufacturing industry in GDP to 20% by 2030 and define the activities to achieve this goal; » The Ministry of Economy should, in cooperation with academia, international organizations (e.g. World Bank, International Monetary Fund, United Nations Conference on Trade and Development [UNCTAD], UN Department of Social and Economic Affairs [UN DESA]) and the civil sector, prepare a study of the efficiency of public investments in Serbia in the last 10 years and make it the starting point for strategic planning in this area. Nationalized sub-goal 9.5: By 2030, increase investments in research and development, improve technological capacities, and encourage innovation, especially in the private sector. Although, according to the Republic Statistical Institutions of Serbia (2019) survey, over 50% of companies in Serbia are innovative, innovations are mostly incremental i.e. refer to small improvements in existing products or services. Business entities record low investments in research and development (R&D), which is best reflected in the low patent activity and the low level of exports of high-tech products in total exports. The structure of the economy, which is dominated by low-tech industries and services, also influences this situation to a certain extent. An important limiting factor is the low percentage of employees with a university degree. Over 15% of small businesses do not have any employees with higher education (RSI, 2019). In addition, the business sector of Serbia is characterized by an unfavorable technological structure and low competitiveness. The key recommendation for Serbia is the adoption of a national development plan with priority development goals, adapted to the national context, and prepared through the participation of all interested parties in the Republic of Serbia. The development plan is the foundation for the initiation and implementation of other processes important for the implementation of the 2030 Agenda and the improvement of the framework for the achievement of individual sustainable development goals. It is very important to position Agenda 2030 as a priority process for managing and implementing development, which would be reflected in the establishment of an institutional framework with a clear division of responsibilities and a strategic approach for its implementation.

FUTURE RESEARCH DIRECTIONS

The results presented in the chapter allowed an insight into the coverage of certain areas to which the goals of sustainable development refer. Mapping of goals, based on four mutually closely related areas, in terms of strategic documents, recommendations were made for research in the following areas: Economic growth (sustainable development goals 9); Development of human resources (sustainable development goals 1,2,3,4,5 and 10); Environment and climate (sustainable development goals 6, 7, 11, 12, 13 and 15); Institutions, finance, and cooperation (sustainable development goals 17). Economic growth, especially in the area of medium-sized and small enterprises, is covered strategically, while in the area of industrial policies and infrastructure development, several important strategies are about to expire. According to the recommendation of the National Program for the Adoption of the Legal Acquis of the European Union - individual documents must be in the process of revision or preparation. These include the Industry Development Strategy with a special focus on production chains in selected sectors of the processing industry, the Smart Specialization Strategy, the Transport Strategy for all modes of transport until 2025, the Mineral and other geological resources management strategy, and finally the Cultural Development Strategy. In the Culture Development Strategy, the development of creative industries and cultures, which should be a lever for the development of tourism, is of particular importance. The development of human resources is covered by several strategic documents, but the National Social Protection Strategy is missing. The field of health is in a transitional period regarding the strategic framework, so there is currently a lack of an umbrella strategy that would deal with the development of public health. Since two strategic documents in the field of health are being prepared, the National Program for the Prevention of Harmful Use of Alcohol and the Strategy for Rare Diseases, the State of Serbia should also bear in mind that certain strategies regarding health are subject to deadlines (Strategies for Mental Diseases were valid until 2017)., already expired, and it is necessary to make them as soon as possible. The field of education is adequately covered by the Education Development Strategy until 2020, however, this is a topic that always needs to be discussed and re-investigated, and since three years have already passed, it is necessary to consult experts from abroad, that is, from the countries which have an organized system of education. The field of environment and climate is strategically defined by numerous strategies related to water management, sustainable use of resources, renewable energy resources and energy efficiency, and risk management. However, an umbrella strategic document is missing for the area of climate, as well as some other important public policy documents in Serbia. The plan is to develop a strategy for combating climate change, an air protection strategy, and a strategy for adaptation to changed climate conditions, and it is necessary to research the development and implementation of these strategies in the country. The horizontal area related to institutions, finance, and cooperation is mostly strategically defined in Serbia, but some key strategies do not have action plans and the achievement of results and goals is not monitored. This primarily refers to the Strategy for the Development of the Free Legal Aid System in the Republic of Serbia and the National Strategy for the Fight against Organized Crime. As part of the sub-goal of a transparent institution, it is necessary to work on the Strategy for the functional organization of affairs in the Republic of Serbia.

CONCLUSION

Judging by the presented results of relevant international and regional sources, it is concluded that there has been no significant progress in terms of reaching the examined sustainable development goals (16 and 8) from the 2030 Agenda. In other words, Serbia has not reached a higher level of democracy, the rule of law, and the quality of institutions in the analyzed period. Moreover, the data point to mostly negative trends or stagnation. It should be noted that the changes in the legal and public policy framework have continued, as stated in the report on the monitoring of goal 16. The Public Administration Reform Strategy, the Action Plan for the Implementation of the Strategy for the Development of the Public Information System, the Strategy for Gender Equality, and the Law on Prohibition of Discrimination are highlighted here., ZRR and the Law on Prevention of Corruption. However, the results of EC assessments, including other objective indicators presented in the text, unequivocally lead to the conclusion that the primary problems lie in the insufficient application of already adopted regulations and measures, as well as insufficient political support for the strengthening of democratic institutions and institutes that lead to a higher level of democracy. the rule of law and the quality of management, which is also a condition for Serbia's accession to the EU. The above data and estimates also indicate that unplanned crises, such as the outbreak of the coronavirus pandemic, additionally illuminate some of the mentioned shortcomings. Therefore, when it comes to priority activities towards reaching SDG 16, i.e. development priority 3, the key measures and interventions that need to be implemented are given in the EC's annual reports. Also, when it comes to the improvement of the legal, institutional, and public policy framework, a series of recommendations was presented in the report on the monitoring of goal 16, and will not be repeated here. Also, from the considered nationalized goal from Agenda 2030, under number 8, which is aimed at the green economy, i.e. the productivity of the workforce, it can be concluded that Serbia is still not on the path to a sustainable - inclusive economy! The reason for this state of affairs lies in the fact that the country was and still is in a multidimensional crisis that has lasted for almost three years. Numerous unresolved political issues, which Serbia is facing today (in 2023), have stopped the implementation of the green economy. Considering that the Republic of Serbia is a small country, which cannot do it alone, it is faced with proving its shaky rating, among other EU member states. The great effort that Serbia, as a country, is making to preserve peace and stability should be welcomed by the world community because the area of the Western Balkans has always been prone to various political unrest and conflicts.

ACKNOWLEDGMENT

This research received no specific grant from any funding agency in the public, commercial, or not-for-profit sectors.

REFERENCES

Andjelic, S., Ilic, B., & Katanic, Z. (2022). Management of education for social entrepreneurship with emphasis on female entrepreneurship (Serbian: Menadžment obrazovanja za socijalno preduzetništvo sa akcentom na žensko preduzetništvo). *Economic signals: business magazine* 7(2), 33-49.

Arandarenko, M. (2007). *Labor market in Serbia - causes of unfavorable trends and new employment policy measures (Serbian: Tržište rada u Srbiji - uzroci nepovoljnih trendova i nove mere politike zapošljavanja). Proceedings: Challenges of Serbia's economic policy in 2007.* Faculty of Economics.

Barisic, A., & Brkic, M. (2021). Acquisition of Competencies for Advocacy in Social Work. *Regional L. Rev.*, 235.

Biermann, F., Hickmann, T., Sénit, C., & Grob, L. (2022). The Sustainable Development Goals as a Transformative Force?: Key Insights. In F. Biermann, T. Hickmann, & C. Sénit (Eds.), *The Political Impact of the Sustainable Development Goals: Transforming Governance Through Global Goals?* (pp. 204–226). Cambridge University Press., doi:10.1017/9781009082945.009

Blewitt, J. (2014). *Understanding sustainable development.* Routledge. doi:10.4324/9781315886459

Bradas, S. (2020). *Youth and active employment policy measures.* Center for Democracy Foundation.

Bradas, S. (2021). *Assessment of the impact of employment policies on the right to decent work, Impact of public policies on society.* Center for Democracy Foundation.

Bradas, S., Djindjic, M., Djurovic, A., Hadzi-Nikovic, L., Ivanovic, L., Mihajlovic, V., Momcilovic, P., Nenadovic, N., Radanovic, M., Savkovic, M., Sekulic, G., & Zivkovic, L. (2022). *Serbia 2030 - Is Serbia managing its (sustainable) development?* Belgrade Open School.

Cauchois, R., Taghipour, A., Kang, D., Zoghlami, N., & Abed, M. (2017). Advanced solutions for a supply chain with stochastic information. *Journal of Advanced Management Science*, *5*(1), 9–13. doi:10.18178/joams.5.1.9-13

Clark, G., Huxley, J., & Mountford, D. (2010). *Organising Local Economic Development: The Role of Development Agencies and Companies.* OECD. doi:10.1787/9789264083530-en

Corruption Perception Index. (2022) Serbian: Indeks percepcije korupcije. *Transparentnost.* https://www.transparentnost.org.rs/images/dokumenti_uz_vesti/CPI_2022_saop%C5%A1tenje.pdf

David, A. (2020). Modeling the pandemic: The simulations driving the world's response to COVID-19. *Nature*, *580*(7803), 316–318. doi:10.1038/d41586-020-01003-6 PMID:32242115

ILO. (1998). *Fundamental principles and rights at work and its application and monitoring*. ILO. https://www.ilo.org/public/english/standards/declaration/declaration_croat.pdf

Dimitrijevic, M. (2021). The importance of the efficiency of the agricultural and food sector for the export of the Republic of Serbia (Serbian: Značaj efikasnosti poljoprivredeno-prehrambenog sektora za izvoz Republike Srbije). *Finance, 76*(1-6), 114–135.

Djukic, G., & Ilic, B. (2020a). Sustainable development, social protection and responsibility. *IzmirJournal of Social Sciences, 2*(2), 83–91.

Djukic, G. P., & Ilic, B. (2021). *Importance of Green Investment and Entrepreneurship for Economic Development*. Emerging Issues in International Business and Global Strategy Contemporary Entrepreneurship Issues in International Business. doi:10.1142/9789811228445_0008

Dobrescu, E. M. (2017). Agenda 2030. New perspectives. [JoDRM]. *Journal of Defense Resources Management, 8*(1), 165–180.

Holmberg, J., & Sandbrook, R. (2019). Sustainable development: what is to be done? In *Policies for a small planet* (pp. 19–38). Routledge. doi:10.4324/9780429200465-1

Ikram, M., Zhang, Q., Sroufe, R., & Ferasso, M. (2020). The social dimensions of corporate sustainability: An integrative framework including COVID-19 insights. *Sustainability (Basel), 12*(20), 8747. doi:10.3390u12208747

Ilic, B., & Djukic, G. (2022). Creating and Designing Sustainable Management on the Global Level. Journal of Economic and Social Development (JESD) –. *Resilient Society, 9*(1), 46–53.

Ilic, B., Djukic, G. & Balaban, M. (2020). Sustainable development directions of rural tourism of Timok region. *The economy of Agriculture, 67*(1), 157-174. doi:10.5937/ekoPolj2001157I

Ilic, B. S. (2019). Renewable Energy Sources Management and Role of Ecological Parks: Improving Quality of Life for Sustainable Development. In U. Akkucuk (Ed.), *Ethical and Sustainable Supply Chain Management in a Global Context* (pp. 220–228). IGI Global., doi:10.4018/978-1-5225-8970-9.ch014

Ilic, B. S. (2022). Poverty and Poverty Indicators in the Republic of Serbia: The Impact of Uneven Regional Development. In N. Baporikar (Ed.), *Handbook of Research on Global Institutional Roles for Inclusive Development* (pp. 261–284). IGI Global. doi:10.4018/978-1-6684-2448-3.ch014

Ilic, B. S., Djukic, G. P., & Balaban, M. M. (2020). Sustainability of Mandatory Pension Insurance in the Circular Economy: A Comparative Analysis. In N. Baporikar (Ed.), *Handbook of Research on Entrepreneurship Development and Opportunities in Circular Economy* (pp. 125–143). IGI Global. doi:10.4018/978-1-7998-5116-5.ch007

Ivic, I., & Pesikan, A. i Kostic, A. (2021). Key data on education in Serbia. Serbian Academy of Sciences and Arts, Belgrade

Ivković, I. N., & Jović, S. B. (2018). Comparative analysis of the unemployment rate obtained based on survey and administrative data (Serbian: Uporedna analiza stope nezaposlenosti dobijene na osnovu anketnih i administrativnih podataka). *Military act journal 70*(4), 310-329.

Jandric, M., & Molnar, D. (2018). Adaptability and security: Key aspects of the quality of employment in the changing labor markets. *Enterprise economics 66*(3-4), 213-225

Labor Force Survey (2021). New Methodology. www.stat.gov.rs

Loivet, W., Taghipour, A., & Kang, D. S. (2020). The rise of green supply chain management: Between complexity and necessity. *Journal of Economics. Business and Management*, *8*(1), 1–7.

Mahfod, J., Canel-Depitre, B., & Taghipour, A. (2019). Quality function deployment-ELECTRE in supplier evaluation. *Journal of Advanced Management Science*, *7*(4), 131–135. doi:10.18178/joams.7.4.131-135

Medic, P., Ivanovic, K., & Mitic, P. (2020). Businesses in Serbia and Agenda 2030 - priorities, challenges and the COVID-19 crisis (Serbian: Preduzeća u Srbiji i Agenda 2030 - prioriteti, izazovi i kriza COVID-19). Center for Advanced Economic Studies, Belgrade

Merimi, M., & Taghipour, A. (2021). Accelerating the digitalization of the supply chain: An empirical research about COVID-19 crisis. In *Digitalization of Decentralized Supply Chains During Global Crises* (pp. 1-24). IGI Global. Moms are the law (Serbian: Mame su Zakon). https://www.mamesuzakon.org/o-nama/vrednosti-i-principi/

Milovanovic, D., Nenadic, N., & Todorovic, V. (2012). *A study on the improvement of the legislative process in the Republic of Serbia*. Dr Mike Falke.

Mnatsakanyan, T., Hayrapetyan, R., & Molnar, D. (2021). Measuring Regional Development Disparities: Some Methodological Contributions And Evidence From Armenia And Serbia. *Regional Science Inquiry*, *13*(2), 327–348.

Nadia, E. N., Beatrice, C. D., & Atour, T. (2020). Luxury hotels' eco-friendly activities & customers' preferences and willingness to pay for green hotels. *Journal of Advanced Management Science*, *8*(1), 7–14.

NALED. https://naled.rs/

National Bank of Serbia. (2023). *Macroeconomic developments in Serbia*. Belgrade Serbia.

Nilsson, M., Griggs, D., & Visbeck, M. (2016). Policy: Map the interactions between Sustainable Development Goals. *Nature*, *534*(7607), 320–322. doi:10.1038/534320a PMID:27306173

Obradovic, 2021. https://www.danas.rs/vesti/drustvo/obradovic-nije-tacno-da-ministarstvo-nije-nista-radilo-odlaganje-objektivno/

Pavlovic-Krizanic, T. (2021). *The path to social consensus around key sustainable goals urban development*. CEVES. Belgrade Permanent Conference of Cities and Municipalities. http://seeurban.net/stalna-konferencija-gradova-i-opstina-skgo/?lang=en

Penev, G. (2021). Demographic summary of Serbia in the first year of the COVID-19 pandemic. *Demographics*, *18*(18), 1–18. doi:10.5937/demografija2118002P

Petovar, K. (2020). *Availability of education in Serbia*. Center for Democracy Foundation.

Pradhan, P. (2019). Antagonists to Meeting the 2030 Agenda. *Nature Sustainability*, *2*(2), 171–200. doi:10.103841893-019-0248-8

Prorok, V., Šerić, N., & Peronja, I. (2019). Analysis of overall and pure technical efficiency of tourism in Europe. *Transactions on Maritime Science Journal, 8*(2), 219–229. doi:10.7225/toms.v08.n02.007

Radomirovic, M., Aleksic, D., & Marinkovic, A. (2020). *Guidelines for development plans of local self-government units*. Belgrade Open School, Belgrade Republic Institute for Statistics of Serbia. https://www.stat.gov.rs/sr-Latn/oblasti/trziste-rada/anketa-o-radnoj-snazi

Roehrl, R. A., Liu, W., & Mukherjee, S. (2020). *The COVID-19 pandemic: A wake-up call for better cooperation at the science–policy–society interface. UNDESA Policy Brief, No. 62*. UNDESA.

Ruiz-Mallén, I., & Heras, M. (2020). What sustainability? higher education institutions' pathways to reach the agenda 2030 goals. *Sustainability (Basel), 12*(4), 1290. doi:10.3390u12041290

Sachs, J. D. (2015). The age of sustainable development. In *The Age of Sustainable Development*. Columbia University Press. doi:10.7312ach17314-016

Sekulovic, I., Bradas, S., & Vuckovic, N. (2020). *Labor Rights are our rights*. Olof Palme International Center.

Shin, M., & Taghipour, A. (2021). Supply Chains Digital Transformation: Automated Underground Logistics Systems. *Underground Construction, 6*(2), 7–18. doi:10.18178/joebm.2021.9.2.651

Stojanović, D. (2017). *Populism the Serbian Way*. Peščanik.

Stojanovic, D., Ilic, B., & Mihajlovi, D. (2017). Foreign direct investments in achieving the goals of sustainable development of local communities in Serbia (Serbian: Strane direktne investicije u ostvarivanju ciljeva održivog razvoja lokalnih zajednica u Srbiji). *Ecologica, 1*(2), 265–270.

Taghipour, A. (2014). *Production Network Planning Based on Constraint Relaxation and Discount Approach* (Vol. 2). Lecture Notes on Information Theory.

Taghipour, A. (2018). A Contemporary Approach to Plan Independent Logistics Actors. In *Contemporary Approaches and Strategies for Applied Logistics* (pp. 337–364). IGI Global. doi:10.4018/978-1-5225-5273-4.ch014

Taghipour, A. (Ed.). (2020). *Demand Forecasting and Order Planning in Supply Chains and Humanitarian Logistics*. IGI Global.

Taghipour, A., Abed, M., & Zoghlami, N. (2015). Design for remanufacturing respecting reverse logistics processes: A review. *In 2015 4th International Conference on Advanced Logistics and Transport (ICALT)* (pp. 299-304). IEEE. 10.1109/ICAdLT.2015.7136602

Taghipour, A., & Beneteau-Piet, C. (2020). Sustainable supply chain management performance. *International Journal of Innovation, Management and Technology, 11*(6), 165–169. doi:10.18178/ijimt.2020.11.6.897

Taghipour, A., & Frayret, J. M. (2011a). A new heuristic search with local optimization to manage a supply chain. *Meta*, 15.

Taghipour, A., & Frayret, J. M. (2011b). *Supply chain coordination planning: A review*. Work paper, École polytechnique de Montréal.

Taghipour, A., Glaa, B., & Zoghlami, N. (2014). Network coordination with minimum risk of information sharing. In *2014 International Conference on Advanced Logistics and Transport (ICALT)* (pp. 184-188). IEEE. 10.1109/ICAdLT.2014.6864115

Taghipour, A., & Merimi, M. (2021). Digital Transformation of Supply Chains during Crisis: COVID-19. In *11th Annual International Conference on Industrial Engineering and Operations Management,* (pp. 7493-7501). IEOM.

Taghipour, A., Murat, S., & Huang, P. (2021). E-supply chain management: A review. International Journal of e-Education, e-Business, e-. *Management Learning*, *11*(2), 51–61.

The European Commission (2020). *Republic of Serbia: Report for 2020*. EC.

The European Commission. (2021). *Republic of Serbia: Report for 2021* The Worldwide Governance Indicators. https://info.worldbank.org/governance/wgi/

Tliche, Y., Taghipour, A., & Canel-Depitre, B. (2019). *Anticipation of Demand in Supply Chains. In Hierarchical Planning and Information Sharing Techniques in Supply Chain Management* (pp. 1-45). IGI Global. Transparency Serbia. https://www.transparentnost.org.rs/index.php/sr/o-nama/trans-srbija

Tliche, Y., Taghipour, A., & Canel-Depitre, B. (2021). Exploring a Downstream Demand Inference Strategy in a Decentralized Two-Level Supply Chain. In *Demand Forecasting and Order Planning in Supply Chains and Humanitarian Logistics* (pp. 1–65). IGI Global. doi:10.4018/978-1-7998-3805-0.ch001

Trumm, S. (2018). The 'New' Wave of Populist Right-Wing Parties in Central and Eastern Europe: Explaining Electoral Support for the Conservative People's Party of Estonia. *Representation (McDougall Trust)*, *54*(4), 331–437. doi:10.1080/00344893.2018.1539028

Udovicki, K., & Medic, P. (2021). The Impact of the COVID-19 Crisis on Employment: A Focus on Vulnerable Categories. Social Inclusion and Poverty Reduction. Team of the Government of the Republic of Serbia, Belgrade.

Vosooghidizaji, M., Taghipour, A., & Canel-Depitre, B. (2020). Information Asymmetry in Supply Chain Coordination: State of the Art. *Journal of Industrial and Intelligent Information, 8*(2).

Vosooghidizaji, M., Taghipour, A., & Canel-Depitre, B. (2022). Coordinating corporate social responsibility in a two-level supply chain under bilateral information asymmetry. *Journal of Cleaner Production*, *364*, 132627. doi:10.1016/j.jclepro.2022.132627

Vrzina, S. (2022). Compliance with value-added tax regulations: The case of the Republic of Serbia (Serbian: Usklađenost sa regulativom poreza na dodatu vrednost: Slučaj republike Srbije). *Finance*, *77*(1-6), 74–91.

Wehrmann, K. C. (2010). Participation in social advocacy: How a professional association can help social workers meet their ethical obligation. *Revista de Asistenţă Socială*, (2), 75–85.

World Bank (2019). *Serbia's New Growth Agenda: Forging a New Future*

World Justice Project. 2022. https://worldjusticeproject.org/rule-of-law-index/global/2022/

World Justice Project Rule of Law Index (2021). The platform of the World Justice Project Rules

Yang, S., Taghipour, A., & Canel-Depitre, B. (2017, August). Cost optimization of reverse logistics: A review. In *Proceedings of the 7th International Conference on Information Communication and Management* (pp. 158-161). 10.1145/3134383.3134393

Zivkovic, P. R. (2022). *Freelancer: The spirit of the globally desirable stateless citizen*: Mirjana Radovic Markovic, Dejan Radulovic, Borislav Djukanovic: Working from Home - Economic, Legal and Socio-Psychological Aspects of Working from Home, Publishing bookstore Zoran Stojanovic, Sremski Karlovci - Novi Sad, 2021. *The Sociological Review*, *56*(2), 724–733.

ADDITIONAL READING

DeRigne, L., Rosenwald, M., & Naranjo, F. A. (2014). Legislative advocacy and social work education: Models and new strategies. *Journal of Policy Practice*, *13*(4), 316–327. doi:10.1080/15588742.2014.929071

Elmaliach-Mankita, H., Weiss-Gal, I., & Gal, J. (2019). Preparing social workers to affect policy: The parliament as a venue for training. *Social Work Education*, *38*(4), 530–543. doi:10.1080/02615479.2018.1542423

Hametner, M. (2022). Economics without ecology: How the SDGs fail to align socio-economic development with environmental sustainability. *Ecological Economics*, *199*, 199. doi:10.1016/j.ecolecon.2022.107490

Ilic, B. S., Djukic, G. P., & Cvetkovski, T. (2022). Global Institutional Roles in Access to Inclusive Education: Comparison of Serbia and Europe. In N. Baporikar (Ed.), *Handbook of Research on Global Institutional Roles for Inclusive Development* (pp. 118–138). IGI Global., doi:10.4018/978-1-6684-2448-3.ch007

Kroll, C., Warchold, A., & Pradhan, P. (2019). Sustainable Development Goals (SDGs): Are we successful in turning trade-offs into synergies? *Palgrave Communications*, *5*(1), 140. doi:10.105741599-019-0335-5

Local quality of life indicators - supporting local communities to become sustainable. (2005). Document - Audit Commission.

Sugiawan, Y., Kurniawan, R., & Managi, S. (2023). Assessing the United Nations sustainable development goals from the inclusive wealth perspective. *Scientific Reports*, *13*(1), 1601. doi:10.103841598-023-28540-0 PMID:36709239

UNDP. (2020). *Human Development Report 2020: The Next Frontier-Human Development and the Anthropocene*. UN.

KEY TERMS AND DEFINITIONS

CPI: The Consumer Price Index is an indicator of the average price change of all products and services used by households for consumption purposes.

EC: The European Commission is a political and main executive body - it is conceived as a body that acts so that its decision-making is independent of the will of the member states (supranational character).

NALED: (Serbian: Nacionalna alijansa za lokalni ekonomski razvoj) is an independent, non-profit and non-partisan association of companies, municipalities and civil society organizations that work together to create better conditions for life and work in Serbia.

PPP: Purchasing Power Parity is the ratio of general price indices among countries that serve to correct official exchange rates.

R&D: Research and Development is an activity that businesses engage in to create new goods, procedures, or services or to enhance those that already exist.

RSI: (Serbian: RSZ, Republički Statistički Zavod) Republic Statistics Institution is a special professional organization in the system of state administration in the Republic of Serbia and the main task of this institution is to perform statistical processing of data related to the state of Serbia.

SDG: Sustainable development Goals se odnose na najveće razvojne izazove sa kojima se suočavaju ljudi u celom svetu. Gobalni poziv na akciju, kako bi se sprečilo siromaštvo, zaštitila životnu sredinu i klimu, i osiguralo da svi ljudi žive u miru i prosperitetu.

UNCTAD: Promoting the interests of developing nations in international commerce is the mission of the United Nations Conference on Trade and Development, an inetrgovernmental institution an housed inside the United Nations Secretariat.

UN DESA –: United Nations Department of Economic and Social Affairs assists nations in overcoming their economic, social, and environmental issues.

VAT -: Value Edit Tax - is a general consumption tax that is calculated and paid on the delivery of goods and the provision of services, in all stages of production and circulation of goods and services, as well as on the import of goods

Chapter 14
The Role of Government in Promoting Sustainable Procurement

Shakerod Munuhwa
Ba Isago University, Botswana

ABSTRACT

This book chapter examines the crucial role of government in promoting sustainable procurement, which is an important tool for achieving sustainable development goals. The chapter provides an overview of sustainable procurement, its benefits, and challenges, and discusses the potential for government to use procurement policies to promote sustainability. The chapter highlights the importance of government leadership, legal frameworks, and institutional capacity for the effective implementation of sustainable procurement practices. The chapter also provides examples of successful sustainable procurement initiatives from around the world and identifies key lessons learned. The chapter concludes with recommendations for government action to promote sustainable procurement, including the need for strategic planning, stakeholder engagement, and ongoing monitoring and evaluation.

OVERVIEW OF SUSTAINABLE PROCUREMENT

According to the European Commission (2020), sustainable procurement is the process of acquiring goods, services, and works in a manner that considers the economic, social, and environmental impacts of the procurement process. Olinga and Gelbman (2013) affirms that sustainable procurement aims to achieve value for money while ensuring that the procurement process supports sustainable development goals. The United Nations defines sustainable procurement as "a process whereby organisations meet their needs for goods, services, works and utilities in a way that achieves value for money on a whole life basis in terms of generating benefits not only to the organisation, but also to society and the economy, whilst minimising damage to the environment" (United Nations Environment Programme, 2017).

The European Commission also defines sustainable procurement as "the integration of environmental and social considerations into all stages of the procurement process with the aim of reducing the envi-

DOI: 10.4018/978-1-6684-9062-4.ch014

ronmental and social impact of the goods and services procured, while also ensuring value for money." (European Commission, 2020).

The three authors converge on the fact that sustainable procurement aims to meet the triple bottom-line requirements and ensure effective value for money to the procuring entity (United Nations Environment Programme, 2017).

Government of South Africa (2017) expounded that the concept of sustainable procurement in government instituitions has gained prominence in recent years as organisations recognise the importance of promoting sustainable development and addressing environmental and social challenges. Sustainable procurement involves considering the full lifecycle of the goods, services, or works being procured, from the extraction of raw materials to the disposal of waste. This involves evaluating the environmental impact of the products being procured, ensuring that they are produced in a sustainable manner, and considering the social and economic impacts of the procurement process (Happaerts & Van de Walle, 2011).

Cauchois et al. (2017) advised that there are several benefits of sustainable procurement for organisations, including reducing costs, improving brand reputation, and contributing to sustainable development goals. By procuring products that are environmentally friendly and socially responsible, organisations can reduce their environmental footprint and enhance their reputation as responsible corporate citizens. Sustainable procurement can also create opportunities for innovation and collaboration with suppliers, leading to the development of more sustainable products and services (El-Nemr et al., 2017).

Sustainable procurement requires a strategic approach and collaboration with suppliers, stakeholders, and customers. Organisations need to establish clear sustainability objectives, integrate sustainability into their procurement processes, and evaluate the performance of suppliers based on their sustainability credentials. This involves setting sustainability criteria and performance indicators, such as the carbon footprint of products and the working conditions of suppliers (El-Nemr et al., 2021).

Several organisations and initiatives have developed frameworks and tools to support sustainable procurement. These include the United Nations Sustainable Development Goals, the ISO 20400 standard for sustainable procurement, and the Global Reporting Initiative's Sustainable Procurement Guidelines (Loivet et al., 2020).

Overall, sustainable procurement is an important approach for organisations to consider in order to promote sustainable development and achieve their environmental, social, and economic objectives. It involves considering the environmental and social impacts of the products being procured, ensuring that they are produced in a sustainable manner, and evaluating the performance of suppliers based on their sustainability credentials. Sustainable procurement can create value for organisations, stakeholders, and the environment, and can contribute to a more sustainable future (Mahfod et al., 2019).

BENEFITS OF SUSTAINABLE PROCUREMENT

According to Sustainable Procurement Charter (2015); The World Bank (2019) and The World Bank (2019), Sustainable procurement has several benefits for organisations, including the following;

Cost savings

Sustainable procurement can lead to cost savings over the long term by promoting the use of more energy-efficient and environmentally friendly products and services. This can result in lower energy costs, reduced waste, and lower operating costs (Merimi & Taghipour, 2021).

Enhanced Reputation

Sustainable procurement can enhance an organisation's reputation by demonstrating its commitment to sustainability and social responsibility. This can improve brand image, attract customers, and help to retain and attract talent (Nadia et al., 2020).

Innovation

Sustainable procurement can drive innovation by encouraging suppliers to develop more sustainable products and services. This can create new business opportunities and help organisations to stay competitive in a rapidly changing market (Shin & Taghipour, 2021).

Improved Supply Chain Management

According to Taghipour and Frayret (2011a), sustainable procurement can improve supply chain management by promoting transparency and collaboration between organisations and their suppliers. This can help to reduce risk, improve efficiency, and enhance resilience in the supply chain.

Compliance with Regulations

Sustainable procurement can help organisations to comply with environmental and social regulations related to the procurement process, including regulations related to energy efficiency, waste management, and labor practices (Taghipour et al., 2021).

Improved Social and Environmental Outcomes

Sustainable procurement can contribute to improved social and environmental outcomes by promoting the use of products and services that are produced in a socially responsible and environmentally friendly manner (Tliche et al., 2021).

Overall, sustainable procurement can create value for organisations, their stakeholders, and the environment. By integrating sustainability into their procurement processes, organisations can achieve cost savings, enhance their reputation, drive innovation, improve supply chain management, comply with regulations, and contribute to improved social and environmental outcomes (Walker, Di Sisto & McBain, 2013).

ROLE OF THE GOVERNMENT IN SUSTAINABLE PROCUREMENT

Policy Development

One of the primary roles of government in promoting sustainable procurement is policy development. Governments can develop policies that encourage the use of sustainable procurement practices by setting sustainability targets, requiring environmental and social considerations in procurement decisions, and promoting the use of sustainable products and services. Sustainable procurement policies can be developed at different levels of government, such as national, regional, or local. For example, the European Union has developed a set of mandatory environmental and social criteria for public procurement, which aims to promote sustainable procurement across member states (European Commission, 2021).

Sustainable procurement policies can also be developed by individual organisations, such as government agencies or private sector companies. For example, the United Nations Global Compact provides guidance on sustainable procurement practices for its signatories, which include businesses and governments (United Nations Global Compact, 2018). Such policies can set out the organisation's commitment to sustainable procurement, provide guidance on how to assess suppliers' sustainability credentials, and promote the use of sustainable products and services (Taghipour & Frayret, 2011b).

Government policies can also encourage the adoption of sustainable procurement practices by establishing standards and certifications. Standards can provide guidance on how to evaluate suppliers' sustainability credentials, while certifications can indicate that a product or service meets specific environmental or social criteria. For example, the Forest Stewardship Council (FSC) certification indicates that a product has been sourced from responsibly managed forests (Forest Stewardship Council, 2021). Governments can require that suppliers meet specific standards or certifications as a condition of participating in procurement processes.

Policy Implementation

Zhang and Parker (2012) contend that implementation of sustainable procurement policies is essential to achieve the sustainability goals set out in policies. Governments can take several steps to implement sustainable procurement policies effectively.

Firstly, governments can include sustainability criteria in procurement processes. Sustainability criteria can include requirements for suppliers to provide evidence of their environmental and social credentials, as well as incorporating life cycle costing into procurement decisions (The World Bank, 2019). Life-cycle costing involves considering the environmental and social impacts of a product or service throughout its entire life cycle, from production to disposal. By incorporating life cycle costing into procurement decisions, governments can identify products or services with the lowest environmental and social impacts over their entire life cycle, rather than just considering the initial cost.

Secondly, governments can educate procurement professionals on sustainable procurement practices. Procurement professionals may not have the necessary knowledge or skills to implement sustainable procurement practices effectively. Therefore, governments can provide training programs, toolkits, and guidance documents to help procurement professionals understand the benefits of sustainable procurement, how to assess suppliers' sustainability credentials, and how to incorporate sustainability criteria into procurement processes (Government of India, 2017).

Thirdly, governments can provide support and resources to help organisations implement sustainable procurement practices. Such resources can include funding, technical assistance, and guidance documents. For example, the United States Environmental Protection Agency provides guidance on sustainable procurement practices and funding for organisations to implement such practices (United States Environmental Protection Agency, 2021).

Fourthly, Ministry of the Environment, Finland (2016) underscores that governments can encourage collaboration between organisations to achieve sustainability goals. Collaboration can help organisations to share knowledge, expertise, and resources, and to develop common standards and certifications. Governments can facilitate collaboration through the establishment of public-private partnerships, industry associations, or other forums for stakeholders to work together towards common sustainability goals.

Include sustainability criteria in procurement processes.

Kweka (2011) emphasizes that governments can include sustainability criteria in procurement processes by requiring suppliers to provide evidence of their environmental and social credentials and incorporating life-cycle costing into procurement decisions.

Requiring suppliers to provide evidence of their environmental and social credentials.

In line with the Ministry of the Environment, Finland (2016), governments can also require suppliers to provide evidence of their environmental and social credentials as part of the procurement process. This evidence can take different forms, such as certifications, reports, or policies. For example, a government agency may require suppliers to provide evidence of their compliance with environmental regulations or their commitment to sustainable production practices. O'Hara (2013) confirmed that governments can also require suppliers to disclose information about their supply chains, such as the origin of raw materials, the use of hazardous substances, or the working conditions of their employees. This information can help governments to assess the environmental and social impacts of products and services throughout their life cycle.

Incorporating life cycle costing into procurement decisions

According to Papoutsis and Pappas (2013) governments can incorporate life-cycle costing into procurement decisions by considering the environmental and social impacts of products and services throughout their entire life cycle, from production to disposal. Life-cycle costing can help governments to identify products or services with the lowest environmental and social impacts over their entire life cycle, rather than just considering the initial cost. For example, a government agency may consider the energy efficiency of a product, the use of hazardous substances in its production, its recyclability, and its disposal at the end of its life. By incorporating life-cycle costing into procurement decisions, governments can encourage suppliers to develop products and services with lower environmental and social impacts, and promote the use of sustainable products and services.

Educate Procurement Professionals

In addition to requiring suppliers to provide evidence of their environmental and social credentials and incorporating life cycle costing into procurement decisions, governments can play a crucial role in ensuring sustainability in procurement processes by educating procurement professionals (Nadia et al., 2020). Procurement professionals are responsible for selecting suppliers, negotiating contracts, and managing procurement processes. They can have a significant impact on the sustainability of government procurement by incorporating sustainability criteria into their decision-making processes. However, many procurement professionals may not be familiar with sustainability concepts and may not know how to integrate them into their work (Reisch & Altstötter-Gleich, 2013); Sustainable Procurement Charter, 2015); (The World Bank. (2019).

To address this gap, governments can provide training and education programs for procurement professionals. These programs can cover a range of topics, including sustainable procurement practices, life-cycle costing, environmental and social regulations, and supplier engagement. Procurement professionals can also benefit from learning about sustainability trends and innovations in their respective industries and markets (Sustainable Procurement Charter, 2015).

According to Venter & Pillay (2011), by educating procurement professionals about sustainability, governments can ensure that procurement decisions are made with a comprehensive understanding of the environmental and social impacts of products and services. They can also help procurement professionals to identify sustainable suppliers and products, negotiate contracts that promote sustainability, and engage with suppliers to improve their sustainability performance.

Provide support and resources.

Welford (2013) elucidates that governments can play a critical role in supporting organisations to implement sustainable procurement practices. By providing guidance documents, toolkits, training programs, and funding, governments can help organisations to overcome barriers to sustainable procurement and effectively integrate sustainability considerations into their procurement processes. Happaerts and Van de Walle (2011) explains the different supporting tool kits as highlighted below;

1. Guidance Documents

Governments can provide guidance documents that offer advice and best practices on sustainable procurement. These documents can provide organisations with practical guidance on how to integrate sustainability considerations into procurement processes, from setting sustainability goals to evaluating supplier sustainability performance. These guidance documents can also provide information on relevant regulations and standards, as well as case studies and examples of successful sustainable procurement practices (Shin & Taghipour, 2021).

2. Toolkits

According to Tliche, et al. (2019), governments can develop toolkits that provide organisations with practical tools to support sustainable procurement. These toolkits can include templates for sustainable procurement policies, guidance on evaluating supplier sustainability performance, and resources for engaging with suppliers on sustainability issues. Toolkits can also provide organisations with information on relevant sustainability certifications and labels, such as Energy Star or Fair Trade, to help them identify sustainable products and services.

3. Training Programs

Vosooghidizaji et al., (2020) posits that governments can develop and providc training programs for organisations to educate employees on sustainable procurement practices. These training programs can include workshops, webinars, or online training courses that cover a range of topics, including sustainable procurement principles, life-cycle costing, and supplier engagement. Training programs can also provide organisations with information on relevant regulations and standards, as well as case studies and examples of successful sustainable procurement practices.

4. Funding

Governments can provide funding to support sustainable procurement initiatives. This funding can take various forms, such as grants, loans, or subsidies. It can be used to support organisations to implement sustainable procurement practices, such as funding for the development of sustainable procurement policies or the implementation of sustainable procurement initiatives (Taghipour & Merimi, 2021). According to Hinrichs-Rahlwes and Zawilska-Florczuk (2011) funding can also be used to support organisations to access sustainable products and services, such as funding for the purchase of renewable energy or sustainable building materials.

Monitoring and evaluating progress towards procurement.

Monitoring and evaluating progress towards procurement sustainability is critical for several reasons. Firstly, it helps to identify areas where the sustainability targets are not being met and where improvements are needed. This could be in terms of the types of products being procured, the suppliers being used, or the criteria used in the procurement process. By identifying these areas, the government can take corrective action to ensure that procurement practices are aligned with sustainability targets (Government of South Africa, 2017).

Secondly, monitoring and evaluation help to measure the effectiveness of sustainability policies and practices. Governments can use performance indicators to measure progress towards sustainability targets and determine whether procurement practices are contributing to sustainable development. This information can help to identify areas where policies and practices need to be strengthened or revised to ensure that sustainability goals are achieved (Ministry of the Environment, Japan, 2015).

Thirdly, monitoring and evaluation can help to promote transparency and accountability in procurement processes. By regularly reporting on progress towards sustainability targets, governments can demonstrate their commitment to sustainability and hold themselves accountable for their procurement practices. This can help to build trust with stakeholders, including the public, suppliers, and civil society organisations (Olinga & Gelbman, 2013); (OECD, 2015).

To monitor and evaluate progress towards procurement sustainability, Schönherr and Schröder (2012) expounded that governments can use various tools and mechanisms. These may include data collection and analysis, stakeholder engagement, performance reporting, and auditing. For example, governments can collect data on the types of products being procured, the suppliers being used, and the environmental and social impacts of procurement practices. They can then use this information to analyze trends, identify areas for improvement, and develop strategies to address any issues (Taghipour, & Beneteau-Piet, 2020).

Walker, Di Sisto and McBain (2013) affirm that stakeholder engagement is also critical in monitoring and evaluating progress towards procurement sustainability. By engaging with suppliers, civil society organisations, and other stakeholders, governments can obtain feedback on their procurement practices and identify areas for improvement. This can help to ensure that procurement practices are aligned with sustainability targets and meet the needs of all stakeholders.

GOVERNMENT STANDARDS AND GUIDELINES FOR SUSTAINABLE PROCUREMENT

Sustainable procurement has become an important consideration for governments around the world as they strive to promote sustainable development and reduce the environmental and social impacts of their procurement activities (De Boer & Baumann, 2013).

Analysis Of Existing Government Standards and Guidelines

According to the Government of South Africa (2017), many governments have developed standards and guidelines for sustainable procurement to provide a framework for organisations to integrate sustainability into their procurement processes and ensure that they are procuring goods and services that meet certain social and environmental criteria. These government standards and guidelines for sustainable procurement include the following;

EU Green Public Procurement (GPP) criteria

The EU Green Public Procurement (GPP) criteria provide guidance on how to integrate environmental considerations into public procurement. The criteria cover a range of product and service categories, such as construction, energy, and transport. The GPP criteria are developed through a process of stakeholder consultation and expert review and are updated regularly to reflect new developments in environmental science and technology (European Commission, 2013). The GPP criteria include both mandatory and voluntary criteria. Mandatory criteria must be met by all public authorities when procuring goods and services in the relevant product or service category. Voluntary criteria are intended to provide additional guidance to public authorities and can be used to further improve the environmental performance of the procured goods and services (European Commission, 2020).

ISO 20400

The International Organisation for Standardization (ISO) developed ISO 20400 as a standard for sustainable procurement. The standard provides guidance on how to integrate sustainability into procurement processes and covers topics such as risk management, supplier engagement, and life cycle thinking. The standard is intended to be applicable to organisations of all types and sizes, and to all stages of the procurement process. ISO 20400 is based on a set of principles and best practices for sustainable procurement. These include integrating sustainability into procurement policies and strategies, engaging with suppliers to promote sustainability, using sustainability criteria in the procurement process, and monitoring and reporting on sustainability performance (Ferrari & Migliarese, 2010).

UN Sustainable Development Goals (SDGs)

The United Nations Sustainable Development Goals provide a framework for sustainable development and include 17 goals, such as no poverty, zero hunger, and climate action (European Commission, 2020). The SDGs are intended to be a universal call to action to end poverty, protect the planet, and ensure that all people enjoy peace and prosperity. Governments can use the SDGs as a reference point when developing sustainable procurement policies and guidelines. For example, a government might prioritize the procurement of goods and services that contribute to SDG 7 (affordable and clean energy) or SDG 12 (responsible consumption and production). By aligning procurement activities with the SDGs, governments can contribute to the achievement of sustainable development goals and demonstrate their commitment to sustainability (Tliche, Taghipour & Canel-Depitre, 2019).

Buy Clean California Act

The Buy Clean California Act is a law that requires state agencies to consider the greenhouse gas emissions of certain building materials when making procurement decisions. The law aims to promote the use of low-carbon building materials and reduce the carbon footprint of public infrastructure projects. Under the Buy Clean California Act, state agencies are required to use a standardized methodology to calculate the greenhouse gas emissions of eligible building materials. The law applies to materials used in the construction of highways, bridges, and other public works projects. By considering the carbon footprint of building materials in procurement decisions, the state of California aims to promote the use of low-carbon materials and reduce the environmental impact of public infrastructure projects (Sustainable Procurement Charter, 2015).

UK Government Buying Standards

According to the European Commission (2013), the UK Government Buying Standards provide guidance on how to integrate sustainability into procurement processes for a range of product and service categories. The standards cover topics such as energy efficiency, sustainable timber, and ethical procurement. The UK Government Buying Standards are intended to be a practical tool for public authorities to use when procuring goods and services. The standards provide guidance on the key sustainability issues that should be considered in the procurement process, as well as practical advice on how to implement sustainable procurement practices.

CASE STUDIES OF SUCCESSFUL IMPLEMENTATION OF GOVERNMENT STANDARDS AND GUIDELINES

Four representative case studies of successful implementation of government standards and guidelines in procurements were chosen. These case studies are explained below;

Case study

The City of Ghent in Belgium implemented a sustainable procurement policy in 2007, which covers sustainable construction, food and catering, and cleaning services. The policy aims to promote sustainable development and reduce the city's environmental impact by prioritizing environmentally and socially responsible products and services. Under the policy, the city has implemented a number of initiatives to promote sustainable construction, including the use of sustainable building materials, energy-efficient heating and cooling systems, and the installation of green roofs. These initiatives have resulted in the construction of several green buildings in the city, which are designed to minimize their environmental impact and promote sustainable living (United Nations Environment Programme, 2017). In addition to sustainable construction, the city has also implemented initiatives to promote sustainable food and catering. The policy requires the use of organic and fair-trade products in city events and encourages the use of local and seasonal products. The city also provides support and guidance to local businesses to help them adopt sustainable practices (Schönherr & Schröder, 2012).

Finally, the policy includes requirements for environmentally friendly cleaning products, which are used in city buildings and facilities. The city has also implemented a program to reduce the use of chemicals in cleaning, which has resulted in significant environmental and health benefits. Overall, the City of Ghent's sustainable procurement policy demonstrates the benefits of government standards and guidelines for sustainable procurement. By prioritizing environmentally and socially responsible products and services, the city has been able to promote sustainable development, reduce its environmental impact, and improve the well-being of its citizens (European Commission. (2020).

Case Study 2

The City of San Francisco's Sustainable Purchasing Ordinance (SPO) was implemented in 2006 and requires all city departments to consider environmental and social factors in their purchasing decisions. The goal of the SPO is to increase the purchase of environmentally preferable products and services and reduce the city's carbon footprint. To implement the SPO, the city created a Sustainable Purchasing Program (SPP) to provide guidance and support to city departments. The SPP developed a list of priority products and services that have a high environmental impact and established criteria for environmentally preferable alternatives. For example, the SPP recommends the use of recycled paper, green cleaning supplies, and energy-efficient lighting (Ferrari & Migliarese, 2010).

The SPO has been successful in increasing the purchase of environmentally preferable products and services. Between 2005 and 2012, the city's purchase of recycled paper increased from 12% to 100%, and the purchase of green cleaning supplies increased from 4% to 71%. In addition, the city has reduced its carbon footprint by purchasing renewable energy and energy-efficient products (Happaerts & Van de Walle, 2011).

The SPO has also had a positive impact on the city's economy and social well-being. The city has encouraged the purchase of products and services from local businesses and small and disadvantaged businesses. This has led to an increase in local economic development and job creation. Overall, the City of San Francisco's Sustainable Purchasing Ordinance and Sustainable Purchasing Program demonstrate the benefits of government standards and guidelines for sustainable procurement. By prioritising environmental and social factors in their purchasing decisions, the city has been able to reduce its environmental impact, support local businesses, and promote social well-being (O'Hara, 2013).

Case Study 3

The Province of Ontario in Canada implemented a sustainable procurement program in 2010, which aims to integrate environmental, social, and economic factors into procurement decisions. The program covers all goods and services purchased by the province and its agencies and includes a number of initiatives to promote sustainability (Taghipour, 2018).

One of the key initiatives of the program is the procurement of renewable energy. The province has implemented a feed-in-tariff program, which encourages the development of renewable energy projects such as wind, solar, and biomass. The program has led to the procurement of renewable energy from various sources, including wind farms, solar panels, and biogas facilities (Taghipour & Beneteau-Piet, 2020).

The program also includes criteria for energy-efficient lighting, which has led to the adoption of LED lighting in government buildings and facilities. The use of LED lighting has resulted in significant energy savings and reduced greenhouse gas emissions. In addition to renewable energy and energy-efficient lighting, the program promotes the use of green cleaning products. The province has developed a list of environmentally friendly cleaning products that meet its criteria for performance and environmental impact. This has led to the adoption of green cleaning products in government buildings and facilities, which has reduced the use of harmful chemicals and improved indoor air quality (Vosooghidizaji et al., 2022).

Overall, the Province of Ontario's sustainable procurement program demonstrates the benefits of government standards and guidelines for sustainable procurement. By integrating environmental, social, and economic factors into procurement decisions, the province has been able to promote sustainability, reduce its environmental impact, and support the development of a green economy (Olinga & Gelbman, 2013).

Case Study 4

The State of Minnesota in the USA implemented a sustainable procurement policy in 2010, which covers environmentally preferable products and services, socially responsible contracting practices, and sustainable transportation. The policy aims to promote sustainability, reduce the state's environmental impact, and improve the health and well-being of its citizens (European Commission, 2020).

Under the policy, the state has implemented initiatives to promote environmentally preferable products and services, such as the procurement of green cleaning supplies. The state has developed a list of environmentally preferable cleaning products that meet its criteria for performance and environmental impact. This has led to the adoption of green cleaning products in state buildings and facilities, which has reduced the use of harmful chemicals and improved indoor air quality (Government of South Africa, 2017).

In addition to environmentally preferable products and services, the policy includes criteria for socially responsible contracting practices. The state encourages contractors to adopt fair labor practices, promote diversity and inclusion, and minimize the use of non-renewable resources in their operations. This has led to the adoption of socially responsible practices by state contractors, which has improved the working conditions of employees and reduced the environmental impact of their operations (Scottish Government, 2018).

The policy also includes criteria for sustainable transportation, which has led to the procurement of electric and hybrid vehicles. The state has implemented a program to encourage the use of electric vehicles by state employees and has installed charging stations in government buildings and facilities. This has reduced the state's dependence on fossil fuels and improved air quality.

Finally, the policy includes criteria for sustainable construction materials, which has led to the adoption of sustainable building practices in state construction projects. The state has implemented a program to encourage the use of sustainable building materials, such as recycled content, and to minimize waste in construction projects. This has resulted in the construction of more environmentally friendly buildings in the state (Scottish Government, 2018).

Overall, the State of Minnesota's sustainable procurement policy demonstrates the benefits of government standards and guidelines for sustainable procurement. By prioritizing environmentally preferable products and services, socially responsible contracting practices, and sustainable transportation, the state has been able to promote sustainability, reduce its environmental impact, and improve the well-being of its citizens.

GOVERNMENT LEADERSHIP IN SUSTAINABLE PROCUREMENT

According to Reisch and Altstötter-Gleich, (2013), government leadership in sustainable procurement is crucial in achieving sustainability goals at local, regional, national, and international levels.

Many governments around the world have recognised the importance of sustainable procurement and have developed policies, guidelines, and standards to promote it. These initiatives are often led by government procurement agencies or sustainability departments, and involve collaboration with other government departments, businesses, and civil society organisations (Ministry of the Environment, Japan, 2015; Ministry of the Environment, Finland, 2016; Government of South Africa, 2017).

Happaerts and Van de Walle (2011) explained that government leadership in sustainable procurement typically involves several key elements, including:

Policy development: Governments develop policies and guidelines that promote sustainable procurement practices and set targets for sustainable purchasing (Tliche et al., 2019).

Capacity building: Governments provide training and support to procurement officials and suppliers to increase their awareness and understanding of sustainable procurement (Vosooghidizaji et al., 2022).

Collaboration: Governments work with businesses, civil society organisations, and other stakeholders to develop sustainable procurement initiatives and improve supply chain sustainability (Taghipour, 2020).

Monitoring and reporting: Governments monitor and report on their sustainable procurement practices to ensure that they are meeting their sustainability goals (Shin & Taghipour, 2021).

Innovation: Governments encourage innovation in sustainable procurement by promoting the use of new technologies, materials, and practices that promote sustainability (Yang et al., 2017).

Overall, government leadership in sustainable procurement is critical to achieving sustainable development goals and creating a more sustainable future for all.

Case studies of successful implementation of sustainable procurement practices by government agencies

According to OECD (2015), there are a number of case studies from different continents representing successful implementation of sustainable procurement practices by government agencies. These include the following;

North America

- City of Portland, Oregon, United States
- Government of Canada, Canada

South America

- Government of Brazil's Sustainable Procurement Program, Brazil
- Municipal Government of Medellin's Sustainable Procurement Program, Colombia

Europe

- City of Helsinki, Finland
- City of Copenhagen, Denmark
- Sustainable Public Procurement Program of the European Union

Africa

- City of Cape Town, South Africa
- City of Durban, South Africa

Asia

- Green Procurement Program of the Tokyo Metropolitan Government, Japan
- South Korea's Public Procurement Service's Green Procurement Program, South Korea
- Sustainable Procurement Program of the Hong Kong Special Administrative Region Government, China

Australia/Oceania

- Sustainable Procurement Program of the Australian Government, Australia
- Sustainable Procurement Program of the Auckland Council, New Zealand

These case studies show that sustainable procurement practices are being implemented successfully in various regions around the world, demonstrating the potential for sustainable procurement to be a global practice. Governments at all levels can play an important role in promoting sustainable procurement practices and contributing to a more sustainable future (Sustainable Procurement Charter, 2015).

CHALLENGES FACED BY GOVERNMENTS IN IMPLEMENTING SUSTAINABLE PROCUREMENT PRACTICES

While government agencies around the world are increasingly adopting sustainable procurement practices, they face several challenges in implementing them effectively. A number of challenges have been identified across the globe and these include;

Resistance to change: Government agencies often face resistance from procurement officials, suppliers, and other stakeholders who are not familiar with sustainable procurement practices. This can create challenges in implementing sustainable procurement practices effectively (Venter & Pillay, 2011).

Lack of capacity and expertise: Procurement officials may not have the necessary expertise and training to implement sustainable procurement practices effectively. This can result in inadequate understanding of sustainability criteria and standards, and difficulties in identifying sustainable products and suppliers (United Nations Environment Programme, 2017).

Limited supplier base: In some cases, there may be a limited number of suppliers that offer sustainable products and services, making it challenging to implement sustainable procurement practices (Tliche et al., 2019).

Cost considerations: Sustainable products and services may be more expensive than non-sustainable alternatives, which can be a barrier for government agencies with limited budgets (Sustainable Procurement Charter, 2015).

Lack of monitoring and reporting: Without proper monitoring and reporting mechanisms, it may be difficult to measure the impact of sustainable procurement practices and identify areas for improvement (European Commission, 2013)

To overcome these challenges, government agencies can work to improve awareness and understanding of sustainable procurement practices among stakeholders, provide training and capacity building for procurement officials and suppliers, develop strong legal and regulatory frameworks to support sustainable procurement practices, and implement effective monitoring and reporting mechanisms to measure progress and identify areas for improvement (The World Bank, 2019).

GOVERNMENT SUPPORT FOR SUSTAINABLE PROCUREMENT

Governments around the world are increasingly recognizing the importance of sustainable procurement and providing support to promote its implementation (Taghipour & Merimi, 2021). Below is an overview of some of the ways in which governments support sustainable procurement:

Policies and guidelines: Many governments have developed policies and guidelines to support sustainable procurement practices. These policies and guidelines provide guidance on how to integrate sustainability considerations into procurement processes and set targets and objectives for sustainable procurement (Walker, Di Sisto & McBain, 2013).

Training and capacity building: Governments provide training and capacity building for procurement officials, suppliers, and other stakeholders to improve their understanding of sustainable procurement practices. This can include workshops, seminars, and online training programs (Welford, 2013).

Standards and certifications: Governments may develop or support the development of sustainability standards and certifications for products and services. These standards and certifications help to identify sustainable products and services and provide a basis for procurement decisions (Zhang & Parker, 2012).

Collaboration and partnerships: Olinga and Gelbman (2013) highlighted that governments may collaborate with other governments, international organisations, and the private sector to promote sustainable procurement practices. These collaborations can lead to the sharing of best practices and knowledge, the development of new procurement solutions, and the identification of opportunities for sustainable procurement.

Incentives: Governments may provide incentives to encourage sustainable procurement practices, such as tax credits or subsidies for sustainable products and services, or preferential treatment for suppliers that meet sustainability criteria (Scottish Government. (2018).

Government Support Mechanisms in procurement

Governments play an important role in promoting sustainable procurement practices, and they provide various support mechanisms such as training, capacity building, and funding to facilitate the implementation of sustainable procurement (Shin & Taghipour, 2021). Such mechanisms are elaborated below

Training and capacity building: Governments provide training and capacity building to procurement officials, suppliers, and other stakeholders to improve their understanding of sustainable procurement practices. This can include workshops, seminars, and online training programs. By investing in training and capacity building, governments can improve awareness and understanding of sustainable procurement practices and build the necessary skills and expertise for effective implementation (Reisch & Altstötter-Gleich, 2013).

Standards and certifications: Governments may develop or support the development of sustainability standards and certifications for products and services. These standards and certifications help to identify sustainable products and services and provide a basis for procurement decisions. By setting clear sustainability criteria and standards, governments can support the procurement of sustainable products and services and provide a level playing field for suppliers (Venter & Pillay, 2011).

Procurement tools and databases: Governments may develop or support the development of procurement tools and databases that provide information on sustainable products and services, suppliers, and best practices. These tools and databases can help procurement officials make informed decisions about sustainable procurement and provide suppliers with access to new markets (Welford, 2013).

Collaboration and partnerships: According to Kweka (2011), governments may collaborate with other governments, international organisations, and the private sector to promote sustainable procurement practices. These collaborations can lead to the sharing of best practices and knowledge, the development of new procurement solutions, and the identification of opportunities for sustainable procurement.

Funding: Most governments are known to have enough funding to support sustainable procurement practices. This funding can be used to support pilot projects, research and development, and the implementation of sustainable procurement practices. By providing funding, governments can help to overcome financial barriers to sustainable procurement and stimulate innovation in sustainable procurement practices (Yang et., 2017).

THE FUTURE OF SUSTAINABLE PROCUREMENT

Sustainable procurement has become increasingly important in recent years, and there are several emerging trends in this area. The key trends are discussed below.

Circular economy: According to United Nations Environment Programme (2017), there is growing interest in the circular economy, which involves designing out waste and pollution, keeping products and materials in use, and regenerating natural systems. Sustainable procurement practices can support the transition to a circular economy by promoting the use of sustainable products and services and encouraging suppliers to adopt circular business models.

Social sustainability: While environmental sustainability has been a focus of sustainable procurement, there is increasing recognition of the importance of social sustainability. This includes issues such as human rights, labor practices, and community engagement. Sustainable procurement practices can support social sustainability by ensuring that suppliers meet social sustainability criteria, and by promoting suppliers that have strong social sustainability practices (Walker et al, 2013).

Digitalization: Digital technologies are increasingly being used to support sustainable procurement practices. For example, digital platforms can be used to provide information on sustainable products and services, and to streamline procurement processes. Digital technologies can also be used to track and monitor the sustainability performance of suppliers (Zhang & Parker, 2012).

Supply chain transparency: Kuosmanen and Mäkitalo-Keinonen (2011) alluded that there is growing demand for greater transparency in supply chains, particularly with regard to environmental and social sustainability. Sustainable procurement practices can support supply chain transparency by requiring suppliers to disclose information on their sustainability performance, and by promoting suppliers that have transparent supply chains.

Collaboration: Hinrichs-Rahlwes and Zawilska-Florczuk (2011) affirmed that sustainable procurement is increasingly being seen as a collaborative effort, involving collaboration between government agencies, suppliers, and other stakeholders. Collaborative approaches can help to build capacity, share knowledge, and develop innovative solutions to sustainability challenges.

THE ROLE OF GOVERNMENT IN SHAPING THE FUTURE OF SUSTAINABLE PROCUREMENT

Governments play a critical role in shaping the future of sustainable procurement, as they have the power to create policies, regulations, and incentives that encourage sustainable procurement practices. Here are some ways in which governments can shape the future of sustainable procurement:

Setting sustainability targets: Governments can set sustainability targets for their own procurement activities and encourage suppliers to meet these targets. This can help to create a market for sustainable products and services, and drive innovation in sustainable procurement (Happaerts & Van de Walle, 2011).

Creating regulatory frameworks: Governments can create regulatory frameworks that require suppliers to meet certain sustainability standards, such as environmental or social sustainability criteria. This can help to ensure that sustainable procurement practices are adopted across a range of industries and supply chains (Government of India, 2017).

Providing guidance and support: De Boer and Baumann (2013) affirm that governments can provide guidance and support to procurement officials and suppliers, helping them to adopt sustainable procurement practices. This can include training programs, toolkits, and other resources that provide information on sustainable procurement best practices.

Creating incentives: Governments can create incentives to encourage suppliers to adopt sustainable procurement practices, such as tax breaks or access to government contracts. This can help to create a market for sustainable products and services and encourage suppliers to invest in sustainable practices (European Commission, 2013).

Collaborating with stakeholders: As highlighted by the Government of Canada (2019) governments can collaborate with stakeholders, including industry groups, non-governmental organisations, and academia, to develop sustainable procurement policies and practices. This can help to build consensus around the importance of sustainable procurement and develop innovative solutions to sustainability challenges.

Conclusively, the role of government in shaping the future of sustainable procurement is crucial. By setting sustainability targets, creating regulatory frameworks, providing guidance and support, creating incentives, and collaborating with stakeholders, governments can promote sustainable procurement practices and contribute to a more sustainable future.

SUGGESTIONS FOR FUTURE GOVERNMENT ACTION ON SUSTAINABLE PROCUREMENT

Governments are expected to still focus on playing a pivotal role in future sustainable procurement. The following measures are recommended to ensure sustainable future of procurement:

Set ambitious sustainability targets: Governments can set ambitious sustainability targets for their procurement activities and encourage suppliers to meet these targets. This can help to drive innovation and create a market for sustainable products and services (Government of South Africa, 2017).

Adopt a life-cycle approach: According to Ferrari and Migliarese (2010) governments can adopt a life-cycle approach to procurement, taking into account the environmental and social impacts of products and services at every stage of their life cycle, from extraction to disposal. This can help to identify opportunities for reducing the environmental and social impact of procurement activities.

Integrate sustainability criteria into procurement processes: Governments can integrate sustainability criteria into procurement processes, such as tender documents and evaluation criteria, to ensure that suppliers meet sustainability standards. This can help to promote sustainable procurement practices across a range of industries and supply chains (European Commission, 2020).

Provide training and capacity building: Governments can provide training and capacity building to procurement officials and suppliers, to help them adopt sustainable procurement practices. This can include training programs, toolkits, and other resources that provide information on sustainable procurement best practices (Government of Australia, 2018).

Encourage collaboration and information sharing: The Federal Ministry for the Environment, Nature Conservation and Nuclear Safety (2019) reiterated that governments can encourage collaboration and information sharing among procurement officials and suppliers, to share knowledge and best practices in sustainable procurement. This can help to build capacity and develop innovative solutions to sustainability challenges.

Promote sustainable innovation: Governments can promote sustainable innovation by supporting research and development in sustainable products and services and encouraging suppliers to invest in sustainable practices. This can help to drive innovation and create a market for sustainable products and services (European Commission, 2020).

CONCLUSION

In conclusion, this book chapter has highlighted the crucial role of government in promoting sustainable procurement as a tool for achieving sustainable development goals. The chapter has provided an overview of sustainable procurement, its benefits, and challenges, and identified the potential for government to use procurement policies to promote sustainability. The importance of government leadership, legal frameworks, and institutional capacity for the effective implementation of sustainable procurement practices has been emphasized, along with examples of successful sustainable procurement initiatives from around the world and key lessons learnt.

Overall, sustainable procurement is an important approach for organisations to consider in order to promote sustainable development and achieve their environmental, social, and economic objectives. Sustainable procurement can create value for organisations, stakeholders, and the environment, and can contribute to a more sustainable future. The chapter concludes with recommendations for government action to promote sustainable procurement, including the need for strategic planning, stakeholder engagement, and ongoing monitoring and evaluation. By working together, government and organisations can make significant progress towards achieving a sustainable future through sustainable procurement.

REFERENCES

Cauchois, R., Taghipour, A., Kang, D., Zoghlami, N., & Abed, M. (2017). Advanced solutions for a supply chain with stochastic information. Journal of Advanced Management Science Vol, 5(1).

De Boer, L., & Baumann, H. (2013). Sustainable procurement: An introduction. In *Sustainable procurement: An introduction* (pp. 1–6). Routledge.

El-NEMR, N., CANEL-DEPITRE, B., & TAGHIPOUR, A. (2021). The determinants of hotel room rates in Beirut: A hedonic pricing model. International Journal of Trade. *Economics and Finance*, *12*(2), 33–42.

El-Nemr, N., Canel-Depitre, B., & Taghipour, A. (2017, September). Determinants of hotel room rates. In Marketing Trends Congress. Luxury Industries Conference London 2017.

European Commission. (2013). *Buying Green! A Handbook on Green Public Procurement*. Publications Office of the European Union.

European Commission. (2020). Green Public Procurement. https://ec.europa.eu/environment/gpp/index_en.htm

European Union. (2014). Public Procurement Directive 2014/24/EU. European Union.

Federal Ministry for the Environment. Nature Conservation and Nuclear Safety. (2019). Guidelines for Sustainable Public Procurement. Federal Ministry for the Environment, Nature Conservation and Nuclear Safety.

Ferrari, S., & Migliarese, P. (2010). Public procurement and sustainable development: A brief review. *Journal of Cleaner Production*, *18*(15), 1440–1446.

Government, N. S. (2018). *NSW Government Sustainable Procurement Policy*. NSW Government.

Government of Australia. (2018). *Sustainable Procurement Guide*. Department of Finance, Government of Australia.

Government of Canada. (2019). *Greening Government Strategy*. Government of Canada.

Government of India. (2017). *Manual for Procurement of Goods 2017*. Ministry of Finance, Department of Expenditure, Government of India.

Government of South Africa. (2017). *Preferential Procurement Policy Framework Act (PPPFA) No.5 of 2000*. Government of South Africa.

Happaerts, S., & Van de Walle, S. (2011). Sustainable procurement in Flemish local governments: An empirical study of the drivers and barriers. *Journal of Public Procurement*, *11*(4), 509–536.

Hinrichs-Rahlwes, R., & Zawilska-Florczuk, M. (2011). Legal frameworks for sustainable public procurement in the European Union. *Journal of Cleaner Production*, *19*(6-7), 975–983.

Kuosmanen, T., & Mäkitalo-Keinonen, T. (2011). Sustainable public procurement practices in Finland. *Journal of Public Procurement*, *11*(4), 537–561.

Kweka, J. (2011). Sustainable procurement practices in the public sector: An international comparative study. *Journal of Public Procurement*, *11*(1), 1–30.

Loivet, W., Taghipour, A., & Kang, D. S. (2020). The rise of green supply chain management: Between complexity and necessity. Journal of Economics. *Business and Management*, *8*(1), 1–7.

Mahfod, J., Canel-Depitre, B., & Taghipour, A. (2019). Quality function deployment-ELECTRE in supplier evaluation. Journal of Advanced Management Science Vol, 7(4).

Merimi, M., & Taghipour, A. (2021). Accelerating the digitalization of the supply chain: An empirical research about COVID-19 crisis. In *Digitalization of Decentralized Supply Chains During Global Crises* (pp. 1–24). IGI Global. doi:10.4018/978-1-7998-6874-3.ch001

Ministry of the Environment. Japan. (2015). Guidelines for Environmental Consideration in Procurement. Ministry of the Environment, Government of Japan.

Ministry of the Environment. Finland. (2016). Guidelines for Green Public Procurement in Finland. Ministry of the Environment, Government of Finland.

Nadia, E. N., Beatrice, C. D., & Atour, T. (2020). Luxury hotels' eco-friendly activities & customers' preferences and willingness to pay for green hotels. Journal of Advanced Management Science Vol, 8(1).

O'Hara, S. (2013). Promoting sustainable procurement: An analysis of government policies and guidelines. *Journal of Cleaner Production*, *56*, 112–119.

OECD. (2015). *Policy Guidance for Greening Government Procurement*. OECD Publishing.

Olinga, T., & Gelbman, A. (2013). A roadmap for sustainable public procurement. *Journal of Cleaner Production*, *55*, 21–29.

Papoutsis, K., & Pappas, P. (2013). The role of government in promoting sustainable procurement. *Journal of Public Procurement*, *13*(2), 152.

Reisch, L. A., & Altstötter-Gleich, C. (2013). Sustainable public procurement: A review of the European legal framework. *European Journal of Sustainable Development*, *2*(3), 15–26.

Schönherr, N., & Schröder, T. (2012). Antecedents and dimensions of sustainable procurement. *Journal of Purchasing and Supply Management*, *18*(4), 232–242.

Scottish Government. (2018). Procurement Reform (Scotland) Act 2014. Scottish Government.

Shin, M., & Taghipour, A. (2021). Supply Chains Digital Transformation: Automated Underground Logistics Systems. *Underground Construction*, *6*(2), 7. doi:10.18178/joebm.2021.9.2.651

Sustainable Procurement Charter. (2015). Sustainable Procurement Charter. https://www.sustainable-procurement.org/about/collaborative-initiatives/sustainable-procurement-charter/

Taghipour, A. (2014). *Production Network Planning Based on Constraint Relaxation and Discount Approach* (Vol. 2). Lecture Notes on Information Theory.

Taghipour, A. (2018). A Contemporary Approach to Plan Independent Logistics Actors. In *Contemporary Approaches and Strategies for Applied Logistics* (pp. 337–364). IGI Global. doi:10.4018/978-1-5225-5273-4.ch014

Taghipour, A. (Ed.). (2020). *Demand Forecasting and Order Planning in Supply Chains and Humanitarian Logistics*. IGI Global.

Taghipour, A., Abed, M., & Zoghlami, N. (2015, May). Design for remanufacturing respecting reverse logistics processes: A review. In 2015 4th International Conference on Advanced Logistics and Transport (ICALT) (pp. 299-304). IEEE. 10.1109/ICAdLT.2015.7136602

Taghipour, A., & Beneteau-Piet, C. (2020). Sustainable supply chain management performance. *International Journal of Innovation, Management and Technology*, *11*(6), 165–169. doi:10.18178/ijimt.2020.11.6.897

Taghipour, A., & Frayret, J. M. (2011a). A new heuristic search with local optimization to manage a supply chain. *Meta*, 15.

Taghipour, A., & Frayret, J. M. (2011b). Supply chain coordination planning: A review. Work paper, École polytechnique de Montréal.

Taghipour, A., Glaa, B., & Zoghlami, N. (2014, May). Network coordination with minimum risk of information sharing. In *2014 International Conference on Advanced Logistics and Transport (ICALT)* (pp. 184-188). IEEE. 10.1109/ICAdLT.2014.6864115

Taghipour, A., & Merimi, M. (2021). Digital Transformation of Supply Chains during Crisis: COVID-19. In 11th Annual International Conference on Industrial Engineering and Operations Management, IEOM (pp. 7493-7501).

Taghipour, A., Murat, S., & Huang, P. (2021). E-supply chain management: A review. International Journal of e-Education, e-Business, e-. *Management Learning*, *11*(2), 51–61.

The World Bank. (2019). *Procuring Infrastructure Public-Private Partnerships*. World Bank Group.

Tliche, Y., Taghipour, A., & Canel-Depitre, B. (2019). Anticipation of Demand in Supply Chains. In *Hierarchical Planning and Information Sharing Techniques in Supply Chain Management* (pp. 1–45). IGI Global.

Tliche, Y., Taghipour, A., & Canel-Depitre, B. (2021). Exploring a Downstream Demand Inference Strategy in a Decentralized Two-Level Supply Chain. In *Demand Forecasting and Order Planning in Supply Chains and Humanitarian Logistics* (pp. 1–65). IGI Global. doi:10.4018/978-1-7998-3805-0.ch001

United Nations Environment Programme. (2017). *Sustainable Public Procurement Implementation Guidelines*. UNEP.

Venter, M., & Pillay, S. (2011). The challenges and benefits of sustainable procurement: The case of South Africa. *Journal of Public Procurement*, *11*(1), 49–83.

Vosooghidizaji, M., Taghipour, A., & Canel-Depitre, B. (2020). Information Asymmetry in Supply Chain Coordination: State of the Art. Journal of Industrial and Intelligent Information Vol, 8(2).

Vosooghidizaji, M., Taghipour, A., & Canel-Depitre, B. (2022). Coordinating corporate social responsibility in a two-level supply chain under bilateral information asymmetry. *Journal of Cleaner Production*, *364*, 132627. doi:10.1016/j.jclepro.2022.132627

Walker, H., Di Sisto, L., & McBain, D. (2013). Drivers and barriers to environmental sustainable procurement in the public sector: A cross-country comparison. *Journal of Public Procurement*, *13*(2), 218–241.

Welford, R. (2013). The future of sustainable procurement. In *Corporate sustainability in Asia* (pp. 317–330). Routledge.

Yang, S., Taghipour, A., & Canel-Depitre, B. (2017, August). Cost optimization of reverse logistics: A review. In *Proceedings of the 7th International Conference on Information Communication and Management* (pp. 158-161). 10.1145/3134383.3134393

Zhang, X., & Parker, D. (2012). Government procurement for sustainability in China: An overview. *Journal of Public Procurement*, *12*(1), 52–82.

KEY TERMS AND DEFINITIONS

Sustainable procurement: The process of acquiring goods, services, and works in a manner that considers the economic, social, and environmental impacts of the procurement process.

Government: A system or group of people responsible for governing and controlling a particular community, country, or territory. It is a political organisation that exercises authority and power over its citizens or subjects, enforces laws and regulations, and provides public services and programs to promote the well-being of its people.

Supply chain management: The management of the flow of goods and services, from raw materials to the final product, including the coordination and collaboration with suppliers.

Sustainable development: A development approach that seeks to meet the needs of the present generation without compromising the ability of future generations to meet their own needs. It is a framework that aims to balance economic growth, social progress, and environmental protection in a way that is sustainable over the long term

Triple bottom line: A business approach that considers the economic, social, and environmental impacts of its operations.

Lifecycle assessment: The evaluation of the environmental impact of a product or service throughout its entire lifecycle, from the extraction of raw materials to the disposal of waste.

Social responsibility: The obligation of an organisation to act in the best interests of society and the environment, beyond its legal obligations.

Chapter 15
Analysis of the Sustainability of Supply Chains and Value Chain Management:
Economy in the Republic of Serbia

Biljana Stojan Ilic
Faculty of Project and Innovation Management "Petar Jovanovic" of Belgrade, Educons University, Serbia

Suncica S. Stankovic
Faculty of Business Economics and Entrepreneurship of Belgrade, Serbia

ABSTRACT

The philosophy of the supply chain concept is aimed at the greatest possible alignment of key business functions of all links in the distribution chain in the process of organizing goods and information flows. Applying the concept of an integrated supply chain between multiple organizations further increases the importance of operational logistics activities, improves process optimizations, and confirms the importance of logistics performance for profitability. Emphasis is placed on the sustainability of the supply chain in Serbia, but also on the broader context of the value chain of economic sectors in the Republic of Serbia. The aim of the chapter is focused on highlighting both positive and limiting factors (the real situation), with the author's wish that the recommendation of good practice and the results of this research be implemented in Serbia.

INTRODUCTION

The implementation of the supply chain idea in one distribution channel has the effect of diminishing the importance of conventional business management and emphasizing the necessity of process management approaches instead, in addition to erasing inter-company barriers. The phrase by Machiavelli that "there is nothing more difficult, dangerous, and with more uncertain success than creating a path to learning

DOI: 10.4018/978-1-6684-9062-4.ch015

something new" (Mansfield, 2023) is one that the authors are aware of. Nevertheless, this assertion serves as further motivation for the authors to make the concept and goals of supply chain implementation more accessible to the book's readers by highlighting important, pertinent global, theoretical, and consulting approaches (Andrijanic & Pavlovic, 2016)(Cauchois et al., 2017). The purpose of the chapter is to help domestic businesses, in this case, firms in Serbia, comprehend the fundamentals of and use the supply chain management concept more quickly. Compared to logistics management, which initially debuted and from which the notion of the supply chain originated, sustainable supply chain management encompasses a strategically positioned and considerably wider range of activities. It also symbolizes a new corporate philosophy. The term "green" is used more frequently in contemporary business practices when referring to management, marketing, reputation management, human resource management, and similar topics (Gordana & Biljana, 2021). The accelerated development of industry and technology has brought humanity into a serious problem - the survival of man on Earth has been called into question, but indirectly the survival of the Earth as well. The climate changes that modern society faces are increasingly pronounced, and as a response to the suppression of harmful consequences, a new concept - on a global level - called Sustainable Development (Biermann et al., 2022) has appeared. This concept originated in the last century, more precisely in 1987, and on that occasion, the United Nations called the report from its summit "Our Common Future" (Brundtland Report). The document defines the concept of sustainable development as development that provides the right to the same resources for future generations, as the current generations have, that is, it promotes development that could harmonize the economic and ecological component with the social component (Ilic et al., 2020). Since then and up to the present, numerous occasions, gatherings, meetings, and agreements have taken place on a global scale in an effort to save the environment and preserve resources. Because everything that is done to attain a certain economic benefit must have the connotation of a green undertaking or sustainable operations, the outcome is that business today has been given the word "green". Green business has permeated every aspect of organizational life, and both green conduct and green supply are being discussed more and more frequently. The idea of "green management" is one that is connected to environmentally friendly behavior. In this context, supply chains known as sustainable supply chains are linked to green management (Djukic & Ilic, 2021; Kostadinovic & Stankovic, 2020). The idea of sustainable supply chains is actually still in the early stages of development since a number of data points indicate that it has not yet reached its zenith, i.e., that the movement of information, money, and other items through a supply chain distribution system is a constant source of issues. However, there are many potential to enhance (daily) business in supply chains that must be sustainable. Even when everything within the organization appears to be in order, the answer to the question of whether there is one final piece necessary for a business process to succeed is frequently in the affirmative. In other words, everything in the organization worked perfectly, but the final, anticipated "excellent success" was mysteriously missing (Tliche et al., 2021; Vosooghidizaji et al., 2020). A similar example can be found in the case of complaints made by users of services or final customers, which (complaints) are related to certain products, which (complaints) are related to certain products, which (complaints) are related to certain products, which should be found on store shelves, at a certain price, under certain conditions of sale, but those products are not available, that is, that they were not delivered on time by the supplier. Examples of this can be seen among regular consumers who are unable to explain to the sales managers what is missing from the purchase in order to be completely satisfied with it. The general manager frequently feels that something is missing in system optimization, in connection with suppliers, and in relation to delivery, but this can also be seen from the perspective of his organization's visionary leader (El-Nemr et al., 2021). The answer lies in timely response, for everything that may be missing in a business process. The answer lies in sustainable supply chains. they lead to sustainable value chains throughout a country's economy.

BACKGROUND

The massive growth of the commodity exchange and all of the information that is shared in this context serve as a major driving force behind the adoption of contemporary logistics and distribution management systems (Loivet et al., 2020). The idea of management throughout the complete supply chain, together with all its methodological tools that have been established so far for the needs of diverse optimizations, is currently at the center of all advancements in the flow of goods and information in the globe. In both absolute and relative aspects, the global economy is evolving quickly. In this regard, it should be noted that problems and methods for overcoming them cannot be the same for all global distribution channels now as they were forty years ago (Mahfod et al., 2019)(Acimovic, 2006). Examples of this can be found in numerous worldwide, statistically relevant data. For example, the value of world merchandise exports in 1963 was more than one hundred and fifty billion dollars. Just nine years ago (2004), the value of world merchandise exports reached over eight thousand billion dollars (WTO, 2004). It is necessary to mention the fact that the structure of the leading countries has also changed to some extent in global world exports. Today, the countries of the European Union have a percentage of slightly more than forty, while the countries of the USA participated with slightly more than nine percent. For the last ten years, China recorded exports of around seven percent - with tendencies to increase its share in world trade, while Japan's share was also slightly above six percent of exports (Merimi & Taghipour, 2021). The rest of the export, up to one hundred percent, belongs to other countries of the world. It can be concluded that it is not the same to organize the delivery of the right goods, to the right place in the right quantity, at the right time, at acceptable costs, and with - as little as possible, errors in the accompanying documentation (Nadia et al., 2020). For goods exported today, it is much more complicated than fifty years ago. In addition, the sensibility and pampering of the modern global consumer impose higher servicing costs, while on the other hand, it differentiates suppliers according to the success of the business and competitive strategy implementation (Taghipour & Beneteau-Piet, 2020). The increased value of commodity exchange contributes to the increase of supply costs, at the level of one company, the entire distribution chain, and all distribution chains within one country. Logistics costs are nowadays a key cost factor in many industries or trade branches. Logistics represents a very important aspect of the functioning of the economy as a whole. And the experience of the USA, as the country where they are most precisely measured and where regular annual studies are conducted, shows that shipping costs are not easy to manage because they can always get out of control. According to Council of Supply Chain Management Professionals (CSCMP) data, the logistics costs of all companies, analyzed through their participation in GDP, have been decreasing over the decades to, for example, in 2005, record a slight percentage - but high absolute increase (CSCMP, 2023)(Shin & Taghipour, 2021). From 1963 to 2005, the share of logistics costs in the GDP of the United States of America increased by more than one hundred and fifty billion dollars. In certain large exporting countries such as China and India - where the logistics infrastructure was insufficiently developed, the share of logistics costs at the macro level was high (ten years ago) (Vollman et al., 2005). On the other hand, the European Union, as a territorially close community of countries that trade a lot within themselves and that generally has a good and developed logistics infrastructure, had in the same period the lowest percentage share of logistics costs in GDP - slightly above seven percent (in 2004). In modern, stormy times, when significant increases in world GDP are expected, which is induced by the still dominant commodity exchange, as well as other factors (politics), it is necessary to find new solutions to optimize world supply chains, i.e. to control distribution costs with a mutually acceptable level of consumer service for both supply and demand (Bozic & Acimovic, 2004). Therefore, developing sustainable supply networks is essential. New supply methods and distribution channels can be developed both within and between companies (in the nation and the world - globally) along with the growth in commodity exchange (Taghipour et al., 2021). New informational technologies, namely the Internet revolution, are the fundamental factor in all of this.

New methodological techniques and technological advancements are quickly replacing outdated methods of managing information and material flows. With new concepts, business practices, innovations, and ideas that aim to move the boundaries between various companies in one distribution channel—from the primary producer to the final consumer—the era of logistics management, which partially optimizes product flows within one system, is changing (Vosooghidizaji et al., 2022; Taghipour et al., 2015)(Pedersen & Shaver, 2011). While the term "sustainable supply chain management," or simply "sustainable supply chain management," is becoming more and more common in corporate practice, there are also an increasing number of relevant theoretical contributions emerging from around the world. Each company and participant in the supply channel is only one link in a sustainable chain in which there are no longer any boundaries between the companies, and the management of sustainable supply chains is situated within the context of a distinctive business process of goods and information flow that follows it along the entire distribution channel (Pham et al., 2020; Tliche et al., 2019). Figure 1 shows sustainable supply chains in the era of new technologies.

Figure 1. Supply chain in the era of new technologies
Source: Pluton Logistics

Due to the limits imposed by the domestic Serbian market and the advent of intense rivalry there, many transport and logistics businesses are searching for strategies to thrive there in today's competitive economic environment. Opening up to the overseas market is one of the ways they can thrive in the highly competitive climate of the world market. In other words, at some point, the domestic local market's potential for growth becomes exhausted, which manifests itself in a decline in the market's appeal for conducting the operations of transport and logistics firms. Additionally, these businesses have the option to increase their commercial operations in foreign markets in order to grow, build their brand, and generate more revenue. In light of this, internationalization has emerged as a crucial term for the survival and growth of transport and logistics businesses in today's cutthroat marketplace. It is mostly used to describe the cross-border activities of these businesses. Previous research works have taken into account the theme of examining the connection between the phenomenon of internationalization and cross-border logistics activities (Trinkuniene & Aksomitiene, 2017; Kedzior-Laskowska, 2020; El-Nemr et al., 2017; Taghipour & Frayret, 2014). Many authors' primary attention was focused on determining whether internationalization had an impact on the expansion of cross-border logistics activities. Their investigation' findings indicated that the performance of cross-border logistics activities is somewhat influenced by the internationalization process. (Kostiuk et al., 2021; Taghipour, 2020; Jarašuniene et al., 2020; Taghipour & Frayret, 2011b). They discovered that the logistics system's features are shifting with regard to distance, delivery time, and the acquisition of commodities, as well as instability in the area of demand forecasting for specific products. On the other hand, international logistics kickstarts the process of internationalization since there is widespread communication among logistics firms and cutting-edge transport systems that enable quick delivery of goods to the customer's destination (Taghipour, 2018; Naevestad et al., 2017)(Taghipour, 2014). Transport and logistics firms may integrate complex cross-border operations into their value chains much more readily because to their presence and the capability that today's global logistics networks offer (Taghipour & Merimi, 2021; Yang, et al., 2017).

MAIN FOCUS - CRITERIA DIMENSIONS IN DESIGNING THE SUPPLY CHAIN IN SERBIA AND COMPETITIVE ADVANTAGE

The goal of this chapter is to examine the significant elements of Serbia's supply chain and to contrast old and contemporary methods. The most significant elements influencing the viability of the Serbian economy are described by the authors. The notion of supply chain management will be redefined in this chapter in the context of contemporary business and the application of sustainability principles. The aspiration is based on the knowledge that the traditional methods of supply and business should be innovated and conceptualized using both new technologies and competitive advantage if the system of sustainable management of Serbia's economic sectors and supply chain achieves effective interactions between participants and improves process performance. The analysis's findings highlight the chain's essential components, or the crucial elements that contribute to Serbia's supply networks being managed sustainably. However, the authors contend that it is impossible to paint a genuine picture of the management of both the Serbian economy and the supply chains without connecting the supply chains and a few key economic sectors. In certain ways, the research serves as a foundation for the construction of modern supply chain management in Serbia, or for the redesign of current management policies. In other words, management is evaluated with an eye toward sustainability, high-quality services, and cost-cutting. The relationships between suppliers and customers strengthen as a result of the usage of new technology in supply chains. However, it is essential to examine a few crucial aspects of the Serbian economy as this will enable the reader to gauge how close or far Serbia is from implementing sustainability, sustainable management, and therefore the use of new technology. The chapter's study has a more theoretical bent. The methodology of scientific research has been synchronized with knowledge from professional and scholarly literature, as well as the approach of comparing the sustainability of supply chains in Serbia and some Western Balkan nations. Serbia might be said to represent a new potential for European production in the area of logistics as a nation still undergoing transformation and attempting to pave the route toward sustainable management and business, to move closer to Europe (Rabrenovic et al., 2020). Serbia is advantageous due to its location, as well as the fact that many foreign businesses that depend on proximity to the European Union market, cheap labor prices, and a skilled workforce, view Serbia as a "potential" on the rise. The creation and management of logistics parks in the Republic of Serbia are both significantly impacted by the nearshoring of supply chains (Lazarevic et al., 2018). The findings of study carried out by the Dutch firm "CTP," one of the pioneers in the field of constructing and issuing business-industrial parks in Central-Eastern Europe, demonstrate the popularization of Serbian logistical assistance. This business made the observation that foreign businesses are increasingly considering the benefits of the Serbian market. The demand for industrial and logistics capacities on the axis of key CTP markets (from the Czech Republic to Romania) is strong due to the increased involvement of the German industrial supply chain in the markets of Central and Eastern Europe and the nearshoring trend, which occurs when companies choose to strengthen the resilience of their global chains by locating production close to the main markets. However, it also causes pressure for wages and other costs to rise. In addition to being close to the markets of European nations (EU), Serbia, a nation outside the European Union, is very competitive in terms of labor prices and a skilled work force (Vukovic et al., 2015). Because CTP parks provide the most cutting-edge, environmentally friendly production and logistics capabilities, an increasing number of businesses are choosing to focus their logistics chains specifically in Serbia. In order to produce its products (motors for electronic window lifters), the German business "Bosch" leased 20,000 square meters in "CTPark" Belgrade West in 2022. At the same time, the logistics company "Milšped" leased a space of sixteen thousand square meters, in the same location. The branch of the CTP company in Serbia handed over a building of over twenty-six thousand square meters to the Japanese company Nidec, at the location "CTPark" Novi Sad (City of Northern Serbia).

At this location, the Nidec-Elesys company is also planning to carry out total works on an area of sixty thousand square meters. Another example of how relevant Serbia is for inclusion in logistics and modern supply chains is the Chinese company "YanFeng", which signed a lease agreement for a third production location of thirty thousand square meters. The construction of this space began at the end of 2022 in the "CTPark" complex in Kragujevac. At the "CTPark Belgrade Sever" location in 2021, approximately twenty-five thousand square meters of logistics space (out of a total of one hundred thousand planned) was provided and put into operation. The Slovenian company "Intereuropa" leased more than fourteen thousand square meters at the location of Novi Banovci (Sremski district of Serbia), for the new distribution center of the company Hisense Gorenje (Pluton Logistics). The World Bank's LPI composite index (Figure 2) provides insight into the current stage of development and is used to evaluate the effectiveness of the logistics system in the Republic of Serbia. This index, which was first released in 2007, provides a biannual evaluation of the quality of the logistics system based on six indicators: customs, infrastructure, international shipments, logistics competence, timeliness, and tracking & tracing. These factors' individual and total evaluations reveal the level of logistics in a country's economy. Based on the graphic presentation, it can be seen that in Serbia, the observed indicators had lower values in the third year of observation (2023) compared to the first two years (2016 and 2018), except for the timeliness score, which had greater values. Serbia's LPI score is at the level of "partial performers" according to the most recent statistics, which suggests that there are considerable logistical constraints and is consistent with the outcomes in lower- and middle-income nations (Arvis et al., 2023). This fact suggests the need for additional development, particularly given the possible effects of those components on businesses from various industries.

Figure 2. Serbia's LPI scores for the period 2016-2023
Source: Arvis et al. (2016; 2018;2023)

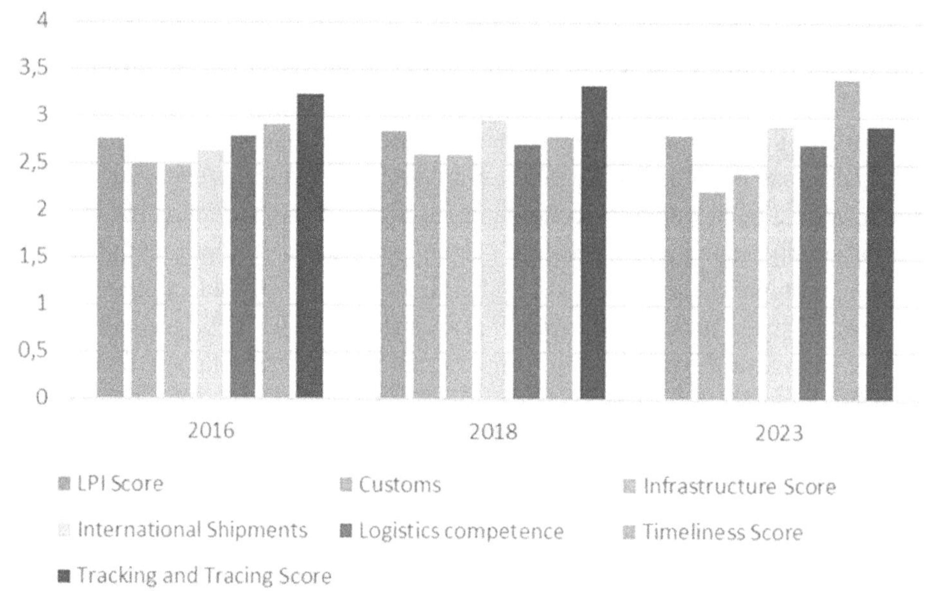

The level of logistics performance development can be determined by comparing the provided indicators to those of other countries, particularly those in the Western Balkans region. Table 1 provides an overview of the rankings and results in the countries of the Western Balkans (Albania, Bosnia & Herzegovina, Montenegro, North Macedonia, and Serbia). The Table shows that North Macedonia (57) had the highest LPI rank among the countries that were observed, followed by Bosnia & Herzegovina (61), Montenegro (73), Serbia (73), and Albania (97). Based on the data presented, it can be noted that each of them has significant space for growth in these areas.

Table 1. LPI score and rank for Western Balkan countries in 2023

Country	LPI Rank	LPI Score	Customs	Infrastructure	International shipments	Logistics competence	Tracking & tracing	Timeliness
Albania	97	2.5	2.4	2.7	2.8	2.3	2.5	2.3
Bosnia and Herzegovina	61	3.0	2.7	2.6	3.1	2.9	3.2	3.2
Montenegro	73	2.8	2.6	2.5	2.8	2.8	3.2	3.2
North Macedonia	57	3.1	3.1	3.0	2.8	3.2	3.5	3.2
Serbia	73	2.8	2.2	2.4	2.9	2.7	3.4	2.9

Source: Author's research

Value chains in Economic Sectors of Serbia

Analyses of the performance and value chain of a few key sectors in the Republic of Serbia are included in the comprehensive report created by the Center for Advanced Economic Studies (CEVES) consortium, in collaboration with the Ministry of Economy, the Secretariat for Public Policy, and the Development Agency of Serbia, as well as with representatives of other ministries, the scientific community, associations, and regional chambers of Serbia. The paper is titled "Analysis of the Performance and Value Chain of Selected Sectors" and examines the competitiveness of four sectors that the Ministry of Economy of the Republic of Serbia chose (CEVES, 2017). The first sector refers to the food and beverage sector, the second to the wood and furniture sector, the third to the rubber and plastic sector, and the fourth to the machinery and equipment sector. The authors will briefly review the summary analysis of the mentioned sectors to bring the readers closer to the state of the Serbian economy and the value chain that these four most important sectors contribute to the Serbian economy. By analyzing the state of the value chain, a broader picture of the state and supply chain in the Republic of Serbia will be provided. Given that Serbia aspires to become a member of the European Union, the Report aimed to provide information relevant to the creation of an industrial development strategy, by the negotiation chapter 20 - Entrepreneurship and industrial policy, which refers to the acceleration of structural adjustments, encouraging the creation of a favorable environment for starting businesses, domestic and foreign investments, promoting small and medium-sized enterprises, as well as entrepreneurship and innovation. Additionally, negotiation chapter 20 focuses on encouraging a more thorough evaluation of the competitiveness of particular sectors and implementing sector-specific efforts, including high-level organizations, policy forums, studies, expert panels, and networking initiatives. Additionally, effective structures for consultation and cooperation are needed for the development and implementation of entrepreneurship and industry policy at the national, regional, and local levels. (Kostadinovic & Stankovic, 2021)(Tanaskovic & Ristic, 2019). The items offered, according to the authors, already show a specific chain of information flow and economic conditions in Serbia. Within Serbia's processing industry, the four chosen sectors exhibit significant comparative advantages, and some relationships within each sector rely on and support one another. The authors wish to draw a distinction between the "traditional" economy and the "new" economy because they have demonstrated utterly different trends in the period after 2009. This distinction is necessary to explain the (somewhat) ambiguous economic trends revealed by Serbia's processing sector.

The term "traditional" economy was used to describe an economy made up of previous state-owned or social companies, regardless of whether they have been privatized or remain part of the state-owned sector. The traditional economy declined and vanished during the observed period, with the exception of a relatively small number of successfully privatized businesses. This had a negative impact on the performance of sectors like machinery and equipment and wood and furniture that had undergone less transformation at the start of the period. However, the new economy, which was made up of new domestic private businesses that debuted on the Serbian economic scene as well as greenfield foreign direct investment, continued to experience robust export-led development after 2009 and 2010. On some aspects of Serbia's defunct traditional economy, one could say, the new economy is based. The behavior of the remaining businesses, which were not owned by well-known foreign companies, fell in between that of the new economy and that of collapsing state-owned corporations. Given the difficult international climate since 2009, diversified export growth has been mostly dependent on the new economy and has remained robust. According to Bozic & Nikolic (2019), growth rates vary more by ownership type (17% for foreign direct investments versus 9% for domestic enterprises) than by sector activity (13% in the manufacturing industry versus 13% for the four sectors stated above). Conquering new markets and boosting participation in existing ones helped many industries see export growth of up to 70%. Even among microbusinesses, this growth was generally faster than the pace of import growth in the major export markets. Due to the failure and disappearance of traditional businesses, the number of large exporting companies decreased from 289 to 265 during this time period (2010), but the number of markets with exports of over one million euros as well as the number of markets with exports of over ten million euros increased (Bozic, & Nikolic, 2017).

A Brief Overview of the Serbian Economic Sector: Key Competitive Advantages and Challenges

The largest export sector in Serbia is the food and beverage industry, accounting for over 12% of all exports from Serbia. Due to both a larger initial base with the indicator of revealed comparative advantage (RCA) of 2.3% and real deficiencies compared to its own potential and supply chains, the increase in its participation in export markets was relatively smaller than in other industries. The capacity of a nation to generate things shifts throughout time as a result of modifications in a variety of variables, including technology and human capital. As a result, a strong dynamic component of comparative advantage exists (Obadi, 2016). On the value of the RCA index over a longer period, more recent research has looked at the effects of a few determinants, including GDP per capita, the number of producers with the designation of protected geographical origin, and the level of direct foreign investment (Balogh et al., 2017). It has also looked at the effects of economic development, support for agriculture, and the diversification of agricultural exports. With total exports of just over 400 million and over 700 million Euros when the agricultural sector is included, the subsector of fruit and vegetable processing is by far the most competitive. Serbia is one of the continent's top producers of raspberries, plums, quinces, and peppers. The RCA indicator of this subsector is around 9. However, there is much room for increased competitiveness through diversification, increased commercialization, and the extension of all value chains as well as supply chains. Although this subsector is characterized by an extremely low concentration of producers, its exports are characterized by low diversification - including frozen raspberries, which make up about seventeen percent of the sector's total exports. The food and beverage sector was privatized early and is predominantly domestically owned. The three largest exporters (eight percent of sectoral exports) are owned by domestic capital. Only fifteen established international companies exported more than ten million euros in 2015 (three hundred million euros in total) (Tomas et al., 2020). International brands are primarily in the beverage sub-sector and targeted at the domestic or regional market, and foreign ownership is typically of a regional nature. In Serbia, the land and climate are incredibly favorable, and the "supplementary work" that contributes to the food and beverage industry's competitiveness is likely unsustainable. The transition from a traditional sector centered on basic subsistence to a modern demand-driven sector is hampered by the fragmentation of land ownership, processing that is primarily carried out by small and medium-sized enterprises, and market intermediaries that are typically local. A large part of the land remains uncultivated (eleven percent in total; nine percent in southern Vojvodina), average yields per hectare of cultivated land are low (thirty-seven percent lower than the EU average for the same portfolio of primary products) and the range of products is relatively low-value and/or short-lived. value chain (SEEDEV, 2017). *The Rubber and Plastics sector* (exports of Euro 982 million) recorded the strongest competitive performance among all sectors and overtook the HiP sector in the position of the sector with the highest RCA – slightly more than 2.7. More than seventy percent of the high export growth in this sector (the annual average is thirteen percent) was achieved by gaining a greater share in several world markets, partly because it is a sector in which the relocation of production (nearshoring) from developed EU markets is especially present. This is a sector of medium concentration of producers and is led by predominantly recognized foreign-owned companies that dominate exports and relatively sustainable supply chains (a total of just over seventy percent of exports, with annual export growth of twenty percent). The top three companies (more than forty percent of exports) are recognized international brands such as Michelin, Cooper Tires, and Viscofa. The rubber and plastic sector is characterized by active small and medium-sized enterprises that have also managed to increase exports significantly faster (fifteen percent per year) than the growth of the market over the years. Serbia was by far the main producer of rubber items in the former Yugoslavia, and today it is the main comparative advantage of the rubber and plastic sector in the available high-quality, highly qualified workforce that is needed for the production and adjustment of often expensive (metal) tools. These are tools that need to be changed/adjusted every time a rubber/plastic product is reshaped. Market opportunities for small and medium-sized enterprises in Serbia have emerged in this sector - in the sub-sector of packaging and packaging materials, which often closely cooperates with the local food industry, producing batches of moderate volume with the possibility of diversifying quality (Kamberovic, et al., 2020).

The *Machinery and Electrical Equipment sector* is the only one taken into consideration here where the RCA is slightly below one, but almost 80% of the rapid growth (just over 12% - average per year) of its diversified exports has been achieved by winning or increasing market share. It can be anticipated that the sector will record steady growth for some time and that it will increase the already significant volume of exports (thousand three hundred milliliters) of goods and services. Additionally, Serbia can anticipate that the growth of this industry will have a considerable impact on the country's processing sector as a whole because it develops and makes use of the same skills and credentials that, by all accounts, are among the country's main competitive advantages.The Machinery and Equipment sector underwent a strong structural change in the observed period, with the share of the traditional economy in exports halved to eleven percent. All three of the largest exporters (which account for thirty percent of the sector's exports), as well as eighteen of the largest twenty, are foreign-owned, mostly in the hands of recognized international brands such as Gorenje, Siemens, Grundfos, manufacturers of household appliances, wind generators, and pumps. Nevertheless, the export of domestic small and medium-sized enterprises is also significant (around three hundred and thirty million Euros), which also records strong growth (slightly more than ten percent for medium and slightly more than eight percent for micro and small). In this sector, the difference between the strengths of the mentioned two types of companies is particularly pronounced - where the highly diversified and dispersed domestic sector is concentrated in general-purpose machines (refrigeration devices, cranes, pumps) for which there is a local demand and it is necessary to adapt to the needs of consumers, especially when it is about the implementation of entire systems, as well as in specialized machines whose production requires a lot of engineering work and relatively little capital (Industrial Policy Strategy of the Republic of Serbia, 2020). The contributions of the *Wood and Furniture sector* are growing, even though exports are lower than those of the other three sectors (total exports of over three hundred million Euros). However, the average annual growth of the sector's exports in the post-crisis period was among the higher - thirteen percent. At the same time, the sector was transforming in this period, with almost the complete disappearance of the previously dominant producer Simpo from Vranje and the difficult situation in the segment of construction carpentry. The wood and furniture sector has significant potential from the point of view of possible long-term development and its social effects (Jakopin, 2011). Of the three largest exporters (sixteen percent of exports), two are domestic de novo companies, and one is an Italian FDI, while of the twenty-five largest companies, only seven are foreign-owned. Comparatively speaking, Serbia is moderately rich in forests but produces very little value per hectare. Interestingly, the part of the value produced that goes to furniture (a little over fifty percent) is higher than in other countries. The key to the achieved success of the furniture industry is in the appropriate combination of elements: quality-price-design. With a high degree of production skills/ knowledge, with limited skills/knowledge in design, marketing, and branding, and with limited access to world markets - Serbia has positioned itself in the lower to lower-middle segment of the price range. About half of the furniture exported from Serbia goes to the region (mainly panel furniture), while the rest (mostly upholstered and solid wood furniture) is oriented toward the east markets and according to the developed EU markets (Lutovac, 2020). All exports outside the region recorded strong growth and high diversification, and in the region, the market continued to expand despite low demand. The main obstacles to the development of this sector are its fragmentation, as well as the unpredictable allocation of primary wood. The proportion of furniture placement through trade chains on the domestic market is lower than that in the food and beverage sector. The policy should mostly support the development of a transparent and predictable market for primary and sawn timber, as well as the integration of producers both in the role of buyers and in positioning on world markets. It seems that the developments of the Foreign Direct Investment (FDI) and domestic small and medium-sized enterprises (SME) sectors moved in parallel, with relatively little integration of the Serbian economy into large FDI value chains (Commission of the European Communities, 2011). While the competitive advantages and disadvantages of the two mentioned types of companies that make up the new economy differ in general, they share a key success factor - a favorable ratio between the level of qualifications and the price of work, whereby the qualifications reflect the existence of "tradition" in the sector. The old traditions of engineering/technical skills, especially in mechanical design and construction as well as in metal processing, are the key to the competitiveness of the machinery and equipment sector and the fabricated metal products sector, but they are also to a large extent the key to the particular success of the rubber and plastics sector. The food and beverage sector is based on an old agricultural tradition, where favorable natural resources play a key role. The strengths of the food and beverage sector are a combination of both qualifications/skills (similar to those in mechanical engineering) and forest resources. Larger foreign companies are successful almost without exception and emphasize investing in larger-scale production. As for MSMEs, given the constraints they usually encounter, they find themselves positioned in two types of circumstances. One is when price differentiation of cheaper quality products is possible, where there is usually also some protection with the costs of transportation and entering the market (food and plastic). Another is when the availability of highly skilled labor at a very low cost creates a strong competitive advantage. This is the case in more technically demanding sectors when a high degree of customization is required or the content of specific services is high. The price of labor in Serbia shows a tendency to be lower than the price in European countries, except in Romania and Bulgaria. The average productivity of the new economy is also lower than in competing countries, but overall it is lower by less than the cost of labor. Nevertheless, the competitiveness of the labor force decreases with the degree of qualification, so the difference is greater with higher than with lower qualifications (Aiginger & Rodrik, 2020).

Issues, Controversies, Problems

The lack of qualified labor in Serbia is a major issue and constraint for both FDI and domestic small and medium-sized businesses, and as a general rule, the employment of qualified personnel increases gradually, with investments and training. Low mobility contributes to the shortage of such a workforce, but it also implies that there are still skilled employees who are unemployed or underemployed. The absence of highly qualified managers with integrated process management and corporate management experience is another obstacle. As a result, supply chain management is challenging in many Serbian economic sectors. The lack of highly skilled personnel poses a substantial barrier to the expansion of domestic SMEs, even while FDI is able to get over it by hiring workers from outside Serbia or by training its domestic workforce. Additionally, a variety of detrimental company development factors that are unrelated to the chapter's topic also have an impact on the competitiveness of both small and large businesses, value chains, and supply networks. As they highlight the effects of fragmentation, particularly in the food and beverage sector (and particularly in the case of fruits and vegetables - which is the area with the greatest comparative advantage otherwise), the usual challenges faced by Serbian SMEs are further exacerbated by the lack of significant market intermediaries in the supply chain as well as by the low level of trust. Serbian SMEs, like those everywhere else, lack access to finance, which prevents them from being able to produce in big quantities, which is both a cause and an effect of supply chain sustainability. Such businesses are significantly more likely to be denied entry to global markets, especially when reputation and branding are crucial. In addition, it's likely that these businesses won't have the skills necessary to open up access to international markets and lengthen supply chains. Additionally, it is highly possible that they won't have the necessary technical, process management, and corporate governance skills to scale up production when/if the chance presents itself. Integration through association or through major intermediaries that may aggregate their products and enter international search engines, so integrating supply and distribution chains outside the borders of Serbia, would considerably reduce these drawbacks. This would make it easier to communicate those industries' comparative advantages on the international market and to bring back signals from the international market to the home economy. This leaves Serbian small and medium-sized businesses to face the challenge of personal market integration, which is fortunately made easier by proximity to the economic hub of the European Union and the growing number of connections with the Serbian diaspora. With its network structure and essential components working together, supply chain management offers a means of establishing improved productivity and, thus, the potential to lower costs. Management is crucial to the success of the supply chain, which necessitates several participant operating modifications. Supply chain optimization should effectively manage a variety of external contacts and the way internal activities are set up. In addition, there is improved cooperation and vertical organization due to the company's wider control radius over its supply chain. In Serbian enterprises, where the authoritarian management style is still in practice, this still happens infrequently. Employee involvement in major organizational decisions on important issues is minimal in this unsustainable management style. Employees in Serbian firms exhibit a high level of uncertainty avoidance, which is partly a result of the national culture in Serbia, where power distance is expressed (Ilic & Djukic, 2021).

Organizations in Serbia, especially small and medium-sized ones, lack managerial optimization throughout all organizational divisions. According to Barac et al. (2011), optimization in the context of supply chains refers to the control of intricate links that aims to synchronize all elements that provide value and are involved in production or distribution. There have been numerous goals for supply chain improvement, according to Mitrovic and Mitrovic. The synchronization of all aspects (participants and activities, managers, and employees) that contribute value to production and distribution as well as the deletion of elements that do not produce or support value stand out among the fundamental objectives (Mitrovic & Mitrovic, 2019). In addition to the two primary objectives, there are auxiliary ones as well

(Kolar, 2014), such as maximizing the productivity of the employed assets and resources (both human and material), maximizing company profit, and maximizing time savings through efficient management, before offering the highest level of customer service and realizing price efficiency. It is important to note that several studies and ideas demonstrate a high correlation between contentment, or customer satisfaction and loyalty, especially if the business practices social responsibility (Rejman-Petrovic, 2016; Ceryno et al., 2013; Acimovic et al., 2018). Customer satisfaction should be achieved while exceeding expectations, including those for responsiveness, in service levels and services. Customers should receive enough value for their money, and goods and services should be more effectively promoted with fewer resources. The simultaneous harmonization of a company's supply and demand sides, both within the company and across the network to which that company or organization belongs, is one of optimization's key objectives (Kostic, 2021). The demand cannot be met right away because to the limited speed of manufacturing, distribution, and transportation.

If the offer is poorly specified, it may take some time to satisfy the end user. In order to increase productivity and gain a competitive edge, optimization aims to hasten material flows "downstream" and information flows "upstream" while simultaneously removing "non-value" items from the chain (Rejman-Petrovic et al., 2012). The supply chain should simply be seen as optimizing the amount of inventory, service, and related logistics activities given that it "cuts" functional areas such as procurement, engineering and design, management at all levels (inventory, employees, material), processing and assembly, storage, and shipping. The fact that acquired components and raw materials make approximately two-thirds of the cost of manufactured items suggests that enhancing supplier quality has a high strategic value. Therefore, a quality-based strategy is intended to continuously improve product quality and reduce costs while focusing on establishing long-term partnerships with important suppliers. It is especially crucial to eliminate product flaws and involve suppliers in the design process. The foundation of process advances like "just-in-time" production is likewise this kind of interaction. Just-in-time production is a little more challenging to execute in Serbia for a variety of factors, but principally technological ones. It is important to note that there are many input elements, including resources, people, equipment, facilities, money, knowledge, and technologies, when the manufacturing process is evaluated from a technological perspective. In order to handle the stated factors sustainably, as required by contemporary society, the management process is again positioned at the center of the analysis.

Given that sustainability encompasses a variety of elements, including employee participation in crucial company choices, the issue of authority-fear is resurfacing in Serbian firms! In the current business climate, businesses are collaborating more closely with their suppliers in order to improve their capacity and responsiveness to the ever-changing needs of their clients. This drastically lowers, and in some cases even completely removes, previously formed protective stocks. The development of a just-in-time model almost eliminates raw material and work-in-progress stockpiles, increasing supplier dependence for businesses. The tendency of the next stage of growth of supply chain management is the selection of one logistics provider who will have the responsibility of overseeing all transport and distribution operations for the company in strong economies—in nations that have led the way for sustainable development. Today's inventive tendencies bring the supplier within the business. Due to the aforementioned, obtaining supplies and providing goods to customers immediately play a crucial part in attaining a competitive edge. Strategic sourcing choices will undoubtedly be distinguished by their commercial significance and organizational financial impact. Therefore, it can be concluded from an analysis of the purpose and fundamental elements of supply chain optimization that value is produced through sustainable management and that optimization offers the essential, i.e., a sound value base. An essential point is that, as is frequently the case in Serbian small and medium-sized businesses, optimization is not achievable without the application of specific activities and the implementation of key variables. Last but not least, the business application needs a few tools that are characterized in a broader perspective as ideas and tactics for sustainable supply chain management that support the optimization process (Hejazi et al., 2023)(Rabrenovic et al., 2020). Depending on the instrument, or method of conducting business, Figures 3 and 4 illustrate two different types of supply chains.

The Generic Supply Chain is depicted in Figure 3. It is clear that the acquisition of raw resources comes first. Raw materials or resources (parts) are delivered to the supplier, who is given the status of a wholesaler, through the logistics provider. The essential raw materials, components, or parts are then given to the manufacturer, who further "creates" the new product(s). Both manufacturers and goods are many. The responsibility of distributing the goods in bulk to "retail" stores falls to the distributors after the products have been provided to them. Customers purchase goods in stores. The cycle is broken by buying the product, yet demand still restarts.

Figure 3. Generic supply-chain
Source: CFI, Supply chain

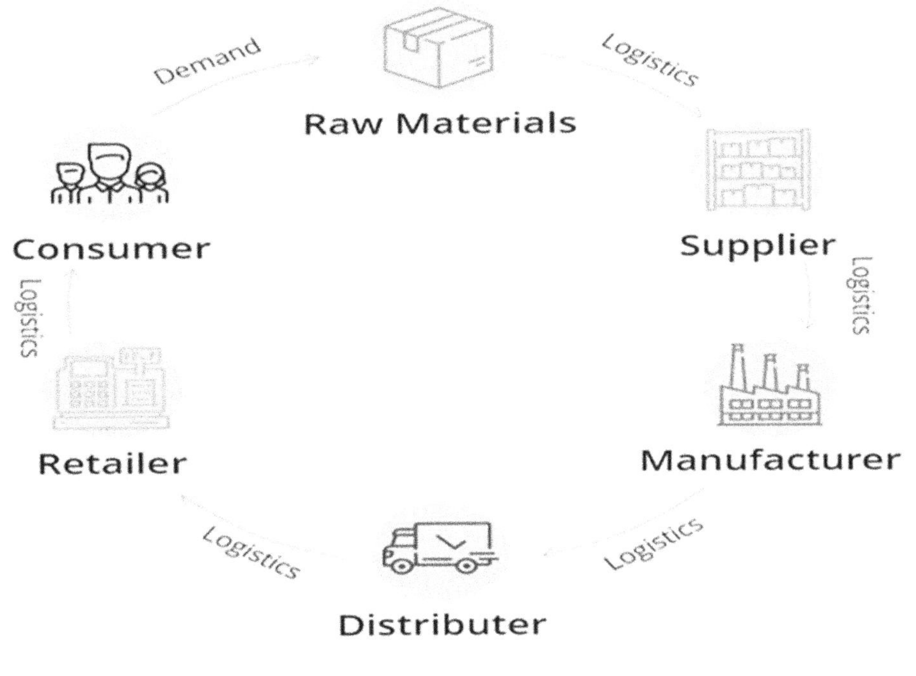

Figure 4 depicts the supply chain for e-commerce businesses. The number indicates that e-commerce businesses have websites where they offer and sell a range of goods. Customers place product orders, which are then processed by a system with a virtual cart using e-technology. Organizations or banks handle online payments (using PayPal or another service). So-called order transactions are the beginning of a new supply chain. The company that markets the product may also use its billing systems in the payment process, although in most situations, banks and other providers have a role in the transaction.

After placing the order, the warehouse gets the merchandise and gets it ready for sale. The storage firm may also be a third-party logistics provider or an internal one. The order is then forwarded to the shipping firm. The company that makes the product, i.e. internally, may deliver it to the client, or another transport company may do so. The order is delivered directly to the customer's address in the form of a package.

Figure 4. e-Commerce company supply chain
Source: CFI, Supply chain

The authors emphasize that the application of e-commerce supply chains is considerably bigger when international companies are participating in the business and have a branch office in Serbia if Serbia is the focus of the development and implementation of new technologies in supply chains. The majority of clothing and small appliance manufacturers operate in this manner, using courier services to deliver goods to the customer's address. On the other hand, if large-scale transportation is involved, traditional supply networks, also known as generic supply chains, are used. In that case, the goods are delivered by large transport trucks.

SOLUTIONS AND RECOMMENDATIONS - OPTIMIZATION OF SUPPLY CHAIN PROCESSES

Two fundamental possibilities are the root of both commercial success and market competition in Serbia. The first is when businesses join the market with a product that is less expensive than rivals' and satisfies minimum requirements and quality standards. Customers will recognize this product as a top domestic option in this way. Another option is to join the market with a product that, because of its caliber and reputation, offers the customer a better value (Mitrovic & Mitrovic, 2019). Because foreign competition is the main source of Serbia's competitiveness, it is necessary to differentiate items in relation to it when developing these two market strategies. The majority of sectors in Serbia and around the world include logistics expenses as a sizeable portion of overall production costs. As a result, by cutting them, bigger savings can be made. Only inside the supply chain is synchronized procurement, inventory optimization, and transportation cost reduction possible, often known as the optimization of goods and information flows. At the same time, competitive advantage and sustainable management form criteria for designing chains (Garipova et al., 2020). According to Werner and Sascha, there are ten important criteria, listed in the section "Supply Chain Management in the Global Context", which can be applied in Serbia as well (Werner & Sascha, 2000). According to these experts, it is important to pay attention to the links between operations inside and outside of the company while creating supply chains.

Even though these tasks may be carried out by several firms (in the same market), they are all interconnected. The supply chain's members are more integrated than before, which makes the company or organizations more competitive. Every firm seeks to lower economies of scale while paying closer attention to the environment because the modern notion of sustainable development encourages this. Only if manufacturing costs are reduced and the burden on the environment is also reduced can the commitment to economies of scale be justified. The overall fixed costs of the entire chain will decrease if it is possible to combine functions within a single supply chain such that one company (as a link in the chain) can take the place of several chain members. As a result, the product's selling price rises, a larger portion of the market is captured, and sustainable business is established. Organizational behavior may have an impact on achieving sustainability with economies of scale. For instance, offering free services to the end user may further enhance the organization's favorable reputation. Because the product's pricing does not fluctuate and the competition cannot take advantage of this advantage, there is also a difference in how customers perceive similar products (Vujicic, et al., 2022). When an organization recognizes a problem, identifies it, and then finally discovers a suitable solution, this phenomena comes to the fore in terms of learning. In this approach, time is saved for several business procedures in addition to cost savings. This will give the company a cost advantage as well as a differentiating advantage over rivals. Transfer of knowledge across firms and supply chain actors is a sign of learning capacity. When knowledge is the goal, it is advised that Serbia strengthen the concept of lifelong learning while disseminating systematic encouragement of the growth of high school education programs in partnership with the economy (Rabrenovic, et al. 2020). It is necessary to improve the responsiveness of the Ministry of Education of the Republic of Serbia, as well as the cooperation between the ministries of economy and education in adapting the programs of secondary vocational schools to the needs of the local economy. Serbia needs to complete and adopt the national qualifications framework. For the Serbian economy, it is necessary to investigate the main reasons for the unavailability of certain secondary school profiles in sub-national regions (Stanković, 2016). It is important to support the mobility of students and the workforce through the subsidization of intercity public transport and to test the establishment of youth accommodation in the country. Introducing vouchers for training students and workers in specific skills, along with a system of testing completed training, is one of the conditions for the return of funds invested in training. Develop programs to support the engagement of experienced professional staff from the Serbian diaspora, especially in management skills processes. Ultimately, Serbia must create cutting-edge academic programs like those that analyze the economics of industrial sectors and organizations since they would provide information that is both economically justified and useful (Kostadinovic & Stankovic, 2020; Popov & Rabrenovic, 2016). The production mix as well as the fixed cost component can be significantly impacted by the usage of one's own capacities (Farrukh & Waheed, 2015). In order to increase confidence and the level of cooperation among participants (the total is greater than the simple sum of the parts), the mutual relations criterion requires the sharing and collaborative use of resources throughout the entire chain. The consolidation of the dispatch function into a single center, which reduces costs and improves chain synchronization, can serve as an illustration of resource sharing throughout the supply chain. Therefore, operations that link parts or various companies must be the main focus of sustainable supply chain management, both worldwide and in Serbia. The final product, which is the outcome of everyone's coordinated efforts, is more competitive on the market than a product made possible by the collaboration of firms outside the supply chain. Time to market is vital for gaining a competitive advantage. Marketing a brand-new, technologically advanced product gives the company an edge over rivals (Micic & Krstic-Randjic, 2022). Because of this, product promotion must be done "as soon as possible". Then competitors are granted a set amount of time. Although a specific organization's or the entire supply chain's discretionary policy has no direct bearing on product production, it can have an impact on how much a product costs (for instance, by requiring the production of environmentally friendly goods or prompt delivery of orders). Although these actions have no impact on the product's functionality, they have a big impact on the cost. The location of a manufacturing facility or service station is particularly crucial since it influences the expenses of the supply chain by affecting the costs of transportation, energy, and professional people (Slogar, 2021)(Taghipour, et al., 2014). If servicing is offered in areas without comparable services, the location may also benefit the organization.

Users or consumers who are satisfied will prefer to purchase goods from a company that values its customers, and this is how a brand is established. However, legislation and a nation's tax structure can have a substantial impact on company and distribution expenses (Vujicic et al., 2021). The industrial policy in Serbia's machinery and electrical equipment sector should place a special emphasis on luring carefully chosen investors, paying close attention to their potential to boost human resource productivity, and supporting their collaboration with domestic suppliers (Stankovic, 2018). Programs that attempt to improve the workforce's knowledge and abilities are also crucial. Finally, more could be accomplished if the benefits of the machinery and electrical equipment sector were presented in a more organized manner on international and foreign markets..

FUTURE RESEARCH DIRECTIONS

Future studies on certain economic sectors and supply chains in the Republic of Serbia are summarized in the "Policy Matrix" at the end of this section. Foreign direct investments (FDI) and support for the MSME sector should be examined and altered in innovative ways. Future study on some of the following topics will need to address some important questions. The influence of MSMEs' development can occasionally be relatively limited, especially because the incentive structure is such that they are more appealing to FDI with lower development potential. However, luring FDI receives ten times more resources than assisting MSMEs. So, in the end, it is vital to look into and discover fresh approaches to draw FDI in a targeted and structured manner in order to boost the consequences of growth. Aid to Serbian MSMEs is typically negligible and dispersed, and as a result, it can only have a little impact. To change that, MSMEs should receive more comprehensive help, integrating a number of factors (advice, access to financial resources, organizational support), i.e., finding ways to dig deeper into the needs of the company for development. One strategy for enhancing the development impact of FDI and advancing the development of MSMEs at the same time is to examine supplier development programs. Investigating the motivation for MMSPa collaboration and their relationship in clusters is one of the research's next topics. The research must be focused on the objectives and direct advantages of the concerned companies, such as the potential for lower material costs as a result of larger orders. to investigate the best approaches to formulate Serbia's industrial policy. Researching the geographical variation in the employment/unemployment profile should receive special emphasis. It is suggested that future research examine every facet of regional development. The best way to improve the reliability of statistics and the accessibility of APR and the Republic Institute of Statistics in Serbia must be found. The competitiveness and growth potential of the sector of exchangeable services, such as the creative industries, IT, tourism, and Belgrade as a regional logistics hub, should be the focus of future research. Look on ways to improve administrative practices so that competent institutions may manage them more efficiently. Examine the government's framework for strategic planning and coordination (and adopt the Planning Law). Future directions may concern strategies to establish or sustain a separate institution for observing macroeconomic economic patterns. Establish strategies for creating independent monitoring programs for Serbia's industrial policy initiatives to promote public-private cooperation and foster public confidence in Serbia's policies. Examine the potential for the establishment in Serbia, in collaboration with the Serbian economy, of centers for the transfer of economic and technological knowledge as well as business and market analytics (business intelligence).

CONCLUSION

The chapter's authors attempted to concentrate on issues relating to the development of the tightly defined concept of the supply chain, but through the broader context of "economic sectors in the Republic of Serbia" and through value chains that should remove bottlenecks within the sector, i.e., support those actors who, by using external factors, can influence the entire economic sector in Serbia. However, the issues, or barriers to competitiveness, are largely shared across all industries. They are primarily caused by the fact that many of these industries are SME's, as well as by the state of Serbia's inadequate effectiveness and serviceability in carrying out (or failing to fully perform) the expected functions. Several reforms and programs are planned as part of the framework of boosting competitiveness prior to joining the European Union. These reforms and programs are the topic of many challenges, particularly problems of economic sustainability, management of value chains, and ultimately supply chains. For instance, it is only possible to permanently develop human capital that will provide it sustained competitiveness, even coming up to the lost ground in the previous ones for decades, with a comprehensive overhaul of the educational system. It is comparable to the issues that should be resolved through public administration reform or public company reform. The business climate in Serbia should dramatically improve as a result of these developments. The investigation of these more significant systemic barriers to competitiveness is outside the purview of this chapter and should be addressed in separate studies. However, the authors want to underline the Republic of Serbia's desire to solve several challenges in governance, particularly sustainability. The fact that Serbia continues to struggle with a poor reputation (that is politically backed) within the context of Europe and the rest of the world is one of the main impediments to paving the path for sustainable growth. Whether the stronger or the weaker has a greater influence on the political landscape must be clarified. Do winners have an impact on history? The answer is obvious!

REFERENCES

Acimovic, S. (2006). *Understanding the supply chain. Economic anals 51* (170), 67-89

Acimovic, S., Mijuskovic, V. M., & Markovic, D. (2018). Segregating The Main Dimensions Of The Green Supply Chain. *Economic Ideas and practice 3*(29), 7-16.

Aiginger, K., & Rodrik, D. (2020). Rebirth of Industrial Policy and an Agenda for the Twenty-First Century. Journal of Industry, Competition and Trade. Springer. doi:10.100710842-019-00322-3

Andrijanic, I., & Pavlovic, D. (2016). *International business*. Libertas – Pleiada Zagreb.

Arvis, J.-F., Ojala, L., Wiederer, C., Shepherd, B., Raj, A., Dairabayeva, K., & Kiiski, T. (2018). *Connecting to Compete 2018: The Logistics in the Global Economy*. TheWorld Bank. doi:10.1596/29971

Arvis, J.-F., Ojala, L., Wiederer, C., Shepherd, B., Raj, A., Dairabayeva, K., & Kiiski, T. (2023). *Connecting to Compete 2023: Trade Logistics in an Uncertain Global Economy*. TheWorld Bank.

Arvis, J.-F., Saslavsky, D., Ojala, L., Shepherd, B., Bush, C., Raj, A., & Naula, T. (2016). *Connecting to Compete 2016: The Logistics in the Global Economy*. The World Bank. doi:10.1596/24598

Balogh, J. M., & Jámbor, A. (2017). Determinants of revealed comparative advantages: The case of cheese trade in the European Union. *Acta Alimentaria, 46*(3), 305–311. doi:10.1556/066.2016.0012

Barac, N., Milovanović, G., & Anđelković, A. (2011). Risk and the resilient supply chain. *Facta universitatis-series. Economics and Organization, 8*(2), 139–151.

Biermann, F., Hickmann, T., Sénit, C., & Grob, L. (2022). The Sustainable Development Goals as a Transformative Force?: Key Insights. In F. Biermann, T. Hickmann, & C. Sénit (Eds.), *The Political Impact of the Sustainable Development Goals: Transforming Governance Through Global Goals?* (pp. 204–226). Cambridge University Press. doi:10.1017/9781009082945.009

Bojnec, S., & Fertő, I. (2017). The duration of global agri-food export competitiveness. *British Food Journal, 119*(6), 1378–1393. doi:10.1108/BFJ-07-2016-0302

Bozic, D., & Nikolic, M. (2017). Serbia's foreign trade exchange and the importance of the agricultural sector. *Themes, 41*(3), 711–730.

Bozic, D., & Nikolic, M. (2019). Foreign trade and comparative advantages of agrarian sector of Serbia and neighbouring countries. *Economics of agriculture 66*(3), 737-754

Bozic, V., & Acimovic, S. (2004). Marketing logistics. Faculty of Economics, Belgrade, Serbia.

Cauchois, R., Taghipour, A., Kang, D., Zoghlami, N., & Abed, M. (2017). Advanced solutions for a supply chain with stochastic information. *Journal of Advanced Management Science, 5*(1), 9–13. doi:10.18178/joams.5.1.9-13

Ceryno, P. S., Scavarda, L. F., Klingebiel, K., & Yuzgulec, G. (2013). Supply chain risk management: A content analysis approach. *International Journal of Industrial Engineering and Management, 4*(3), 141.

CEVES - Center for Higher Economic Studies. (Serbian: Centar za Visoke ekonomske studije). (2017). *Performance and value chain analysis of selected sectors*. Serbian Chamber of Commerce, Belgrade, Serbia. https://corporatefinanceinstitute.com/resources/management/supply-chain/

Commission of the European Communities. (2011). *Innovation Union Scoreboard*. The Innovation Union's performance scoreboard for Research and Innovation /1 February 2011

Djukic, G. P., & Ilic, B. (2021). Importance of green investment and Enerprenuership for Economic development. in: Jasovska, P., Logue, D. & Rammal, G.D. (Ed.), Contemporary Enterprenuership Issues in International Business World (pp. 195-220). World Scientific Publishing Co. Pte. Ltd.

El-Nemr, N., Canel-Depitre, B., & Taghipour, A. (2017). Determinants of hotel room rates. In *Marketing Trends Congress. Luxury Industries Conference London 2017*

El-Nemr, N., Canel-Depitre, B., & Taghipour, A. (2021). The determinants of hotel room rates in Beirut: A hedonic pricing model. International Journal of Trade. *Economics and Finance*, *12*(2), 33–42.

Farrukh, M., & Waheed, A. (2015). Learning Organization and Competitive Advantage: An Integrated Approach. *Journal of Asian Business Strategy*, *5*(4), 73–79. doi:10.18488/journal.1006/2015.5.4/1006.4.73.79

Garipova, E. N., Kulik, E. N., & Nabieva, L. G. (2020). Assessment of the influence of innovation and IT markets on the parameters of the regional economy. *International Review (Steubenville, Ohio)*, *3*(4), 29–40. doi:10.5937/intrev2003029G

Gordana, D. P., & Biljana, I. S. (2021). Sustaining SME Management and Innovations in the Post-COVID Era. In N. Baporikar (Ed.), *Handbook of Research on Strategies and Interventions to Mitigate COVID-19 Impact on SMEs* (pp. 588–608). IGI Global., doi:10.4018/978-1-7998-7436-2.ch029

Hejazi, M. T., Al Batati, B., & Bahurmuz, A. (2023). The Influence of Green Supply Chain Management Practices on Corporate Sustainability Performance. *Sustainability (Basel)*, *15*(6), 5459. doi:10.3390u15065459

Ilic, B., & Djukic, G. (2021). Cultural dimensions - the impact of differences and similarities on business in the era of COVID-19. In: *Proceedings 11th International Symposium on Natural Resources Management, ISNRM 2021*. Faculty of Management, Zajecar Megatrend University, Belgrade, 169-176

Ilic, B., Djukic, G., & Balaban, M. (2020). Sustainable development directions of rural tourism of Timok region. *Economics of agriculture* *67*(1), 157-174. https://doi.org/ doi:10.5937/ekoPolj2001157I

Jakopin, E. (2011). The framework of new Serbian industrial policy. *Business Economics (Cleveland, Ohio)*, *59*(1-2), 73–88.

Jarašūnienė, A., Sinkevičius, G., Čižiūnienė, K., & Čereška, A. (2020). Adaptation of the management model of internationalization processes in the development of railway transport activities. *Sustainability (Basel)*, *12*(15), 6248. doi:10.3390u12156248

Just in time production. www.samuderanaga.com/zara-just-in-timeproduction-k.html

Kamberovic, S., Mitrovic, S., & Arno Behrens, A. (2020). *GAP analysis of opportunities for economic strengthening by applying sustainable business models after the COVID-19 pandemic in the Republic of Serbia*. OSCE Mission in Serbia. Belgrade, Serbia.

Kędzior-Laskowska, M. (2020). Polish road freight transport and process of internationalisation–selected effects for quality and competitiveness. *Entrepreneurship and Sustainability Issues*, *7*(3), 2481–2493. doi:10.9770/jesi.2020.7.3(68)

Kolar, N. (2014). Working capital management in Dell Inc. *Economía: Teoría y Practica*, *7*(4), 1–20.

Kostadinović, I., & Stanković, S. (2020). Innovation clusters as an association model of the small and medium-sized enterprises: the context of regional development. In *Proceedings 6th Leadership, Innovation, Management and Economics: Integrated Politics of Research* (pp. 47–56). Association of Economists and Managers of the Balkans. doi:10.31410/LIMEN.S.P.2020.47

Kostadinović, I., & Stanković, S. (2020). The analysis of the regional disproportions in the labor market in the Republic of Serbia. *Economics*, *66*(1), 25–35.

Kostadinović, I., & Stanković, S. (2021). Organizational learning and innovation in the tourism industry as a basis for creating value for tourists. *Economic Themes*, *59*(1), 153–172. doi:10.2478/ethemes-2021-0009

Kostic, I. (2021). *Financial management of supply chain risks in order to maximize company value*. Faculty of Economics, University of Kragujevac, Serbia.

Kostiuk, Y., Kalinova, E., & Kučera, J. (2021). Impact of Globalization and Internationalization Processes on Added Value in EU Countries, SHS Web of Conferences: Globalization and its Socio-Economic Consequences, 92, 09008. 10.1051hsconf/20219209008

Lazarevic-Moravcevic, M., Eric, D., & Kamenkovic, S. (2018). The influence of the business environment on the performance of the SME sector in Serbia. *Business Economics (Cleveland, Ohio)*, *12*(1), 33–53.

Loivet, W., Taghipour, A., & Kang, D. S. (2020). The rise of green supply chain management: Between complexity and necessity. *Journal of Economics. Business and Management*, *8*(1), 1–7.

Lutovac, D. M. (2020). New industrial policy as a prerequisite for efficient development of Serbian industry. Faculty of Economics, Belgrade, Serbia.

Mahfod, J., Canel-Depitre, B., & Taghipour, A. (2019). Quality function deployment-ELECTRE in supplier evaluation. *Journal of Advanced Management Science*, *7*(4), 131–135. doi:10.18178/joams.7.4.131-135

Mansfield, H. (2023). *Niccolò Machiavelli. Encyclopedia Britannica*. https://www.britannica.com/biography/Niccolo-Machiavelli

Merimi, M., & Taghipour, A. (2021). Accelerating the digitalization of the supply chain: An empirical research about COVID-19 crisis. In *Digitalization of Decentralized Supply Chains During Global Crises* (pp. 1–24). IGI Global. doi:10.4018/978-1-7998-6874-3.ch001

Micic, I., & Krstic-Randjic, J. (2022). Establishing the competence framework with the aim of strengthening the strategic performance of the organization. *Economía: Teoría y Practica*, *15*(1), 61–77.

Mitrovic, V., & Mitrovic, I. (2019). Modern concept of supply chain management using information and communication technologies. *Economic Signals 14*(2), 081-096

Nadia, E. N., Beatrice, C. D., & Atour, T. (2020). Luxury hotels' eco-friendly activities & customers' preferences and willingness to pay for green hotels. *Journal of Advanced Management Science*, *8*(1), 7–14.

Nævestad, T. O., Phillips, R. O., Meyer Levlin, G., & Hovi, I. B. (2017). Internationalisation in road transport of goods in Norway: Safety outcomes, risk factors and policy implications. *Safety (Basel, Switzerland), 3*(4), 22. doi:10.3390afety3040022

Obadi, S.M. (2016). Revealed comparative advantage and competitiveness in the EU-28 and the USA. *Ekonomické Rozhl'ady / Ecomomic Review 45*(2), 243–259.

Pedersen, T., & Shaver, J. M. (2011). Internationalization revisited: The big step hypothesis. *Global Strategy Journal, 1*(3-4), 263–274. doi:10.1002/gsj.20

Pham, V. Q., Nguyen, B. K. Q., & Le, T. Q. (2020). Success factors affecting internationalization process of large Vietnamese companies: A conceptual framework. *Journal of Asian Finance. Economics and Business, 7*(11), 905–913.

Popov, D., & Rabrenović, M. (2016). A look at the optimization problem in consumer theory. *Megatrend Review, 13*(1), 46–56. doi:10.5937/MegRev1601035P

Rabrenovic, M., Popov, D., & Stamenovic, M. (2020). The degree of liberalization of Serbia's economy in the process of accession to the World Trade Organization. *Megatrend review 17*(3), 65-78

Rabrenovic, M., Simonovic, P., & Cogoljevic, D. (2020). Optimization strategies for the organization of mental healthcare. *International Journal for Quality in Health Care, 32*(6), 412–413. doi:10.1093/intqhc/mzaa061 PMID:32484888

Rabrenovic, M. D., Mitrovic, R., & Kovacevic, B. (2020). The relationship between strategic management and public relations and their implications for financial operations. *International Review (Steubenville, Ohio), 1*(2), 89–93. doi:10.5937/intrev2001089R

Rejman-Petrovic, D. (2016). Business process improvement in e-supply chains. *Economic horizons 18*(3), 215-232.

Rejman-Petrovic, D., Milanovic, I., & Kalinic, Z. (2012). Supply chain architectures in an e-environment. *Economic horizons 14*(1), 37-50

SEEDEV. (2017). Competitiveness of Serbian agriculture. SEEDEV. https://www.seedev.org/

Shin, M., & Taghipour, A. (2021). Journal of Economics. *Business and Management, 9*(2), 36–40.

Slogar, H. (2021). Relationship between market orientation and innovativeness in companies. *International Review (Steubenville, Ohio), 3*(4), 1–29.

Stankovic, S. (2016). The transformation of the Serbian labour market from a gender perspective. *Economic Themes, 54*(4), 587–604. doi:10.1515/ethemes-2016-0030

Stankovic, S. S. (2018). *Application of dependency methods in the analysis of differences in earnings between the sexes in the Republic of Serbia*. Economics Faculty, University of Nis, Serbia.

Taghipour, A. (2014). Production Network Planning Based on Constraint Relaxation and Discount Approach. *Lecture Notes on Information Theory, 2*(3), 279–282. doi:10.12720/lnit.2.3.279-282

Taghipour, A. (2018). A Contemporary Approach to Plan Independent Logistics Actors. In *Contemporary Approaches and Strategies for Applied Logistics* (pp. 337–364). IGI Global. doi:10.4018/978-1-5225-5273-4.ch014

Taghipour, A. (Ed.). (2020). *Demand Forecasting and Order Planning in Supply Chains and Humanitarian Logistics*. IGI Global.

Taghipour, A., Abed, M., & Zoghlami, N. (2015). Design for remanufacturing respecting reverse logistics processes: A review. In *2015 4th International Conference on Advanced Logistics and Transport (ICALT) (pp. 299-304)*. IEEE. 10.1109/ICAdLT.2015.7136602

Taghipour, A., & Beneteau-Piet, C. (2020). Sustainable supply chain management performance. *International Journal of Innovation, Management and Technology*, *11*(6), 165–169. doi:10.18178/ijimt.2020.11.6.897

Taghipour, A., & Frayret, J. M. (2011b). *Supply chain coordination planning: A review*. École polytechnique de Montréal, Canada.

Taghipour, A., & Frayret, J. M. (2014). A new heuristic search with local optimization to manage a supply chain. *Lecture Notes on Information Theory*, *2*(1), 78–84. doi:10.12720/lnit.2.1.78-84

Taghipour, A., Glaa, B., & Zoghlami, N. (2014). Network coordination with minimum risk of information sharing. In *2014 International Conference on Advanced Logistics and Transport (ICALT)* (pp. 184-188). IEEE. 10.1109/ICAdLT.2014.6864115

Taghipour, A., & Merimi, M. (2021). Digital Transformation of Supply Chains during Crisis: COVID-19. In *11th Annual International Conference on Industrial Engineering and Operations Management, IEOM* (pp. 7493-7501).

Taghipour, A., Murat, S., & Huang, P. (2021). E-supply chain management: A review. *International Journal of e-Education, e-Business, e-. Management Learning*, *11*(2), 51–61.

Tanaskovic, S., & Ristic, B. (2019). *Competitive position of Serbia in 2019 according to the report of the World Economic Forum*. Foundation for the Development of Economic Science (FREN), Belgrade, Serbia.

Tliche, Y., Taghipour, A., & Canel-Depitre, B. (2019). Anticipation of Demand in Supply Chains. In *Hierarchical Planning and Information Sharing Techniques in Supply Chain Management* (pp. 1–45). IGI Global.

Tliche, Y., Taghipour, A., & Canel-Depitre, B. (2021). Exploring a Downstream Demand Inference Strategy in a Decentralized Two-Level Supply Chain. In *Demand Forecasting and Order Planning in Supply Chains and Humanitarian Logistics* (pp. 1–65). IGI Global. doi:10.4018/978-1-7998-3805-0.ch001

Tomas Simin, M., Glavas-Trbic, D., & Djuric, K. (2020). Organic agriculture and the common agricultural policy of the EU. *Agricultural Economics*, *49*(87), 13–25.

Trinkuniene, S., & Aksomitiene, J. (2017). *International transport companies in the Baltic countries: internationalization motives and barriers*. In: Proceedings of the International Scientific Conference: Society. Integration. Education. (4) 414-426. Rēzeknes Tehnoloģiju akadēmija. 10.17770ie2017vol4.2373

Vollman T., Berry W., Whabark C., & Jocobs R. (2005). *Manufacturing, Planning and Control for Supply Chain Management*. McGraw-Hill Co.

Vosooghidizaji, M., Taghipour, A., & Canel-Depitre, B. (2020). Information Asymmetry in Supply Chain Coordination: State of the Art. *Journal of Industrial and Intelligent Information*, *8*(2), 38–43. doi:10.18178/jiii.8.2.38-43

Vosooghidizaji, M., Taghipour, A., & Canel-Depitre, B. (2022). Coordinating corporate social responsibility in a two-level supply chain under bilateral information asymmetry. *Journal of Cleaner Production*, *364*, 132627. doi:10.1016/j.jclepro.2022.132627

Vujicic, S., Ravic, N., & Nikolic, M. (2021). The influence of planning on the development of innovations in small and medium-sized enterprises. *Trends in business* *9*(1), 78-83

Vujicic, S., Staletovic, M., Stevanovic, M., & Gavrilovic, M. (2022). Organizational structures of companies in modern business environment. *Economía: Teoría y Practica*, *15*(4), 25–41.

Vukovic, A., Ubiparip, D., Radovanovic, M., & Jacimovic, S. (2015). Fresh tomato: Promissing export product for Serbia? *Industry*, *43*(3), 171–189. doi:10.5937/industrija43-9166

Werner, D., & Sascha, A. (2000). *Supply Chain Management in Global Context.* Arbeitsbericht Nr.102/Working Paper No. 102. pdfs.semanticssholar.org/bf0e/53 58acf4631c92ed877fla116e9db 1a cef.pdf

World Trade Organisation Statistics. 2004. www.wto.org

Yang, S., Taghipour, A., & Canel-Depitre, B. (2017, August). Cost optimization of reverse logistics: A review. In *Proceedings of the 7th International Conference on Information Communication and Management* (pp. 158-161). 10.1145/3134383.3134393

ADDITIONAL READING

Altay, N., Prasad, S., & Sounderpandian, J. (2009). Strategic planning for disaster relief logistics: Lessons from supply chain management. *International Journal of Services Sciences*, *2*(2), 142–161. doi:10.1504/IJSSCI.2009.024937

Chopra, S., & Meindl, P. (2001). Strategy, planning, and operation. *Supply Chain Management*, 13–17.

Hametner, M. (2022). Economics without ecology: How the SDGs fail to align socio-economic development with environmental sustainability. *Ecological Economics*, *199*, 199. doi:10.1016/j.ecolecon.2022.107490

Hasibuan, A., Arfah, M., Parinduri, L., Hernawati, T., Harahap, B., Sibuea, S. R., & Sulaiman, O. K. (2018, April). Performance analysis of supply chain management with supply chain operation reference model. [). IOP Publishing.]. *Journal of Physics: Conference Series*, *1007*(1), 012029. doi:10.1088/1742-6596/1007/1/012029

Huan, S. H., Sheoran, S. K., & Wang, G. (2004). A review and analysis of supply chain operations reference (SCOR) model. *Supply Chain Management*, *9*(1), 23–29. doi:10.1108/13598540410517557

Jacobs, F. R., Chase, R. B., & Lummus, R. R. (2014). *Operations and supply chain management.* McGraw-Hill/Irwin.

Mishra, R., Singh, R. K., & Rana, N. P. (2022). Developing environmental collaboration among supply chain partners for sustainable consumption & production: Insights from an auto sector supply chain. *Journal of Cleaner Production, 338*, 130619. doi:10.1016/j.jclepro.2022.130619

Winch, J. K. (2003). Supply chain management: Strategy, planning, and operation. *International Journal of Quality & Reliability Management, 20*(3), 398–400. doi:10.1108/02656710310461350

KEY TERMS AND DEFINITIONS

RCA: Index: This is the indicator of revealed comparative advantage, which measures the export of one product of a country in relation to the total export of that country and to the corresponding performance of the total world export.

SME: Small and medium enterprises whose number of employees does not exceed a certain number. In addition to the number of employees, the criteria for the size of the company can be gross income and the value of assets. The criteria in Serbia for SMEs are that the number of employees is less than 50, the gross income is up to 2.5 million euros and the value of assets is 1 million euros for small, and for medium the number of employees is less than 250, the gross income is up to 10 million euros, and the value of assets is up to 5 million euros.

FDI: Foreign Direct Investment: means the investment of foreign capital by an investor resident (enterprise) of one country in a resident (enterprise) of another country in order to achieve common interests.

MSMEs: Abbreviation that stands for Micro, Small, and Medium Enterprises. The law of the state and the economy of a certain state prescribes categories based on the number of employees and gross income.

CFI: This is the leading provider of practical learning and productivity tools for finance and banking professionals.

SEDEV: Serbian organization, composed of a team of experts in the field of agriculture, economics and biotechnical sciences, which analyzes trends in production and trade, competitiveness of agricultural and food products, market chains.

LPI: Indeks: Provides a biannual evaluation of the quality of the logistics system based on six indicators: customs, infrastructure, international shipments, logistics competence, timeliness, and tracking and tracing.

Compilation of References

Abe, M., & Ye, L. (2013). Building Resilient Supply Chains against Natural Disasters: The Cases of Japan and Thailand. *Global Business Review, 14*(4), 567–586. doi:10.1177/0972150913501606

Abu el Ata, N., Drucbert, A., Abu el Ata, N., & Drucbert, A. (2017). Case# 3: Managing Operational Risk: Global Supply Chain. *Leading from Under the Sword of Damocles: A Business Leader's Practical Guide to Using Predictive Emulation to Manage Risk and Maintain Profitability*, 191-196.

Acimovic, S. (2006). *Understanding the supply chain. Economic anals 51* (170), 67-89

Acimovic, S., Mijuskovic, V. M., & Markovic, D. (2018). Segregating The Main Dimensions Of The Green Supply Chain. *Economic Ideas and practice 3*(29), 7-16.

Agus, A. (2011). Supply chain management, supply chain flexibility and business performance. *Journal of Global Strategic Management., 5*(1), 134–145. doi:10.20460/JGSM.2011515818

Ahn, S. H., Lee, Y. H., & Hwang, M. K. (2010). A framework for measuring performance of service SCM. The *40th International Conference on Computers & Indutrial Engineering, 62*(3), 801-818. 10.1109/ICCIE.2010.5668196

Aiginger, K., & Rodrik, D. (2020). Rebirth of Industrial Policy and an Agenda for the Twenty-First Century. Journal of Industry, Competition and Trade. Springer. doi:10.100710842-019-00322-3

Aitken, J., Childerhouse, P., Deakins, E., & Towill, D. (2016). A comparative study of manufacturing and service sector supply chain integration via the uncertainty circle model. *International Journal of Logistics Management, 27*(1), 188–205. doi:10.1108/IJLM-03-2014-0047

Ajinmoto Group. (2022). *Ajinomoto Group ASV Report 2022.* Ajinmoto. https://www.ajinomoto.co.jp/company/en/ir/library/annual/main/08/teaserItems1/01/linkList/0/link/ASV%20Report%202022_E_A4.pdf

Akinlar, S., & Fraunhofer, I. M. L. (2014). *Logistics 4.0 and challenges for the supply chain planning and IT.* IIS. https://www.iis.fraunhofer.de/content/dam/iis/tr/Session%203_5_Logistics_Fraunhofer%20IML_Akinlar.pdf

Akono, D., & Fernandes, V. (2009). Impacts du développement durable sur les organisations logistiques. *Revue management et avenir*, (6), 241-255.

Albertini, E. (2013). Does environmental management improve financial performance? A meta-analytical review. *Organization & Environment, 26*(4), 431–457. doi:10.1177/1086026613510301

Al-Doori, J. A. (2019). The impact of supply chain collaboration on performance in automotive industry: Empirical evidence. *Journal of Industrial Engineering and Management, 12*(2), 241–253. doi:10.3926/jiem.2835

Aliakbari Nouri, F., Shafiei Nikabadi, M., & Olfat, L. (2019). Developing the framework of sustainable service supply chain balanced scorecard (SSSC BSC). *International Journal of Productivity and Performance Management, 68*(1), 148–170. doi:10.1108/IJPPM-04-2018-0149

Ali, I., & Shukran, K. (2016). Managing supply chain risks and vulnerabilities through collaboration: Present and future scope. *Journal of Developing Areas, 50*(5), 335–342. doi:10.1353/jda.2016.0027

Alla, L., Bentalha, B., & Bouhtati, N. (2022a). Assessing Supply Chain Performance in the Covid 19 Context: A Prospective Model. In *2022 14th International Colloquium of Logistics and Supply Chain Management (LOGISTIQUA)* (pp. 1-6). IEEE.

Alla, L., Bentalha, B., & Elyoussfi, A. (2023). Intelligence territoriale et positionnement stratégique des regions au Maroc: Le cas de la région de Fès Meknes en perspective. *Le concept de l'intéligence en sciences juridiques, économiques et sociales*, 215-237.

Alla, L., Bentalha, B., Megzari, G., & Hmioui, A. (2022b). The effects of COVID-19 on supply chains: A qualitative analysis. *Reconfigurations du tourisme en contexte de la crise du Covid-19: Quelles démarches pour quelles résiliences au Maroc et ailleurs, 1* (1), pp.130-153

Almeida, F. L. F., & Calistru, C. (2013). The main challenges and issues of big data management. *International Journal of Research Studies in Computing, 2*(1). Advance online publication. doi:10.5861/ijrsc.2012.209

Alvarado, U. Y., & Kotzab, H. (2001). Supply chain management: The integration of logistics in marketing. *Industrial Marketing Management, 30*(2), 183–198. doi:10.1016/S0019-8501(00)00142-5

Amblee, N., & Bui, T. (2011). Harnessing the influence of social proof in online shopping: The effect of electronic word of mouth on sales of digital microproducts. *International Journal of Electronic Commerce, 16*(2), 91–114. doi:10.2753/JEC1086-4415160205

Amoore, L. (2006). Biometric borders: Governing mobilities in the war on terror. *Political Geography, 25*(3), 336–351. doi:10.1016/j.polgeo.2006.02.001

Amoore, L. (2018). Cloud geographies: Computing, data, sovereignty. *Progress in Human Geography, 42*(1), 4–24. doi:10.1177/0309132516662147

Anadon, M., & Savoie-Zajc, L. (2009). L'analyse qualitative des données. *Association pour la recherche qualitative, 28*(1). [En ligne] www.recherche-qualitative.qc.ca/revue.html consulté le 07/01/2020

Anand, A. (2015). Securing android code using white box cryptography and ob-fuscation technique. *International journal of computer science and mobile1295computing 4*(4), 347–352.

Anand, N., & Grover, N. (2015). Measuring retail supply chain performance: Theoretical model using key performance indicators (KPIs). *Benchmarking, 22*(1), 135–166. doi:10.1108/BIJ-05-2012-0034

Andjelic, S., Ilic, B., & Katanic, Z. (2022). Management of education for social entrepreneurship with emphasis on female entrepreneurship (Serbian: Menadžment obrazovanja za socijalno preduzetništvo sa akcentom na žensko preduzetništvo). *Economic signals: business magazine 7*(2), 33-49.

André, Q., Carmon, Z., Wertenbroch, K., Crum, A., Frank, D., Goldstein, W., Huber, J., van Boven, L., Weber, B., & Yang, H. (2018). Consumer choice and autonomy in the age of artificial intelligence and big data. *Customer Needs and Solutions, 5*(1-2), 28–37. doi:10.100740547-017-0085-8

Andrijanic, I., & Pavlovic, D. (2016). *International business.* Libertas – Pleiada Zagreb.

Angeles, R. (2005). RFID technologies: Supply-chain applications and implementation issues. *Information Systems Management*, *22*(1), 51–65. doi:10.1201/1078/44912.22.1.20051201/85739.7

Arandarenko, M. (2007). *Labor market in Serbia - causes of unfavorable trends and new employment policy measures (Serbian: Tržište rada u Srbiji - uzroci nepovoljnih trendova i nove mere politike zapošljavanja). Proceedings: Challenges of Serbia's economic policy in 2007*. Faculty of Economics.

Arvis, J.-F., Ojala, L., Wiederer, C., Shepherd, B., Raj, A., Dairabayeva, K., & Kiiski, T. (2018). *Connecting to Compete 2018: The Logistics in the Global Economy*. TheWorld Bank. doi:10.1596/29971

Arvis, J.-F., Ojala, L., Wiederer, C., Shepherd, B., Raj, A., Dairabayeva, K., & Kiiski, T. (2023). *Connecting to Compete 2023: Trade Logistics in an Uncertain Global Economy*. TheWorld Bank.

Arvis, J.-F., Saslavsky, D., Ojala, L., Shepherd, B., Bush, C., Raj, A., & Naula, T. (2016). *Connecting to Compete 2016: The Logistics in the Global Economy*. The World Bank. doi:10.1596/24598

Asahi. (2021). *Annual sustainability report*. Ashai.

Ash, J., Kitchin, R., & Leszczynski, A. (2018). Digital turn, digital geographies? *Progress in Human Geography*, *42*(1), 25–43. doi:10.1177/0309132516664800

Asif, M. S. (2018). An appraisal of issues faced by manufacturing companies, when selecting an enterprise resource planning (Erp) system. *International Journal of Business and General Management*, *7*(1), 1–8.

Asif, M. S., & Gill, H. (2022). Blockchain technology and green supply chain management (GSCM)–improving environmental and energy performance in multi-echelon supply chains. IOP Conference Series: Earth and Environmental Science. IOP Publishing. doi:10.1016/j.jclepro.2020.124191

Asif, M. S., Lau, H., Nakandala, D., Fan, Y., & Hurriyet, H. (2022). Case study research of green life cycle model for the evaluation and reduction of scope 3 emissions in food supply chains. *Corporate Social Responsibility and Environmental Management*, *29*(4), 1050–1066. doi:10.1002/csr.2253

Association for Supply Chain Management. (2015). *What is supply chain management?* ASCM. https://www.ascm.org/scm/#:~:text=What%20is%20supply%20chain%20management,information%2C%20physical%20distribution%20and%20cash

Athey, S., Parashkevov, I., Sarukkai, V., & Xia, J., (2016). *Bitcoin pricing, adoption, and usage: theory and evidence*. Stanford University.

Atlam, H. F., Alenezi, A., Alassafi, M. O., & Wills, G. (2018). Blockchain with Internet of Things: Benefits, challenges, and future directions. *International Journal of Intelligent Systems and Applications*, *10*(6), 40–48. doi:10.5815/ijisa.2018.06.05

Auchois, R., Taghipour, A., Kang, D., Zoghlami, N., & Abed, M. (2017). Advanced solutions for a supply chain with stochastic information. *Journal of Advanced Management Science*, *5*(1).

Bag, S., Wood, L. C., Xu, L., Dhamija, P., & Kayikci, Y. (2020). Big data analytics as an operational excellence approach to enhance sustainable supply chain performance. *Resources, Conservation and Recycling*, *153*(1), 104559. doi:10.1016/j.resconrec.2019.104559

Bai, C., & Sarkis, J. (2020). A supply chain transparency and sustainability technology appraisal model for blockchain technology. *International Journal of Production Research*, *2020*(58), 2142–2162. doi:10.1080/00207543.2019.1708989

Balogh, J. M., & Jámbor, A. (2017). Determinants of revealed comparative advantages: The case of cheese trade in the European Union. *Acta Alimentaria*, *46*(3), 305–311. doi:10.1556/066.2016.0012

Baltacioglu, T., Ada, E., Kaplan, M. D., And, O. Y., & Kaplan, Y. C. (2007). A New Framework for Service Supply Chains. *Service Industries Journal*, *27*(2), 105–124. doi:10.1080/02642060601122629

Banerjee, M., & Mishra, M. (2017). Retail supply chain management practices in India: A business intelligence perspective. *Journal of Retailing and Consumer Services*, *34*(1), 248–259. doi:10.1016/j.jretconser.2015.09.009

Barac, N., Milovanović, G., & Anđelković, A. (2011). Risk and the resilient supply chain. *Facta universitatis-series. Economics and Organization*, *8*(2), 139–151.

Barak, B., Goldreich, O., Impagliazzo, R., Rudich, S., Sahai, A., Vadhan, S., & Yang, K. (2001). On the (im) possibility of obfuscating programs. Annual International Cryptology Conference. Springer.

Bardhan, P., & Ray, I. (2008). The Contested Commons: Conversations Between Economists and Anthropologists. Blackwell Publishing.

Baret, P. (2006), L'évaluation contingente de la Performance Globale des Entreprises: Une méthode pour fonder un management sociétalement responsable? 2ème journée de recherche du CEROS, 1-24.

Barhhan, P. (2003). *International Trade Growth and Development: Essays*. Wiley-Blackwell. doi:10.1002/9780470752777

Barisic, A., & Brkic, M. (2021). Acquisition of Competencies for Advocacy in Social Work. *Regional L. Rev.*, 235.

Barney, J. B. (2012). Purchasing, Supply Chain Management and Sustained Competitive Advantage: The Relevance of Resource-based Theory. *The Journal of Supply Chain Management*, *48*(2), 3–6. doi:10.1111/j.1745-493X.2012.03265.x

Baro, E., Degoul, S., Beuscart, R., & Chazard, E. (2015). Toward a literature-driven definition of big data in healthcare. *BioMed Research International*, *2015*, 2015. doi:10.1155/2015/639021 PMID:26137488

Barshefsky, C. (2001). Trade policy for a networked world. *Foreign Affairs*, *80*(2), 134–146. doi:10.2307/20050070

Basheer, M. F., Siam, M. R. A., Awn, A. M., & Hussan, S. G. (2019). Exploring the role of TQM and supply chain practices for firm supply performance in the presence of information technology capabilities and supply chain technology adoption: A case of textile firms in Pakistan. *Uncertain Supply Chain Management*, *7*(1), 275–288. doi:10.5267/j.uscm.2018.9.001

Beamon, B. M., & Chen, V. C. P. (2001). Performance analysis of conjoined supply chains. *International Journal of Production Research*, *39*(14), 3195–3218. doi:10.1080/00207540110053156

Beniger, J. R. (1986). *The Control Revolution: Technological and Economic Origins of the Information Society*. Harvard University Press.

Benko, G. (2001). *Développement durable et systèmes productifs locaux. POMRNIER, P. Réseaux d'entreprises et territoires. Regards sur les systemes productifs locaux*. La Documentation Française.

Bentalha, B., & Hmioui, A. (2022). Smart Service Supply Chain and Just Walk Out Technology: A Netnographic Approach. In *Innovations in Smart Cities Applications Volume 5: The Proceedings of the 6th International Conference on Smart City Applications* (pp. 223-236). Cham: Springer International Publishing. 10.1007/978-3-030-94191-8_18

Bentalha, B., Hmioui, A., & Alla, L. (2020). Digital service supply chain management: current realities and prospective visions. In *Innovations in Smart Cities Applications Edition 3: The Proceedings of the 4th International Conference on Smart City Applications 4* (pp. 808-822). Springer International Publishing. 10.1007/978-3-030-37629-1_58

Bentalha, B., Hmioui, A., & Alla, L. (2021). The global performance of a service supply chain: a simulation-optimization under arena. In *Innovations in Smart Cities Applications Volume 4: The Proceedings of the 5th International Conference on Smart City Applications* (pp. 489-502). Springer International Publishing. 10.1007/978-3-030-66840-2_37

Bentalha, B., Hmioui, A., & Alla, L. (2023). Green Transportation Balanced Scorecard: A VIKOR Fuzzy Method for Evaluating Green Logistics Initiatives. In *Digital Technologies and Applications: Proceedings of ICDTA'23,* (pp. 916-925). Cham: Springer Nature Switzerland. 10.1007/978-3-031-29857-8_91

Bentalha, B. (2022). Smart Technologies for a Sustainable Service Supply Chain: A Prospective Perspective. *Journal of Environmental Issues and Climate Change*, *1*(1), 77–89. doi:10.59110/jeicc.v1i1.81

Bentalha, B. (2023). Les fondements théoriques du supply chain management: Une analyse critique. *Alternatives Managériales Economiques*, *5*(2), 1–22.

Bentalha, B., Hmioui, A., & Alla, L. (2019). The digitalization of the supply chain management of service companies: a prospective approach. In *Proceedings of the 4th International Conference on Smart City Applications* (pp. 1-8). ACM. 10.1145/3368756.3369005

Bhagwat, R., & Sharma, M. K. (2007). Performance measurement of supply chain management: A balance scorecard approach. *Computers & Industrial Engineering*, *53*(1), 43–62. doi:10.1016/j.cie.2007.04.001

Bhalerao, S., Agarwal, S., Borkar, S., Anekar, S., Kulkarni N., & Bhag- wat, S. (2019) *Supply Chain Management using Blockchain.* 2019 International Conference on Intelligent Sustainable Systems (ICISS), Palladam, India. . doi:10.1109/ISS1.2019.8908031

Biermann, F., Hickmann, T., Sénit, C., & Grob, L. (2022). The Sustainable Development Goals as a Transformative Force?: Key Insights. In F. Biermann, T. Hickmann, & C. Sénit (Eds.), *The Political Impact of the Sustainable Development Goals: Transforming Governance Through Global Goals?* (pp. 204–226). Cambridge University Press., doi:10.1017/9781009082945.009

Blanco, C., Caro, F., & Corbett, C. J. (2016). The state of supply chain carbon footprinting: Analysis of CDP disclosures by US firms. *Journal of Cleaner Production*, *135*, 1189–1197. doi:10.1016/j.jclepro.2016.06.132

Blecker, T., Kersten, W., & Meyer, C. (2015). *Development of an Approach for Analyzing Supply Chain Complexity.* Hamburg University of Technology.

Blewitt, J. (2014). *Understanding sustainable development.* Routledge. doi:10.4324/9781315886459

Bohnsack, R., Kolk, A., & Pinkse, J. (2015). Catching recurring waves: Low-emission vehicles, international policy developments and firm innovation strategies. *Technological Forecasting and Social Change*, *98*, 71–87. doi:10.1016/j.techfore.2015.06.020

Bojnec, S., & Fertő, I. (2017). The duration of global agri-food export competitiveness. *British Food Journal*, *119*(6), 1378–1393. doi:10.1108/BFJ-07-2016-0302

Boone, T., Ganeshan, R., Jain, A., & Sanders, N. R. (2018). Forecasting sales in the supply chain: Consumer analytics in the big data era. *International Journal of Forecasting*, *35*(1), 170–180. doi:10.1016/j.ijforecast.2018.09.003

Boonitt, S., & Pongpanarat, C. (2011). Measuring service supply chain management processes: The application of the Q-sort technique. *International Journal of Innovation, Management and Technology*, *2*(1), 217–221.

Boon-itt, S., Wong, C. Y., & Wong, C. W. Y. (2017). Service supply chain management process capabilities: Measurement development. *International Journal of Production Economics*, *193*, 1–11. doi:10.1016/j.ijpe.2017.06.024

Bouhtati, N., Hmioui, A., Alla, L., & Bentalha, B. (2022). Logistique et performance touristique: Une étude comparative des principales destinations en Afrique. *Alternatives Managériales Economiques, 1*, 116–132.

Bourguignon, A. (1997). Sous les pavés la plage… ou les multiples fonctions du vocabulaire comptable: l'exemple de la performance. *Comptabilité - Contrôle - Audit, tome 3*(1), 89-101. . doi:10.3917/cca.031.0089

Bourguignon, A. (1995). Peut-on définir la performance? *Revue Française de Comptabilité*, (juillet- août), 61–66.

Bourguignon, A. (2000). *Performance et contrôle de gestion, encyclopédie de comptabilité, contrôle de gestion et audit*. Ed Economica.

Bouzembrak, Y., Klüche, M., Gavai, A., & Marvin, H. J. P. (2019). Internet of Things in food safety: Literature review and a bibliometric analysis. *Trends in Food Science & Technology, 2019*(94), 54–64. doi:10.1016/j.tifs.2019.11.002

Bowman, P., Ng, J., Harrison, M., Lopez, S., & Illic, A. (2009). Sensor based condition monitoring. B*uilding Radio frequency IDentification for the Global Environment, (Bridge) Euro RFID project.*

Bozic, D., & Nikolic, M. (2019). Foreign trade and comparative advantages of agrarian sector of Serbia and neighbouring countries. *Economics of agriculture 66*(3), 737-754

Bozic, V., & Acimovic, S. (2004). Marketing logistics. Faculty of Economics, Belgrade, Serbia.

Bozic, D., & Nikolic, M. (2017). Serbia's foreign trade exchange and the importance of the agricultural sector. *Themes, 41*(3), 711–730.

Bradas, S. (2020). *Youth and active employment policy measures*. Center for Democracy Foundation.

Bradas, S. (2021). *Assessment of the impact of employment policies on the right to decent work, Impact of public policies on society*. Center for Democracy Foundation.

Bradas, S., Djindjic, M., Djurovic, A., Hadzi-Nikovic, L., Ivanovic, L., Mihajlovic, V., Momcilovic, P., Nenadovic, N., Radanovic, M., Savkovic, M., Sekulic, G., & Zivkovic, L. (2022). *Serbia 2030 - Is Serbia managing its (sustainable) development?* Belgrade Open School.

Bradley, S. P., & Nolan, R. L. (1998). *Sense and Respond: Capturing Value in the Network Era*. Harvard Business School Press.

Bravi, L., Santos, G., Pagano, A., & Murmura, F. (2020). Environmental management system according to ISO 14001: 2015 as a driver to sustainable development. *Corporate Social Responsibility and Environmental Management, 27*(6), 2599–2614. doi:10.1002/csr.1985

Bredenoord, A. L., Mostert, M., Isasi, R., & Knoppers, B. M. (2015). Data sharing in stem cell translational science: Policy statement by the international stem cell forum ethics working party. *Regenerative Medicine, 10*(7), 857–861. doi:10.2217/rme.15.42 PMID:26506014

Bremmer, I. (2005). Managing risk in an unstable world. *Harvard Business Review, 83*(6), 51–54. PMID:15938438

Brinker, S. (2020). Martech 5000—Really 8,000, but who's counting?. *Marketing technology landscape supergraphic.*

Brulhart, F., & Moncef, B. (2010). L'impact des pratiques de SCM sur la performance de l'entreprise: Une étude empirique dans le contexte français. Finance Contrôle Stratégie. *Association FCS, 13*(1), 33–66.

Burgess, K., & Singh, P. J. (2006). A proposed integrated framework for analysing supply chains. *Supply Chain Management, 11*(4), 337–344. doi:10.1108/13598540610671789

Cadet, I. (2010). La norme ISO 26000 relative à la responsabilité sociétale: une nouvelle source d'usages internationaux. *Revue internationale de droit économique*, (4), 401-439.

Callebaut, B. (2022). *Forever Chocolate Progress Report 2021/2022*. Barry Callebaut. https://www.barry-callebaut.com/en-AU/group/forever-chocolate/sustainability-reporting/forever-chocolate-progress-report-202122

Cao, M., & Zhang, Q. (2011). Supply chain collaboration: Impact on collaborative advantage and firm performance. *Journal of Operations Management*, *29*(3), 163–180. doi:10.1016/j.jom.2010.12.008

Cao, S., Bryceson, K., & Hine, D. (2021). Collaborative risk management in decentralised multi-tier global food supply chains: An exploratory study. *International Journal of Logistics Management*, *32*(3), 1050–1067. doi:10.1108/IJLM-07-2020-0278

Capocasale, V., Musso, S., & Perboli, G. (2022). Interplanetary File System in Logistic Networks: a Review. *2022 IEEE 46th Annual Com- puters, Software, and Applications Conference (COMPSAC)*. IEEE. 10.1109/COMPSAC54236.2022.00268

Capron, M. & Quairel, F. (2006). Évaluer les stratégies de développement durable des entreprises: l'utopie mobilisatrice de la performance globale. *Revue de l'organisation responsable, 1*(1), 5-17. doi:10.3917/ror.001.0005

Capron, M., & Quairel-Lanoizelée, F. (2020). *L'entreprise dans la société*. La Découverte.

Carter, C. R., Kosmol, T., & Kaufmann, L. (2016). Toward a Supply Chain Practice View. *The Journal of Supply Chain Management*, *53*(1), 114–122. doi:10.1111/jscm.12130

Carvalho, V. M., Nirei, M., Saito, Y. U., & Tahbaz-Salehi, A. (2021). Supply chain disruptions: Evidence from the great east japan earthquake. In Quarterly Journal of Economics, 136(2), 1255–1321. Oxford University Press. doi:10.1093/qje/qjaa044

Casado-Vara, R., Prieto, J., De la Prieta, F., & Corchado, J. M. (2018). How Blockchain improves the supply chain: Case study alimentary supply chain. *Procedia Computer Science*, *134*, 393–398. doi:10.1016/j.procs.2018.07.193

Cassivi, L. (2006). Collaboration planning in a supply chain. *Supply Chain Management*, *11*(3), 249–258. doi:10.1108/13598540610662158

Castka, P., & Balzarova, M. A. (2018). An exploration of interventions in ISO 9001 and ISO 14001 certification context– A multiple case study approach. *Journal of Cleaner Production*, *174*, 1642–1652. doi:10.1016/j.jclepro.2017.11.096

Catalini, C., & Gans, J. S. (2016). *Some simple Economics of the Blockchain*. National Bureau of Economic Research. doi:10.3386/w22952

Cauchois, R., Taghipour, A., Kang, D., Zoghlami, N., & Abed, M. (2017). Advanced solutions for a supply chain with stochastic information. Journal of Advanced Management Science Vol, 5(1).

Cauchois, R., Taghipour, A., Kang, D., Zoghlami, N., & Abed, M. (2017). Advanced solutions for a supply chain with stochastic information. *Journal of Advanced Management Science, 5*(1).

Cauchois, R., Taghipour, A., Kang, D., Zoghlami, N., & Abed, M. (2017). Advanced Solutions for a Supply Chain with Stochastic Information. *Journal of Advanced Management Science, 5(*1).

CDP. (2019a). Cascading Commitments: Driving ambitious action through supply chain engagement. In: CDP Carbon Trust. CDP.

CDP. (2019b). MAJOR RISK OR ROSY OPPORTUNITY; Are companies ready for climate change? *CDP Carbon Trust*. CDP. https://6fefcbb86e61af1b2fc4-c70d8ead6ced550b4d987d7c03fcdd1d.ssl.cf3.rackcdn.com/cms/reports/documents/000/004/588/original/CDP_Climate_Change_report_2019.pdf?1562321876

Ceryno, P. S., Scavarda, L. F., Klingebiel, K., & Yuzgulec, G. (2013). Supply chain risk management: A content analysis approach. *International Journal of Industrial Engineering and Management*, *4*(3), 141.

CEVES - Center for Higher Economic Studies. (Serbian: Centar za Visoke ekonomske studije). (2017). *Performance and value chain analysis of selected sectors*. Serbian Chamber of Commerce, Belgrade, Serbia. https://corporatefinanceinstitute.com/resources/management/supply-chain/

Chanchaichujit, J., Balasubramanian, S. & Charmaine, N.S.M.(2020). A systematic literature review on the benefit-drivers of RFID implementation in supply chains and its impact on organizational competitive advantage. *Cogent Bus. Manag.*

Chanegrih, T., & Creusier, J. (2019). L'élargissement du lean aux acteurs de la supply chain : Vers plus de performance? *Logistique & Management*, *27*(3), 182–191. doi:10.1080/12507970.2019.1586457

Chang, Y., Iakovou, E., & Shi, W. (2020). Blockchain in global supply chains and cross border trade: A critical synthesis of the state-of-the-art, challenges and opportunities. *International Journal of Production Research*, *58*(7), 2082–2099. doi:10.1080/00207543.2019.1651946

Chan, J.-T., & Yang, W. (2004). Advanced obfuscation techniques for Java bytecode. *Journal of Systems and Software*, *71*(1-2), 1–10. doi:10.1016/S0164-1212(02)00066-3

Chen, I. J., & Paulraj, A. (2004). Understanding supply chain management: Critical research and a theoretical framework. *International Journal of Production Research*, *42*(1), 131–163. doi:10.1080/00207540310001602865

Chen, J., Chen, Y., Du, X., Li, C., Lu, J., Zhao, S., & Zhou, X. (2013). Big data challenge: A data management perspective. *Frontiers of Computer Science*, *7*(2), 157–164. doi:10.100711704-013-3903-7

Chen, J., Sohal, A. S., & Prajogo, D. I. (2013). Supply chain operational risk mitigation: A collaborative approach. *International Journal of Production Research*, *51*(7), 2186–2199. doi:10.1080/00207543.2012.727490

Chen, X., Xi, Z., & Jing, P. (2017). A Unified Framework for Evaluating Supply Chain Reliability and Resilience. *IEEE Transactions on Reliability*, *66*(4), 1144–1156. doi:10.1109/TR.2017.2737822

Chin, T. A., Hamid, A. B. A., Raslic, A., & Heng, L. H. (2014). The Impact of Supply Chain Integration on Operational Capability in Malaysian Manufacturers. *Procedia: Social and Behavioral Sciences*, *130*(1), 257–265. doi:10.1016/j.sbspro.2014.04.030

Cho, D. W., Lee, Y. H., Ahn, S. H., & Hwang, M. K. (2012). A framework for measuring the performance of service supply chain management. *Computers & Industrial Engineering*, *62*(3), 801–818. doi:10.1016/j.cie.2011.11.014

Choi, S., Kim, B. H., & Noh, S. D. (2015). A diagnosis and evaluation method for strategic planning and systematic design of a virtual factory in smart manufacturing systems. *International Journal of Precision Engineering and Manufacturing*, *16*(6), 1107–1115. doi:10.100712541-015-0143-9

Choi, T. M., Cai, Y. J., & Shen, B. (2019). Sustainable Fashion Supply Chain Management: A System of Systems Analysis. *IEEE Transactions on Engineering Management*, *66*(4), 730–745. doi:10.1109/TEM.2018.2857831

Choon Tan, K., Lyman, S. B., & Wisner, J. D. (2002). Supply chain management: A strategic perspective. *International Journal of Operations & Production Management*, *22*(6), 614–631. doi:10.1108/01443570210427659

Chow, S., Eisen, P., Johnson, H., & Van Oorschot, P. C. (2002). A white-box des im-plementation for drm applications. *ACM Workshop on Digital RightsManagement*. Springer.

Chow, W., Madu, C., Kuei, C., Lu, M., Lin, C., & Tseng, H. (2008). Supply chain management in the U.S. and Taïwan: An empirical study. *Omega*, *36*(5), 665–679. doi:10.1016/j.omega.2006.01.001

Christopher, M., & Peck, H. (2004). *Building the resilient supply chain.*

Christopher, M., & Peck, H. (2004). *Building the resilient supply chain.* Emerald Insight.

Christopher, M., & Peck, H. (2004). Building the Resilient Suply Chain. *International Journal of Logistics Management*, *15*(2), 1–13. doi:10.1108/09574090410700275

Ciliberti, F., de Haan, J., de Groot, G., & Pontrandolfo, P. (2011). CSR codes and the principal-agent problem in supply chains: Four case studies. *Journal of Cleaner Production*, *19*(8), 885–894. doi:10.1016/j.jclepro.2010.09.005

Cimato, S., De Santis, A., & Ferraro Petrillo, U. (2005). Overcoming the obfuscation of Java programs by identifier renaming. *Journal of Systems and Software, 78*(1). Elsevier BV. . doi:10.1016/j.jss.2004.11.019

Ciuffo, J., Jones, S. S., & Groom, F. M. (2019). Artificial Intelligence in Marketing. In Artificial Intelligence and Machine Learning for Business for Non-Engineers (pp. 71-76). CRC Press, Taylor & Francis Group. doi:10.1201/9780367821654-6

Clark, G., Huxley, J., & Mountford, D. (2010). *Organising Local Economic Development: The Role of Development Agencies and Companies.* OECD. doi:10.1787/9789264083530-en

Coca-Cola. (2022). *Refresh the world. Make a difference.* Coca-Cola. https://www.coca-colacompany.com/content/dam/journey/us/en/reports/coca-cola-business-and-sustainability-report-2022.pdf

Colin, J. (2005). Le supply chain management existe-t-il réellement? *Revue française de gestion*, (3), 135-149.

Commission of the European Communities. (2011). *Innovation Union Scoreboard.* The Innovation Union's performance scoreboard for Research and Innovation /1 February 2011

Conick, H. (2017). The past, present and future of AI in marketing. *Marketing News*, *51*(1), 26–35.

Cook, L., Heiser, D., & Sengupta, K. (2011). The moderating effect of supply chain role on the relationship between supply chain practices and performance: An empirical analysis. *International Journal of Physical Distribution & Logistics Management*, *41*(2), 104–134. doi:10.1108/09600031111118521

Copacino, W. C. (1997). *Supply chain management: The basics and beyond* (1). CRC Press.

Corruption Perception Index. (2022) Serbian: Indeks percepcije korupcije. *Transparentnost.* https://www.transparentnost.org.rs/images/dokumenti_uz_vesti/CPI_2022_saop%C5%A1tenje.pdf

Crampton, J. (2016). Assemblage of the vertical: Commercial drones and algorithmic life. *Geographica Helvetica*, *7*(12), 137–146. doi:10.5194/gh-71-137-2016

CRED. (Centre for Research on the Epidemiology of Disasters). (2023). *Explanatory Notes.* CRED. https://www.emdat.be/explanatory-notes

Crosby, M., Pattanayak, P., Verma, S., & Kalyanaraman, V. (2016). Blockchain technology: Beyond Bitcoin. *Appl. Innov.*, *2*, 6–10.

Cui, A. P., & Liu, W. (2009). Study on capability coordination in logistics service supply chain with options contract. *Chin. J. Manage. Sci.*, *17*(2), 59–65.

Da Silveira, G., & Arkader, R. (2007). The direct and mediated relationships between supply chain coordination investments and delivery performance. *International Journal of Operations & Production Management, 27*(2), 140–158. doi:10.1108/01443570710720595

Dabbene, F., Gay, P., & Tortia, C. (2014). Traceability issues in food supply chain management: A review. *Biosystems Engineering, 120*, 65–80. doi:10.1016/j.biosystemseng.2013.09.006

Dai, B., Nu, Y., Xie, X., & Li, J. (2020). Interactions of Traceability and Reliability Optimization in a Competitive Supply Chain with Product Recall. *European Journal of Operational Research, 290*(1), 116–131. doi:10.1016/j.ejor.2020.08.003

Dangelico, R. M., & Pontrandolfo, P. (2015). Being 'green and competitive': The impact of environmental actions and collaborations on firm performance. *Business Strategy and the Environment, 24*(6), 413–430. doi:10.1002/bse.1828

Dania, W. A. P., Xing, K., & Amer, Y. (2018). Collaboration behavioural factors for sustainable agri-food supply chains: A systematic review. *Journal of Cleaner Production, 186*, 851–864. doi:10.1016/j.jclepro.2018.03.148

Danone Group. (2022). *Integrated Annual Report - Danone's Sustainability Performance*. Danone Group. https://www.danone.com/content/dam/danone-corp/danone-com/rai/2022/danone-integrated-annual-report-2022.pdf

Danskin, P., Englis, B. G., Solomon, M. R., Goldsmith, M., & Davey, J. (2005). Knowledge management as competitive advantage: Lessons from the textile and apparel value chain. *Journal of Knowledge Management, 9*(2), 91–102. doi:10.1108/13673270510590245

Danzi, P., Kalor, A. E., Stefanovic, C., & Popovski, P. (2018). Analysis of the communication traffic for blockchain synchronization of IoT devices. In *2018 IEEE International Conference on Communications (ICC)*. IEEE. 10.1109/ICC.2018.8422485

Daumas, J. C. (2006). Consommation de masse et grande distribution: Une révolution permanente (1957-2005). *Vingtieme Siecle (Paris, France), 91*(3), 57–076. doi:10.3917/ving.091.76

Davenport, T., Guha, A., Grewal, D., & Bressgott, T. (2020). How artificial intelligence will change the future of marketing. *Journal of the Academy of Marketing Science, 48*(1), 24–42. doi:10.100711747-019-00696-0

David, A. (2020). Modeling the pandemic: The simulations driving the world's response to COVID-19. *Nature, 580*(7803), 316–318. doi:10.1038/d41586-020-01003-6 PMID:32242115

De Boer, L., & Baumann, H. (2013). Sustainable procurement: An introduction. In *Sustainable procurement: An introduction* (pp. 1–6). Routledge.

De Bruyn, S., Ahdour, S., Bijleveld, M., de Graaff, L., Schep, E., Schroten, A., & Vergeer, R. (2018). Environmental Prices Handbook 2017: Methods and Numbers for Valuation of Environmental Impacts. CE Delft, Delft.

Decker, C., Berchtold, M. L., Chaves, W. F., Beigl, M., Roehr, D., & Riedel, T. (2008). Cost benefit model for smart items in the supply chain. The Internet of Things, 155–172. Springer. doi:10.1007/978-3-540-78731-0_10

Deng, J., Tang, Y., & Zhang, T. (2021). The Deeping Research on the Enterprise's Green Competitiveness under the "Environmental Protection Tax Law" in China. *Technoeconomics & Management Research, 7*, 51–55.

Deshpande, A. R. (2012). Supply Chain Management Dimensions, Supply Chain Performance and Organizational Performance: An Integrated Framework. *International Journal of Business and Management, 7*(8), 2–19. doi:10.5539/ijbm.v7n8p2

DeSimone, L. D., & Popoff, F. (2000). *Eco-efficiency: the business link to sustainable development*. MIT Press.

Developer Community for Android. (n.d.). *Meet android studio &Android Developers*. Android. https://developer.android.com/studio/intro

Devins, C., Felin, T., Kauffman, S., & Koppl, R. (2017). The Law and Big Data. *Cornell Journal of Law and Public Policy*, *27*(2), 3. https://scholarship.law.cornell.edu/cjlpp/vol27/iss2/3

Dewick, P., Foster, C., & Webster, S. (2017). Facilitating a more sustainable food and farming sector in the UK. In *System Innovation for Sustainability 3* (pp. 46–58). Routledge. doi:10.4324/9781351279369-3

Diallo, C., Venkatadri, U., Khatab, A., & Bhakthavatchalam, S. (2016). State of the art review of quality, reliability and maintenance issues in closed-loop supply chains with remanufacturing. *International Journal of Production Research*, *55*(5), 1277–1296. doi:10.1080/00207543.2016.1200152

Diemer, A., & Labrune, S. (2007). L'écologie industrielle: quand l'écosystème industriel devient un vecteur du développement durable. *Développement durable et territoires. Économie, géographie, politique, droit, sociologie.*

Dimitrieska, S., Stankovska, A., & Efremova, T. (2018). Artificial intelligence and marketing. *Entrepreneurship*, *6*(2), 298–304.

Dimitrijevic, M. (2021). The importance of the efficiency of the agricultural and food sector for the export of the Republic of Serbia (Serbian: Značaj efikasnosti poljoprivredeno-prehrambenog sektora za izvoz Republike Srbije). *Finance*, *76*(1-6), 114–135.

Dixon, J. R., Nanni, A. J., & Volmann, T. E. (1990). *The new performance challenge: measuring operations for world class competition*. Dow Jones-Irwin.

Djukic, G. P., & Ilic, B. (2021). Importance of green investment and Enerprenuership for Economic development. in: Jasovska, P., Logue, D. & Rammal, G.D. (Ed.), Contemporary Enterprenuership Issues in International Business World (pp. 195-220). World Scientific Publishing Co. Pte. Ltd.

Djukic, G. P., & Ilic, B. (2021). *Importance of Green Investment and Entrepreneurship for Economic Development*. Emerging Issues in International Business and Global Strategy Contemporary Entrepreneurship Issues in International Business. doi:10.1142/9789811228445_0008

Djukic, G., & Ilic, B. (2020a). Sustainable development, social protection and responsibility. *IzmirJournal of Social Sciences*, *2*(2), 83–91.

Dobrescu, E. M. (2017). Agenda 2030. New perspectives. [JoDRM]. *Journal of Defense Resources Management*, *8*(1), 165–180.

Donlon, J. P. (1996). Maximizing value in the supply chain. *Chief Executive*, *117*, 54–63.

Drozdibob, A., Sohal, A., Nyland, C., & Fayezi, S. (2022). Supply chain resilience in relation to natural disasters: Framework development. *Production Planning and Control*, 1–15. doi:10.1080/09537287.2022.2035446

Dubuisson-Quellier, S. (2009). La consommation engagée. *Lectures, Les livres.*

Eksoz, C., Mansouri, S. A., & Bourlakis, M. (2014). Collaborative forecasting in the food supply chain: A conceptual framework. *International Journal of Production Economics*, *158*, 120–135. doi:10.1016/j.ijpe.2014.07.031

Elgazzar, S., & Elzarka, S. (2017) Supply chain management in the service sector: an applied framework. In: *ABRM - AASTMT 2nd International Conference (Entrepreneurship, Supply Chain Management & Information Systems),* 121 – 134.

Elkington, J. (1997). The triple bottom line. *Environmental management: Readings and cases, 2*, 49-66.

Elkington, J. (1998). Partnerships from cannibals with forks: The triple bottom line of 21st-century business. *Environmental Quality Management, 8*(1), 37–51. doi:10.1002/tqem.3310080106

Ellram, L. M., Tate, W. L., & Billington, C. (2004). Understanding and Managing the Services Supply Chain. *The Journal of Supply Chain Management, 40*(4), 17–32. doi:10.1111/j.1745-493X.2004.tb00176.x

Ellram, L. M., Tate, W. L., & Billington, C. (2007). Services Supply Management: The Next Frontier for Improved Organizational Performance. *California Management Review, 49*(4), 44–66. doi:10.2307/41166405

Elluru, S., Gupta, H., Kaur, H., & Singh, S. P. (2019). Proactive and reactive models for disaster resilient supply chain. *Annals of Operations Research, 283*(1–2), 199–224. doi:10.100710479-017-2681-2

El-Nemr, N., Canel-Depitre, B., & Taghipour, A. (2017, September). Determinants of hotel room rates. In *Marketing Trends Congress. Luxury Industries Conference London 2017*, London, England.

El-Nemr, N., Canel-Depitre, B., & Taghipour, A. (2017, September). Determinants of hotel room rates. In Marketing Trends Congress. Luxury Industries Conference London 2017.

El-Nemr, N., Canel-Depitre, B., & Taghipour, A. (2017, September). Determinants of hotel room rates. In *Marketing Trends Congress. Luxury Industries Conference London 2017*. Research Gate.

El-Nemr, N., Canel-Depitre, B., & Taghipour, A. (2017, September). Determinants of hotel room rates. In *Marketing Trends Congress*. Luxury Industries Conference.

El-Nemr, N., Canel-Depitre, B., & Taghipour, A. (2021). The determinants of hotel room rates in Beirut: A hedonic pricing model. International Journal of Trade. *Economics and Finance, 12*(2), 33–42.

El-Nemr, N., Canel-Depitre, B., & Taghipour, A. (2017, September). Determinants of hotel room rates. In *Marketing Trends Congress. Luxury Industries Conference London 2017*. ACM.

Essid, M., & Berland, N. (2011). Les impacts de la RSE sur les systèmes de contrôle. *Comptabilité-contrôle-audit, 17*(2), 59–88. doi:10.3917/cca.172.0059

European Chemical Agency. (2021). REACH – Regulation (EC) No 1907/2006. ECHA. https://echa.europa.eu/regulations/reach

European Commission. (2013). *Buying Green! A Handbook on Green Public Procurement*. Publications Office of the European Union.

European Commission. (2020). Green Public Procurement. https://ec.europa.eu/environment/gpp/index_en.htm

European Union. (2014). Public Procurement Directive 2014/24/EU. European Union.

Fang, C., Liu, X., Pardalos, P. M., & Pei, J. (2016). Optimization for a three-stage production system in the Internet of Things: Procurement, production and product recovery, and acquisition. *International Journal of Advanced Manufacturing Technology, 83*(5-8), 689–710. doi:10.100700170-015-7593-1

Fang, J., & Ma, A. (2020). IoT application modules placement and dynamic task processing in edge-cloud computing. *IEEE Internet of Things Journal, 8*(6), 12771–12781.

Fang, J., Qu, T., Li, Z. G., Xu, G., & Huang, G. Q. (2013). Agent-based gateway operating system for RFID-enabled ubiquitous manufacturing enterprise. *Robotics and Computer-integrated Manufacturing, 29*(4), 222–231. doi:10.1016/j.rcim.2013.01.001

Farouk, A., & Zhen, D. (2019). Big data analysis techniques for intelligent systems. *Journal of Intelligent & Fuzzy Systems, 37*(3), 3067–3071. doi:10.3233/JIFS-179109

Farrukh, M., & Waheed, A. (2015). Learning Organization and Competitive Advantage: An Integrated Approach. *Journal of Asian Business Strategy, 5*(4), 73–79. doi:10.18488/journal.1006/2015.5.4/1006.4.73.79

Federal Ministry for the Environment. Nature Conservation and Nuclear Safety. (2019). Guidelines for Sustainable Public Procurement. Federal Ministry for the Environment, Nature Conservation and Nuclear Safety.

FEMA (Federal Emergency Management Agency). (2003). *Citizen Corps*. FEMA.

Ferrari, S., & Migliarese, P. (2010). Public procurement and sustainable development: A brief review. *Journal of Cleaner Production, 18*(15), 1440–1446.

Field, J. M., & Meile, L. C. (2008). Supplier relations and supply chain performance in financial services processes. *International Journal of Operations & Production Management, 28*(2), 185–206. doi:10.1108/01443570810846892

Filippini, R., & Forza, C. (2016). The Impact of the Just-in-Time Approach on Production System Performance: A Survey of Italian Industry. *A Review and Outlook. A Journey through Manufacturing and Supply Chain Strategy Research,* (19–39). Springer. doi:10.1007/978-3-319-31104-3_2

Fitzsimmons, J., & Fitzsimmons, M. (2010). *Service Management: Operations. Strategy, and Information Technology* (7th ed.). McGraw-Hill.

Fouilleux, È., & Goulet, F. (2012). Firmes et développement durable: Le nouvel esprit du productivisme. *Etudes Rurales,* (190), 131–146. doi:10.4000/etudesrurales.9708

Fraisse, R. (1996). In Robert Rochefort, La Societe Des Consommateurs. Quinzaine Litteraire, 26-26.

Francis, V. (2008). Supply chain visibility: Lost in translation? *Supply Chain Management, 13*(3), 180–184. doi:10.1108/13598540810871226

Friday, D., Ryan, S., Sridharan, R., & Collins, D. (2018). Collaborative risk management: A systematic literature review. *International Journal of Physical Distribution & Logistics Management, 48*(3), 231–253. doi:10.1108/IJPDLM-01-2017-0035

Fujimoto, T., Kato, Y., & Iwao, S. (2019). *The Evolution of Disaster-Response Capabilities: The Case of Toyota.*

Fujita, M., Nobuaki, H., Sagara, J., & Adam, B. (2012). *The economics of disaster risk, risk management, and risk financing*. World Bank. https://documents1.worldbank.org/curated/en/175611468044671950/pdf/793950BRI0drm000Box377374B00Public0.pdf

Fukuyama, F. (2015). After neoconservatism. In *Paradoxes of Power* (pp. 130–139). Routledge.

Fu, N., Flood, P. C., Bosak, J., Morris, T., & O'Regan, P. (2013). Exploring the Performance Effect of HPWS on Professional Service Supply Chain Management. *Supply Chain Management, 18*(3), 292–307. doi:10.1108/SCM-04-2012-0118

Gabriel, P. (2003). Le marketing comme moyen de légitimation des, entreprises dans une perspective de développement durable. *Décisions marketing*, 67-76.

Garipova, E. N., Kulik, E. N., & Nabieva, L. G. (2020). Assessment of the influence of innovation and IT markets on the parameters of the regional economy. *International Review (Steubenville, Ohio), 3*(4), 29–40. doi:10.5937/intrev2003029G

Garske, B., Stubenrauch, J., & Ekardt, F. (2020). Sustainable phosphorus management in European agricultural and environmental law. *Review of European, Comparative & International Environmental Law*, *29*(1), 107–117. doi:10.1111/reel.12318

General Office of the People's Government of Shenzhen Municipality. (2022, December 30). *Notice of the General Office of Shenzhen Municipal People's Government on the Issuance of Several Measures to Promote the High-Quality Development of Green and Low-Carbon Industries in Shenzhen--Policy and Regulations.* General Office of the People's Government of Shenzhen Municipality. http://www.sz.gov.cn/cn/xxgk/zfxxgj/zcfg/content/post_10364326.html

Germain, C., & Trébucq, S. (2004), La performance globale de l'entreprise et son pilotage: quelques réflexions, pp. 35-41. Semaine sociale Lamy.

Ghisellini, P., Cialani, C., & Ulgiati, S. (2016). A review on circular economy: The expected transition to a balanced interplay of environmental and economic systems. *Journal of Cleaner Production*, *114*, 11–32. doi:10.1016/j.jclepro.2015.09.007

Giannakis, M. (2011). Conceptualizing and managing service supply chains. *Service Industries Journal*, *31*(11), 1809–1823. doi:10.1080/02642069.2010.503879

Global, C. (2020). CDP Climate Change. In Yearly. United Kingdom: Carbon Disclosure Project.

Global, C. (2021). CDP Climate Change. In Yearly. United Kingdom: Carbon Disclosure Project.

Goffetti, G., Böckin, D., Baumann, H., Tillman, A. M., & Zobel, T. (2022). Towards sustainable business models with a novel life cycle assessment method. *Business Strategy and the Environment*, *31*(5), 2019–2035. doi:10.1002/bse.3005

Golinelli, G. M., & Volpe, L. (2012). *Consonance, value, sustainability. Toward sustainable enterprise*. Cedam.

Gordana, D. P., & Biljana, I. S. (2021). Sustaining SME Management and Innovations in the Post-COVID Era. In N. Baporikar (Ed.), *Handbook of Research on Strategies and Interventions to Mitigate COVID-19 Impact on SMEs* (pp. 588–608). IGI Global., doi:10.4018/978-1-7998-7436-2.ch029

Government of Australia. (2018). *Sustainable Procurement Guide*. Department of Finance, Government of Australia.

Government of Canada. (2019). *Greening Government Strategy*. Government of Canada.

Government of India. (2017). *Manual for Procurement of Goods 2017*. Ministry of Finance, Department of Expenditure, Government of India.

Government of South Africa. (2017). *Preferential Procurement Policy Framework Act (PPPFA) No.5 of 2000*. Government of South Africa.

Government, N. S. (2018). *NSW Government Sustainable Procurement Policy*. NSW Government.

Govindan, K., Azevedo, S. G., Carvalho, H., & Cruz-Machado, V. (2014). Impact of supply chain management practices on sustainability. *Journal of Cleaner Production*, *85*, 212–225. doi:10.1016/j.jclepro.2014.05.068

Green, K. W. Jr, Zelbst, P. J., Meacham, J., & Bhadauria, V. S. (2012). Green supply chain management practices: Impact on performance. *Supply Chain Management*, *17*(3), 290–305. doi:10.1108/13598541211227126

Grenier, C., & Martin, V. (2013). Performance des organisations et bien-être des usagers: Quels modes de pilotage et d'intervention? *Management & Avenir*, *61*(3), 129–145. doi:10.3917/mav.061.0129

Grönroos, C., & Ojasalo, K. (2004). Service productivity. *Journal of Business Research*, *57*(4), 414–423. doi:10.1016/S0148-2963(02)00275-8

Guangzhou Port Authority. (2022, September 19). Notice on the Issuance of the Implementation Measures of Guangzhou Port Ship Emission Control Subsidy Funds. Guangzhou Port Authority. https://www.gz.gov.cn/gfxwj/sbmgfxwj/gzsgwj/content/post_8576369.html

Gubbi, J., Buyya, R., Marusic, S., & Palaniswami, M. (2013). Internet of Things (IoT): A vision, architectural elements, and future directions. *Future Generation Computer Systems*, *29*(7), 1645–1660. doi:10.1016/j.future.2013.01.010

Guilbert, L. (2007). Ethnologie collaborative: Elaboration et analyse d'espaces de médiation en contexte de migration. *Recherches Qualitatives*, *4*(1), 14–36.

Gunasekaran, A., Patel, C., & Tirtiroglu, E. (2001). Performance measures and metrics in a supply chain environment. *International Journal of Operations & Production Management*, *21*(1/2), 71–87. doi:10.1108/01443570110358468

Gunningham, N. (2013). Managing the energy trilemma: The case of Indonesia. *Energy Policy*, *54*, 184–193. doi:10.1016/j.enpol.2012.11.018

Guo, Y., Xia, X., Zhang, S., & Zhang, D. (2018). Environmental regulation, government R&D funding and green technology innovation: Evidence from China provincial data. *Sustainability (Basel)*, *10*(4), 940. doi:10.3390u10040940

Guoyou, Q., Saixing, Z., Chiming, T., Haitao, Y., & Hailiang, Z. (2013). Stakeholders' influences on corporate green innovation strategy: A case study of manufacturing firms in China. *Corporate Social Responsibility and Environmental Management*, *20*(1), 1–14. doi:10.1002/csr.283

Gu, Y., Wu, Y., Xu, M., & Zuo, T. (2016). Waste Electrical and Electronic Equipment (WEEE) Recycling for a Sustainable Resource Supply in the Electronics Industry in China. *Journal of Cleaner Production*, *127*, 331–338. doi:10.1016/j.jclepro.2016.04.041

Habib, A., & Bhuiyan, M. B. U. (2017). Determinants of monetary penalties for environmental violations. *Business Strategy and the Environment*, *26*(6), 754–775. doi:10.1002/bse.1947

Habib, M. A., Sardar, M. B., Jabbar, S., Faisal, C. M. N., Mahmood, N., & Ahmad, M. (2020). Blockchain-based Supply Chain for the Automation of Transaction Process: Case Study based Validation. In *Proceedings of the 2020 International Conference on Engineering and Emerging Technologies, ICEET 2020*, Lahore, Pakistan. 10.1109/ICEET48479.2020.9048213

Happaerts, S., & Van de Walle, S. (2011). Sustainable procurement in Flemish local governments: An empirical study of the drivers and barriers. *Journal of Public Procurement*, *11*(4), 509–536.

Hart, O., & Zingales, L. (2017). *Companies should maximize shareholder welfare not market value.* ECGI-Finance Working Paper, (521).

Hasan, H., AlHadhrami, E., AlDhaheri, A., Salah, K., & Jayaraman, R. (2019). Smart contract-based approach for efficient shipment management. *Computers & Industrial Engineering*, *136*, 2019. doi:10.1016/j.cie.2019.07.022

Hausman, H. (2004). Supply chain performance metrics. In *The practice of supply chain management: Where theory and application converge* (pp. 61–73). Springer. doi:10.1007/0-387-27275-5_4

He, Q., Guan, N., Lv, M., & Yi, W. (2018). On the consensus mechanisms of blockchain/dlt for internet of things. In *2018 IEEE 13th International Symposium on Industrial Embedded Systems (SIES)*. IEEE. 10.1109/SIES.2018.8442076

Heale, R., & Twycross, A. (2018). *What is a case study?* (Vol. 21). Royal College of Nursing.

Hejazi, M. T., Al Batati, B., & Bahurmuz, A. (2023). The Influence of Green Supply Chain Management Practices on Corporate Sustainability Performance. *Sustainability (Basel)*, *15*(6), 5459. doi:10.3390u15065459

Hemilä, J., & Vilko, J. (2015). The development of a service supply chain model for a manufacturing SME. *International Journal of Logistics Management*, *26*(3), 517–542. doi:10.1108/IJLM-01-2014-0001

Henrich, J., Li, J. D., Mazuera, C., & Perez, F. (2022). *Future-proofing the supply chain with supply chains in the spotlight, three new long-term transformation priorities form a fresh focus for competitive advantage*. McKinsey.

Hinrichs-Rahlwes, R., & Zawilska-Florczuk, M. (2011). Legal frameworks for sustainable public procurement in the European Union. *Journal of Cleaner Production*, *19*(6-7), 975–983.

Hmioui, A., & Bentalha, B. (2020). Service Supply Chain Management et performance commerciale: Esquisse d'une synthèse théorique. *Revue ame, 2,* 1-21.

Hmioui, A., Bentalha, B., & Alla, L. (2020). Service supply chain: A prospective analysis of sustainable management for global performance. In 2020 *IEEE 13th International Colloquium of Logistics and Supply Chain Management (LOGISTIQUA)* (pp. 1-7). IEEE. 10.1109/LOGISTIQUA49782.2020.9353940

Hmioui, A., Alla, L., & Bentalha, B. (2017). *Impact des pratiques de la RSE sur la performance commerciale des entreprises touristiques: Cas des établissements hôteliers de Fès. Le tourisme au Maghreb: Économie et Management, Laboratoire de recherche en entrepreneuriat et management des organisations*. ENCG de Fès.

Hmioui, A., & Bentalha, B. (2021). Service supply chain management: A literature review. *International Journal of Logistics Systems and Management*, *40*(3), 332–353. doi:10.1504/IJLSM.2021.120253

Hoa Vo, T. L., & Bironneau, L. (2011). Systèmes d'information et gestion globale de la chaîne logistique: un état de l'art. 2ème journée thématique SILOGIN - Système d'information, logistique, innovation, Nantes, France.

Hoenicke, J. 2002. Java optimize and decompile environment. *Source Forge.* ¡https://jode.sourceforge.net/¿

Hollmann, R. L., Scavarda, L. F., & Thomé, A. M. T. (2015). Collaborative planning, forecasting and replenishment: A literature review. *International Journal of Productivity and Performance Management*, *64*(7), 971–993. doi:10.1108/IJPPM-03-2014-0039

Holmberg, J., & Sandbrook, R. (2019). Sustainable development: what is to be done? In *Policies for a small planet* (pp. 19–38). Routledge. doi:10.4324/9780429200465-1

Honda. (2011). *About the major earthquake in northeastern Japan*. Honda. https://global.honda/newsroom/news/2011/c110314eng.html

Hong, J., Zhang, Y., & Shi, M. (2017). The impact of supply chain quality management practices and knowledge transfer on organisational performance: An empirical investigation from China. *International Journal of Logistics*, *21*(3), 259–278. doi:10.1080/13675567.2017.1394992

Hong, J., Zheng, R., Deng, H., & Zhou, Y. (2019). Green supply chain collaborative innovation, absorptive capacity and innovation performance: Evidence from China. *Journal of Cleaner Production*, *241*, 118377. doi:10.1016/j.jclepro.2019.118377

Hosseini, S., Ivanov, D., & Dolgui, A. (2019). Review of quantitative methods for supply chain resilience analysis. *Transportation Research Part E, Logistics and Transportation Review*, *125*, 285–307. doi:10.1016/j.tre.2019.03.001

Huang, H., Liu, X., Lu, X., Li, J., & Lu, L. (2022). 250g tea with a 1kg package, it is time to get at the root of overpackaging. *Xinhua Daily*, 1–3.

Huo, B., Ye, Y., Zhao, X., & Shou, Y. (2016). The impact of human capital on supply chain integration and competitive performance. *International Journal of Production Economics, 178*(1), 132–143. doi:10.1016/j.ijpe.2016.05.009

Hussain, M., & Al-Aomar, R. (2017). A model for assessing the impact of sustainable supplier selection on the performance of service supply chains. *International Journal of Sustainable Engineering, 11*(6), 366–381. doi:10.1080/19397038.2017.1414898

Ibrahim, S. E., & Ogunyemi, O. (2012). The effect of linkages and information sharing on supply chain and export performance: An empirical study of Egyptian textile manufacturers. *Journal of Manufacturing Technology Management, 23*(4), 441–463. doi:10.1108/17410381211230394

Ikram, M., Zhang, Q., Sroufe, R., & Ferasso, M. (2020). The social dimensions of corporate sustainability: An integrative framework including COVID-19 insights. *Sustainability (Basel), 12*(20), 8747. doi:10.3390u12208747

Ilic, B., Djukic, G. & Balaban, M. (2020). Sustainable development directions of rural tourism of Timok region. *The economy of Agriculture, 67*(1), 157-174. doi:10.5937/ekoPolj2001157I

Ilic, B. S. (2019). Renewable Energy Sources Management and Role of Ecological Parks: Improving Quality of Life for Sustainable Development. In U. Akkucuk (Ed.), *Ethical and Sustainable Supply Chain Management in a Global Context* (pp. 220–228). IGI Global., doi:10.4018/978-1-5225-8970-9.ch014

Ilic, B. S. (2022). Poverty and Poverty Indicators in the Republic of Serbia: The Impact of Uneven Regional Development. In N. Baporikar (Ed.), *Handbook of Research on Global Institutional Roles for Inclusive Development* (pp. 261–284). IGI Global. doi:10.4018/978-1-6684-2448-3.ch014

Ilic, B. S., Djukic, G. P., & Balaban, M. M. (2020). Sustainability of Mandatory Pension Insurance in the Circular Economy: A Comparative Analysis. In N. Baporikar (Ed.), *Handbook of Research on Entrepreneurship Development and Opportunities in Circular Economy* (pp. 125–143). IGI Global. doi:10.4018/978-1-7998-5116-5.ch007

Ilic, B., & Djukic, G. (2021). Cultural dimensions - the impact of differences and similarities on business in the era of COVID-19. In: *Proceedings 11th International Symposium on Natural Resources Management, ISNRM 2021.* Faculty of Management, Zajecar Megatrend University, Belgrade, 169-176

Ilic, B., & Djukic, G. (2022). Creating and Designing Sustainable Management on the Global Level. Journal of Economic and Social Development (JESD) –. *Resilient Society, 9*(1), 46–53.

ILO. (1998). *Fundamental principles and rights at work and its application and monitoring.* ILO. https://www.ilo.org/public/english/standards/declaration/declaration_croat.pdf

Iraten, S. (2014). La Supply Chain management un levier pour améliorer la performance de l'entreprise. *Revue Reformes Economiques et Intégration En Economie Mondiale, 17*(1), 135–159.

Issor, Z. (2017). La performance de l'entreprise: un concept complexe aux multiples dimensions. *Projectics / Proyéctica / Projectique, 17*(2), 93-103. . doi:10.3917/proj.017.0093

Ivic, I., & Pesikan, A. i Kostic, A. (2021). Key data on education in Serbia. Serbian Academy of Sciences and Arts, Belgrade

Ivković, I. N., & Jović, S. B. (2018). Comparative analysis of the unemployment rate obtained based on survey and administrative data (Serbian: Uporedna analiza stope nezaposlenosti dobijene na osnovu anketnih i administrativnih podataka). *Military act journal 70*(4), 310-329.

Jabbour, A. B. L., Filho, A. G. A., Viana, A. B. N., & Jabbour, C. J. C. (2011). Measuring supply chain management practices. *Measuring Business Excellence, 15*(2), 18–31. doi:10.1108/13683041111131592

Jakopin, E. (2011). The framework of new Serbian industrial policy. *Business Economics (Cleveland, Ohio), 59*(1-2), 73–88.

Jandric, M., & Molnar, D. (2018). Adaptability and security: Key aspects of the quality of employment in the changing labor markets. *Enterprise economics 66*(3-4), 213-225

Jarašūnienė, A., Sinkevičius, G., Čižiūnienė, K., & Čereška, A. (2020). Adaptation of the management model of internationalization processes in the development of railway transport activities. *Sustainability (Basel), 12*(15), 6248. doi:10.3390u12156248

Jarek, K., & Mazurek, G. (2019). Marketing and Artificial Intelligence. *Central European Business Review, 8*(2).

Jesús Sáenz, M., & Revilla, E. (2014). *Creating More Resilient Supply Chains*. MIT Sloan Management Review. https://sloanreview.mit.edu/article/creating-more-resilient-supply-chains/

Jiang, J., Li, Z., Tian, Y., & Al-Nabhan, N. (2020). A review of techniques and methods for IoT applications in collaborative cloud-fog environment. *Security and Communication Networks, 2020*, 1–15. doi:10.1155/2020/8849181

Jianglong, L., & Min, X. (2016). A Mobile Social App for College Students Based on Perceived Similarity and Trust. 2016 8th International Con- ference on Information Technology in Medicine and Education. ITME. doi:10.1109/ITME.2016.0090

Jin, L. Y. (2006). Service Supply Chain Management, Customer Satisfaction and Business Performance. *Chinese Journal of Management Science, 14*(1), 100–106.

Johnson, J. C., & Wood, D. F. (1990). *Contemporary logistics*. Macmillan.

Johnston, R., Glark, G., & Shulver, M. (2012). *Service operations and management* (4th ed.). Pearson.

Jourdan, A. (2014). McDonald's to boost China supplier audits after food safety scandal. *Reuters*.

Just in time production. www.samuderanaga.com/zara-just-in-timeproduction-k.html

Jüttner, U., & Maklan, S. (2011). Supply chain resilience in the global financial crisis: An empirical study. *Supply Chain Management, 16*(4), 246–259. doi:10.1108/13598541111139062

Kagermann, H. (2015). Change through digitization—value creation in the age of Industry 4.0. Management of Permanent Change, 23–45. Springer.

Kaliani Sundram, V. P., Chandran, V., & Awais Bhatti, M. (2016). Supply chain practices and performance: The indirect effects of supply chain integration. *Benchmarking, 23*(6), 1445–1471. doi:10.1108/BIJ-03-2015-0023

Kamalahmadi, M., & Parast, M. M. (2016). A review of the literature on the principles of enterprise and supply chain resilience: Major findings and directions for future research. *International Journal of Production Economics, 171*, 116–133. doi:10.1016/j.ijpe.2015.10.023

Kamberovic, S., Mitrovic, S., & Arno Behrens, A. (2020). *GAP analysis of opportunities for economic strengthening by applying sustainable business models after the COVID-19 pandemic in the Republic of Serbia*. OSCE Mission in Serbia. Belgrade, Serbia.

Kamble, S. S., Gunasekaran, A., & Gawankar, S. A. (2020). Achieving sustainable performance in a data-driven agriculture supply chain:A review for research and applications. *International Journal of Production Economics, 2020*(219), 179–194. doi:10.1016/j.ijpe.2019.05.022

Kamble, S., Gunasekaran, A., & Arha, H. (2019). Understanding the Blockchain technology adoption in supply chains-Indian Context. *International Journal of Production Research, 57*(7), 2009–2033. doi:10.1080/00207543.2018.1518610

Kane, E., (2017). *Is Blockchain a General Purpose Technology?*

Kanjilal, J. (2021, June 8). *How java is used in Android App Development.* Developer.com. https://www.developer.com/mobile/java-mobile/java-mobile- pr ogramming-for android/

Karimi, E., & Rafiee, M. (2014). Analyzing the Impact of Supply Chain Management Practices on Organizational Performance through Competitive Priorities (Case Study: Iran Pumps Company). International Journal of Academic Research in Accounting, Finance and Management Sciences, 4(1), 1-15. doi:10.6007/IJARAFMS/v4-i1/503

Kashiwagi, Y., & Todo, Y. (2020). *Propagation of Positive Effects of Postdisaster Policies through Supply Chains: Evidence from the Great East Japan Earthquake and Tsunami.* ADB. doi:10.22617/WPS200003-2

Kathawala, Y., & Abdou, K. (2003). Supply chain evaluation in the service industry: A framework development compared to manufacturing. *Managerial Auditing Journal, 18*(2), 140–149. doi:10.1108/02686900310455137

Kaur, H., & Singh, S. P. (2019). Sustainable procurement and logistics for disaster resilient supply chain. *Annals of Operations Research, 283*(1–2), 309–354. doi:10.100710479-016-2374-2

Kędzior-Laskowska, M. (2020). Polish road freight transport and process of internationalisation–selected effects for quality and competitiveness. *Entrepreneurship and Sustainability Issues, 7*(3), 2481–2493. doi:10.9770/jesi.2020.7.3(68)

Ketzenberg, M., Bloemhof, J., & Gaukler, G. (2015). Managing perishables with time and temperature history. *Production and Operations Management, 2015*(24), 54–70. doi:10.1111/poms.12209

Khanchanapong, T., Prajogo, D., Sohal, A., Cooper, B., Yeung, A., & Cheng, T. (2014). The Unique and Complementary Effects of Manufacturing Technologies and Lean Practices on Manufacturing Operational Performance. *International Journal of Production Economics, 153*(1), 191–203. doi:10.1016/j.ijpe.2014.02.021

Kitchin, R., & Dodge, M. (2011). *Code/Space: Software and Everyday Life.* MIT Press. doi:10.7551/mitpress/9780262042482.001.0001

Knudsen, J. S., Moon, J., & Slager, R. (2015). Government policies for corporate social responsibility in Europe: A comparative analysis of institutionalisation. *Policy and Politics, 43*(1), 81–99. doi:10.1332/030557312X656016

Kolar, N. (2014). Working capital management in Dell Inc. *Economía: Teoría y Practica, 7*(4), 1–20.

Kolcava, D. (2023). Greenwashing and public demand for government regulation. *Journal of Public Policy, 43*(1), 179–198. doi:10.1017/S0143814X22000277

Kostadinović, I., & Stanković, S. (2020). Innovation clusters as an association model of the small and medium-sized enterprises: the context of regional development. In *Proceedings 6th Leadership, Innovation, Management and Economics: Integrated Politics of Research* (pp. 47–56). Association of Economists and Managers of the Balkans. doi:10.31410/LIMEN.S.P.2020.47

Kostadinović, I., & Stanković, S. (2020). The analysis of the regional disproportions in the labor market in the Republic of Serbia. *Economics, 66*(1), 25–35.

Kostadinović, I., & Stanković, S. (2021). Organizational learning and innovation in the tourism industry as a basis for creating value for tourists. *Economic Themes, 59*(1), 153–172. doi:10.2478/ethemes-2021-0009

Kostic, I. (2021). *Financial management of supply chain risks in order to maximize company value*. Faculty of Economics, University of Kragujevac, Serbia.

Kostiuk, Y., Kalinova, E., & Kučera, J. (2021). Impact of Globalization and Internationalization Processes on Added Value in EU Countries, SHS Web of Conferences: Globalization and its Socio-Economic Consequences, 92, 09008. 10.1051hsconf/20219209008

Kranz, S. (1996). *What is it?* Purchasing Today.

Kshetri, N. (2018). Blockchain's roles in meeting key supply chain management objectives. *International Journal of Information Management*, *39*(April), 80–89. doi:10.1016/j.ijinfomgt.2017.12.005

Kumar, S., & Havey, T. (2013). Before and after disaster strikes: A relief supply chain decision support framework. *International Journal of Production Economics*, *145*(2), 613–629. doi:10.1016/j.ijpe.2013.05.016

Kuner, C., Cate, F. H., Millard, C., & Svantesson, D. J. B. (2012). The challenge of « big data » for data protection. *International Data Privacy Law*, *2*(2), 47–49. doi:10.1093/idpl/ips003

Kuosmanen, T., & Mäkitalo-Keinonen, T. (2011). Sustainable public procurement practices in Finland. *Journal of Public Procurement*, *11*(4), 537–561.

Kweka, J. (2011). Sustainable procurement practices in the public sector: An international comparative study. *Journal of Public Procurement*, *11*(1), 1–30.

Labor Force Survey (2021). New Methodology. www.stat.gov.rs

Lambert, D. M., Cooper, M. C., & Pagh, J. D. (1998). Supply Chain Management: Implementation Issues and Research Opportunities. *International Journal of Logistics Management*, *9*(2), 1–20. doi:10.1108/09574099810805807

Lam, C. Y., & Ip, W. H. (2019). An Integrated Logistics Routing and Scheduling Network Model with RFID-GPS Data for Supply Chain Management. *Wireless Personal Communications*, *2019*(105), 803–817. doi:10.100711277-019-06122-6

Lamsiah, A., & Bentalha, B. (2022). Economic Diplomacy and Economic Intelligence Amalgamation: The Moroccan-Nigerian Economic Exchange as a Case Study. *Alternatives Managériales Economiques*, *4*(4), 582–603.

Lan, H. (2022). *Grab the opportunity of low carbon and speed up energy transformation*, 5. Shandong Provincial State-owned Assets Supervision and Administration Commission.

Lansiti, Marco, & Lakhani, K. (2017). The truth about Blockchain. *Harvard Business Review*.

Larson, P. D., & Rogers, D. S. (1998). Supply Chain Management: Definition, Growth and Approaches. *Journal of Marketing Theory and Practice*, *6*(4), 1–5. doi:10.1080/10696679.1998.11501805

Lasi, H., Fettke, P., Kemper, H.-G., Feld, T., & Hoffmann, M. (2014). Industry 4.0. *Business & Information Systems Engineering*, *6*(4), 239–242. doi:10.100712599-014-0334-4

Laukkanen, M., Manninen, K., Huiskonen, J., & Kinnunen, N. (2021). Sustainable Value Creation for Advancing Sustainability Transition: An Approach to Integrate Company-and System-Level Sustainability. In Business Models for Sustainability Transitions: How Organisations Contribute to Societal Transformation (pp. 89-121). Springer.

Laville, É. (2009). *L'entreprise verte: le développement durable change l'entreprise pour changer le monde*. Pearson Education France.

Lazarevic-Moravcevic, M., Eric, D., & Kamenkovic, S. (2018). The influence of the business environment on the performance of the SME sector in Serbia. *Business Economics (Cleveland, Ohio)*, *12*(1), 33–53.

Lebosse, S., Taghipour, A., & Canel-Depitre, B. (2017). Quick response to fluctuations in supply chains: A review. *Journal of Advanced Management Science*, *5*(5), 394–400. doi:10.18178/joams.5.5.394-400

Lemtaoui, M., & Rochdi, M. H. (2017). Le management de la chaine logistique entre efficience et réactivité. *Revue d'Etudes en Management et Finance d'Organisation*, *2*(6), 1–13.

Lenny Koh, S. C., Demirbag, M., Bayraktar, E., Tatoglu, E., & Zaim, S. (2007). The impact of supply chain management practices on performance of SMEs. *Industrial Management & Data Systems*, *107*(1), 103–124. doi:10.1108/02635570710719089

Lentine, K., Lam, N. & Segev, D. L. (2019). Risks of Living Kidney Donation. *Clinical Journal of the American Society of Nephrology, 14*(4). Ovid Technologies (Wolters Kluwer Health). . doi:10.2215/CJN.11220918

Leończuk, D., Ryciuk, U., Szymczak, M., & Nazarko, J. (2019). Measuring Performance of Adaptive Supply Chains. In A. Kawa & A. Maryniak (Eds.), *SMART Supply Network. EcoProduction (Environmental Issues in Logistics and Manufacturing)*. Springer. doi:10.1007/978-3-319-91668-2_5

Lezoche, M., Panetto, H., Kacprzyk, J., Hernandez, J. E., & Alemany Díaz, M. M. E. (2020). Agri-food 4.0: A survey of the Supply Chains and Technologies for the Future Agriculture. *Computers in Industry*, *2020*(117), 103187. doi:10.1016/j.compind.2020.103187

Li, B., Yang, C., & Huang, S. (2014). Study on supply chain disruption management under service level dependent. *Journal of Networking*, *9*(6), 1432–1439. doi:10.4304/jnw.9.6.1432-1439

Li, D. (2016). Perspective for smart factory in petrochemical industry. *Computers & Chemical Engineering*, *91*, 136–148. doi:10.1016/j.compchemeng.2016.03.006

Li, G., Fan, H., Lee, P. K., & Cheng, T. (2015). Joint supply chain risk management: An agency and collaboration perspective. *International Journal of Production Economics*, *164*, 83–94. doi:10.1016/j.ijpe.2015.02.021

Li, R., & Xu, C. (2019). Develop deep-sea green cultivation, and establish deep-sea creature research center. *Fisheries Science & Technology Information*, *46*(06), 350.

Li, S., Ragu-Nathan, B., Ragu-Nathan, T. S., & Subba Rao, S. (2006). The impact of supply chain management practices on competitive advantage and organizational performance. *Omega*, *34*(2), 107–124. doi:10.1016/j.omega.2004.08.002 PMID:17876965

Li, S., Rao, S., Ragunathan, T., & Ragunathan, B. (2005). Development and validation of a measurement instrument for studying supply chain management practices. *Journal of Operations Management*, *23*(6), 618–641. doi:10.1016/j.jom.2005.01.002

Liukkonen, M., & Tsai, T. N. (2016). Toward decentralized intelligence in manufacturing: Recent trends in automatic identification of things. *International Journal of Advanced Manufacturing Technology*, *87*(9-12), 2509–2531. doi:10.100700170-016-8628-y

Livolsi, L. (2007), Le Supply Chain Management: synthèse et propositions. *Actes de la XVIIIème Conférence Internationale de Management Stratégique de l'AIMS*. Grenoble.

Loivet, W., Taghipour, A., & Kang, D. S. (2020). The rise of green supply chain management: Between complexity and necessity. *Journal of Economics. Business and Management*, *8*(1), 1–7.

Loivet, W., Taghipour, A., & Kang, D. S. (2020). The Rise of Green Supply Chain Management: Between Complexity and Necessity. Journal of Economics. *Business and Management*, *8*(1), 1–7.

Lom, M., Pribyl, O., & Svitek, M. (2016). Industry 4.0 as a Part of Smart Cities, *Smart Cities Symposium Prague (SCSP)*, 2016. IEEE, 1–6. 10.1109/SCSP.2016.7501015

Lotfi, Z., Sahran, S., Mukhtar, M., & Zadeh, A. T. (2013). The relationship between supply chain integration and product quality. *Procedia Technology*, *11*(2), 471–478. doi:10.1016/j.protcy.2013.12.217

Lummus, R. R., Duclos, L. K., & Vokurka, R. J. (2003). Supply Chain Flexibility : Building a New Model. *Global Journal of Flexible Systems Managment*, *4*(4), 1–13. www.giftsociety.org

Lutovac, D. M. (2020). New industrial policy as a prerequisite for efficient development of Serbian industry. Faculty of Economics, Belgrade, Serbia.

Macchion, L., Moretto, A., Caniato, F., Danese, P., & Vinelli, A. (2020). Static supply chain complexity and sustainability practices: A multitier examination. *Corporate Social Responsibility and Environmental Management*, *27*(6), 2679–2691. doi:10.1002/csr.1992

Madu, C. N., & Kuei, C. H. (2014). Disaster relief supply chain quality management (DRSCQM). *International Journal of Quality & Reliability Management*, *31*(9), 1052–1067. doi:10.1108/IJQRM-08-2013-0136

Mahfod, J., Canel-Depitre, B., & Taghipour, A. (2019). Quality function deployment-ELECTRE in supplier evaluation. *Journal of Advanced Management Science Vol, 7*(4).

Mahfod, J., Canel-Depitre, B., & Taghipour, A. (2019). Quality function deployment-ELECTRE in supplier evaluation. *Journal of Advanced Management Science, 7*(4).

Mahfod, J., Canel-Depitre, B., & Taghipour, A. (2019). Quality function deployment-ELECTRE in supplier evaluation. *Journal of Advanced Management Science*, *7*(4), 131–135. doi:10.18178/joams.7.4.131-135

Manders, J. H. M., Caniëls, M. C. J., & Ghijsen, P. W. T. (2017). Supply chain flexibility. *International Journal of Logistics Management*, *28*(4), 964–1026. doi:10.1108/IJLM-07-2016-0176

Mansfield, H. (2023). *Niccolò Machiavelli. Encyclopedia Britannica.* https://www.britannica.com/biography/Niccolo-Machiavelli

Marinagi, C., Trivellas, P., & Reklitis, P. (2015). Information quality and supply chain performance: The mediating role of information sharing. *Procedia: Social and Behavioral Sciences*, *175*(1), 473–479. doi:10.1016/j.sbspro.2015.01.1225

Marquès, G., Thierry, C., Lamothe, J., & Gourc, D. (2010). A review of vendor managed inventory (VMI): From concept to processes. *Production Planning and Control*, *21*(6), 547–561. doi:10.1080/09537287.2010.488937

Martindale, W. (2010). Food supply chain innovations. *Aspects of Applied Biology*, *102*, 1–6.

Martínez, C., Paraskevas, J. P., Grimm, C., Corsi, T., & Boyson, S. (2020). The Impact of Environmental Risks in Supply Chain Resilience. In *Supply Chain Management and Logistics in Emerging Markets* (pp. 11–39). Emerald Publishing Limited. doi:10.1108/978-1-83909-331-920201002

Martin, J. Y. (Ed.). (2014). *Développement durable?: Doctrines, pratiques, évaluations*. IRD Éditions.

Martin, P. R., & Patterson, J. W. (2009). On measuring company performance within a supply chain. *International Journal of Production Research*, *47*(9), 2449–2460. doi:10.1080/00207540701725604

Matharu, G. S., Upadhyay, P., & Chaudhary, L. (2014). *The Internet of Things: Challenges & security issues*. In *Proceedings of the 2014 International Conference on Emerging Technologies, ICET 2014*, Islamabad, Pakistan. 10.1109/ICET.2014.7021016

Matsuo, H. (2015). Implications of the Tohoku earthquake for Toyota's coordination mechanism: Supply chain disruption of automotive semiconductors. *International Journal of Production Economics, 161*, 217–227. doi:10.1016/j.ijpe.2014.07.010

Mazda. (2011). Mazda production schedule update for 4 April onward in wake of major earthquake in northeast Japan. *Newsroom.* https://newsroom.mazda.com/en/publicity/release/2011/201103/110331a.pdf

Mbiatem, J., Taghipour, A., & Canel-Depitre, B. (2018). Supplier selection approaches for decision makers. In *Proceedings of the 8th International Conference on Information Communication and Management,* (pp. 108-112). ACM. 10.1145/3268891.3268895

Medic, P., Ivanovic, K., & Mitic, P. (2020). Businesses in Serbia and Agenda 2030 - priorities, challenges and the COVID-19 crisis (Serbian: Preduzeća u Srbiji i Agenda 2030 - prioriteti, izazovi i kriza COVID-19). Center for Advanced Economic Studies, Belgrade

Mello, M. H., Gosling, J., Naim, M. M., Strandhagen, J. O., & Brett, P. O. (2016). Improving coordination in an engineer-to-order supply chain using a soft systems approach. *Production Planning and Control, 28*(2), 89–107. doi:10.1080/09537287.2016.1233471

Meng, S., Dong, W., Hu, H., & Li, Y. (2021). Analysis of supply chain's resilience in crowd networks. *International Journal of Crowd Science, 5*(2), 166–184. doi:10.1108/IJCS-02-2021-0004

Mentzer, J. T., DeWitt, W., Keebler, J. S., Min, S., Nix, N. W., Smith, C. D., & Zacharia, Z. G. (2001). Defining Supply Chain Management. *Journal of Business Logistics, 22*(2), 1–25. doi:10.1002/j.2158-1592.2001.tb00001.x

Mentzer, J. T., Rutner, S. M., & Matsuno, K. (1997). Application of the means-end value hierarchy model to understanding logistics service value. *International Journal of Physical Distribution & Logistics Management, 27*(9/10), 630–643. doi:10.1108/09600039710188693

Merimi, M., & Taghipour, A. (2021). Accelerating the digitalization of the supply chain: An empirical research about COVID-19 crisis. In *Digitalization of Decentralized Supply Chains During Global Crises* (pp. 1-24). IGI Global. Moms are the law (Serbian: Mame su Zakon). https://www.mamesuzakon.org/o-nama/vrednosti-i-principi/

Merimi, M., & Taghipour, A. (2021). Accelerating the digitalization of the supply chain: An empirical research about COVID-19 crisis. In *Digitalization of Decentralized Supply Chains During Global Crises* (pp. 1–24). IGI Global. doi:10.4018/978-1-7998-6874-3.ch001

Meunier, C., & Zéroual, T. (2006). Transport durable et développement économique. *Développement durable et territoires. Économie, géographie, politique, droit, sociologie.*

Micic, I., & Krstic-Randjic, J. (2022). Establishing the competence framework with the aim of strengthening the strategic performance of the organization. *Economía: Teoría y Practica, 15*(1), 61–77.

Miecznikowski, J., & Hendren, L. (2002). Decompiling java bytecode: problems, traps and pitfalls. In: *Compiler Construction, 11th International Conference, 2304 of Lecture Notes in Computer Science.* Springer-Verlag.

Miemczyk, J., Howard, M., & Johnsen, T. E. (2016). Dynamic development and execution of closed-loop supply chains: A natural resource-based view. *Supply Chain Management, 21*(4), 453–469. doi:10.1108/SCM-12-2014-0405

Milovanovic, D., Nenadic, N., & Todorovic, V. (2012). *A study on the improvement of the legislative process in the Republic of Serbia.* Dr Mike Falke.

Min, H. (2019). Blockchain technology for enhancing supply chain resilience. *Business Horizons, 2019*(62), 35–45. doi:10.1016/j.bushor.2018.08.012

Ministry of Industry and Information Technology, Ministry of Finance, Development and Reform Commission, & Ministry of Science and Technology. (2021, December 31). *Notice on the financial subsidy policy for the promotion and application of new energy vehicles in 2022*. China Government Network. https://www.gov.cn/zhengce/zhengceku/2021-12/31/content_5665857.htm

Ministry of the Environment. Finland. (2016). Guidelines for Green Public Procurement in Finland. Ministry of the Environment, Government of Finland.

Ministry of the Environment. Japan. (2015). Guidelines for Environmental Consideration in Procurement. Ministry of the Environment, Government of Japan.

Min, S., & Mentzer, J. T. (2004). DEVELOPING AND MEASURING SUPPLY CHAIN MANAGEMENT CONCEPTS. *Journal of Business Logistics*, *25*(1), 63–99. doi:10.1002/j.2158-1592.2004.tb00170.x

Mitrovic, V., & Mitrovic, I. (2019). Modern concept of supply chain management using information and communication technologies. *Economic Signals 14*(2), 081-096

Mnatsakanyan, T., Hayrapetyan, R., & Molnar, D. (2021). Measuring Regional Development Disparities: Some Methodological Contributions And Evidence From Armenia And Serbia. *Regional Science Inquiry*, *13*(2), 327–348.

Morgan, S. (2021). *Report: Cyberwarfare in the C-suite*. Cybercrime Magazine.

Muduli, K., Barve, A., Tripathy, S., & Biswal, J. N. (2016). Green practices adopted by the mining supply chains in India: A case study. *International Journal of Environment and Sustainable Development*, *15*(2), 159. Advance online publication. doi:10.1504/IJESD.2016.076365

Muhammad, L., & Gul-E-Rana. (2020). Mediating role of customer forgiveness between perceived justice and satisfaction. *Journal of Retailing and Consumer Services*, *52*(1), 101886. doi:10.1016/j.jretconser.2019.101886

Mukaddes, A. M. M., Abul, C., Rashed, A., & Abdul, A. M. (2010). Developing an Information Model for Supply Chain Information Flow and its Management. *International Journal of Innovation and Technology Management.*, *1*(2), 226–231.

Nadia, E. N., Beatrice, C. D., & Atour, T. (2020). Luxury hotels' eco-friendly activities & customers' preferences and willingness to pay for green hotels. Journal of Advanced Management Science Vol, 8(1).

Nadia, E. N., Beatrice, C. D., & Atour, T. (2020). Luxury hotels' eco-friendly activities & customers' preferences and willingness to pay for green hotels. Journal of Advanced Management Science Vol, 8(1). Merimi, M., & Taghipour, A. (2021). Accelerating the digitalization of the supply chain: An empirical research about COVID-19 crisis. In Digitalization of Decentralized Supply Chains During Global Crises (pp. 1-24). IGI Global.

Nadia, E. N., Beatrice, C. D., & Atour, T. (2020). Luxury hotels' eco-friendly activities & customers' preferences and willingness to pay for green hotels. *Journal of Advanced Management Science, 8*(1).

Nadia, E. N., Beatrice, C. D., & Atour, T. (2021). The Determinants of Hotel Room Rates in Beirut: A Hedonic Pricing Model. *International Journal of Trade, Economics and Finance, 12*(2).

Nadia, E.-N., Beatrice, C.-D., & Atour, T. (2020). Luxury hotels' eco-friendly activities & customers' preferences and willingness to pay for green hotels. *Journal of Advanced Management Science, 8*(1).

Nadia, E. N., Beatrice, C. D., & Atour, T. (2020). Luxury hotels' eco-friendly activities & customers' preferences and willingness to pay for green hotels. *Journal of Advanced Management Science*, *8*(1), 7–14.

Nævestad, T. O., Phillips, R. O., Meyer Levlin, G., & Hovi, I. B. (2017). Internationalisation in road transport of goods in Norway: Safety outcomes, risk factors and policy implications. *Safety (Basel, Switzerland)*, *3*(4), 22. doi:10.3390afety3040022

Naím, M. (1994). Latin America: The second stage of reform. *Journal of Democracy, 5*(4), 32–48. doi:10.1353/jod.1994.0057

Nakamoto, S. (2008). *Bitcoin: A peer-to-peer electronic cash system.* Bitcoin.

Nakandala, D., & Lau, H. C. (2019). Innovative adoption of hybrid supply chain strategies in urban local fresh food supply chain. *Supply Chain Management, 24*(2), 241–255. doi:10.1108/SCM-09-2017-0287

NALED. https://naled.rs/

Nanjing Intermediate People's Court of Jiangsu Province. (2021, March 10). Nanjing Intermediate People's Court - Nanjing Trial Network. NJFY. https://www.njfy.gov.cn/www/njfy/xwzx_mb_a39210310136710.htm

Narayanan, A. (2015). Private Blockchain' is just a confusing name for a shared database. *Freedom to Tinker.* https://freedom-to-tinker.com/2015/09/18/private-blockchainis-just-a-confusing-name-for-a-shared-database/

National Bank of Serbia. (2023). *Macroeconomic developments in Serbia.* Belgrade Serbia.

National Bureau of Statistics. (2022, October 8). *The 14th Report on Achievements of Economical Society Development.* Information Disclosure, National Bureau of Statistics. http://www.stats.gov.cn/xxgk/jd/sjjd2020/202210/t202

Neri, A., Cagno, E., Lepri, M., & Trianni, A. (2021). A triple bottom line balanced set of key performance indicators to measure the sustainability performance of industrial supply chains. *Sustainable Production and Consumption, 26*, 648–691. doi:10.1016/j.spc.2020.12.018

Ng, I. C., & Wakenshaw, S. Y. (2017). The Internet-of-Things: Review and research directions. *International Journal of Research in Marketing, 34*(1), 3–21. doi:10.1016/j.ijresmar.2016.11.003

Niesten, E., Jolink, A., de Sousa Jabbour, A. B. L., Chappin, M., & Lozano, R. (2017). Sustainable collaboration: The impact of governance and institutions on sustainable performance. *Journal of Cleaner Production, 155*, 1–6. doi:10.1016/j.jclepro.2016.12.085

Nilsson, M., Griggs, D., & Visbeck, M. (2016). Policy: Map the interactions between Sustainable Development Goals. *Nature, 534*(7607), 320–322. doi:10.1038/534320a PMID:27306173

Nishitani, K., Nguyen, T. B. H., Trinh, T. Q., Wu, Q., & Kokubu, K. (2021). Are corporate environmental activities to meet sustainable development goals (SDGs) simply greenwashing? An empirical study of environmental management control systems in Vietnamese companies from the stakeholder management perspective. *Journal of Environmental Management, 296*, 113364. doi:10.1016/j.jenvman.2021.113364 PMID:34399553

Nizami, A., Ali, J., & Nguyen-Khoa, S. (2021). Government-industry partnership for sustainable water use: Insights from Pakistan. *Sustain. Ind. Water Use Perspect. Incent. Tools, 115*, 115–126. doi:10.2166/9781789060676_0115

Nye, J. S. (2011). Power and foreign policy. *Journal of Political Power, 4*(1), 9–24. doi:10.1080/2158379X.2011.555960

O'Hara, S. (2013). Promoting sustainable procurement: An analysis of government policies and guidelines. *Journal of Cleaner Production, 56*, 112–119.

O'Reilly Radar Team. (2012). *Planning for big data: A CIO's handbook to the changing data landscape* (E. Dumbill, Ed.; 1st ed.). O'Reilly Media Inc.

Obadi, S.M. (2016). Revealed comparative advantage and competitiveness in the EU-28 and the USA. *Ekonomické Rozhl'ady / Ecomomic Review 45*(2), 243–259.

Obradovic, 2021. https://www.danas.rs/vesti/drustvo/obradovic-nije-tacno-da-ministarstvo-nije-nista-radilo-odlaganje-objektivno/

OECD. (2015). *Policy Guidance for Greening Government Procurement*. OECD Publishing.

Okongwu, U., Brulhart, F., & Moncef, B. (2015). Causal linkages between supply chain management practices and performance. *Journal of Manufacturing Technology Management*, *26*(5), 678–702. doi:10.1108/JMTM-01-2013-0002

Olinga, T., & Gelbman, A. (2013). A roadmap for sustainable public procurement. *Journal of Cleaner Production*, *55*, 21–29.

Omar, I. A., Jayaraman, R., Salah, K., Debe, M., & Omar, M. (2020). Enhancing vendor managed inventory supply chain operations using blockchain smart contracts. *IEEE Access : Practical Innovations, Open Solutions*, *8*, 182704–182719. doi:10.1109/ACCESS.2020.3028031

Ono, T., & Watanabe, K. (2015). Application of natural disaster information for supply chain resilience. *Journal of Disaster Research*, *10*(sp), 783–786. doi:10.20965/jdr.2015.p0783

Ounnar F. (2018). *Une formulation multicritère pour le choix de prestataires de services logistiques dans un réseau partenarial auto-organisé*. Logistique & Management. doi:10.1080/12507970.2018.1528902

Ozbekler, T. M., & Ozturkoglu, Y. (2020). Analysing the importance of sustainability-oriented service quality in competition environment. *Business Strategy and the Environment*, *29*(1), 1504–1516. doi:10.1002/bse.2449

Padhee, S., & Nandan, D. (2021). Design of Automated Visual Inspection System for Beverage Industry Production Line. *TS. Traitement du Signal*, *38*(2), 461–466. doi:10.18280/ts.380225

Pagell, M., & Wu, Z. (2009). Building a more complete theory of sustainable supply chain management using case studies of 10 exemplars. *The Journal of Supply Chain Management*, *45*(2), 37–56. doi:10.1111/j.1745-493X.2009.03162.x

Paksoy, T., Karaoğlan, I., Gökçen, H., Pardalos, P. M., & Torğul, B. (2016). Experimental research on closed loop supply chain management with internet of things. *Journal of Economics Bibliograph.*, *15*(3), 1–20.

Pal, K. (2018). A Big Data Framework for Decision Making in Supply Chain. In P K Gupta, Tuner Oren, Mayank Singh (eds.) Predictive Intelligence Using Big Data and the Internet of Things. IGI Global Publication.

Pal, K. (2019). Algorithmic Solutions for RFID Tag Anti-Collision Problem in Supply Chain Management. *The 9th International Symposium on Frontiers in Ambient and Mobile Systems (FAMS)*. Procedia Computer Science, 929-934.

Pal, K. (2019). Quality Assurance Issues for Big Data Applications in Supply Chain Management, in P K Gupta, Tuner Oren, Mayank Singh (eds). Predictive Intelligence Using Big Data and the Internet of Things. IGI Global Publication.

Pal, K. (2023). Security Issues and Solutions for Resource-Constrained IoT Applications. Using Lightweight Cryptography, in Cybersecurity Issues, Challenges, and Solutions in the Business World. IGI Global Publication.

Pal, K., & Karakostas, B. (2014). A Multi Agent-Based Service Framework for Supply Chain Management. In *Proceedings of the 5th International Conference on Ambient Systems, Networks and Technologies (ANT14)*. Procedia Computer Science.

Pal, K., & Yasar, A. (2023). Internet of Things Impact on Supply Chain Management, in *Proceedings of the 14th International Conference on Ambient Systems, Networks and Technologies (ANT23)*. Procedia Computer Science.

Pal, K. (2017). Supply Chain Coordination Based on Web Services. In H. K. Chan, N. Subramanian, & M. D. Abdulrahman (Eds.), *Supply Chain Management in the Big Data Era* (pp. 137–171). IGI Global Publication. doi:10.4018/978-1-5225-0956-1.ch009

Pal, K. (2020). Internet of Things and Blockchain Technology in Apparel Supply Chain Management. In H. Patel & G. S. Thakur (Eds.), *Blockchain Applications in IoT Security*. IGI Global Publication.

Pal, K. (2021). Privacy, Security and Policies: A Review of Problems and Solutions with Blockchain-Based Internet of Things Applications in Manufacturing Industry. *Procedia Computer Science*, *191*, 176–183. doi:10.1016/j.procs.2021.07.022

Pal, K., & Yasar, A. (2020). Internet of Things and Blockchain Technology in Apparel Manufacturing Supply Chain Data Management. *Procedia Computer Science*, *170*, 450–457. doi:10.1016/j.procs.2020.03.088

Panigrahi, S. S., Bahinipati, B., & Jain, V. (2019). Sustainable supply chain management: A review of literature and implications for future research. *Management of Environmental Quality*, *30*(5), 1001–1049. doi:10.1108/MEQ-01-2018-0003

Papoutsis, K., & Pappas, P. (2013). The role of government in promoting sustainable procurement. *Journal of Public Procurement*, *13*(2), 152.

Paradas, A. (2011). Développement durable en petites entreprises: de la sensibilisation à l'engagement. *La Revue des sciences de gestion*, (1), 129-137.

Paradas, A. (2006). Perception du développement durable par des dirigeants de petites entreprises: résultats d'enquêtes. *actes du 8ème Congrès international francophone en entrepreneuriat et PME, Fribourg, Suisse*.

Pargaien, S., Pargaien, A. V., Chilwal, B., Tripathi, N., Joshi, H., & Negi, H. (2021). Urge To Implement IOT For Monitoring and Preventing Blood Bank System Crisis. *2021 First International Conference on Advances in Computing and Future Communication Technologies (ICACFCT)*, Meerut, India. 10.1109/ICACFCT53978.2021.9837377

Park, Y. W., Hong, P., & Roh, J. J. (2013). Supply chain lessons from the catastrophic natural disaster in Japan. *Business Horizons*, *56*(1), 75–85. doi:10.1016/j.bushor.2012.09.008

Paschen, J., Kietzmann, J., & Kietzmann, T. C. (2019). Artificial intelligence (AI) and its implications for market knowledge in B2B marketing. *Journal of Business and Industrial Marketing*, *34*(7), 1410–1419. doi:10.1108/JBIM-10-2018-0295

Pavlovic-Krizanic, T. (2021). *The path to social consensus around key sustainable goals urban development*. CEVES. Belgrade Permanent Conference of Cities and Municipalities. http://seeurban.net/stalna-konferencija-gradova-i-opstina-skgo/?lang=en

Pearce, D. W., & Turner, R. K. (1990). *Economics of Natural Resources and the Environment*. JHU Press.

Pedersen, T., & Shaver, J. M. (2011). Internationalization revisited: The big step hypothesis. *Global Strategy Journal*, *1*(3-4), 263–274. doi:10.1002/gsj.20

Penev, G. (2021). Demographic summary of Serbia in the first year of the COVID-19 pandemic. *Demographics*, *18*(18), 1–18. doi:10.5937/demografija2118002P

Petovar, K. (2020). *Availability of education in Serbia*. Center for Democracy Foundation.

Pham, V. Q., Nguyen, B. K. Q., & Le, T. Q. (2020). Success factors affecting internationalization process of large Vietnamese companies: A conceptual framework. *Journal of Asian Finance. Economics and Business*, *7*(11), 905–913.

Phan, T., Doan, X., & Nguyen, T. (2020). The impact of supply chain practices on performance through supply chain integration in textile and garment industry of Vietnam. *Uncertain Supply Chain Management*, *8*(1), 175–186. doi:10.5267/j.uscm.2019.7.006

Plessis, M. D. (2007). Knowledge management: What make complex implementations successful? *Journal of Knowledge Management*, *11*(2), 91–101. doi:10.1108/13673270710738942

Ponis, S. T., & Koronis, E. (2012). Supply Chain Resilience: Definition Of Concept And Its Formative Elements. *Journal of Applied Business Research*, *28*(5), 921. https://www.cluteinstitute.com/. doi:10.19030/jabr.v28i5.7234

Ponomarov, S. Y., & Holcomb, M. C. (2009). Understanding the concept of supply chain resilience. *International Journal of Logistics Management*, *20*(1), 124–143. doi:10.1108/09574090910954873

Popov, D., & Rabrenović, M. (2016). A look at the optimization problem in consumer theory. *Megatrend Review*, *13*(1), 46–56. doi:10.5937/MegRev1601035P

Pournader, M., Shi, Y., Seuring, S., & Koh, S. C. L. (2020). Blockchain applications in supply chains, transport, and logistics: A systematic review of the literature. *International Journal of Production Research*, *2020*(58), 2063–2081. doi:10.1080/00207543.2019.1650976

Pradhan, P. (2019). Antagonists to Meeting the 2030 Agenda. *Nature Sustainability*, *2*(2), 171–200. doi:10.103841893-019-0248-8

Prajogo, D., & Sohal, A. (2013). Supply chain professionals. *International Journal of Operations & Production Management*, *33*(11/12), 1532–1554. doi:10.1108/IJOPM-08-2010-0228

Prendeville, S., Cherim, E., & Bocken, N. (2017). Circular cities: Mapping six cities in transition. *Environmental Innovation and Societal Transitions*.

Prorok, V., Šerić, N., & Peronja, I. (2019). Analysis of overall and pure technical efficiency of tourism in Europe. *Transactions on Maritime Science Journal*, *8*(2), 219–229. doi:10.7225/toms.v08.n02.007

Quinn, F. J. (1997). What's the buzz. *Logistics Management*, *36*(2), 43–47.

Rabrenovic, M., Popov, D., & Stamenovic, M. (2020). The degree of liberalization of Serbia's economy in the process of accession to the World Trade Organization. *Megatrend review 17*(3), 65-78

Rabrenovic, M. D., Mitrovic, R., & Kovacevic, B. (2020). The relationship between strategic management and public relations and their implications for financial operations. *International Review (Steubenville, Ohio)*, *1*(2), 89–93. doi:10.5937/intrev2001089R

Rabrenovic, M., Simonovic, P., & Cogoljevic, D. (2020). Optimization strategies for the organization of mental healthcare. *International Journal for Quality in Health Care*, *32*(6), 412–413. doi:10.1093/intqhc/mzaa061 PMID:32484888

Radomirovic, M., Aleksic, D., & Marinkovic, A. (2020). *Guidelines for development plans of local self-government units*. Belgrade Open School, Belgrade Republic Institute for Statistics of Serbia. https://www.stat.gov.rs/sr-Latn/oblasti/trziste-rada/anketa-o-radnoj-snazi

Rahman, M. (2020). Performance Measurement of Service Supply Chain Management of Steel Industry on Dealers' Perspective -The Case of Bangladesh. 22. *International Journal of Research in Humanities and Social Studies*, *7*(1), 22–28.

Ramanathan, R. (2010). The moderating roles of risk and efficiency on the relationship between logistics performance and customer loyalty in e-commerce. *Transportation Research Part E, Logistics and Transportation Review*, *46*(6), 950–962. doi:10.1016/j.tre.2010.02.002

Rashmitha, M., Babu, R. J., Sumathi, B., Mories, M. S., Sravani, V., & Madhuri, C. R. (2021). Covid Contentment Contribution. *2021 5th International Conference on Electrical, Electronics, Communication, Computer Technologies and Optimization Techniques (ICEECCOT)*, Mysuru, India. 10.1109/ICEECCOT52851.2021.9708001

Reisch, L. A., & Altstötter-Gleich, C. (2013). Sustainable public procurement: A review of the European legal framework. *European Journal of Sustainable Development*, *2*(3), 15–26.

Rejman-Petrovic, D. (2016). Business process improvement in e-supply chains. *Economic horizons 18*(3), 215-232.

Rejman-Petrovic, D., Milanovic, I., & Kalinic, Z. (2012). Supply chain architectures in an e-environment. *Economic horizons 14*(1), 37-50

Ren, Z., Taghipour, A., & Canel-Depitre, B. (2016). Information sharing in the supply chain under uncertainty. In *2016 6th International Conference on Information Communication and Management (ICICM)*, (pp. 67-71). IEEE. 10.1109/INFOCOMAN.2016.7784217

Reyna, A., Martin, C., Chen, J., Soler, E., & Diaz, M. (2018). On blockchain and its integration with IoT, Challenges and opportunities. *Future Generation Computer Systems*, *28*, 173–190. doi:10.1016/j.future.2018.05.046

Reynaud, E. (2003). *Développement durable et entreprise: vers une relation symbiotique, Journée AIMS, Atelier développement durable*. ESSCA Angers.

Riikkinen, M., Saarijärvi, H., Sarlin, P., & Lähteenmäki, I. (2018). Using artificial intelligence to create value in insurance. *International Journal of Bank Marketing*, *36*(6), 1145–1168. doi:10.1108/IJBM-01-2017-0015

Ritchie, B., & Brindley, C. (2007). Supply chain risk management and performance: A guiding framework for future development. *International Journal of Operations & Production Management*, *26*(3), 303–322. doi:10.1108/01443570710725563

Rizhao. (2023). A 3-Year PLAN to Promote Green, Low-Carbon Development. *Rizhao Daily*, 1–15. doi:10.28662/n.cnki.nrzrb.2023.000051

Roehrl, R. A., Liu, W., & Mukherjee, S. (2020). *The COVID-19 pandemic: A wake-up call for better cooperation at the science–policy–society interface. UNDESA Policy Brief, No. 62*. UNDESA.

Rogers, J. (2008). Sustainability and the'world class' city: what is being sustained and for who? In World Cities and Urban Form: Fragmented, Polycentric, Sustainable? (pp. 57-70). Routledge.

Rojo, A., Stevenson, M., Lloréns Montes, F. J., & Perez-Arostegui, M. N. (2018). Supply chain flexibility in dynamic environments. *International Journal of Operations & Production Management*, *38*(3), 636–666. doi:10.1108/IJOPM-08-2016-0450

Roth, A., Cattani, K., & Froehle, C. (2008). Antecedents and performance outcomes of global competence: An empirical investigation. *Journal of Engineering and Technology Management*, *25*(1-2), 75–92. doi:10.1016/j.jengtecman.2008.01.003

Ruiz-Mallén, I., & Heras, M. (2020). What sustainability? higher education institutions' pathways to reach the agenda 2030 goals. *Sustainability (Basel)*, *12*(4), 1290. doi:10.3390u12041290

Rust, R. T. (2020). The future of marketing. *International Journal of Research in Marketing*, *37*(1), 15–26. doi:10.1016/j.ijresmar.2019.08.002

Sachs, J. D. (2015). The age of sustainable development. In *The Age of Sustainable Development*. Columbia University Press. doi:10.7312ach17314-016

Saeed, M., & Kersten, W. (2019). Drivers of Sustainable Supply Chain Management: Identification and Classification. *Sustainability (Basel)*, *11*(4), 1137. doi:10.3390u11041137

Sahay, B. S., & Mohan, R. (2003). Supply chain management practices in Indian industry. *International Journal of Physical Distribution & Logistics Management*, *33*(7), 582–606. doi:10.1108/09600030310499277

Sahraoui, A., Tran, N. K., Tliche, Y., Kacem, A., & Taghipour, A. (2023). Examining ICT Innovation for Sustainable Terminal Operations in Developing Countries: A Case Study of the Port of Radès in Tunisia. *Sustainability (Basel)*, *15*(11), 9123. doi:10.3390u15119123

Sajdik, M. (2011). Rendre la justice sur le terrain: Les défis de la lutte contre la corruption aux niveaux national et international. *Chronique ONU*, *49*(4), 19–21. doi:10.18356/4170e8b4-fr

Sampson, S. E., & Spring, M. (2012). Customer Roles in Service Supply Chains and Opportunities for Innovation. *The Journal of Supply Chain Management*, *48*(4), 30–50. doi:10.1111/j.1745-493X.2012.03282.x

Santoso, T., Ahmed, S., Goetschalckx, M., & Shapiro, A. (2005). A stochastic pro- gramming approach for supply chain network design under uncertainty [H. Mohammadi Bidhandi, M.Y.]. *European Journal of Operational Research*, *167*(1), 96–115. doi:10.1016/j.ejor.2004.01.046

Sarkis, J., Gonzalez-Torre, P., & Adenso-Diaz, B. (2010). Stakeholder pressure and the adoption of environmental practices: The mediating effect of training. *Journal of Operations Management*, *28*(2), 163–176. doi:10.1016/j.jom.2009.10.001

Savy, M. (2011). *Le transport de marchandises*. Editions Eyrolles.

Schmidt, C. G., & Wagner, S. M. (2019). Blockchain and supply chain relations: A transaction cost theory perspective. *Journal of Purchasing and Supply Management*, *25*(4), 100552. doi:10.1016/j.pursup.2019.100552

Schoenherr, T., & Speier-Pero, C. (2015). Data science, predictive analytics, and big data in supply chain management: Current state and future potential. *Journal of Business Logistics*, *36*(1), 120–132. doi:10.1111/jbl.12082

Scholten, K., & Schilder, S. (2015). The role of collaboration in supply chain resilience. *Supply Chain Management*, *20*(4), 471–484. doi:10.1108/SCM-11-2014-0386

Schönherr, N., & Schröder, T. (2012). Antecedents and dimensions of sustainable procurement. *Journal of Purchasing and Supply Management*, *18*(4), 232–242.

Science Based Targets. (2023). *Ambitious Corporate Climate Action*. Science Based Targets. https://sciencebasedtargets.org/

Scottish Government. (2018). Procurement Reform (Scotland) Act 2014. Scottish Government.

Securities Times. (2022, November 9). Insights on the new energy vehicle value chain: The improvement of the upper steam and the rise of the track in thermal management. *Securities Times*. https://baijiahao.baidu.com/s?id=1748972321314236306&wfr=spider&for=pc

SEEDEV. (2017). Competitiveness of Serbian agriculture. SEEDEV. https://www.seedev.org/

Sekulovic, I., Bradas, S., & Vuckovic, N. (2020). *Labor Rights are our rights*. Olof Palme International Center.

Selviaridis, K., & Norrman, A. (2014). Performance-based contracting in service supply chains: A service provider risk perspective. *Supply Chain Management*, *19*(2), 153–172. doi:10.1108/SCM-06-2013-0216

Sengupta, K., Heiser, D. R., & Cook, L. S. (2006). Manufacturing and Service Supply Chain Performance: A Comparative Analysis. *The Journal of Supply Chain Management*, *42*(4), 4–15. doi:10.1111/j.1745-493X.2006.00018.x

Serdarasan, S. (2013). A review of supply chain complexity drivers. *Computers & Industrial Engineering*, *66*(3), 533–540. doi:10.1016/j.cie.2012.12.008

Seuring, S., & Müller, M. (2008). From a literature review to a conceptual framework for sustainable supply chain management. *Journal of Cleaner Production*, *16*(15), 1699–1710. doi:10.1016/j.jclepro.2008.04.020

Sezen, B. (2008). Relative effects of design, integration and information sharing on supply chain performance. *Supply Chain Management*, *13*(3), 233–240. doi:10.1108/13598540810871271

Sgarbossa, F., & Russo, I. (2017). A proactive model in sustainable food supply chain: Insight from a case study. *International Journal of Production Economics*, *183*, 596–606. doi:10.1016/j.ijpe.2016.07.022

Shahin, A. & Mehrparvar, H. & Karbasian, M. (2016). *An Integrated Framework for Selecting Performance Indicators Based on ELECTRE Method and SMART Criteria With a Case Study in Single Level Bidirectional Service Supply Chain*. Social Science Research Network.

Shahin, Arash & Jamshidian, Mehdi. (2020). *Indicators of Supply Chain Management (SCM): Performance and Supplier Selection*. Online conference logistic, Tahran, Iran.

Sharma, D. K., Pradhan, R., Kumar, V., & Gupta, Y. (2016). *Big data and analytics. Work paper*. GLA University India.

Sharma, M. J., Moon, I., & Bae, H. (2008). Analytic hierarchy process to assess and optimize distribution network. *Applied Mathematics and Computation*, *202*(1), 256–265. doi:10.1016/j.amc.2008.02.008

Sharma, P. K., Moon, S. Y., & Park, J. H. (2017). Block-VN: A distributed Blockchain based vehicular network architecture in smart city. *Journal of Information Processing Systems*, *13*(1), 84.

Sheena, A., & Sachin, A. (2017). Machine learning and its applications: A review. In *International Conference on Big Data Analytics and Computational Intelligence (ICBDAC)* (Vol. 10).

Shelton, T., Poorthuis, A., & Zook, M. (2015). Social media and the city: Rethinking urban socio-spatial inequality using user-generated geographic information. *Landscape and Urban Planning*, *142*, 198–211. doi:10.1016/j.landurbplan.2015.02.020

Shibin, K., Dubey, R., Gunasekaran, A., Hazen, B., Roubaud, D., Gupta, S., & Foropon, C. (2020). Examining sustainable supply chain management of SMEs using resource based view and institutional theory. *Annals of Operations Research*, *290*(1-2), 301–326. doi:10.100710479-017-2706-x

Shin, M., & Taghipour, A. (2021). Journal of Economics. *Business and Management*, *9*(2), 36–40.

Shin, M., & Taghipour, A. (2021). Supply Chains Digital Transformation: Automated Underground Logistics Systems. *Underground Construction*, *6*(2), 7. doi:10.18178/joebm.2021.9.2.651

Shin, T. H., Chin, S., Yoon, S. W., & Kwon, S. W. (2011). A service-oriented integrated information framework for RFID/WSN-based intelligent construction supply chain management. *Automation in Construction*, *20*(6), 706–715. doi:10.1016/j.autcon.2010.12.002

Simchi-Levi, D., Chen, X., & Bramel, J. (2005). *The Logic of Logistics: Theory, Algorithms, and Applications for Logistics Management* (2nd ed.). Springer.

Singh, D., & Reddy, C. K. (2014). A survey on platforms for big data analytics. *Journal of Big Data*, *2*(1), 8. Advance online publication. doi:10.118640537-014-0008-6 PMID:26191487

Sirieix, L., & Le Borgne, G. (2016). *Vers de nouveaux modèles de consommation?* (No. hal-01595649).

Slogar, H. (2021). Relationship between market orientation and innovativeness in companies. *International Review (Steubenville, Ohio)*, *3*(4), 1–29.

Smith, B. G. (2008). Developing sustainable food supply chains. *Philosophical Transactions of the Royal Society of London. Series B, Biological Sciences*, *363*(1492), 849–861. doi:10.1098/rstb.2007.2187 PMID:17766237

Solakivi, T. (2014). *The connection between supply chain practices and firm performance-Evidence from multiple surveys and financial reporting data*. Turku School of Economics.

Son, B. G., Chae, S., & Kocabasoglu-Hillmer, C. (2020). Catastrophic supply chain disruptions and supply network changes: A study of the 2011 Japanese earthquake. *International Journal of Operations & Production Management*, *41*(6), 781–804. doi:10.1108/IJOPM-09-2020-0614

Sony. (2011). *Status of Sony group manufacturing operations in Japan affected pacific coast of Tohoku earthquake, tsunami and related power outages*. Sony. https://www.sony.com/en/SonyInfo/News/Press/201103/11-0322E/

Spina, D., Di Serio, L. C., Brito, L., & Duarte, A. (2015). The Influence of Supply Chain Management Practices in the Enterprise Performance. *American Journal of Management*, *15*(2), 54–63.

Stahl, B., Cerinšek, G., Colombo, F., & Taisch, M. (2012). Development of competence for sustainable manufacturing by using serious games. *Transactions of FAMENA*, *36*(4), 63–72.

Stalidis, G., Karapistolis, D., & Vafeiadis, A. (2015). Marketing decision support using Artificial Intelligence and Knowledge Modeling: Application to tourist destination management. *Procedia: Social and Behavioral Sciences*, *175*, 106–113. doi:10.1016/j.sbspro.2015.01.1180

Standing Committee of the National People's Congress. (2018, October 26). *Taxation Law of the People's Republic of China on Environment Protection*. State Taxation Administration. http://www.chinatax.gov.cn/chinatax/n610/c5178958/content.html

Stankovic, S. S. (2018). *Application of dependency methods in the analysis of differences in earnings between the sexes in the Republic of Serbia*. Economics Faculty, University of Nis, Serbia.

Stankovic, S. (2016). The transformation of the Serbian labour market from a gender perspective. *Economic Themes*, *54*(4), 587–604. doi:10.1515/ethemes-2016-0030

State Administration for Market Regulation, & the National Standardization Administrative Committee. (2021, August 10). *Requirements of Restricting Excessive Package—Foods and Cosmetics*. China GB Standard. https://openstd.samr.gov.cn/bzgk/gb/newGbInfo?hcno=30366DF41D69DA50E3EEABC0CE18A241

Sterne, J. (2017). *Artificial intelligence for marketing: practical applications*. John Wiley & Sons. doi:10.1002/9781119406341

Stevenson, G. W., & Pirog, R. (2013). Values-based food supply chains: Strategies for agri-food enterprises-of-the-middle. *Techincal Report. Accessed*, (June), 22.

Stiglitz, J. (2017). *Globalization and its Discontents Revisited: Anti-Globalization in the Era of Trump*. Penguin.

Stojanović, D. (2017). *Populism the Serbian Way*. Peščanik.

Stojanovic, D., Ilic, B., & Mihajlovi, D. (2017). Foreign direct investments in achieving the goals of sustainable development of local communities in Serbia (Serbian: Strane direktne investicije u ostvarivanju ciljeva održivog razvoja lokalnih zajednica u Srbiji). *Ecologica*, *1*(2), 265–270.

Sundram, V. P., Ibrahim, A. R., & Govindaraju, V. G. R. (2011). Supply chain management practices in the electronics industry in Malaysia: Consequences for supply chain performance. *Benchmarking*, *18*(6), 834–855. doi:10.1108/14635771111180725

Sunstein, C. R. (2002). *Risk and reason: Safety, law, and the environment*. Cambridge university press.

Sun, Z., & Zhang, W. (2019). Do government regulations prevent greenwashing? An evolutionary game analysis of heterogeneous enterprises. *Journal of Cleaner Production*, *231*, 1489–1502. doi:10.1016/j.jclepro.2019.05.335

Sustainable Procurement Charter. (2015). Sustainable Procurement Charter. https://www.sustainable-procurement.org/about/collaborative-initiatives/sustainable-procurement-charter/

Taghipour, A. (2009). Évaluation de la collaboration dans une chaîne d'approvisionnement. *Revue française de gestion industrielle*, *28*(1), 26-42.

Taghipour, A., & Frayret, J. M. (2010). Negotiation-based coordination in supply chain: model and discussion. In *2010 IEEE International Conference on Systems, Man and Cybernetics*. IEEE. 10.1109/ICSMC.2010.5642397

Taghipour, A., & Frayret, J. M. (2011). Supply chain coordination planning: A review. *Work paper, École polytechnique de Montréal.*

Taghipour, A., & Frayret, J. M. (2011b). *Supply chain coordination planning: A review.* École polytechnique de Montréal, Canada.

Taghipour, A., & Frayret, J. M. (2011b). Supply chain coordination planning: A review. *Work paper, École polytechnique de Montréal.*

Taghipour, A., & Frayret, J. M. (2011b). *Supply chain coordination planning: A review.* Work paper, École Polytechnique de Montréal.

Taghipour, A., & Frayret, J. M. (2013). An algorithm to improve operations planning in decentralized supply chains. In *2013 International Conference on Advanced Logistics and Transport*. IEEE. 10.1109/ICAdLT.2013.6568442

Taghipour, A., & Frayret, J.-M. (2011). Supply chain coordination planning: A review. *Work paper, École polytechnique de Montréal.*

Taghipour, A., & Merimi, M. (2021). Digital Transformation of Supply Chains during Crisis: COVID-19. In *11th Annual International Conference on Industrial Engineering and Operations Management,* (pp. 7493-7501). IEOM.

Taghipour, A., & Merimi, M. (2021). Digital Transformation of Supply Chains during Crisis: COVID-19. In *11th Annual International Conference on Industrial Engineering and Operations Management, IEOM* (pp. 7493-7501).

Taghipour, A., & Merimi, M. (2021). Digital Transformation of Supply Chains during Crisis: COVID-19. In *11th Annual International Conference on Industrial Engineering and Operations Management, IEOM* (pp. 7493-7501). IEOM.

Taghipour, A., & Merimi, M. (2021). Digital Transformation of Supply Chains during Crisis: COVID-19. *In 11th Annual International Conference on Industrial Engineering and Operations Management.* IEOM.

Taghipour, A., Abed, M., & Zoghlami, N. (2015, May). Design for remanufacturing respecting reverse logistics processes: A review. In 2015 4th International Conference on Advanced Logistics and Transport (ICALT) (pp. 299-304). IEEE. 10.1109/ICAdLT.2015.7136602

Taghipour, A., Murat, S., & Huang, P. (2021). E-supply chain management: A review. *International Journal of e-Education, e-Business, e-Management, and e-Learning, 11*(2), 51-61.

Taghipour, A. (2014). Improving the Plan of a Manufacturing Network with Non-Integrated Business Units. [IJAL]. *International Journal of Applied Logistics*, *5*(2), 1–11. doi:10.4018/ijal.2014040101

Taghipour, A. (2014). *Production Network Planning Based on Constraint Relaxation and Discount Approach* (Vol. 2). Lecture Notes on Information Theory.

Taghipour, A. (2014). Production Network Planning Based on Constraint Relaxation and Discount Approach. *Lecture Notes on Information Theory*, *2*(3), 279–282. doi:10.12720/lnit.2.3.279-282

Taghipour, A. (2018). A Contemporary Approach to Plan Independent Logistics Actors. In *Contemporary Approaches and Strategies for Applied Logistics* (pp. 337–364). IGI Global. doi:10.4018/978-1-5225-5273-4.ch014

Taghipour, A. (Ed.). (2020). *Demand Forecasting and Order Planning in Supply Chains and Humanitarian Logistics.* IGI Global.

Taghipour, A., & Beneteau-Piet, C. (2020). Sustainable supply chain management performance. *International Journal of Innovation, Management and Technology*, *11*(6), 165–169. doi:10.18178/ijimt.2020.11.6.897

Taghipour, A., Fooladvand, A., Khazaei, M., & Ramezani, M. (2023). Criteria Clustering and Supplier Segmentation Based on Sustainable Shared Value Using BWM and PROMETHEE. *Sustainability (Basel)*, *15*(11), 8670. doi:10.3390u15118670

Taghipour, A., & Frayret, J. M. (2011a). A new heuristic search with local optimization to manage a supply chain. *Meta*, 15.

Taghipour, A., & Frayret, J. M. (2014). A new heuristic search with local optimization to manage a supply chain. *Lecture Notes on Information Theory*, *2*(1), 78–84. doi:10.12720/lnit.2.1.78-84

Taghipour, A., Glaa, B., & Zoghlami, N. (2014, May). Network coordination with minimum risk of information sharing. In *2014 International Conference on Advanced Logistics and Transport (ICALT)* (pp. 184-188). IEEE. 10.1109/ICAdLT.2014.6864115

Taghipour, A., Khazaei, M., Azar, A., Rajabzadeh Ghatari, A., Hajiaghaei-Keshteli, M., & Ramezani, M. (2022). Creating shared value and strategic corporate social responsibility through outsourcing within supply chain management. *Sustainability (Basel)*, *14*(4), 1940. doi:10.3390u14041940

Taghipour, A., & Merimi, M. (2021). Digital Transformation of Supply Chains during Crisis: COVID-19. In *11th Annual International Conference on Industrial Engineering and Operations Management, IEOM* (pp. 7493-7501).

Taghipour, A., Murat, S., & Huang, P. (2021). E-supply chain management: A review. International Journal of e-Education, e-Business, e-. *Management Learning*, *11*(2), 51–61.

Taghipour, A., Murat, S., & Huang, P. (2021). E-Supply Chain Management: A Review. International Journal of e-Education, e-Business, e-. *Management Learning*, *11*(2), 51–61.

Taghipour, A., Ramezani, M., Khazaei, M., Roohparvar, V., & Hassannayebi, E. (2023). Smart Transportation Behavior through the COVID-19 Pandemic: A Ride-Hailing System in Iran. *Sustainability (Basel)*, *15*(5), 4178. doi:10.3390u15054178

Taghipour, A., Rouyendegh, B. D., Ünal, A., & Piya, S. (2022b). Selection of suppliers for speech recognition products in IT projects by combining techniques with an integrated fuzzy MCDM. *Sustainability (Basel)*, *14*(3), 1777. doi:10.3390u14031777

Tanaskovic, S., & Ristic, B. (2019). *Competitive position of Serbia in 2019 according to the report of the World Economic Forum*. Foundation for the Development of Economic Science (FREN), Belgrade, Serbia.

Tang, C. S. (2006). Perspectives in supply chain risk management. *International Journal of Production Economics*, *103*(2), 451–488. doi:10.1016/j.ijpe.2005.12.006

Tang, C. S., & Veelenturf, L. P. (2019). The strategic role of logistics in the industry 4.0 era. Transp. Res. Part E Logist. *Transport Reviews*, *2019*(129), 1–11.

Tan, J., & Koo, S. (2014). A survey of technologies in internet of things, in IEEE. *Computers & Society*, 269–274.

Tan, K. C., Kannan, V. R., & Handfield, R. B. (1998). Supply chain management: Supplier performance and firm performance. *International Journal of Purchasing and Materials Management*, *34*(3), 2–9.

Tanriverdi, H. (2006). Performance effects of information technology synergies in multibusiness firms. *Management Information Systems Quarterly*, *30*(1), 57–77. doi:10.2307/25148717

Taschner, A. (2016). Improving SME logistics performance through benchmarking, Benchmarking. *Benchmarking*, *23*(7), 1780–1797. doi:10.1108/BIJ-03-2015-0029

Taxation Law of the People's Republic of China on Environment Protection. (2018). *Environmental Protection Tax Law of the People's Republic of China*. State Taxation Administration. http://www.chinatax.gov.cn/chinatax/n610/c5178958/content.html

Team, T. (2014). McDonald's faces declining sales in Asia after China food scandal. *Forbes*.

Techopedia.com. (2018). What is an Artificial Neural Network (ANN)? *Technopedia*. https://www.techopedia.com/definition/5967/artificial-neural-network-ann

Temri, L. (2011). Innovations technologiques environnementales dans les petites entreprises: Proposition d'un modèle d'analyse. *Innovations (Paris)*, *34*(1), 11–36. doi:10.3917/inno.034.0011

The European Commission (2020). *Republic of Serbia: Report for 2020*. EC.

The European Commission. (2021). *Republic of Serbia: Report for 2021* The Worldwide Governance Indicators. https://info.worldbank.org/governance/wgi/

The State Council. (2018, March 27). *A Provisional Regulation For Express Delivery*. The State Council, The People's Republic of China. https://www.gov.cn/zhengce/content/2018-03/27/content_5277801.htm

The State Council. (2022). *China to deepen institutional reform in the electrical and electronics industry*. The State Council. english.www.gov.cn/policies/latestreleases/202209/23/content_WS632d9fdac6d0a757729e06e0.html

The State Council. (2022). *China to further curb over-packaging*. The State Council. english.www.gov.cn/policies/latestreleases/202209/08/content_WS6319ae19c6d0a757729dfc18.html

The Supreme People's Court of The People's Republic of China. (2021, November 2). *Authoritative Release - The Supreme People's Court of The People's Republic of China*. Supreme People's Court of the People's Republic of China. https://www.court.gov.cn/fabu-xiangqing-329821.html

The World Bank. (2019). *Procuring Infrastructure Public-Private Partnerships*. World Bank Group.

Tiwari, S., Wee, H., & Daryanto, Y. (2018). Big data analytics in supply chain management between 2010 and 2016: Insights to industries. *Computers & Industrial Engineering*, *115*, 319–330. doi:10.1016/j.cie.2017.11.017

Tixier, D., Mathe, H., & Colin, J. (1996). *La logistique d'entreprise: vers un management plus compétitif*. Éditions Dunod.

Tliche, Y., Taghipour, A., & Canel-Depitre, B. (2019). *Anticipation of Demand in Supply Chains. In Hierarchical Planning and Information Sharing Techniques in Supply Chain Management* (pp. 1-45). IGI Global. Transparency Serbia. https://www.transparentnost.org.rs/index.php/sr/o-nama/trans-srbija

Tliche, Y., Taghipour, A., & Canel-Depitre, B. (2019). Anticipation of Demand in Supply Chains. In *Hierarchical Planning and Information Sharing Techniques in Supply Chain Management* (pp. 1–45). IGI Global.

Tliche, Y., Taghipour, A., & Canel-Depitre, B. (2020). An improved forecasting approach to reduce inventory levels in decentralized supply chains. *European Journal of Operational Research*, *287*(2), 511–527. doi:10.1016/j.ejor.2020.04.044

Tliche, Y., Taghipour, A., & Canel-Depitre, B. (2021). Exploring a Downstream Demand Inference Strategy in a Decentralized Two-Level Supply Chain. In *Demand Forecasting and Order Planning in Supply Chains and Humanitarian Logistics* (pp. 1–65). IGI Global. doi:10.4018/978-1-7998-3805-0.ch001

Tolkamp, J., Huijben, J., Mourik, R., Verbong, G., & Bouwknegt, R. (2018). User-centred sustainable business model design: The case of energy efficiency services in the Netherlands. *Journal of Cleaner Production, 182*, 755–764. doi:10.1016/j.jclepro.2018.02.032

Tomas Simin, M., Glavas-Trbic, D., & Djuric, K. (2020). Organic agriculture and the common agricultural policy of the EU. *Agricultural Economics*, *49*(87), 13–25.

Toyota. (2011). *The Great East Japan Earthquake*. Toyota. https://www.toyota-global.com/company/history_of_toyota/75years/text/leaping_forward_as_a_global_corporation/chapter5/section5/item1.html

Trinkuniene, S., & Aksomitiene, J. (2017). *International transport companies in the Baltic countries: internationalization motives and barriers*. In: Proceedings of the International Scientific Conference: Society. Integration. Education. (4) 414-426. Rēzeknes Tehnoloģiju akadēmija. 10.17770ie2017vol4.2373

Trumm, S. (2018). The 'New' Wave of Populist Right-Wing Parties in Central and Eastern Europe: Explaining Electoral Support for the Conservative People's Party of Estonia. *Representation (McDougall Trust), 54*(4), 331–437. doi:10.1080/00344893.2018.1539028

Tseng, M.-L., Chen, C.-C., Wu, K.-J., & Tan, R. (2020). Eco-efficient sustainable service supply chain management hierarchical model based on qualitative information and quantitative data. *Management of Environmental Quality, 31*(4), 961–984. doi:10.1108/MEQ-08-2019-0179

Tukamuhabwa, B. R., Stevenson, M., Busby, J., & Zorzini, M. (2015). Supply chain resilience: Definition, review and theoretical foundations for further study. *International Journal of Production Research, 53*(18), 1–32. doi:10.1080/00207543.2015.1037934

U.S. Department of Energy. (n.d.). *Energy Policy and Conservation Act (EPCA)*. USDE. https://www.energy.gov/laws-policies/energy-policy-and-conservation-act-epca

Udovicki, K., & Medic, P. (2021). The Impact of the COVID-19 Crisis on Employment: A Focus on Vulnerable Categories. Social Inclusion and Poverty Reduction. Team of the Government of the Republic of Serbia, Belgrade.

UNDRR. (United Nations Office for Disaster Risk Reduction) (2023). *Terminology Disaster*. UNDRR. https://www.undrr.org/terminology/disaster

United Nations Environment Programme. (2017). *Sustainable Public Procurement Implementation Guidelines*. UNEP.

United Nations Global Compact. (n.d.). *About the Global Compact*. UN. https://www.unglobalcompact.org/what-is-gc

Van Hoek, R. I. (2001). The contribution of performance measurement to the expansion of third party logistics alliances in the supply chain. *International Journal of Operations & Production Management, 21*(1-2), 15–29. doi:10.1108/01443570110358431

Vanichchinchai, A., & Igel, B. (2011). The impact of total quality management on supply chain management and firm's supply performance. *International Journal of Production Research, 49*(11), 3405–3424. doi:10.1080/00207543.2010.492805

Velter, M., Bitzer, V., & Bocken, N. (2022). A boundary tool for multi-stakeholder sustainable business model innovation. *Circular Economy and Sustainability*, *2*(2), 401–431. doi:10.100743615-021-00103-3 PMID:34888576

Venter, M., & Pillay, S. (2011). The challenges and benefits of sustainable procurement: The case of South Africa. *Journal of Public Procurement*, *11*(1), 49–83.

Verdouw, C. N., Wolfert, J., Beulens, A., & Rialland, A. (2016). Virtualization of food supply chains with the internet of things. *Journal of Food Engineering*, *176*, 128–136. doi:10.1016/j.jfoodeng.2015.11.009

Veza, I., Mladineo, M., & Gjeldum, N. (2015). Managing innovative production network of smart factories. *IFAC-PapersOnLine*, *48*(3), 555–560. doi:10.1016/j.ifacol.2015.06.139

Vickery, S. K., Jayaram, J., Droge, C., & Calantone, R. (2003). The Effects of an Integrative Supply Chain Strategy on Customer Service and Financial Performance: An Analysis of Direct versus Indirect Relationships. *Journal of Operations Management*, *21*(5), 523–539. doi:10.1016/j.jom.2003.02.002

Vogel-Heuser, B., & Hess, D. (2016). Guest editorial Industry 4.0–prerequisites and visions. *IEEE Transactions on Automation Science and Engineering*, *13*(2), 411–413. doi:10.1109/TASE.2016.2523639

Vollman T., Berry W., Whabark C., & Jocobs R. (2005). *Manufacturing, Planning and Control for Supply Chain Management*. McGraw-Hill Co.

Vosooghidizaji, M., Taghipour, A., & Canel-Depitre, B. (2020). Information Asymmetry in Supply Chain Coordination: State of the Art. *Journal of Industrial and Intelligent Information Vol, 8*(2).

Vosooghidizaji, M., Taghipour, A., & Canel-Depitre, B. (2020). Information Asymmetry in Supply Chain Coordination: State of the Art. *Journal of Industrial and Intelligent Information, 8*(2).

Vosooghidizaji, M., Taghipour, A., & Canel-Depitre, B. (2020). Information Asymmetry in Supply Chain Coordination: State of the Art. *Journal of Industrial and Intelligent Information*, *8*(2), 38–43. doi:10.18178/jiii.8.2.38-43

Vosooghidizaji, M., Taghipour, A., & Canel-Depitre, B. (2022). Coordinating corporate social responsibility in a two-level supply chain under bilateral information asymmetry. *Journal of Cleaner Production*, *364*, 132627. doi:10.1016/j.jclepro.2022.132627

Vrzina, S. (2022). Compliance with value-added tax regulations: The case of the Republic of Serbia (Serbian: Usklađenost sa regulativom poreza na dodatu vrednost: Slučaj republike Srbije). *Finance*, *77*(1-6), 74–91.

Vujicic, S., Ravic, N., & Nikolic, M. (2021). The influence of planning on the development of innovations in small and medium-sized enterprises. *Trends in business* *9*(1), 78-83

Vujicic, S., Staletovic, M., Stevanovic, M., & Gavrilovic, M. (2022). Organizational structures of companies in modern business environment. *Economía: Teoría y Practica*, *15*(4), 25–41.

Vukovic, A., Ubiparip, D., Radovanovic, M., & Jacimovic, S. (2015). Fresh tomato: Promissing export product for Serbia? *Industry*, *43*(3), 171–189. doi:10.5937/industrija43-9166

Wagner, S. M., & Bode, C. (2008). An empirical examination of supply chain performance along several dimensions of risk. *Journal of Business Logistics*, *29*(1), 307–325. doi:10.1002/j.2158-1592.2008.tb00081.x

Wahdan, M. A., & Emam, M. A. (2017). The Impact of Supply Chain Management on Financial Performance and Responsibility Accounting Agribusiness Case from Egypt. *Accounting and Finance Research*, *6*(2), 136. doi:10.5430/afr.v6n2p136

Wakolbinger, T., & Cruz, J. M. (2011). Supply chain disruption risk management through strategic information acquisition and sharing and risk-sharing contracts. *International Journal of Production Research, 49*(13), 4063–4084. doi:10.1080/00207543.2010.501550

Walker, H., Di Sisto, L., & McBain, D. (2013). Drivers and barriers to environmental sustainable procurement in the public sector: A cross-country comparison. *Journal of Public Procurement, 13*(2), 218–241.

Walker, P. H., Seuring, P. S., Sarkis, P. J., & Klassen, P. R. (2014). Sustainable operations management: Recent trends and future directions. *International Journal of Operations & Production Management, 34*(5). doi:10.1108/IJOPM-12-2013-0557

Wang, T., Zhang, Y., & Zang, D. (2016) Real-time visibility and traceability framework for discrete manufacturing shopfloor. In Proceedings of the 22nd International Conference on Industrial Engineering and Engineering Management, (pp. 763–772). Springer. 10.2991/978-94-6239-180-2_72

Wang, B., Kang, Y., Childerhouse, P., & Huo, B. (2018). Service supply chain integration: The role of interpersonal relationships. *Industrial Management & Data Systems, 118*(4), 828–849. doi:10.1108/IMDS-02-2017-0062

Wang, G., Gunasekaran, A., Ngai, E. W., & Papadopoulos, T. (2016). Big data analytics in logistics and supply chain management: Certain investigations for research and applications. *International Journal of Production Economics, 176*, 98–110. doi:10.1016/j.ijpe.2016.03.014

Wang, L., Laszewski, G. V., Young, K. M., & Tao, J. (2010). Cloud Computing: A Perspective Study. *New Generation Computing, 28*(2), 137–146. doi:10.100700354-008-0081-5

Wang, X., White, L., & Chen, X. (2015). Big data research for the knowledge economy: Past, present, and future. *Industrial Management & Data Systems, 115*(9). Advance online publication. doi:10.1108/IMDS-09-2015-0388

Ward, J. S., & Barker, A. (2013). Undefined by data: a survey of big data definitions. *arXiv preprint arXiv:1309.5821.*

Wehrmann, K. C. (2010). Participation in social advocacy: How a professional association can help social workers meet their ethical obligation. *Revista de Asistenţă Socială*, (2), 75–85.

Weidema, B. P. (2015). Comparing three life cycle impact assessment methods from an endpoint perspective. *Journal of Industrial Ecology, 19*(1), 20–26. doi:10.1111/jiec.12162

Welford, R. (2013). The future of sustainable procurement. In *Corporate sustainability in Asia* (pp. 317–330). Routledge.

Werner, D., & Sascha, A. (2000). *Supply Chain Management in Global Context.* Arbeitsbericht Nr.102/Working Paper No. 102. pdfs.semanticssholar.org/bf0e/53 58acf4631c92ed877f1a116e9db 1a cef.pdf

Williams, H., Wikström, F., & Löfgren, M. (2008). A life cycle perspective on environmental effects of customer focused packaging development. *Journal of Cleaner Production, 16*(7), 853–859. doi:10.1016/j.jclepro.2007.05.006

Wirth, N. (2018). Hello marketing, what can artificial intelligence help you with? *International Journal of Market Research, 60*(5), 435–438. doi:10.1177/1470785318776841

Wisner, J. D. (2003). A structural equation model of supply chain management strategies and firm performance. *Journal of Business Logistics, 24*(1), 1–26. doi:10.1002/j.2158-1592.2003.tb00030.x

Wognum, P. M., Bremmers, H., Trienekens, J. H., Van Der Vorst, J. G. A. J., & Bloemhof, J. M. (2011). Systems for sustainability and transparency of food supply chains—Current status and challenges. *Advanced Engineering Informatics, 2011*(25), 65–76. doi:10.1016/j.aei.2010.06.001

World Bank (2019). *Serbia's New Growth Agenda: Forging a New Future*

World Cocoa Foundation. (2023). *CocoaAction Brasil*. World of Cocoa Foundation. https://www.worldcocoafoundation.org/initiative/cocoaaction-brasil-por/

World Justice Project Rule of Law Index (2021). The platform of the World Justice Project Rules

World Justice Project. 2022. https://worldjusticeproject.org/rule-of-law-index/global/2022/

World Trade Organisation Statistics. 2004. www.wto.org

Xie, Y., Yin, Y., Xue, W., Shi, H., & Chong, D. (2020). Intelligent supply chain performance measurement in Industry 4.0. *Systems Research and Behavioral Science*, *37*(1), 711–718. doi:10.1002res.2712

Xing, B., Gao, W. J., Battle, K., Nelwamondo, F. V., & Marwala, T. (2012). e-RL: the Internet of things supported reverse logistics for remanufacture-to-order, *International Conference in Swarm Intelligence: Advances in Swarm Intelligence*, (pp. 519–526). IEEE.

Xu, B., Chen, W., Zhang, G., Wang, J., Ping, W., Luo, L., & Chen, J. (2020). How to achieve green growth in China's agricultural sector. *Journal of Cleaner Production*, *271*, 122770. doi:10.1016/j.jclepro.2020.122770

Xuewen, T. (2007). *The Sustainability of Food Supply Chain in China: Review and Comment.* Rural Development Institute of Chinese Academy of Social Sciences.

Xu, J., Pero, M. E. P., Ciccullo, F., & Sianesi, A. (2021). On relating big data analytics to supply chain planning: Towards a research agenda. *International Journal of Physical Distribution & Logistics Management*, *51*(6), 656–682. doi:10.1108/IJPDLM-04-2020-0129

Yalabik, B., & Fairchild, R. J. (2011). Customer, regulatory, and competitive pressure as drivers of environmental innovation. *International Journal of Production Economics*, *131*(2), 519–527. doi:10.1016/j.ijpe.2011.01.020

Yan, B., & Huang, G. (2009). Supply chain information transmission based on RFID and internet of things in Computing. In: *Communication, Control, and Management, ISECS International Colloquium on*, (pp. 166–169). Springer.

Yang, C.-S., & Lirn, T.-C. (2017). Revisiting the resource-based view on logistics performance in the shipping industry. *International Journal of Physical Distribution & Logistics Management*, *47*(9), 884–905. doi:10.1108/IJPDLM-05-2017-0184

Yang, S., Taghipour, A., & Canel-Depitre, B. (2017, August). Cost optimization of reverse logistics: A review. In *Proceedings of the 7th International Conference on Information Communication and Management* (pp. 158-161). ACM. 10.1145/3134383.3134393

Yao, J., & Liu, L. (2009). Optimization analysis of supply chain scheduling in mass customization. *International Journal of Production Economics*, *117*(1), 197–211. doi:10.1016/j.ijpe.2008.10.008

Yasuda, J. K. (2015). Why food safety fails in China: The politics of scale. *The China Quarterly*, *223*, 745–769. doi:10.1017/S030574101500079X

Yazan, D. M., Yazdanpanah, V., & Fraccascia, L. (2020). Learning strategic cooperative behavior in industrial symbiosis: A game-theoretic approach integrated with agent-based simulation. *Business Strategy and the Environment*, *29*(5), 2078–2091. doi:10.1002/bse.2488

Yin, R. K. (2009). *Case study research: Design and methods*, *5*. Sage.

Yli-Huumo, J., Ko, D., Choi, S., Park, S., & Smolander, K. (2016). Where is current research on Blockchain technology?—A systematic review. *PLoS One*, *11*(10), 1–27. doi:10.1371/journal.pone.0163477 PMID:27695049

Youngdahl, W. E. (1996). An investigation of service-based manufacturing performance relationships. *International Journal of Operations & Production Management*, *16*(8), 29–43. doi:10.1108/01443579610125769

Yusuf, R., & Shehu, A. U. (2017). The review of supply chain management systems and firm performance. *International Journal of Management Research and Reviews*, *7*(2), 113–122.

Yu, T. (2003). Supplier selection in constructing logistics service supply chain. Syst. Eng.-. *Theory into Practice*, *23*(5), 49–53.

Yuvaraj, S., & Sangeetha, M. (2016). Smart supply chain management using internet of things (IoT) and low power wireless communication system. *Wireless Communication, Signal Processing and Networking, International Conference*, (pp. 555-558). Springer.

Zailani, S., Iranmanesh, M., Foroughi, B., Kim, K., & Hyun, S. S. (2019). Effects of supply chain practices, integration and closed-loop supply chain activities on cost-containment of biodiesel. *Review of Managerial Science*, *14*(1), 1299–1319. doi:10.100711846-019-00332-9

Zawadzki, P., & Zywicki, K. (2016). Smart product design and production control for effective mass customization in the industry 4.0 concept. *Management of Production Engineering Review*, *7*(3), 105–112. doi:10.1515/mper-2016-0030

Zhang, X., & Parker, D. (2012). Government procurement for sustainability in China: An overview. *Journal of Public Procurement*, *12*(1), 52–82.

Zhang, Y., & Kitsos, P. (2016). *Security in RFID and Sensor Networks* (1st ed.). Auerbach Publications.

Zhao, Z., Cheng, Z., Wu, F., & Lv, D. (2023). Impact of China's Environmental Protection Tax Law on Corporate Employment. *Zhongguo Renkou Ziyuan Yu Huanjing*, *33*(1), 61–73.

Zhou, K., Liu, T., & Zhou, L. (2015). Industry 4.0: towards future industrial opportunities and challenges. In: *2015 12th International Conference on Fuzzy Systems and Knowledge Discovery (FSKD)*. IEEE.

Zhou, H., & Benton, W. Jr. (2007). Supply chain practice and information sharing. *Journal of Operations Management*, *25*(6), 1348–1365. doi:10.1016/j.jom.2007.01.009

Zhou, J., & Jin, S. (2013). *Food safety management in China: A perspective from food quality control system*. World Scientific. doi:10.1142/8689

Zhu, Z., Chu, F., Dolgui, A., Chu, C., Zhou, W., & Piramuthu, S. (2018). Recent advances and opportunities in sustainable food supply chain: A model-oriented review. *International Journal of Production Research*, *56*(17), 5700–5722. doi:10.1080/00207543.2018.1425014

Zimmermann, F., & Foerstl, K. (2014). A Meta-Analysis of the "Purchasing and Supply Management Practice–Performance Link". *The Journal of Supply Chain Management*, *50*(1), 37–54. doi:10.1111/jscm.12051

Zivkovic, P. R. (2022). *Freelancer: The spirit of the globally desirable stateless citizen*: Mirjana Radovic Markovic, Dejan Radulovic, Borislav Djukanovic: Working from Home - Economic, Legal and Socio-Psychological Aspects of Working from Home, Publishing bookstore Zoran Stojanovic, Sremski Karlovci - Novi Sad, 2021. *The Sociological Review*, *56*(2), 724–733.

Zwitter, A. (2014). Big Data ethics. *Big Data & Society*, *1*(2), 205395171455925. doi:10.1177/2053951714559253

About the Contributors

Atour Taghipour is a professor and the head of two international management master programs at Normandy University (Le Havre) in France. He holds a PhD in Industrial Engineering from the Polytechnic School of Montreal in Canada. He received two masters' degrees, one in Management, Logistics & Strategy and other in Industrial Engineering. He has more than ten years of experiences as a manager in automobile industries. He has published four books and many research papers in international journals. His areas of research are supply chain and operations management.

***

Muhammad Salman Asif is a sessional lecturer at Western Sydney University and an active researcher in industrial supply chain management with a particular emphasis on improving the environmental footprint and energy performance of food manufacturing firms. His research involves developing innovative methods to measure the environmental and energy footprint of these firms and their external suppliers. One of his notable contributions is the creation of an integrated architecture of Blockchain Technology (BT) and Life Cycle Assessment (LCA), which aids companies in gaining control over their extended supply chain emissions. Salman has made significant contributions to his field, having published research papers in esteemed journals and presented his findings at various international conferences.

Yassamine Belrhazi is a master candidat at Normandy University. She's studing the master of international management- international purchaisng. Her domain of interest is resilient sustainable supply chain management.

Nouhaila Damoum is a master candidat at Normandy University. She's studing the master of international management- international purchaisng. Her domain of interest is resilient sustainable supply chain management.

YiJiao Du is currently an undergraduate student at United International College in the Faculty of Business Management. She is taking a Bachelor's in accounting. Her business interests are managerial accounting and corporate governance.

Youssef Elhaoussine is a researcher and professional from France. He has a scientific background in Physics, Chemistry, and Analytical Chemistry, as well as a background in Marketing and Entrepreneurship. He has worked in China for over 5 years as a production manager for a French printing consumables retailer, where he developed a network of manufacturers and monitored production in China and Europe. In 2013, he decided to pursue an academic career, focusing his research on consumer behavior in China. Subsequently, he became a researcher at the Sun Yat-sen International School of Business and Finance, specializing in B2B branding strategies for Chinese factories and the Belt Road Initiative. He is regularly invited by trade organizations to provide the latest developments in brand strategies. Currently, he holds the position of Assistant Professor at the Faculty of Business and Management of Beijing Normal University - Hong Kong Baptist University United International College.

Biljana Ilić, PhD in Management and Business, was born in Zaječar, Eastern Serbia. She graduated from the Higher Business School of the University of Belgrade. She continued further education at the Faculty of Management Zaječar, Megatrend University in Belgrade, where she obtained the title of Master - Manager after completing the Academic Studies of Management. She also defended doctoral dissertation titled "Strategic directions of regional economic and ecological development of the tourist potential of Gamzigrad spa" at the Faculty of Management. She was elected to the position of associate professor in 2021, in the subjects Management, Intercultural Management, Research and Development, Entrepreneurship (Professional Studies), Business Decision-Making (Master's Studies) and Natural Resource Management (Doctoral Studies). Since 2023, she has been working at the Faculty of Project and Innovation Management "Petar Jovanović" in Belgrade, Educons University, as an associate professor, for the scientific field of Management and Project Management. The areas of interest, as well as the scientific competences of PhD Biljana Ilić, are related to Sustainable Development, Human Resource Management and Natural Resource Management. PhD Biljana Ilić is the author and co-author of more than a hundred scientific and professional papers, published in national and international scientific journals, as a chapter in foreign books - in cooperation with professors from the country and abroad. She has also been hired as a reviewer by numerous international, high-ranking magazines. She participated in the Swiss-Pro - Gender Equality project of the Swiss government, actively advocating for gender equality and the position of women in modern society. Highlighted references of PhD Biljana Ilić can be found in the Web of Science database of researchers, ID: ABA-7870-2021, in the ORCID database - link: , Google Scholar database, as well as on Researchgate.

Huan Chen Jia is currently an undergraduate student at Beijing Normal University and Hong Kong Baptist University United International College in Zhuhai, China. He is pursuing a bachelor's degree in applied economics. His business interests are in responsible investing, ESG, and sustainable regulations on tax and subsidies.

Erdinç Koç completed his PhD in Business Administration at Ankara University in 2017. He continues his academic activities as an associate professor in Department of Business Administration at Bingöl University. He works in the fields of supply chain management, innovation management and operations management.

XiaoWen Lu is a PhD candidate at Normandy University. Her domain of research is Supply Chain Management and Digitalization. She has many publications in these domains.

Shakerod Munuhwa is a seasoned supply chain management and logistics practitioner with more than 12 years experience in both industry and academic. He has held senior positions in Distribution and

Contract transport logistics with various industries including Cocacola. Currently Dr Munuhwa is the head of department for Business Management where supply chain management programes are housed. Dr Munuhwa has the following qualifications; PhD in Logistics, Msc Supply chain management, BTech International Purchasing, Logistics and Transport, Chartered member of CILT-UK

Kamalendu Pal is with the Department of Computer Science, School of Science and Technology, City, University of London. Kamalendu received his BSc (Hons) degree in Physics from Calcutta University, India, Postgraduate Diploma in Computer Science from Pune, India, MSc degree in Software Systems Technology from the University of Sheffield, Postgraduate Diploma in Artificial Intelligence from Kingston University, MPhil degree in Computer Science from the University College London, and MBA degree from the University of Hull, United Kingdom. He has published over hundred international research articles (including book chapters) widely in the scientific community with research papers in the ACM SIGMIS Database, Expert Systems with Applications, Decision Support Systems, and conferences. His research interests include knowledge-based systems, decision support systems, teaching and learning practice, blockchain technology, software engineering, service-oriented computing, sensor network simulation, and supply chain management. He is on the editorial board of an international computer science journal and is a member of the British Computer Society, the Institution of Engineering and Technology, and the IEEE Computer Society.

Damodharan Palaniappan Completed Ph.D in Anna University, Chennai. At Present working as an Associate Professor & Head of Information Technology Department, Marwadi University.

Sunčica Stanković was born in 1970 in Požarevac. She graduated from the Management School in Zajčar in 2005. She graduated from the Faculty of Business Studies in Belgrade in 2007. She enrolled in doctoral studies in 2015 at the Faculty of Economics, University of Niš, majoring in Macroeconomics. After taking the exam, provided by the plan and program of academic - doctoral studies, she registered the topic of her doctoral dissertation. In October 2018, she defended her doctoral dissertation entitled: Application of dependency methods in the analysis of gender differences in earnings in the Republic of Serbia. With this, she earned the title of Doctor of Science. She was elected to the position of assistant professor on 11.10. in 2021 at the Faculty of Management, Zaječar, Megatrend University, Belgrade, for a narrower scientific field: Mathematical Economics. From 2022, he works at the Faculty of Business Economics and Entrepreneurship, as an assistant professor for the narrower scientific field: Applied Mathematics.

Premavathi T earned an M.E from Anna University-Chennai, Now the Research Scholar at Marwadi University

Mohamad Zreik is a distinguished scholar in international relations. His broad academic background focuses primarily on International Relations, China's foreign policy, and the geopolitics of Eurasia, with special attention to the Arab region. His academic credentials include a PhD from Central China Normal University and double MA degrees in International Relations, Political Science, and International Law from Paris University. Dr. Zreik's academic journey started with a BA in Translation and Interpretation, which has profoundly influenced his research path. Throughout his career, Dr. Zreik has penned numerous acclaimed publications, predominantly focused on the Belt and Road Initiative and its impact on Middle Eastern and Asian nations. His groundbreaking work has marked him as a respected authority in his field and his research is not only expected to yield new theoretical insights, but it also has real-world implications for legislators and business strategists. His scholarship and commitment to his research make him an essential voice in understanding international relationships in the modern world.

Index

F

G

I

L

M

N

P

R

S

T

U

V

W

www.ingramcontent.com/pod-product-compliance
Lightning Source LLC
LaVergne TN
LVHW060410300926
849162LV00006B/1393
* 9 7 8 1 6 6 8 4 9 0 6 2 4 *